Celebration
Proceedings of the Oxford Symposium on Food and Cookery 2011

Celebration

Proceedings of the Oxford Symposium on Food and Cookery 2011

Edited by Mark McWilliams

Prospect Books
2012

First published in Great Britain in 2012 by Prospect Books, Allaleigh House, Blackawton, Totnes, Devon, TQ9 7DL.

© 2012 as a collection Prospect Books.
© 2012 in individual articles rests with the authors.

The authors assert their moral right to be identified as authors in accordance with the Copyright, Designs & Patents Act 1988. No part of this publication may be reproduced, stored in a retrieval system or transmitted in any form of by any means, electronic, mechanical, photocopying, recording or otherwise, without the prior permission of the copyright holders.

ISBN 978-1-903018-89-7

The illustration on the front cover is of a New Year greetings card sent from Metz (then in Germany) to Paris: toasting midnight with a glass of *Silversterpunsch*. See the paper by Elizabeth Gabay, below.
The illustration on the back cover is of the front cover of the Symposium anniversary volume, designed by Jake Tilson and edited by Jill Norman.

Design and typesetting in Gill Sans and Adobe Garamond by Tom Jaine and Lemuel Dix.

Printed and bound in Great Britain by Jellyfish Solutions.

Contents

Foreword   9
   Mark McWilliams

The Celebratory and the Everyday: Guinea Pigs, Hamburgers
   and the Performance of Food Heritage in Highland Ecuador   13
   Emma-Jayne Abbots

Celebrating Solitude: M.F.K. Fisher on Dining Alone   23
   Robert Appelbaum

Celebration and Japanese Food   31
   Kimiko Barber

Transylvanian Lambs and Easter Tables: Celebrations in Danger of
   Extinction   37
   Rosemary Barron and Kate Hawkings

It Was Divine … Gods and their Food in the Ancient Greek World   49
   Kim Beerden

Sukkot: The Paradigmatic Harvest Festival   56
   Jonathan Brumberg-Kraus

Chi vuol godere la festa, digiuni la vigilia: On the Relationship
   between Fasting and Feasting   66
   Anthony F. Buccini

A History of the Wassail Bowl: From Pagan Brew to Christian Custard   76
   Joanna Crosby

Celebrating Hellenism far from Hellas: Feasts and Festivals of
   Ptolemy II of Egypt   86
   Andrew Dalby

The 'Floating Feasts' of Ancient Rome   95
   John F. Donahue

Celebration

The Great Aussie Barbecue   105
Len Fisher

Celebrating Christmas and New Year with Punch   112
Elizabeth Gabay

Long Life to You! Drinking and Celebrating in Ancient Rome in the Festival of Anna Perenna   123
Christopher Grocock

Celebrating with Altamiras: The Spirit of Fiesta Food   133
Vicky Hayward

Buttering Up the Sun: Russian Maslenitsa from Pagan Practice to Contemporary Celebration   141
Sharon Hudgins

Celebrating with Sweets in Ottoman Turkey   151
Priscilla Mary Işın

Royal Pomp: Viceregal Celebrations and Hospitality in Georgian Dublin   163
Máirtín Mac Con Iomaire and Tara Kellaghan

The Unavoidable Ham Biscuit   174
Mark McWilliams

North and South: Two Banquets Given to Promote the Great 1851 Exhibition   184
Valerie Mars

Dining with the Drapers: The Drapers' Company 1564 Election Day Feast as a Map of Elizabethan London   199
Sarah Ann Milne

Feast for a King: The Wine and Food Society's Carême Banquet at the Royal Pavilion, Brighton   209
Joan Navarre

Keeping Kosher: Cause for Celebration?   217
Felicity Newman

Celebration

The Midwinter Celebration in Antarctica: Feeding Body and Soul 228
Diana Noyce

The Bull's Head Breakfast in Old Los Angeles 242
Charles Perry

Underground Restaurants – A New Way to Celebrate with Strangers 248
Heike Pethe and Sabine Cikic

On *Mfúúmbu, Nkasa,* and Whisky: A Wedding Celebration in Kimbonga-Louamba (Congo-Brazzaville) 258
Birgit Ricquier

Tableware and Taste: Ceramic Production and the Presentation of Banquet Food 267
Gillian Riley

Þorrablót – Icelandic Feasting 277
Nanna Rögnvaldardóttir and Michael R. Leaman

Celebrating Life in Multicultural Rotterdam: A Visual Approach 284
Linda Roodenburg

M.F.K. Fisher, W.H. Auden, and *Thanksgiving for a Habitat* 297
Seth Rosenbaum

Cake: The Centrepiece of Celebrations 308
Marietta Rusinek

Celebrating Purim and Passover: Food and Memory in the Creation of Jewish Identity 316
Georg Schäfer and Susan Weingarten

Prints Charming: Nineteenth-Century New York Cake Boards and New Year's Cake 326
Kimberly Sorensen

The Festive Fruit: A History of Figs 335
David C. Sutton

Celebration

Be Merry, Around a Wheat Berry! The Significance of Wheat
    in Anatolian Rituals and Celebrations   346
    Aylin Öney Tan

The Rise of Taste and the Rhetoric of Celebration   356
    Viktoria von Hoffmann

Celebrations and the Torrid Pleasures of an Ice-Cream and
    Sorbet Tree in Rome in August 1714   364
    Robin Weir

The Origins of the Celebration of St Cosmas and St Damian
    in Rio de Janeiro   373
    Marcia Zoladz

Foreword

For three decades, the Oxford Symposium on Food and Cookery has celebrated the best in food studies by gathering together scholars, writers, chefs, and all those interested in food and foodways – including experts from chemists to artisan producers – to discuss a given theme each year. It is only fitting, therefore, that in our thirtieth year the Symposium devoted itself to the theme of Celebrations.

This is the latest of thirty such volumes and the first produced under my editorship as I attempt to follow in the footprints of former editors Helen Saberi, Susan Friedland, and Richard Hosking. In addition to my predecessors, I would like to thank Elisabeth Luard, Ursula Heinzelmann, Harlan Walker, Cathy Kaufman, and Tom Jaine for all their help during the transition.

The best testimony to the continuing strength of the Symposium, nevertheless, is the gathering itself, and from the very beginning this year was no exception. The Symposium opened with The Jane Grigson Memorial Lecture delivered by Richard Wrangham on the history of fire in cooking, after which symposiasts were entertained by a brief film on the Symposium's theme by Barbara and Joe Wheaton. Dinner featured a celebratory meal prepared by Shaun Hill, of The Walnut Tree in Wales, working with Tim Kelsey and his staff at St Catherine's. A tequila-tasting rounded off the evening, along with the opening of 'an altar of remembrance to symposiasts past' assembled by celebrated performance-artist and long-time symposiast Alicia Rios.

On Saturday morning, business started with introductory remarks by Co-Chairs Paul Levy and Claudia Roden and Trustee Director Elisabeth Luard. The prestigious Sophie Coe Prize in Food History was awarded to Eileen White for her elegantly constructed who-done-it, 'On Watty's birthday, a gentry family celebrates in 1763'.

The day's presentations began with a plenary talk delivered by the *New Yorker*'s Jane Kramer on the importance of culinary rituals in celebrations, which was followed by Joelle Balhoul on exchanges between Jewish and Muslim communities in North Africa. Thereafter, the first group of parallel sessions obliged symposiasts to make difficult choices, as always, between topics including sweets in Ottoman Turkey, a history of confetti, M.F.K. Fisher's thoughts on dining alone, the festivals of Ptolemy II in Egypt, feasts afloat and ashore in ancient Rome, the integral relationship between fasting and feasting, black banquets and funerary feasts, and the rituals traditional to the celebration of saints' days in Rio de Janeiro.

Celebration

Lunch commemorated the 150th anniversary of the unification of Italy. Hosted by Claudia Roden and supported by the Italian Trade Commission's Antonietta Kelly, a Risorgimento feast moved from antipasti to zabaglione, with each course accompanied by Italian wines and beer to stimulate conversation among symposiasts gathered from around the world.

Afternoon sessions discussed the Italian *Credenziere*, ceramic production, underground restaurants, Antarctic banquets, feasts in Elizabethan and Victorian England as well as Georgian Dublin, followed by the construction on stage of an elaborate ice-cream tree by Robin Weir. Parallel sessions resumed after tea with papers on a banquet inspired by Carême, the 'radical little cookbook' of Altamiras, the culinary discourse of celebrations, Anatolian wheat, Icelandic feasts, and children's celebrations in both real life and fairy tales.

Saturday ended with a traditional Mexican fiesta prepared by Fernando de la Cruz (chef at London's Santo), Sage Bernard Conran and Tom Conran and hosted by Caroline Conran, Bruce Kraig and Jan Thompson. The meal took the form of foods prepared in celebration of the Day of the Dead and on each plate symposiasts found little sugar skulls handmade by Caroline Conran and Beth Coventry.

The Symposium's final day began with Paul Levy's presentation of the Raymond Blanc Scholarship to young chef Anna Colquhoun. Business continued as the president of the American Friends, Cathy Kaufman, awarded the Cherwell Prize to Seth Rosenbaum for his paper on W. H. Auden's debt to M. F. K. Fisher. Oswyn Murray then shed light on the history of the Greek symposium, followed by a Greek Clean Monday lunch organized and introduced by Aglaia Kremezi which took the form of the meatless feast traditionally served on the first day of Lent, including marinated octopus and several excellent Greek wines.

The final set of parallel sessions considered the ancient Roman feast of Anna Perenna, figs, supernatural celebrations in ancient Greece, the ham biscuits of the American South, elaborately carved cake-boards, wedding rituals in Congo-Brazzaville, the wassail bowl, and the central role of cake and punch in many celebrations.

Theodore Zeldin, one of the Symposium's founders, opened the closing plenary session with reflections on the changing nature of the annual gathering. Participants then planned for the Symposium's future by debating and choosing the topic for 2014, *Food and Markets*.

In addition to the present volume, the Symposium's lively history forms the subject of a series of reflections gathered in a publication entitled *Celebration: 30 Years of the Oxford Symposium on Food and Cookery*. Introduced by Theodore Zeldin, designed by Jake Tilson, and edited by Jill Norman, the book includes recipes and memories from the Symposium's informal potluck roots at St Antony's College in 1982 as well as those which reflect the more formally organized, college-catered meetings that now take place at St Catherine's.

Celebration

Methods of accessing past papers are also changing to reflect the Trustees' desire to increase the Symposium's outreach, with previous volumes formerly available only in printed form increasingly being made available online through the generous support of Friends of the Oxford Symposium encouraged by William Rubel.

Mark McWilliams
Editor, Oxford Symposium on Food & Cookery

The Celebratory and the Everyday: Guinea Pigs, Hamburgers and the Performance of Food Heritage in Highland Ecuador

Emma-Jayne Abbots

This paper examines changing food and foodways among the peasant classes in the greater Cuenca region of the Ecuadorian Andes, with a specific focus on the manner in which food expresses and constitutes both modernity and tradition. Initially, I address the celebratory dish of *cuy* (roast guinea pig), examining the ways in which members of peasant households actively seek to maintain *cuy* traditions by restricting its consumption to ritual and festive occasions and upholding strict rules concerning the exchange, slaughter, butchery, cooking and eating of the meat. These practices are notable because the Cuencano peasantry are generally outward-looking, have rejected a number of established food practices and have an inclination towards embracing change and 'modernity'. Moreover, fast-food chains, which are located in the region's capital city, are popular haunts for peasant actors, who continue to live in the rural environs and villages rapidly being incorporated into the city's urban sprawl.

My purpose in this paper is to demonstrate that, contrary to the views posited by advocates of McDonaldization theory (Ritzer 2010) and Cuenca's privileged classes, the peasantry's embracing of modernity, in the form of global fast-food chains, is not tantamount to the wholesale rejection of their food heritage. Rather, I suggest that while their consumption of prepared foods is, in part, motivated by the peasantry's desire for upward mobility and modernity, this is balanced and contained by their continuing need to remain rooted to their rural subjectivities. I contend that celebratory food is one of the key mechanisms through which this rootedness is realized. The tensions between being outward- and inward-orientated, modern and traditional, socially mobile and lower class, and urban and rural are at the heart of what it means to be a member of the peasant class in the Cuenca region today, and I demonstrate that individuals manage these tensions by distinguishing celebratory food from the everyday. Thus I show that through their cooking and eating practices the Cuencano peasantry draw protective boundaries around *cuy*, treating it as a distinct heritage dish, while categorizing the hamburgers, french fries, rice, bean stew and pre-prepared chicken procured through global and national fast-food outlets and supermarkets as 'everyday'. Moreover, I suggest this is a self-conscious act of heritage protection and, echoing Bourdieu (1977), contend that it is only through the introduction of new possibilities and new foods that existing foodways become realized, categorized, and valorized as 'tradition'.

The Celebratory and the Everyday

The two categories thereby interplay and mutually reinforce each other, and I explore the processes through which, rather than leading to a loss of food heritage, the presence of the fast-food chains is negotiated in a manner which facilitates the protection and reproduction of heritage dishes. I thus aim to contribute an enhanced understanding of the ways in which specific celebratory foodways are continually performed and categorized as 'traditional' in relation to 'everyday' prepackaged and imported foods. In highlighting this dialectic relation, I question theories of McDonaldization in addition to indicating the import of both categories of food to the constitution of complex, multi-faceted subjectivities.

Performing tradition and being modern: the relative merits of *cuy* and KFC

The consumption of *cuy*, which are native to the Andean region, has a long history, with archaeological records demonstrating that the animals were possibly domesticated as early as 5000 BC (Wing 1986: 260), and widely distributed before the Spanish conquest (Archetti 1997: 30–1). Unlike alpacas and llamas, guinea pigs were not owned by the Incan state, although records show that *cuy* was never a quotidian dish during this era but was rather reserved for ritual consumption (Archetti ibid.; Cobo 1990; Gade 1967; Poma de Ayala 1978). This indigeneity has led a number of commentators to claim that *cuy* is a lower class 'Indian' food, the most notable of whom is Weismantel (1988) who, drawing on Lévi-Strauss (1968), structurally opposes the dish to the higher status 'white / *mestizo* (mixed-race)' foods of rice and chicken. More recent accounts have called for a rather more dynamic interpretation, with Bourque (2001) asserting that the status of *cuy* is dependent upon the subject position of the consumer and is therefore rather more ambiguous than structurally determined. Her description of *mestizo* attitudes to *cuy* meat demonstrates that the status of 'Indian and peasant' food is relational to the social status and ethnicity of the individual consumer, and as a result she shows that its classificatory status is not immovable but rather shifts across contexts and subjectivities. Thus, *mestizos* in the city do not regard the consumption of *cuy* as compromising their *mestizo*-ness, while those in a 'peasant' village take steps to distance themselves from the meat (Bourque 2001: 95).

The ambiguous status of *cuy* is further heightened by the manner in which its production and consumption has changed considerably in recent years, specifically in terms of its commodification. Large-scale *cuyerias* (guinea pig farms) and restaurants that specialize in marketing the delicacy to tourists and the middle classes have been introduced and, as a consequence, the dish has been refined, elevated, and presented as the heritage dish *par excellence*. Yet, despite its increasing availability as an everyday commodity and enhanced status among the upper classes, members of peasant households in the greater Cuencano region continue to treat *cuy* as a 'special' dish and uphold established prohibitions regarding its production and consumption. In this context, *cuy* is only ever eaten on ritual occasions, including life-cycle events and Catholic fiestas, and, in contrast to the production of other Cuencano foods, the home-rearing, preparation and cooking of *cuy* is a labour-intensive, non-mechanized process in which only kin and intimate friends are involved. Slaughtering, butchering, and roasting *cuy* is a skilled and time-consuming practice in which members of the household communally kill, prepare and then spit-roast the meat over a fire located in the private spaces at the back of the home. This private practice, which contrasts to the manner in which pigs are publically butchered and consumed at the front of the house, indicates that, although celebratory, for the peasantry *cuy* remains understood as a low-status food that can potentially reinforce their household's low subject position vis-à-vis the professional and privileged classes. Moreover, on the occasions they do not have sufficient *cuy* in their own household, members of the peasantry rely on their personal exchange networks to acquire additional animals for the table rather than purchasing them on the open market; a form of limited distribution which can be understood as representing a distinct sphere of circulation (cf. Bohannan 1967). Sharing *cuy*, therefore, acts to reaffirm and define social relations between households, and between individuals within those households (Bourque 2001: 90). Consequently the dish is understood as inherently social. As Weismantel states, 'to kill a *cuy* for someone ... is an open declaration that you would like to deepen and formalize the relationship between your household and theirs' (1988: 131). Peasant households thus make concerted efforts to continue performing *cuy* foodways in the same manner as their ancestors, and look to render this timeless by valorizing these eating and cooking performances as 'tradition'.

The Cuencano peasantry, across all generations, are also enthusiastic consumers of dishes purchased from global and national fast-food chains. During a period of fieldwork in Cuenca's two major malls, which are situated on the city's margins, it became evident that KFC and Burger King are particularly popular concessions, especially on Sundays, when families visit the malls with the specific purpose of eating at one of these restaurants. When not in one of these global chains, members of the peasant class can also be commonly observed in one of the regional chains that specialize in spit-roasted chicken that are located in both the city centre and its outskirts. A comparative observation has been made by Oldakowski & McEwen (2010), whose study of the major fast-food chains in the Ecuadorian coastal city of Guayaquil indicate that KFC is second only to McDonald's in terms of popularity and frequency of visits.[1] This success and market penetration of the global fast-food chains has been attributed to a number of factors that can be characterized as efficiency, predictability, control and calculability (Ritzer 2010: 16–17). Low prices are factored into the latter, yet, outside of the US and Europe, prices can be higher than in comparative local restaurants (Lozada 2000). This is the case in Cuenca, and my comparison of the global chains' to local restaurants' prices suggests that a meal in the former is significantly, and potentially two to three times, more costly than in the latter. My research participants noted this price differential and not only emphasized the relatively high prices of the global chains, but also indicated that high pricing contributed to their popularity, as they were consequently perceived as more prestigious. This view is illustrated by Elena who, in response to my statement that KFC was generally regarded as lower status in the UK, explained:

> It is exactly the opposite here, exactly the opposite. It is because they are so expensive, and they come from the US too – they are foreign, not Ecuadorian – so they are prestigious. It is good to be seen there. I can't eat there, it's too expensive, but I can pay for a coffee, just a coffee. And people will see me there and talk – it's all about status here; I only need to go once or twice.

Other members of the peasantry commonly echoed Elena's perspective on the prestige of KFC and Burger King, while also indicating that they are locally interpreted as symbols of modernity, wealth, and urbanization. As Conchetta explained, 'It's here because we want it, and yes it is globalization and modernization, but we want it here'. This symbolic capital of global fast-food chains has also been noted elsewhere; Oldakowski & McEwen state that they are locally regarded as 'upscale restaurants' located in middle-class suburbs (2010: 37), while both Watson (1997, 2000) and Yan (2000) demonstrate that consumers of McDonald's in China are commonly drawn from the middle-classes, who symbolically associate the chain with modernity. Thus it becomes evident that, dependent on the subject position of the consumer, fast-food can be regarded as distinctly more prestigious than indigenous dishes although, as I explain below, in the Cuencano context, there is no direct correlation between prestige and 'celebratory'.

'We don't eat these foods every day': classifying the celebratory and the everyday

The popularity of global fast-food chains among the peasantry is not lost on the professionals, expatriates, and political élites who comprise Cuenca's upper and middle classes, all of whom roundly condemn this perceived McDonaldization and regard it as a threat to the cultural food heritage of the region. The presence and the local popularity of the fast-food chains is a source of constant dismay; a perspective exemplified by Andria who told me 'Colonel Saunders is everywhere: all the traditions were dying' and by Leala who, gesticulating to a branch of Burger King, stated, 'we get the worst of American culture here; it's embarrassing'. Embedded within this discourse is a clear sense of paternalism in which the peasantry's enthusiasm for fast-food is regarded as rather childlike and naïve. This is illustrated by Mariana who exclaimed, 'they just don't know any better', and Ricardo who explained, 'it's an education thing, these people just don't know how and what to eat'. Furthermore, Leonara stated, 'they're just not as far along as we are in realizing the dangers of these foods'. A resonant perspective, that rationalization and globalization, as epitomized by the proliferation of the global chains, will lead to the loss of indigenous culinary heritage and create a homogenous global culture, is found in the work of scholars whose understanding of fast-food consumption is framed by the McDonaldization thesis (Ritzer 2010). However, the resulting notion

The Celebratory and the Everyday

that McDonald's is a force for cultural imperialism is challenged by those who stress localization and demonstrate that consumers adapt, modify, and integrate the global fast-food chains into their own cultural realities (cf. Caldwell 2004; Turner 2003; Yan 2000; Watson 1997, 2000). This process of localization is more akin to the Cuencano context, although rather than being understood as a process of hybridization, I suggest the Cuencano peasantry manage the presence of the global fast-food chains through differentialism and classification.

When I asked my research participants if they felt that fast-food chains were eroding their food traditions, the answer was a clear and resounding 'no', with many offering the additional explanation that they believed the two aspects of their culinary lives could live alongside each other. 'We don't eat these things everyday, so we still eat our traditional food, especially during fiestas', was a common response, and it became evident through our discussions that my participants clearly define and classify foods into different categories; two of which are 'the everyday' and 'the celebratory'. Falling into the category of 'everyday' are those foods purchased for general consumption, such as rice, beans, vegetables, and some meats. Pre-prepared foods, such as the hamburgers, fries, and chicken purchased from the fast-food chains also fall within this category. These foods are often, although not always, associated with modernity and globalization, and subsequently they can be understood as prestigious and/or low status, dependent on the subjectivity and class position of the consumer. These foods may also, in some contexts, be social, as the central role that KFC plays in Sunday's family meals exemplifies, but they are not classified as such by members of the peasantry; this categorization seems founded on the way these foods are always commoditized, and are either pre-prepared in restaurants, or prepared at home by a single cook, often a domestic servant.

As my participants' comments in the paragraph above show, everyday foods are clearly not consumed every day, and the peasantry's acceptance of fast-foods is premised on the notion that they are balanced with other categories of food, included the 'celebratory'. *Cuy*, which is not only inherently social, but is also regarded as such by the peasantry, epitomizes this category, and hence its commoditization is resisted and the meat can only be acquired through personal exchange networks. Furthermore, in contrast to everyday foods, when the use of technology in their preparation is sanctioned, *cuy* must be prepared communally and by hand following a prescribed method in which the use of technology and exogenous – particularly waged – assistance is prohibited. Thus, peasant households make a clear distinction between everyday and celebratory foods, and this division is maintained, not because of the material qualities of the dish, but through the discourse and practices of peasant actors. By treating *cuy* as a unique food, and following specifically culturally prescribed cooking and eating customs, *cuy* becomes segregated from everyday foods and valorized as traditional and celebratory. Peasant actors thereby draw protective boundaries around the dish, which they continually renew and affirm through their own practices. Moreover, these eating, cooking, and exchanging performances are not enacted every day, but only on the sole occasions which are demarcated as ritual and/or festive on the household's social calendar. Therefore specific time designated as celebratory is set aside for the preparation and consumption of *cuy*. Food and event can consequently be seen to mutually reinforce each other's unique classificatory status; *cuy* becomes celebratory because it is consumed on festive occasions, and the occasion is marked as celebratory because *cuy* is consumed. Thus, temporalities serve to further reiterate the boundary between the everyday and the celebratory.

'Fast-food protects our traditions': the interplay between the celebratory and the everyday

Notions of time further inform the classificatory process of foods, with the relation between past and present, and tradition and modernity, playing a central role. As theorists of modernity have highlighted, the modern condition brings an inherent contradiction in which social actors become increasingly aware of a rupture with the past while also seeking to (re)create continuities (Bauman 2000; Habermas 1987). This temporal consciousness and the emergence of a new presentness, which derives from an opposition between past and future, can create uncertainty and anxiety as actors are faced with the 'agonies of choice' (Bauman 1998: 74) and become aware that tradition is invented. The tension between stability and choice is, as Simmel (1978) argued, one of the intrinsic characteristics of modernity. However, the appearance of new possibilities – and potential threats – throws the existing order of things and taken-for-granted practices into sharp relief, which in turn can initiate and facilitate the valorization of these practices as 'tradition' (Bourdieu 1977). Applying this theoretical framework to foodways in Cuenca, it can be argued that traditional, celebratory *cuy* becomes valorized as such *because* of the presence of the global fast-food chains, rather than despite of them; a theoretical assertion borne out by the perspectives of members of the Cuencano peasantry.

As I indicated above, the Cuencano peasantry are rather more relaxed about the presence of global fast-food chains and their potential impact on the region's culinary traditions than members of the middle and upper classes. It quickly emerged in our group discussions that the reason behind this is not only peasant actors' ability to compartmentalize and classify the foods as everyday and celebratory, but also because they regard these two distinct categories as mutually reinforcing. The general consensus among the groups with whom I worked was that, in the last two to three years, there had been a greater level of promotion and recognition of local gastronomy and the region's food heritage, and they noted this had developed alongside an increasing number of fast-food outlets and greater availability of imported and processed foods. As Sara told me, 'fast-food helps us protect our traditions, because it makes us more aware of them, it highlights them', and Jose explained, 'in Cuenca, we are very conservative, the most conservative in all of Ecuador, so we protect our traditions; we like fast-food, you know, I love KFC, but our traditions are important too; so we need to look after them'. Thus, echoing modernity theorists, members of the peasantry understood that

The Celebratory and the Everyday

the presence of global fast-food chains and 'exogenous' dishes were helping preserve their culinary heritage. We thereby see the interplay between the everyday and the celebratory: one category, it appears, cannot exist without the other. Moreover, this theme was particularly pronounced among teenagers, suggesting that while young people may drive demand for the products of the global fast-food chains (Bugge 2011, Lozada 2000, Yan 2000), they are also developing nuanced and sophisticated understandings of the relation between new and established eating practices. However, it also becomes evident, through my participants' discourse and their self-conscious performances of cooking and eating *cuy* as 'tradition', that fast-food does constitute a threat and the boundaries between the everyday and celebratory are perceived as potentially permeable. Yet, it also appears that my participants are highly aware of this potential threat and recognize that boundaries have to be remade and reaffirmed through their own actions. Consequently they look to valorize *cuy* as 'traditional' and 'celebratory', and look to reinforce the distinction in order to minimize potential loss and cross-contamination (cf. Douglas 2002).

This became particularly clear when I asked my participants whether they thought that hamburgers could become 'celebratory' food in the future; a question which created the greatest level of disagreement and discussion, with a number stating that this clearly could not happen as 'our food traditions are protected', while others argued that, as celebratory food is the 'food of the ancestors', in 'four to five generations time' the ancestors will be today's consumers and 'we are eating hamburgers'. Individuals in this latter group drew on the history of the region to support their cause, explaining that, as some foods introduced during Spanish colonization are now regarded as typical of the region, foods from the USA could be interpreted in the same way in the not-so-distant future. Yet this process was not understood as a uni-directional globalizing force originating in the North and homogenizing the South, but was rather constructed as a dialogue between the different forms of cuisine. This perspective is further evidenced by Oldakowski and McKewen (2010), who note that KFC's success outside of the USA has been built on a strategy based on adaptation to local cuisine and tastes, and demonstrate that their research respondents understand that, out of all of the chains, KFC offers a menu closest to Ecuadorian cuisine.

My research participants made a similar observation, but stressed that the presence of rice, shrimp, and *menestra* on the KFC menu should not be regarded as a cynical ploy to exploit local tastes for commercial gain. Rather it is seen as evidence of the strength of their own food traditions. As Rafe forcibly stated, 'our traditions, our food is very strong – they [KFC] are having to adapt to us'. This adaptation is, however, limited, and my participants expressed horror at the thought of *cuy* being on the menu at the global fast-food chains. I suggest that this is because of its classification as a 'celebratory' dish, and the consequent associations of sociality and gift giving, as opposed to commoditization, that this classificatory status brings. The foods which can acceptably form part of the KFC menu, and which Rafe takes pride in, may be classified as 'local' and in some contexts be defined as 'traditional', but they are also classified as 'everyday' foods and are therefore able to shift across different dining settings and temporal contexts. In contrast, I contend, *cuy* has to remain rooted to a specific context – that of a celebratory event – and the prospect of this rootedness being undermined and challenged, by situating the dish in an everyday commoditized context, cannot, and will not, be considered.

The strength of this reaction stems, at least in part, from the role that *cuy*, and celebratory food in general, plays in shaping the identities of the Cuencano peasantry. When Cristián informed me '*cuy* is part of my culture; it is who I am', and Maria took immense pride in the way that her son 'loved his *cuy*' and explained that this was because 'he is a son of Jima',[2] they echoed the voices of many of my participants, young and old, who use the dish to define their rural personhood. At a time of immense social change and new possibilities of being and eating, *cuy*, and the celebratory events in which the dish plays a pivotal role, offers a groundedness to members of the peasantry who are faced with the 'agonies of choice' that modernity presents. Yet, being 'traditional' and 'rural' is just one aspect of being a member of the Cuencano peasantry, and individuals within this social group have multiple relative subjectivities. Aspirations of social mobility, founded on global rather than local symbols, outward orientation, and conceptions of modernity, are dominant characteristics of social life for this group, and play a significant role in informing shifting eating and consumption practices. I have demonstrated that these tensions between rural and urban, outward and inward orientation, and tradition and modernity are managed through a process of classification, but further suggest that the presence of the global fast-food chains, among other 'modern' symbols, enables this process to occur not only by throwing the traditional into sharp relief, but by also creating a new subject position from which the protective boundaries around *cuy* can be drawn. By acknowledging that fast-food outlets are high in social capital, I argue that they help facilitate the class mobility of the peasantry and thus, building on Bourque's (2001) assertion that the relative status of *cuy* is shaped by the relative status of the consumer, contend that *cuy*, in turn, can also become elevated from its 'Indian / peasant' connotations in this social context. The dish consequently becomes less potentially damaging to the upwardly mobile aspirations of the peasantry. Thus, by providing a site through which they can enhance their social status, the global fast-food chains provide the foundations through which members of the Cuencano peasantry can celebrate and value rather than diminish their food heritage. As Julia surmised, 'I may be here with my laptop and modern clothes and go to Burger King but I will still teach my children our traditions – my daughters will still know how to cook and eat *cuy*.'

Conclusion

The Cuencano peasantry's classification of foods into the everyday and the celebratory can be seen to be their method of negotiating and managing the tension between stability and choice that is characteristic of the modern condition (Simmel 1978).

Consequently, celebratory dishes, for example *cuy*, have to be distinctly bounded and segregated from everyday foods. Yet, this boundary is understood to be constantly under threat and therefore has to reaffirmed and maintained through specific culturally prescribed exchange, cooking and eating practices. These practices not only provide a sense of stability at a time of dramatic social change, but are also consistently valorized as performances of 'tradition'; a valorization that can, paradoxically, only occur, following Bourdieu (1977) and Habermas (2000), when new possibilities appear. Thus, far from resulting in an eradication of culinary heritage, the presence of global and regional fast-food chains can be seen to facilitate the self-conscious protection of particular food 'traditions'.

An analysis of the relation between celebratory and everyday foods shows us how the Cuencano peasantry are negotiating and constituting new subjectivities that are simultaneously traditional and modern, lower and higher status, and rural and urban, and elucidates the process through which they keep both grounded and explore new culinary opportunities. Thus, contrary to the views of some scholars and the Cuencano privileged classes, the peasantry have a nuanced understanding of relations between global and local and are not adopting fast-food with a childlike naivety, but are rather negotiating their increased presence through a classificatory process. I suggest much can be learnt from the Cuencano peasantry's approach to both the global fast-food chains and their culinary heritage, for they remind us not to view these topics through the lens of our own culinary values and biases.

Notes
1. Cuenca does not currently have a McDonald's branch, although a Facebook page entitled 'I wish there was a McDonald's in Cuenca', with 5,770 'likes', indicates its potential popularity.
2. Jima is a small 'peasant' village located in the centre of the greater Cuenca region.

Bibliography
Archetti, Eduardo P. 1997: *Guinea-pigs: Food, Symbol and Conflict of Knowledge in Ecuador* (Oxford, Berg).
Bauman, Zygmunt 1998: 'Postmodern Religion?' in Heelas, P. (ed.), *Religion, Modernity and Postmodernity* (London, Blackwell), 55–79.
Bauman, Zygmunt 2000: *Liquid Modernity* (Cambridge, Polity Press).
Bohannan, Paul 1967 [1959]: 'The Impact of Money on an African Subsistence Economy', in Dalton, G. (ed), *Tribal and Peasant Economies: Readings in Economic Anthropology* (Texas, University of Texas Press), 123–135.
Bourdieu, Pierre 1977: *Outline of a Theory of Practice*, translated by Richard Nice (Cambridge, Cambridge University Press).
Bourque, Nicole 2001: 'Eating Your Words: Communicating with Food in the Ecuadorian Andes', in

Hendry J. and C.W. Watson (eds), *An Anthropology of Indirect Communication* (London, Routledge), 85–100.

Bugge, Anenchen B. 2011: 'Lovin' It?: A Study of Youth and the Culture of Fast Food', *Food, Culture & Society* 14(1), 71–89.

Caldwell, Melissa L. 2004: 'Domesticating the French Fry: McDonald's and Consumerism in Moscow', *Journal of Consumer Culture* 4(1), 5–26.

Cobo, Bernabe 1979 [1653]: *History of the Inca Empire: An Account of the Indians' Customs and their Origins together with a Treatize on Inca Legends, History and Social Institutions*, translated and edited by Roland Hamilton (Austin, University of Texas Press).

Douglas, Mary 2002 [1966]: *Purity and Danger: An Analysis of Concepts of Pollution and Taboo* (London, Routledge and K. Paul).

Gade, Daniel W. 1967: 'The Guinea Pig in Andean Folk Culture', *Geographical Review* 57(2), 213–224.

Habermas, Jurgen 1987: *The Philosophical Discourse of Modernity: Twelve Lectures,* translated by F. Lawrence (Cambridge, Polity Press).

Lévi-Strauss, Claude 1968: *Structural Anthropology*, Volume 1, translated by C. Jacobson and B. Grundfest Schoepf (London, Allen Lane, Penguin Press).

Lozada Jr., Eriberto P. 2000: 'Globalized Childhood? Kentucky Fried Chicken in Beijing', in Jing, J. (ed.), *Feeding China's Little Emperors: Food, Children and Social Change* (Stanford, CA, Stanford University Press), 114–134.

Oldakowski, Ray and John McEwen 2010: 'The Diffusion of American Fast Food in Ecuador', *Material Culture* 42(2), 28–49.

Poma de Ayala, Guaman 1978 [1613]: *Nueva Coronica y Buen Gobierno* (London, Allen & Unwin).

Ritzer, George 2010: *McDonaldization: The Reader* (LA, Pine Forge Press).

Simmel, Georg 1978: *The Philosophy of Money,* translated by T. Bottomore and D. Frisby (London, Routledge and Kegan Paul).

Turner Bryan S. 2003: 'McDonaldization: Linearity and Liquidity in Consumer Cultures', *American Behavioral Scientist* 47(2), 137–153.

Watson, James L. 2000: 'China's Big Mac Attack', *Foreign Affairs* 79(3), 120–134.

Watson, James L. (ed.) 1997: *Golden Arches East: McDonald's in East Asia* (Stanford, CA, Stanford University Press).

Weismantel, Mary J. 1988: *Food, Gender and Poverty in the Ecuadorian Andes* (Philadelphia, University of Pennsylvania Press).

Wing, Elizabeth 1986: 'Domestication of Andean Mammals', in Vuilleumier F. and M. Monasterio (eds.), *High Altitude Tropical Biogeography* (Oxford, Oxford University Press), 246–264.

Yan, Yunxiang 2000: 'Of Hamburger and Social Space: Consuming McDonald's in Beijing', in David, D. S. (ed.) *The Consumer Revolution in Urban China* (Berkeley, University of California Press), 201–225.

Celebrating Solitude: M.F.K. Fisher on Dining Alone

Robert Appelbaum

Performance theory has its origins in a number of academic disciplines, among them sociology, anthropology, theatre studies, and philosophy. Erving Goffmann, in his seminal work *The Presentation of the Self in Everyday Life,* taught sociologists to take seriously the expression in Shakespeare, which Shakespeare himself found in classical sources, that 'all the world is a stage'. Our social lives are performances within what Shakespeare and his contemporaries liked to call 'the theatre of the world'. Similarly, the anthropologist Victor Turner stressed that collective behaviour commonly took the form of 'dramas' where a groups of individuals improvised structured actions in response to social crises, at once making things up as they went along and obeying unwritten codes of ritualistic behaviour. Meanwhile, theatre director and critic Richard Schechner, a founder of *The Drama Review*, encouraged the view that drama was politics and politics was drama, and then went on, with Turner's cooperation, to make 'performance studies' a new discipline, or rather an inter-discipline where social theory was combined with the analysis of drama and other kinds of performative art and practice. And in philosophy, both Anglo-American and Continental traditions have inclined toward elaborations of performance theory with regard to linguistic and epistemological inquiry. The analytic philosopher J.L. Austin demonstrated how language itself was inherently 'performative': one could not only make statements, one could also 'do things' with words. Speech included a number of 'speech acts', and to say 'I do' at a wedding ceremony was not only to assert a proposition but to transform oneself and others. Jacques Derrida and other deconstructive philosophers developed Austin's theory in a radical direction, devising the term 'performativity' to indicate how even the most inward forms of behaviour, including the realization of one's gender identity, operate as reiterations of scripts, performances in keeping with previously devised and often unconscious codes; even sexuality, on this head, is a kind of drama.

The relevance of performance theory to the idea of a 'celebration' and the topic of this conference almost goes without saying. A celebration is a kind of ritual, and any celebration which features food is a kind of food ritual. Sometimes celebrations take on religious or quasi-religious meanings and process what Turner calls 'liminality', that is, the transition from one state of affairs to another. The first cutting of a wedding cake is one such liminal celebration. Even after the necessary parties say 'I do', the marriage still hasn't completely taken place until the cake is cut. But other celebrations are not so much liminal as reiterative. Thanksgiving meals, for example, going back to ancient Hebrew times, commemorate. They commemorate in an expression of gratitude and conviviality and confirm a covenant. But they do not *change* anything. The celebrants are the same people, with the same social and religious status, that they were before the meals began.

But performance theory encourages us to think of celebratory meals in the abstract, as 'dramas' of one kind or another, whether liminal, commemorative, or otherwise ceremonial. In addition, the theory encourages us to try to think of such social rites from a value-neutral position, a position oriented toward a social grammar, as it were, rather than a social semantics. What matters for performance theory, in the first place, is the structure of the performance, not its meaning. Following Schechner, and momentarily putting aside questions of meaning and value, we can therefore think of any celebratory meal as exemplifying at least these five structural characteristics:

1. The act involves a special ordering of time.
2. The act attaches a special value to objects.
3. The act is economically non-productive.
4. The act requires that participants abide by rules specific to the act.
5. Participants act, abiding by their rules, as if (or as in fact really) performing before an audience.[1]

Thus the grammar of the celebratory meal, in five of its most important aspects. No doubt, other aspects could be cited, but these may do for our purposes here. Any celebratory meal, in keeping with these structural qualities, will in the first place order time in a way that is different from the norm of everyday life: and so a Thanksgiving meal in America, or a Passover Seder in Jewish tradition, or a Christmas meal in most of Europe, will entail an *elongation* of the meal time, as well as a *prescription of sequence*. And in the second place, such a meal will attach special values to foodstuffs and the paraphernalia that accompany them. The turkey, the lamb, the goose, the cranberry dressing, the *charoset*, the Christmas pudding, along with the special plates, decorations and ritual objects: all of these things are objects which have a performative value specific to the occasion, and they take their meaning on this occasion from it. And in the third place, then, the meal is *non-productive*; that is, it does not involve work or the creation of wealth; the celebratory meal may entail symbolic work and symbolic exchange, but it is above all an occasion of consumption and expenditure. Fourthly, all of these transformations of the everyday, the ordering of time, the special valuing of objects and the non-productivity of the meal, follow according to certain rules, whether unwritten (as in the case of Thanksgiving) or written (as in the case of Passover). And finally, when participants engage in these celebrations, they know that they are performing in front of one another, whether well or badly; they show themselves to be abiding by the rules or not, to express the decorum appropriate to the occasion or not, to be enjoying themselves appropriately or not, and so forth. One can imagine someone having a Thanksgiving, a Passover, or a Christmas dinner alone, with all the trappings; one can even imagine someone having such a dinner in front of a television, watching other people having a celebratory meal, or watching

Celebrating Solitude: M.F.K. Fisher on Dining Alone

a film about Thanksgiving, or Passover, or Christmas. But we are inclined not only to think that such a thing would be sad and alienated, but also to observe that such a meal would not be quite the real thing. It would lack community, and for lack of community it could not be completely *performed*. A celebratory meal is a performance because it orders time in a special way, because it attaches special value to the objects it employs, because it is a non-productive rather than productive activity, because it follows according to certain written or unwritten rules, and perhaps above all because it requires a community of performers, each of whom is performing the meal in front of the others.

* * * * *

Now all of this might seem to make dining alone, the subject of this essay, not only sad and alienated, but also lacking in form and drama. A celebratory meal is a performance of community, within a community and by a community. But a dinner of one, even on a ceremonial occasion, cannot seem to be *performed*; it is not *performable*. At best, a dinner of one, undertaken in a ceremonial spirit, would seem to be a *simulacrum* of a celebration. This would seem to be the case even if we broaden our understanding of what constitutes a celebration to include occasions like dinner parties or romantic suppers. Dinner parties and romantic suppers, too, can be regarded as performances where time is ordered in a special way and so forth. For that matter even a family meal can be celebratory. To make a meal into a celebration, all one seems to need to do is to make it into a performance, whatever the occasion: to use the meal as a momentary transformation of the structure of time and matter, of economy and behaviour, and above all of community. A celebratory meal is any meal of form and drama, where the participants are consciously involved in the reproduction of form and the performance of a drama. But a dinner of one, then, would seem to be incapable of fulfilling a celebratory function. For it cannot be performed in the full sense of the word.

There is something socially important about the apparent inability of the solitary meal to fulfil a celebratory function. For never in modern history have so many people in the developed world gotten into the habit of taking their meals alone, and apparently without ceremony. In Britain today, according to a report from a few years ago, nearly half of all meals taken at home are eaten alone. I quote from the BBC account of the 2004 report, for the language is revealing:

> Nearly half the meals eaten in the UK are now eaten alone, research found last year. In the past 20 years, the number has soared from 4bn to 12bn, much of which is due to the explosion in 'meals for one'. One analyst said: 'We have reached the situation where people no longer even buy dining tables because they have effectively become redundant.' Half of all the money spent on ready-meals in the EU is spent in the UK, a report last year found, with Brits shelling out £7,000 a minute on them.[2]

Celebrating Solitude: M.F.K. Fisher on Dining Alone

Dining tables are 'redundant', of course, because the meals are eaten in front of the television set, where individuals dining alone enjoy the simulacra of community that television broadcasting provides. Although the BBC report is a bit obsessed with the economic aspects of dining alone – how much is *spent* on this and that – it is much more important to think about what this phenomenon means for the quality of life in the United Kingdom. In that vein, it would be interesting to find out how many people in Britain enjoy their evening meal, alone, while watching programmes like *Come Dine with Me*, where a group of four people on camera take turns providing celebratory meals for one another, in a competition to see which of them is the best host. Certainly, it would seem that the majority of the people eating their meals alone in the United Kingdom today are still supplementing their experience with a form of entertainment that simulates, in the space of one's dining area, the physical and dramatic presence, the bodies, movements, voices and emotions of other people. This is a quality of life issue indeed. Raising the issue in this way already implies a critique of the phenomenon in question, already suggests the idea that we in the modern world are *too* alone, and even that there is something wrong with the grammar of aloneness. And perhaps we need not be so negative about the phenomenon. But we do need to address it: people are dining alone, surrounding themselves with the simulacra of togetherness; and they are not, by and large, dining particularly well. They are eating ready-meals.

Yet there would seem to be an alternative to this alienated form of dining alone – a dining alone which recognizes that aloneness need not be rejected, and that both aloneness and the dining experience of aloneness can be celebrated. And it turns out that a great advocate of dining alone is that most innovative and influential of food writers M.F.K. Fisher (1908–1992). Dining alone is a recurrent theme in her work, especially the early work compiled in a collection known as *The Art of Eating* (originally published in 1954). It would seem that the meaning of dining alone – the significance of it, the value and the joy it – is a crucial problem for the ethics of gastronomy that Fisher tries to construct. To put the question in the terms of performance theory, one may ask, along with Fisher, whether dining alone can involve a special ordering of time, a special valuation of objects, a mode of non-productivity, an observance of rules and a kind of dramatics performed as in front of an audience? And if so, what would it look like? And what would it mean?

Fisher answers yes to the first question, and fleshes out answers to the other two questions, in her early essay in *Serve It Forth*, entitled 'On Dining Alone'. She begins the essay by retelling a story (with considerable poetic liberty, as we will see) from Plutarch's *Parallel Lives*:

> Lucullus, the Roman host whose dinners are still talked about for their elaborate menus and their fabulous cost, grew tired one day of dining with other men.
>
> He ordered a meal for one person. When it was served to him, he was conscious of a certain slackness: the wine was perhaps a shade too cold, and the

sauce for the carp, which certainly was less succulent than usual, lacked that tang for which the chef was justly famed.

Lucullus frowned and summoned the major-domo.

'Perhaps, perhaps', that official agreed, with a flood of respectful salutations. 'We thought that there was no need to prepare a fine banquet for my lord alone–'

'It is precisely when I am alone', the great gourmet answered, icily, 'that you must pay special attention to the dinner. At such times, you must remember, Lucullus dines with Lucullus.'³

Fisher calls attention, in this passage, to what might be called a ceremony of the self. She thinks it is a valuable thing for even the most average of people: 'An occasional meal with himself is very good for Mr Doe.' She does not think that dining alone is the best way to dine, but imagines that it has its place in the larger scheme of the art of eating. For Mr Doe, 'It gives him an opportunity to look about him; quiet in which to savour his present mouthful; opportunity to broil his steak a new way or try again those dishes his wife hates'.⁴ What would seem to be missing in this sort of dining are two things: a ceremonial occasion and an audience. But the implication is that a person can provide his or her own occasion, that one can momentarily celebrate one's self, and even one's solitude, by taking a good meal alone. Moreover, a person can play the role of one's own audience. Lucullus dines with Lucullus. Lucullus can *perform* the act of dining in front of himself, given the special occasion of dining alone. And when he does so, he will have before him objects of a special value, a 'special attention' being paid to what he eats. He may even find himself following special rules of dining.

Fisher, however, neglects one of the other aspects of the Lucullus ceremony of the self, although it is implied in what she says: she neglects the fact that the Lucullus ceremony is 'non-productive'. It is never just to feed himself and fulfil a biological need so he can go on with his business in the world that Lucullus wants on occasion to dine alone, and it is never just to do so economically. On the contrary, it is important to Lucullus that he be fed with a surplus of expenditure, of time, effort, and money. Moreover, it is important that he command this expenditure in view of a kind of bargain with himself, as if he were the guest of himself, the recipient of the hospitality of his self. The original version of this story, in Plutarch, makes this a little clearer, and in the course of the story forefronts an idea that Fisher possibly deliberately avoids, the notion of pride:

> [T]hat Lucullus took not only pleasure but pride in this way of living, is clear from the anecdotes recorded of him. It is said, for instance, that he entertained for many successive days some Greeks who had come up to Rome, and that they, with genuinely Greek scruples, were at last ashamed to accept his invitation, on the ground that he was incurring so much expense every day on their account; whereupon Lucullus said to them with a smile, 'Some of this expense, my

Grecian friends, is indeed on your account; most of it, however, is on account of Lucullus.' And once, when he was dining alone, and a modest repast of one course had been prepared for him, he was angry, and summoned the servant who had the matter in charge. The servant said that he did not suppose, since there were no guests, that he wanted anything very costly. 'What sayest thou?' said the master, 'dost thou not know that today Lucullus dines with Lucullus?'[5]

This 'pride', or 'glory', as another translator might put it, in a 'way of living' – σεμνυνόμενος τῷ βίῳ τούτῳ δῆλος – is a condition of that self-mirroring that is necessary in order for Lucullus to dine with himself ceremonially; it is also a chief cause, along with what Plutarch simply calls 'pleasure' (ἡδόμενος) for the sake of which the gastronome, though dining alone, will insist on excessive expenditure. Pride and non-productivity go hand in hand in the life of someone like Lucullus because he operates in a world of patronage, where power consists in one's ability to be generous to others; and where therefore it follows that one of the highest expressions of power may come in the form of generosity to oneself, shown in all its glory to oneself.

In fact, in 'On Dining Alone', Fisher embraces this sort of generosity to the self, embraces the celebration of solitude it enables, embraces the idea that when, even alone, one can arrange to eat as if in the midst of a ceremonial occasion, one has arrived at a moment of self-gratification. But Fisher also stresses that solitary diners celebrating their own solitude should not be trying to impress themselves, to indulge in something like self-glorification. Plutarch implies that that is what Lucullus was doing. Plutarch is not in fact an admirer of Lucullus' gastronomy, and he thinks the kind of self-mirroring involved as something more or less frivolous and vain.[6] Fisher, however, imagines that Lucullus and his modern imitators are doing something essential, not to impress themselves but to express themselves, not to accomplish something for which they may be proud to reveal to themselves but to explore a part of themselves that they need to come to terms with. We need, Fisher asserts, to be a spectacle of ourselves to ourselves, if only in order to know ourselves; and this spectacle entails not only something we do in our mind's eye but also something we do with our hands, mouths, and tongues.

So according to Fisher there is, or can be, an alternative to both that dining in company which is properly ceremonial and that un-ceremonial dining alone which is sad, alienated, and phony. There is a the celebration of solitude by way of the special occasion of a solitary meal. And Fisher has examples to demonstrate what she means. But the examples are bit strange; they take place not in solitude but in busy restaurants. In one of them, in Los Angeles, a young woman sits for four hours in a Viennese kosher delicatessen, dawdling over a cup of coffee and pastries; in another, also in Los Angeles, an old man dines on the same meal every night, alone, complete with a sugared, liquor-drenched avocado for dessert. Fisher claims that these people were 'happy' as they ate and drank alone, and perhaps they were. But there seems to something fragile about their happiness, and something not entirely alone about it either.

Celebrating Solitude: M.F.K. Fisher on Dining Alone

In other essays in *Serve It Forth* and the other books compiled in *The Art of Eating*, Fisher provides the reader with a number of glances of herself eating alone. The emphasis is frequently on an enjoyment that is also self-exploratory and self-assertive. But it is hard to escape the impression that a lingering sadness underlies her solitary enjoyments. Sitting in a small flat in depression-era Strasbourg, alone, with nothing to do, on an afternoon when her husband has gone away to teach or study, treating herself to 'magical' tangerines, heated and plumped on the radiator; adventuring alone on an ocean liner, returning to America to tell her parents about her decision to divorce her husband and marry another man, who was terminally ill; learning how to make a spectacle of herself and independence in the ship's dining-room, ordering her own lone table, making herself the cynosure of waiters, cooks, and fellow passengers – in such situations she finds a happiness that serves as a defence against impending tragedy.

Then comes a final essay, opening her *Alphabet for Gourmands*, 'A is for dining Alone'. Her second husband is dead now, a victim of suicide in response to the agony of his illness, and she is working as a script consultant in Hollywood, living alone in a flat too small to have a proper hob and oven, or even a dining table. 'And so I am', she begins – dining alone, that is – 'if a choice must be made between most people I know and myself. This misanthropic attitude is one I am not proud of, but it is firmly there, based on my increasing conviction that sharing food with another human being is an intimate act that should not be indulged in lightly.'[7] Aloneness has been imposed upon Fisher. For the purposes of this essay being alone is always second best; the first best thing, as she puts it, would be to have the 'One' with her at her side. For want of 'One', solitude may be best because togetherness is never sufficient. But solitude has to be struggled with and mastered. One has to learn how to feed oneself when one is alone, how to make a celebration out of it. One has to learn how to eat in restaurants alone, and nourish oneself. And more important, one has to learn to eat alone in the solitude of one's apartment. 'Never be daunted in public', Fisher remembers Ernest Hemingway having once said. But now she has teach herself another principle: 'Never be daunted in private'.[8]

In pursuit of this ceremony of the self, the solitary diner has no occasion to appeal to except her own conviction that she needs to take care for herself. She has no special objects to enjoy, except those which she has chosen out of concern for pleasure, convenience and nourishment, for what she calls her 'own chemical pattern'. She does not have the luxury of suspending her need to be productive, except so far as she is determined not to surrender to the merely practical, and allow herself whatever surplus expenditure she can afford. As for rules, she has to make them up as she goes along, eating and drinking what she finds her hungers incline her to eat and drink. And as for performance – well, she will have to be aware of acting in front of herself, for the benefit of herself. 'If *One* could not be with me', she concludes, ' … then I was my best companion'.[9] But to be one's own companion takes special effort too.

* * * * *

Celebrating Solitude: M.F.K. Fisher on Dining Alone

What performance theory may alert us to is that even our most intimate moments involve 'performativity'. In the case of communal celebratory meals, some of the performance is unthinking and some thinking. When Thanksgiving comes, Americans already know what they are supposed to do; they can take the form of the ceremony for granted. Yet they know that they have to live up to the form of the ceremony, they have to take responsibility for it; in a word, they have to *do* Thanksgiving. Thinking and unthinking then, the participants in a celebratory, communal meal are both reflective and unreflective, active and passive, inventive and uninventive.

If M.F.K. Fisher is our guide in these matters, dining alone in a mode of celebration is even more difficult. One celebrates one's solitude, yes. But doing so is difficult. There is always a suspicion that dining alone is second best; there may always be an absence present when one eats alone. The solitude may often be incomplete: there are waiters in the dining-room, and fellow diners. Even when at home, there may be voices from the apartment next door, or from the radio on the shelf. But dining alone in a mode of celebration is a way of caring for oneself, a way of thinking, of being reflective, active, and inventive. The ready-meal, heated in a microwave, eaten on a sofa in front of a television with *Come Dine With Me* on the screen, may present the very picture of passivity, along with simulation and alienation. But according to Fisher, when one dines with oneself, when one allows oneself to perform a celebratory meal in front of oneself, when in effect one performs one's own performativity, one is inevitably reflective, active, and inventive. Even if *One* is not there, there is nevertheless a companion in the room, and a special meal with which to entertain her.

Notes

1. Richard Schechner, *Performance Theory*, second edition (London and New York: Routledge, 1988), esp. 8–14. Also see Victor Turner, 'Social Dramas and Stories about Them', *Critical Inquiry*, 7.1 (1980): 141–168, and Turner, *The Anthropology of Performance* (New York: PAJ Publications, 1986).
2. 'Portrait of the "Meal for One" Society'. *BBC News* 30 January 2004: http://news.bbc.co.uk/1/hi/magazine/3445091.stm (accessed 20 April 2011).
3. M.F.K. Fisher, *The Art of Dining* (Hoboken, NJ: Wiley, 2004): 96.
4. Fisher 96.
5. Plutarch, *Parallel Lives*, Loeb edition (Cambridge, MA: Harvard, 1914), vol. 2: 603. http://penelope.uchicago.edu/Thayer/E/Roman/Texts/Plutarch/Lives/Lucullus*.html (accessed 20 April 2011).
6. Plutarch 599.
7. Fisher 577.
8. Fisher 580.
9. Fisher 581.

Celebration and Japanese Food

Kimiko Barber

On the day of the one-month anniversary of the magnitude 9.0 earthquake and tsunami that devastated the north-eastern part of Japan it was hard to think how, or whether, I could rework this paper based on the theme of 'celebration'. The natural disaster quickly turned into a man-made nuclear crisis when the Fukushima Dai-ichi nuclear power plant was crippled and began spreading radioactive contamination first into the atmosphere and then into the ocean, raising huge health concerns not just within the country but also internationally. The disaster has not only reshaped the landscape of the region but has shaken the whole nation to the core and badly damaged the image of Japanese food on a global scale.

The news from the stricken nuclear plant is still far from clear, and many countries continue to impose import bans on Japanese food. Although Japanese food export accounts for only one per cent of GDP and the export ban will have minimal economic effect, it is the reputation that has been questioned. Japanese fresh fruits and vegetables sold abroad in places such as in Hong Kong, Taiwan, and Korea were known for their high quality and safety and commanded a premium status. The nuclear disaster changed all that with no immediate prospect of improvement, and in fact there seems little to celebrate in my country's food scene.

But let's pause here for a moment. Japan is a mountainous archipelago that is peculiarly vulnerable to natural calamity – typhoons, floods, landslides, earthquakes, and of course tsunamis. Yet its extremes of longitude and geographical features mean that Japan is also one of the most climate-diverse places on the planet. And the special character of Japanese food culture is its closeness to nature and its fundamental appreciation of seasonality.

Japanese 'food celebration' has its origins in sacred ritual and ceremony and contains important elements of appeasement to mother nature / the gods as well as gratitude for the seasonal gifts, which come and go irrespective of nature's caprices. And so at the time of a national tragedy such as this, the celebration of Japanese food holds all the more poignant significance.

Cooks in Japan aspire to 'draw out natural tastes from each season's offerings'; because they believe nature is best. Seasonal foods reflect Japan's cultural attitudes as well as define its cuisine. Japan has four distinctive seasons and every food has its *shun* that loosely translates as 'the season when food is bountiful and tastes at its best'. Eating *shun no mono* – food in season – ensures that Japanese tastes are in harmony with nature and also the freshest possible seasonal ingredients. *Shun* can last weeks or even a few months; alternatively it can be a fleeting moment of just a matter of a few hours. Each season is associated with particular foods; symbolic foods of spring are bonito fish and bamboo shoot, followed by rape flower and various wild mountain plants such as *warabi* (bracken) and *zenmai* (fiddleheads). In summer it is eel, *edamame*, cucumber, and water melon; while *sanma* (Pacific saury), sweet chestnuts, persimmon, and wide varieties of mushrooms symbolize autumn; and in winter blowfish, yellowtail, giant white radish, and *hakusai* (Chinese cabbage) abound.

However, this can be a difficult concept to grasp nowadays when supermarket shelves are filled with fruits and vegetables flown in from far-flung countries almost all year round with little respect for the season. The seasonality of produce has become blurred, and it seems that our senses have become blunted and the pleasures of anticipation diminished. When a new seasonal food first appears on the market, it is generally in short supply, the price is always high (if not extreme), and it doesn't necessarily taste its best. But Japanese gourmets and top-class restaurateurs are eager to catch the first of any seasonal delicacies, and there is a saying in Japan that every time you eat *hatsu-mono* (first season food), you lengthen your life by 75 days. In contrast, when a meal includes *nagori-mono* (end of season food), it is said to be enriched with the sentiment of a prolonged farewell, knowing it will be another year before that food appears on the table once again.

The Japanese calendar is studded with seasonal and religious celebrations and festivals that call for certain special foods; pale pink sweets and rice cakes are served for the Dolls' Festival on 3 March to celebrate the well-being of little girls, while sweet rice dumplings are prepared for the Spring and Autumn Equinox. Japanese festive celebrations are closely tied to the season in particular with rice farming, and many have Chinese/Buddhist origins and form the basic structure of the yearly calendar. At the beginning of the seventh century, the Japanese imperial court adopted Buddhism and with it came many things including the lunar calendar. Imperial festivals slowly spread throughout the country, steadily influenced by the samurai warrior class who became dominant from the twelfth century onwards. But it was under the powerful Tokugawa clan who ruled throughout the Edo period (1603–1868) that food culture was further enriched by many regional folk traditions and spread nationwide.

By far the most important and the first seasonal celebration in Japan is the New Year, on the first three days of January. There are four key foods associated with the New Year celebration – *kagami-mochi* (two large disc-size rice cakes), *o-toso* (herbal infused sweet sake), *o-zoni* (a special New Year soup with *mochi*, rice cake – its tastes and styles differ according to region, and each family has its own traditional recipe) and a cooked preserved food called *o-sechi* – an abbreviation for *o-sechi-ku*, which means season or a significant day of one's life. Originally *o-sechi* cuisine came from China and was adapted by the imperial court in the ancient capital of Kyoto during the Heian period (794–1185). It was originally prepared at five seasonal celebrations but later became confined to the New Year. Here the emperor worshipped his ancestral Sun Goddess, the legendary creator of Japan, to pray for a good harvest and a healthy, prosperous year with offerings of food and drink.

Each Japanese New Year food has its own meaning and symbolism or is used for auspicious word play. For example, the two large disc-size rice cakes called *kagami-mochi*, which means 'mirror rice cake', are said to represent heart/life and to symbolize the sun and the moon. It is called mirror because legend has it that the Sun Goddess hid herself in a rock cave after an argument with her wayward brother and the world descended into darkness, so the ancient Japanese people forged a large mirror as an offering and sang and danced just outside the cave to entice her out.

O-sechi cuisine is always presented in highly stylized forms in four-tiered special lacquered boxes. The contents of the top tier differ between the eastern Tokyo region and the western Kyoto style – in the east, black soybeans/*kuro-mame* (*mame*/bean also means 'diligence'), salted herring roe/*kazunoko* (*kazu* means 'numerous' and *ko* means 'child', symbolizing a wish for being blessed with many children) and caramelized baby sardines/*tazukuri* (literally meaning 'rice paddy maker' as the fish were traditionally used for fertilizing rice fields); while in the western, Kyoto style, burdock replaces the sardines. Cooked sweet chestnuts, rolled sweet omelettes, as well as broiled red and white fish cakes are other common occupants of the top tier.

The second tier contains grilled fish such as yellowtail, salmon, and the essential *tai* (sea bream) – the Japanese name *tai* contains the same sound as *medetai*, meaning 'auspicious', and no celebratory table is complete without this fish. The third tier is for simmered vegetables such as burdock, carrot, and rolled, seasoned seaweeds. In the bottom, fourth tier sit vinegar-preserved items such as sardine, sierra, turnip, and lotus root.

The universal rule of New Year *o-sechi* foods is that they are all cooked to preserve and to last for several days, because Japanese housewives traditionally abstained from cooking and using fire in the kitchen during the first three-day celebration in deference to the kitchen fire god. The only exception is the cooking of *o-zoni*/New Year soup with *mochi*, rice cake. Although today many housewives buy in ready-prepared *o-sechi* food from shops, especially in large cities, traditionally it was prepared at home during the second half of December. As in the West, the run-up to the New Year is the busiest time for households in Japan and the month is traditionally called *shiwasu*, meaning 'rushing priests', because even normally calm and serene priests are in a hurry.

On the seventh day of the New Year, Japanese people eat the seven-herb rice porridge according to an ancient Chinese tradition, in the belief that it wards off evil spirits and keeps them healthy. In the old days, housewives rose at daybreak and foraged for herbs in nearby fields and cooked the porridge for breakfast. The traditional practice is based on a sound health principles – rice porridge is easy to digest and is a welcome respite for the over-worked stomach after the rich New Year festive food, while the herbs provide scarce fresh vegetables.

During *hina matsuri*, the Dolls' Festival on 3 March that celebrates and prays for young girls, families adorn special sets of dolls that depict the old imperial court on a step-altar and make offerings of pale-coloured rice cakes. Setting up the *hina* dolls is an elaborate affair that can take the good part of a day, but it is an elegant and enjoyable seasonal activity, which is traditionally done by mothers and daughters sometime around the second half of February. First the doll set has to be taken out of storage and the step-altar has to be erected and covered with the special crimson red cloth before the dolls can be positioned. The emperor and the empress dolls sit on the top tier, the three ladies-in-waiting on the second level, followed by five court musicians with their tiny instruments, and on the fourth level the two grand chamberlains guard miniature table displays. Below are the three court jesters seated between model trees of mandarin and peach, and finally the two bottom levels display a collection of miniature furniture, a model palanquin, and an ox-drawn carriage. Food for the occasion varies from region to region and family to family but the traditional must-haves are; pink-, white-, and pale green-coloured rice cakes cut into diamond shapes called *hishi mochi*; opaque non-alcoholic sweet sake; and pale pink and white puffed rice sweets. My mother and grandmothers always added to the festivity with consommé-style soup with clams and a big platter of colourful scattered sushi with pink fish flakes and bright yellow scrambled eggs.

Cherry-blossoms are Japan's favourite bloom and signal the arrival of spring. Diners in top restaurants, especially in Kyoto, may be served a cup of slightly salty and fragrant cherry-blossom tea. Cherry-blossom viewing parties are a favourite seasonal must-do in Japan, and every year the Meteorological Agency provides daily updates of the *sakura zensen* (cherry-blossom front) in its weather report. There is no fixed menu for the occasion; people pack lunch boxes with whatever food they like, but always featuring seasonal favourites like succulent bamboo shoots, soft squid, and shellfish, all to be consumed under fragrant blossoms with copious amounts of sake.

The fifth of May is the traditional Boys' Festival, but since 1948 the day has been called *kodomo-no-hi* (Childrens' Day) to celebrate the well-being of all young children. Families hoist large cloth carp streamers outside, and samurai warrior dolls in miniature armour are displayed by the entrance alcove. The sight of colourful carp streamers flying high in the wind against the backdrop of a clear blue sky is marvellous. The celebration is not complete without special foods: *chimaki*, steamed rice wrapped in bamboo leaves, and *kashiwa-mochi,* oak-leaf-wrapped sweet rice dumplings with adzuki bean jam inside. Other seasonal food like bamboo shoots and bonito fish are also featured on the festive table.

Tanabata, the Star Festival on the seventh of July, also traces its origin to an ancient Chinese legend but has become distinctively Japanese over the centuries and reflects Japanese values and the aspiration for technical achievements and hard work. The legend is based on a story of Princess Shukujo the weaver (represented by Vega), and her husband Kengyu, the ox-herd (represented by Altair), who lived on the west side of the Heavenly River, which is also known as the Milky Way. The princess was a hard working and skilled weaver, making beautiful cloth for the gods in her imperial father's mansion on the eastern side of the river, and the emperor chose Kengyu to be her groom. But the young couple's honeymoon lasted far too long, and they both neglected their duties, angering the gods and the emperor. So the emperor decided to punish them by separating the couple on opposite sides of the river and only allowing them to meet one night every year. Today people throughout Japan celebrate the day by writing their wishes on colourful strips of paper and tying them onto freshly cut bamboo branches, which are floated down rivers. Other common decorations are colourful paper streamers, which are said to symbolize the weaving of threads, and fishing nets that mean good luck for fishing and farming. Many towns and cities hold festivals and display decorations in main streets. Seasonal vegetables such as cucumbers and aubergines are prepared and chilled fine-strand somen noodles are eaten.

The city of Sendai is particularly famous for its *Tanabata* festival – it is said to have been started some 400 years ago by the local warlord Masamune Date (1567–1636), and is held for three days between 6 and 8 August in accordance with the lunar calendar. Today, local business and shops sponsor the event, displaying huge elaborate decorations made with bamboo all around the city as if in a beauty contest. Unique to Sendai are the Seven Ornaments, which embody prayers for progress in studies, calligraphy, family happiness and wellbeing, good health and longevity, prosperous business, a large fish catch, and a good harvest. The event became more and more grandiose in style, especially after the end of the Second World War, aiming to revitalize the local community. And in keeping of the spirit of recovery from the tsunami, the city authority has announced that they are resolutely going ahead with the festival this summer.

Early July through mid-August marks the hottest days in Japan, and since the eighteenth century Japanese people have been eating grilled freshwater eels to gain energy and to help them survive the sticky humid summer weather. On the 'Day of the ox in the midsummer Dog Days period' defined by ecliptic longitudes of the sun and therefore changing in date slightly every year – 27 July this year – nearly a quarter of the annual eel consumption takes place. This culinary habit is believed to have been started by an eighteenth-century doctor, writer, inventor, and artist called Gennai Hiraga, who came up with a sales slogan to help his eel restaurateur friend, encouraging people in Edo (old Tokyo) to eat eel on the day. Indeed, eels are highly nutritious; rich in vitamins A, B1, B2, E and calcium. Many old restaurants have their own secret and delicious sweet eel-basting sauces that have been kept for generations. Eel is commonly glaze-grilled over charcoals, and fat from the fish drips and burns, creating an irresistible mixture of the basting-sauce-infused smoke which seduces many customers into the restaurants every summer.

The ninth day of the ninth month was traditionally the chrysanthemum festival, but it is hardly celebrated nowadays; instead many horticultural events, especially showing chrysanthemums, are held throughout the country. By mid-September the summer heat begins to give way to quieter, longer evenings, and farmers pray for dry autumn weather for rice to ripen. In ancient times Japanese people adopted an old Chinese custom of holding *tsukimi*, a moon-viewing evening on 15 August in the lunar calendar when the moon is said to be at its brightest, but not necessarily full. A stack of fifteen ping-pong-sized rice dumplings on a tray, cooked taro, *edamame*, and seasonal fruits such as sweet chestnuts and grapes are offered with a vase decoration of pampas grass and other autumn flowers. *Tsukimi* evenings are traditionally celebrated quietly at home.

Autumn is a season of plenty. Fish such as Pacific saury, sardine, and mackerel, and other foods such as Japanese pear, persimmon, sweet chestnuts, aubergine, and corn – just to name a few – are at their best. But by far the single most sought-after autumn taste is *matsutake* mushroom: Japan's equivalent of white truffle in its rarity, expense, taste and aroma. Japan's home demand far outstrips its domestic supply, and imports from China, Korea, and Canada fill the gap, but connoisseurs and top restaurant chefs always prefer home produce and are prepared to pay as much as £100 per pound or more. Like cherry-blossom viewing parties in the spring, Japanese people go out to the countryside to enjoy autumn leaves or to forage for mushrooms and sweet chestnuts.

The onset of winter brings fish like yellowtail, sierra, plaice, bluefin tuna, and (the most awaited) blowfish, which must be prepared expertly by a licensed chef. The cold season's favourite cooking is *nabe*, hot-pot stews that guarantee to warm up the body and soul. *Nabe* is the most convivial and relaxed way of cooking that brings people together. If a Japanese person invites another to share a *nabe* with him, this is an ultimate invitation to friendship; he likes you enough to dip his chopsticks into a communal hot-pot. *Nabe* is the season's most popular method of cooking and probably the first choice for end-of-year parties. There are numerous regional variations featuring local ingredients.

And finally, on New Year's Eve, families traditionally gather round tables to eat hot bowls of soba noodles – *toshi-koshi soba* – that literally means year-crossing soba, as the noodle symbolizes a long healthy life in the upcoming year. The choice of soba noodle also has a pragmatic reason because traditional Japanese housewives would have been busy cooking and cleaning for the New Year celebration and would prefer to make something quick, simple, and nourishing for the last evening meal of a year.

And so the annual cycle begins again. This spring, when I was in Japan shortly after the earthquake and tsunami, there was much talk of national *jishuku* – self-restraint – and the cancellation of *o-hanami*, cherry-blossom viewing parties. In a nation of stoics, the most patient quiet sufferers, by common consent, are from the poor north-eastern region where the earthquake and tsunami struck. They are renowned for their gritty *gaman*, endurance, even by Japanese standards. But in the end, the seasonal festivals and celebrations centred on seasonal foods will continue and provide a measure of comfort in adversity, especially in the worst-hit areas, and provide a ray of hope for the future to the whole nation.

Transylvanian Lambs and Easter Tables: Celebrations in Danger of Extinction

Rosemary Barron and Kate Hawkings

Spring, a time of renewal and rebirth, reassures us of life's bounty. It's a time to celebrate life in the very best way we can think of, to finish up the previous year's carefully stored produce, to spread our tables lavishly with the finest foods of the moment, with brilliant, spirit-lifting colours.

European city-dwellers have long grown used to being separated from the rhythms of the land, and many today may have some difficulty explaining why lamb, young vegetables, eggs, and fresh cheese have pride of place on their country's traditional, celebratory spring tables. For the people of southern Transylvania, however, where living in harmony with the seasons is still a way of life, these are the foods that are central to celebrating the welcome arrival of spring. Here, the production of lamb and cheese is at the core of a profound and symbiotic relationship between the land and the people. It has provided food and employment throughout hundreds of politically turbulent years and has shaped the landscape into an area of outstanding natural beauty with ecosystems of remarkably rich, but fragile, biodiversity. The purpose of this paper is to celebrate not only the Easter feast itself, but also the landscapes and livelihoods of those communities in which the food is produced: landscapes and livelihoods that are now in danger of disappearing.

Central to the production of lamb and cheese in Transylvania is the practice of transhumance – the movement of animals between winter and summer pastures. Sheep and goats were the first animals to be domesticated, and documents dating back to Aristotle's time record this semi-nomadic seasonal activity. Two types of transhumance are practised locally. Pendulation, or short-distance transhumance, refers to the system whereby animals are fed on hay and kept in lowland barns or other shelters in winter then moved to nearby mountain slopes for summer grazing. This type of transhumance, enabling small flocks to be kept to provide food for local households, is in little immediate danger of disappearing.

The same cannot be said for the second type practised in this unique landscape – long-distance transhumance. Its purpose is to provide year-round grazing for large flocks of sheep. In summer, they are grazed on high meadows and semi-natural grasslands, then taken by shepherds to lowland arable stubbles and pastures for the winter. Often, the shepherds move their flocks distances of 500 km or more in the autumn, returning to the summer pastures in time for lambing in the spring.

Transylvanian Lambs and Easter Tables

Transylvanian Lambs and Easter Tables

Long-distance transhumance in Transylvania can be traced back to at least to the twelfth century; lack of records from earlier centuries makes it impossible for us to establish a more precise time. However, Transylvanian shepherd communities date to the pre-Roman Dacians, so we can probably assume, since climate and terrain have changed little, that transhumance has been practised since then.

Modern Transylvania, roughly the same size it was when part of the medieval Hungarian kingdom, became part of Romania by treaty in 1918, after the First World War. However, Romanians have always regarded this beautiful and intriguing region as their true heartland. The Romans (106–271 AD) coveted Transylvania for its precious metals, especially gold, and made use of it as a route to northern Europe. It's thought that it was used too as a place of exile for dissidents, many of whom remained to live in relative peace with the local population of Dacians after the legions withdrew. During the following centuries, Transylvania was invaded by Huns, Avars, Slavs and Bulgars, amongst others, as they migrated westwards from Asia into Europe.

In the ninth century, Szekelers (a Magyar people from the east) settled in eastern Transylvania while other Magyars settled in Hungary. A century later, in 997, the Hungarian Magyars invaded Transylvania, beginning a 900-year occupation. During these centuries of threats, the semi-nomadic pastoralists of the mountain areas kept their distance, and their way of life. Surrounded by the Apuseni and Carpathian mountains, the curved, sweeping landscape of fertile valleys and verdant forests acted as a natural barrier to those intent on sacking the Hungarian empire to the north. Even so, frequent invasions, or the threat of them, gave the Magyars and, later, the Habsburgs cause to put in place resettlement programmes that have shaped present-day Transylvania. In the twelfth century, King Geza II of Hungary, his empire under threat from the east by the Cumans, a Turkic people from the northern Caucasus, offered land and tax concessions to German farmers (Saxons) if they would establish cities and villages in southern Transylvania. So many accepted his offer that whole villages in Germany lost their populations in a very short time, a moment in history that is thought to have given birth to the story of the pied piper of Hamelin. The Saxons, with their superior knowledge of early medieval agricultural innovations, thrived and established powerful cities (known as the Siebenburgen, or 'seven citadels': Bistrita, Cluj, Medias, Sighisoara, Sibiu, Sebes, and Brasov), wealthy market towns and highly self-sufficient villages, whose dual purpose for the Hungarians was to act as an early-warning system and as a protective shield from enemies from the east.

Thirteenth-century documents relating to deeds for hay meadows and pastures indicate that livestock production in these settled communities was well established by this time, and shepherds from remote mountain villages in Transylvania were selling their products in port towns along the Danube delta and the Black Sea. In the fourteenth century, demand for wool rapidly expanded as the textile industries, particularly in the cities of Sibiu and Brasov, flourished. This led to an increase in flock sizes and thus a need, literally, to seek pastures new.

Transylvanian Lambs and Easter Tables

For this purpose, transhumant shepherds from the Sibiu region travelled to the north-west, to the Tisa plains, while those from the county of Brasov found winter grazing around the Danube floodplains. Due to their physical remoteness, many mountain communities did not fall under Hungarian rule, and Transylvanian shepherds from 'free' villages were able to continue their transhumance while other populations in Transylvania were forced into serfdom as their lands were seized and the movement of animals was strictly controlled. These routes continued successfully well into the nineteenth century, when Transylvania was still part of the powerful Habsburg empire.

Throughout the eighteenth and nineteenth centuries, the Habsburgs encouraged other groups of people to move into the region to join the Romanians, Hungarians, Saxons and Roma (who, since the fifteenth century, had served the Transylvanians as musicians, wood-carvers, metal-workers and slaves) already living there. They brought in Ukranians to work the land and Poles to help build the railroads and roads, and they encouraged Jews and Armenians to come west, from Ottoman-held territories. After 1918, Romanian immigration into Transylvania rapidly increased. Today, a world war, several revolutions and forty years of Ceausescu's communism later, the entire population follows the cultural mores of the majority Romanian group.

By the end of the nineteenth century, long-distance transhumance was in decline. Agrarian reforms in the lowlands resulted in the conversion of pastures into arable land, mostly for the production of wheat. This caused an exodus of some transhumance flocks

Transylvanian Lambs and Easter Tables

from Transylvania to the Crimea, the Caucasus, Wallachia, the areas bordering Serbia and Hungary, and to Bulgaria and Greece. In addition, political changes at the end of the century meant shepherds' movements were restricted within the boundaries of the Carpathians. The need for more grazing land led to deforestation within the region and the creation of the mountain grasslands that still exist today.

Transhumance mostly survived the consequences of Ceausescu's devastating agricultural policies as Transylvania's mountains, difficult terrain, and harsh climate provided some protection from Bucharest's long arm of officialdom. Although some flocks and land were confiscated, and there was some collectivization, it was impossible even for this government to fully monitor the transhumant shepherds in these remote communities or to limit the number of sheep kept by each household. In any case, the wool, meat, and cheese from these large flocks were essential for domestic and export markets. Production quotas for households were introduced and, although allowed to grow crops and hay on smallholdings, villagers were left relatively little for their own consumption.

With the fall of Ceausescu in 1989 came the loss of these protected markets and competition for the shepherds from cheap imported lamb, wool and cheese. Landowners who had had their land confiscated were returning, and some blocked the movement of the transhumant flocks travelling between the seasonal pastures. Many shepherds have been forced to find new routes or, in some cases, simply sell their flocks and find employment elsewhere. Sheep numbers in Romania drastically declined, from

16.5 million in 1989 to 6.9 million in 2005. While there had been a slight increase, to 7.6 million, in 2008, this was solely due to increased production in regions other than Transylvania.

Transhumance has over the centuries led to extensive cultural exchanges as the shepherds travelled long distances in search of grazing, and many contemporary traditions – in food, literature and song – have their roots in this practice. A defining work of Romanian culture, as important to the country's self-consciousness, or identity, as the *Iliad* is for the Greeks, or *Beowulf* for the Anglo-Saxons, is the poem, *Miorița*, a story of a shepherd being warned by his lamb of a plot to murder him. It is, however, quite different from the stories at the core of other European civilizations: it is short (most versions contain fewer than 140 very brief lines), with minimal action (it takes place in the length of time that's needed to recite the ballad) and narrative (two shepherds plan to kill a third for his wealth). There are none of the usual heroic tales, battles, and long sieges here, nor mention of warriors, slaves, kings and nobles. Instead, human relationships are quite fleeting. It is the shepherd-victim's relationship with the *Miorița* lamb, and the natural world of birds, stars, mountains and forests, that is at its heart.

The *Miorița* is far from being a description of Utopia – in fact, it is a story of avarice and greed. Its full meaning is best understood by considering the society that created it: from sixteenth-century documents we know that, throughout Europe, thefts of flocks were common occurrences in the lives of shepherds; even the Bible attests that such disputes were a part of pastoral life. The significance of the *Miorița* story is that of conflict-resolution at a level of emotional creativity, and how this is reflected in the Romanian outlook through long periods of the country's history.

Today, above Copsa Mare, a Saxon-founded village in the county of Sibiu, a shepherd, Mihai Mihalache, tends a flock of over 1000 sheep in the summer mountain pasture. He owns most of the sheep, but several hundred belong to different people from nearby villages. To keep track of this side of his business, their coats are splashed with different colour paints. A horse and cart, four-wheel drive, or hardy old Romanian-made Dacia car make easy work of the journey from Copsa Mare to the pasture along a 6 km dirt track that crosses a shallow river and cuts through forests of deciduous and pine to the flower- and butterfly-filled high meadow. There, Mihai lives with his wife and a handful of shepherds and farmhands in a simple but workmanlike compound along with about 40 magnificent pigs; a half dozen handsome goats; flocks of chickens, geese, and guinea fowl; a few donkeys; two horses; and a pack of sheep dogs that both round up the sheep for milking and keep the more dangerous inhabitants of the forest – wolves, lynx, and bears – at bay. These predators have become extinct almost everywhere else in Europe.

The ewes are herded from their pastures and milked by hand twice daily. Mihai makes *cas* and *urda*, two fresh cheeses similar in texture, respectively, to Cretan *manouri* and *mizythra*, and *cascaval*, a semi-hard cheese that's kept for up to three months, from the milk. Later in the summer, when the milk has a higher fat content, he makes a feta-like cheese called *telemea*. These cheeses are made in a makeshift dairy fashioned from an old caravan; he salts the curds, wraps them into cheesecloth orbs, and hangs them for 24 hours before placing them on slatted wooden shelves to settle into heavy discs of mountain cheese. The nutrient-rich whey is given to the pigs and sheepdogs. Mihai allocates some of the cheeses to the other sheep-owners; the remainder are sold at local markets.

When winter arrives, in October, Mihai and six of his men set off with their sheep, goats, donkeys and dogs on their 500 km transhumance trek while his wife, the remaining farmhands and the animals return to the village. The shepherds travel to rented pastures around Satu Mare, near the Ukranian border, a journey that takes five weeks. Wearing long sheepskin cloaks and striking woollen hats, and carrying crooks with curved horn handles which they carve with incredibly intricate patterns during the long cold nights, they sleep in spartan huts – somewhat like large rabbit hutches – or under open skies, while their flocks are herded into corrals and watched over by the fearsome dogs. Donkeys carry their basic provisions, and the shepherds make *urda* along the way, which forms the major part of their diet.

During the journey the sheep graze on arable stubble and whatever other pastures the shepherds can find, with maize supplementing their diet when grazing is sparse. This process enriches the landscapes they cross by fertilizing the soils in the migratory corridors with sheep dung, and encourages biodiversity by transporting fruits and seeds on the wool as well as in the dung. The sheep are mated when they reach Satu Mare, and then they return to the summer pastures in time for lambing in February or March, depending when Easter falls (as the perfect size for an Easter lamb is around 10 kg, it needs to be eight to ten weeks old).

For the Easter celebration Romania follows the Orthodox calendar, where the Easter Saturday midnight meal of *ciorba de miel* (lamb bone broth) breaks a six-week Lenten fast. A great deal of preparation precedes the Easter Sunday feast. Work begins the week before; the house and kitchen are thoroughly cleaned, cookies and bread are baked on the Wednesday and Thursday, and eggs are prepared for painting. These are all enjoyable communal tasks for family and friends, young and old – a perfect opportunity to exchange news. For Mihai, this is his busiest time, as he processes and fulfils orders for lamb and cheese. Wednesday and Thursday are egg-painting days for some of the women and for the children, with much friendly competition and laughter. No work is done on the Friday (Good Friday) – this a time for rest and contemplation.

On Easter Saturday, Nicoleta and Nicolai Nevodar, in nearby Biertan, prepared their lamb for Easter. The family is Romanian, though living in one of the most Saxon of Transylvania's villages, for Biertan's sixteenth-century fortified Saxon church is a UNESCO-protected site. Nicolai used to work in the local glass factory, until it closed down; he now has a smallholding while Nicoleta is a cook in one of Biertan's two old peoples' homes. My day started with coffee and cake in their spotless house, enjoying the view of the towering, and slightly foreboding, church just metres away.

Transylvanian Lambs and Easter Tables

In the kitchen, the lamb, its innards removed and cleaned the day before, was waiting for us on the cleared and cleaned kitchen table. Two months old, it weighed 10 kg. First, Nicolae removed its head with a quick action and heavy, sharp knife, and neatly severed the four leg joints. He wrapped and refrigerated the two forelegs for later that week. Then Nicoleta cut along the ribcages each side of the backbone and severed the neck and the head from the top of the spine. Well-cleaned in cold water, the joints were divided up for the dishes they were to be used in. The neck was cut into pieces and split between the *ciorba de miel cu cherval* (lamb broth with chervil) and *tocanita de miel* (lamb stew with paprika), the hind legs were put aside for *friptura miel* (roast lamb), and one half-ribcage for *miel umplut* (stuffed lamb). The second ribcage was put aside for later in the week. Meanwhile, Nicolae was setting up their splendid old-fashioned grinder – of the sort used in England in the 1950s – for the *drob de miel* (lamb terrine), and their son, Vlad, who had been peacefully sleeping until his mother decided he was needed in the kitchen, prepared the twenty cloves of garlic that were required for the *friptura*. The scene was one of speed but not haste, work but not labour, and much good-tempered anticipation.

Over the following two hours, the innards were minced with onions, herbs, smoked pork fat and seasonings into a large bowl, an egg added, and all mixed by hand until the texture resembled curds. Nicoleta then lined a 5-centimetre-deep pan with cleaned stomach caul, filled it with the *drob* mixture, and covered it with the remaining caul. Later, it would be baked in a low oven and served sliced, with pickles and radishes.

Transylvanian Lambs and Easter Tables

Nicolae, meanwhile, made twenty slits in the two legs and pushed a garlic clove into each, then rubbed the legs with plenty of salt and pepper and arranged them (legs) in a roasting pan containing a half-inch of pork fat. This fragrant *friptura* would be served at room temperature as an appetizer, or warm with mashed potatoes or spinach. On the stove the head and bones were simmering in a large saucepan. For the soup broth, tiny dice of carrot, celery root, parsley root and onion were stewed in sunflower oil before adding the well-skimmed broth and chopped meat from the head (Nicoleta broke it in half with an expert swipe of a small axe) and skinned tongue. Later, handfuls of chervil would be added, and thick *smantana* (fresh soured sheep cream). In another saucepan, the meaty neck pieces were simmering gently with the same choice of vegetables and plenty of sweet paprika. This delicious stew would be eaten later in the week, as it only improved on keeping for a day or two.

The last of the dishes to be prepared during this enjoyable morning was the *miel umplut*. Nicoleta carefully removed the skin from the ribcage, leaving it attached along the side away from the spine, to create a packet. She stuffed this with some set-aside *drob* mixture that had been enriched with a handful of finely chopped parsley and spring onion. Vlad was once again brought into action, this time to thread a needle with twine and sew up the 'packet'. The next day the baked dish would take pride of place on the Easter table alongside a beautiful fresh *cas* cheese and a huge loaf of bread with half a dozen red eggs nestling at its centre. All this work was done with minimum fuss, very quickly, in a small kitchen that was kept spotlessly clean. Nothing was thrown away

– the bones went to the dog, the vegetable scraps to the chickens. The family had five beautifully prepared dishes to enjoy over the next two days, and another three joints, prepared and waiting in the refrigerator, for later in the week.

This rhythmic way of life – both in the kitchen, with a fresh, whole celebratory lamb and in the mountain grazing pastures – is now under threat from our way of life in the modern European world. The living conditions of the shepherds are harsh, and the communities supporting the shepherds are very poor; many young people have left the villages to find work in cities or abroad, so skills are being lost, and markets for the shepherds' produce are reduced. Some parts of the landscape have already been severely damaged by poorly controlled hunting, forestry and mineral exploitation, and changes to land tenure are putting great strain on the shepherds' ability to move their flocks.

But perhaps the biggest threat comes from the European Union (EU) which Romania joined in 2007. Blanket regulations that have been designed for sedentary and intensive livestock production are often entirely inappropriate in this area, and targets to halt biodiversity decline have not been met. As there is still no clear legal framework regulating the practice of transhumance, the shepherds are now operating within uncertain legal boundaries. Although they have long been used to this (mistrust of officialdom amongst shepherds is historic), the reach of the EU's regulations draws ever nearer and, for less remote communities, has already started to take effect. Currently, broad regulations include disallowing movements of animals across major roads, strictly regulating milk and cheese production and compulsory vaccination and parasite treatments, with accompanying documentation. Although some shepherds now move their flocks by truck, this is both costly and environmentally unsound. It is still quite usual for an autumn or spring car trip in southern Transylvania to be halted for several hours while a flock of a thousand sheep cross the road, much to the annoyance of motorists. Inevitably, shepherds are becoming more cautious, choosing to cross roads at night or diverting along railway lines or river banks.

The mountain 'dairies' are rudimentary in the extreme – there is no refrigeration, no running water, little protection from contamination, and the cheeses are transported in unrefrigerated vehicles, often in hot weather. The cost of installing infrastructure that complies with EU regulations in these remote compounds would be prohibitive. Poorly educated and with no historical culture of self-determinism or empowerment, it's hard for people to form associations through which their voices can be heard or to challenge a bureaucracy whose policies favour distant intensive systems and not the work of pastoralists. Recent years have seen some improvement in the representation of shepherds at local level, largely through the work of some NGOs, but the future for many is still looking precarious.

One hope for the future of the land and its people lies in tourism – not the more traditional kind where visitors briefly stop by before moving on to the next 'site', but one where the attraction is the experience itself, of the place and of its artisan food products and those who make them. This kind of tourism brings money and jobs into a community and provides a reason to maintain the landscape. This will only happen if transhumance is allowed to continue. Without tourist-generated income, the population will continue to dwindle and this unique medieval landscape is likely to return to wild scrubland.

The form of pastoralism that's practised in southern Transylvania, and the ecosystems it supports, is fundamental to a culture that has, for centuries, flourished by developing in close harmony with its environment. We fear that recognition of the transhumant pastoral systems of Transylvania being 'lighthouses of sustainable agriculture' by those who wield power will come too late, if it comes at all, for our modern world is moving fast. In some other parts of Europe, similar transhumance practices have become extinct in the face of generously supported intensive and industrialized agricultural systems where sheep production is associated with environmental damage due to overgrazing and soil erosion. In Transylvania, transhumance is essential to maintaining extraordinary biodiversity; the ecosystems that have evolved here over centuries have resulted in landscapes and habitats that are now unique in Europe. For, as Mihai the shepherd told us, 'If cheese is not made here, we don't have the sheep and this landscape would change completely.' And in the words of Nicoleta, the cook: 'This is the life that we know; we have much to celebrate.'

Field research
Easter celebrations and spring transhumance, Biertan and Copsa Mare: Rosemary Barron, April 2011.
Summer transhumance, Viscri/Mesendorf and Copsa Mare: Rosemary Barron & Kate Hawkings, September 2005 and July 2010.

With thanks to
Nicoleta Nevodar and her family, Biertan, Romania, for their generosity in sharing their skills.
Mihai Mihalache, the shepherds. and villagers of Copsa Mare, Romania, for their hospitality.
Giovanna Bassetti, of Copsa Mare Guesthouses, Copsa Mare, Romania, for her introduction to the shepherds and people of the surrounding area.

Bibliography
Arnold, E. R., Greenfield, H. J. 2006: 'The Origins of Transhumant Pastoralism in Temperate South Eastern Europe', http://umanitoba.academia.edu/HaskelGreenfield/Papers/187233/The_Origins_of_Transhumant_Pastoralism_In_Temperate_Southeastern_Europe_a_Zooarchaeological_Perspective_From_the_Central_Balkans

Barron, R. 2011: 'Transylvania Charcoal-Coated Bread: From village staple to local hero', *Cured, Fermented and Smoked Foods: Proceedings of the Oxford Symposium on Food & Cookery, 2010* (Prospect Books).

Beaufoy, G., Jones, G., de Rijck, K. & Y. Kazakova, 2008: 'High Nature Value Farmlands: Recognising the Importance of South East European landscapes' (*WWF Danube-Carpathian Programme/European Forum on Nature Conservation and Pastoralism*).

Harrop, S.R, 2009: 'Globally Important Agricultural Heritage Systems', *Journal of International Wildlife Law and Policy*, 12 (3). pp. 127–165.

'High Nature Value Grasslands: Securing the ecosystem services of European farming post-2013', 2010: (Conference Conclusions Fundatia ADEPT).

Huband, S., McCracken, D. I., Mertens, A., 2010: 'Long and Short-Distance Transhumant Pastoralism in Romania: past and present drivers of change', *Pastoralism*, vol. 1, no. 1.

Latham, Husar & Salzman, 1999: *Miorita: An Icon of Romanian Culture* (Iasi, Oxford, Portland, The Center for Romanian Studies).

PASTORAL (2003) Project, EU Commission of European Communities RTD Programme QLRT-20000–00559, page 3.

Photographs
Cordell Barron.

It Was Divine … Gods and their Food in the Ancient Greek World

Kim Beerden

The ancient Greek world of the divine was thought to feast together, and these divine celebrations had more than one thing in common with human feasts.[1] Take, for example, the following parallel celebrations from Homer's *Iliad*, one human and one divine. During their feast the gods sit with one another, they eat, drink, and are entertained:

> Then Hephaistos drew sweet nectar from the mixing-bowl, and served it round among the gods, going from left to right; and the blessed gods laughed out a loud approval as they saw him bustling about the heavenly mansion. Thus through the livelong day to the going down of the sun they feasted, and every one had his full share, so that all were satisfied. Apollo struck his lyre, and the Muses lifted up their sweet voices, taking turns.[2]

Odysseus and his men are involved in roughly the same activities at their banquet:

> then, when they had finished their work and the feast was ready, they ate it, and every man had his full share, so that all were satisfied. As soon as they had had enough to eat and drink, pages filled the mixing-bowl with wine and water and handed it round, after giving every man his drink-offering. Thus all day long the young men worshipped the god with song, hymning him and chanting the joyous paean, and the god took pleasure in their voices.[3]

Human and divine feasts cannot be seen independently from one another: after all, the divine feast – and, also, the existence of the divine as such – was created by the ancient Greek man, who thought his gods celebrated *like* himself, as appears from the fragments quoted above. Both gods and man participated in 'a sumptuous meal or entertainment, given to a number of guests; a banquet, *esp.* of a more or less public nature.'[4] All feasts revolve, in their way, around social relationships which needed to be created and maintained.[5]

However, food also divided gods and man.[6] The gods celebrated *like* us, but not in completely the same way. Gods were conceived to be different from man in nature, and consequently in behaviour. This behaviour including feasting. As the fragments above show, gods were thought to consume different foods than did men. While men drank wine and water, the gods drank nectar; while man ate meat from the sacrifice, we know from other sources that the gods ate ambrosia. With regards to the consumption of food, different needs or preferences seem to have been attributed to the divine than to humans – at least according to the traditional picture, into which the above passages from the *Iliad* fit neatly.[7]

Yet, this traditional picture of the differences between divine and human feasting – but especially the food they consumed during these celebrations – is much less clear-cut than it appears. On closer inspection, an inconsistency becomes visible: while the Greek supernatural is thought to feast on nectar and ambrosia, it nevertheless seems to be inclined to eat human foods, too. There are two particular gods who seem to be the hungriest and thirstiest among their colleagues. Take the god Hermes, the messenger of the other gods. He was considered to be the most human god of all, always on the move between man and gods. Furthermore, the sources depict him as craving meat (as humans would do) and at the same time as not giving in to this desire:

> Next glad-hearted Hermes dragged the rich meats he had prepared and put them on a smooth, flat stone, and divided them into twelve portions distributed by lot, making each portion wholly honourable. Then glorious Hermes longed for the sacrificial meat, for the sweet savour wearied him, god though he was; nevertheless his proud heart was not prevailed upon to devour the flesh, although he greatly desired.[8]

Eating meat would impair his divine status, a status Hermes is not prepared to give up. But why would Hermes crave meat in the first place? This seems rather ungodly according to the traditional picture as outlined above. It has been argued that Hermes appears to be a special god, a blend of two natures – divine and man – leading to this problem of wanting meat but not being able to eat it. While Hermes is the prime example, this inconsistency can also be found in other gods – most prominently in Dionysus (the god of wine and ecstasy).[9] On many Greek images, Dionysus is shown while he is at a banquet. He is drinking something on these occasions, and we know it must have been wine: the state in which Dionysus is depicted after the feast testifies to this.

Although the two passages from the *Iliad* suggest that boundaries between gods and man were clear, Hermes and Dionysus present complications: an inconsistency with regard to divine consumption of food has appeared. This inconsistency can be further investigated by analyzing human celebrations where the gods were supposed to be present or involved. They relate to the ancient-Greek-on-the-street's ideas about the nature of the supernatural. This is not a new subject: past scholarship has paid attention to Greece's 'eating gods'.[10] Here, however, I will attempt to relate these insights to wider questions about the nature of Greek gods.

An inconsistency in Greek religion

There are a number of occasions where the gods were thought to join humans during their feasts: *thysia, splánchna, trapezomata*, and *theoxenia*.[11] *Thysia* consist of the sacrifice of an animal and its aftermath. Man, naturally, needs to eat nourishing foodstuffs. For most Greeks, most of their nourishment would be derived from a small number of staple foods, especially grain. Luxurious foods, such as meat, were probably only eaten by ordinary men after this communal sacrifice:

> Then, when they had prayed, and had sprinkled the barley grains, they first drew back the victims' heads, and cut their throats, and flayed them, and cut out the thighs and covered them with a double layer of fat, and laid raw flesh thereon. And the old man burned them on stakes of wood, and made libation over them of gleaming wine; and beside him the young men held in their hands the five-pronged forks. But when the thigh-pieces were wholly burned, and they had tasted the entrails, they cut up the rest and spitted it, and roasted it carefully, and drew all off the spits.[12]

Except for the fact that sacrifice provided a – for most citizens – fairly rare opportunity to eat meat, the Greek sacrificial ritual served a multitude of other purposes, one of which was to provide the gods with offerings. Yet, this divine meal did not consist of sacrificial meat but of smoke ('the thigh-pieces were wholly burned'). This practice is explained by means of myth: Hesiod relates that Prometheus sacrificed an animal and made two piles of meat, one looking unappetizing on the outside but with nutritious and tasty meat inside and the other pile consisting of inedible bones but it looked good because Prometheus had covered the pile with fat: 'Before the rest he set flesh and inner parts thick with fat upon the hide, covering them with an ox paunch; but for Zeus he put the white bones dressed up with cunning art and covered with shining fat.'[13] Zeus let himself be tricked and chose the bones and fat. These were then burned to make them fit for divine consumption. This myth mirrors ancient practice, and in Greece, then, pieces of meat were meant for man and smoky smells were consumed by the gods. Although the gods were very fond of them, they did not need them for nourishment in the human sense of the word.[14] The practice of *thysia* fits into the traditional idea that gods ate their own, divine foodstuffs.[15]

Here are more occasions of human feasting where the divine was thought to join in. The *splánchna*, or entrails, were eaten immediately after sacrificing the animal, while still warm, by a limited group of people. It was thought that the gods perhaps joined in on this occasion. It should, however, be noted that these included only Hermes and the barbarian gods: except for Hermes, Greek Olympians did not eat of the *splánchna*.[16]

Trapezomata are that part of the sacrificial meat which was called the 'gods' portion'. The meat was put on a special table after the sacrifice for the gods to eat while man was engaged in the communal meal. Yet, H.S. Versnel notes that this 'gods' portion' in fact may have been another name for the 'priests' portion'.[17] In that case this meat would either not be meant for the gods at all, or for the gods in name but in practice for their human functionaries. It is, then, not quite clear if and in which way the supernatural engaged with *trapezomata*.

At *theoxenia*, particular members of the supernatural (mostly heroes) were perceived to participate in human banquets. A banqueting couch was put in place for the divine guest and food was set in front of him, after which he was perceived to join in the banquet. Were *theoxenia* the place where this particular set of supernatural beings was really thought to join humans in their meal? It appears to be so, yet still there was a difference in preparation between human and divine meat: whereas meat meant for humans was, in classical times, normally boiled, meat for the divine was either grilled or left unprepared.

It has been shown in the above, in a very brief manner, that there is enough evidence to argue that there is something problematic going on with the Greek supernatural and its food – the sources are inconsistent. The gods seem to eat human food sometimes, but there is always some reason why their food is still 'not quite human'. Greek humans apparently could not imagine their gods without some kind of anthropomorphic consumption taking place, but gods were not thought to actually *need* to eat. This appears to have been one of those matters which did invite reflections by individuals (as the sources show), whereas, in the end, they were perfectly happy to look the other way and accept the situation as it was, although they were aware that something was not completely logical. It has been argued that this was possible on the basis of a so-called 'model of dissonance': any individual's ideas about the world are likely to be inconsistent and he or she finds this perfectly acceptable, not giving it a second thought. This can also be applied to the patterns of consumption of Greek gods: a god may be thought to actually eat one day, and the other day he does not and would never. Greek individuals accepted both one and the other, at the same time.

Problem and comparison

Greek gods were possibly in need of more than a sniff of smoke to survive, or at least there was no consensus on this matter. Gods are different, and they are the same. Gods are like us: they eat. Gods are other: 'if they eat, they do not eat human food,' because then they would be humans.[18] This last statement might seem like a pretty normal idea to us: the Christian God is not known for his appetite, for example (except when He was on earth as a man). Yet, a comparison with another ancient culture can help us to reach a better understanding of the particular nature of this inconsistency in Greek thought.

Mesopotamian conceptions of divine eating were straightforward. The divine was thought to eat human food by looking at it, and gods were given their own meals by humans.[19] Humans provided food for divine feasts – based on their own local diet, but more luxurious – as an offering and placed it in the appropriate place near the statue of the god at a particular temple. In earlier periods, man could even place a statue of himself near the statue of the god which allowed man to feast together with the gods.[20] This is the daily (!) menu at one sanctuary:

21 top-grade sheep, fattened and without flaw, fed on barley for two years; 4 specially raised sheep, fed on milk; 25 second-grade sheep not fed on milk; 2 large steers; 1 milk-fed calf; 8 lambs; 30 *marratu* (?)birds; 20 turtledoves(?); 3 mash-fed geese; 5 ducks fed on flour mash; 2 second-grade ducks; 4 dormice; 3 ostrich eggs and 3 duck eggs.[21]

The background to these divine meals was that man was thought to exist in order to provide services to the gods – running the divine household (the 'temple') and providing the divine with meals was one of man's duties.[22] The cult statue of a god was thought to be 'alive'. From myths, we know the supernatural would starve without human offerings: the Babylonian *Epic of Creation* (*Enuma Elish*) tells us that the god Marduk was in charge of supplying food and drink, which he made the responsibility of man. They would be those who provisioned the shrines.[23] Mesopotamian man, in short, lived in a *Gottes-Ernährungsgemeinschaft* (a god-feeding society).[24]

What is important to note is that there is no trace of the Greek inconsistency: the Mesopotamian gods were simply perceived to have eaten the same food as humans did, prepared like human food, and there are no contradictory or inconsistent reports on this matter. These Mesopotamian gods did not eat 'other' foods like ambrosia, they did not receive particular parts of sacrificial animals, they did not eat raw meat and so on: they were simply eating human meals, but rather more extensive ones.

To conclude

So what was the Greek divine feast all about, and why should we care? What has emerged from the comparison is that Mesopotamian gods must have perceived their Greek neighbours as peculiar beings with strange appetites. Whereas the Mesopotamian god ate human meals, but in large quantities, the Greek god was at times perceived to feast like man and at the same time either could not eat human foods or preferred to eat differently prepared foods to man's – resulting in an inconsistency in terms of the divine diet.

Why did this inconsistency exist specifically in Greece? This must have to do with the Greek view of the nature of their gods. The contrast between Greek and Mesopotamian gods at table implies that, at least on the basis of their dinner, Mesopotamian gods were seen as a kind of *super*humans – 'bigger-than-life humans' – whereas this was more complicated in the Greek world. The inconsistency with regards to food implies that the gods were been perceived as *super*human and non-human at the same time. They were like humans, but they were at the same time thought to be completely different from, and elevated above, Greek man.

A subsequent question is the following: why do these conflicting ideas on the nature of the gods become so very clear when discussed in terms of food? Why is food so especially appropriate for expressing inconsistent views of the nature of the divine? It must be that preparing food and eating it in a social setting is an activity that makes us human. Food was, then, a suitable vehicle for the ancient Greek man-on-the-street to engage in thinking about the nature of the supernatural. This remained a subject about which there were many views, which were all generally accepted in this ancient society, shrugging its shoulders where this inconsistency was concerned.

Supernatural celebrations must have been divine occasions to Greek gods – for modern scholars it remains a topic of blood, sweat and tears without easy solutions. Yet, it leads to questions about what may be the most fundamental issue of ancient Greek religion: the nature of its gods.

Notes

1. I thank Dr F.G. Naerebout for his comments on a first draft of this article. The following title appeared after this paper was submitted and is not incorporated here: V. Pirenne-Delforge & F. Prescendi (eds.), *'Nourrir les dieux?' Sacrifice et représentation du divin* (Liège 2011).
2. Homer, *Iliad* 1.597–604. Trans. by Samuel Butler. Edition: Teubner. αὐτὰρ ὁ τοῖς ἄλλοισι θεοῖς ἐνδέξια πᾶσιν | οἰνοχόει γλυκὺ νέκταρ ἀπὸ κρητῆρος ἀφύσσων· | ἄσβεστος δ' ἄρ' ἐνῶρτο γέλως μακάρεσσι θεοῖσιν | ὡς ἴδον Ἥφαιστον διὰ δώματα ποιπνύοντα. | ὣς τότε μὲν πρόπαν ἦμαρ ἐς ἠέλιον καταδύντα | δαίνυντ', οὐδέ τι θυμὸς ἐδεύετο δαιτὸς ἐΐσης, | οὐ μὲν φόρμιγγος περικαλλέος ἣν ἔχ' Ἀπόλλων, | Μουσάων θ', αἳ ἄειδον ἀμειβόμεναι ὀπὶ καλῇ.
3. Homer, *Iliad* 1.467–474. Trans. by Samuel Butler. Edition: Teubner. αὐτὰρ ἐπεὶ παύσαντο πόνου τετύκοντό τε δαῖτα | δαίνυντ', οὐδέ τι θυμὸς ἐδεύετο δαιτὸς ἐΐσης. | αὐτὰρ ἐπεὶ πόσιος καὶ ἐδητύος ἐξ ἔρον ἔντο, | κοῦροι μὲν κρητῆρας ἐπεστέψαντο ποτοῖο, | νώμησαν δ' ἄρα πᾶσιν ἐπαρξάμενοι δεπάεσσιν, | οἳ δὲ πανημέριοι μολπῇ θεὸν ἱλάσκοντο | καλὸν ἀείδοντες παιήονα κοῦροι Ἀχαιῶν | μέλποντες Ἑκάεργον• ὁ δὲ φρένα τέρπετ' ἀκούων.
4. 'feast 3', *Oxford English Dictionary Online*, last modified December 2010, accessed on 15 March 2011.
5. Brian Hayden, 'A Prolegomenon to the Importance of Feasting', in *Feasts: Archaeological and Ethnographic Perspectives on Food, Politics, and Power*, ed. Michael Dietler and Brian Hayden (Washington: Smithsonian Institution Press, 2001): 23–64 (30); Michael Dietler and Brian Hayden, 'Digesting the Feast: Good to Eat, Good to Drink, Good to Think', in *Feasts*, ed. Dietler and Hayden: 1–20 (3).
6. Gunnel Ekroth makes this argument in 'Burnt, cooked, or raw? Divine and human culinary desires at Greek animal sacrifice', in *Transformations in Sacrificial Practices: from Antiquity to Modern Times*, ed. Eftychia Stavrianopoulou, Axel Michaels, and Claus Ambos (Berlin: Lit Verlag, 2008): 87–111 (87).
7. See, e.g., Lucian, *On Sacrifice* 9.
8. *Homeric hymn to Hermes*, 127–133. Trans. by Hugh G. Evelyn-White (Loeb). Edition: Oxford Classical Texts. Ἑρμῆς χαρμόφρων εἰρύσατο πίονα ἔργα | λείῳ ἐπὶ πλαταμῶνι καὶ ἔσχισε δώδεκα μοίρας | κληροπαλεῖς• τέλεον δὲ γέρας προσέθηκεν ἑκάστῃ. | ἔνθ' ὁσίης κρεάων ἠράσσατο κύδιμος Ἑρμῆς• | ὀδμὴ γάρ μιν ἔτειρε καὶ ἀθάνατόν περ ἐόντα | ἡδεῖ'• ἀλλ' οὐδ' ὥς οἱ ἐπείθετο θυμὸς ἀγήνωρ | καί τε μάλ' ἱμείροντι περῆν' ἱερῆς κατὰ δειρῆς.
9. Henk S. Versnel, *Coping with the Gods: Wayward Readings in Greek Theology* (Leiden: Brill, 2011): 322–325.
10. Apart from many articles, a few of the main publications are: *La cuisine du sacrifice en pays grec*, ed. Marcel Detienne and Jean-Pierre Vernant (Paris: Gallimard, 1979); Pauline Schmitt Pantel, *La cité au banquet: histoire des repas publics dans les cités grecques* (Rome: École Française de Rome, 1992); Gunnel Ekroth, *The Sacrificial Rituals of Greek Hero-cults in the Archaic to the Early Hellenistic period* (Liège:

Centre International d'Étude de la Religion Grecque Antique, 2002).
11. Another seemingly divine meal is the human food that gods ate when they were thought to appear in an epiphany. Yet, there is a logic in this: if a god appeared in the body of a human, he could eat human foods – although he was still an immortal god. I have therefore not included epiphanic meals here.
12. Cf. Folkert T. van Straten, *Hierà kalá: Images of Animal Sacrifice in Archaic and Classical Greece* (Leiden: Brill, 1995); Homer, *Iliad* 1.458–466. Trans. by Augustus T. Murray (Loeb). Edition: Teubner. αὐτὰρ ἐπεί ῥ' εὔξαντο καὶ οὐλοχύτας προβάλοντο, | αὐέρυσαν μὲν πρῶτα καὶ ἔσφαξαν καὶ ἔδειραν, | μηρούς τ' ἐξέταμον κατά τε κνίσηι ἐκάλυψαν | δίπτυχα ποιήσαντες, ἐπ' αὐτῶν δ' ὠμοθέτησαν. | καῖε δ' ἐπὶ σχίζηις ὁ γέρων, ἐπὶ δ' αἴθοπα οἶνον | λεῖβε· νέοι δὲ παρ' αὐτὸν ἔχον πεμπώβολα χερσίν. | αὐτὰρ ἐπεὶ κατὰ μῆρ' ἐκάη καὶ σπλάγχν' ἐπάσαντο, | μίστυλλόν τ' ἄρα τἆλλα καὶ ἀμφ' ὀβελοῖσιν ἔπειραν, | ὤπτησάν τε περιφραδέως, ἐρύσαντό τε πάντα.
13. Hesiod, *Theogony* 538–541. Trans. by Hugh G. Evelyn-White (Loeb). Edition: Oxford Classical Texts. τῷ μὲν γὰρ σάρκάς τε καὶ ἔγκατα πίονα δημῷ | ἐν ῥινῷ κατέθηκε, καλύψας γαστρὶ βοείῃ, | τοῖς δ' αὖτ' ὀστέα λευκὰ βοὸς δολίῃ ἐπὶ τέχνῃ | εὐθετίσας κατέθηκε, καλύψας ἀργέτι δημῷ.
14. See a recent article for a publication which does seem to speak of eating (or at least does not problematize this): Edoarda Barra-Salzédo, 'À la table des dieux en Grèce ancienne', *Food and History* 8 (2011): 23–37 (27–32).
15. There are always exceptions, like, for example, Ares as described in Homer's *Iliad*. See Tamara Neal, 'Blood and Hunger in the Iliad', *Classical Philology* 101 (2006): 15–33 (28).
16. Versnel, 353–355.
17. Versnel, 359.
18. Versnel, 388–9.
19. Jean-Jacques Glassner, 'Mahlzeit. A', *Reallexikon der Assyriologie*, ed. Erich Ebeling et al. (Berlin: De Gruyter 1932-): 7, 259–66 (261); Denise Schmandt-Besserat, 'Feasting in the Ancient Near East', in *Feasts*, ed. Dietler and Hayden: 391–403 (400).
20. Frans A.M. Wiggerman, 'Theologies, Priests and Worship in Ancient Mesopotamia', in *Civilizations of the Ancient Near East*, ed. Jack M. Sasson et al., 4 vols (New York: Charles Scribner's Sons, Macmillan Library Reference USA, 1995): 3:1857–70 (1863).
21. See Jean Bottéro, *The Oldest Cuisine in the World: Cooking in Mesopotamia*, trans. Teresa L. Fagan (Chicago: University of Chicago Press, 2002): 114.
22. See for other myths Lambert, 'Donations of food and drink', in *Ritual and Sacrifice*, ed. Quaegebeur: 193–201 (197–8); Marcel Sigrist, 'Sacrifice, Offerings, and Votives: Mesopotamia', in *Religions of the Ancient World: A Guide*, ed. S.I. Johnston (Cambridge, MA: Belknap Press, 2004): 330–2; Tzvi Abusch, 'Sacrifice in Mesopotamia', in *Sacrifice in Religious Experience*, ed. Albert I. Baumgarten (Leiden: Brill, 2002): 39–43.
23. Gilgamesh tablet 11.155–163.
24. Stefan M. Maul, 'Den Gott ernähren. Überlegungen zum regelmäßigen Opfer in altorientalischen Tempeln', in *Transformations in Sacrificial Practices, ut sup.*: 75–86 (82).

Sukkot: The Paradigmatic Harvest Festival

Jonathan Brumberg-Kraus

The Jewish harvest festival of Sukkot, 'Tabernacles,' is the quintessential Jewish holiday celebration. The tradition itself recognizes this liturgically, by calling it *He-Hag* – '*The Holiday*,' *z'man simhateynu* – 'the season of our rejoicing,' in comparison to the other two pilgrimage festivals on the Jewish calendar, *Pesah* (Passover) and *Shavuot* ('the Festival of Weeks'). But besides these explicit declarations of Sukkot's pre-eminence as 'The Holiday,' I will show how the specific foods and food practices associated with Sukkot implicitly mark and cultivate experiences of *simhah* – which designates both the emotional state of 'joy' and the ritual celebration intended to effect it.

My analysis starts with Mary Douglas' famous insight in 'Deciphering a Meal,' that in a culture's system of meals, 'meals are ordered in scale of importance and grandeur throughout the week and the year. The *smallest, meanest meal metonymically figures the structure of the grandest*, and each unit of the grand meal figures again the whole meal – or the meanest meal.'[1] But I go beyond her point that the patterned multiplication of the basic dishes of 'the meanest meal' distinguishes the festive 'grand meals,' that is, in this study, the holiday meals of Sukkot, from ordinary meals. There are multiplications of other aspects of Sukkot meals besides the foods actually eaten that are intended to bring about the emotional state of joy. All of them depend upon some kind of expression of extravagance, through activities involving different sorts of superabundant 'consumption.' By adding to a basic, ordinary meal these five things or practices: (1) superabundant foods eaten during the seven days of Sukkot, (2) superabundant sensory experiences of Sukkot 'foods', (3) superabundant expenditures for Sukkot ritual objects, (4) superabundant number of guests ('*Ushpizin*') for Sukkot meals, and (5) superabundant memories of Sukkot celebrations past and to come even after we die, Sukkot is distinguished from all other festival celebrations in the Jewish system of meals. I will explain each of these in what follows.

Superabundant foods

The patterned *multiplication* of the dishes of lesser or non-festive meals distinguishes the festive meals of Sukkot from other Jewish meals, as do Sukkot's characteristic stuffed foods or other 'one-dish meals' with multiple ingredients. We can see this both in the idealized prescriptions of *halakhah*, Jewish law, defining what and how to eat and drink on the holiday, and the internalization of this 'grammar of meals' in the improvisations of it in actual Jewish meal practice for Sukkot. According to *halakhah*, the 'fixed meals' one should eat in the *sukkah* consist minimally of bread, cake, or other dishes made

Sukkot: The Paradigmatic Harvest Festival

from grains.[2] So for festivals in general, not just Sukkot, according to Jewish Talmudic and post-Talmudic prescriptions, one must eat meat and drink wine in order to enjoy a festival. This is what distinguishes '*Yom Tov*' (holiday) meals from ordinary meals.[3] So if adding things to it makes an ordinary meal a festive meal, i.e. meat and wine to bread, then it seems that the stuffed foods and rich stews customarily eaten on Sukkot (e.g. in Ashkenazic Jewish cuisine – stuffed cabbage, a meaty *tzimmes*, or brisket cooked with dried fruit and root vegetables), are conscious expressions and improvisations of this halakhic grammar of meals to make Sukkot even 'more festive' than other Jewish festival meals. We can see this in at least four ways: in the attention called to adding 'side dishes' to the main course; or to main entrees that include the sides in one dish (according to what I call the 'chicken Marengo principle' *à la* Mary Douglas); adding ingredients that make the base foods seem richer, and modern Jewish cookbook authors' recommendation of other dishes (Jewish or not) previously not associated with Sukkot as 'Sukkot foods' because they fit these principles. The Ashkenazic dish *tzimmes*, a sweet cooked dish of root vegetables and dried fruits, is pretty much universally designated as a Sukkot dish by modern Jewish cookbooks, no doubt in part due to its seasonally appropriate harvest ingredients, and its sweetness symbolizing a hope for a 'sweet New Year.' However, even its name calls attention to its being an 'added dish,' if Gil Marks' suggested etymology for *tzimmes*, from the Yiddish, *zum essen,* is correct.[4] In other words, *tzimmes* basically means 'side dish.' Marks also suggests that the carrots in *tzimmes*, *mehren* [meaning both 'carrots' and 'more' in Yiddish] also symbolize abundance, and that the Yiddish expression *machen a tzimmes fun …* ('making fuss about something') refers the extra effort and added ingredients Eastern European housewives devoted to their Sukkot *tzimmeses*.[5] In other words, to use another Yiddish expression, a Sukkot *tzimmes* is more *ongepotscht* than other ordinary foods. Hence, typically, one adds meat, usually brisket, to a *tzimmes* for Sukkot to make it richer, like the recipe for a *fleishig* 'meat' *tzimmes* Marks provides in the entry 'tzimmes' his *Encyclopedia of Jewish Food*.[6] Thus, *tzimmes* exemplifies the practice of adding ingredients to simpler dishes to make them more festive according to the grammar of Jewish meals. Similarly, raisins or other dried fruits are often added to the challah for Sukkot and the High Holidays. Thus, these festival challahs, which are often baked in a round shape, are differentiated from 'ordinary' Sabbath challahs (the classic oblong braided 'Jewish' egg twists), which are themselves differentiated from ordinary daily bread made from coarser, darker flours. In addition, one should place *two* whole loaves of challah on the festive table in the *sukkah*.[7] Yes, the doubled challah loaves and their raisins symbolize 'plenty,' and the round shape the seasonal cycle, but at base Sukkot bread is a variation and expansion of ordinary bread.[8]

Typical Sukkot foods are often stuffed or, especially, one-dish meals or casseroles because they too symbolize abundance more or less according to what I'm calling the 'chicken Marengo principle.' According to Mary Douglas, 'the features which a single copious dish would need to display before qualifying as a meal … would be

Sukkot: The Paradigmatic Harvest Festival

something like the famous chicken Marengo served to Napoleon after his victory over the Austrians,' which earned its fame precisely because it 'combine[d] the traditional soup, fish, egg, and meat courses of a French celebratory feast in a *plat unique*.'[9] Thus an Ashkenazic meaty *tzimmes* of brisket, carrots, dried fruit, sweet and white potatoes like the one for which Gil Marks provides a recipe is not just a side, but a 'main course' for Sukkot,[10] because it basically recapitulates the Jewish festive meal of meat, savory vegetable side, starch, and sweet side in a single dish. Similarly, the variation with *knaidlach* (matzo balls), a specialty which my wife's *bubbe* used to make for Passover – *tzimmes mit a knaidl* ('Because,' as she explained deadpan, 'it's a *tzimmes* with a *knaidl*'), includes the 'bread course,' appropriately replacing the leavened bread with a starch made of matzo meal and eggs. The Moroccan *pastilla*, a phyllo dough pie, filled with chicken, sweet ground nuts, beaten eggs, and a mixture of savory and sweet spices, is a Sephardic one-dish meal made also especially for Sukkot and other Jewish holidays.[11] Of course, pies like this and 'meal-in-one stews' are popular for Sukkot also because they can be conveyed outside to the *sukkah* and kept hot easily.[12] Stuffed foods are characteristic fare for Sukkot, just as indeed they signify the idea of abundance in the foods of harvest celebration banquets in many other cultures. Marks lists numerous stuffed foods from a variety of Jewish cultures around the world as typical Sukkot foods, such as 'Ashkenazic ... stuffed veal breast or poultry, knishes, filled dumplings, fruit and cabbage strudels ... Sephardic ... filled phyllo pastries ... and Bukharan ... *oshee tos kadoo* (stuffed pumpkin) and *samsa* (turnovers).' And under 'Sukkot' in his index, Marks lists among others such stuffed foods as '*boreka, bulemas, dolma, fluden, knedliky, sambusak*, strudel, stuffed cabbage, and stuffed peppers.'[13] Even if these stuffed dishes don't always recapitulate the whole meal (like *pastilla*), they still signify abundance by combining other components of the meal: bread/starch and sweet and savory sides, bread/starch and meats, vegetable sides and meat and/or starch, etc.

Finally, I think the most telling expression of the internalized grammar of Sukkot meals appears in modern Jewish cookbooks when they suggest adapting and applying the 'rule' for appropriate Sukkot foods to dishes that previously were not part of the Sukkot or even Jewish culinary repertoire. Thus for example, Gloria Kaufer Greene in her Jewish *Holiday Cookbook* recommends one Cuban Jewish family's recipe for *Papas Rellenas* (Meat-stuffed Mashed Potato Croquettes) 'because they are in keeping with the tradition of eating stuffed foods on Sukkot [though the family] often eat[s] them on Shabbat as well.'[14] And I particularly like her rationale for including 'Orange Glazed Turkey with Fruit–Nut Stuffing' as a Sukkot dish. She explains,

> Some say that the American holiday of Thanksgiving may have been influenced by the Jewish one of Sukkot. As both are festivals celebrating an abundant fall harvest, this is indeed possible. Interestingly, modern American Jews have turned the tables (so to speak) on the Pilgrims, and now serve many typical Thanksgiving foods, particularly stuffed turkey, during Sukkot ... The following

turkey recipe features a unique fruit–nut stuffing and orange glaze that are quite in keeping with the Sukkot tradition eating fruit and nuts.[15]

Greene's 'translation' of the 'language' of American festive meals into the language of Jewish festive meals works because the 'syntax' of adding or stuffing ingredients to signify 'abundance' is so similar in both, not to mention the shared seasonal and 'sweet' symbolism of the ingredients. To be sure, there are other things going on here in Greene's *Jewish Holiday Cookbook*, which reflect the complex strategies of negotiation of modern American Jewish identities.[16] One is the assimilation of 'Jewish' food *per se* to 'Jewish holiday food.' That is, American Jews often eat stereotypically *Jewish* food on *Jewish* holidays, 'American' or other ethnic foods on all other days. Or when Jews eat stereotypically American holiday foods – like stuffed turkey – that in effect makes them *Jewish* holiday foods. A second is the exoticization of Sephardic Jewish foods by many American Jews who come primarily from Ashkenazic, Eastern European Jewish backgrounds. Thus, eating and cooking Sephardic Jewish foods allow Jews to eat 'ethnic' (the other's) food and Jewish (our 'own') food at the same time. So 'adding' Sephardic foods to the 'default' Ashkenazic culinary repertoire, and especially for Jewish holiday meals, is another way to mark them as special, and different from other 'ordinary' Jewish meals. For example, though my family is Ashkenazic, I know I often cook 'foreign' Middle Eastern or Sephardic Jewish dishes (such as a rich savory vegetarian couscous with end-of-summer vegetables and a sweet garnish of caramelized onions and raisin for Sukkot)[17] when we invite guests to our Jewish holiday meals. But there's more to making Sukkot the pre-eminently festive festival than the variation and multiplication of the courses and components of the foods we *eat*.

Superabundant sensory experiences: more than food that *tastes* good

Certain rituals specific to Sukkot alone are added to signify abundance or extravagance beyond the way the special foods and practices of other Jewish holidays do. There are 'foods' specifically prescribed in the Bible for Sukkot, the citron or '*etrog*' (called the *pri etz hadar*, 'the fruit of the beautiful tree' in the Bible),[18] and the leaves of the date palm, the *lulav*, to be enjoyed not through the sense of taste, but through their fragrant smell, visual beauty, feel, and sound when they are waved together with the other two of 'the four species,' myrtle and willow leaves. Indeed the following midrash brought by the modern Israeli Jewish educator Ephraim Kitov to explain their symbolism stresses not only that their taste is not their sole pertinent quality, but also that they are 'metonymic foods:'[19]

Our Sages expounded (Vayikra Rabbah 30):

The fruit of a beautiful tree – this refers to Israel, for just as the *esrog* [sic] has both taste and scent, so too are there Jews who both possess Torah learning and good deeds.

> *The branch of the palm tree* – This refers to Israel, for just as the *lulav* has taste [i.e. dates] but lacks scent, so too are there Jews who possess Torah learning but lack good deeds.
>
> *A bough from the 'avos' tree* – This refers to Israel, for just as the *hadas* has scent but lacks taste, so too are there Jews who possess good deeds but lack Torah learning.
>
> *Willows of the stream* – This refers to Israel, for just as the *aravah* lacks both taste and scent, so too are there Jews who lack both Torah learning and good deeds.
>
> What does God do with them … God says, 'Bind them together, and they will atone for each other!'[20]

These foods which stand for the different components of the Jewish people, are brought together and 'consumed' not through the mouth and the sense of taste, but by smelling, touching, seeing, and hearing them when one holds them together and waves them in six different directions.[21] In this ritualized metaphor, it is a prerequisite to bring the Jewish people together symbolically 'to atone for one another' each day before one eats their meal in the *sukkah*. That is, one must perform the ritual of taking and waving the four species before one is even permitted to eat a festive meal in the *sukkah*.[22]

Where one eats the festive Sukkot meals enhances them by drawing attention to their visual appeal as well as to their taste. To fulfil the scriptural verse 'This is my God and I shall exalt Him' (*anvayhu*, literally, I shall make Him *naveh* – 'beautiful', Ex 15:2), Jews are encouraged to decorate the *sukkah*, the booth they build for the holiday, with colorful seasonal foods (like gourds, Indian corn, and cranberries where I live in New England).[23] The post-biblical commandment to make the *sukkah* and the other ritual objects beautiful is called *hiddur mitzvah*, 'beautification of the commandment,' and the criteria that make them beautiful are especially features of their visual appearance, which Jewish tradition carefully specifies.[24] Taking these visual aesthetic experiences together with the other special tastes, scents, textures, and sounds of Sukkot, one enjoys the festival when abundance and extravagance is to be experienced in multi-sensory, synaesthetic ways.

Superabundant expenditure

One can spend even beyond one's means for the sake of *hiddur mitzvah*.[25] The plot of the 2004 Israeli movie *Ushpizin* turns on this tradition. The protagonist, Moshe Bellanga, a poor Hasidic Jewish man living in the ultra-Orthodox neighborhood Mea Shearim in Jerusalem with his childless wife, Malli, doesn't have enough money to purchase food for the week of Sukkot, not to mention a *sukkah* and the other ritual items for the holiday. They pray for a miracle and one occurs. They're given an anonymous donation of $1000 and a *sukkah*. But then Moshe uses up most of the money to buy an expensive, perfectly formed *etrog* (unbeknownst to his wife, who becomes furious at him when she discovers this), only to have one of his guests in the *sukkah* cut it up and put it in a salad in his unwittingly disastrous attempt to reciprocate his host's hospitality.[26]

Superabundant guests: *ushpizin*

The very custom of going out of one's way to entertain '*ushpizin*' – guests both invisible (the ancestors Abraham, Isaac, Jacob, Moses, etc., and the mystical divine *sefirot* to which they correspond) and visible (the poor, those without a place to celebrate) – is also a ritual expression of extravagance. For the invisible *ushpizin*, there are ritual formulas to 'invite' each supernatural guest into the *sukkah* on their appropriate day: some set a chair at the table, or put up pictures of them in the *sukkah* to suggest their presence.[27] Our family custom is to improvise on this. We paint and post pictures not only of the traditional male *ushpizin*, but also female biblical heroines (like Miriam, Esther, Sarah, etc., to suit our egalitarian perspective), and at the table ask our guests to think of people whom they would wish to have at our meal if they could choose them from any place or time. As for the visible guests, Jewish tradition suggests inviting the supernatural guests not with the expectation that it's not necessary to feed them, but rather, one prepares extra food for them, and invites the actual poor in to eat it.[28] Moreover, for these real *ushpizin*, another tradition urges that the host be personally involved in the preparation of the food for these meals in the *sukkah*, even if he or she has many servants.[29]

The movie *Ushpizin* dramatizes the how far out of their way observant Jews might go to in their efforts to observe the *mitzvah* of entertaining guests for Sukkot. As the movie review in the *New York Times* describes,

> The guests arrive just in time for dinner. Chowing down like famished dogs, they proceed to eat and drink the Bellangas out of house and home. *But the hosts are thrilled. The appearance of guests during a holiday celebrating hospitality must be another sign of divine beneficence.* And when Eliyahu and Yossef make no signs of leaving, the hosts adjust their thinking and gratefully accept the boorish behavior of the men who came to dinner as a divine test with a reward at the end.
>
> Unbeknownst to the Bellangas, Eliyahu and Yossef have just escaped from prison and are actually hiding from the police. Eventually, the guests go too far. After demanding money from Malli to buy meat, they set up an outdoor grill, blast pop music on a portable sound system and dance around wildly, incensing the neighbors.[30]

And as I mentioned, these impossible guests cut up the exorbitantly priced *etrog* in a salad for their host. But the point is that, at least at first, Moshe and Malli believed that the addition of guests to their meals in the *sukkah* 'during a holiday celebrating hospitality must be another sign of divine beneficence.'[31]

Sukkot: The Paradigmatic Harvest Festival

Superabundant memories

On Sukkot, it is also customary to evoke certain parts of what I shall call for the purpose of this paper 'the Jewish collective memory' that speaks of the loss or fleetingness of abundance, namely *Simhat Bet Ha-Sho'evah,* the water-libation festival imagined nostalgically to have been celebrated at Sukkot long past in the time of the Temple, and the reading of the world-weary book of Ecclesiastes (Koheleth) said to have been written by an old King Solomon, on the Sabbath that falls during the seven days of Sukkot. In many observant Jewish communities it is the custom to gather in synagogues and houses of study on the nights of Sukkot 'to rejoice together through music, song, and remembrance of the *simchas beis ha-sho'evah.*'[32] Why this long-past celebration in particular? The rabbis praised this celebration of *Simhat Bet Ha-Sho'evah* superlatively: 'Whoever never witnessed *Simhat Beit Hasho'evah* has never in his life seen true joy,' and with hyperbolic accounts of people singing in the streets, dancing atop magnificent pillars, lamps lit and shining so brightly from one end of Jerusalem to the other, that the night seemed like the day.[33] By celebrating with water, sustenance common to all, this festival called for God to spread His blessing of the fruitful rains to all the inhabitants of the world, Jew and non-Jew alike. We add to our joy by recalling past experiences of exceedingly abundant joy, though with that memory comes an undercurrent of regret and loss, at the remembrance of abundance *past.*

Finally, the prescribed Sukkot synagogue reading of Ecclesiastes (an almost desperate summons to enjoy feasting in the shadow of death), expresses the mood of the harvest season. It's an explicit *memento mori*, a parable calling our attention to the meaning of the harvest's abundance in the face of the impending chill of the winter, the precarious construction of the *sukkah* exposing its diners to the elements, and the last gasp of autumn's colorful leafy exuberance: 'Leaves become most beautiful when they're about to die.'[34] Or as Ecclesiastes itself puts it, 'To every thing there is season … a time to be born, a time to die,' and therefore, 'Go, then, eat your food and enjoy it, and drink your wine with a cheerful heart: for God has already accepted what you have done … Enjoy life with a woman you love all the days of your allotted span here under the sun, futile as they are.'[35] One might think the sentiments of Ecclesiastes put a limit on the joy in our temporary abundance. Not so! Paradoxically, evoking death in the midst of feasting is the ultimate symbol of abundance, of extravagance, and excess – intimating that our joy transgresses even the boundary of our own mortality. As George Bataille says in his essay 'Joy in the Face of Death':

> Those who look at death and rejoice are no longer the individuals destined for the body's rotten decay, because simply entering into the arena with death already projected them outside themselves, into the heart of the glorious community of their fellows where every misery is scoffed at. Every instant dispelling, and annihilating the preceding one, the triumph of time seems to them bound up in their own people's conquering action. Not that they imagine they can thus escape

their lot by substituting a community that is more durable than their persons. Quite the contrary ... the feeling of cohesion with those who have chosen each other to share their great intoxication is ... only the means of perceiving all of the glory and conquest signified by the loss, all of the renewed life, the rebounding, the 'alleluia' signified by the dead person's fall ... One must have experienced, at least once, this excess of joy to know to what extent the fertile prodigality of the sacrifice is expressed in it.[36]

In other words, when we celebrate, our *awareness* of less, is *more*. The grammar of joy, the syntax and symbolism of abundance, can be spoken even in the language of memory, the memories of meals (and those with whom we shared them) we missed and still miss.

Conclusion

Extravagance and variety of food and guests, *multi*sensory enjoyment of festive 'foods', the impulse to beautify, the impulse to sacrifice, and 'joy in the face of death,' are what make Sukkot the most festive of Jewish feasts. But wouldn't these components make any meal festive, not just Jewish ones? The rabbinic discussion of how to be joyous (and the passage that was my original impetus for the idea of this paper) is instructive. In the Babylonian Talmud some time back in the fourth to six centuries CE,

> The Rabbis taught: A person is obligated to make his children and the members of his household happy on Yom Tov, as the verse says, and you shall be joyous in your holiday. And how does he make them happy? With wine. Rebbe Yehuda said: men with what is appropriate for them and women with what is appropriate for them. Men with what is appropriate for them – with wine. And women with what? Rav Yosef taught: in Bavel with colored clothing and in Eretz Yisrael with pressed flax clothing. We learned in a Braita: Rebbe Yehuda ben Beteira said: when the Beit Hamikdash is standing simcha is only with meat, as the verse says and you shall slaughter peace offerings and eat them there and be joyous in front of Hashem your God, and when the Beit Hamikdash is not standing simcha is only with wine, as the verse says, and wine shall gladden the hearts of man.[37]

Even in the Jewish legal discussions of joy, there's room for improvisation, as long as one knows how to express joy in one's particular language of meals. Jewish meal language clearly employs a syntax and symbolism of abundance to signify joy and celebration. But I think this is also the 'generative grammar' as it were of Mary Douglas' 'grandest meals,' and so, I suspect, of harvest festivals in general, like the North American Thanksgiving feast. In short, Sukkot is not only the paradigmatic Jewish celebration feast, but also, can be a paradigm for understanding how to express joy in the languages of other meal systems in other cultures.

Sukkot: The Paradigmatic Harvest Festival

Notes

1. Mary Douglas, 'Deciphering a Meal,' *Daedalus* 101, no. 1 (1 January 1972): 67.
2. Jewish law defines the word 'dwell' in the biblical commandment 'Dwell in sukkot for seven days' (Lev. 23:42) to mean one should eat all their *meals* in the *sukkah*, drink in the *sukkah*, and have convivial conversations with one's friends in the *sukkah*. Eliyahu Kitov explains that Jewish law not only defines the basic 'fixed meal' as bread, or some other baked grain product, but also 'drinking': namely, 'sitting down with friends in a formal manner to drink wine, beer, or some other beverage' (*The Book Of Our Heritage: The Jewish Year And Its Days Of Significance*, ed. Dovid Landesman, trans. Nachman Bulman, 3-volume pocket ed. [Jerusalem: Feldheim Publishers, 1999]: 1:130–1).
3. R. Isaiah Horowitz, *Shnay Luhot Ha-Brit: M.Sukkah Ner Mitzvah* 31. There is no *simhah* ['joy' or 'celebration'] without meat, or wine. But see also Rabbi Michoel Zylberman, 'The Mitzvah of Simcha on Yom Tov,' *YU Torah Online – Sukkot To-Go 5769* (2008): 59–62. http://www.yutorah.org/togo/5769/sukkot/. In his opinion, the commandment to 'rejoice in your festivals … and you should be exceedingly happy' [Dt. 16:14,15: *ve-samahta ve-hagekha … ve-hayita akh sameah*, the signature phrase and song typically sung during Sukkot] refers to a 'subjective' experience of joy, for which eating meat is but one of several means to that end. He says, 'Everyone has to attain a state of joy, but the way that one does so may depend on his ability, wealth, and personal preferences. For men it may be through eating meat and drinking wine; for women it may be through getting new clothing; and for children it may be through new toys' (60), and infers 'that if a person enjoys other kinds of food more than meat, he may fulfill his obligation of simchat Yom Tov with the foods that he enjoys' (61).
4. Gil Marks, *Encyclopedia of Jewish Food* (Hoboken, N.J: John Wiley & Sons, 2010), 598.
5. Marks, 599–600. In other words, *tsimmes* can be a pretty basic dish, 'as simple as cooked carrots and honey,' but one *potschkies* with it by adding lots of extra ingredients to make it special for the holidays.
6. Marks, 600.
7. Kitov, 1:178.
8. The two loaves, which are also required for Sabbath meals, are also an allusion to the double portion of manna, the miraculous bread from heaven the Israélites received in the desert on the day before the Sabbath, so that they wouldn't violate God's prohibition against work on the Sabbath, that is, by 'harvesting' the fallen manna resting on the ground (Ex 16:22–26ff).
9. Douglas, 'Deciphering a Meal,' 68.
10. Marks, 599.
11. Marks, 448–9.
12. Marks, 569; Gloria Kaufer Greene, *The Jewish Holiday Cookbook: An International Collection Of Recipes And Customs*, 1st ed. (New York: Times Books, 1985), p. 107.
13. Marks, 654.
14. Greene, 115. She points out that they are very similar to an Iraqi-Jewish recipe.
15. Greene, 121–2. I'm guessing from the sentence concluding the quotation that this recipe is her own invention or innovation.
16. See Laurence Roth, 'Toward a Kashrut Nation in American Jewish Cookbooks, 1990–2000,' *Shofar: An Interdisciplinary Journal of Jewish Studies* 28, no. 2 (2010): 65–91, for an incisive account of identity formation and strategies of acculturation in modern American Jewish cookbooks, though what I say about them is my own interpretation of how they're played out in the 'language' of Jewish holiday meals.
17. A sort of hybrid derived from recipes in Gil Marks, *Olive Trees And Honey: A Treasury Of Vegetarian Recipes From Jewish Communities Around The World* (Hoboken, NJ: Wiley, 2005) and Sally Pasley, *The Tao Of Cooking* (Berkeley, Calif.: Ten Speed Press, 1982).
18. The types of citrons used on Sukkot look like lemons, and are not the Buddha's hand citron, though they are related and have a similar assertively pleasant fragrance. See Marks, *Encyclopedia of Jewish Food*, 180.

19. On 'metonymic foods' and the formation of group identities, see Jordan Rosenblum, *Food and Identity in Early Rabbinic Judaism* (New York, N.Y: Cambridge University Press, 2010) pp. 45–75, based on Emiko Ohnuki-Tierney, *Rice as Self: Japanese Identities Through Time* (Princeton, N.J: Princeton University Press, 1993).
20. Kitov, 1:161–2.
21. Kitov, 1:157.
22. Kitov, 1:150.
23. Kitov, 1:129.
24. Kitov, 1:153–156: e.g. the etrog 'completely clean of spots, the *pitom* [its nipple-like protuberance],' unbroken and 'centered on the top … and parallel to the *oketz* [the pointed end where the fruit was originally connected to the tree]'; the lulav (palm branch) 'should be green and no evidence of dryness from top to bottom … straight like a rod without twists or bends on any side,' etc.
25. Kitov, 1:157–160. To illustrate his point, Kitov tells a story not unlike the one dramatized in the movie *Ushpizin*.
26. This is more or less the basic plot-line of the story Kitov tells, too.
27. Kitov, 1:139.
28. Kitov, 1:144.
29. Kitov, 1:109.
30. Stephen Holden, 'Guess Who is Coming for Sukkot? Unbelievers,' *New York Times*, 19 October 2005, sec. Movie Review, http://movies.nytimes.com/2005/10/19/movies/19ushp.html, emphasis mine.
31. Holden.
32. Kitov, 1:176.
33. B. Sukkah 51a.
34. Regina Spektor, 'Time is All Around', *Far* (Sire Records, 2009).
35. Ecclesiastes 3:1–2; 10:7,9.
36. Georges Bataille, 'Joy in the Face of Death,' in *The College of Sociology (1937–39)*, ed. Denis Hollier, trans. Betsy Wing (Minneapolis: University of Minnesota Press, 1988, Theory and History of Literature, vol. 41): 322–28.
37. B. Pesahim 109a.

Chi vuol godere la festa, digiuni la vigilia:[1]
On the Relationship between Fasting and Feasting

Anthony F. Buccini

Historically in the Roman Catholic tradition and still today in the Orthodox tradition roughly half the days of the year are to some degree fast-days. Given that, fasting represents a central – and generally sorely neglected – aspect of the culinary history of Christian societies. The need for culinary historians to examine with care the rules for fasting and abstinence is, however, not to be understood merely in a straightforward manner; rather, the sobriety of fast-days is to be seen in relation both to the 'ordinary' days of the year and, perhaps more interestingly, in relation to the feasting of celebrations and holy days, to which the fast-days are typically juxtaposed: fasting and feasting in the Christian world are two sides of a single coin of spiritual and bodily nourishment, the one giving meaning to the other.

In this paper, I examine the rules for Christian fasting generally and argue that they are to be understood in a complex way, involving: 1) theological issues; 2) social issues, which include matters that pertain, for example, to ethno-historical identities; 3) practical or economic issues, involving, among other things, the general and seasonal availability of foods; and 4) aesthetic issues, which lie at the very heart of a given culture's culinary life. All of these aspects of fasting stand, moreover, in relation to contrasting aspects of feasting. As a case study, I investigate the Greek Orthodox tradition of abstaining periodically from the use of olive oil, a practice that has no analogue in the Roman Catholic tradition.

Culinary culture and the Christian calendar
Christianity was reared within the confines of the Roman Empire, born of Judaism and flourishing strongly in the Hellenistic culture of the eastern Mediterranean, before gradually spreading thence to Italy and the Latinized western parts of the Empire. With regard to the new religion's relationship to food, Christianity took from the start its own stance over against those of Judaism and the Græco-Roman mainstream, rejecting altogether the Hebrews' inviolable dietary restrictions of Mosaic law but also embracing in a fashion the Jewish tradition of making fasting a key element in the human dialogue with God, while at the same time developing its own particular conception of the meaning of sacrificial feasting in terms of the Eucharist. In the course of its first few centuries, Christianity differentiated itself further in terms of its culinary culture from its forebears and rivals through its development of the practice of fasting, in terms both of the extent to which fasting was required and of the significance of the act itself.[2]

On the Relationship between Fasting and Feasting

While Christian fasting at first surely maintained its Jewish character – short periods of abstaining totally from food (and drink) with an essentially penitential or propitiatory purpose and an often communal orientation – it began already by Late Antiquity to broaden and drift in the direction that was then fully developed in the Middle Ages. This more familiar Christian approach involves for the general population both short periods of fasting in the narrow sense – i.e. total abstinence – alongside longer periods of sustained partial abstinence – i.e. the setting aside of specific foods for more or less protracted spans of time.[3] The specific rules regarding when the short, full fasts and the various kinds of partial abstinence were to take place, as well as the rules regarding what foods were to be abstained from, show considerable variation between different branches of Christianity, with further significant variation found sometimes across time and space even within a given denomination. In the present context, a detailed discussion of these rules is neither possible nor necessary and so I will focus on the traditional practices among the Roman Catholics of southern Italy and members of the Orthodox Church in Greece which are most relevant for our discussion.

Christian fasting is associated in most people's minds primarily, if not exclusively, with the traditions surrounding Lent; and rightly so insofar as the Lenten fast was likely the very first one observed by early Christians and has always remained the most important one, both in terms of the scale of the dietary restrictions involved and, more significantly, in terms of its spiritual value. Indeed, today in the Roman Catholic Church and among most Protestant denominations, to the limited degree that community sanctioned fasting is carried out at all, it is in association with Lent. From an historical perspective, however, Lent is only part of a series of occasions when fasting by Christians is or was considered necessary, a series which spans the entire year.

As backdrop to the schedule of the various specific fasts and feasts of the Christian calendar, there has been in both Roman Catholic and Greek Orthodox tradition a related dietary rhythm to the days of the week. Sunday has been considered in both west and east an inherently joyous day, associated with the resurrection and habitually celebrated at table, and it stands then in contrast to the more solemn days when fasting is appropriate, namely, the days of Wednesday, associated with the betrayal of Christ by Judas, and especially Friday, associated with the crucifixion. There is an interaction between this weekly frame of joyous and solemn days and the extended periods of fasting and celebration in the liturgical year: Sundays during solemn periods are marked by a break from fasting or a reduced level of fasting, while Wednesdays and especially Fridays have tended to be marked by particularly rigorous forms of fasting during solemn periods of the calendar; on the other hand, the inherent solemnity of Wednesdays and Fridays and their strong association with fasting can be overridden by the concurrence of a major feast-day.

Over this underlying frame of the days of the week, the main traditional fasts and feasts in the Roman Catholic Church were as follows. Coinciding with the beginning of the Catholic liturgical year was the beginning of Advent season, which includes four

Sundays and historically involved a fast during the three to four weeks leading up to Christmas. With the feast-day of the Nativity of Jesus comes an extended celebration of the twelve days of Christmas itself which continues on to the immediately following Epiphany (6 January) and thence on to the minor feast of the Baptism of Jesus (13 January), after which begins a period of 'ordinary time' that concludes ultimately with the beginning of Lent. Though not a liturgical event, at the popular level in Catholic lands, people have long celebrated and feasted to various degrees at 'Carnival' in the period immediately preceding the onset of Lent, achieving in many places a level of revelry and indulgence that corresponds well to the solemnity and sobriety of the longest and most rigorous of the extended periods of fasting and abstinence. This Lenten fast in the Catholic Church traditionally begins on Ash Wednesday, ends on Holy Saturday, and so – setting aside the intervening Sundays, when one is obliged not to fast but rather to be joyous – comprises a total of 40 lean-days.

Further fast-days in the Catholic tradition are the so-called 'Ember days' or *Quattuor Tempora*: in the week beginning each of the year's four seasons strict fasts were to be held on the Wednesday, Friday and Saturday. The Rogation Days – Major Rogation on 25 June and Minor Rogation being the three days preceding the Feast of the Ascension – were also observed with fasts. Finally, the vigils of other feast-days were also to be marked by fasting from early in Church history, especially the vigils of Christmas (i.e. Christmas Eve), the Assumption and the Apostles (28 June); to these were later added the vigils of Pentecost, St John the Baptist, St Lawrence and All Saints.[4]

The Eastern Orthodox liturgical calendar is in all general ways similar to its Catholic counterpart, with a combination of fixed and moveable feasts, the inclusion of extended fasts and the general juxtaposition of fast-days to feast-days. The two also shared until recently the underlying weekly pattern throughout the year of regular fasting on Wednesdays and Fridays, with Sunday also being set aside as a sort of weekly feast-day. Fasting practices in the Orthodox world have certainly been maintained to a greater degree than they have among Roman Catholics but from an historical perspective one notes too that Orthodox fasting has been stricter with regard to the range of food restrictions, more complicated in its rules, and more broadly in effect across the calendar. In particular one notes that in the Eastern Orthodox calendar there are four periods of extended fasts, with the longest being, of course, the Great Lent or Easter Fast in the spring, which is followed by the Apostles' Fast – of very variable length – in May/June, then the Dormition or Virgin Mary's Fast in the first half of August (Dormition corresponding to the Catholic Assumption), and finally the Nativity Fast, which corresponds to Advent but involves forty days of fasting (as opposed to the four weeks of fasting in the Catholic Church). In addition, there are some further short fasts that are required (Eve of Theophany, Beheading of John the Baptist, etc.) and four periods when fasting is proscribed and which stand in association with the fasting seasons mentioned above. All told, the Eastern Orthodox calendar includes 180–200 fast-days per year (Trepanowski & Bloomer 2010).

On the Relationship between Fasting and Feasting

For present purposes, we need to consider briefly the specific rules of abstinence observed in the Greek Orthodox tradition. Here there are several levels of restricted eating between the extremes of days when no restrictions apply whatsoever and those few days when total or near-total abstinence from food is expected, with the intermediary levels involving:

1. abstinence from meat;
2. abstinence from meat and other animal products (esp. eggs and dairy);
3. abstinence from all animal products plus fish (with backbones);
4. abstinence from all animal products plus fish, wine and olive oil.

The first three levels are observed on days of fasting that coincide with occasions that are in some sense or to some degree festive and so mitigate the level of fasting required. The fourth level of fasting is known as *xerophagy* or 'dry eating' and is the level of abstinence appropriate not only to the bulk of the days during the extended fasting seasons but also generally on Wednesdays and Fridays throughout the year. Xerophagy involves the consumption only of foods cooked in water with salt, especially grains, pulses and vegetables, as well as fruits and invertebrates, most especially crustaceans and molluscs.

The degree to which all of the fasts and specific rules of abstinence are followed by members of the Greek Orthodox Church is declining but it is worth noting that these rules are still in place and that a significant number of people do engage in fasting to some degree (Trichopoulou et al. 1998, 218). In the Roman Catholic Church, however, since 1966 required fasting has been reduced to a mere two days, namely Ash Wednesday and Good Friday, and there are relatively few Roman Catholics who still voluntarily observe the traditional regulations in strict fashion. For the purposes of the discussion in the following section of this paper, we need to look back to the time when a robust set of regulations still obtained in southern Italy.

In 1906, the rules of fasting that were in effect for all of Italy (and Malta) were as follows (Palombelli 1906, 230–1):

A limitation of one full meal per day was in effect:

> for all of Lent, Sundays excepted;
> on Fridays and Saturdays in Advent;
> on the Ember days;
> on the vigils of Pentecost, the Apostles Peter and Paul, the Assumption, All Saints and the Nativity;
> and for all of the above, including the Sundays of Lent, the taking of fish and meat together at the same meal was forbidden.

In addition to the above, abstinence from meat and all animal products (eggs, dairy, lard, etc.) was to be observed:

on Ember Friday in Lent;
Good Friday;
the vigils of the Assumption and the Nativity.

But on the following days abstinence from animal products was limited to meat and meat-broth while eggs and dairy and animal-derived condiments (butter, etc.) were permitted:

on Fridays and Saturdays of Lent;
on Fridays and Saturdays of Advent;
on Ember days (other than Friday in Lent);
on the vigils of Saint Joseph, the Annunciation, Pentecost, Apostles Peter and Paul, and All Saints.

Abstinence from meat or meat-broth but not from eggs and dairy (or animal-derived condiments) was to be observed on all other Fridays of the year.

The general trend in the Roman Church since the Middle Ages, and especially after the Reformation, has been a gradual relaxation of the rules for fasting and abstinence, but the just-listed rules for Italy issued in 1906, which represent a response by the Church to numerous requests from the Italian bishops for mitigation, nonetheless are striking in their conservatism (Palombelli 1906, 230).[5] The most significant difference between these rules and those in effect in earlier times is the more liberal rule regarding the consumption of eggs and dairy, which had formerly been forbidden, broadly, for Lent, Advent, Wednesdays and Fridays in general, etc., in accordance with the precepts adumbrated most notably by Aquinas (2006, 799).

Thus, before these mitigations the Roman and Eastern Orthodox rules for abstinence from meat and all other animal products were quite similar; the most noteworthy differences in western and eastern practices involved rather the treatment of fish and olive oil. Whereas in the Roman Church, fish and olive oil were – depending upon availability – quintessential elements of the lean-day diet, in the Orthodox Church these were treated also as special foods, forbidden on basic fast-days and allowed instead only on occasions that are deemed to fall between a basic fast-day and a day with no dietary restrictions.

The relationship between fasting and feasting

The theological underpinnings of Christian fasting and abstinence are several and there exists room for differing interpretations of what is the most important reason for dietary discipline. According to some, the primary purpose of fasting is to make the individual conscious of his or her dependence upon God and with this to evoke a sense of contrition. Fasting has also been viewed as a means of developing spiritual discipline which finds application beyond issues of the table and can be extended to control of other desires of the flesh, in particular the sexual; this conception of the role of fasting was especially prevalent in the past. In more recent times, greater emphasis seems to be laid upon the traditional notion of the discipline of fasting as part of a generally heightened awareness of the need to lead a pious life and in particular to shun all forms of sin and to practise good deeds, especially almsgiving. In this last regard, many people have felt that the fasting of those who in life generally have enough is an opportunity to give to those who have less and in this way it can serve as a means by which the different levels of society can be drawn together.

Christian fasting regulations clearly focus first and foremost on the consumption of meat and when that is taken into account alongside the theories of ancient and medieval medicine about the effects of different foods on the body, the old notional connection with sexual desires and their suppression makes perfect sense. Beyond that, however, meat-eating has other associations that support its special status: the association with blood and violence comes immediately to mind but, especially in the context of the Mediterranean world, where meat has historically been more often than not in short supply, an association with power and wealth. But above these is the more basic association of meat-eating with pleasure, with feelings of satiety and well-being, and with the joy of sharing in the goodness of flesh and fat in the context of sacrificial feasting on holidays, a kind of feasting that characterized Jewish practice but also the traditions of the Greek, Roman and other Mediterranean societies in which Christianity flourished early on. Finally, within the Christian context, there is the specific symbolism of Christ as the sacrificial Paschal lamb, the hunger and appreciation for which one nurtures in the extended fasts that precede Christmas and Easter, occasions that mark His birth and resurrection, which make possible the consumption of His flesh that in turn makes everlasting salvation possible. In this way, Christian abstinence from meat becomes the necessary complement to the celebration of Christ Himself.

Xerophagy and abstinence from olive oil in the Orthodox tradition

In the Roman Catholic Church, the traditional rules for abstinence can all be derived in straightforward fashion from the core notion of abstinence from meat: flesh-meat and broth made from it constitute the basic category of foods to be set aside on fast-days, with other animal products – eggs, cheese, butter – allowed on lesser fast-days but also banned on more serious occasions. The ambiguity of these products makes sense, in that they are not really flesh-meat, by any reasonable definition of the term, and yet they do derive from animals, contain animal fat and provide, moreover, a measure of satiety and pleasure akin to that derived from actual meat.[6] The injunction that meat and fish not be taken together at the same meal is a late (eighteenth-century) accretion to the rules directed against excess at table and still involves meat; it is then related to the long-standing call for the faithful to forego the consumption of costly or luxurious items, whatever their nature, on fast-days.

In the Eastern Orthodox tradition abstinence extends, however, beyond the category of flesh-meat and other animal products.[7] As mentioned above, there is additionally a ban placed on the use of both wine and olive oil on the many days when the strictest abstinence is required and one is constrained to engage in xerophagy. While the question of the exclusion of wine and other alcoholic beverages is an important one deserving of detailed treatment, given limitations on space we focus here on the Orthodox abstinence from olive oil.

While there may well be a single correct explanation in terms of the reasoning of the church fathers who first decided to make abstinence from olive oil an integral part of Orthodox practice, the reason now seems to have become obscure to many and a source of speculation among some. There are three explanations which I have encountered:

> 1. biblical precedent: In the Old Testament, fasting on some occasions appears to involve abstinence from the use of olive oil, as in Daniel 10.2–3: 'In those days I Daniel was mourning three full weeks. I ate no pleasant bread, neither came flesh nor wine in my mouth, neither did I anoint myself at all, till three whole weeks were fulfilled.'

> 2. practical historical explanation: Some claim that the rule of abstinence from both olive oil and wine arose in reaction to the widespread old practice of transporting these substances in goat skins, by which the liquids became contaminated and unsuitable for strict fasting.

> 3. inner spiritual effect: According to some, abstinence from olive oil is necessary on the strictest days for the additional sacrifice of something inherently filling and delicious; dressing foods with oil or frying them in oil renders the fast ineffective.

Of these, only the last is at all convincing. The first seems problematic, given that Daniel's mourning involves no mention of abstinence from the consumption of olive oil but rather only from its external use as an ointment, refreshing and beautifying. The second explanation seems perhaps plausible at first blush but leaves one wondering why, in a land such as Greece, where wine and oil are so common and have been stored since ancient times in receptacles other than just goat skins, why people would not have developed ways to avoid or work around to some degree the alleged contamination. The third of these explanations does, however, seem to ring true, in that it places the abstinence from olive oil logically in the overall scheme of Orthodox fasting, as one of the elements (along with wine) which distinguish a further intermediate level between strictest fasting and non-fasting.

There is, however, a problem with accepting the third explanation without further qualification or discussion. Whereas it works perfectly well to explain the total ban on the consumption of oils on days calling for xerophagy that one finds in some Eastern Orthodox communities, such as the Russian Orthodox, it works less well to explain the practice of the Greek Orthodox community, in which the ban on oil involves only olive oil and not other vegetable oils. And the Greek Orthodox practice looks even more curious if one considers that the ban on olive oil on strict fast-days does not extend to olives themselves as a food. In other words, for the Greek Orthodox, it is not something inherent about olives nor something generally about the nutritional and aesthetic qualities of vegetable oils, it is something specific about olive oil (and wine) that triggers, as it were, their exclusion from the most solemn fast-days.

It seems most reasonable to me to explain this special status of olive oil in terms of its specifically Christian use (albeit with clear Jewish antecedents) to anoint individuals in Church sacraments. And the close association of olive oil and wine in one and the same rule of abstinence makes then good sense, in that wine is also a spiritually-charged and sacramental substance. Here one notes too that the differing treatment of table olives and olive oil is exactly paralleled in the differing treatments of grapes and wine.

The question remains: why is it that the Greek Orthodox Church accords olive oil a special status which neither the Russian Orthodox nor the Roman Catholic Church does? In the case of the Russian Orthodox Church, native to a land in which the olive and olive oil are purely foreign imports and probably always only seldom used, a specific rule of abstinence from olive oil made little sense and instead the rule was interpreted in a general way, with the general spiritual effect (see explanation 3 above) uppermost in mind.

In the case of the Roman Catholic Church, the situation is rather different.[8] At the time Christianity established itself and became widespread in Italy, olive oil was very much a widely produced and consumed item and just as in Greece, both olive oil and wine were surely from the earliest days integral to the administration of the sacraments. But were they equally spiritually charged for the broader population of Italy as they were for the Greeks? I would say not and in the case of olive oil, the difference seems clear and makes good historical sense. For the Greeks, olive oil was from (seemingly) time immemorial a part of their culture and, indeed, given the intimate association of the olive tree and olive oil with Athena, the quintessential Greek deity, and Athens, the pre-eminent Greek city, it seems clear that both tree and oil together were elements of the Greeks' ethnic identity.[9] For the Italic peoples of Italy, relative to the Greeks latecomers to the Mediterranean, the olive and olive oil were consciously thought of as imports to their land, believed to have been introduced by the Greeks. And whereas the olive figures prominently in Greek myth and custom, its place in Roman religion and popular culture does indeed seem marginal or secondary in comparison. All this is not to say that olive oil was not very important to the Romans: it was highly prized and widely enjoyed, but it was not already imbued with a deeply felt spiritual worth at the time Christianity arrived in Italy, nor was it felt to be an ancient part of Roman ethnic identity, though it has become that for Italians in later times.

There seems also to be a practical aspect, itself related to culinary culture, to the differing treatment of olive oil in Greek Orthodox and Roman Catholic rules of abstinence. In Greece, with its closer connexions to the cultures of the eastern Mediterranean, the use of vegetable oils other than olive oil may very well have been more prominent than it has been in central or southern Italy, where items such as sesame and nut oils have never been widely used. In central and southern Italy, where already in classical times the consumption of pork was relatively massive, lard has been an especially common and popular fat for cooking and seasoning (King 1999). In the context of Christian rules of abstinence, it was simple and natural to make a binary distinction in fats that coincided with the treatment of meat – when meat was proscribed, so too was lard, and the natural alternative for lean-day eating was olive oil. In Greece and the Aegean region generally, lard was also used but with the added factors of the special status of olive oil and the availability of other vegetable oils, the particular Greek Orthodox rule of abstinence pertaining to olive oil could make sense both from a spiritual and a practical standpoint.

Conclusion

There are a great many similarities between the cuisines of Greece on the one hand and those of central and southern Italy on the other, similarities which go well beyond the basic level of shared raw ingredients from a common physical environment and climate. Indeed, waves of strong cultural influences have repeatedly gone in both directions, bringing the cuisines of the two lands closer together. And yet, in many respects these cuisines are also quite distinct, in part thanks to differing influences from elsewhere but also in part due to differences in the rules for fasting and abstinence in these lands' religions. Though at first glance these differing rules of fasting may seem of little importance, they have a considerable impact on the actual patterns of culinary expression in the two countries throughout the year. I consider these differences, as elements of the deeply ingrained rhythm of ordinary vs. lean vs. festive days that marks both the weekly pattern of meals and the yearly calendar, to exist at a fundamental level of the culinary grammar of the respective cuisines, with cultural roots extending remarkably far into the past.

Notes

1. *Chi vuol godere la festa, digiuni la vigilia*: an Italian proverb meaning 'He who wishes to enjoy the feast should observe the preceding fast.' This paper is intended as the first in a series of pieces exploring different aspects of the relationship between feasting and fasting. Many thanks to Amy Dahlstrom for her comments.
2. For a recent detailed discussion of the development of fasting in early Christianity and its relationship to contemporary Jewish and Græco-Roman practices, see Grimm 1996 (with extensive further references).
3. In the west, there was traditionally a distinction between 'fasting' (*ieiunus*) and 'abstinence (*abstinentia*), a distinction not normally observed in modern English outside of Roman Church regulations. In this regard, N.B.: 'Prior to the Second Vatican Council, the Roman Catholic Church made a clear distinction between the two terms: abstinence concerned the types of food eaten, irrespective of

quantity, whereas fasting signified a limitation on the number of meals or the amount of food taken' (*Lenten Triodion* 1977: 16–7). For a discussion of the Latin and corresponding Greek terms relating to fasting/abstinence, see Arbesmann (1929, 3ff.)

4. See 'abstinence' in *Catholic Encyclopedia, Vol. I*, pp. 67ff.
5. Cf. the roughly contemporaneous abstinence rules for the United States, which are significantly more lax regarding all animal-derived foods (*Catholic Encyclopedia* 1913, 69).
6. The question of which creatures are classified as meat and which as fish is interesting and at times amusing but it falls outside our present focus. See Parra Herrera (1935, 86–8).
7. Aglaia Kremezi (p.c.) notes the basis of the differing treatments of fish with backbones and other seafood in Orthodox tradition is the presence/absence of blood. In the west, no such distinction is made and all creatures considered 'aquatic' are permitted as food on fast-days.
8. Here I draw on material in Buccini (forthcoming), where there will appear extensive references to the primary and secondary literature.
9. In Buccini (2010, 61), I suggest that oleïculture was a cultural borrowing for the Greeks from an Anatolian people and that already from the start the olive took on religious significance for them; the topic will be treated in detail in Buccini forthcoming.

References

Aquinas, Thomas [2006]: *Summa Theologica II-II*. Fathers of the English Dominican Province (trans.), D. McClamrock (ed.). (Project Gutenberg Ebook #18755).
Arbesmann, P.R. 1929: *Das Fasten bei den Griechen und Römern* (Giessen, Alfred Töpelmann).
Buccini, Anthony F. 2010: 'The Anatolian Origins of the Words 'Olive' and 'Oil' and the Early History of Oleïculture', in Hosking, Richard (ed.), *Food and Language. Proceedings of the Oxford Symposium on Food and Cookery 2009* (Totnes: Prospect), 52–117.
———. Forthcoming: *From Green to Gold. A History of Olive Oil* (New York: Columbia University Press.)
The Catholic Encyclopedia Vol. I. 1913: C.G. Herbermann et al. (eds.), (New York: Encyclopedia Press).
Grimm, Veronika E. 1996: *From Feasting to Fasting, the Evolution of a Sin. Attitudes to food in late antiquity* (London: Routledge).
King, Anthony 1999: 'Diet in the Roman world: a regional inter-site comparison of the mammal bones.', *Journal of Roman Archaeology* 12, 168–202.
The Lenten Triodion 1977: Mother Mary & Archimandrite Kallistos Ware (trans.), (Faber & Faber: London).
Parra Herrera, Antonio 1935: *Legislacion eclesiastica sobre el ayuno y la abstinencia* (Washington, D.C.: Catholic University of America).
Palombelli, Pietro 1906: 'Cose romane (Cronaca contemporanea).' *La Civiltà Cattolica* (Anno 57, vol. 4), 229–32.
Trichopoulou, A., S. Andreadaki & K. Botsi 1998: 'Religious Fasting in Greece. Yesterday and Today', *Rivista di Antropologia* 76, 217–8.
Trepanowski, John F., & Richard J. Bloomer 2010: 'The impact of religious fasting on human health', *Nutrition Journal* 9, 7 (on-line: http://www.nutritionj.com/content/9/1/57).

A History of the Wassail Bowl: From Pagan Brew to Christian Custard

Joanna Crosby

The wassail is a British folk tradition that has clung on into the present day as the subject of a carol and as a warming seasonal drink. Some people serve a 'wassail bowl' over the Christmas period, usually a drink of hot, spiced cider or apple juice. Although specific pottery bowls were popular for the wassail, the term 'wassail bowl' applies to the drink or contents of the bowl, not just to the vessel. In apple-growing areas the wassail celebration is still practised. The community goes out into the orchards 'wassailing' or blessing the trees with singing, dancing, and loud noises. At this ritual the wassail bowl is poured around the roots of each tree and shared among the participants.

The origins of the wassail celebration are found in the rites of fertility and harvest celebration, although it must be noted that many of these rites were re-worked and re-invented by antiquarians to suit societal and cultural agendas. However, there is no doubt that apples and orchards acquired a mythical significance in British folkloric tradition, and fruit trees have long been celebrated at the darkest time of winter to encourage a good crop the next season. The wassail celebration, and the mysterious drink that was shared by celebrants, is a point of connection between tradition and our modern secular and Christian celebrations of winter.

Considering the practice of wassailing allows an exploration of drinking customs, apples and winter rituals. Examining the ingredients in the bowl – the drink itself – and the variations in the recipe over region and time gives rise to exploration of the social and historical significance of its changing ingredients. By Victorian times the wassail bowl in certain cookery books is unrecognizable from the ale-based drink of its original conception, and has become a dessert – something very like a modern trifle – of custard poured over cake and biscuits. This tamed dish formed part of the Christmas or Twelfth Night buffet spread.

The word wassail comes from the Norse and Old English traditional drinking salute; 'Was hael' meaning 'good health'. The response is 'Drinc hael!' which is equivalent to 'Cheers!' This toast has been used in England since at least the time of Vortigen, King of South Britain, in 449. Geoffrey of Monmouth, writing in the twelfth century, describes Vortigen being saluted with these words by the daughter of the Viking leader, Hengist.[1] She, and Vortigen, would have been drinking ale, or possibly mead. There are many variations in the spelling of 'wassail', and it seems to have been muddled with the word 'vessel' in some places. Anything from 'warzail' (Cornish dialect) to 'washeall' (Samuel Pepys) can be found.

A History of the Wassail Bowl

The British have always liked their drink, and the 'was hael' salute or toast became synonymous with revelry and drunkenness. Nigellus Wireker, writing around 1190, records that the English students at the University of Paris were too fond of their 'wessail and dringail'.[2] But from being a general drinking salute, the word wassail soon attaches itself to a distinct drink served on Twelfth Night. This was a bowl of hot spiced ale, brought into the hall of the house with some ceremony, and making a warming end to the Christmas revelry. The household records of Henry VII and of Henry VIII both reference this custom; 'the wassail or banket was brought in, and so brake up Christmas.'[3]

Meanwhile, in the countryside, the wassail was being enjoyed communally in the villages, and young women were processing and singing from door to door, bearing a wassail bowl full of spiced, sweetened ale, decorated with ribbons, rosemary, and evergreens. This decoration of wassail bowls with rosemary and evergreens accounts for the 'leaves so green' in the wassail carol sung by girls in Leeds, Yorkshire, which dates from the beginning of the seventeenth century and continued until Victorian sensibilities dispensed with the bowl of liquor. By the 1850s the girls were wassailing with a bough of evergreens decorated with oranges, ornaments and a wax representation of Christ:[4]

> Here we come a wassailing
> Among the leaves so green,
> Here we come a wassailing
> So fair to be seen
> Love and Joy come unto you
> And to you your wassail too
> And God bless you and send you
> A happy New Year[5]

During the seventeenth century wassailing or carolling was practised in towns as well as in the countryside. Samuel Pepys records on 26 December 1661, 'We went into an alehouse and there a washeall-bowle woman and girle came to us and sung to us.'[6] During this period, the wassail bowl drink is undergoing a change from the more punch-like spiced, sweetened ale, to something richer, and with more connection to apples:

> Bands of comely damsels, escorted by their sweethearts, went from house to house bearing huge brown bowls dressed with ribands and rosemary, and filled with a drink called Lambswool, composed of sturdy ale, sweetened with sugar, spiced with nutmeg, and having toasts and crabs floating within it. Such was the vigil of the year 1600.[7]

'Lambswool, ... having toasts and crabs', requires some decoding. The term lambswool appears in records of wassail celebrations from across the country, not just from apple-growing areas. Putting toasted bread into wine was a common practice, thought to improve the flavour. Crabs are crab apples, roasted in a pan in the fire, or on a string over the fire, until they sizzle. They are then dropped, still hot, into the warmed, spiced, sweetened ale. This is the basic recipe for lambswool; although, like any fashionable recipe, it quickly acquired variations. In Gerard's *Herbal* (1633), it is described as a drink of warmed, spiced ale or cider, in which bob roasted apples: 'Sometimes, eggs or cream, or both, are whisked in, and sometimes it is served poured over small fruit cakes'.[8] Lambswool in this form continued to be enjoyed at wassail celebrations until the mid-nineteenth century. P.G. Bond, giving a personal account of a wassail he attended as a boy in 1860, in the South Hams, Devon, recalls, 'The drink offered was warmed cider in which were placed baked apples. The cake offered was good currant cake…the cider cup was passed to all and sundry (including the boys) with the cake.'[9]

Nell Heaton, writing in the late 1940s, notes that 'At Jesus College Oxford the wassail bowl holds ten gallons, and the ladle half a pint. "Lambs Wool" is drunk in this College on November 1st; it derives its name from the day which is dedicated to the Angel presiding over fruits and seeds, which was originally called 'La Masu bal' which was corrupted to Lambs Wool.'[10]

Leaving aside the angel, the curious name may derive from the Middle Irish *La Mas abnal* (in Gaelic, *ubhail*). This phrase has the root-word *Lannas* and may mean 'day of the apple fruit'.[11] Or it could simply be a reference to the fluffy appearance of the pulp of the roast apples, bobbing about in the warm brew. Some recipes require the roasted apples to be skinned and beaten, so that only the pulp is used. The pulp rises to the top, and gives a more fleece-like appearance to the drink. The Victorian writer, Hervey, is certain that the name is on account of the 'delicate and harmonious qualities' of the apples in the bowl, which make the drink mild and harmless.[12] If the drink 'lambswool' derives its name from a day celebrating the apple, this raises the questions of why Britain, or at least England, Ireland and Wales, had a 'day of the apple fruit' at all, and in what ways has the apple been celebrated, even before the wassailers arrived in the orchards.

Barrie E. Juniper and David J. Mabberley, in their extensive history of the apple, note that 'the sweet apple, unlike almost every other alien fruit, appears to have received a degree of adulation in the West unprecedented, except possibly for the rose.'[13] However, it is something of a stretch these days for British residents to think of the apple as an alien invader. D.T. Fish, writing in 1847 with the particular certainty of a Victorian gardener, tells us:

> The apple, as is pretty well known, is in its wild state, as the crab, (*Pryus malus*) indigenous to Britain and most parts of Europe, and probably affords one of the most striking examples of the variation and improvement of a species under domestication. We have no direct proof that our present varieties of apple are the direct descendent from the acid crab of our woods. On the contrary,

it is generally supposed that our present race of apples, or rather their more immediate progenitors, might have been introduced by the Romans. If so, they were probably lost when the imperial conquerors left their British possessions to lapse again into semi-barbarism. The degeneration of species and varieties of fruit simultaneously with the decadence of nations is a curious subject, and it would almost seem at times as if the condition of peoples and their cultivated plants rose and fell together. And this would be the more likely to be the case with a fruit so dependent on man's care and skill as the apple.[14]

The apple in folklore, however, pre-dates the Romans. The apples mentioned in the Bible were probably any other kind of fruit – citrons or pomegranates have been put forward as better translations of the Hebrew *tappuah*. The Greeks had a confusing habit of labelling every round fruit they encountered as some kind of apple; this has led to the descriptions of golden apples and so on in Greek myths.[15]

But the folklore of northern Europe contains a bushel of genuine apples. The apple is a magical object in the myths of Scandinavia, Ireland, Iceland, Germany, Brittany and England. There were apples that sang, apples that cried, and apples that nourished people for long periods of time. In Norse myth, the warrior King Volsung was conceived by an apple, eaten by his mother, which contained the seed or essence of the god Odin. To commemorate his parentage, Volsung grew a living apple tree in the centre of his feasting hall. So valuable are apple trees that in these ancient stories they are often guarded by dragons or serpents.[16]

It would appear that celebrating orchards, and offering libations to the apple trees, has behind it at least an awareness of the sacred importance of the fruit, not just its value as a crop. However the cash value of apples was at times considerable, which partly accounts for why so many different varieties were developed and cultivated. George Johnson states that 'in the Remembrance Office a MS exists in Henry VII (1485–1509)'s own handwriting, in which he records that on one occasion apples were from one to two shillings each, a red fetching the highest price.'[17]

Back to our wassailers, gathered round the largest apple tree in the orchard, with a tumbler of hot lambswool in their hand, and probably several more in their bellies. What were they doing out there in the cold, on any night between Christmas Eve and Twelfth Night? (The spread of wassailing from a specific Twelfth Night custom, to one that could take place across Christmastide, was partly due to the increasing importance of Christmas Eve as a time for major community celebrations, and partly due to the replacement of the Julian calendar with the Gregorian in 1752, which left 'old' Christmas Day on 6 January – Twelfth Night.)

Victorian writers, especially those sympathetic to the Romantic movement, took an interest in quaint survivals of 'Merrie England' and began to write accounts of rustic wassailing. Other writers then quoted these accounts, so that it is now difficult to determine the exact date and place on which the celebrations as described took place, but the accounts are variations on a theme and these two examples will serve for the whole body:

> Let it rain, hail, blow or snow, this very essential and interesting ceremony is always commenced at twelve o'clock at night, a tremendous fire being kept up for several hours afterwards. They repeat or sing the following interesting song, with all the might which their lungs will permit. The juice of the fruit is generally made use of for many hours, pretty freely, previously to this interesting ceremony, so that a perfect ripeness of address and expertise in gunnery is the result. Guns and firelocks long laid by are on this remarkable occasion brought forward. The following is what I have heard sung on these occasions, although much more is added in some localities:
>
> Here's to thee, old apple tree
> Whence thou mayest bud, and whence thou mayest blow
> And whence thou mayest bear apples enow
> Hats full, caps full
> Bushel, bushel sacks full
> And my pockets full too [18]

> In some places the parishioners walk in procession visiting the principal orchards of the Parish. In each orchard one tree is selected as the representative of the rest; this is saluted with a certain form of words, which have in them the air of an incantation, and then the tree is either sprinkled with cider, or a bowl of cider is dashed against it, to ensure its bearing plentifully the ensuing year. In other places, the farmer and his servants only assemble upon the occasion, and after immersing cakes in cider, they hang them on the apple trees ... after this the men dance round the tree, and retire to the farmhouse to conclude, with copious draughts of cider, these solemn rites, which are undoubtedly relics of Paganism.[19]

Steve Roud reminds us that 'Victorians had an uncanny knack of clothing their inventions and re-modelled traditions in an aura which implied that they were traditional and ancient,'[20] and this is certainly the case with many aspects of the Christmas festivities. It is doubtful that wassailing the orchards had continued as a completely unbroken celebration since pre-Christian times, especially when Cromwell made Christmas illegal. The Victorians recorded wassailing celebrations and championed wassailing as an example of the open-handed hospitality which the Victorians saw and respected in the sixteenth and seventeenth centuries, when 'the gentry and nobility knew their responsibilities, took them seriously, and took having fun seriously. They were at the heart of society and ensured that the ordinary people had a good time too.'[21]

However, the Victorians had some qualms about the excesses of Anglo-Saxon feasting and the Tudor court, in particular, with the amount of alcohol consumed.

Victorian commentators, especially that mouthpiece of Victorian values, the mass-circulation *Illustrated London News*, turned their focus towards 'the sanctities of home', and began to concentrate on 'domestic rites';[22] family celebrations of the season. In this re-modelled Christmas, there was no room for the wassail cup that held gallons of alcohol, or for frightening the neighbours with gunshot and loud caroling: 'The picturesque ceremonies and rude festivities that distinguished the Christmas of bygone times have passed away, and, for ourselves, we can regard the loss of them without regret. We are too thankful to have lighted upon a more civilized age.'[23]

Given this cultural climate, the next transformation of the wassail bowl, a sublimation of the alcoholic drink into a sweet, milk-based dessert, makes sense. Mrs Beeton championed milk-based dishes as a remedy for almost everything, noting, 'this bland and soothing article of diet is excellent for the majority of thin, nervous people, especially for those who have suffered high emotional disturbance.' In her cookery book there are over a hundred dessert and pudding recipes. The Victorian diet reflected the British love of sweetness; Britain used almost half of the sugar beet consumed in Europe, as well as the greatest proportion of imported cane sugar.[24] The recipe that most clearly demonstrates this change in the wassail bowl appears in *Warne's Model Housekeeper* by Ross Murray:

> One bottle of sherry, half a pint of cold water, six or seven eggs, according to size, quarter of a pound of powdered sugar, a little nutmeg, and a few cloves, half a pound of macaroons, half a pound of ratafias, twelve spongecakes, one lemon.
>
> Grate the biscuits into an old china bowl, and squeeze a lemon over them; beat the eggs thoroughly with the sugar and spice; pour the wine and water into an enamelled saucepan; stir till they boil; then pour them by degrees over the eggs, stirring one way all the time. If it does not thicken put it on the fire and stir till it does; then pour it hot over the cakes.
>
> Or: Ingredients: One pound of macaroons, one pound of ratafias, twelve sponge cakes, one lemon, one bottle of sherry, one quart of custard. Crumble the cakes altogether and squeeze the lemon juice on them, pour over them the greater part of the bottle of wine, at least enough thoroughly to saturate them; lay on the top a rich custard.
>
> Make this sweet dish in an old china bowl. It makes an excellent pair with the punchbowl.[25]

The second recipe seems to be a convenience-food version of the first. Using a whole bottle of sherry, this is by no means a teetotal recipe, and is exceedingly rich. With macaroons, ratafias, and spongecakes, this would make a very solid sort of trifle, especially in the first recipe where the hot custard would soak all the way through the biscuits.

This wassail-bowl dessert, while seeming so far removed from the drink of hot spiced ale and bobbing crab apples, is a glorious mixture of tradition with Victorian innovation. The egg custard is reminiscent of another celebratory drink, the 'posset'; the cakes hark back to the 'bride cakes' of the Middle Ages, and the ready-made biscuits are a triumph of Victorian consumer society.

Recipes for 'ratafie' biscuits and macaroons had been published since the Regency era.[26] Although the ratafia biscuit is unhelpfully defined in the *OED* as 'a macaroon', it is made with bitter almonds, whereas the macaroon is sweeter, so it would seem that the ratafias provided extra flavour to the recipe. By the time of 'the model housekeeper' ready-made biscuits, the natural companion to the cup of afternoon tea, were widely available to the middle classes, and could have been used for this recipe.

The sponge cake could have been supplied by a local baker, but was more likely to have been made at home. Better quality flour and more predictable raising agents – baking powder sold in tins – meant a lighter sponge was easily obtainable in the Victorian kitchen. Farming and transport technology extended the laying season of hens and brought fresh eggs (and milk) into town, allowing this recipe to be made in the middle of winter.

Specifying cake as the bottom layer of the dish echoes the use of cakes at various important celebrations across the calendar. Ivan Day notes 'there was a time when we marked the progress of our year with cakes'. The force behind offering toast, or cakes, to the apple trees during a wassail becomes clearer when we learn that the earliest known English record of a cake or loaf used in a ritual context occurs in a complex twelfth-century remedy, written in Old English and Latin, designed 'to amend thine acres if they wax not well' during which the loaf, kneaded with holy water, was buried under the first furrow cut by the plough. Day has also written a masterly history of the bride-cake, which I shall not duplicate, except to point out the associations between the wedding cake, the wedding posset, and Mrs Warne's wassail bowl recipe.[27] Possets have been consumed since Elizabethan times, especially at celebrations such as weddings, Christmas, or even funerals. Day describes the wedding or benediction posset as:

> a blend of eggs, cream and sack or ale, … used to toast the bride and groom before they retired to the nuptial bed. This intoxicating nightcap consisted of a frothy head of aerated custard floating on a draught of highly alcoholic liquor. The custard was eaten with a spoon, while the liquid was sucked piping hot through the spout of the posset pot. As a wedding night pick-me-up, it had universal appeal and was consumed by all classes with a great deal of elbow nudging and mirth.[28]

As Peter Brears notes, however:

> Since the possets … were traditional drinks, regularly made by the local community, there was no need to record their recipes in written form, particularly at a time when many people were illiterate. For this reason relatively few recipes for ale possets have survived through to the present day. However, from those which are available, we can see how the ale was either fortified with rum, added

to roasted apples, tempered with milk or thickened with bread, cake, oats or eggs. It was always served piping hot. In many parts of the country, from Yorkshire down to Cornwall, the hot ale was enriched with rum, sugar and spices.[29]

In the wassail bowl the cakes, apples, and the hot custard were often brought together, as in this description from 1823:

> An old custom among the Welsh on Twelfth Night was the making of wassail, namely, cakes and apples baked and set in rows on top of each other, with sugar between, in a kind of beautiful bowl which had been made for the purpose and which had twelve handles. Then warm beer, mixed with hot spices from India, was put in the Wassail, and friends sat around in a circle near the fire and passed the Wassail bowl from hand to hand, each drinking in turn. Lastly the wassail (namely the cakes and apples after the beer covering them had been drunk) was shared among the whole company.[30]

Fine earthenware wassail bowls were made in Wales and elsewhere from the beginning of the nineteenth century, and it is interesting to note that the Mrs Warne's recipe specifies 'an old china bowl' in a seeming continuance of this tradition.

Before getting carried away with Victorian visions of merry villagers wassailing from Christmas Eve to Twelfth Night, it is worth considering the costs of the ingredients of a wassail bowl, and the Victorian dessert. Like the Elizabethan 'trifle', which was in fact anything but trifling, being made from thickened cream, sweetened with rare sugar, perfumed with rosewater and exotic spices, the wassail denoted celebration by the cost and scarcity of its ingredients. Certainly lambswool, thick with eggs and cream, would have been fanciful at Christmas time, in the depths of winter, when for centuries the labouring rural poor were scraping through on potatoes and burnt toast grated up to make 'tea'. At that time of year the milk would not have been thick enough for much cream, and the hens would have stopped laying regularly.

G.E. Fussell, studying the diet of the English rural labourer, remarks 'Legendary history is rarely so apparent anywhere else as it is in discussion of people's food. Feasts are easier to remember than the orderly procession of normal days; cake is more memorable than bread and its recipes more extensive in cookery books…so that it is difficult for contemporaries to record anything but the festivals.'[31] In other words, wassailing is not representative, and must be all the more remarkable for the demands it would have made on the villagers' provisions.

The labourer's diet as recorded was mainly bread, a little bacon in the West Country especially, and a little cheese. Canon Tuckwell, estimating the expenditure of a family in 1885, gives them only bread, flour, bacon, potatoes, cheese, sugar, tea, butter, milk, and treacle to eat. Even supposing they were 'growing their own' and had access to some apples, this is a poor diet and liable to be much scanter in the winter. The Canon acknowledges that 'Dreary England had taken the place of Merrie England'.[32]

A History of the Wassail Bowl

Today there is once again an increase in interest in folk traditions, and a desire among some parts of society to reconnect to rural traditions. There is a revival of interest in 'growing your own'; this time as a lifestyle choice rather than from harsh necessity. This has provoked interest in orchards and, in particular, in 'heritage varieties' of apples. In 1990 the organization Common Ground initiated Apple Day,[33] and as a result of this many people have become interested in celebrating their local orchards. Wassailing has been heard again, from Somerset to East Anglia.

Three years ago the members of the Trumpington Community Orchard Project, myself included, organized an informal wassail at short notice to celebrate the Cambridgeshire apple trees we had recently planted. The noise of pots and pans being banged together, and our spirited singing of the Leeds wassail carol (the only one I knew) brought out about twenty local inhabitants to celebrate with us and drink spiced warmed apple juice. This year we held a wassail that started with a lantern procession, and included folk musicians and singers. Over one hundred people joined in.[34]

The wassail is a celebration that has survived, in some form, throughout the centuries. It has often been feared to have died out altogether, but it has adapted and survived changes of calendar, religious observance and local economic circumstances. The ingredients of the bowl have reflected these and the societal changes from community to home. Whether modern wassailers drink apple juice, hot ale, spiced cider, or a rich frothy draught of lambswool thickened with eggs and cream, they are in touch with a ritual that has embraced whole communities of celebrants, from urban wassailers in town taverns to village folk firing shot-guns in orchards at midnight. If there is no tradition of wassailing in your community, perhaps you might like to 'invent' one, drawing on the materials, both culinary and cultural, that have been passed down. At the very least, on Christmas Eve, or on Old or New Twelfth Night, wish your neighbours a hearty 'Was hael'.

Notes

1. Andrew Barr, *Drink: A Social History of America* (London: Pimlico, 1995): p. 386. Vortigen then asks for the price of the Viking princess's hand in marriage, and is told it is the whole of Thanet, which he gives up willingly.
2. Peter Brears, 'Wassail: Celebrations in Hot Ale,' *Liquid Nourishment: Potable Foods and Stimulating Drinks*, ed. C. Anne Wilson (Edinburgh: Edinburgh University Press, 1993): p. 106.
3. Ibid. p. 108.
4. Ibid. p. 114.
5. Ibid. p. 114.
6. Ibid. p. 109.
7. W. Harrison Ainsworth, 'Auriol, the Elixir of Life,' qtd. Ruth Ward, *A Harvest of Apples* (London: Penguin, 1988): p. 221.
8. Quoted in Barrie E. Juniper and David J. Mabberley, *The Story of the Apple* (Portland Oregon: Timber Press, 2006): p. 165.

9. A letter from Mr Bond is an appendix to J. Rendel Harris, *Origin and Meaning of Apple Cults* (London, Longman, Green and Co. 1919): p. 49.
10. Nell Heaton, *Traditional Recipes of the British Isles* (London: Faber and Faber, 1950): p. 91.
11. Hogg, 1851, qtd. Juniper and Mabberley, p. 165.
12. Thomas K. Hervey, *The Book of Christmas*, 1888 (reprint by the Folklore Society, London: Wordsworth 2000): p. 169.
13. Juniper and Mabberley p. 136.
14. D. T. Fish, *The Apple: Its History, Varieties and Cultivation* (London: The Country Periodical, 1847): p. 1.
15. Juniper and Mabberley discuss both attributions. They note that although apple cultivation goes back three thousand years in Israel, the translation of *tappuah* as 'apple' is incorrect (p. 87).
16. The Norse goddess, Idun, kept a basket of the apple of eternal youth, which she dished out to the gods and goddesses. When the basket was stolen, the immortals began to age. These and other myths are discussed in Tamra Andrews, *Nectar and Ambrosia: An Encyclopedia of Food in World Mythology* (Santa Barbara, CA: ABC-Clio, 2000).
17. George W. Johnson and R. Errington, *The Gardener's Monthly Volume, November: The Apple; its culture, uses and history*, Volume One (London: Simpkin Marshall and Co, 1847) p. 8.
18. Ibid. vol 1 p. 10.
19. Richard Folkard Jun., *Plant Lore* (London: Sampson Low, Marston, Searle and Rivington, 1884): p. 219.
20. Steve Roud, Introduction, *The Book of Christmas*, by Thomas K. Hervey, 1888, reprint by the Folklore Society (London: Wordsworth, 2000): p. 23.
21. Mark Connelly, *Christmas: A Social History* (London: I.B. Tauris, 1999): p. 9.
22. *Illustrated London News*, qtd. ibid. p. 11: '…it would seem to be a special characteristic of the Teutonic race to watch with the deepest interest and tenderest solicitude over the sanctities of home, and Christmas has been consecrated by them, from time immemorial to the performance of domestic rites.'
23. H. V., 'Christmas with the Poets', 1852, qtd. ibid. p. 24.
24. Colin Spencer, *British Food: An Extraordinary Thousand Years of History* (London: Grub Street with Fortnum and Mason, 2002): pp. 275–277.
25. Ross Murray, *Warne's Model Housekeeper* (London: Frederick Warne & Co, 1882): http://chestofbooks.com/food/household/Housekeeper/WassailBowl.html.
26. For example, in 'A collection of Above Three Hundred Receipts' [details unknown, date given as 1734], see image of the recipe online at: http://historyhoydens.blogspot.com/2008/06/regency-refreshment-sratafia-biscuits.html.
27. Ivan Day, 'Bride Cake', in *Food and the Rites of Passage*, ed. Laura Mason (London: Prospect Books, 2001): p. 35 and following.
28. Ivan Day, ed., *Eat, Drink and Be Merry: The British at Table 1600–2000* (London: Philip Wilson, 2000): p. 19.
29. Brears, p. 122.
30. Ibid., p. 119.
31. G. E. Fussell, *The English Rural Labourer – His Home, Furniture, Clothing and Food from Tudor to Victorian Times* (London: Batchworth Press, 1949): p. 82.
32. Ibid., p. 85
33. http://www.england-in-particular.info/cg/appleday/index.html.
34. http://www.trumpingtonorchard.blogspot.com/.

Celebrating Hellenism far from Hellas: Feasts and Festivals of Ptolemy II of Egypt

Andrew Dalby

Ptolemy II in his time and place

The year is 271 BC. Alexandria, most famous of the foundations of Alexander the Great, has been in existence for just sixty years, and it is already one of the three greatest cities in the world, the other two being Pataliputra in India and Chang'an, modern Xi'an, in China. Alexandria is growing more rapidly than either.

The city walls enclose a roughly rectangular area, an area shaped like a cloak, according to a geographer more imaginative than his colleagues (evidently the cloaks in his wardrobe were rectangular). The road pattern is perfectly regular, centred on a very wide road, the Platea, that runs from the Sun Gate in the east to the Moon Gate in the west. North of this road the land falls away towards the sea front and the two harbours, beyond which the great lighthouse, the Pharos, the new wonder of the world, guides the many ships that now cross the Mediterranean from Rhodes, the Aegean and mainland Greece. The central harbour is closed off by the Promontory, covered with royal palaces, temples, and gardens, divided from the rest of the city by a monumental gateway. The gates stand open.

Alexander the Great founded this capital city; he also re-founded the kingdom of Egypt, of which he took possession in the course of his conquest of the vast Persian Empire. The Egyptians may well have seen the Greeks as liberators. Alexander himself felt a special affinity with the valley kingdom, regarding the Egyptian god Amun as his divine father.

Egypt until Alexander's conquest had looked inward; a civilization at least three thousand years old and as fertile and self-sufficient as any. By its site on the Mediterranean coast, Alexandria signalled that Egypt would henceforth look outwards.

Ptolemy son of Lagos was Alexander's most trusted lieutenant, so he said. He wrote a history of Alexander's conquests; what he wrote forms the basis of the standard histories. Alexander died young, and Ptolemy, eleven years older, was among the generals who gathered in Babylon to decide what to do next. Ptolemy, unlike the others, knew what he wanted. He took and kept Egypt. He also took the embalmed body of Alexander, which was eventually to lie in a golden sarcophagus in Alexandria.

Several of Alexander's successor generals were killed during the wars that followed his death. Ptolemy was among the four survivors who declared themselves kings in 305 BC. The Ptolemaic kingdom of Egypt dates from that year, and Ptolemy I, the 'Saviour', ruled as king for twenty years. In 285 BC he handed power to his 23-year-old son.

Feasts and Festivals of Ptolemy II of Egypt

Ptolemy II inherited a fertile kingdom, prosperous trade routes, and a full treasury. He had only one wife, but he was shortly to marry a second, Arsinoe, the most powerful and dangerous woman of the third century BC. This was the first brother-sister marriage in that famously incestuous family of the Macedonian kings of Egypt. Ptolemy II ruled for forty prosperous years. Arsinoe died in 270 BC: thereafter Ptolemy presided over the worship of Arsinoe Philadelphos, 'Arsinoe who loved her brother', in the confident knowledge that when he died he, too, would necessarily become a god, to keep her company. He did so, in 246 BC, and was henceforth known as Ptolemy Philadelphos, 'Ptolemy who loved his sister'.

There was much to celebrate during this reign, and there are rich sources for Ptolemy II's celebrations: descriptions of a royal banqueting pavilion, of a religious carnival in honour of Dionysos, of the festival of Adonis directed by Queen Arsinoe. There is a fictional but not unrealistic narrative of a symposium hosted by Ptolemy himself; from a later generation there is a sketch of the royal kitchens of Ptolemaic Alexandria. We begin with contemporary glimpses of Ptolemy himself.

Ptolemy II, seen from afar: Theokritos, *Idylls* 14.58–68
One unlikely Sicilian shepherd addresses another.

> 'If you are really inclined to emigrate, then Ptolemy is the best paymaster for a free man.'
> 'Oh? And what's he like in other ways?'
> 'The very best – kindly, cultured, gallant [*erotikos*], as nice as can be; knows his friends, and knows his enemies even better. As a king should be, he's generous to many, and doesn't refuse when asked, but you mustn't be always asking, Aischinas. So if you fancy pinning your cloak-end on your right shoulder, if you're brave enough to stand firm on both feet against a strong man's attack, then off with you to Egypt.'

> *Notes:*
> 'Gallant': an allusion to Ptolemy's wives and mistresses.
> 'Cultured': he inherited the newly created Museum, the first institution that ever had this name. The Museum was in reality a research centre: attached to it, and founded by Ptolemy II himself, was the Alexandrian Library. He worked assiduously to enlarge the library, to the extent of confiscating books from travellers' luggage.

Ptolemy II, seen from close at hand: Theokritos, *Idylls* 15.46–49
Two Alexandrian women chat on their way to the festival of Adonis somewhere in the palace grounds.

> 'You've done some good things, Ptolemy, since your father became an immortal. Nowadays no ruffian slips up to you in the street in the Egyptian way and does you a mischief. The tricks those rascals used to play!'

Notes:
   'Since your father became an immortal': Ptolemy II had taken control at his father's invitation in 285 BC; Ptolemy I became an immortal in 283 BC.

Ptolemy II, a later view: Athenaios, *Deipnosophistai* 576e–f

Then again the second king of Egypt, the one called Philadelphos, had a great many lovers (so says Ptolemy Euergetes in his *Historical Notes*): Didyme, an indigenous woman who was extremely beautiful, also Bilistiche and Agathokleia and Stratonike, to whom a big memorial still stands beside the sea near Eleusis, and Myrtion and a great many more. He was quite unusually amorous. Polybios says in *Histories* book 14 that in Alexandria are to be seen numerous images of the girl who poured wine for Ptolemy, Kleino, wearing only a tunic and holding a drinking-horn in her hands. Isn't it true, Polybios adds, that the finest houses are named after Myrtion, Mnesis and Potheine? Yet Mnesis was a flute-player, also Potheine, while Myrtion was notoriously a common showgirl.

Notes:
   'Ptolemy Euergetes': this author, quoted by Athenaios, was himself a member of the dynasty. He ruled as Ptolemy VIII and was Ptolemy II's great-great-grandson.
   'Eleusis': in Egypt near Alexandria (not the Eleusis in Greece).
   'Numerous images': as I argue in another paper, the great historian Polybios is wrong here: what he saw were images of Queen Arsinoe in Egyptian style.

How Ptolemy II traced his ancestry to Dionysos: Satyros quoted by Theophilos of Antioch, *To Autolykos* book 2

There are at least three reasons why the Greek wine god Dionysos figured so largely in the great procession soon to be described. First, Dionysos was said to have led a conquering expedition to India long ago, just as Alexander the Great (heroic founder of Ptolemaic Egypt) had recently done. Second, Dionysos was likened to and identified with the new Egyptian god Serapis, whose worship was assiduously encouraged by Ptolemy I and his successors. Third, the Ptolemies were themselves descendants of Dionysos. This text, part of a 'mythology' of the demes and tribes of Alexandria, gives a semi-official version of the royal family tree.

Satyrus, in his list of the demes of Alexandria, starts out with Ptolemy IV Philopator and his descent from Dionysos, because this explains why the first tribe to be founded was Dionysia. Here is the text: 'Dionysos slept with Thestios' daughter Althaia. She gave birth to Deianeira, who was the wife of Zeus' son Herakles and bore Hyllo, whose son was Kleodaios, whose son was Aristomachos, whose son was Temenos, whose son was Kisos, whose son was Maron, whose son was Thestios, whose son was Akoos, whose son was Aristodamidas, whose son was Karanos, whose son was Koinos, whose son was Tyrimmas, whose son was Perdiccas, whose son was Philippos, whose son was Aëropos, whose son was Alketas, whose son was Amyntas, whose son was Bokros, whose son was Meleagros, whose daughter was Arsinoe, who married Lagos and bore Ptolemy [I] who is called "Saviour", who married Berenike [I]: their son was Ptolemy [II] Philadelphos, who married Arsinoe: their son was Ptolemy [III] Euergetes, who married Berenike [II] the daughter of Magas King of Cyrene: their son was Ptolemy [IV] Philopator. This is the genealogy that connects Dionysos to the kings of Egypt.'

Notes:
'Dionysos slept with Thestios' daughter Althaia': according to the usual version of the myth this happened immediately after Dionysos' return from India. Althaia's husband, Oineus, King of Kalydon in Greece, looked the other way. His reward was the gift of wine, *oinos*: thus Oineus is the mythical founder of the Greek wine-making tradition.

'Berenike the daughter of Magas King of Cyrene': Berenike, the second lady of this name in the Egyptian royal family, Ptolemy II's daughter-in-law, is the one whose shorn hair became the constellation Coma Berenices.

The main questions

Major questions that demand to be answered – this paper offers evidence towards the answers – are these. Do these public celebrations recreate older traditions? If so, are these the traditions familiar from earlier Egypt, or from elsewhere in Alexander's empire, or from earlier Greece, or an imaginary Greece of the idealized past? Ptolemaic Egypt was, however, a new state, and its celebrations are also new: they mark the beginnings of a new cultural synthesis, as seen, soon afterwards, in bilingual religious documents such as the Rosetta Stone.

The great procession: Kallixeinos of Rhodes, *On Alexandria* quoted by Athenaios, *Deipnosophistai* 197c–203b

This is an extended description of a religious carnival procession through the streets of Alexandria. It began an hour before dawn, with displays dedicated to the morning star, and ended an hour after sunset, with a sequence dedicated to the evening star, but the god principally honoured was Dionysos. Only brief extracts are quoted here.

> Then came floats pulled by mules: the floats displayed scenes of foreign countries, and Indian and other women sat on them, dressed like prisoners of war. There were also she-camels loaded with 300 minas of frankincense, 300 minas of myrrh, and 200 minas each of saffron, cassia, cinnamon, iris-root and other spices.
>
> A four-wheeled cart 30 feet long and 24 feet wide was pulled along … by 300 men. A wine-press 24 cubits high … full of grapes had been built on top of it: 60 satyrs were trampling the grapes and singing a grape-pressing song to the accompaniment of pipes, and Silenos was supervising them: the grape-must ran everywhere in the street. Immediately after it came a four-wheeled cart 37

feet long and 28 feet wide, pulled by 600 men. On this was a wineskin with a capacity of 3000 amphoras, stitched together from leopard skins; it too flooded the street as it was slowly allowed to empty out.

Notes:
'Indian women': Ptolemy had never fought in India. But he had developed seaports along the length of the Red Sea, far south of the existing borders of his kingdom, and this enabled him to encourage the spice trade – a source of ever-increasing wealth through import and export duties – and to begin the taming of African elephants, his newly-developed weapon, a substitute for the Indian elephants that had been accessible to the mythical Dionysos and the real Alexander. The Red Sea bases brought him the elephants; trading links with India allowed him to display the costly spices and pretended prisoners of war, all of which showed him to be a worthy successor to Dionysos and Alexander.
'300 minas': roughly 300 pounds, 150 kilograms.
'24 cubits': 36 feet, nearly 12 metres.
'The satyrs', led by Silenos, were the traditional companions of Dionysos. Satyrs are often depicted treading the grapes in paintings on Greek vases.
'Wineskins': a bag-in-a-box without the box, typically made from a single whole ox-skin with a standard capacity of 20 amphoras, i.e. 115 gallons or 525 litres. The one described here is 150 times the usual size.

Adonis dead: Theokritos, *Idylls* 15.64–65, 77, 106–120

The same two women arrive to see the festival of Adonis. They take advice from an old woman on her way home ('Women know everything, even what Zeus did with Hera. Look, Praxinoa, what a crowd around the gates!') and squeeze in through the monumental gateway that marks off the palace quarter from the rest of the city ('Everybody's in, as the man said, locking the bedroom door'). They admire the tapestries, and listen to a professional singer performing the Adonis song. Its lyrics tell first of Queen Arsinoe, and then of the divine Adonis who is to spend one day with Aphrodite before his descent to the underworld:

Lady of Cyprus, child of Dione, you changed Berenike from mortal to immortal, so men say, dropping ambrosia into her womanly breast. For your sake, Lady of many names and many shrines, Berenike's daughter Arsinoe, as lovely as Helen, cossets Adonis with all good things. Around him in their season are all that fruit-trees bear, and delicate gardens placed in silver baskets, and golden flasks of Syrian perfume, and all the delicacies that women fashion on their kneading-trays, mixing every colour with fine white wheat-flour, and all that they make with sweet honey and glistening olive oil. All creatures of the earth and air are there too, and green bowers have been built, heavy with tender dill.

Notes:
'What Zeus did with Hera': the king and queen of the Greek gods had a brother-sister marriage, just like Ptolemy, and this interesting parallel was noticed in Egypt.
'Lady of Cyprus, child of Dione ... Lady of many names and many shrines': Aphrodite, the Greek goddess of love, often identified by Egyptians with their goddess Isis. The myth of Aphrodite and Adonis, which caught the imagination of many later poets, arises from a

mixture of Greek and Near Eastern stories: Adonis is a form of the Semitic god Tammuz and could be identified by Egyptians with their god Osiris.

Berenike I, mother of Ptolemy II and Arsinoe, became a god some time between 279 and 274 BC. Arsinoe herself died in 270 BC, so the dramatic date (and probably the real date of Theokritos' poem) must be in the mid- to late-270s BC. Arsinoe was already being linked with Aphrodite in the dynastic cult, hence it is appropriate to see her (and not just Aphrodite) cosseting Adonis. On the everyday level the words mean that Arsinoe is responsible for the arranging the festival.

'Gardens of Adonis' were delicately made from living plants and artfully arranged around the central scene. They were thrown into the sea next day in mourning for Adonis.

Dill is 'heavy' because of its aroma, which came to Linnaeus' mind when he named this species *Anethum graveolens*, 'dill with the heavy aroma'.

The symposium pavilion: Kallixeinos of Rhodes, *On Alexandria,* quoted by Athenaios, *Deipnosophistai* 196a–197b

A description of a wooden dining pavilion, set up in the palace gardens on some unspecified occasion, that was big enough to hold 130 couches arranged around a central space. The pillars around this central area were 75 feet high; outside them was a peristyle or concourse, with a lower roof, where the diners' attendants could gather.

> The entire floor had been strewn with flowers of every kind; for the fact that the air in Egypt is temperate, and the gardeners there cultivate plants that grow elsewhere only in limited quantities and in particular seasons, means that the country produces enormous quantities of flowers at every time of year, and the general rule is that no flower, including roses, white violets, or anything else, ever completely stops blooming. The fact that the party took place in midwinter meant that the guests were astonished by what they saw, because flowers that could not easily have been found combined in a single garland in any other city had been arranged in garlands in immense numbers for the large crowd of guests and strewn in heaps on the floor of the pavilion, making it look as if it were truly a divine meadow … A hundred gold couches with feet shaped like sphinxes were set along the two sides of the pavilion; the front end of the hall was left open … Smooth Persian carpets with fine designs of living creatures worked into them covered the space in the centre where people walked. Two hundred gold tables on silver tripods were set out, two per couch; behind them were set 100 silver ewers and an equal number of water-jugs for them to wash with. Another couch had been set up facing the symposium to display the cups and drinking vessels and the other utensils needed; these were all made of gold, studded with jewels, and were of extraordinary workmanship.
>
> *Notes:*
> 'Gardeners there cultivate plants that grow elsewhere only … in particular seasons': Alexander and his successors had been keen to introduce plants to new habitats; Egypt had already been famous in earlier Greece as a place where seasonal fruits and flowers were available throughout the year.

'The guests were astonished by what they saw': evidently they are visitors to Egypt. Egyptians would think it normal to see flowers that were grown by local gardeners: overseas guests, particularly from Greece with its well-marked seasons, would be surprised. Probably the occasion is the first Ptolemaiia, the four-yearly festival inaugurated by Ptolemy II to celebrate his dynasty, in midwinter 279/278 BC.

'Persian carpets': I know no evidence for the early trade in Persian carpets, but I would suggest that they became known in Egypt when it was part of the Persian empire, before Alexander's conquest.

'A hundred gold couches': there is room for 130 couches but for this event only a hundred couches are arranged. One hundred was a classic number in this context. Alexander the Great's travelling banqueting pavilion would accommodate 100 couches. The sources differ on how many Macedonian officers were married to Persian ladies at the mass marriage celebrated by Alexander: somewhere between 80 and 100.

'Two hundred gold tables on silver tripods': notice the generosity and the practicality. Two small tables per couch, and all in precious metal, but only three legs per table. In a temporary construction, to expect small four-legged objects to stand flat would be to expect too much.

'Open': so that ordinary citizens might see what was going on (as the two women were able to crowd into the palace precincts to see the Adonia).

A symposium: *Letter of Aristeas* 180–294

We know what Ptolemy II talked about at his symposia if we believe the *Letter of Aristeas*, which was written to explain how the Greek translation of the Old Testament came to be made during Ptolemy's reign. Sadly, we cannot believe it. Written at least a hundred years after the event, it is a historical novel, not a piece of history. But the setting seems accurate.

The seventy translators were given accommodation on Pharos Island, because it was more peaceful than the city and caught the sea breezes, but before they set to work Ptolemy invited them to a symposium in the palace quarter. Since they were all present, together with Ptolemy himself and other guests, the total numbers would have been 100 or more and the scene would necessarily have been very much like the pavilion just described. The couches were arranged 'in two rows, so that Ptolemy would have half of them on his right and half behind him'. This could be another way of describing the arrangement of couches in a circle, open at one end, in the symposium pavilion. The fine foods that Ptolemy had ordered for them were admirably served under the orders of the royal steward Dorotheos. Ptolemy turned to the first translator on his right and said: 'How may a king keep his kingdom, with justice, until his last day?' The symposium continued through seventy questions and seven days until the last translator faced his challenge: 'What is the greatest achievement of a ruler?' The answer was, 'To ensure that his subjects are always at peace, and always, without delay, receive just verdicts in the courts.' This echoes the praise of Ptolemy by the two ladies of Theokritos' dialogue. Finally Ptolemy raised his cup and drank a toast to the translators, and sent each of them back to their lodgings with a messenger carrying three talents of silver. After which 'the king gave himself over to festivities unreservedly.'

Feasts and Festivals of Ptolemy II of Egypt

The royal kitchens: Plutarch, *Life of Mark Antony* **28**
Nothing more is known of the royal steward Dorotheos mentioned in the *Letter of Aristeas*. For a glance into the palace kitchens we go to a still-later source, but one we can trust. Plutarch, author of the *Parallel Lives*, narrates at length the tragic love affair of Mark Antony and Cleopatra, who was Ptolemy II's great-great-great-great-great-great-granddaughter. Plutarch resorts to his own family tradition for this anecdote.

> My grandfather had a friend named Philotas who was a doctor in a neighbouring city. As Philotas used to tell the story, he had been a medical student in Alexandria in Cleopatra's time. He had made friends with one of the royal cooks, and was persuaded, as was natural enough in a young man, to come and see the lavish preparations which were made for a royal dinner. He was taken into the kitchens of the palace, and after he had seen the enormous abundance of provisions and watched eight wild boars being roasted, he expressed his astonishment at the size of the company for which this vast hospitality was intended. The cook laughed aloud and explained that this was not a large party, only about a dozen people, but that everything must be cooked and served to perfection, and that the whole effect could be ruined by a moment's delay. It might happen that Antony would call for the meal as soon as the guests had arrived, or a little later he might postpone it and call for a cup of wine, or become absorbed in some conversation. 'So we never prepare one supper,' he explained, 'but a whole number of them, as we never know the exact moment when they will be sent for.'

Notes:
'Medical student': Alexandria was one of the main centres for medical education in the ancient Mediterranean.
'Expressed his astonishment': as a resident of Alexandria he might have already seen a symposium pavilion as just described, and observed public banquets like the one honouring the seventy translators.

Consequences

Ptolemaic Egypt had a vast influence on later cultures. Like the other Hellenistic kingdoms it impressed the Romans deeply at the period when they were conquering an empire in the eastern Mediterranean and learning to enjoy their new-found wealth and luxuries. Egypt was the last of these kingdoms to fall to Rome. By reputation it was the wickedest and the most luxurious of all. The Roman emperor Augustus and his successors were rich with the spices that came by way of Egypt.

Epilogue: Plutarch, *Life of Mark Antony* **75**
The end of Ptolemaic Egypt came suddenly: the botched suicide of Antony and the skilful and romantic suicide of Cleopatra left a vacuum that Augustus was ready to fill.

Plutarch here describes Antony's last dinner, on the evening before he clumsily turned his dagger on himself.

> He told his slaves to fill his cup and serve him more generously than usual, for no man could say whether on the next day they would be waiting on him or serving other masters, while he himself would be lying dead, a mummy and a nothing ... That evening, so the story goes, about the hour of midnight, when all was hushed, suddenly there was heard a marvellous sound of music, which seemed to come from a consort of instruments of every kind, and voices chanting in harmony, and at the same time the shouting of a crowd in which the cry of bacchanals and the ecstatic leaping of satyrs were mingled, as if a troop of revellers were leaving the city, shouting and singing as they went. The procession seemed to follow a course through the middle of the city towards the outer gate which led to the enemy's camp, and at this point the sounds reached their climax and then died away. Those who tried to discover a meaning for this prodigy concluded that the god Dionysos, with whom Antony claimed kinship and whom he had sought above all to imitate, was now abandoning him.
>
> *Notes:*
> 'The outer gate': the gate of the Sun.
> 'With whom Antony claimed kinship': as did Cleopatra and her ancestors, see the grand procession described above. Dionysos was abandoning the Egyptian royal dynasty too.

Bibliography

Bevan, E.R. *The House of Ptolemy*. London: Methuen, 1927.
Casson, Lionel. 'Ptolemy II and the hunting of African elephants', *Transactions of the American Philological Association* vol. 123 (1993) pp. 247–260.
Chauveau, Michel. 'Ptolémée II, le Philadelphe', in Jacob and Polignac 1992 (below) pp. 138–151.
Dalby, Andrew. *Bacchus: a Biography*. London: British Museum Press, 2003.
Gow, A.S.F., ed. *Theocritus*. Cambridge: Cambridge University Press, 1952.
Hölbl, Günther. *A History of the Ptolemaic Empire*. London: Routledge, 2001.
Hunter, Richard, ed. *Theocritus: Encomium of Ptolemy Philadelphus*. Berkeley: University of California Press, 2003.
Jacob, C. and François de Polignac, eds. *Alexandrie IIIe siècle av. J.-C.: tous les savoirs du monde ou le rêve d'universalité des Ptolémées*. Paris, 1992.
McKechnie, Paul and Philippe Guillaume, eds. *Ptolemy II Philadelphus and his World*. Leiden: Brill, 2008.
McKenzie, Judith. *The Architecture of Alexandria and Egypt, c. 300 BC to AD 700*. New Haven: Yale University Press, 2007.
Olson, S. Douglas, ed. *Athenaeus: The Learned Banqueters*. Cambridge: Harvard University Press, 2006.
Pelling, C.B.R., ed. *Plutarch: Life of Antony*. Cambridge: Cambridge University Press, 1988.
Rice, E.E. *The Grand Procession of Ptolemy Philadelphus*. Oxford: Oxford University Press, 1983.
Tarn, W.W. 'Ptolemy II', *Journal of Egyptian Archaeology* vol. 14 (1928) pp. 246–260.
Tarn, W.W. 'Ptolemy II and Arabia', *Journal of Egyptian Archaeology* vol. 15 (1929) pp. 9–25.
Thompson, Dorothy J. 'Philadelphus' procession: dynastic power in a Mediterranean context', in L. Mooren, ed., *Politics, Administration and Society in the Hellenistic and Roman World* (Louvain, 2000) pp. 365–388.

The 'Floating Feasts' of Ancient Rome

John F. Donahue

Feasting was an essential thread in the celebratory fabric of Roman social life. In recent years, scholarly interest in this topic has been both intense and wide ranging, with the result that, from the private dining-room to the public square, we are now much better informed about the rich complexity of this activity.[1] Largely overlooked, however, have been those feasts that occurred near or upon bodies of water. Indeed, much of the evidence is quite provocative. Nero, for example, is said to have celebrated one of his many public theatrical performances by feasting the people in boats on an artificial canal at Rome in 59 CE. Five years later, with the help of his debauched accomplice Tigellinus, he staged his infamous feast upon an artificial lake in Rome, where he and his associates enjoyed the finest foods and wines, while on shore the populace sampled the pleasures of temporary cook shops and brothels amid exotic flora, fauna and wildlife imported solely for the occasion.[2]

How can we begin to interpret evidence of this sort? On the one hand, the public's reaction against imperial excess as filtered through a later literary tradition is never far from the surface in these accounts. We also need to be mindful that the ancient sources, especially imperial biography, were keen to utilize criteria such as festal comportment in order to draw contrasts between the 'good' and the 'bad' emperor.[3] While these features are important to recognize, the 'floating feast' deserves careful scrutiny in its own right, especially for what it can reveal about two interconnected themes: the Romans' ability to adapt Eastern traditions of celebration and display for their own use; and, the emperor's capacity to display his majesty, however novel or excessive, while reinforcing the social and political distance between ruler and ruled. Both of these themes have their basis in the Hellenistic world: the first, through the festal ship, the *thalamegos*, and its relationship to later Roman pleasure craft; the second, in the nature of the Eastern monarch himself and his influence on the behavior of the Roman emperor. I shall examine both of these themes in turn with the hope of showing that, far from being a perverse curiosity, the floating feast provides a useful interpretative lens through which to view both the concept of celebration and the workings of imperial power and display in the early decades of the Roman Empire.

The *thalamegos* of Ptolemaic Egypt

When we turn to the historical evidence for celebrating on ships, most compelling is the testimony from the reign of Ptolemy IV Philopator, who ruled in Egypt from 221 to 204 BCE as a member of the Ptolemaic dynasty that succeeded Alexander the Great. Philopator, whose name means 'lover of his father,' is portrayed in the sources as a devotee of Dionysius, god of wine, and generally as a ruler who preferred private pleasures to public duties.[4] While some scholars have reassessed this harsh judgment in recent years,[5] what is not in dispute during his reign is the appearance of the *thalamegos*, his palatial Nile barge. *Thalamegoi* were common in Egypt; in fact, the Greek historian Appian records that the Ptolemaic fleet included 800 of these vessels which, with their gilded sterns and prows, were typically deployed to ferry government officials up and down the river.[6] What sets Philopator's vessel apart, however, is its conversion from a business to a pleasure craft and the fact that it seems to have initiated the long tradition of floating festal palaces in the ancient world.

Our source for this vessel is Kallixenos, a contemporary historian whose account is preserved in the *Deipnosophistae* (*The Learned Banqueters*), a witty, third-century collection of excerpts and anecdotes on food and a wide range of other subjects preserved as a dinner conversation among a group of learned men in Rome. Kallixenos takes us on a vivid tour of this grandiose vessel, which was nearly 300 feet long, 45 feet wide at its broadest point, and 60 feet above the water. Especially noteworthy was the amount of space devoted to dining:

> The dining-room featured a beautiful coffered ceiling of cypress-wood, its ornamentation carved and gilded. A bedroom large enough for seven couches was next to this dining-room. Connected to this room was a narrow passageway that spanned the width of the ship and divided off the women's quarters; in this area was a dining-room large enough for nine couches, which was decorated as richly as the large one, and a bedroom large enough for five couches. This was how the first deck was arranged.[7]

Kallixenos is no less descriptive of the ship's upper deck where the reader, now working from the rear of the ship to the front, encounters another room large enough for five couches and with a rhombus shape. Close to it was a:

> rotunda-like shrine of Aphrodite in which there was a marble statue of the goddess. Opposite this was another luxurious peripteral dining-room with columns of Indian marble. Bedrooms decorated like the areas described above were alongside this dining-room. As you advanced toward the prow, there was a peristyle room dedicated to Dionysius large enough for 13 couches; running around this room was a cornice that was gilded up to the level of the architrave. The ceiling was appropriate to the character of the god. On the right side of the room a cave had been built; on the outside was stonework of genuine jewels and gold. Placed inside it were portrait-statues of the royal family made of translucent marble. Situated directly above the largest room was another very pleasant dining-room arranged like a tent. It did not have a roof, but crossbeams extended high above in a bow-shape, and purple curtains were suspended from them when the ship was sailing. Next was an atrium that filled the area above

the vestibule one deck below. Next to this was a winding staircase that led to an enclosed walkway, and a dining-room large enough for nine couches.[8]

In closing, Kallixenos provides a further description of this final dining-room with its many columns and the additional information that there were many other rooms in the space in the center of the ship's hold and in every other part of it.

This account is important in several respects. In an architectural context, the dining-room designed like a tent recalls the famous feasts held in tents by Ptolemy's grandfather, Ptolemy Philadelphos, and suggests that by the later third century BC Ptolemaic engineering and ingenuity had perfected the transfer of these tented feasts to a nautical setting. Furthermore, the colonnaded basilica reflects an architectural form that the Romans would later adapt quite widely. Finally, on a religious level, the space devoted to Aphrodite and Dionysius on the upper deck underscores the dynasty's close connection to these tutelary deities, a link that was reinforced by statues of the royal family to form a kind of dynastic sanctuary.[9]

What is clearly most striking, however, is the emphasis on banqueting, which followed the élite model of diners reclining to eat and drink on couches, with one guest per couch. Kallixenos claims that the main hall on the lower deck alone contained twenty couches, far above the range of five to eleven couches in the typical purpose-built dining-room of Attica during the classical period.[10] We can suppose that the large tented space above the main hall held an equal number of diners. Elsewhere, dining couches on both decks were plentiful, and banqueting space was even included in the men's and women's bedrooms. This evidence is consistent with the lavish dining associated with Hellenistic monarchs and, even if nothing on board this ship equaled the hundred-couch dining tent that Alexander brought with him to Asia, the numbers are still quite impressive and confirm the centrality of celebration on this remarkable vessel.[11]

Given this reality, it is difficult to come to a conclusion other than that the primary function of this magnificent ship, fashioned to resemble a grand villa, was to provide a unique and lavish venue for imperially sponsored celebrations. Unlike the Roman evidence to be considered later, we have no testimony of an actual banquet held on this vessel. Even so, Kallixenos' description is detailed enough to suggest that the ship was well known in the later third century, and we are left to wonder if he himself had witnessed this wondrous *thalamegos*. In many ways it was the perfect vessel for a king so devoted to luxury and to Dionysius.

Cleopatra and Antony at the Cydnus River

The Ptolemaic fascination with elaborate festal ships reappeared most colorfully some two hundred years after the reign of Ptolemy Philopator in the highly dramatic meeting between Antony and Cleopatra in 41 BC, when the Queen answered Antony's call to meet him at Tarsos in Asia Minor by sailing up the Cydnus River in her own *thalamegos*.

Antony himself was no stranger to maritime pleasures. He was well known in Italy for his picnics in groves and on riverbanks, and later continued to pursue this interest in Egypt through his escapades with Cleopatra on the banks of the Canopus and Taposiris rivers.[12] It should come as no surprise then that he chose the Cydnus as the setting for their first meeting, although he could never have foreseen that her approach would become one of the most celebrated events in Roman history.

Our sources are Athenaeus and the Greek biographer Plutarch, although the ultimate source may have been a member of Antony's own entourage, perhaps even his chronicler Dellius or the historian Sokrates of Rhodes.[13] This would help to explain the vivid emphasis on sight, smell, and sound in this episode. Cleopatra reclines beneath a canopy of cloth and gold, dressed as Venus and surrounded by attendants in the guise of Cupids, who cool her with their fans. Her all-female crew is attired as Nereids and Graces, while rich perfume wafts to the riverbanks from censers onboard her ship. Concerning the ship itself, we know only that it featured a gilded poop, purple sails, and silver oars manned by rowers, who kept time to the music of flute, pipe, and lyre.[14]

Antony too is carefully presented. He is finely dressed and awaits the Queen upon his tribunal, only to be abandoned by the crowd, which rushes up river to view the approaching Queen. Cleopatra first invites Antony on board with his commanders and entourage to enjoy a royal drinking party that is unspeakably lavish. The walls are hung with purple tapestries woven with threads of gold, the drinking vessels are made of gold and precious stones, and the guests are accommodated at twelve *triclinia*, couches arranged in groups of three, with each couch holding as many as three diners. Most magnificent is the extraordinary number of lights, which are let down from the roof and displayed all at once in various and creative patterns that produce a shimmering spectacle of beauty. The following evening, a more opulent banquet ensues, at the conclusion of which the Queen encourages her guests to take away many of her furnishings as gifts. Not yet finished, Cleopatra entertains Antony a final time, on which occasion she expends a large sum of money on roses, which cover the floor of her dining-room to a depth of two feet and which she arranges in spiral decorations all over her ship. Plutarch relates that at one point Antony attempts to reciprocate with a feast of his own but quickly realizes that he is hopelessly outdone.[15] The crude soldier is no match for the stylish and seductive queen.

Cleopatra's challenge was to win over Antony while absolving herself of supporting Cassius in the recent civil war. What better way to accomplish this than to rely in part on the *thalamegos*, which had long been associated in Egypt with both luxury and official state business? After all, Cleopatra was already well acquainted with the Roman appetite for Eastern splendor and in this instance she was intent on surpassing whatever it was that Antony might have known about her; at the same time, she was probably well aware of Antony's own predilection for extravagance and excessive behavior.[16] I would suggest that the *thalamegos* provided the Queen with the perfect opportunity to recreate in Tarsus the luxury of her Alexandrian court in order to help her to achieve her aims. As our sources confirm, she accomplished all of this brilliantly and in the process no doubt affirmed the value of this unique vessel as a highly effective instrument for advertising her power and status.

This was not the end of the *thalamegos*, however. In its Roman form it figured prominently among certain emperors, who, as we shall now see, would exploit it to display their own status in a manner that was every bit as memorable as that of Cleopatra and her Ptolemaic predecessors.

Caligula and Nero: perversity and excess

While it is difficult to establish a direct connection between the Ptolemaic *thalamegos* and the later Roman version, the very existence of the latter suggests that the Romans were well aware of such vessels and the possibilities they offered for imperial display. Moreover, the appearance of the festal ship during the Principate fits nicely with Rome's enthusiastic assimilation of Hellenistic culture in general, a phenomenon that was well established by the time we first hear of these vessels in the first century. In order to make this connection more securely, we must first turn to the literary evidence and then to the archaeological record. Neither category is completely satisfactory in itself, but taken together they can provide a framework for understanding that is more broadly based than an inquiry forced to rely on only one type of source material at the exclusion of the other.

The literary evidence for festal vessels focuses on the Julio-Claudian emperors, especially Caligula, about whom Suetonius reports the following:

> And he built Liburnian galleys, with ten banks of oars, jeweled sterns, multi-colored sails, and with huge baths, colonnades, and banqueting halls on board – not to mention vines and fruit trees of different varieties. In these vessels he used to take cruises along the Campanian coast, reclining on his couch and listening to songs and choruses.[17]

The passage, with its emphasis on sight and sound, is reminiscent of Plutarch's earlier description of Cleopatra's cruise up the Cydnus River. Here, however, Caligula relies on a Liburnian galley, the name given by the Romans to a ship built after a model borrowed from the Liburni, an Illyrian people on the north-east coast of the Adriatic, who were famous as seafarers and pirates. Originally a light, fast ship with a single bank of oars, the Romans outfitted the *liburnica* with a second set of oars and utilized it with great success in the Battle of Actium, where Octavian defeated the fleet of Antony and Cleopatra in 31 BC.[18] It would appear that Caligula lavishly retrofitted this popular warship for purely private pleasures, much like his predecessor Ptolemy had done centuries earlier.

A second piece of evidence, this coming from the Greek historian Cassius Dio, is equally intriguing. Here, Caligula attempted to build a bridge across the Bay of Baiae by fashioning ships together. Once completed, he celebrated an undeserved triumph, gave money to the friends, associates, and soldiers on hand for the occasion and, for the rest of the day – and into the night – feasted with them, he on the bridge, the rest on boats anchored close by. Recalling Cleopatra's first feast for Antony, Dio relates that torches were set up everywhere, in accordance with Caligula's wish 'to make the night day, as he had made the sea land.' The event took a turn for the worse, however, when Caligula, having eaten and drunk heavily, threw many of his guests to their death from the bridge and killed many others by attacking them with beaked ships.[19]

What it lacks in terms of providing a possible motive, the passage makes up for in its lurid exposition of imperial debauchery. In this aspect it recalls the similarly infamous episode involving the floating feast of Nero in 64 CE as mentioned above. This event took place on the Stagnum Agrippae, the great artificial lake or pool in the Campus Martius, one of the key centers for public entertainment in Rome. Tacitus and Dio record that Nero floated not on the luxury yacht of the Ptolemies or Caligula but on a makeshift vessel of planks fixed on empty wine casks and covered with purple carpets and soft bedding, all of which was towed around the pool by other vessels of gold and ivory. Temporary taverns and brothels, crowded with people, lined the banks of the pool and sexual licence of all kinds was practised in the open. Similar to Caligula's celebration at Baiae, Nero's orgy filled the night with light but also with chaos, as the drunken Romans, both men and women, caroused and fought, many to their own deaths. Nero surveyed it all from the lake, where he dined in splendor among his invited guests.[20]

Both of these accounts are stunning in that they portray emperors who seem to recognize the Hellenistic appeal of the extravagant ship and its power to advance personal interests, however perverse those interests may be. Furthermore, all of this takes place within a maritime setting which, like the ship itself, the emperor has the power to manipulate for his own ends. I shall propose some possible explanations for such behavior in the final section of this paper. In the meantime, it will be useful to conclude the first theme by turning to the famous ships of Lake Nemi and their value in providing a material basis for understanding the Roman festal ship and its connection to earlier Hellenistic models.

The Nemi ships

Situated in a volcanic crater in a heavily wooded area about 20 miles south of Rome, Nemi was well known in antiquity as a haven from the noise and the crowds of the imperial capital. Julius Caesar was said to have had a villa near the lake; it also served as a religious sanctuary for worshippers of Diana, goddess of the woods and hunt, to whom a temple was dedicated in the surrounding grove. The presence of ships at the bottom of the lake had been known since at least the sixteenth century. It was not until 1929, however, under the direction of Mussolini, whose Fascist government had an abiding interest in the grandeur of ancient Rome, that operations were undertaken to drain the lake in order to recover the ships. By the early 1930s the remains of two ships had revealed themselves amid the receding waters. They were then carefully moved to a museum built on the shores of the lake, where they were housed until 1944, when a fire destroyed them during the Nazis' advance through the area.[21]

Despite this tragedy, the loss was not completely catastrophic in that many artifacts had already been acquired by the National Museum in Rome; the archaeological site plans and technical drawings of the ships done by the Italian navy also escaped destruction. As a result, we possess a record of two ships that is truly remarkable in several aspects. First, both ships were quite large. The first vessel to be rescued, a sailing ship, measured some 230 feet long, with the second, an oared galley, slightly longer. Although smaller than the *thalamegos* of Ptolemy II, these ships were still twice as long as the *trireme*, the most popular warship in antiquity. Second, both ships were elaborately decorated and displayed a high degree of quality workmanship. The sailing ship provided evidence of splendid wall and floor mosaics in *opus tessellatum* (cubes in mortar) and *opus sectile* (cut marble inlay), bronze faucets, and gilded copper roof tiles. Also of interest were hundreds of terracotta pipes and tiles, evidence that not only running water but also heated water in conjunction with a Roman bath was available on board. Indeed, the discovery of similar lead water pipes from Pompeii, thought to be used for fountains and baths, provides additional support for viewing the Nemi ships as luxury vessels.[22] Equally luxurious, the second ship included the remnants of a structure thought to be a temple, as well as fluted columns, additional copper roof tiles and terracotta roof ornaments, and many pieces of marble and ivory. Third, on the basis of lead water pipes stamped with his name, it is virtually certain that Caligula built the ships. Finally, closer analysis of the mosaics and numismatic evidence suggest that the Nemi ships were later redecorated under Nero. Why they eventually sank remains hard to know.[23]

Given all of this evidence, it is not surprising that the Nemi ships are commonly recognized as the floating palaces of Caligula and Nero. The security of the dating and the fact that the artifacts are consistent with the tenor of luxury and excess preserved in the literary sources for these two emperors is quite striking, even if the archaeological remains do not conform in every detail to Suetonius' description of Caligula's Liburnian galleys, much less to the account of Nero's floating barrels in the Campus Martius. Nevertheless, the Nemi ships contribute enormously to our understanding of imperial behavior by providing material corroboration for the literary depiction of extravagant maritime display during the first century.

And what of feasting? Unlike the *thalamegos* in Athenaeus' account, with its emphasis on multiple dining areas, the Nemi ships preserved only their massive wood-framed hulls and the materials mentioned earlier. Nevertheless, based on this lavish décor and the survival of various drinking implements and amphorae typically used to hold wine, it is clear that these ships were intended as pleasure craft, the likes of which, in fact, were never to be seen again in antiquity.[24]

The 'Floating Feasts' of Ancient Rome

Cast thy bread upon the waters?

At Ecclesiastes 11.1–3 we find the well-known but enigmatic verses: 'Cast thy bread upon the waters: for thou shalt find it after many days. Give a portion to seven and also to eight; for thou knowest not what evil shall be upon the earth.' According to one interpretation, the meaning is that spontaneous deeds like the release of bread upon the water may, despite the odds, yield benefits many times over.[25] The gesture then is essentially one of liberality. Of course, we must be mindful of the difficulties of interpreting Roman imperial behavior in general, especially through the lens of biblical wisdom-literature. Nevertheless, might this be one way of understanding what these floating celebrations were all about? Of emperors literally 'casting their bread upon the waters' out of spontaneity and generosity? The explanation is tempting in some ways but it is perhaps too easy. I would suggest that a more nuanced approach, one that takes into consideration the nature of leadership itself in antiquity and the way in which a ruler was compelled to interact with his people, might prove more useful.

Among their many duties as leaders, monarchs and emperors were also benefactors, not only of institutions but also of individuals. This was certainly true in the Hellenistic world, and it was a lesson that was later embraced by Roman dynasts of the Republic and subsequently by the emperors as well. Chief among such beneficiaries were members of the leader's inner circle, whose loyalty was always critical to his success and well-being. Here, gifts were typically related to the social class of the beneficiary. At his famous fourfold triumphal celebration of 46 BC, Julius Caesar provided a feast that included lampreys, a delicacy, for his inner circle, while the masses celebrated simultaneously throughout the city on lesser fare. In the same way, senators feasted on better food and drink than the general public at shows in the Colosseum.[26] Such accounts are telling for what they reveal about motive and expectation when it came to imperially-sponsored acts of generosity and perhaps help us to envision more fully the social reality of who was on board the luxury vessels with Caligula and Nero and how they interacted on these occasions. For the *populus* who ate apart from the emperor, they too were well provided for on these occasions, although they were often left to view the emperor from afar, underscoring both the physical and social distance between ruler and ruled.

Closely related to this reality is the fact that, as Graham Shipley has recently reminded us in the case of the Hellenistic king, a celebration among his subjects provided the leader with an important opportunity for positive self-representation.[27] In the Roman world, Nero, who possessed a shrewd understanding of what the people wanted, especially recognized this, and his extravagantly staged maritime feasts fitted perfectly with such aims.[28] At the same time, such opportunities for self-representation could easily become transgressive events of barbarity and bloodshed, especially in the hands of young and excessively cruel emperors like Nero and Caligula whose monstrous behavior could not be easily checked.

In the final analysis, as with so many other things in their world, it was from the East that the Romans appropriated the floating feast and made it their own. Furthermore, for the likes of Caligula and Nero, wisdom-literature virtues like generosity and spontaneity perhaps did not matter so much. What mattered much more were display, ego, fantasy, and festivity, all of which found ready expression in the luridly fascinating spectacle that was the floating feast of ancient Rome.

Notes

1. See, e.g., Roller (2006), Dunbabin (2003), Donahue (2004).
2. On the maritime feast of 59 CE, see Tac. *Ann.* 14.15 and Dio Cass. 61.20.5. On the banquet with Tigellinus in 64 CE, see Tac. *Ann.* 15.33–37, with Dio Cass. 62.15.1–6 (all citations of Greek and Roman sources follow the abbreviations found in the *Oxford Classical Dictionary*). For the discrepancies between these two accounts, see Champlin, *Nero* (2003, 311, note 23).
3. Donahue (2004, 66).
4. Polyb. 5.34 and 14.11–12; see also Errington (2008, 166).
5. On this reassessment, see Shipley (2000, 205).
6. App. *Praef.* 10. For the principal modern studies, see Caspari (1916, 1–74), Pfrommer (1999, 93–124).
7. Ath. 5.205c–d (all translations of Greek and Latin are my own).
8. Ath. 5.205d–206a.
9. On the famous feasts of Ptolemy Philadelphos, see Rice (1983); on the adaptation of Ptolemaic architectural elements in a Roman setting, see Wilson (2005, 129–140); on the religious aspect, see Nielsen (1994, 136).
10. Dalby (1996, 14).
11. Ibid., 15.
12. Plut. *Ant.* 9.8; *Demetr. and Ant.* 3.3.
13. Roller (2010, 78).
14. Plut. *Ant.* 26.
15. Ibid., 26–27.
16. Roller (2010, 79).
17. Suet. *Cal.* 37.
18. Casson (1991, 218 and plate 39).
19. On the bridge at Baiae, see Dio Cass. 59.17 and Kleijwegt (1994, 652–671).
20. See note 2.
21. For the principal study, see Ucelli (1950); see also G.C. Speziale (1929, 333–346); Denham (1929, 347–350); G. Rubin de Cervin (1955, 38–42).
22. On size and décor, see Carlson (2002, 29–30); on similar lead water pipes at Pompeii, see Andersson (1990, 207–236).
23. On the mosaics, see V.M. Strocka (1984, 135, note 4); on some traditional explanations for the sinking of the ships, none of which is very convincing, see Rubin de Cervin (1955, 40–41).
24. For the drinking implements, see Ucelli (1950, 133–134); for amphorae (421–422, nos. 323 and 324).
25. Seow (1997, 334–336).
26. On Caesar, see Dio Cass. 43.21; Suet. *Caes.* 26, 27; Plut. *Caes.* 55; more recently, Beard (2007, 102–104, 145, 154); on the Colosseum feast, see Stat., *Silv.* 1.6.28–34 and Donahue (2004, 16–23).
27. Shipley (2000, 67).
28. Champlin (2003, esp. 145–177).

Bibliography

Andersson, E.B. 1990. 'Fountains and the Roman Dwelling: Casa del Torello in Pompeii,' *Jahrbuch des Deutschen Archäologischen Instituts* 105, 207–236.
Beard, M. 2007. *The Roman Triumph* (Cambridge, Harvard University Press).
Carlson, D N. 2002. 'Caligula's Floating Palaces,' *Archaeology* 55, 26–31.
Caspari, F. 1916: 'Das Nilschiff Ptolemaios IV,' *Jahrbuch des Kaiserlich Deutschen Archäologischen Instituts* 31, 1–74.
Casson, L. 1991. *The Ancient Mariners: Seafarers and Sea Fighters of the Mediterranean in Ancient Times* (Princeton, Princeton University Press).
Champlin, E. 2003. *Nero* (Cambridge, Harvard University Press).
Dalby, A. 1996. *Siren Feasts: A History of Food and Gastronomy in Greece* (London, Routledge).
Denham, H. 1929. 'Caligula's Galleys: Notes on a Short Visit, Especially with Regard to Their Construction,' *Mariner's Mirror* 15, 347–350.
Donahue, J. 2004. *The Roman Community at Table during the Principate* (Ann Arbor, University of Michigan Press).
Dunbabin, K.M.D. 2003. *The Roman Banquet: Images of Conviviality* (Cambridge, Cambridge University Press).
Errington, R. M. 2008. *A History of the Hellenistic World, 323–30 BC* (Malden, MA, Blackwell).
Hornblower, S. and Spawforth, A. (eds.), 1996. *Oxford Classical Dictionary* (Oxford, Oxford University Press).
Kleijwegt, M. 1994. 'Caligula's 'Triumph' at Baiae,' *Mnemosyne* 47, 652–671.
Nielsen, I. 1994. *Hellenistic Palaces: Tradition and Renewal* (Aarhus, Aarhus University Press).
Pfrommer, M. 1999. *Alexandria: Im Schatten der Pyramiden* (Mainz, Verlag Philipp von Zabern).
Rice, E.E. 1983. *The Grand Procession of Ptolemy Philadelphus* (Oxford, Oxford University Press).
Roller, D.W. 2010. *Cleopatra: A Biography* (Oxford, Oxford University Press).
Roller, M. 2006. *Dining Posture in Ancient Rome: Bodies, Values, and Status* (Princeton, Princeton University Press).
Rubin de Cervin, G. 1955. 'Mysteries and Nemesis of the Nemi Ships,' *Mariner's Mirror* 41, 38–42.
Seow, C.L. (ed. and comm.), 1997. *Anchor Bible, Ecclesiastes: A New Translation* (New York, Doubleday), vol. 18C.
Shipley, G. 2000. *The Greek World after Alexander 323–30 BC* (London, Routledge Press).
Speziale, G.C. 1929. 'The Roman Galleys in the Lake of Nemi,' *Mariner's Mirror* 15, 333–346.
Strocka, V.M. 1984. 'Ein Missverstandener Terminus des Vierten Stils. Die Casa del Sacello iliaco in Pompeji (I 6,4),' *MDAI(R)* 91, 125–140.
Ucelli, G. 1950. *Le Navi di Nemi* (Rome, Libreria dello Stato).
Wilson, R.J.A. 2005. 'On the Origin of the Roman Civic Basilica: The Egyptian Connection,' in Mols, S.T.A.M. and Moormann, E. (eds.), *Omni Pede Stare: Saggi architettonici e circumvesuviani in memoriam Jos de Waele* (Naples, Electa Napoli), 129–140.

The Great Aussie Barbecue

Len Fisher

The Aussie barbecue is a unique celebratory institution. From humble beginnings, with meat cooked on a ploughshare over an outback campfire, or on a shovel in the firebox of a steam locomotive, the Aussie barbecue has now reached iconic status. It forms the focus of many of our national and personal celebrations. To give just one example, the 2009 award of 'Australian of the Year' at the National Parliament House in Canberra on Australia Day was accompanied by a barbeque for some 650 invited VIPs where 'chefs manned barbeques cooking Australian produce – beef, lamb, chicken, seafood and vegetables.'[1] According to organizer Nicole Lieschke,[2] the 2010 award ceremony followed a similar pattern, with eight chefs manfully manning four giant barbecues. Even more impressively, the Queen was farewelled from her 2011 visit to Australia with a giant barbecue attended by over 100,000 people, where more than 600 volunteers cooked over 130,000 sausages, with celebrity chefs contributing their own barbecued dishes for the royal visitors.[3]

The Aussie barbecue is clearly here to stay.

Two out of three Australian homes possess a barbecue, and more than half a million new ones are sold each year.[4] We celebrate birthdays, christenings, anniversaries, and even weddings and funerals[5] around them. Think of Australia, and as likely as not you will visualize the alpha Australian male (the one holding the tongs), dressed in shorts and a loud Hawaiian shirt, standing under a bright blue sky as he turns the sausages, steaks, and prawns on an oiled metal plate heated from below by a bed of glowing coals or bottled gas.

How does the Aussie barbecue differ from barbecues in other countries? What is its history? How does the flavour of its products differ from simply frying the food indoors on a stove? Why do we bother to construct elaborate contraptions to perform essentially the same process out of doors? What is it that gives the Aussie barbecue its mystique? How has it become such a national icon?

How is the Aussie barbecue different?

The traditional Aussie barbecue consists of a flat metal plate and/or a set of metal bars, open to the air and heated from below by a wood fire, hot coals, or, in more recent times, a propane gas flame.[6]

This arrangement is similar in principle to the French-style barbecue, where meat is also cooked on a griddle over hot coals. There the similarity ends. In an Australian wood-fired barbecue we traditionally use whatever dry wood is to hand, from the eucalypt tree branches that litter my back garden to old railway sleepers 'rescued' by a friend. This casual tradition is becoming refined in some quarters, with long-burning desert hardwoods such as mulga and gidgee (a type of acacia) being preferred by serious barbecue *aficionados*, and cooking over charcoal also coming back into favour.[7] The refinement has not reached the level suggested by *Larousse Gastronomique*, however, whose editors claim that barbecued entrecôte steak only tastes good if cooked over glowing Cabernet vine shoots.[8]

The Aussie barbecue is very different from its American counterpart, where 'barbecuing' means the low-temperature, slow heating of meat in a closed chamber by means of hot air from smouldering wood coals.[9] A rotating spit (rotisserie) above the grill is also common. In Australia, the meat is out in the open, and the slow heating is not infrequently replaced by blazing flames fueled by dripping fat from the sausages or lamb chops above. Instead of a slow infusion of aromas from the wood, the result can too often be a coating of charcoal. I have personally seen people eating the charcoal in preference to the sausages.

This traditional image of the Aussie barbecue is changing rapidly, however. While gastronomic disasters are still a not-infrequent occurrence, the barbecue also has culinary advantages that are increasingly being recognized and exploited by serious amateur cooks and professional chefs.

The history of the Aussie barbecue

Mankind has cooked meat over open fires since prehistoric times. The earliest known European example[10] was discovered in the Czech Republic by archaeologists who uncovered a 31,000-year-old barbecue pit containing the remains of not one, but two woolly mammoths (a mother and calf). The beasts had been cooked *luau*-style, buried along with heating stones.

The history of open-fire cooking in Australia goes back even further, with ancient middens and charcoal from hearths having been discovered from as long ago as 40,000 years.[11] Middens are waste dumps from cooking, and often consist primarily of burnt shells from oysters and other seafood – an ancient forerunner of the present-day 'throw another shrimp on the barbie'. This well-known phrase was actually an invention of the Australian Tourism Commission, and was used in a 1984 advertising campaign featuring Paul Hogan and aimed at Americans.[12] Before that campaign, the modern Aussie barbecue was primarily used for cooking red meats. Now, almost any food seems to be fair game, including fish, pizzas, vegetables, tofu, and even soufflés.[13]

The modern Aussie barbecue had its inception with the arrival of nearly 1,500 European convicts, soldiers, and settlers in a fleet of eleven ships (the 'First Fleet') in Port Jackson (now called Sydney Harbour) in 1788.[14] The new arrivals had little choice at first but to cook their food in the open air over a fire. The earliest recorded description of the European invaders cooking in something approximating a barbecue style was given in 1790 by one Captain Watkin Tench, who described how salted pork sent from England had to be treated.[15] 'We soon left off boiling the pork, as it had become so old and dry [through being preserved in salt for several years] that it shrunk to one half of its dimensions when so dressed. Our usual method of cooking it was to cut off the daily morsel, and toast it on a fork before the fire, catching the drops which fell on a slice of bread …'

From the earliest times of European settlement, however, the aim of middle-class families was to emulate the cooking and food styles of their native England.[16] Emigrants to the new country were advised[17] to bring as much as possible of 'Domestic ironmongery [and] all useful cooking utensils of the same kinds as are common in England [including ovens],' and were told that, 'There has been a general want of coarse crockery in the colony. Dinner and breakfast services most colonists have remembered, but almost all have forgotten milk-pans, covered jars and pans, and things of that kind. You will find it expedient to purchase jugs and vessels in which liquids and stores are kept, *with covers* to them; the number of flies which seem to claim a right to everything consumable by man is extraordinary.'

With the kitchen thus equipped, an imitation of English practices could prevail.[18] Even when eating outdoors, the whole box and baggage was brought along, including a tablecloth to lay on the grass.[19] An open fire was nowhere to be seen. Cooking outdoors over an open fire was looked down on as the province of rough and uncultured itinerants and farm workers, often accompanied by their dogs. A typical scene is described by Henry Lawson in his wonderful humorous short story 'The Loaded Dog'.[20] The principle human characters are three gold prospectors called Andy, Dave, and Jim. Dave and Jim have been out prospecting, while Andy looks after the camp:

> Andy saw them coming, and put a panful of mutton-chops on the fire. Andy was cook to-day; Dave and Jim stood with their backs to the fire, as Bushmen do in all weathers, waiting till dinner should be ready. The retriever went nosing round after something he seemed to have missed.

The men stood next to the smoky fire, not just to keep warm, but also to keep the mosquitoes away. The pan would have contained water to boil the chops; the practice of using an oiled metal plate to cook the meat at a higher temperature was still far from common, perhaps because oils and fats were scarce, valuable commodities in 1901, when this story was written.

It is very difficult to track down just when the practice of cooking meat on a metal plate over the fire started. There are anecdotal accounts of train drivers cooking on shovels in the firebox of the engine, and dish-shaped ploughshares (like a giant wok with a hole in the middle) have often been used as barbecue plates. This latter practice was common in the Australian outback in the 1950s, with the fat running out through the square sprocket hole onto the fire producing a spectacular jet of flame.

How this sort of cooking became a socially acceptable middle-class activity is also something of a mystery. The transition began in the early nineteen-thirties, and the first published record of a socially acceptable middle-class barbecue appeared in a newspaper of 1933.[21] It was recorded that Sir George Fairbairn and Lady Fairbairn graciously made their grand home 'Greenlaw' available for a 'chop picnic' in aid of the Animal Welfare League. 'At this unique party,' says the article 'chops were grilled in the open and grilled in picnic style out of doors.' It is worth noting, however, that 'Lady Fairbairn also provided a cold luncheon in the dining-room for those who preferred it.'

The idea of outdoor meals cooked over a fire as a means of hospitality rapidly caught on. At the same time the description 'chop picnic' began to be displaced by the pithier 'barbeque'.[22] It is unclear why this spelling was preferred to the American 'barbecue', since American barbecues had been referred to in Australian newspapers for a century or so. The earliest reference was in a 1855 article entitled 'A Timeless Speech', quoting a Texas Methodist preacher who advertised a 'barbecue, with better liquors than are generally furnished'. Hopeful imbibers who turned up found that the 'liquor' referred to was water.[23]

Perhaps the British spelling 'barbeque' was preferred because it was thought to carry a connotation of English gentility, rather than American brashness. Following the Second World War, and increasing contact with visiting American servicemen, the American spelling began to take over. It was soon abbreviated in typical Australian fashion to 'Barbie', and in the 1970s to the even shorter 'BBQ'. The very first appearance of this latter abbreviation in print was in an advertisement in the *Australian Women's Weekly* for 6 June 1973[24] which was headlined 'How to B.B.Q. chump chops': 'Season 4–6 lamb chump chops with salt and pepper. Barbecue quickly and serve immediately with 1 can Masterfoods hot Mushroom Sauce.' I remember my mother following this actual recipe. Unfortunately, she overlooked the word 'quickly', and the strong-tasting sauce failed to obscure the flavour of the over-cooked meat buried beneath it.

The physical barbecue

During the 1970s the quintessential suburban barbecue became a more-or-less elaborate permanent structure of brick, stone, or Besser blocks[25] occupying a prominent position in the back garden or even on the verandah or deck. My younger brother even built one with a chimney the height of the house. Owners took considerable pride in these structures – far more pride, in fact, than they did in the cooking itself, which could become a burnt offering of biblical proportions.

The barbecue plate was generally made of cast iron, which is prone to rust. 'Cranking up the barbie' became a ritual, where the plate was heated, scraped and wire-brushed. The finishing touch was steam-cleaning with a splash of the ubiquitous beer or, in sophisticated households, white wine.

In the nineteen-nineties, such barbecues fell out of fashion, to be largely displaced by portable barbecues[26] with names like 'Turbo Classic', 'Cordon Bleu', or 'Patiomaster', and stainless steel replacing the cast iron. These barbecues are generally gas-fuelled, easy to use and easy to clean. There is also a burgeoning industry in barbecue cookbooks (e.g. ref. 13), many with innovative recipes that reflect the current popularity of TV cooking shows. There are, in addition, forums such as the Aussie BBQ Forum,[27] where enthusiasts exchange recipes and cooking practices.

All of these changes have meant that the culinary standard of the Aussie barbecue has been on the rise, in some quarters at least. While there are still plenty of examples where over-cooked steaks and sausages are piled up on one side of the barbecue and left to cool and congeal while people file past to collect them on cold plates, there is also a serious foodie revolution in progress. It is not uncommon, according to barbecue historian Mark Thomson,[28] to 'find fairly average blokes willing to have a complex discussion about marinating fish with lime juice and shredded ginger. That was rarely the case 10 or 15 years ago. The carbonized snags are now the exception rather than the rule.'

Another trend has been the rugged individuality of some people in manufacturing individually crafted barbecues out of the most unlikely-sounding materials. Washing machines, lawnmowers, old hot-water systems, forty-four gallon drums, the blast-resistant floor of an armored personnel carrier, and even discarded loudspeaker enclosures from public address systems have all been put to good use in this way.

Barbecue flavours

Just *why* barbecued food cooked on a hot plate or griddle has its unique flavour is rarely discussed in culinary literature. One author has suggested (on the basis of no evidence whatsoever) that 'juices vaporizing on a hot surface underneath the meat [are] thrown back onto it'.[29] Others believe that the aroma of wood smoke (from eucalyptus branches in most Aussie barbecues or mesquite, hickory, or applewood in the US) contributes (although this hardly applies to the presently popular gas barbecues).

According to Mark Thomson, founder of the iconically Australian 'Institute of Backyard Studies',[30] the simple act of cooking and eating outdoors creates an ambience that contributes to the perceived flavour. 'Because you're outside' he says 'all your senses are alert: the sight of the meat cooking, the sound of it sizzling. The smell is fantastic, your mouth is salivating (quick, put some beer in it to prevent stressing your saliva [*sic*] glands …)'.

There is likely to be some truth in this; certainly there is plenty of evidence that environmental factors have a significant role in our perception of food flavours.[31] The major factor, though, is surely the temperature of the meat surface during cooking. When meat is grilled in a frying-pan, moisture released during cooking tends to be retained and to act as a coolant. On a barbecue (especially one with open bars), the meat surface is hotter and dryer. The Maillard reactions between protein amino acids and reducing sugars in the meat, which contribute to the flavour[32] but which require temperatures in excess of 150°C, can occur more readily.

The increasing popularity of barbecuing has been accompanied by a corresponding increase in the availability of flavour-enhancing accompaniments in the way of sauces and seasonings, marinades and dry rubs, pastes and seasonings. Some of these are constructed from uniquely Australian ingredients such as wattleseed, lemon myrtle and alpine pepper. The best of them can enhance or complement Maillard products, although many contain sugars that caramelize rapidly at barbecue temperatures, producing a visual illusion that Maillard reactions have been taking place without the corresponding complex flavours.[33]

Conclusion

Overall, the Aussie-style barbecue provides a wealth of culinary opportunities in the right hands, although it can also produce culinary catastrophes. Its primary role in Australian celebrations, however, has little to do with its culinary attributes.

The real value of the Aussie barbecue is as a focus for celebrations, regardless of the quality of the cooking. As my correspondent 'Davo' from the Aussie BBQ Forum has pointed out '[In the 1970s when we were young] we didn't care much what was being cooked ... all the food was one colour ... BLACK ... but stuck between a couple of slices of white bread ... and heaps of tomato sauce ... Bloody bewdy mate!!'

The quality of the cooking may have improved since those days, but it remains true that 'the Australian barbecue is a universal one-size-fits-all celebration that is religious worship, tribal bonding and ritual ceremony all rolled into one. It's the place where big lies and truths are converted into myth and legend'.[34] It is, in other words, a place where the suburban Australian male can still imagine that he is out in the wilderness, fighting and taming nature in the way that his pioneering forebears were doing for real as they cooked over their outback campfires.

References

1. Ratcliffe, Carli, 'Australia Day'. *SBS Food* (http://www.sbs.com.au/food/occasion/3385/Australia_Day), 23 January (2009).
2. Nicole Lieschke, personal communication 1 March 2011.
3. Tony Barrass, 'More then 100,000 people in Perth farewell the Queen', *The Australian*, 29 October 2011 (http://www.theaustralian.com.au/national-affairs/more-than-100000-people-in-perth-farewell-the-queen/story-fnapmixa-1226180291017).
4. Anon., 'Why Do Men Hang Around the Barbecue?' http://health.ninemsn.com.au/whatsgoodforyou/theshow/694078/why-do-men-hang-around-the-barbecue (December 2 2009).
5. See, for example, http://www.allsuburbs.com.au/event-catering-funeral-catering.php
6. Thomson, Mark, *Meat, Metal and Fire: The Legendary Australian Barbecue*. HarperCollins, Sydney (1999).
7. Thomson, Mark, personal communication.
8. [Montagné, Prosper], *Larousse Gastronomique: The New American Edition of the World's Greatest Culinary Encyclopedia*, edited by Jennifer Harvey Lang. Crown, New York (1988), 418.
9. McGee, Harold, *On Food and Cooking*. 2nd edn, Scribner, New York (2004), 157–158.
10. Jiri Svoboda et al., 'Pavlov VI: an Upper Paleolithic living unit', *Antiquity* vol. 83 (2009), 282–295; http://www.msnbc.msn.com/id/31085915/ns/technology_and_science-science/.
11. Presland, Gary, *Aboriginal Melbourne: the Lost Land of the Kulin People*, 2nd edn, McPhee Gribble, Melbourne (1994), p. 128.
12. http://www.youtube.com/watch?v=Xn_CPrCS8gs
13. Howard, Peter, *Peter Howard's BBQ Collection*. New Holland Australia (2009).

14. Dunn, Cathy & McCreadie, Marion, 'The First Fleet', *Australian History Research* (http://www.australianhistoryresearch.info/the-first-fleet/).
15. Daunton-Fear, Richard & Vigar, Penelope, *Australian Colonial Cookery*. Rigby, Adelaide (1977), 7.
16. Ibid., 8; D.H. Borchardt, *Australians: A Guide to Sources*. Fairfax, Syme & Weldon Associates, Sydney (1987), 327.
17. Gouger, Robert, *South Australia in 1837*. Harvey & Darton (London), 1838.
18. Daunton-Fear, op. cit., 23.
19. Picture, 'Christmas Day – A Picnic at Studley Park', *Illustrated Melbourne Post*, 22 December 1864, reproduced in Daunton-Fear, op. cit., 18.
20. Lawson, Henry, 'The Loaded Dog', in *Joe Wilson and His Mates* (1901) (http://freeread.com.au/ebooks/e00025.txt). The dog very soon comes into the story when he picks up a stick of dynamite and trails the fuse in the fire, then follows the terrified prospectors as they try to get away from his playful antics while still holding onto the dynamite.
21. 'Chop Picnic for Animal Welfare League', *The Argus*, 2 November 1933, 4.
22. The earliest reference appears to be in *The West Australian* of 17 May, 1933 (http://trove.nla.gov.au/ndp/del/article/32479007?searchTerm=barbeque&searchLimits=l-australian=y|||sortby=dateDesc).
23. 'A Timeless Speech', *The Moreton Bay Courier*, 28 July 1955 (http://trove.nla.gov.au/ndp/del/article/3709069?searchTerm=barbecue&searchLimits=sortby=dateAsc|||l-australian=y).
24. http://trove.nla.gov.au/ndp/del/article/47224914?searchTerm=bbq&searchLimits=sortby=dateAsc|||l-australian=y
25. Taylor, Peter, *All About Barbecues*. Methuen of Australia, Sydney (1979); Whelan, Rob & Sue, *Building Barbecues*. Bay Books, Sydney, n.d. (1984?).
26. See, for example, 'Barbeques Galore' website (http://www.barbequesgalore.com.au/products/barbeques.aspx).
27. http://www.aussiebbq.info/forum/
28. Mark Thomson, personal communication.
29. Taylor, Peter, *All About Barbecues*, 8.
30. http://www.ibys.org/shed/
31. Auvray, Malika & Spence, Charles, 'The Multisensory Perception of Flavour', *Consciousness and Cognition* Vol. 17 (2008), 1016–1031.
32. Martins, Sara I.F.S., Jongen, Wim M.F. & van Boekel, Martinus A.J.S. 'A review of Maillard reaction in food and implications to kinetic modeling', *Trends in Food Science and Technology* Vol 11 (2001), 364–373.
33. Vic Cherikoff, 'A Taste of the Bush' (http://www.atasteofthebush.com.au/). Cherikoff, a chef and tireless promoter of Australian-based flavours, also comments (personal communication, 8 May 2011) that: 'Considering the BBQ often features high-fat meats (sausages, cheaper cuts such as ribs and pork belly, chicken etc) and sugary sauces and rubs, the popularity can also be ascribed to a response to our instinctive, evolutionary taste-drives towards fat and sweetness. In hunter-gatherers, quenching the drive for fat delivers proteins and fat soluble (lipophilic) antioxidants (including some fibre from sinew and skin and vitamin C in the livers of game animals). The drive for sweetness expends significant calories in attainment and delivers dietary fibre, slow release carbohydrates, micro-sugars and water soluble (hydrophilic) antioxidants (although wild Australian fruits have also been shown to be extremely rich in lipophilic antioxidants in contrast to modern fruits). The significance of micro-sugars is in their ability to up-regulate the cellular absorption of beneficial nutrients. Perhaps the modern BBQ is a logical extension of our hunter-gatherer skill of cooking with an open fire increasing the absorption of food nutrients by appealing to innate taste drives for a balance of the 10 building blocks of flavour – sweet, salt, sour, bitter, aromatic, pungent, umami, Maillard, metallic and fat.'
34. Thomson, Mark 1999, pp. viii–ix.

Celebrating Christmas and New Year with Punch

Elizabeth Gabay

While collecting old postcards depicting punch bowls and punch drinking, I have been fascinated by the number of Christmas and New Year greetings cards dating from the late nineteenth century to the 1940s that feature punch. Looking further into the role played by punch at these celebrations has highlighted some interesting differences over time across countries, resulting in punches with little similarity to each other but which share certain defining features – a common heritage, conviviality around a punch bowl containing a blend of varying ingredients, and a festive symbolism associated with certain recipes and customs.

Punch has been drunk in many countries over the past 450 years at family life-cycle celebrations, national, patriotic and political events. Robert Burns celebrated occasions 'such as new-year's day, a christening, or the kirn-night, when my punch bowl is brought from its dusty corner and is filled up in honor of the occasion.'[1] In modern times 'champagne' is often synonymous with celebration, but during the eighteenth and nineteenth centuries punch was often the celebratory drink of choice. To be 'drunk with great animation, not in champagne, but in rum punch' was not unusual.[2] An advantage of punch has always been that it can be made in large quantities to serve a crowd with ease.

Before looking further into these festive punches, some definition and history of punch is required. The first recorded mention is in a letter to an English East India merchant, Thomas Colley, in eastern India in 1632 from another merchant, Robert Adams, encouraging him to 'drincke punch by no allowance'. Over the next century, as it spread to the Caribbean, the eastern seaboard of America and Europe, punch was widely written about and mutated into subtly different concoctions, reflecting the availability of ingredients, cost and season.

One theory for the origin of 'punch' is that it means 'five', deriving from the Hindi *panch*, due to the five ingredients (water, alcohol, fruit juice, sugar, and spice) supposedly included in punch. However, one of the earliest descriptions, from 1638, describes punch as having only four ingredients: eau-de-vie, rose water, lemons, and sugar.[3] The name may also be a corruption of the name for a drinks barrel on board ship – a puncheon.

The earliest published English recipe, based on wine and including no water, comes from Hannah Woolley's *The Queene-like Closet* (1670): 'Take one Quart of Claret Wine, half a pint of Brandy, and a little Nutmeg grated, a little sugar, and the juice of a Limon, and so drink it'. Toast, raisins, cinnamon, nuts, ambergris (a perfumed secretion of sperm whales, regarded as an aphrodisiac), and 'other ingredients' could also be added.[4]

Celebrating Christmas and New Year with Punch

In Britain, an increase in alcohol-related problems was noticed during the second half of the seventeenth century as the population moved away from drinking weak beer, cider, and wine to spirits such as brandy, rum and eau-de-vie, drunk straight or in punch, cordials and 'waters'. The arrival of cheap gin in the early eighteenth century exacerbated the problem. In an attempt to reduce alcoholism, taxes and licensing laws were introduced and the amount of water, tea, or milk added to punch began to increase, partly to avoid the higher costs of spirits, but also due to a change in fashion for lighter punches.

By the first decades of the eighteenth century, punch developed a consistent style base on four main ingredients: acid (lemon, lime or orange juice), sweet (sugar), strong (alcohol in the form of brandy, rum, arrack [distilled palm wine] and sometimes wine), and weak (water, tea, milk or eggs). Recipes frequently followed a set proportion between these elements: one (measure) of sour, two of sweet, three of strong, and four of weak which resulted in the 'ideal' punch of a balance between the four ingredients.

By the nineteenth century, punch recipes were changing again. The fixed proportions were no longer always followed; many different fruits, liqueurs, wines and even beer were added, and generally punches became less acidic and more sweet and rich. At the same time, the nature of Christmas and New Year celebrations changed, becoming more dramatic and ritualized. Enjoying the same punch every year became an essential part of the festivity. Punch bowls, sometimes with matching cups, decorated appropriately for Christmas (Christmas scenes, evergreens, and Father Christmas) or New Year (words and music of 'Auld Lang Syne') set the scene.

In northern Europe, the cold season led to hot, mulled, or flaming punches. From the early 1800s, English writers reminisced about the passing of old customs, including the country custom of visiting neighbours carrying the wassail bowl. An 1826 nostalgic portrait of a country squire depicted him as celebrating feast days such as Christmas with 'a bowl of strong brandy punch, garnished with a toast and nutmeg' with neighbours 'round a glowing fire, and told and heard the ... tales of the village'.[5]

The middle decades of the nineteenth century in Britain were the heyday of hot Christmas punch, popularized in fiction with descriptions of a white Christmas with familial cheer around a fire, plentiful food and drink. In Dickens' *A Christmas Carol* (1843) Scrooge 'sees' a vision of how Christmas should be, where the feast is topped by 'seething bowls of punch, that made the chamber dim with their delicious steam'. This novel had a major impact in both Britain and America on the Christmas image. In a letter from 1847, Dickens gave his recipe for Christmas punch, which included brandy and rum (which was set alight and allowed to burn for three or four minutes), boiling water, lemons and sugar. He warns that an old bowl is recommended in case it gets damaged! In the novel *Christmas at the Cross Keys* (1853), the Christmas punch included port and is not flamed: 'He put in port wine, lemons, sugar, brandy, spice, and rum, and hot water at discretion'.[6] The Frenchman Louis Blanc, writing in January 1863, marvelled at the opulence of an English Christmas at which were served 'flaming bowls

Celebrating Christmas and New Year with Punch

of punch'.[7] The December 1863 issue of *The What-Not*, before giving their punch recipe, indicated why punch was so appropriate: 'The Convivial custom of drinking toasts is one which is practised whenever any particular occasion brings a party together which is interested in the same subject: Christmas being the season par excellence'.[8] The punch has half a lemon, sherry, brandy, rum and boiling water, with extra water and sugar for younger drinkers.

Juleglögg, traditionally regarded as Denmark's Christmas punch, includes red wine, brandy and port and is seasoned with orange peel, cardamom, cloves, and cinnamon, with raisins and almonds added. Just before serving, 'a fine wire mesh [is placed] over the kettle' to hold the sugar cone. Brandy is poured over the sugar and set alight. Once the sugar has all melted, the *Juleglögg* is served hot.[9] In Germany this punch is known as *Feuerzangenbowle* ('fire-tong punch'). Part of the theatre is that while the sugar cone is burning, the lights are dimmed and the flames are a focus of attention. For some, the ceremony is more important than the drink: celebrating the gathering of friends and conveying a notion of *Gemütlichkeit* (warm, cosy geniality).[10] The camaraderie around the bowl of flaming punch was celebrated in the film *Feuerzangenbowle* (1944).

Warm punch or 'glee wine' was, and is, popular in Germany. An account of Christmas and New Year in Nuremburg in 1842 describes how the warm punch was served on Christmas Eve at 'their feast of punch and their great gingerbread hearts'. The gingerbread was decorated with almonds and was 'peculiar, being mixed with honey, and often flavoured with aniseeds'.[11]

Christmas punch in the Americas developed along different lines. On Christmas Day 1795, Theophilus Bradbury wrote to his daughter Harriet about his Christmas dinner with George Washington. They ate 'roast beef, veal, turkeys, ducks, fowls, hams &c.; puddings, jellies, oranges, apples, nuts, almonds, figs, raisins, and a variety of wines and punch.'[12] The type of punch is not specified, but Washington did write down his recipe for eggnog, which included rye whiskey, Jamaican rum, sherry, eggs, sugar, cream and milk. The egg whites were beaten up and folded in.[13] In 1815, an English observer noted 'a liquor with which the Americans used to treat their friends on Christmas Day, and which is called egg-nog'.[14] In 'the South it is almost indispensible at Christmas time, and at the North it is a favourite at all seasons'.[15] Eggnog has more eggs than an egg punch, making it more custard-like, and was regarded by many as a healthy and innocuous drink for all the family. The temperance movement struggled to convince people that it was indeed alcoholic.[16] A more alcoholic version with extra brandy was called 'Tom and Jerry' and was said to have been inspired by Pierce Egan in the 1820s in his journal *Life in London*.[17] Egg punches (although not necessarily for Christmas) are also found in England and in the Netherlands and Germany (*Eier Punsch*). Dutch bottled advocaat is part of this same tradition of festive eggnog.

To toast mid-winter with a punch made from fresh milk or eggs was a major celebration. Milk and egg punches were normally reserved for the summer, as milk and eggs were less readily available in winter and expensive. To mark the start of the season, the first Sunday in May is called Milk-a-Punch Sunday in the Channel Islands. Condensed milk in tins was available from the late 1850s, pasteurized milk and evaporated milk in tins from the 1890s, followed by bottled milk in the early 1900s. *The Practical Housewife* (1860) has a 'Milk Punch for Christmas Day' made with lemons, rum and milk. As with a posset, where the milk was curdled by ale or wine, the milk was curdled by adding lemon juice; the strained punch, made from the whey, is mild and delicate.[18]

In 1847 an eggnog maker noted how he had, the previous May, stored his eggs when they were,

> four cents per dozen; and this morning, I took them out to make egg nog for the ladies (Lord bless them; for they must all have egg nog on Christmas, in Kentucky), when I found them as fresh as the day when they were put up. … My neighbors wish to know where I get eggs at four cents per dozen, while they are paying this morning forty cents a dozen – or no egg nog.[19]

A classic eggnog recipe from Croly's (1866) book included egg yolks beaten up with sugar and nutmeg, rum and brandy or Madeira, whisked egg whites and creamy milk, served uncooked.[20]

Christmas Day often started with eggnog, as a Philadelphian bride, living in Eutaw, Alabama, noted in 1842 in a letter home: 'Before breakfast, at Christmas time, everyone

Christmas greeting card (1900s) sent to Florida with Father Christmas serving a glass of eggnog with cherries or cranberries. (Author's Collection)

takes a glass of egg-nog and a slice of cake. ... As Christmas was kept during four days egg-nog was drank regularly every morning.'[21]

Making the Christmas eggnog was often a family affair, directed by a grandparent, symbolizing the continuation of tradition. In a Virginian description from 1827, every person was given a task in the preparation and the recipe included the southern variant of 'old peach brandy'.[22] In *Christmas Reminiscences*, the grandfather directs preparation in 'the gigantic china punch-bowl, relic of ancestral feasts across seas in "ye old Countrie",' further emphasizing the family tradition. Once ready, 'the flaming sconces were lighted, and the eggnog bowl, surrounded by pyramids of tumblers, was placed upon it. Then we proceeded to "drink in Christmas".'[23]

Eudora Welty remembered her childhood Christmases in 1920s Mississippi, when she awoke to the sound of her mother beating eggnog, made with Bourbon whiskey:

> It was ladled from the punch bowl into punch cups and silver goblets, and had to be eaten with a spoon. It stood up in peaks. It was rich, creamy and strong. Mother gave full credit for the recipe to Charles Dickens. But its taste was simply, and absolutely, the taste of Christmas Day ...[24]

That Dickens was associated with the eggnog recipe is interesting, as his recipe for Christmas punch, as we have seen, was quite different.

In Texas, December 1872, it was noted that 'Most of the Austin saloons will "make merry" in a genteel way on Christmas morning, and will treat friends and patrons to excellent egg-nog.' A list of the saloons, and times when free eggnog would be served, was given.[25]

Punch evolved to suit taste and the ingredients available. During the American Civil War (1861–65), Federal prisoners of war made their Christmas eggnog: 'And such egg-nog! – made without milk.' It was made with beaten eggs, whiskey or brandy, nutmeg, and sugar, but with water replacing the milk, resulting in 'a delicious egg-nog, without its usual deleterious qualities', though what he means by the bad effects of an eggnog made with milk is hard to say.[26]

Similar traditions are found in the Caribbean. In a 1788 Jamaican Christmas, the slaves visited 'the white people during the festivity, and are treated with punch'.[27] After emancipation, American traditions were seen as 'superior', civilized and 'Christian', and drinking egg and milk punch at Christmas was adopted: 'It was usual to rise early on Xmas morning and mix [a] huge bowl of egg punch which the elders enjoyed.'[28] Recipes vary from island to island, use tinned milk due to the lack of fresh milk, and are generally cooked. In Dominica, *Ponche de Ron* is sweet and unctuous, made with evaporated milk, condensed milk, rum and egg yolks cooked together and served chilled.[29] In Trinidad *Punch de Crème* is made by whisking eggs flavoured with lime zest, then cooked slowly with condensed milk and evaporated milk until the mixture thickens, then seasoned with nutmeg, cinnamon, ground cloves and vanilla. When cool, Angostura bitters and rum are added before bottling; it is served cold. Its part in

Christmas tradition is immortalized in Lord Kitchener's *parang* (calypso), 'Drink Ah Rum and a Punch de Crème'.[30]

On the Hispanic islands and South America, recipes for Christmas punch also included eggs – either following the North American tradition or a Spanish tradition of egg-yolk-based punch. In Venezuela, the *ponche Navideño* (Christmas punch) is made with evaporated milk, eggs, rum, and the unusual addition of anise. Don Eliodoro's bottled *ponche* first appeared in 1900 and continues to be successful; the company's motto is '*Navidad es compartir!*' (Christmas is for sharing).[31]

Puerto Rican writer Esmeralda Santiago remembers her childhood Christmases when ripe coconuts were split open; the children grated the meat and squeezed it for coconut milk 'to be used for arroz con dulce and tembleque [a type of blancmange]. Some of the coconut milk was mixed with sweet evaporated milk, sugar, egg yolks and rum to make coquito,' to be served during Christmas and New Year celebrations.[32] In Honduras a *ponche infernal* or *Ponche de Piña Navideño* is served 'hot and contains pineapple and aguardiente [local eau-de-vie] … On Christmas Eve, families prepare punch and other foods, including tamales'.[33]

In South America, a festive eggnog punch called *rompope* is made, as well as fruit-based punches. An Argentinian *Ponche Navideño* recipe from 1951 has no specific quantities, so would vary from maker to maker, and has little to show it is Argentinian: 'In a punch bowl, place several slices pineapple, lemons, oranges, Benedictine to taste, drops bitters, sugar, stir – add a little soda, ice, add Cognac, Whisky or Rum. Allow to stand a moment then add the Champagne and serve'.[34]

In Mexico recipes using local and seasonal ingredients developed within families, although apparently not published until the 1980s.[35] Both of the following punches are served hot. *Ponche Navideño*, is served at midnight on Christmas Eve and throughout the season. Its three basic ingredients are *tejocote* (*Crataegus pubescens stipulacea*, similar to a crab apple, which ripens in December) added whole or quartered, guava and sugar cane. Tamarind, hibiscus flowers and *piloncillo* (dark brown sugar cone) are also traditional. Almost any available fruit can be added and stewed until soft. Tequila or rum can be added when serving, making it a *Ponche con Piquete* (punch with a sting).

Guatemalan *Ponche Navideño* contains dried fruit such as pineapple, papaya, mango and peaches, but not guavas or *tejocote*.[36] It can also contain cinnamon, cloves, black peppercorns, mamey (*Mammea americana* – South American apricot) and coconut.[37]

Sometimes the same punch is drunk throughout the winter season, with variations according to the occasion. A Louisiana Creole eggnog in 1900 was made with boiling milk and whisked egg whites and 'served cold by the Creoles at New Year's receptions. At the famous Christmas and New Year Reveillons it is served hot.'[38]

In some countries a different punch is served to mark the New Year. While a Christmas punch can be prepared for any time of day, a New Year's Eve Punch has to be ready to toast the New Year as the clock strikes midnight. Many New Year cards show toasting midnight with a glass of punch. Coleridge, on 1 January 1796, complained that

Celebrating Christmas and New Year with Punch

he was 'desired to drink only one glass of Punch in honour of the departing Year – and after twelve, one other in honour of the new year.' Travellers maintained the tradition: 'We greeted the entrance of the New Year in the good old English fashion. A bowl of punch was prepared, and whilst the clock, striking the hour of midnight, tolled the knell of the expiring year, we drank to the health of our dear distant friends, with fondest wishes for their welfare and happiness'.[39]

A British army officer fighting in South Africa celebrated New Year's Eve 1899–1900 with 'a fine bowl of punch, with slices of pine-apple in it, which we shared with our men on watch, wishing them all a happy New Year'.[40] In 1860s Denmark, a milk punch was traditional, 'it would be advisable to fetch some milk punch to drink the old year out'.[41] Many New Year punches are variations of the fruity Christmas punch. A modern Danish recipe for 'New Year's Eve Punch' includes warm spiced cider and tea.

31 December is St Sylvester's Day, so Central European punches are often called Sylvester Punch. Polish *Poncz Sylwestrowy* is made with white wine, sugar, arrack, vodka or rum, lemons, and oranges.[42] German *Silvesterpunsch* is made with mulled wine, lemon juice, sugar, spices, and rum.[43] (The cover image of this volume depicts a New Year greetings card sent from Metz (then in Germany) to Paris: toasting midnight with a glass of *Silversterpunsch*. The lid on the punch bowl served to keep it warm.) *Silvesterpunsch* was dramatized in the East German musical comedy *Silvesterpunsch* (1960) and in the television series *Ein Herz und eine Seele* episode 'Silvesterpunsch' (2008). Hungarian Sylvester Punch or *Krampampuli* is served hot and contains chopped dried figs, candied ginger, and fruit peel infused in brandy, red wine, orange and lemon juice, tea and some vinegar. Austrian Sylvester Punch is a mulled mixture of red wine, tea, cinnamon and cloves, served with jam doughnuts.

Austria invaded Italy during the 1850s and 1860s and during this time may well have introduced the tradition of drinking Sylvester Punch at New Year's Eve. Lady Isabel Burton described the celebrations for New Year in Genoa when 'as the clock struck twelve on St Sylvester's night, 1857, as we all shook hands and drank each other's health in a glass of punch at the Café de la Concorde'.[44] Helen Barolini describes family celebrations in Vicenza in north-east Italy, greeting the New Year and chasing away the demons which brought bad luck. Family heirlooms were brought out, including the 'silver punch bowl ... set out on the old credenza'; a traditional dish of lentils is accompanied by 'the Saint Sylvester punch bowl for laughter and merriment'. Barolini's version includes tea, rum, brandy, lemons, and an Italian addition of sparkling Lambrusco wine.[45]

Different punches were traditionally served on New Year's Day, when timing is less precise. A New York tradition was drinking punch and eggnog as part of the New Year's Day visiting ritual. Gentlemen visited friends, who held open-house with drinks and food on New Year's Day, regarded as the most important day of the year, when 'The mayor of the city, and others ... advertise, two or three days before, that they will reciprocate the compliments of the season with the inhabitants at their house on

Celebrating Christmas and New Year with Punch

New Year's Day'. John Lambert visited the mayor, where he found him in a crowded room with visiting gentlemen eating and drinking from 'a large table spread with cakes, wine, and punch.' Lambert offered his 'compliments of the season, a happy new year, and drank a glass of excellent punch,' before leaving for the next house.[46] Pride was taken in the making of a good bowl of punch with which to start off the year. In a 1868 description of New York:

> Punch is seen in all its glory on this day and each household strives to have the best of this article. There are regular punch-makers in the city, who reap harvest at this time. Their services are engaged long beforehand, and they are kept busy all the morning going from house to house, to make this beverage which is nowhere so palatable as in this city.[47]

Not everyone was enthusiastic about this tradition. New Year's Day collations are discussed in *The Token* (1837). Mrs T. offers oysters, sandwiches, chocolate, coffee, wines, and whiskey punch – but the whiskey punch is regarded as vulgar, and Lizzy thought it was 'banished from all refined society'. Refined offerings were considered to be champagne and cake.[48] Books on household management and cookery gave advice to New Year's Day hosts. 'Jennie June' (1870) gave advice on what drinks to offer. Although in favour of non-alcoholic drinks, she conceded that 'Cherry, old Bourbon, and claret punch are in great demand where they are to be found'.[49] Mrs Shepherd (1887) suggested punch be served with tea or coffee, but bouillon was best, explaining that punch was falling out of favour due to the groups of unruly men roaming the streets, having consumed too much punch 'and so, from fear of causing one's brother to sin, many have banished the familiar punch-bowl'.[50]

Eggnog is also part of the Creole New Year's Day festivities, while in New Orleans a traditional finish to the day was *brulé* – a flaming punch of 'brandy, kirsch, cinnamon, allspice, and sugar, or *café brulot*, coffee fortified with brandy, spices, and orange and lemon peel'.[51]

That punch, even if missing key ingredients, has become so much part of the ritual associated with these mid-winter festivals can be see in an account by anthropologist Nancy Pollock of Christmas in the outer Marshall Islands. There was very little food, but 'The party centrepiece of Christmas fare for all fourteen families of the islet, or 230 people in total, was three 10-gallon pots of Hawaiian punch, made from packets of crystals mixed with rainwater and additional sugar … Hawaiian punch was Christmas dinner for the assembled community'.[52] The concoction may not have answered any strict definition of punch, but the important point, as with all the celebrants above, is that in the eye of the drinkers, they are gathered around a bowl of punch, sharing their festivity. Celebratory Christmas and New Year punches had different ingredients and preparation methods. They included expensive or rare ingredients such as champagne or pineapple, unseasonal ingredients such as milk or eggs, or seasonal fruit such as *tejocote* and cranberries to emphasize the unique time of year. They could be flamed, emphasizing the mid-winter element of the festivity. One feature that remains constant is the atmosphere created when people gather around a punch bowl, sharing a communal drink which has developed a symbolism associated with festivity.

Notes

1. Burns, *The Complete Works of Robert Burns*, p. 334.
2. Atkinson, *Gertrude the Emigrant*, chapter XXIV.
3. von Mandelslo, 'Albrecht Mandelslo's Travels into the Indies', p. 13.
4. Phillips, *The New World of English Words*.
5. Hone, *The Every-Day Book*, p. 811.
6. Deene, *Christmas at the Cross Keys*, p. 18.
7. Blanc, *Letters on England*, Letter CXIV, p. 279.
8. *The What-Not or Ladies Handy Book*, p. 27.
9. Allan-Christensen, *Tak for Mad*, p. 267.
10. Fairfield, '*Gemutlichkeit* in Harlem'.
11. Howit, *The Rural and Domestic Life of Germany*, p. 178.
12. Letter from Theophilus Bradbury to his daughter Harriet.
13. Bauer, *Capitol Hill Cooks*, p. 259.
14. *Niles' Weekly Register*, Volume VIII: March–September 1815.
15. Thomas, *How to Mix Drinks*, p. 40.
16. Sargent, 'Wild Dick and Good Little Robin'.
17. 'Tom and Jerry'.
18. Philp, *The Practical Housewife*, p. 260.
19. Allen, ed., *The American Agriculturalist*, p. 61.
20. Croly, *Jennie June's American Cookery Book*, p. 275.
21. Rutledge, *The Carolina Housewife*, p. xxiv.
22. Mitchell, 'A Christmas in Jo Tank', p. 168.
23. 'Christmas Reminiscences'.
24. Polk, *Eudora Welty*, p. 401.
25. Silverthorne, 'Texas Celebrates: Late Nineteenth Century 1870–1900', p. 15.
26. Harris, 'Prison Incidents', p. 99.
27. Marsden, *An Account of the Islands of Jamaica*, p. 33.
28. Moore and Johnson, 'Celebrating Christmas in Jamaica 1865–1920: From Creole Carnival to "Civilised" Convention', p. 163.
29. 'Ponche de Ron (Rum Eggnog)'.
30. 'Punch de Crème'.
31. 'Ponche Crema'.
32. Santiago, 'Letters from New York', p. 161.
33. Bertelsen, *Food Cultures of the World Encyclopedia*, p. 189.
34. Clave, *El Barman Practico*.
35. Fernández, *La Cocina Mexicana*, p. 59.
36. Knowles, 'Ponche de Navidad (Christmas Punch) for Share Our Strength'.
37. Boobbyer, *Guatemala Handbook*, p. 53.
38. The Picayenne, *The Picayenne's Creole Cook Book*, p. 360.
39. Melina, *Leaves from a Lady's Diary of her Travels in Barbary*, p. 89.
40. Burne, *With the Naval Brigade in Natal 1899–1900*, chapter III.
41. Scharling, *Nöddebo Parsonage*, p. 146.
42. Vitz, 'Christmas Day and the Christmas Season'. p. 159.

43. 'Silvesterpunsch – New Year's Eve Punch Bowl Recipe'.
44. Burton, *The Romance of Isabel, Lady Burton*, p. 104.
45. Barolini, *Festa*, pp. 82, 89.
46. Lambert, *Travels through Canada, and the United States of North America*, p. 111.
47. Martin, *The Secrets of the Great City*, p. 136.
48. Hawthorne, 'New Year's Day', p. 27.
49. Croly, *Jennie June's American Cookery Book*, p. 310.
50. Sherwood, *Manners and Social Usages*, pp. 229–230.
51. Laborde and Magill, 'Creole New Year's Reveillon', p. 144.
52. Pollock, 'Nor Any Drop to Drink: Drinking Habits in Pacific and New Zealand Societies', p. 42.

Bibliography

Allan-Christensen, Leah. *Tak for Mad*. Lulu.com, 2005.
Allen, A.B., ed. *The American Agriculturalist*. Vol. VII. New York: C.M. Saxton, 1848.
Atkinson, Caroline Louisa. *Gertrude the Emigrant: A Tale of Colonial Life*. Sydney; J.R. Clarke, 1857. Chapter XXIV. www.adc.library.usyd.edu.au/data-2/p00076.pdf.
Barolini, Helen. *Festa: Recipes and Recollections of Italian Holidays*. Univ. of Wisconsin Press, 1988.
Bauer, Linda. *Capitol Hill Cooks: Recipes from the White House, Congress, and All of the Past Presidents*. Lanham: Taylor Trade Publications, 2010.
Bertelsen, Cynthia D. *Food Cultures of the World Encyclopedia*. Ed. Ken Albala. Greenwood, 2011.
Blanc, Louis. Letter CXIV. *Letters on England*. Trans. James Hutton, revised by the author. Vol. II. London: Sampson, Low, Son & Marston 1866.
Boobbyer, Claire. *Guatemala Handbook: the Travel Guide*. Bath: Footprint Travel Guides, 2002.
Bradbury, Theophilus. Letter to Harriet Bradbury. 26 December 1795. 'The President's House in Philadelphia – First-Person Accounts: The Washington Years'. *Independence Hall Association*. 2001–2010. http://www.ushistory.org/presidentshouse/history/quotes.htm Letter from Massachusetts congressman Theophilus Bradbury, to his daughter Harriet.
Burne, Lieutenant R.N. *With the Naval Brigade in Natal 1899–1900 – Journal of Active Service kept during the relief of Ladysmith and subsequent operations in northern Natal and the Transvaal, under General Sir Redvers Buller, V.C., G.C.B*. London: Edward Arnold, 1902.
Burns, Robert. *The Complete Works of Robert Burns*. Edinburgh: William P. Nimmo, 1867.
Burton, Lady Isabel. *The Romance of Isabel, Lady Burton*. Ed. W. H. Wilkins. Vol. I. New York: Dodd Mead & Company, 1897.
'Christmas Reminiscences'. *Ladies' Home Journal*. December 1889.
Clave, Julio Cesar. *El Barman Practico*. Buenos Aires: 3rd edition 1951.
Croly, Jane Cunningham. *Jennie June's American Cookery Book*. New York: American News Co., 1866.
Deene, Kenner (Charlotte Smith). *Christmas at the Cross Keys*. London: T. Cautley Newby, 1853.
Fairfield, John. '*Gemutlichkeit* in Harlem: Modern Liberalism and the City.' American Studies Association. 12 Oct. 2006.
Fernández, Adela. *La Cocina Mexicana*. Panorama, 1985.
Harris, Lieut. Wm. C. 'Prison Incidents.' *Prison Life in the Tobacco Warehouse at Richmond by a Ball's Bluff Prisoner*. Philadelphia: George W. Childs, 1862.
Hawthorne, Nathaniel. 'New Year's Day.' *The Token and Atlantic Souvenir. A Christmas and New Year's Present*. New York: Charles Bowen, 1837.
Hone, William. *The Every-Day Book or Everlasting Calendar of Popular Amusements*. Vol 1. London: Hunt and Clarke, 1826.
Howitt, William. *The Rural and Domestic Life of Germany*. London: Longman, Brown, Green and Longmans, 1842: Chapter XIII.
Knowles, Brian. 'Ponche de Navidad (Christmas Punch) for Share Our Strength'. *The Gringo Chapin:*

Discover the Flavors of Guatemala. 7 December 2010. http://www.thegringochapin.com/2010/12/ponche-de-navidad-christmas-punch-for-share-our-strength.html.

Laborde, Peggy Scott and John Magill. 'Creole New Year's Reveillon'. *Christmas in New Orleans*. Louisiana: Pelican Publishing, 2009.

Lambert, John. *Travels through Canada, and the United States of North America in the years 1806, 1807 and 1808*. Vol. II. London: C. Cradock and W. Joy, 1814.

Mandelslo, Johann von. 'Albrecht Mandelslo's Travels into the Indies'. *The Voyages and Travells of the Ambassadors sent by Frederick Duke of Holstein into Muscovy, Tartary and Persia*. N.p.: John Starkey and Thomas Basset, 1669.

Marsden, Peter. *An Account of the Islands of Jamaica by a Gentleman Lately Resident on a Plantation*. Newcastle: S. Hodgson 1788.

Martin, Edward Winslow (James D McCabe). *The Secrets of the Great City: A work Descriptive of the Virtues and the Vices, the Mysteries and Crimes of New York City*. Philadelphia: Jones Brothers and Co., 1868.

Melena, Elpis. *Leaves from a Lady's Diary of her Travels in Barbary*. Vol 1. London: H. Colburn, 1850.

Mitchell, Stephen T. 'A Christmas in Jo Tank'. *The Spirit of the Dominion*. Richmond: Shepherd & Pollard, 1827.

Moore, Brian L. and Michele A. Johnson. 'Celebrating Christmas in Jamaica 1865–1920: From Creole Carnival to "Civilised" Convention'. *Jamaica in Slavery and Freedom: History, Heritage and Culture*. Eds. Kathleen E.A. Monteith and Glen Richards. Jamaica: The University of West Indies Press, 2002.

Morris, Desmond. *Social and Cultural Aspects of Drinking: A Report to the European Commission*. Oxford: SIRC (Social Issues Research Centre for the Amsterdam Group), 1998.

Niles' Weekly Register. Volume VIII: March–September. Baltimore: 1815.

Philp, Robert Kemp. *The Practical Housewife A Complete Encyclopedia of Domestic Economy and Family Medical Guide'*. London: Houlston & Wright and Philadelphia; J.B. Lipincott, 1860.

Phillips, Edward. *The New World of English Words or a General Dictionary*. London: 1658.

The Picayune. *The Picayenne's Creole Cook Book*. New York: Dover, 2002.

Polk, Noel. *Eudora Welty: A Bibliography of Her Work*. Oxford, MS: UP of Mississippi, 1994.

Pollock, Nancy J. 'Nor Any Drop to Drink: Drinking Habits in Pacific and New Zealand Societies'. *Drinking: Anthropological Approaches*. Eds. Igor and Valerie De Garine. Berghahn Books, 2001.

'Ponche Crema'. *Complejo Licorero Ponche Crema*. 2012. http://www.ponchecrema.com/.

'Ponche de Ron (Rum Eggnog)'. *Aunt Clara's Kitchen: Dominican Cooking*. 2 Jan 2011. http://www.dominicancooking.com/905-ponche-de-ron-rum-eggnog.html.

'Punch de Crème'. *TriniGourmet.com*. 11 December 2011. http://www.trinigourmet.com/index.php/punch-de-creme/.

Rutledge, Sarah. *The Carolina Housewife*. Columbia: U. South Carolina P., 1979.

Santiago, Esmeralda. 'Letters from New York.' *When I was Puerto Rican*. Cambridge, MA: Da Capo, 2006.

Sargent, Lucius Manlius. 'Wild Dick and Good Little Robin'. *The Temperance Tales*. Vol. 1. Boston: Whipple and Damrell, 1840.

Scharling, Henrik. *Nöddebo Parsonage: A Story of Country Life in Denmark*. Vol. 2. London: R. Bentley 1867.

Sherwood, Mary. *Manners and Social Usages*. New York: Harper & Brothers, 1887.

Silverthorne, Elizabeth. 'Texas Celebrates: Late Nineteenth Century 1870–1900'. *Christmas in Texas*. College Station, TX: Texas A&M UP, 1994.

'Silvesterpunsch – New Year's Eve Punch Bowl Recipe'. The German Kitchen: German Food and German Culture. 13 December 2010. http://www.thegermankitchen.com/.

Thomas, Jerry. *Bartender's Guide*. New York: Dick & Fitzgerald, 1862.

Thomas, Jerry. *How to Mix Drinks, or the Bon-Vivants Companion*. New York: Dick and Fitzgerald, 1862.

'Tom and Jerry'. *Merriam-Webster Dictionary*: http://www.merriam-webster.com/dictionary.

Vitz, Evelyn Birge. 'Christmas Day and the Christmas Season'. *A Continual Feast: A Cookbook to Celebrate the Joys of Family and Faith Throughout the Christian Year*. New York: Ignatius Press, 1991.

'*The What-Not or Ladies Handy Book*.' Vol. IV. London: Kent & Co. 1863.

Long Life to You! Drinking and Celebrating in Ancient Rome in the Festival of Anna Perenna

Christopher Grocock

The topic of this paper is the festival of Anna Perenna, an extremely obscure Roman female deity whose festival is – despite her obscurity – recorded in some detail in the third book of his poems calendaring the festivals of Rome, the *Fasti*, by the Roman poet Ovid (43 BC–AD 17 or 18).[1] Traditionally, the Roman new year began on 1 March, and 15 March – the *Ides* – was also the new moon festival. It is attested as an 'addition in red' on the *Fasti Antiates maiores*, a Roman calendar dated to 84–55 BC (Scheid 2003: 52 fig. 1, Wiseman 2004: colour plate 6, 68). According to the *Vatican Calendar*, it took place at 'the first milestone on the *Via Flaminia*' (Frazer 1929: 110),[2] while Ovid gives a location by the Tiber, probably somewhere near the present-day Porta del Populo (Warde Fowler 1911: 50), which fits in with his statement in *Fasti* iii. 524 (see below).

The date of the festival of this goddess – the Ides of March (15 March) – is of course overshadowed by the fact that it was also on this day in 44 BC that Julius Caesar, suspected of aiming at supreme power for himself, was assassinated by Brutus and the various other conspirators who saw in Caesar a threat to their own potential advancement. It is perhaps unusual that none of the biographical or historical accounts of his death, which include numerous references to portents and the religious contexts, make any mention of her.[3] This is rather surprising, as the link between Anna Perenna and the *annus perennis* or 'everlasting circle of years' would have lent itself well to Caesar's death – after all, it came to an abrupt halt on a most unpropitious day in his case!

Ovid and the *Fasti*

Ovid wrote the *Fasti* in order to celebrate the many and varied religious festivals to be found in the Roman calendar. Bailey points out that it mirrors Horace *Odes* iii in its focus on the traditional cults of Rome, and may have been written to show that, in contrast to his other more lascivious works, Ovid showed a genuine interest in the revival of traditional religion which was such a hallmark of the Augustan regime.[4] It was composed in the middle period of Ovid's life, in about 2 and 1 BC, though it probably underwent some revisions after Augustus' death in AD 14 while Ovid languished in exile in Tomi. Only the first six books were completed; sadly, we have nothing treating July to December, and this is a major loss to our knowledge about the detail of Roman celebrations in the early imperial era. The *Fasti* provoke a variety of reactions: Bailey regarding *Fasti* iii as illustrating 'his power of arresting attention by vivid detail and exciting narrative' (Bailey 1921: 7); A.S. Hollis regards them as poems in which his 'talent for narrative', breaking free from the 'slight restrictions of the elegiac couplet' found its fulfilment (Binns 1973: 104–5), though there is but scant reference to the collection by the contributors to Binns' volume as a whole. In contrast, E.J. Kenney commented dismissively that 'it lacks the spontaneity of his other work, and the elegiac couplet, though employed with astonishing virtuosity, is not a suitable medium for sustained narrative' (Kenney 1972: 764).

The most recent edition of the text is that of E.H. Alton, D.E.W. Wormell, and E. Courtney (Teubner, Leipzig, 1978); the easiest to access is the Loeb edition, edited and translated by Sir J.G. Frazer (Heinemann: Harvard and London, 1931), and Frazer also produced the most detailed commentary on the work in his five volumes published in 1929 (Frazer 1929), though Frazer, like his predecessors, 'exploited it solely as an antiquarian curiosity' (Herbert-Brown 1994: vii). The commentary by Bömer (Bömer 1958) is of a purely linguistic and philological nature, with some discussion on the light it sheds on Roman religion in general; Herbert-Brown 1994 focuses on historical issues raised in the *Fasti* and does not examine the passages discussed here.

In Ovid's accounts, which are set out below in my own translations, the festival seems to have had two aspects. In the first of these, it seems to have been a festival celebrated exclusively by the elderly, in a kind of apotropaic activity intended to prolong their (already) long life. In addition it acts as a deliberate evocation in a town of country living out-of-doors on the banks of the Tiber (with similarities in this regard, but only in this regard, to the Hebrew Feast of Tabernacles);[5] and finally, this part of the celebration of the goddess incorporates sanctioned, deliberate drunkenness.

Ovid provides us with a fairly detailed description of what happened at the festival itself and who took part in it, and goes on to supply a range of explanations for the origin of the celebration, based on Roman mythology and fairly basic (though interesting) attempts at etymology. Harrison 1993 seems to be the most recent scholar to have discussed this celebration, though his focus is not on the passage under discussion here. Ovid combines a number of aspects of the celebration associated with Anna Perenna, and in so doing he seems to be making use of a range of data in an attempt to explore the aetiological arguments which may be associated with the festival; thus after the passage which is under consideration (*Fasti* iii. 523–42) he goes on to outline some explanatory stories: the first links this goddess with the Anna who was sister of Dido, who famously was the lover of Aeneas and who committed suicide after that hero abandoned her in Carthage (told by Vergil in *Aeneid* iv; *Fasti* iii 543–656, a lengthy episode in which Ovid seems to delight in filling out some missing narrative from Vergil); then in *Fasti* iii. 657–60 two alternative explanations, dealt with briefly: Anna is either the moon, 'because she fills the years with months', or the nymph Hagno, daughter of Atlas who was the first to give food to the infant Jupiter, or to Io, in ancient mythology the horned moon-goddess and daughter of Iachus of Argos, or an obscure character called Anna of Bovillae (*Fasti* iii. 661–74) who – in a story he has heard which,

Ovid claims, has some plausibility (*Fasti* iii. 662) – made *rustica liba* or 'rustic cakes' for the plebs on the occasion of the Aventine secession, a protest against patrician injustice, traditionally dated to 494 BC. Bailey notes that although this is another aetiological myth, it does indicate that there *must have been* a cult of Anna Perenna at Bovillae (Bailey 125–6). Wiseman comments that 'the combination of Mars and Minerva, close to Liber in the archaic calendar, suggest an early date [for the festival]'(Wiseman 2004: 84). Adkins & Adkins 2000 content themselves with the briefest of paraphrases of Ovid's account, without critical assessment.

This is the account given of the festival of Anna Perenna by Ovid in *Fasti* iii. 523–542:

> On the Ides is the genial festival of Anna Perenna,
> not far from your banks, Tiber, you incomer.
> Ordinary folk come and, strewn all over the place on the green grass,   525
> they drink, and each reclines with his partner.
> Some rough it in the open air, a few pitch tents,
> there are those whose leafy shack is made from branches,
> and some, when they have stood up reeds in place of firm columns,
> lay their togas stretched out on them.   530
> But they are warm with the sun and the wine and they pray
> for as many years as the cups they can drink, and they drink up to that many.
> You will find there a man who was drinking Nestor's years,
> (and) a woman who might have made into the Sybil by her wine-cups.
> There they also sing whatever they have learned in the theatres,   535
> and they throw their hands about in a lively way to their words,
> and putting the wine-bowl down they lead rough and ready dances,
> and the 'smart girlfriend' leaps about with her hair let loose.
> When they return, they stagger and they are a right show for the public,
> and the crowd which bumps into them calls them the 'lucky ones'.   540
> Recently there was a procession – it seemed to me worth the telling –
> a drunken old duck was dragging along her drunken old man!

The passage needs some comment, since much of what was familiar to a contemporary reader of Ovid may be lost on us. In particular, his vocabulary is redolent with significant meaning. Anna Perenna is (as Bailey points out) the *numen* or presiding spirit of the recurring year ('genial' in l. 523 is Latin *geniale*, which may be linked with the *genius* of the year, a cognate form with the *numen* or 'spirit', an essential characteristic in ancient Roman religion, but it might also carry the meaning 'genial', allowing for more licence and merrymaking than would normally be allowed, and this is the interpretation which Bailey prefers);[6] Anna recalls Latin *annus* 'year', and *anulus* 'ring', but also *anus* 'old woman' – a pun Ovid plays on in this passage and in the other stories he tells about her. 'Ordinary folk' (Latin *plebs*) in l. 525 makes it clear that this was a popular, rather than a priestly, celebration, and ordinary folk are involved – though, it seems, only the elderly, in the passage which we are considering at the moment, perhaps under the influence of the pun *anus/annus*? They are old, but not necessarily poor – some of them have togas to use as shading (see l. 530), which shows that they are 'respectable',[7] and *plebs* is perhaps used as a contrast to *patrician* – this is a genuinely 'popular' festival. However, Ovid appears to expect his readers to be familiar with the event, and the appeal to his eye-witness testimony at the end indicates that he is describing something which is common knowledge. From line 526 it appears to be celebrated by couples – which may allow for a connection with a fertility rite, but given the age of the participants, this seems unlikely.

Others take part in the celebration of Anna Perenna in different ways later on in *Fasti* iii, but in these lines, which seem to be describing the core of the event, only older members of Roman society seem to be involved. Here, there are four main features of the celebration:

1. It is held in the open air, in ad hoc, temporary shelters. There is a similar passage in Tibullus ii. 5. 95–8, but almost certainly refers to another festival, the *Parilia*, held on 21 April. As mentioned above, this aspect of Anna Perenna resembles the Jewish Feast of Tabernacles, and may recall some country origins, as does the timing of the festival; note 'roughing it' (Latin *durat*) in l. 527, implying some hardship for the participants.

2. Drinking to excess, quite deliberately – not only do the participants drink 'many happy returns of the year',[8] but as they are affected by the mixture of spring sunshine and alcohol (*sole tamen vinoque calent*, l. 531) another motif is interpreted, whereby they hope they live for as many years as they can down cups of wine – the kind of games seen in Mediterranean night clubs or at rugby celebrations. Dalby (2003a: 123) comments of the imperial period that 'examples of communal drunkenness are less frequent … excessive drinking … becomes an example of excess.' Ovid uses mythical examples to illustrate this, saying that they use Nestor (the veteran Homeric hero) and the Sibyl (the ageless prophetess of Cumae on the Bay of Naples).[9] However, the wine is not drunk neat (there is a *crater* or mixing-bowl present, and they drink from *cyathi* and *calices*, by no means large cups: a *cyathus* is nominally one-twelfth of a *sextarius*, hence about 1½ fl oz, or 0.045 litres. If they drank as many as 100 cups (for every year of a long, but not unknown life in the ancient world), their consumption would equate to 4.5 litres – eight pints, give or take, of liquid! However, if the wine was mixed with water in the ratio 2:3 then little more than a litre of wine (1.76 pints) is consumed – and that, one presumes, at a leisurely rate (Davidson 1997: 61–9, Dalby 2003a: 351, 354; Dalby 2003b: 87; Grocock & Granger 2006: 84–5) but it has an inebriating effect all the same. Frazer (1929: 113) has a nice rendering of l. 534, 'a woman who would live to the Sibyl's age if cups could do the trick.'

3. This then leads to singing and dancing, using popular songs and 'letting your hair down'. The songs in l. 535 are probably those included in the *mimi* or *fabular riciniatae* of popular theatre; Hallam (ad. loc.) notes that Decimus Laberius, who made these low forms of entertainment 'respectable' by raising them to respected forms of literature, composed one on the subject of Anna Perenna – perhaps based on the second story Ovid tells about her, discussed below.[10] L. 537 *posito cratere* probably means that they put the wine mixing-bowl on the ground and dance around it, as in Greek folk-dancing; I think the *choreas* refer to the men, while in l. 538, the *culta amica* dances a solo. There is some sarcasm in Ovid's juxtaposition of the *duras choreas*, 'rough and ready dances', with the *culta amica* – she is nothing of the kind, or so it seems, especially with her hair flying about! Bailey thinks it means 'dressed up' or 'in her best'.[11]

4. A lack of care about what others think! Once the celebration is over, the parties return home; Ovid's choice of *titubant* is deliberate – they are not utterly wasted or comatose from drink, since they can still walk, but they 'stagger' or 'totter'; they are also a *spectacula volgi*, a 'spectacle for vulgar eyes', as Frazer renders it; *spectaculum* indicates something eye-catching or a performance, open to the gaze of everyone, while the crowd which runs into them calls them the 'lucky ones', *fortunati*: then as now, 'happy' or 'merry' was a suitable slang epithet for someone under the influence of alcohol, and Hallam renders it 'drunk as a lord'; the point seems to be that they are doing no harm to themselves or to anyone else, and it is worth stressing that those who encounter them have *not* taken part in the celebration – reinforcing the idea that only the *elderly* get drunk in this way. There is further irony in the use of the term *pompa*, a triumphal procession, used to describe two inebriated old folk on their way home.

In these lines, Ovid demonstrates both his skill in conveying subtle detail, and also his predilection for the grotesque, especially linguistically; he is a poet who cannot resist a pun and delights in visual incongruity. The stress on old age need not necessarily surprise us: there are attested instances, such as Ummidia Quadratilla (Pliny the Younger, *Letters* vii.24), whose seventy-nine years are nothing compared to Iuilius Valens, veteran of Legion II Augusta, whose tombstone at Caerleon asserts that he lived to be a hundred (*RIB* 363), like the Roman statesman and hero Valerius Corvus (or Corvinus: so Cicero, *De Senectute* 60).

More to our point considering 'celebration', the festival he describes focuses on wine and drinking. The consumption of wine makes us invariably think of Bacchus/Liber: already introduced by Ovid into his poem in *Fasti* iii. 469 ff., the story of Ariadne. The stress Ovid places on drinking is probably not coincidental, then; and after *Anna Perenna* he goes on in *Fasti* iii. 713 – with only a brief interlude discussing the death of Julius Caesar – to the 'very popular celebration of Bacchus' or *Liber*, the *Liberalia*, on 17 March. This has obvious seasonal links to other Bacchic revels in the ancient world, such as the Athenian Great Dionysia, which took place in 'Elaphebolion, a month which answers to the last half of March and the first half of April. It must have terminated on the 15th, and begun on the 10th or 11th. It could hardly have lasted less than five days' (Haigh 1898: 9–21).

However, this was a *new wine* festival, and Rome had its own counterpart, the Vinalia, held on 23 April (and also described in Ovid *Fasti* iv. 863–900 – so Anna Perenna cannot be part of this – it is a month early). Dalby (3003a: 352) points out that fermentation might have been completed within a month of the vintage, which was taken later than in modern times; so the new wine might well have been ready by 15 March, but the *opening* of the jars of new wine was a specific feature of the Vinalia, a month later (Scheid 2003: 49). ... have the old folk been consuming *old* wine? Was there some need to – apart from its delicious qualities?

Were they perhaps drinking imported wine? Tchernia notes that while the supply shifted first from purely local produce to wines imported via Ostia, which then themselves were in decline after a recovery in the output of vineyards in Latium and Etruria in about the middle of the first century AD, the consumption of wine in ancient Rome remained constant, citing Moses Finlay's description of Rome as 'a fabulous consumer of wine' (Finlay 1973: 206, n.24; Tchernia 1986: 21, 251.) This was largely due to the sheer demand of Rome: von Reden comments that even in ancient Greece at least, per capita consumption of wine was 'probably significantly higher than, for example, in mediaeval times' (von Reden in Scheidel et al. 2007: 393).

The old folk Ovid describes are not criticized in any way; Ovid's language is indifferent to the ethics of their drinking, and since it forms part of a religious festival (however strange that may seem to us), it is sanctioned drunkenness – as it seems to have been in the Athenian Dionysia. The behaviour of the old folk – drinking, singing, dancing – are all inherent parts of Dionysiac ritual from its earliest times, despite its overthrowing of social norms: 'The madness which is called Dionysus is no sickness, no debility in life, but a companion of life at its healthiest' (Otto 1981: 143). This is quite different to the views expressed about drunkenness generally in the ancient world: 'the consumption of wine (in opposition to beer) was not only socially castigated but could also be seen as a chance for foreign merchants to exploit their social partners, and was thus part of a wider discourse about freedom and subordination' (von Reden in Scheidel et al. 2007: 393). The terms in which Ovid describes the drunken couple at the end of the passage may therefore be taken to imply that this was not an ordinary occurrence, unlike (for example) British high streets on Saturday nights. For example, Pliny the Elder (*HN* xiv. 89–90) claims that in its earliest days, women were not allowed to drink wine, and that Romulus refused to find one Egnatius Rufus guilty of a murder charge when the latter found his wife sneaking wine from the vat and clubbed her to death! Speaking of later times, Pliny repeats what sounds like common knowledge of his own day, that 'drunkards shorten their lives. Tippling brings a pale face and hanging cheeks, sore eyes, shaky hands that spill the contents of vessels when they are full, and the condign punishment of haunted sleep and restless nights, and the crowning reward of drunkenness, monstrous licentiousness and delight in iniquity… This is what they call "snatching life as it comes!", when, whereas other men daily lose their yesterdays, these people lose tomorrow also' (*HN* xiv. 142, trans Rackham in the Loeb series – this is quite the opposite of the intention of the Anna Perenna festival).

Other aspects of Anna Perenna

This is not all that we have from Ovid: after the aetiological discussion about various Annas (discussed above), he includes in his final section a quite separate aspect of the celebration. Here the stress is on ribald verses sung by *puellae* perhaps meaning 'girls' in a general sense (as used nowadays, e.g. for the participants in a hen party?), or perhaps embracing a younger set of participants – though they only take advantage of the general change, and do not get involved in the drinking. The gender limitation makes this very close to the Dionysiac ritual celebrated in Euripides' play *Bacchae*, and to the deliberate, state-sponsored, and utterly outrageous humour found in Old Comedy:

> Now it remains for me to tell why it is that girls sing obscene songs: 675
> for they gang together and sing songs which are definitely disgusting.
> (Anna) had just become a goddess; Mars Gradivus ('Mars-on-the-march') came
>   to Anna
> and taking her aside he uttered words like these:
> 'You will be worshipped in my month, I have joined my times to yours;
> my great hope depends on you doing your duty 680
> Smitten with love for Minerva, one warrior for another,
> I am on fire, and I've been feeding this wound for a long time.
> Find a way for we two gods with such similar interests to come together:
> you should be able to play these parts well, you kindly old duck.'
> He finished speaking. She tricked the god with an empty promise 685
> and dragged out his silly hope, keeping him wondering for ages.
> When he pressed her more often she said 'I have carried out your orders!
> She is defeated, and has only just raised her hands in surrender.'
> The lover believed her and got the marriage-bed ready.
> (But) Anna was led there covering her face, just like a newly-wed. 690
> Mars was just going to give her a kiss when he recognised Anna;
> shame and anger fought for control of the god.
> The new goddess laughed at the lover of his darling Minerva,
> and there was never a joke played more pleasing to Venus than this one.
> From this, old jokes and filthy stories are sung, 695
> and people love to recall how she ticked off the mighty god.

This aspect of the festival concerns the younger generation – not with wine, either, or at least it is not mentioned – but with sanctioned coarseness. Again there are similarities to what was allowed in Dionysiac revels – the 'official' status of women in ancient Rome did not allow for such behaviour as a rule, and the festival as a whole hardly chimes with the general tone of the Augustan age (cf. Suetonius *Divus Augustus* 31).

There are other references to the festival, mentioned by Frazer 1929 and the other commentators following him, which indicate that there were other aspects to this festival: Martial iv. 64: 16, discussing the little estate of Julius Martialis, on the Janiculum, mentions 'the fruitful grove of Anna Perena that rejoices in the blood of virgins' (trans. Shackleton Bailey, who comments that 'the reference to virgin's blood (i.e. deflowering?) is unexplained, and the text has been suspected.' Frazer 1929: 111–12 comments 'the celebration of the festival, as described by Ovid, was a thoroughly popular one. The pairing of sweethearts, lying on the grass, trolling out ribald staves, and drinking themselves drunk, points to customs like those formerly observed on May Day and Midsummer Eve in many parts of Europe, when the licence accorded to the sexes was a relic of magical rites performed for the purpose of maintaining the fertility of nature alike in the greenwoods and the fields, in man and beast.' There is also the suggestion made in 1920 by E.H. Alton that lines 541–2 indicate not a real old woman but an effigy, a *Petreia* mentioned in Festus along with a male companion *Petro*, and that this 'procession' might have indicated the replacing of the old year by New Year.[12] The early fifth-century collector of curiosities Macrobius recorded in his *Saturnalia* i.12.6 that in the month of March 'both public and private sacrifice is offered to Anna Perenna, so that we might propitiously pass the year (*annare*) and many years after (*perennare*)' (Kaster 2011: i. 139); the use of the present tense should not mislead us, however, as by the time that Macrobius was writing Christianity had long been dominant at Rome, and the battle over the Altar of Victory had been lost by the pagans a generation before; Anna Perenna was by this time surely a matter of interest only for antiquarians.

It makes one wonder whether the authors writing about Caesar, some 100 years after Ovid, knew about Anna Perenna – or whether her cult had died out by then, perhaps because of its connotations with licentiousness and the opportunities it provided for outrageous behaviour (something which would not have fitted in well with Augustan morality, or the political paranoia of Nero and Domitian in later times). It is possible that Ovid includes the festival for completeness' sake in his poetic discussion of all the items in the Roman calendar (though he only got as far as the end of June) but he does seem to find the festival and its associated celebrations interesting on a number of counts, not least because of its sheer quirkiness.

Notes

1. Editions: Teubner, ed. Wormell, Alton, Courtney, 1997; Loeb with (very archaic) facing translation, ed. and trans. Sir J.G. Frazer, Harvard, Heinemann, 1931; Frazer also commented on the work as a whole; Ovid, *Fasti*, ed. G.H. Hallam (Macmillan, London, 1881); C. Bailey, *P. Ovidi Nasonis Fastorum Liber III* (Oxford, OUP, 1921). See also s.v. 'Ovid', 'Fasti' in the *Oxford Classical Dictionary*.
2. *Corpus Inscriptionum Latinorum* i. pp. 242, 311, *Feriae Annae Perennae via Flam. ad lapidem prim.*, cited by Frazer 1929: 110.
3. See the very full accounts in Suetonius, *Divus Iulius* 81, Plutarch, *Caesar* 63–6.
4. Bailey, pp. 7–9;
5. See Bailey, p. 121.
6. Bailey, p. 120.
7. See Suetonius, *Divus Augustus* 40.3 for Augustan (and therefore contemporary) insistence on formal dress in and around the Forum, part of the general conservatism of Augustus' rule.
8. See Bailey on ll. 531–4, p. 121.
9. See e.g. Ovid *Fasti* iv. 875; *Met.* xiv. 130–153; *Ex Ponto* ii. 8. 41; Petronius, *Satyricon* 48.
10. Hallam, p. 249; *Oxford Classical Dictionary*, art. 'Laberius'.
11. For *culta* see *Oxford Latin Dictionary* (OUP Oxford 1982), p. 467, s.v. *cultus , -a, -um*; all the four basic senses noted imply some kind of care or grooming; Bailey, ad loc.
12. p. 281, ed. Lindsay, 'Petreia vocabatur, quae pompam praecedens in colonis aut municipiis imitatur avum ebrium, ab agri vitio, scilicet petris, appelata[m]'; p. 226, 'petrones rustici fere dicuntur propter vetustatem.'

Bibliography

Adkins & Adkins 2000: Lesley Adkins, Roy A. Adkins, *Dictionary of Roman Religion*. New York and Oxford: Oxford University Press (reprint).

Bailey 1921: Cyril Bailey, *P. Ovidi Nasonis Fastorum Liber III, ed. with an introduction and commentary* (Oxford, Clarendon Press, 1921)

Binns 1973: James W. Binns (ed.), *Ovid. Greek and Latin Studies. Classical Literature and its Influence*. London and Boston: Routledge & Kegan Paul.

Bömer 1958: Franz Bömer, *P. Ovidius Naso. Die Fasten*. 2 vols. Heidelberg, Carl Winter Universitätslag.

Dalby 2003a: Andrew Dalby, *Food in the Ancient World from A to Z*. London, Routledge

Dalby 2003b: Andrew Dalby, *Bacchus: a Biography*. London: British Museum Press.

Davidson 1997: James Davidson, *Courtesans and Fishcakes: the consuming passions of classical Athens*. London: HarperCollins.

Frazer 1929: Sir James G. Frazer, *Publii Ovidii Nasonis Fastorum Libri Sex: The Fasti of Ovid*, 5 vols: London, Macmillan.

Frazer 1931: Sir James G. Frazer, Ovid: *Fasti* (Loeb Classical Library, Cambridge, Mass. and London, Harvard University Press, 1976 (so my copy; but preface written in 1931).

Grocock & Grainger 2006: Christopher W. Grocock, Sally Grainger (ed. and trans.), *Apicius*. Totnes: Prospect Books.

Haigh 1898: A. E. Haigh, *The Attic Theatre*. Oxford: Clarendon Press.

Hallam 1881: G. A. Hallam, *The Fasti of Ovid. Edited with Notes and Indices* (London, Macmillan).

Harrison 1993: S. J. Harrison, 'A Roman Hecale: Ovid Fasti 3. 661–74', *Classical Quarterly* 43.2 (1993), 455–7.

Herbert-Brown 1994: Geraldine Herbert-Brown, *Ovid and the* Fasti. *An Historical Study*. Oxford: Clarendon Press.

Kaster 2011: Robert A. Kaster (ed. and trans.), Macrobius, *Saturnalia*, 3 vols; Cambridge, Mass., and London: Loeb Classical Library, Heinemann.

Kenney 1971: Edward J. Kenney, article 'Ovid', in *Oxford Classical Dictionary* (Oxford, OUP, 2nd edn with corrections, 1972), 763–4.

Otto 1981: Walter F. Otto, *Dionysus: Myth and Cult*. Translated with an introduction by Robert B. Palmer. Dallas, Texas: Spring Publications.

Panella & Tchernia 2002: Clementina Panella, André Tchernia, 'Agricultural Products transported in Amphorae: Oil and Wine', in Scheidel & von Reden 2002, 173–89.

Scheid 2003: John Scheid, *An Introduction to Roman Religion*. Edinburgh: Edinburgh University Press.

Scheidel et al. 2007: Walter Schiedel, Ian Morris, Richard Saller (eds.), *The Cambridge Economic History of the Greco-Roman World*. Cambridge: Cambridge University Press.

Scheidel & von Reden 2002: Walter Scheidel, Sitta von Reden (eds.) *The Ancient Economy*. Edinburgh Readings on the Ancient World. Edinburgh: Edinburgh University Press.

Tchernia 1986: André Tchernia, *Le Vin de l'Italie romaine: essai d'histoire économique d'après les amphores*. Rome: École Française de Rome.

von Reden 2007: Sitta von Reden, 'Classical Greece: consumption' in Scheidel et al. 2007, 385–408.

Warde Fowler 1911: W. Warde Fowler, *The Religious Experience of the Roman People from the Earliest Times to the Age of Augustus*. London: Macmillan.

Wiseman 2004: T. P. Wiseman, *The Myths of Rome*. Exeter: Exeter University Press.

Celebrating with Altamiras: The Spirit of Fiesta Food

Vicky Hayward

French cuisine held sway at Madrid's Bourbon court when Juan Altamiras, an Aragonese friar, wrote his radical little cookbook. Turning his back on court cookery, he wrote for home and monastic cooks hard-pressed by economic crisis. This he spelled out clearly in his book's title: *New Art of Cookery, Drawn from the School of Economic Experience* (1745).[1] But for him eating in 'times of calamity and misery' did not mean eating badly. It meant rethinking refinement and, when it came to celebration dishes, replacing banquets with fiesta food that rich and poor could enjoy alike.

Altamiras, who ran the kitchen of a university college in Zaragoza, Aragon's cosmopolitan capital, was not ignorant of courtly food. Quite the opposite. He emulated its art and architecture playfully for friary guests, tagging the recipes for them as he saw fit. Old-fashioned game sops, layered high, perhaps topped by a gilded hen, were, he wrote, fitting for a Spanish Grandee. A Guardian Father who inspected the friars' lifestyle could be served marzipan-stuffed eggshells. These were elegant but not extravagant dishes since most of the ingredients were sourced outside the cash economy. One mutton pie he tagged for 'people of distinction' and 'a great treat for the poor.' In other words, he wanted no hungry spectators at his feasts.[2]

Such dishes help sketch the friars' world for us. Social floaters, they depended on alms, but moved easily between prisons and palaces. They lived close to the poor, but visited the rich. In Altamiras' lifetime their radius of reach grew. By the late 1740s the Franciscans were moving north from New Mexico to explore California for the Spanish crown. This gave the friars clout at court. When Charles III, Franciscan by sympathy, inherited the throne in 1759, their ascendancy was sealed.[3]

So, when Altamiras turned his back on court cookery, he did so knowingly. 'For surely,' he wrote, justifying his theme of economical cookery, 'a Cook who pitches his voice in any other tone will provoke a storm of curses and anger …'.

Why would the anger be so stormy? Travellers' accounts help to explain. A French diarist described one 1755 supper, the best he could find on the Aragonese plains. It consisted of a scrawny chicken 'that you would say had been killed by dogs', four half-formed eggs (yolk-only, from inside the chicken) and a black bread and olive oil soup. This meal drew a crowd of crying children 'all naked and dying of hunger who… tore out our entrails.' Historians support the drama of such accounts. Cyclical drought brought failed harvests on poor land and, in the winters that followed, the hungry flocked to the cities to live off monastic kitchens' soup and bread, doled out at lunchtime every day. Even so, food shortages and high prices led to food riots. Against that backdrop, courtly cooking's 'ostentation and squander' was likely to turn a friary cook's stomach.[4]

Small wonder, then, that *New Art* seems mute on celebration. The idea of luxury fiesta food, as we know it, was alien to everyday Spanish homes then and for the next two centuries. Everyday scarcity made much fiesta food a humble affair in most homes. 'There's no chicken or a turkey, but a good rabbit's the best of all,' says Juan, putting a brave face on a bare Christmas table in Carmen Laforet's novel *Nothing* (1945). Laforet's generation, who lived through the Spanish Civil War, were to echo Altamiras' anger about hunger: Luis Bunuel's documentary *Tierra Sin Pan* (1932), Miguel Hernández's poetry and Camilo José Cela's fiction, to give just a few examples, all described modern hunger in searingly dark works.

Oral accounts of these years suggest that Christmas belonged to a fiesta calendar very different from our own times. Holy Week was the most deeply felt moment of the Church year; the pig killing and Carnival, twinned food feasts, were its biggest popular family fiestas; the local patron saint's or Virgin's day was the community party.[5]

If we return to reading *New Art* with that old calendar in mind and take British chef Mark Hix's approach to historic cookbooks – that they can be read like poetry – we then find that Altamiras was not mute on celebration. He simply did things his own way.

Monastic 'holy days': *los días grandes*

Altamiras' first snapshot of feasting falls in the book's opening pages. He neatly sidesteps courtly cookbooks' banquet menus and ornate table plans to discuss a simpler friars' feast for a 'holy day' or *día grande*. 'When you need to feed many mouths, e.g. three hundred men,' he wrote,

> govern the occasion thus. On the eve of the feast cut up the rations of meat, lay them in their dishes, then, when midnight has tolled, put your fire in order, prepare your stews, and roasts, and if you are making *pepitoria*, have it laid out on tablecloths so it does not turn sour: take care to skim off any foam and, once your dishes are seasoned, put them to one side near the hearth, sitting on a few embers, to finish cooking; then, with your fire free, cook your rabbit and chicken *cazuelas*. Give them a little boil and finish them on a gentle fire, taking care to feed the flames when they languish; then, a small fire is enough for your soupmaking. If your kitchen is cramped find an open field where you can cook; heed me, for one Cook I knew did not do so and was suffocated by the smoke.

The friars' meal, then, was not so different to today's open-air pilgrimage lunches of rice or a lamb stew, *calderetas*, cooked up over a fire built out in the countryside. Altamiras' focus was not the food, but how to manage a cooking fire for many hours of unbroken cooking.[6]

His feast's 'stews and roasts' we find later in the book. He gave recipes for stewed or roast chicken alongside a *pepitoria*, or little stew of chicken wings, necks, giblets and

Celebrating with Altamiras: The Spirit of Fiesta Food

livers. He gave a trio of lamb or kid dishes together – pluck pie, testicles and pot-roasted meat on the bone – and stewed or pot-roast veal close to calf's head and tongue. These, then, are families of dishes, like those for old country weddings, designed to make use of whole birds or beasts.[7]

Friary accounts suggest this meat came from home-slaughtered livestock. One eighteenth-century Zaragoza friary cook noted the cost of hay among his kitchen outgoings and, on 13 May 1795, '*un cabrito pa el dia de la Ascensn*', a kid for Ascension day, though it is not clear whether this was late payment for that year's Easter lunch or early buying to fatten a kid for the following year. In all, that winter and spring, the friars bought twelve kids, eight calves and one lamb.[8]

We also learn a lot from what Altamiras chose to leave out of his book. The *olla podrida*, the famous Spanish dish enriched by various meats, poultry, game and sausages, is nowhere to be found. Nor are wood-roasted baby lamb or kid, so often written about as classic Spanish country food. Instead slow-cooked stews and pot roasts simply seasoned with garlic, parsley and white wine become celebration food when set against the pulses and vegetables that make up an unprecedented quarter of his book.[9]

We forget how despised these monkish vegetables and beans were. As late as 1880 novelist Emilia Pardo Bazán pointed out how startlingly true that was in her novel *The House of Ulloa*, set in rural Galicia. '"Vegetables indeed!" the Cebre priest's housekeeper would have cried, laughing with all her heart and all her ribcage too, "Vegetables on the patron saint's feast-day! They'll do for the pigs."'[10]

But of course the friars did eat vegetables on feast-days during Lent and Holy Week. Then lunch would be beans and greens as normal, but rounded out with an almond milk rice pudding or fish.[11] Here again Altamiras stuck close to what humble kitchens could afford. He knew very well how to cook eel, salmon, trout and sturgeon, river fish that abounded on the tables of wealthy old monasteries with royal fishing rights, but he chose to lead with salt cod.

Why? As Altamiras wrote himself, salt cod was 'a matter of little substance'. On the other hand fresh fish was a rare luxury in friaries far from the sea and cheap salt cod, an easy traveller, allowed everyone to celebrate Lent, Holy Week, and other meatless fiestas. The Church encouraged that: food, like processions or sculpture, made the sacred real. Altamiras, then, had good reasons to put Spain's first salt cod recipes into print – just a dozen, but remarkably diverse in flavour and technique.[12]

One of these dishes captures *New Art*'s resonance. Altamiras threw 'hard saltcod heads', garlic bulbs, and perhaps a few chopped greens into a well-simmered pot of chickpeas. A humble throwaway idea, it holds the origins of today's much loved Lenten chickpea stew, or *potaje de vigilia*, still served at high and low tables alike. Sometimes it is a homely potful, and other times it is a chef's dazzling avant-garde dish. Whichever it may be, the richly satisfying flavours, as a kind of universal fiesta food, are those put into print by Altamiras.[13]

Celebrating with Altamiras: The Spirit of Fiesta Food

Popular fiestas: pig killing and carnival

Breathless and lively, Altamiras' pig killing was also new to a Spanish cookbook. In his priorities, he made clear where his heart lay. He gave six lines to what he called 'the salting of the joints' – that is, ham making – and four pages to sausages, lard, and crackling.[14]

Why include a pig killing at all, one might ask? His reasons were largely practical: the monasteries made their own hams and sausages till modern times. But he also threw in attitude. Cultural historian América Castro, writing in exile, has tracked how ham-eating was used by Spanish writers to position themselves on religious purity in a Christian society that hounded those with hidden Muslim and Jewish identities revealed through such food habits. Seventeenth-century poet and dramatist Francisco de Quevedo, for example, mistrusted anyone who did not want to eat ham. Miguel de Cervantes was protectively ironic: he gave a meat-stripped ham bone, 'something suckable for safe-conduct'[15] to Ricote, a Christianized Muslim character in *Don Quixote*.

What, then, was Altamiras' position? He fled from piety with his whacky title – 'How to Dress a Pig, from Killing it to Hanging the Hams and Sausages: Of Special Use for Nuns'[16] – and shrugged off orthodoxy. His pig killing was instead a celebration of Carnival, the most hedonistic food fiesta of them all. Altamiras could not join in its fleshy revels, but he could give a complicit wink at its world-upside-down fun, the year's highlight for his family and friends. Our times of plenty and Franco's forty-year ban make it hard for us to grasp the importance of Carnival then, but Altamiras would have understood. As Lope de Vega wrote, putting his words in a countryman's mouth, '*Por pascua garrovillas como, / y por carnestolendas, longaniza.*' For Easter Day I eat carob twigs, / and, for Carnival, longaniza sausage.[17]

Which would you choose if you were a food-lover? Altamiras surely shared Lope de Vega's position.

So Altamiras went out of his way to open and close his pig killing with fiesta spirit. He opened with an irreverent nun joke, one of several in the book, and ended with a recipe for the sweet lardy sweetbread still eaten to celebrate the end of the pig killing. In between he fully described the dirty work of washing the pig's guts and soaking them in herb water. He also remained loyal to local flavours like aniseed, cinnamon, pepper, and cloves in his sausages. When it came to the recipes using these products he made a little go a long way. Court cooks might open banquets with luxurious platefuls of sliced ham, just as caterers open cocktail parties today, but Altamiras spread the flavour of diced lean and fat through dozens of dishes. It would not have given a bacony twang, as so often described in eighteenth-century flavours, but the subtle flavour of air-dried ham, even, perhaps, black-footed Iberico.[18]

What, then, of Altamiras' Carnival food? No dishes were flagged up, or rather, I failed to spot them, till a chance conversation led me to the family-owned Hostal Castellote in the Aragonese countryside. When I talked to Mariano Lechal, who runs

Celebrating with Altamiras: The Spirit of Fiesta Food

the *hostal*, we discovered that Altamiras' *rellenos de pan y grasa* were the *hostal*'s Carnival bread dumplings. When I asked Mariano Lechal to write something about these dumplings this is what he sent me:

> Our dumplings, or *pellas*, were born in the countryside where most people used to make sausages and ham from their own pigs. They are our big Carnival dish. We eat them only two days a year, Lardy Thursday, the day when Carnival starts, and the following Saturday, and the wait to enjoy them through the year, always as if for the first time, gives them the special feel of fiesta dishes. Our family have made them year in and year out, right through the ban on Carnival, though without commenting on it. You'll rarely find the recipe written down: grandmothers and mothers pass it on, from memory, as part of a bigger tradition of transforming humble food into a dish that gathers the whole family round the table, converting simplicity into a fiesta.'[19]

Altamiras could not have put it better himself. Food shortages might limit feasting. There might be a ban on world-upside-down fun inside friary walls or the outside world. But the taste of dumplings, handed down and put in print by Altamiras, kept alive the popular spirit of fiesta: inclusive, humble, between-the-lines, resistant.

Saints' days: sweet things

Beyond the poor lay a marginalized world well known to Altamiras. Aragonese medieval law had defined 'widows, orphans, all penurious folk, Jews, Moors' as one class.[20] But that group was shattered and fragmented by the time Altamiras wrote his book. The Jews had been forcibly converted or expelled at the end of the fifteenth century and the last Aragonese Christianized Muslims, known as Moriscos, some 300,000 people, were sent into exile between 1609 and 1614. In the mid-eighteenth century Gypsy persecution became acute and the Inquisition kept working.

Nonetheless, somewhat remarkably, in *New Art* Altamiras decided to take on board Muslim and Jewish flavours, techniques and recipes. These crypto-Jewish and Morisco dishes were not new to Iberian cookbooks. For example, in the famous Aragonese-Catalan *Llibre del Coc*, published under the name of Mestre Robert (or Ruperto de Nola), dishes entitled 'Morisco' sat alongside those identified as Jewish in earlier cookery manuscripts.[21]

The debate on how such continuity occurred is a lively one. Were recipes and techniques shared between medieval communities for reasons of health, safety and economy? Or did Christians seek out what attracted them in Morisco lifestyle? There are many points of view.[22] Whichever – and probably the process varied on the ground from one region, valley or town to the next – what Altamiras' recipes did was to reveal they had even become part of Christian celebration foods.

Take, for example, *New Art*'s deep-fried puffs or *bunuelos*, a dish with Muslim origins. Altamiras knew perfectly well that Montiños, author of Spain's baroque court cookery bible, the reference book of the time, was at pains to fry his puffs in pork lard or use it in the dough, the Christian way. Altamiras, though, flipped back to the Muslim formula: he deep-fried fatless *bunuelo* dough in olive oil, just as frying stalls had done in al-Andalus, and flavoured the puffs with anis and honey, as in medieval Arabic courtly recipes. Today, the continuity with that tradition can still be seen when fiestas come around. Just two of the best known among many examples are Zaragoza's Torta del Pilar pastries and Catalonia's anis-sprinkled fritters for All Saint's Day.[23]

Altamiras' cheese making is another case in point. To make fresh white cheese he warmed milk 'in a new pot, used for nothing else' then turned his back on his contemporary court confectioner Juan de la Mata's advice that lamb's or kid's rennet was the only kind to use. Instead he told readers to stick to wild thistle or artichoke rennet. Some have seen such vegetarian cheese-making, effectively kosher, as Altamiras declaring Jewish origins, but that diminishes the bigger story: how Sephardism contributed 'almost invisibly' to Spanish culture, as historian Henry Kamen has put it. Significantly, too, he did not use his cheese sparingly, as it would be even in a wealthy household. Instead he conjured it up as a celebratory dish sprinkled with cinnamon and sugar, perhaps for a feast or a gift for patrons.[24]

Unblinded by faith, then, Altamiras intertwined the sweet things of persecuted faiths with Christianity's own white dishes. This was all the more radical given his resounding silence on chocolate. By the time *New Art* was published it was not just a popular craze: it had become a favourite liquid breakfast among priests and monks. Yet Altamiras found no space for it, and friary accounts show that cocoa was bought, if ever, once a year, just before Christmas. Did Altamiras do this to keep a distance from the wealthy religious orders? Or did he simply prefer the older rural flavours of many faiths?

Hard to know. The friars were ambivalent on many subjects. One was the Inquisition itself. 'How can there be justice if some are despised and humiliated from generation to generation?' wrote Fray Luis de León, poet, theologian and Franciscan friar, who, like Teresa of Avila, a Carmelite, came from a converted Jewish family which got into trouble with the Inquisition.[25] Perhaps Altamiras, writing two hundred years later, when waves of trials and imprisonments of crypto-Jews and Gypsies were still going on around him, felt it was time not only to acknowledge the food of the exiled, but also celebrate it as it deserved.

When *New Art* first reached readers in 1745, it must have seemed an unlikely bestseller, but it turned out to be one of the most influential cookbooks of its time. It ran through some twenty editions and stayed in print for over 150 years. While French cuisine ruled the day in wealthy homes, it kept the flame of Spanish cooking burning in popular kitchens. Food historians have explained that success through the book's simplicity.[26] True, Altamiras was chattily clear about his simple kitchen, his respect for both social etiquette and the poor, his love of a good laugh and big flavours. His celebration dishes did contain all these elements. But he slipped in other ingredients, too, between the lines: regional loyalties, the foods of other faiths, a certain animosity

Celebrating with Altamiras: The Spirit of Fiesta Food

to palace cooking and straight-laced piety. Perhaps these values, inclusive, inviting Everyman to the table, a new art of refinement, were what really made *New Art* a lasting bestseller.

Notes

1. I have used Spaniards' affectionate name for Altamiras' cookbook, *New Art*, throughout this article. Translations are my own, drawn from the forthcoming English edition of the book.
2. Most friary produce came from its own kitchen garden, hen house and orchard or was paid for by city-hall alms. Cane sugar was relatively cheap in Spain.
3. For a good resumé of the Franciscans and their world in eighteenth-century Spain, see *The Sacred Made Real*, 2010 (London, Yale University Press).
4. I am indebted to Gillian Riley for pointing me towards Barnabite de Livoy, P. 1772: *Voyage d'Espagne fait en l'Année 1755* (Paris, chez Cotard), also quoted by Sophie Coe on chocolate drinking. On subsistence crises see Anes, G. 1970: *Las crisis agrarias en la España moderna* (Madrid, Taurus). On the Aragonese bread riots see Peiró Arroyo, A. 1981–82: 'La Crisis de 1763–66 en Zaragoza y el Motín del Pan', *Cuadernos Aragoneses de Economía*, 239–50. On aristocratic ostentation, see Terrón, E. 1992: *España Encrucijada de Culturas Alimentarias* (Madrid, Ministerio de Agricultura).
5. Laforet, C. 1999: *Nada* (Barcelona, Ediciones Destino). Thankyou to Dolores Campayo Sánchez (Albacete province, Sierra de Ayna) and Miguel Oñoro Alonso (León province) for personal communications on the annual feast-day cycle.
6. For typical court banquet menus see Martínez Montiño F. 1992: *Arte de Cocina, Pasteleria, Vizcocheria, y Conserveria* (Valencia, Librerías Paris-Valencia S.L.), 14–22, which was still in use when Altamiras was writing. Juan de la Mata's 1741 *Arte de Repostería* included ten engravings of table decorations (1992, Burgos).
7. Vidal, D. 2003: *Flor de Cardo Azul* (Teruel, Instituto de Estudios Turolenses), 79.
8. Archivo Historico Nacional, Clero Secular Regular, Libro 18782, 38. The meats bought each year varied slightly.
9. Pulses or vegetables are the main ingredient in nearly fifty of *New Art*'s dishes, which number just over 200.
10. Pardo Bazán, E. 1990: *The House of Ulloa* (London, Penguin), 70.
11. Sundays in Lent, when the friars preached, were often *días grandes*.
12. See Casey, J. 1993, *Early Modern Spain, A Social History* (London, Routledge) 230, for a brief but telling account of the Church's need to secure its tenuous hold on Spain.
13. Ortega, S. 1978: *Mil ochenta recetas de cocina* (Madrid, Ed. Alianza) gives a recipe for home cooks; BACALAO, *monográficos de cultura y gastronomía, tabula 01*, Barcelona, 2004, gives a chef's dish (Andra Mari).
14. Alonso de Herrera, G. 1996: *Agricultura General* (Madrid, Ministerio de Agricultura) and Sierra Rigal, J.V. 1987: *La Cocina Aragonesa* (Zaragoza, Mira Editores S.A.).
15. Castro, A. 1974: *Cervantes y los casticismos españoles* (Madrid, Ed. Alianza).
16. The Spanish title of the pig killing was '*Modo de componer un Lechon, desde que se deguella hasta colgarse: servirà en especial para Religiosas.*'
17. See Lope de Vega, F. 2008: *Rimas humanas y divinas del licenciado Tomé de Burguillos* (Catedra S.A.). Franco's ban on Carnival ran in parallel with Mussolini's ban on Venetian Carnival, reborn in 1979.
18. Lean or fat ham, or both, were used sparingly in over 60 recipes: this is one of various flavours giving Altamiras' cooking a lot of *umami*, as Gillian Riley has pointed out.

19. Personal communication, March 2011.
20. See Harvey, L.P., 1990: *Islamic Spain, 1250–1500* (London, The University of Chicago Press) on the 1247 Fueros, or laws, promulgated by Jaime I.
21. See De Nola, R. 1994: *Libro de Guisados*, (Huesca, Val de Onsera) and Huici Miranda, A. 2005: *La cocina hispano-magrebí durante la época almohade* (Gijón, Trea).
22. See Henry Kamen, op. cit. (bibliography) and Gitlitz D.M. and Davidson L.K., 1999: *A Drizzle of Honey, The Lives and Recipes of Spain's Secret Jews* (New York, St Martin's Press).
23. On al-Andalus's fritters see García Sánchez, E, 1997: 'La tríada mediterránea en al-Andalus', in *Con Pan, Aceite y Vino…* . On Christian lard-fried fritters see Francisco Martínez Montiños, op. cit, 198–203. For contemporary olive-oil fried fritters see Ruscalleda, C. 2005: *Cocinar para ser feliz* (Barcelona, Viena Ediciones) 64.
24. On Altamiras' Jewish origins see Aguilera Pleguezuelo, J. 2002: *Las cocinas árabe y judía y la cocina española* (Malaga, Arguval), 115, and on the larger Arab contribution see Henry Kamen, op. cit., 9. On fresh milk gift dishes in convents see De Sagastizabal, J. (ed), 1995: *La Cocina Monacal* (Barcelona, Planeta), 259.
25. Casey, J. 1993: *Early Modern Spain, A Social History* (London, Routledge), 231
26. Martínez Llopis, M. 1995: *Historia de la gastronomía española* (Huesca, Val de Onsera).

Bibliography

Altamiras, J. 1994: *Nuevo Arte de Cocina, Sacado de la Escuela de la Experiencia Economica* (Huesca, Val de Onsera)

Kamen, H. 2007: *The Disinherited, The Exiles Who Created Spanish Culture* (London, Penguin)

Serrano Larráyoz, F. 2008: 'Confitería y cocina conventual Navarra del siglo XVIII. Notas y precisiones sobre el "Recetario de Marcilla" y el *Cocinero Religioso* de Antonio Salsete', *Revista Principe de Viana* 243, 141–181

Buttering Up the Sun: Russian Maslenitsa from Pagan Practice to Contemporary Celebration

Sharon Hudgins

From prehistoric times to the present, people in many parts of the world have developed rituals for celebrating the changing of the seasons at the spring and autumn equinoxes and at the summer and winter solstices. In both Eastern and Western Europe, the period immediately preceding the vernal equinox has been a time for bidding farewell to winter and welcoming the return of spring, with rituals designed to encourage the fertility of animals and the soil as the days lengthen and the weather warms, to promote the regeneration of life and ensure a bountiful harvest in the months ahead.

These practices cross many cultures and date to pre-Christian times, when people in the northern hemisphere observed the spring equinox at or near the actual time of its occurrence, in the third week of the month we know as March, the third month of the year on the contemporary Western Gregorian calendar.[1] For some agrarian cultures in northern Europe, March was also the beginning of the new year: as winter died, spring was born, the frozen soil began to thaw, and crops could soon be planted again. In the Christian era, however, the timing of this specific seasonal celebration shifted somewhat, becoming associated with the period preceding Lent in the Christian religion, i.e. the six or seven weeks immediately before Easter, which itself is a moveable holiday that can occur between late March and early May, depending on the phases of the moon and the calendrical calculations used by different Christian churches.[2]

In both Eastern and Western Europe, this previously pagan celebration of the vernal equinox has expanded into a secular festival of several days, weeks, or even months leading up to the beginning of Lent. Known as Shrovetide in Britain, *Fasching* (*Fasnacht*, *Fasnet*) in Germanic countries, and Carnival in many Latin countries, this is a period of feasting and merrymaking before the fasting and solemnity of Lent. In Russia, this pre-Lenten celebration is known as Maslenitsa (Butter Week), from the Russian word for butter and oil (*maslo*), since the consumption of butter is an important part of the festivities before being prohibited during Lent.[3] It is also called Pancake Week because celebrants devour huge quantities of *bliny*, yeast-raised pancakes shaped like golden rounds symbolizing the sun and made with eggs, milk, and butter, all ingredients soon to be proscribed during Lent. Another term for this same festival is Cheesefare Week. The fasting guidelines of the Russian Orthodox Church prohibit the consumption of meat during the week preceding the start of Lent, so cheese is one of the primary sources of protein during Maslenitsa – and a food that must be abstained from (along with all other dairy products) during the next seven weeks of Russian Great Lent and Holy Week.[4]

Pagan roots, Christian overlay

Like people in many other cultures and societies around the world, the Eastern Slavs celebrated the waning of winter and coming of spring with rituals designed to banish the short, dark, cold days of the preceding months and encourage the return of longer days illuminated by the sun's light, reviving the earth with its life-giving warmth.

Before Prince Vladimir of Kiev converted to Christianity in 988, the Eastern Slavs were polytheists and in some regions shamanists.[5] Since they did not have a written language, little is actually known about their ancient folk rituals except what can be deduced from certain archaeological finds, texts written by medieval monks, and ethnographical observations in the modern era of the non-Christian rites still practised around the time of the vernal equinox. These include lighting bonfires to honor the sun and encourage its return, to banish bad spirits and as a ritual purification ceremony; dancing in a circle moving in the same direction as the sun to protect against evil; dressing as demons, devils, and witches to banish bad spirits, invoke benign ones and mediate between the upper and lower worlds; dressing as bears, believed to possess protective and healing powers, and as animal symbols of fertility like goats, mares and bulls; eating ritual foods, such as round flat breads symbolizing the sun; indulging in ritual gluttony to ensure future bounty of crops and animals; offering food to the earth and/or the sun and to dead ancestors; parading a straw effigy of an old woman or sometimes a man around the village, then carrying it out to a field, burning it, and scattering the ashes on the earth.[6] These pre-Christian rituals, performed to placate the spirits of the underworld and please the sun above, were clearly associated with fears and hopes concerning the fertility of the earth and fecundity of animals: without a good harvest later in the year, and without animals to provide food and labor, people would go hungry or even starve to death.[7]

While Byzantine Christianity was adopted by Russia's ruler in 988, the process of Christianizing the rest of Russia extended over several centuries, up to the 1600s or even later in some places, primarily because of the geographical and cultural isolation of the Russian peasantry in so vast a land. Different social strata converted to the new religion at different times, starting with the nobility and only later filtering down. The lower classes kept many of their pagan beliefs and rituals, which they grafted onto, or intertwined with, the Christian traditions they ultimately accepted, resulting in a dual belief system described by the Russian word *dvoeverie* (dual or double faith).[8]

As the Russian Orthodox Church tried to replace pagan beliefs and practices with Christian beliefs and rituals, it partially absorbed the pagan celebration of the vernal equinox into the Church calendar, tying it to the variable dates of Lent and Easter, hence replacing the fixed holiday of the solar equinox in March with a moveable feast that could occur, depending on the year, at a time from early February to late March.

Buttering Up the Sun: Russian Maslenitsa

Known in earlier times as Komoeditsy, this celebration of spring morphed into the festival called Maslenitsa, in reference to the last period in which butter and oil could be consumed before the strict fast of Lent and Holy Week, when devout believers abstained from eating meat, dairy products, eggs, fish, animal fats, all (or certain kinds of) oils, alcohol, and sometimes sugar (with a few exceptions to these rules on certain feast days during Lent). Meat was even prohibited during the last seven days of Maslenitsa itself, because the Church intended Maslenitsa to be a period of spiritual and physical preparation for Lent. But most people still considered Maslenitsa to be an end-of-winter-welcome-to-spring festival, a time for eating, drinking, singing, dancing and licentiousness, a last fling before the dietary and social strictures of the Lenten season.

The number of days during which people celebrated this spring festival has varied over time. The pagan festival is said to have lasted for seven days before and seven days after the vernal equinox. During different periods in the Christian era, Maslenitsa has been celebrated for twenty-one, fourteen, ten, eight, seven, or even fewer days (especially in Soviet and early post-Soviet times). In a seventeenth-century effort to suppress the pagan aspects of the festival, the Church reduced the length of Maslenitsa from fourteen to seven days, but many accounts from the following two centuries describe it as a ten-day (or longer) festival, replete with rituals from the pre-Christian past. As sociologist Christel Lane noted, 'Shrovetide never became thoroughly Christianized and has always been distinguished by its focus on pagan ritual as well as on pleasure and popular entertainment.'[9]

Popular festival

Despite the Church's attempt to give Maslenitsa a more religious focus as a prelude to Lent, by the nineteenth century the celebration of this festival had become more secular, especially in cities and towns, while village celebrations still retained many elements of their pagan past. Accounts from the eighteenth through nineteenth centuries describe the festivities in St Petersburg and Moscow as a period of nearly non-stop merrymaking. Traditional amusements included troika rides and sleigh parades; giant ice slides, rides on seesaws and big swings (even Peter the Great liked to swing with his officers at the opening of Maslenitsa); ferris wheels and carousels; fireworks; organized fist fights, snowball fights and wrestling matches (originally symbolizing the struggle between winter and spring); and storming a snow fort (a symbolic conquering of winter). Long rows of wooden booths, outdoor stages, and temporary theaters (some seating up to 5,000 people) were set up in public places as venues for performances by mimes, jugglers, clowns, fire-eaters, gypsies, dancing bears, circuses, musicians and the Petrushka puppet shows that became a Maslenitsa tradition. People dressed in fancy or outrageous costumes to attend private parties and masked balls. This was also a time for personal socializing, weddings, commercial fairs and many public events where all classes could mix together, from peasants to princes. And as a threshold between the seasons, Maslenitsa was also a period in which rules could be broken – a time of gluttony, alcoholic exuberance and sexual licence.[10]

In the villages, vestiges of pagan practices persisted in the lighting of big bonfires and rolling wheels of fire down hillsides; parading a decorated cart wheel atop a tall pole as a symbol of the sun; dressing in animal costumes and masks and making loud noises; jumping high, swinging high and riding down tall ice slides to make the flax grow high in the summer; and climbing tall poles to reach prizes on top. And in both rural and urban areas, Maslenitsa always ended with the burning of a straw witch, to symbolize the banishing of winter, and the scattering of her ashes to fertilize the soil – a combination of pagan and Christian beliefs in the rebirth of life through sacrifice and death.[11]

Maslenitsa was also a major event on the culinary calendar. Vendors set up stands selling nuts and gingerbreads, pastries and confections, hot tea and *sbiten'* (a warm drink made from honey and spices), and of course vodka, often flavored with caraway or anise seeds, orange or lemon zest, berries, hot peppers, buffalo grass, and tree buds, barks and leaves. On 9 March (which sometimes occurred during Maslenitsa), people also baked small semi-sweet yeast buns shaped like larks to celebrate the day on which the larks returned after winter, heralding the arrival of spring.

But the iconic food of Maslenitsa was, and still is, the sun-symbol *blin*. Round pancakes, neither thick nor thin, *bliny* are made with a leavened batter that produces a somewhat spongy textured, porous product perfect for soaking up plenty of melted butter.[12] Traditionally made of buckwheat flour leavened with yeast, *bliny* can also be made from wheat or rye flour, finely ground barley or oats, even (more rarely) cornmeal, or a mixture of these flours, and leavened with baking soda or stiffly beaten egg whites. Many Russians believe that the best *bliny* are those made with buckwheat flour and yeast, the batter allowed to rise three times before being cooked in a hot iron skillet. Making perfectly shaped *bliny* is an art. A Russian proverb admits that 'The first *blin* is always a lump' – a way of saying, 'If at first you don't succeed, try again,' or 'Practice makes perfect.'

Maslenitsa was a time for gorging on *bliny*, sometimes dozens at one sitting. *Bliny*-eating contests were popular, too. (A Russian saying advises, 'Eat as many *bliny* as the number of times a dog wags its tail.') But *bliny* aren't eaten on their own. Besides melted butter, typical toppings for *bliny* include sour cream, smoked or pickled fish, red or black caviar, creamed or preserved mushrooms, fresh farmer's cheese, chopped hard-cooked eggs, and chopped scallions, as well as honey, fruit and berry jams, preserves, syrups, and even sweetened condensed milk.

The amount of melted butter consumed during Maslenitsa was a source of amazement to foreign observers. One American noted in 1804, 'In Europe, the Russians are, as far as I know ... the only people that drink melted butter, like brandy, in what they call the butter week.'[13] A European visitor to Maslentisa wrote in 1782, 'In this week their extravagancies exceed almost all belief ... they employ it in the most extravagant

Buttering Up the Sun: Russian Maslenitsa

excess in drinking brandy and melted butter, which they pour down their throats in such amazing quantities, that one would imagine the least spark of fire would set their bodies in a flame; nay, they are very often obliged to quench this inflammation with milk to prevent their dying on the spot, which frequently happens.'[14]

Writing about the history and traditions of Maslenitsa, Natalya Sokolova points out that there were also regional differences in *bliny* and other foods for this celebration:

> in the south of the Nizhny Novgorod region, people baked different pastries depending on the day of Maslenitsa week. From Monday to Thursday this was pancakes, starting from Thursday – drop scones, on Sunday – *kokurki*, small wheat rolls with egg stuffing. In the Kaluga region, people ate rye pancakes at the beginning of Maslenitsa week, wheat yeast pancakes at the end of the week, and sour pancakes [presumably sour-dough pancakes or those leavened with baking soda and soured milk or *kefir*] all week long. In the Ryazan region, housewives baked better quality *bliny* with the progress of Maslenitsa week – starting from rye and finishing by wheat pancakes, made of pure wheat flour. Other popular dishes were *pryazhentsy*, small fried pies with a variety of stuffing; 'nuts' made of unleavened dough, or *malinki* – small cube-shaped pastries similar to 'nuts,' which were fried in oil and crunched pleasantly when eaten.[15]

Each day of the Maslenitsa season had its own special rituals, many of them focused on foods. On Meatfare Sunday, the day before Maslenitsa week began, men invited their sons-in-law to help devour the remaining meat in the house, since the consumption of meat was forbidden from the beginning of Maslenitsa until Easter Sunday. People also visited the gravesites of their ancestors for a special meal in memory of the departed, where *bliny* were eaten as a symbol of the cycle of life, their roundness representing the circular trajectory from birth to death.

On Maslenitsa Monday the first *blin* was traditionally given to a beggar, since beggars, as 'outsiders,' were viewed as intermediaries between the worlds of the living and the dead. On Tuesday friends and relatives were invited to sample *bliny* at one's home. Wednesday was a day of feasting, 'sweet tooth day,' when tents and stalls were erected to sell foods at the local fairs, and when men visited their mother-in-law to sample her own *bliny*. Thursday was a time for even more revelry, often the day when the Maslenitsa celebrations got into full swing, and when a wife's parents would bring butter and buckwheat flour to her home for a *bliny* party on Friday, to which the husband was obligated to invite his mother-in-law. (Presumably the husband had to cook the *bliny* for that feast.) On Saturday newly wed wives were supposed to invite their sisters-in-law (traditional family rivals) to the couple's home for a meal with more *bliny*, followed by gift-giving.

The last day of Maslenitsa was known as Cheesefare Sunday, because it was the final day on which dairy products could be consumed before Lent. This was also Forgiveness Sunday, when people went to church to confess their sins before the beginning of Lent, and a day of reconciliation when they set aside old grievances with friends, relatives, and neighbors so they could start Lent with an open heart and a clean slate. *Bliny* were left on the graves of their ancestors to bid farewell to the dead, and leftover *bliny*, butter, and other foods, as well as rags and household junk, were thrown into the bonfire on which the Maslenitsa effigy was burned – all as a way of purging the past in preparation for Lent. Then Maslenitsa came to an end – for the strictly devout, at the conclusion of the vesper service at church that Sunday, and for last-minute revelers when the church bells chimed at midnight.[16]

Decline and revival

The great public celebrations of Maslenitsa in the nineteenth century declined in the twentieth century. Long before the Bolsheviks came to power in 1917, the huge outdoor festivals held in St Petersburg's squares had already subsided, for a number of reasons, including Russia's temperance movement.[17] Yet Maslenitsa continued to be celebrated in various ways, privately and in public; early Soviet accounts from the 1920s complain about an increase in worker absenteeism and drunkenness on the job during Maslenitsa.

Although many sources claim that Maslenitsa was suppressed under the anti-religious Soviets – because of its calendrical connection to Lent – others point out that some people still observed it privately, with *bliny* parties in their homes, and that some villages continued to celebrate Maslenitsa as a secular spring festival, complete with many elements of its pagan past. In the early 1980s, sociologist Christel Lane described how some holidays of religious origin that had been forbidden during Stalin's reign were later revived by the Soviets in the 1960s and 1970s as traditional folk holidays. Maslenitsa became 'Farewell to Winter,' a festival that retained its original secular dimensions, but with contemporary socialist elements grafted onto it by the official organizers of the event. However, Lane also pointed out,

> While [Maslenitsa] was once a holiday organized by the small community for itself, it is now being celebrated in big towns as well as in villages, and impersonal organizations [e.g. the Municipal House of Culture] rather than the community itself stage the holiday … Consequently this traditional folk holiday, although colourful and offering plenty of entertainment, has not got a fixed date and is not being celebrated universally in Russian areas. Nor does it attract widespread participation in those big towns where it is staged regularly.[18]

After the collapse of the Soviet Union in 1991, religious and semi-religious holidays could once more be celebrated openly, and several old holidays were revived or reinvigorated, including Maslenitsa – slowly in some cases, more rapidly in others, in various locations around the country.

On Forgiveness Sunday in mid-March 1994, I attended the Maslenitsa celebration in Irkutsk, Siberia, the first major public observance of that festival within memory of all the Russians I knew there. Outdoor activities had been organized at several places around the city. Municipal parks were decorated with images of the sun shining atop tall poles and with brightly painted plywood murals depicting sun symbols, birds and flowers, Carnival characters, and religious references. Children bundled up in parkas and snow boots shrieked in delight as they whooshed down ice slides, while a succession of shirtless men and boys tried to climb a tall wooden pole, to grab the prizes attached to the top: an electric samovar, a fringed paisley shawl, a mystery prize inside a plastic bag.

Throngs filled the public square in front of the municipal sports stadium downtown where the main events were being held. Hundreds of people in fur hats and fur coats, their breath forming clouds of condensation in the frosty air, milled about in front of an outdoor stage set up on the square. Over the stage, a row of huge animal masks made of red-painted papier-mâché perched above big signs advertising furniture, clothing, sports events, and investment companies. Folk dancers in colorful costumes from different parts of eastern Siberia performed to live and recorded music, while jesters and clowns worked the crowd. Handsome horses with brass bells on their harnesses provided rides for the kids and pulled sleighs full of revelers. And towering over the multitude was a giant effigy of Maslenitsa – the Old Witch of Winter herself – constructed of paper, cloth, and wood, her grotesque form covered with long red ribbons and straw streamers that rustled like whispered warnings in the chilly wind.

Opposite the stage, a long row of gaily decorated food stalls provided portable sustenance for the merrymakers. Children and adults wandered from one display to the next, dividing their attention between the wares being hawked and the entertainers on stage – their ears tuned to the sounds of celebration, their noses turned toward the aromas of freshly cooked foods.

At one stall, a hefty woman in a karakul-lamb coat cooked *bliny* on a tiny four-burner gas stove that looked like it belonged in a museum of early twentieth-century kitchen appliances. Fresh from the skillet, the hot *bliny* were slathered with butter, sour cream, or jam, then handed to the customers on squares of hand-cut paper, while the vendor totaled up the bills on a wooden abacus. Nearby, aluminum trays full of extra *bliny* awaited reheating on the stove, while other trays held *bliny* rolled into cones and filled with sweetened pastry cream.

Women wrapped in floral-print shawls sold the most extensive array of baked goods I had ever seen in Irkutsk: sweet and savory pastries, small rolls and buns, giant cookies and gooey layer cakes, all displayed on folding tables set up in the snow. Other food stalls offered meat products traditionally prohibited by Russian Orthodox fasting guidelines during Maslenitsa week: skewers of *shashlyk* grilled over hot coals, small meatballs and large rissoles, savory buns with bits of fried bacon on top, cylinders of bread dough with a forcemeat filling. One vendor sold shiny boxes of commercially made candies. Another stood stoically beside several cardboard boxes of unwrapped chocolate ice cream cones with no fear of their melting in the frigid air. From the back of a truck, a woman handed out hot pizzas baked in a portable oven. And all this festive fare was washed down with cans of Coca-Cola for the kids, cups of hot tea for the women, and shots of vodka for the men.

Suddenly, at 2:30 in the afternoon on that snowy square in Irkutsk, a big bonfire was set ablaze at the foot of the Maslenitsa witch, and five minutes later all that remained of the frightening figure was a pile of harmless ashes. That entire day, the sky had been gray and cloudy, the weather cold and windy. But just after the witch's effigy burned to the ground, the clouds suddenly parted, the sun came out, and the snow began to melt, as if cued by God himself. That Maslenitsa Sunday, on 13 March, was the first day the temperature had risen above freezing in Irkutsk that year – once again confirming the ancient Russians' belief that banishing the barren Witch of Winter will indeed bring the onset of fertile and felicitous spring.[19]

Modern Maslenitsa

Today the date of Maslenitsa is once again determined by the date of Russian Orthodox Great Lent, and the holiday is celebrated for up to a week in many parts of the Russian Federation, as well as in several other countries with large Russian immigrant populations.[20] Some travel agencies now even offer special Maslenitsa tours to Russia.

St Petersburg celebrates with special performances of Igor Stravinsky's 1911 ballet, *Petrushka*, which is set during the Maslenitsa festival in Russia's capital in the 1830s. Since 2005, St Petersburg's Mariinsky Theatre has hosted an annual Maslenitsa music festival, featuring both classical and folk music. Other activities throughout the city include troika rides, masked balls, fireworks, and plenty of *bliny* eating.

Every year since 2002, the city of Moscow has staged a Maslenitsa carnival just off Red Square on the Vasilievsky Spusk, the slope behind St Basil's Cathedral that leads down to the Moscow River. Smaller Maslenitsa events are held at other venues in Moscow, too. The festival now attracts 300,000 visitors annually to the carnival rides, parades, games, fireworks, folk dances, and other amusements traditionally associated with Maslenitsa, some of them updated for twenty-first-century tastes. Food stalls still sell stacks of buttery *bliny*, but these iconic pancakes now also star in modern record-breaking feats and competitions: in 2002, the world's largest pancake (although not a round one), 1 kilometer long and weighing 300 kilograms; in 2003, a 7-meter-high tower of *bliny* threaded on a pole, succeeded by a 14.58-meter pancake tower in 2004; a weight-lifting tournament with pancake-loaded weights in 2005; a *bliny*-making speed contest in 2006, and a *bliny*-eating competition the following year; in 2008, a map of the world made of pancakes, with national boundaries delineated by chocolate chips; in 2009, a *bliny*-cooking contest for disabled people; and record-breaking thick and thin pancakes cooked at Moscow's Maslenitsa in 2010.[21]

In recent years the city has banned the burning of the Maslenitsa effigy so near to the Kremlin because of the fire hazard. Instead, the traditional straw witch has been replaced with a floodlit ice sculpture of Lady Maslenitsa and videos of an effigy

Buttering Up the Sun: Russian Maslenitsa

immolation shown on giant screens. Moscow officials have also tried to discourage the traditional Maslenitsa fist-fights in public places, but with only limited success – leading locals to conclude that Maslenitsa in Moscow today is still best characterized as it was in the past: 'a week of partying, pancakes, and punch-ups.'

Notes

1. The Gregorian calendar was a new calendar introduced by Pope Gregory XIII in 1582, which corrected errors in the older Julian calendar that had been introduced by Julius Caesar in 45 BC and was still in use by the Catholic Church in the 1500s. The new Gregorian calendar was gradually adopted by most European countries over the next two centuries, although Russia did not adopt it until 1918. Today the Gregorian Calendar is the civil calendar used by most of the world's nations, although some Eastern Orthodox churches, including the Russian Orthodox Church, still adhere to some form of the older Julian Calendar, which, in this century, is thirteen days behind the Gregorian Calendar.
2. Differences in the dates on which Western and Eastern churches observe Easter are based on calculations too complex to discuss here, including the phases of the moon, the type of calendar used (Julian or Gregorian) and the date of Jewish Passover. In some years the date of Easter coincides for Eastern Orthodox and Western Christian churches (as it did in 2011, when both celebrated Easter on 24 April), whereas in other years the dates of Easter for Western and Eastern churches may be from one to five weeks apart, with Easter occurring on a Sunday between late March and early May. When the dates of Easter do not coincide, the Eastern Orthodox holiday is always later than Western Easter.
3. The Russian word for 'to cajole' is *umaslivat'*, from the root word *maslo* (butter, oil) – i.e., figuratively, 'to butter someone up.'
4. Russian Orthodox Great Lent begins on the Monday after the last Sunday of Maslenitsa and extends over a period of 40 consecutive days through Friday, six weeks later, followed by Lazarus Saturday, then Palm Sunday, the beginning of Holy Week (or Passion Week). The seven days of Holy Week precede Easter Sunday, which begins a new period on the church calendar. Thus the entire Russian Orthodox Great Lent and Holy Week season extends over a period of 48 days between the end of Maslenitsa and the arrival of Easter.
5. Pagan is not used here in a pejorative sense; it merely refers to the polytheistic religious beliefs of the Eastern Slavs before they converted to Christianity.
6. An early name for this straw effigy was 'Kostroma,' possibly from the Russian word for 'bone' (*kost*), in reference to the sacrifice of the effigy on a bonfire. Later the effigy came to be called 'Maslenitsa,' or 'Lady Maslenitsa,' a name deriving from this festival's connection to the Christian calendar and the last eating of butter (*maslo*) and certain kinds of oil before the beginning of Lent, when they were prohibited.
7. Ivanits, Linda J. 1989: *Russian Folk Belief* (Armonk, NY, M.E. Sharpe), 3–8; Veletskaia, N.N. 1992: 'Forms of Transformation of Pagan Symbolism in the Old Believer Tradition,' in Balzer, Marjorie Mandelstam (ed.) 1992: *Russian Traditional Culture* (Armonk, NY, M.E. Sharpe), 62–67.
8. Vlasov, V.G. 1992: 'The Christianization of the Russian Peasants,' in Balzer, op. cit., 16–31.
9. Lane, Christel 1981: *The Rites of Rulers: Ritual in Industrial Society: the Soviet Case* (Cambridge, Cambridge University Press Archive), 132.
10. Several travelers to Russia in the nineteenth and early twentieth centuries wrote detailed accounts of the Maslenitsa festivities in Moscow and St Petersburg (although some of the later accounts seem to have been partially adopted from earlier published versions by the other authors cited here). See Kohl, Johann Georg 1844: *Russia* (Ayer Publishing; reprinted by Arno Press, 1970), 149–159; Marquis

de Custine, Astolphe 1844: *Russia*, Volume 1 (London, Longman, Brown, Green, and Longmans), 149–153; Ker, David 1871: 'Easter in the Far North,' *The Churchman's Shilling Magazine & Family Treasury*, (London, Houlston and Sons,), 143–150; Whishaw, Frederick 1893: *Out of Doors in Tsarland: A Record of the Seeings and Doings of a Wanderer in Russia* (London, Longmans, Green & Co.), 69–76; and Rappoport, A. S. 1913: *Home Life in Russia* (New York, Macmillan), 55–57. The English writer Charles Dickens vividly described a devastating fire he witnessed at a wooden theater in St Petersburg during Maslenitsa in 'On Fire,' *All the Year Round: A Weekly Journal*, Vol. 11, 27 February 1864 (London, Chapman and Hall), 69–72. In *Land of the Firebird: The Beauty of Old Russia* (New York, Touchstone, 1982), 366–370, Suzanne Massie also provides a good summary description of this colorful festival.

11. For an interesting account of Maslenitsa in several Siberian villages, see Minenko, N.A. 1992: 'The Living Past: Daily Life and Holidays of the Siberian Village in the Eighteenth and First Half of the Nineteenth Centuries,' in Balzer, op.cit., 207–210.
12. *Bliny* differ, in both thickness and width, from two other kinds of Russian pancakes, *olad'i* and *blinchiki*. *Olad'i* are the smallest and thickest, about 3 to 4 inches in diameter, whereas *blinchiki*, the Russian version of crêpes, are the largest and thinnest, about 7 to 8 inches in diameter. *Bliny* are in between, with a diameter of approximately 5 to 7 inches. For a variety of *bliny* recipes (and additional descriptions of Maslenitsa celebrations), see Chamberlain, Lesley 1982: *The Food and Cooking of Russia* (London, Allen Lane), 222–227; Volokh, Anne, with Mavis Manus 1983: *The Art of Russian Cuisine* (New York, Macmillan), 462–470; Goldstein, Darra 1983: *A La Russe: A Cookbook of Russian Hospitality* (New York, Random House), 135–137; von Bremzen, Anya, and John Welchman 1990: *Please to the Table: The Russian Cookbook* (New York, Workman), 511–515; Toomre, Joyce 1992: *Classic Russian Cooking: Elena Molokhovets' A Gift to Young Housewives* (Bloomington, Indiana University Press), 319–322; and Sacharow, Alla 1993: *Classic Russian Cuisine* (New York, Arcade), 192–195.
13. Brown, Charles Brockden 1804: 'On the Propensity of Several Nations to Greasy Meats and Drinks,' *The Literary Magazine and American Register for 1804*, Volume II (Philadelphia, John Conrad & Co.), 48.
14. Bruce, Peter Henry 1782: *Memoirs of Peter Henry Bruce* (privately printed), 106–107.
15. Sokolova, Natalya 2011: 'Maslenitsa: Pancake Week from beginning to end,' Russian Geographical Society, http://int.rgo.ru/news/maslenitsa-pancake-week-from-beginning-to-end/ (3 March 2011).
16. Sokolova, Natalya 2009: 'Maslenitsa'; 'Maslenitsa: Russia's taste-fest,' http://rt.com/news/prime-time/maslenitsa-russia-s-taste-fest/ (1 March 2009).
17. Vorobei, Andrei 2003: 'A Wrap on the City's Holidays,' *The St Petersburg Times*, Issue #877 (45), Friday, 20 June 2003 http://www.sptimes.ru/index.php?action_id=100&story_id=10306; Taruskin, Richard 1996: *Stravinsky and the Russian Traditions: A Biography of the Works through Mavra*, Vol. I (Berkeley, University of California Press), 692.
18. Lane, op. cit., 133–134.
19. Adapted from Hudgins, Sharon 2003: *The Other Side of Russia: A Slice of Life in Siberia and the Russian Far East* (College Station, Texas A & M University Press), 198–200; and Hudgins, Sharon 2003: 'A Trinity of Siberian Easter Season Meals,' *Anthropology of East Europe Review*, Vol. 17, No. 1, 17–26.
20. Several documentary videos of contemporary Maslenitsa celebrations are posted on YouTube. See also the videos posted on http://angelanilsson.wordpress.com/2011/03/04/maslenitsa-pancake-weekbutter-weekrussian-carnival/
21. Sokolova, 'Maslenitsa: Russia's taste-fest,' op. cit.

Celebrating with Sweets in Ottoman Turkey

Priscilla Mary Işın

Associating sweetness with joy, good fortune, and well-being can be traced far back in history, to the Sumerians, the biblical land of milk and honey, and the rivers of honey in the Koran.

In the Islamic world this phenomenon reached new heights, perhaps because the burgeoning of the sugar industry in western Asia coincided with the expansion of Islam. Sugar and sweetmeats acquired an extraordinary symbolic importance in Islamic culture, as illustrated by two *hadith*, or traditional sayings of the Prophet Muhammed, recorded in the seventeenth century by the Turkish writer Evliyâ Çelebi: 'Loving sweets is an article of faith' and 'The faithful are like *halwâ*' (1996–2007 1, 248).

Sweet foods became a feature of celebratory occasions, both private and public, sacred and secular, particularly in the Islamic world and its sphere of influence. This paper looks at the history of such traditions in Turkey and the extent to which they have survived into the twenty-first century. In Ottoman Turkey sweetmeats were an integral part of celebratory and commemorative events, including rites of passage, religious events, ancient festivals, and official ceremonies.

Birth

In eighth-century Samarkand mothers fed their newborn babies with 'stone honey … desiring that [they] speak sweetly when grown up' (Schafer 1985, 153). This Central Asian custom continued in Turkey, where midwives in Istanbul rubbed sugar on the mouths of newly born babies (Ali Rıza Bey, n.d., 106). In rural areas of Turkey today, a little sweetened water is rubbed on the lips of newborn babies in the wish that they not only be sweet-tongued, but also enjoy a life of health and happiness.

The new mother was given red-tinted sherbet flavoured with cinnamon and cloves, known as *lohusa şerbeti*, to give her strength and increase her milk. As in the past this sherbet is still made from square sherbet tablets purchased from confectioners' shops. A fifteenth-century Turkish poem by Süleyman Çelebi describes how Amine, mother of the Prophet Muhammed, is given sherbet to quench her thirst during labour (Onay 2000, 425):

> As I burned with raging thirst
> They handed me a glassful of sherbet
>
> Cold it was and whiter than snow
> Sugar could not compare for flavour

Jugs of *lohusa şerbeti* were also sent to friends and relatives to inform them of the happy event. These were wrapped in gauze, the lid of the jug left unwrapped if the child was a boy, and wrapped if a girl (Ali Rıza Bey n.d., 106).

Six days after the child's birth the bowl beneath the cradle was filled with sugared almonds and given to the midwife (Ali Rıza Bey n.d., 108).

Until the late eighteenth century births of royal children had been an occasion for expensive public celebrations, but when Abdülhamid I's (r. 1774–1789) second son was born he abandoned this tradition, only sending gifts to dervishes and school teachers, and distributing money and a meal of pilaf and *zerde* (saffron-flavoured rice pudding) to school children in the city (Uzunçarşılı 1988, 109).

When a child cuts its first tooth, a dish of boiled whole wheat grains known as *diş buğdayı* ('tooth wheat') was, and often still is prepared, either sweet or savoury, and eaten with family or friends. At a time when infant mortality was high, *diş buğdayı* was a way for the mother to express her joy that her child had survived the first dangerous year of its life (Ahmed Cavid 2006, 34). Claudia Roden describes a similar custom among Syrian Jews: 'cooked green wheat and barley grains in syrup were decorated with nuts and silver balls and offered to visitors when a baby cut its first tooth' (Roden 1997, p. 494).

Circumcision

Of all Turkish rites of passage, a boy's circumcision was the most important. Royal circumcision celebrations sometimes continued for several weeks. Sweets were an important part of the banquets given on these occasions. At the circumcision of Mehmed II's sons Bâyezid and Mustafa, held in the city of Edirne in 1457, the guests were served with sherbet followed by almond, pistachio, coriander, pine-nut, cinnamon, and clove comfits (Tursun Bey 1977, 89). The guests were also presented with boxes of crystallized fruit in boxes to take home (Ünver 1952, 16; Hammer 1917, 3/35).

When Sultan Süleyman the Magnificent's sons Bâyezid and Cihângîr were circumcised in 1539, one of the numerous banquets consisted solely of sweets and puddings, 58 varieties in all: including *sabuni* (in various colours flavoured with tamarind), white and red pulled sugar sticks, pistachio and almond brittle, lemon balls, *zelabiyye, güllaç, paluze, mergubi, levzine, helva-yı kırma bademi, peşmine* (helva in fine threads made of flour, butter and honey or sugar), yellow helva, *lokma* (doughnuts in syrup), *çavariş* (fondant in pistachio, cherry, almond, lemon and coconut flavours, and another with gold leaf), preserves (citrus fruit, gourd, watermelon, quince, apple, cornelian cherry, aubergine, green walnut, pear, peach, sour cherry, cherry, carrot, melon), *perverde* (jelly preserve of carrot, bottle gourd, quince), *akîde* (boiled sweets, 'diamond' and apple varieties), comfits, and various sweet pastries (Tezcan 1998, 7–8).

Ottoman royal circumcisions and weddings featured sculpted sugar models of gardens, buildings, and animals made by the palace confectioners which were paraded, then broken up and eaten by the crowd (Âlî 1996, 105–106; And 1982, 93–151; Nutku

1987, 73). In 1457 sugar mosques, castles, pavilions, and meadows with a myriad flowers and fragrant herbs were made for the circumcision of Mehmed the Conqueror's sons Bâyezid and Mustafa (Tursun Bey 1977, 89).

At the 52-day circumcision celebrations for Murad III's sons in 1582, hundreds of sculpted sugar figures of animals were carried in procession through the streets. These included lions, lion cubs, tigers and tiger cubs, elephants and elephant calves, horses and mules, camels, buzzards, vultures, falcons, partridges, peacocks, cockerels, ducks and geese (Âlî 1978, 105–106):

> The ground was transformed into a new world
> With wild animals and birds all of sugar.

There were even backgammon and chess sets made of sugar (Âlî 1996, 219). Reinhold Lubenau of Konigsberg, who watched these festivities, mentions sugar giraffes, monkeys, mermaids, fish, watermelons, grapes, peaches, pomegranates, oranges, lemons, apricots, candlesticks, and pools with fountains and castles (And 1982, 218).

Three sugar gardens made for the 1675 wedding of Hatice Sultan, the eldest daughter of Mehmed IV, contained sugar nightingales and other birds, lions, roe deer, fish, and camels, according to the poet Nâbî (Nutku 1987, 64). Another observer (Covel 1893, 228–229) recorded:

> Then followed, in two files on each side of the way, 120 sugar-works, borne on frames by two slaves a piece, sedan wise, made from 2½ foot to a yard and a half high, some more or less as the fancy required. They were Ostridges, Peacocks, swans, Pelicans etc., Lyons, Beares, greyhoundes, dear (deer), horses, Elephants, Rams, Buffaloes etc.

Miniature paintings illustrate eight sugar gardens made in 1720 for the sons of Ahmed III. These contain pools with boats or fountains, pavilions, fruit trees, flowers, and birds in cages. From contemporary accounts we know that the pools were filled with sherbet; the soil was made of sugar and musk, and the pebbles were sugared almonds. Miniatures illustrating the sugar sculptures show a lion, leopard, camel, elephant, giraffe, horse, mythological creatures, storks, geese, and fish (Koçu 1952, 83; And 1982, 120; Hâfız Mehmed Efendi 2008, 31).

Zerde, a pudding made with rice, tinted yellow with saffron or turmeric, and sprinkled with pine-nuts and currants was always served with pilaf at celebrations, whether circumcisions, weddings, victory celebrations, or religious holidays.

School

Starting school was another opportunity for celebrating with sweets, this time *lokma* (Abdülaziz Bey 1995, 58). On the appointed day the children followed the teacher in procession to the home of the new pupil, and after a ceremony were served doughnuts (Koç Keskin 2010, 152). Memorizing a *sûrah* of the Koran for the first time was commemorated with a gift of baklava to the teacher. When the Turkish novelist Aziz Nesin (1915–1995) learnt his first *sûrah* at the age of five, his mother was ashamed because she could not afford to bake baklava for the school mistress, but had to make do with *börek* instead (Nesin 1998, 32).

Engagements

The preliminary step towards engagement in Turkey is *kız isteme* (asking for the girl's hand in marriage). The boy's family present some kind of sweet confection or pastry in the hope of getting a favourable answer.

The actual engagement also required gifts of sweetmeats to the bride. When Sultan Abdülmecid's (1839–1861) daughter Münire Sultan was engaged to İbrahim İlhami Paşa in 1858, one of his gifts to his future bride was European sweetmeats in porcelain dishes (Saz 1974, 158).

Sweet dishes made for engagement parties in provincial Turkey vary enormously: for example, *demir tatlısı* (the pastry known as rosette fritters in Scandinavia and the United States) in the village of Keramet in Bursa, and shortcakes in the shape of pears in the city of Bursa.

Weddings

One of the earliest examples of sweetmeats served at weddings is the feast held for the daughter of the Abbasid caliph in 807, at which 40,000 kilograms of sugar were consumed (Geerdes 1966, 10).

When the Ottoman statesman Siyavuş Paşa married the sister of Murad III in 1575, sugar models of towns, forts, and figures of elephants and other animals were carried in the bridal procession (Gerlach 2007, 199). Another bridal procession witnessed by Gerlach, this time of a wealthy but non-royal couple, also featured sugar models that the bride afterwards distributed to her friends (Gerlach 2007, 319):

> Those who followed carried perhaps fifty statues made of sugar. At the front were six or seven figures of elephants each ridden by a negro, then came two lions, three horses, four strange sea creatures, a peacock, stork, falcon and other diverse birds, cups, jugs, candlesticks and innumerable other objects, all made of sugar and colourfully painted, so that one might have thought that they were made of wood or some other material ... After the wedding the bride distributes these sugar works to her friends, giving one a lion, one an elephant, and thereby gratifying them all.

When Hatice Sultan, the daughter of Mehmed IV (r. 1648–1687) married Musahib Mustafa Paşa the groom's gifts to the bride included '30 mules laden with sugar-plums and sweet-meats' (Coke 1676, 366). Of the 50 *nahıl*s – artificial trees symbolizing plenty and long life – carried in the wedding procession of Hatice Sultan, eldest daughter of Mehmet IV, eight were made of sugar (Nutku 1987, 67).

Celebrating with Sweets in Ottoman Turkey

Zerde was an essential feature of the wedding banquet, as noted by English portraitist Mary Walker, who attended numerous weddings with her Ottoman patronesses during her years in Istanbul (Walker 1886, 1/10–11): 'the inevitable "zerdè pillaw", made of boiled rice, ornamented with cinnamon, saffron, and pomegranate-seeds … an indispensable delicacy at every marriage feast.' In Konya and other parts of Turkey *zerde* remains an essential feature of wedding feasts (Halıcı n.d., 198).

Showering the bride with sweets, cereal grains, or small coins was a widespread custom (Kalafat 2005, 51, 66; Çetin 2008, 119). Garnett notes that Greek brides were showered with sugared almonds (Garnett 1893, 1/85). These customs deriving from ancient fertility rituals were common around the world. Among the Karakhanid Turks (840–1212) of Central Asia, grain or coins were scattered over the bride (Kurtoğlu 2009, 90). The Crimean Tatars poured millet over the bride (Tott 1785, 1–2/213):

> A Dish, of about a foot in Diameter, was placed on the Head of the Bride; over this a veil was thrown, which covered the Face and descended to the Shoulders; Millet then was poured upon the Dish, which, falling and spreading all round her, formed a Cone, with a Base corresponding to the height of the Bride. Nor was her Portion complete till the Millet touched the Dish, while the Veil gave her the power of respiration. This Custom was not favourable to small People, and, at present, they estimate how many measures of Millet a Daughter is worth. The Turks and Armenians, who make their Calculations in money, still preserve the Dish and the Veil, and throw Coin upon the Bride, which they call spilling the Millet. Have not the Crown and the Comfits the same Origin?

In Ottoman Turkey gifts of sweets from the bridegroom to the bride included bergamot and mastic-flavoured *çevirme* (fondant), sherbet tablets, and syrups (Abdülaziz Bey 1995, 1/111). Gifts presented to the Ottoman princess Refia Sultan by her husband-to-be Ethem Paşa included 500 Dresden china pots of diverse fruit preserves (Fontmagne 1902, 146). Sweetmeats were also among the gifts to Mihrimâh Sultan, daughter of Sultan Mahmud II (r. 1808–1839) when she married Admiral of the Fleet Mehmed Said Paşa in 1836 (Pardoe, 1838, 2/111). Poorer bridegrooms sent their bride a gift of coffee-bean comfits and ground coffee (Saz 1974, 256.)

Hollow lollipops in the form of animals, trains, and other figures are traditionally sold at weddings in some parts of Turkey. Vendors produce them at home and usually sell them in the streets during the day and at wedding receptions in the evenings, where guests buy them as a treat for their children.

Death

The most common funeral food in Turkey is helva made at home with flour or semolina. This is reflected in such regional vernacular names as 'soul helva' or 'pick and spade helva' (Güzel n.d., 91). It is made on the day of the funeral in the home of the bereaved family, and again at memorials held on the fortieth day following the death.

Celebrating with Sweets in Ottoman Turkey

In the Aegean region of western Turkey doughnuts known as *lokma*, either in the form of small balls or rings soaked in syrup, are the main funeral food. These are distributed to mourners and passers-by on the street outside the mosque. In the city of Balıkesir there is a firm specializing in making *lokma* and tombstones, a strange combination that reflects just how closely doughnuts and death go together in this region (www.mezarcicemalusta.com).

In Ottoman times, a type of helva made with flour, clarified butter, and sugar called *gaziler helvası* (warriors' helva) was made in the memory of soldiers killed in action. The seventeenth-century courtier Evliyâ Çelebi describes how the survivors of a sea battle between a Turkish ship and enemy galleons near the island of Sönbeki (Syme), off the Mediterranean port of Marmaris, cooked *gaziler helvası* and recited prayers for the souls of their dead comrades (Evliyâ Çelebi 1996–2007, 9/121).

Mevlit

Ceremonies known as Mevlit were held to commemorate the birth of the Prophet, and the births and deaths of ordinary people. Small paper cones filled with a mixture of pulled sweets (*peynir şekeri*) and boiled sweets (*akîde*) were distributed to the guests. In 1817 a woman retainer in the royal harem called Mihrivefa Hatun left a legacy of two thousand piastres for the provision of sherbet, coffee and mixed sweets in paper cones at an annual Mevlit ceremony in memory of herself and her friend Durnab Hatun (Abdurrahman Şerif 1910, 336–337).

In her memoirs Ayşe Osmanoğlu (1887–1960), daughter of Abdülhamid II, describes Mevlit ceremonies held at the palace (Osmanoğlu 1984, 65–66):

> During the Mevlid large silver trays of *akîde* sweets, each carried by two cellarers, were brought and first offered to my father, and then by turns to everyone in the salon. Each person took one sweet. The gentlemen-in-waiting brought the trays to the Harem side of the room, and everyone took one from these heaps of diverse sweets. When the Mevlid was over … decorated baskets and boxes of sweets would be given to all the guests. These were purchased from Hacı Bekir Efendi.

The custom of giving paper cones of sweets at Mevlits continues today. In the town of İncesu in Kayseri, lumps of pulled sugar called *Mevlüt şekeri* or *Konya şekeri* were traditionally given, although today a mixture of boiled sweets, Turkish delight, chocolate, and mint-flavoured pulled sugar is more common, and some people even offer cake (Özen 2006, 126).

Ramazan

During the month of Ramazan people break their fast in the evening with a meal called *iftar*, and eat an early meal called *sahur* before daybreak. Light puddings such as stewed fruit and milk puddings are preferred, above all *güllaç*, made with tissue-thin starch wafers, soaked in milk or syrup, and ground nuts. *Güllaç* used to be made exclusively for Ramazan, and the wafers were unobtainable at other times of year. The Ottoman composer and poet Leyla Saz (1850–1936) relates in her memoirs how housewives served *güllaç* to their guests at the evening *iftar* meal (Saz 1974, 124).

Baklava was also closely associated with Ramazan and in the second half of the fifthteenth century was made for palace officials during this month (Barkan 1979, 275). At the *imaret* (public kitchen) founded by Sultan Bayezid II (r. 1481–1512) in Amasya, baklava for Ramazan was flavoured with saffron (Ottoman Archive, Defter 2113, 179). Well-off families sent trays of baklava as gifts to friends, neighbours, their children's schoolteachers, and to college students who had been unable to return home for Ramazan (Abdülaziz Bey 1995, 76, 273). Turkish novelist Hüseyin Rahmi Gürpınar (1864–1944) recalled being given baklava as a reward for fasting for one day at the age of nine, although in fact he had secretly eaten meatballs, jam, and stewed fruit in the kitchen (Gürpınar 1973, 19–20).

At an annual ceremony held at Topkapı Palace on 15 Ramazan hundreds of trays of baklava were distributed to the janissaries, one tray for each squad of ten soldiers (Esad Efendi 1979, 32–3). Two soldiers from each squad would hang their tray of baklava on a pole carried on their shoulders, then they marched out of the palace in a procession known as the Baklava Alayı (Baklava Procession). The following day the empty copper trays and cloths were returned to the palace kitchens (Ali Rıza 2001, 200–201; Koçu 1958–1973, 2/1939–1940). In later years the janissaries stopped returning the trays and cloths, claiming insolently that they had eaten those too (Ortaylı 1994, 2/5). Until the Janissary Corps was liquidated in 1826, the Baklava Procession was a popular public spectacle, as recorded in the following verses from a watchman's rhyme:

As the sun and moon revolve
May divine aid be your company
The sultan gave baklava
To his loyal janissaries

I watched the procession
And look what I did
I saw the ceremony
And relate it to you

Other sweets associated with Ramazan are *zerde*, which was served to the employees of the mosque complex and *medrese* students during Ramazan (Ünver 1952, 81–83), and *un kurabiyesi* (shortbread) and *un helvası* (flour helva), which were prepared by cooks in wealthy households on the last evening of Ramazan (Abdülaziz Bey 1995, 2/262):

In grand houses the chief cook would prepare *un kurabiyesi* (shortbread cakes) and *un helvası* decorated with gold leaf. These would be arranged on a decorated tray with burning wax tapers around the edge and sent into the harem. The tray would be sent back to the kitchen with a red purse for the head cook and gauze pouches containing tips for the other cooks in place of the dishes.

In Turkey the three-day *bayram* that followed Ramazan was so closely associated with sweets that by the late eighteenth century it had become popularly known as the Şeker Bayram (Sugar Bayram). Abdülaziz Bey describes how this *bayram* was celebrated by a well-off Ottoman family in the late nineteenth century (Abdülaziz Bey 1995, 1/151):

> That day the mistress of the house sent decorated baskets of many coloured sweets to her midwife, friends, children's teachers and former servants who had married. Then guests would begin to arrive to offer bayram greetings to the master of the house. If these guests included ministers or state officials, they would be welcomed by the steward himself, who would take the guest's arm and accompany him to the room where the master of the house was waiting. Each guest would be offered small pieces of mastic-flavoured *râhat-ı hulkum* (Turkish delight), marzipan and musk-flavoured *akîde* sweets on decorated silver trays by the chief cellarer and his underlings.

Muharrem

The tenth day of Muharrem is when Shiite and Alevî Muslims mourn the death of Hüseyin at Kerbela. *Aşûre* (wheat berry pudding), associated since ancient times with death and rebirth, was traditionally prepared on this occasion. The Umayyads, in contrast, celebrated the day that Hüseyin was killed because of his refusal to pay allegiance to the Caliph Yezîd of the Umayyad dynasty (*İslâm Ansiklopedisi* 1989–2010, 4/26). The upshot was that Sunni Muslims continued to prepare *aşûre*, but not in mourning for Hüseyin. Instead various other legends grew up around this wheat pudding: Adam's penitence, Abraham's escape from the fire, the reunion of Jacob and his son Joseph, and the grounding of Noah's Ark (Hançerlioğlu 2000, 28; Sertoğlu 1986, 21–22).

However, traces of the link between *aşûre* and death survived among Turkish Sunni Muslims into the late Ottoman period. While the *aşûre* was cooking the Yâ Sîn and Al Mulk *sûrah*s from the Koran were recited for the souls of dead ancestors (Abdülaziz Bey 1995, 1/246). A related tradition among Orthodox Christians is the wheat berry dish, called *koliva*, prepared for funerals, Christmas, and Lent.

State occasions

Victories were also celebrated with sweets. A banquet held in 1522 to celebrate the conquest of Rhodes included *murabbâ* (fruit jelly), *zerde*, *peşmîne*, *şeker börek* (fried pastry packages filled with nuts), *güllaç*, *palude* (pudding of fruit juice thickened with starch), and *helva* (Günay Kut, 1986, x–xi). Following victories, common soldiers were served a feast consisting of *yahni* (boiled mutton stew), pilaf, and *zerde* (Pakalın 1983, 1/149).

Celebrating with Sweets in Ottoman Turkey

When the Ottoman army set out on campaign it was accompanied by artisans who provided behind-the-lines services. As the army marched out of Edirne on its way to Poland on 4 May 1672, these artisans put on entertainments for the watching crowds. Galland describes that of the helva makers (Galland 1881, 1/118–119):

> What was most amusing was a man who preceded the corps of confectioners who wore a chemise that descended to his heels and was covered all over with *alva*, that is to say sweetmeat, from top to bottom, and grabbed handfuls from his buttocks that he ate and flung at the crowd. His beard, which was very long, was so covered that it could not be seen and his bonnet was made of sweetmeat.

At the three-monthly distribution of salaries to the janissaries, they were given a meal of pilaf and *zerde*, after which the Muhzır Ağa, one of the highest ranking janissary officers, would present a dish of *akîde* sweets to the grand vizier and other statesmen as a symbol of the Janissary Corps' allegiance to state and sovereign (Esad Efendi 1979, 77).

Civil celebrations

Helva and *zerde* played a symbolic role on many different occasions, such as guild ceremonies for journeymen graduating to the rank of master (Göncüoğlu 2009, 41).

Helva was also central to meals held to reconcile friends on bad terms (Ahmed Câvid, 2006, 7): 'When friends are estranged their friends arrange a reconciliation meal. They cook helva and invite them both to dinner, and persuade them to patch up their quarrel.'

In the mountain village of Şıhlar in southern Turkey, a type of helva called *külük helvası* (a sweetmeat with a texture of fine threads made of honey, butter, and flour, similar to *peşmîne*, known today as *pişmaniye*) was traditionally made to mark the return from the mountain pastures at the end of the summer. According to local legend this helva was introduced from Khorasan in the thirteenth century by the founder of the village, a religious scholar named Pirce Alaaddin.

Nevrûz

Nevrûz (literally 'new day' in Persian) was the first day of the new year in the pre-Islamic calendar, celebrated by Turks and Persians on 22 March (Pakalın 1983, 2/636–638). The eleventh-century Islamic scholar Birûnî relates several legends relating to Nevrûz. According to one of these, the Prophet Muhammed was presented with helva on a silver tray on Nevrûz and distributed it to his followers declaring, 'the day that God gave life to this sleeping world' (Maksetof 1996), and, according to another, the mythological ruler of ancient Persia, Jamshid, discovered the sugar cane on Nevrûz and commanded the first sugar to be made.

In Turkey and Iran a kind of sweet paste called *Nevrûz macunu* or *nevrûziyye* was made by pharmacists and physicians. This contained forty or more ingredients, such as ambergris, musk, rosewater, cloves, cochineal, almond oil, cinnamon, sandalwood, cardamom, nutmeg, coconut, ginger, coriander, angelica, and sugar (Baylav 1968, 172–179). It was tinted red with cochineal and topped with gold leaf. Confectioners also prepared a conserve called *Nevrûz şerbeti* in the form of crunchy sugar squares flavoured with musk and ambergris and again decorated with gold leaf (Unger 2003, 81).

At the Ottoman palace the chief physician presented crystal or porcelain pots of *Nevrûz macunu* to the sultan, members of the royal family, and official dignitaries. Ayşe Osmanoğlu remembers gifts of *Nevrûz macunu* being sent to the sultan by the Persian ambassador (Osmanoğlu 1984, 106):

> At Nevrûz the Persian Embassy would send *macun* and diverse Persian sweetmeats in precious porcelain vessels and decorative boxes placed on trays wrapped in fabric as a gift for my father. The Nevrûz sweets were decorated with small Persian gold coins bearing the portrait of the Shah of Persia arranged to spell my father's name. My father would give these to us or send them to other people.

In the western Turkish city of Manisa *Nevrûziyye* (known as *mesir macunu*) has been distributed at Nevrûz for centuries. Every year thousands of people gather in the city centre while the governor, mayor, and local MPs toss three tons of *mesir macunu* wrapped in coloured cellophane packages from the roof of Sultan Mosque to the crowds below.

As such examples reveal, many traditions relating to sweetmeats and their symbolic role still survive in Turkey today, although they are being steadily eroded by modern changes in life style, even in rural communities. The symbolic importance of sweetmeats and sweet pastries in Ottoman and earlier west Asian cultures has ancient roots in ideas of fertility and rebirth, symbolized by wheat and other cereals that can be traced back to rituals associated with Tammuz, the Babylonian god of wheat and fertility, combined with those of joy and good fortune symbolized by sweet foods like honey, manna, and sugar.

Bibliography

Abdurrahman Şeref 1910–1911: 'Topkapı Saray-ı Hümâyûn', *Tarih-i Osmanî Encümeni Mecmuası* (Istanbul).

Abdülaziz Bey 1995: *Osmanlı Âdet, Merasim ve Tabirleri*, eds. Kâzım Arısan and Duygu Arısan Günay, 2 vols. (Istanbul, Tarih Vakfı).

Ahmed Câvid 2006: *Tercüme-i Kenzü'l-İştiha*, eds. Seyit Ali Kahraman and Priscilla Mary Işın (Istanbul, Kitap Yayınevi).

Ali Rıza, Balıkhane Nazırı, n.d: *Bir Zamanlar İstanbul*, ed. Niyazi Ahmet Banoğlu (Istanbul, Tercüman 1001 Temel Eser).

And, Metin 1982: *Osmanlı Şenliklerinde Türk Sanatları* (Ankara, Kültür ve Turizm Bakanlığı)

Baylav, Naşid 1968: *Eczacılık Tarihi* (Istanbul, Yörük Matbaası).

Coke, Thomas 1676: 'A true Narrative of the great Solemnity of the Circumcision of Mustapha, Prince of Turky, eldest Son of Mahomet, Present Emperor of the Turks…', *Harleian Miscellany* 5 (London, 1810), 365–366.

Çetin, Cengiz 2008: 'Türk Düğün Gelenekleri ve Kutsal Evlilik Ritüeli', *Ankara Üniversitesi Dil ve Tarih-Coğrafya Fakültesi Dergisi* 48/2.

Esad Efendi 1979: *Osmanlılarda Töre ve Törenler (Teşrifât-ı Kadîme)*, ed. Yavuz Ercan (Istanbul, Tercüman 1001 Temel Eser).

Evliyâ Çelebi 1996–2007: *Evliyâ Çelebi Seyahatnâmesi*, 10 vols., eds. Seyit Ali Kahraman, Yücel Dağlı, Robert Dankoff et al. (Istanbul, Yapı Kredi).

Fontmagne, Baronne Durand de 1902: *Un Séjour a l'Ambassade de France a Constantinople sous le Second Empire* (Paris, Librairie Plon).

Galland, Antoine 1881: *Journal d'Antoine Galland pendant son sejour de Constantinople (1672–1673)* (Ernest Leroux, Paris).

Garnett, Lucy 1893: *The Women of Turkey and their Folklore*, 2 vols. (London, David Nutt).

Geerdes, Thomas 1966: *Ana Besin Maddelerinden Şeker ve Tarihi*, tr. Cihad Gökdağ (Ankara, Türkiye Şeker Fabrikaları).

Âlî, Gelibolulu Mustafa 1978: *Ziyâfet Sofraları (Mevâidü'n-nefâis fi kavâidi'l mecâlis)*, 2 vols., ed. Orhan Şaik Gökyay (Istanbul, Tercüman 1001 Temel Eser).

Gerlach, Stephan 2007: *Türkiye Günlüğü 1573–1576*, 2 vols. (Istanbul, Kitap Yayınevi).

Göncüoğlu, Süleyman Faruk 2009: 'İstanbul'un Fethi Sonrası Kurulan İlk Semt: Saraçhane', *Atatürk Üniversitesi Güzel Sanatlar Enstitüsü Dergisi* (accessed 3 May 2011).

Güzel, Abdurrahman 1990: 'Türk Kültürü'nde Mevlid ve Yoğ Gelenekleri Etrafında Teşekkül Eden Folklorik Unsurlar', *Üçüncü Milletlerarası Yemek Kongresi, 7–12 Eylül 1990* (Ankara, Konya Kültür ve Turizm Vakfı), 80–93.

Hâfız Mehmed Efendi 2008: *1720, Şehzadelerin Sünnet Düğünü*, ed. Seyit Ali Kahraman (Istanbul, Kitap Yayınevi).

Hammer-Purgstall, Joseph von 1917: *Devlet-i Osmaniye Tarihi*, tr. Mehmed Âta (Istanbul, Evkaf-ı İslamiye Matbaası).

Hançerlioğlu, Orhan 2000: *İslâm İnançları Sözlüğü*, 3rd edn. (Istanbul, Remzi Kitabevi).

İslâm Ansiklopedisi 1989–2010: 38 vols. (Istanbul, Türkiye Diyanet Vakfı).

Kalafat, Yaşar 2005: *Balkanlardan Uluğ Türkistan'a Türk Halk İnançları II* (Ankara, Ebabil).

Koç Keskin, Neslihan 2010: 'Abdülhamit'in Sehzadelerinin Bed'-i Besmele Törenini Anlatan Enderûnlu Fâzıl'ın Sûrnâme-i Sehriyâr'ı Üzerine', *Selçuk Üniversitesi Türkiyat Araştırmaları Dergisi*, 27, 149–186.

Koçu, Reşat Ekrem 1952: *Tarihimizde Garip Vakalar* (Varlık Yayınları, Istanbul).

Kurtoğlu, Orhan 2009: 'Klasik Türk Şiirinde Saçı Geleneği', *Milli Folklor* 81, 89–99.

Maksetof, Kabil 1996: 'Ebû Reyhan Beyrûnî ve Nevrûz Hakkında', *Nevrûz ve Renkler* (Ankara, Atatürk Kültür Merkezi).

Nutku, Özdemir 1987: *IV. Mehmet'in Edirne Şenliği 1675*, 2nd edn. (Ankara, Türk Tarih Kurumu).

Onay, Ahmet Talât 2000: *Eski Türk Edebiyatında Mazmunlar ve İzahı*, (Ankara, Akçağ).

Osmanoglu, Ayşe 1984: *Babam Sultan Abdulhamid* (Istanbul, Selçuk).
Ottoman Archive, Defter 2113.
Özen, Aysel 2006: unpublished book, *Tarihin İzleri ile İncesu Yemek Kültürü* (İncesu).
Pakalın, Mehmet Zeki 1983: *Osmanlı Tarih Deyimleri ve Terimleri Sözlüğü*, 3 vols. (Istanbul, Milli Eğitim Bakanlığı).
Redhouse, James W. 1890: *A Turkish and English Lexicon* (Constantinople, American Mission).
Schafer, Edward H. 1985: *The Golden Peaches of Samarkand, A Study of T'ang Exotics* (Berkley, University of California).
Sertoğlu, Midhat 1986: *Osmanlı Tarih Lûgatı* (Istanbul, Enderun Kitabevi).
Tezcan, Semih 1998: *Bir Ziyafet Defteri* (Istanbul, Simurg).
Tott, Francois 1785: *Memoirs of Baron de Tott: Containing the State of the Turkish Empire and the Crimea, During the Late War with Russia; with Numerous Anecdotes, Facts, and Observations, on the Manners and Customs of the Turks and Tartars*, (G.G.J. and J. Robinson).
Tursun Bey 1977: *Târîh-i Ebü'l-Feth*, (Istanbul, Baha Matbaası).
Uzunçarşılı, İsmail Hakkı 1988: *Osmanlı Devletinin Saray Teşkilâtı* (Ankara, Türk Tarih Kurumu).
Ünver, Süheyl 1952: *Fatih Devri Yemekleri* (Istanbul, İstanbul Üniversitesi Tıp Tarihi Enstitüsü).
Walker, Mary Adelaide 1886: *Eastern Life and Scenery with Excursions in Asia Minor, Mytilene, Crete, and Roumania* (London: Chapman and Hall, 1886).

Royal Pomp: Viceregal Celebrations and Hospitality in Georgian Dublin

Máirtín Mac Con Iomaire and Tara Kellaghan

The viceroy: chief host of the nation

During the successive reigns of the Hanoverian kings in England (1714–1830), a total of thirty-seven different viceroys were sent to Ireland as representatives of the British Crown (Table 1). The position of viceroy (also referred to as lord lieutenant) was awarded as a matter of political expediency, but the viceroy's role was one of social as much as political significance. The viceroy and his vicereine played the roles of the British monarchs *in absentia,* and the Protestant minority ruling class, often referred to as the Ascendancy, expected the viceregal court at Dublin Castle to not merely mirror, but to outshine that of St James's Palace in London. The standards of hospitality set by the Irish themselves ensured that no incoming lord lieutenant would long be in doubt as to what was expected of him as the chief host of the Irish nation, and, perhaps even more importantly, as the leader of Dublin society.

Table 1: Listing of Irish Lords Lieutenant and dates of appointment to office (1714–1830)

1. Charles Spencer, Earl of Sunderland	September 1714
2. Charles, Viscount Townshend	February 1717
3. Charles Polwett, 2nd Duke of Bolton	April 1717
4. Charles Fitroy, 2nd Duke of Grafton	June 1720 (returned August 1723)
5. John Carteret, 2nd Baron Carteret	May 1724
6 (i). Lionel Cranfield Sackville, 1st Duke of Dorset	June 1730
7. William Cavendish, 3rd Duke of Devonshire	April 1737 (returned March 1740 and Sept. 1741)
8. Philip Dormer Stanhope, 4th Earl of Chesterfield	January 1745
9 William Stanhope, 1st Earl of Harrington	November 1747
6 (ii) Lionel Cranfield Sackville, 1st Duke of Dorset	December 1750
10. William Cavendish, Marquis of Hartington, 4th Duke of Devonshire	April 1755

11. John Russell, 4th Duke of Bedford	January 1757 (returned October 1759)
12. George Montague Dunk, Earl of Halifax	April 1761
13. Hugh Percy, 2nd Duke of Northumberland	April 1763
14. Thomas Wynne, 3rd Viscount Weymouth	June 1765
15. Francis Seymour-Conway, Earl of Hertford	August 1765
16. George William Hervey, 2nd Earl of Bristol	October 1766
17. George Townshend, 4th Viscount Townshend	August 1767
18. Simon Harcourt, 1st Earl of Harcourt	October 1772
19. John Hobart, 2nd Earl of Buckinghamshire	December 1776
20. Frederick Howard, 5th Earl of Carlisle	November 1780
21. William Henry Cavendish Bentick, 3rd Duke of Portland	April 1782
22 (i). George Nugent-Temple-Grenville, 3rd Earl Temple	August 1782
23. Robert Henley, 2nd Earl of Northington	May 1783
24. Charles Manners, 4th Duke of Rutland	February 1784
22 (ii). George Nugent-Temple-Grenville, Marquis of Buckingham	November 1787
25. John Fane, 10th Earl of Westmorland	October 1789
26. William Wentford Fitzwilliam, 2nd Earl of Fitzwilliam	December 1794
27. John Jeffreys Pratt, 2nd Earl of Camden	March 1795
28. Charles Cornwallis, 1st Marquis Cornwallis	June 1798
29. Philip Yorke, 3rd Earl of Hardwicke	March 1801
30. Edward Clive, 1st Earl of Powis	November 1805
31. John Russell, 6th Duke of Bedford	February 1806
32. Charles Lennox, 4th Duke of Richmond	April 1807
33. Charles Whitworth, 1st Baron Whitworth	June 1813
34. Charles Chetwynd Talbot, 2nd Earl of Talbot	September 1817
35. Richard Wellesley, 1st Marquis Wellesley	December 1821
36. Henry William Paget, 1st Marquis of Anglesey	February 1828
37. Hugh Percy, 3rd Duke of Northumberland	February 1829

Celebrations and Hospitality in Georgian Dublin

Ireland's élite consisted at this time of 'politicians, lawyers, divines, Huguenot merchants, bankers and landowners', all of whom looked to Dublin Castle to provide entertainment superior to the routs, plays, concerts, balls, gaming, and masquerades available throughout the city (Somerville-Large 1996: 128). Although the actual government salary for the viceroy rose from £12,000 at the start of the eighteenth century to £20,000 by its end, funding the opulent entertainments considered *de rigueur* by Ireland's élite usually required reaching into one's own private purse to the tune of several thousand pounds. Consequently, only a very wealthy individual could afford to take up the position of lord lieutenant. To adequately represent the absent monarch, it was necessary to make 'the grand figure', something very much appreciated by the Irish (Barnard 2004). Luxurious garments, coaches drawn by numerous fine horses, liveried servants, and splendid repasts – all of these served as distractions from the political dissatisfaction evident at all levels of society. In 1701, the sight of the Earl of Rochester travelling in a magnificent carriage hauled by 'eight greys' awed the populace. They were offended to an equal degree, however, when the Marquis of Hartington elected to appear in 'informal civilian garb' at an official function in 1755 (Barnard 2004: 9).

Vinous hospitality at the Castle

Many different wines, from Canary to Rhenish, were available in Georgian Dublin, but the upper echelons of society were awash with claret. Lord Chesterfield (1745–1746), who distinguished himself amongst viceroys of this era by his abstemiousness, cited the vast amount of claret imported into Ireland annually as shocking evidence of its over-consumption by 'those of superior rank'. Maxwell (1946: 101) observed that 'no one of any position in Dublin would have thought himself truly hospitable unless he provided large quantities of claret for his guests'.

Quantity, nevertheless, was expected to be allied with quality, and there is copious evidence that the Irish gentry considered themselves to be wine connoisseurs. A letter to the *Hibernian Magazine* (February 1780: 85) heaps opprobrium upon a fictional couple of social climbers for serving cloudy wine to aristocratic guests. The Irish travelling in England were demanding oenophiles, frequently commenting on the ubiquity of inferior claret. In 1725, an Irish visitor and his companions fell upon an Irish-owned eating house as an oasis. Identifying his group to the proprietor as compatriots, he observed that they were consequently served 'excellent wine; and indeed it was a rarity as I had tasted none good since my coming to England' (Huth and Carew Hazlitt 1869: 125). Another group of visiting Irish roundly upbraided the owner of a London chophouse in 1761; upon being served poor quality wine they assured him that they 'belonged to the kingdom that knew the difference between good and bad claret' (Barnard 2004: 332).

Faced with such a high degree of native expertise, it was fortunate that the vast majority of viceroys managed to impress Dublin society with the quality and scale of their wine consumption. It was standard practice to allow members of parliament

– who were well in with the Castle – to select wine from any hogshead in the lord lieutenant's cellar and drink to their individual limit. The 2nd Duke of Ormond, twice viceroy in the early 1700s, managed to impose a flexible cap on such consumption by stipulating that no chairs would be provided, thereby ensuring that no man would drink longer than he could remain standing (Robins 2001: 40). Other viceroys were more liberal: after the Marquis of Hartington presided over a spectacular drinking session that followed a Castle ball in 1755, the eminent Lord Kildare wrote his wife, 'I don't think I ever drank so hard and fast in my life: everyone of the company complain today' (Fitzgerald 1949: 16). Lord Carteret (1724–1730) was deemed a success as lord lieutenant, his heavy drinking weighing in his favour with public opinion. Not all hard-drinking viceroys endeared themselves to Dublin's citizens, however. Dublin Castle was viewed as 'a glorified tavern and brothel' during the tenure of the Duke of Wharton (1708–1710), with the Duke himself often spotted careening around Dublin at night like 'a drunken madman' (O'Mahoney 1912: 131). The Marquis of Townshend may, inadvisably, have taken Wharton for a role model. As Townshend departed at the end of his term as viceroy in 1772, a local journal aimed the following farewell volley: 'Drunkards ... go mourn: Townshend never shall return' (*Faulkner's Dublin Journal*, September 1772: 188).

Flowing wine was a feature of all viceregal banquets, but on red-letter days such as the king's birthday or the commencement of a viceroy's term of office, splendour and lavish generosity was obligatory. Throughout the two viceroyalties of Lionel Sackville, 1st Duke of Dorset, the customary approach to royal anniversaries was observed, i.e. they were marked by day-long festivities culminating in a Castle ball. Dorset and his Duchess, however, strove to reach new heights of hospitality with the calibre of their entertainment. A font that flowed with wine all through the night was set up in the Castle's council chamber. Even the commonalty was not neglected, as wine for its consumption was ducted to a courtyard below. In 1745, Chesterfield refined these methods of wine distribution. For the king's birthday that year, Dublin Castle's supper-room was partly transformed into a temple of Minerva in which a continuous flow of wine spouted from sundry statues. Again, some of this was piped to a lower yard for the benefit of the king's less exalted citizens (Robins 2001: 27). By 1770, an Irish military correspondent reckoned the Castle's official celebrations on the queen's birthday superior to those he had experienced at St James's the previous year (Barnard 2001: 189).

In terms of gastronomic connoisseurship, the Duke of Rutland (1784–1787) stands out amongst Georgian-era lord lieutenants. *The Hibernian Magazine* (March 1784: 164) reported details of the first ball he hosted at the Castle as viceroy. A particularly fine impression was made by the stunning silver and gold plate Rutland and his Duchess put on display, and the supper provided, 'consisted of every curiosity that art could procure, imagination suggest, or the season furnish'. Tantalizingly, this report neglects to list specific dishes. However, it can be assumed that they were indeed of the highest gastronomic standard as the Duke was a most exacting epicure. Upon his orders, the chief cook at Dublin Castle was despatched to France. The cook's brief was to expand his culinary repertoire by undertaking *stages* at French courts, such as those of the renowned gourmets the Franco-Irish Archbishop of Narbonne, Arthur Richard Dillon, and the Duc d'Orléans. Rutland's quest for gustatory perfection naturally required superior wines. In 1786, he sent another member of staff on a quest to France to source the finest available. A resulting consignment to the Castle cellars included '500 bottles of the very best quality Sillery champagne', as well as '300 bottles of Hautevillers champagne, the growth preferred in Paris to any other' (Robins 2001: 72).

Toasting

In a nation where claret was quaffed 'cold, mulled, or buttered' (Barrington 1826: 43), it cannot surprise that toasting provided an ideal excuse for downing multiple glasses at any given sitting. In the delightful *Recollections of Jonah Barrington*, the aptness of the title for one chapter – 'Irish Dissipation in 1778' – is soon evident. Detailing a convivial get-together, the author notes:

> numerous toasts ... as was customary in those days, intervened to prolong and give zest to the repast – every man shouted forth his fair favourite, or convivial pledge; and each voluntarily surrendered a portion of his own reason in bumpers to the beauty of his neighbour's toast ... one songster chanted the joys of wine and women; another gave ... the pleasures of the fox and chase ... claret flowed. (Barrington 1826: 45)

Claret must have flowed, likewise, at a celebratory dinner in a Dublin Masonic Lodge in 1741. Many of the Castle grandees were members of the fraternity, and the tenor and number of toasts proposed likely bears some resemblance to the style of toasting favoured at the Castle. On this occasion, nine specific toasts were prescribed, headed by one to 'The King and the Craft' and including 'Masons and Masons' Bearns & those that lye in Masons Arms wch. some Folks have wth. Curious Impert' (Parkinson 1957: 101). Even taking into consideration the fact that toasting glasses of the period had thick bowls that magnified the appearance of a small amount of wine, the cumulative effect of multiple glasses could not have been insignificant.

An even more onerous toasting session evolved at Dublin Castle. After an annual banquet given there to fête the lord mayor of the city, the latter was conducted, along with his officials, to the cellars. There, a large glass of wine, constantly replenished, was passed from man to man. Not only was each obliged to propose the lord lieutenant's good health, but he was expected to drop a gold coin into the glass! This ritual continued till the 1760s when a sitting lord mayor begged to be excused from the demands on his purse and, presumably, his constitution (Robins 2001: 40). Maxwell (1946: 101) confirms that festive occasions at the Castle witnessed the most intensive drinking sessions with 'the chief stimulating agent being the interminable toasts that were given, in accordance with the fashion of the times'.

Celebrations and Hospitality in Georgian Dublin

Private and public dining at Dublin Castle

The Duke of Shrewsbury is credited with modelling the viceregal household on that of the court of St James's, where he served as court chamberlain. During his term of office in Dublin (1713–1714), an ordinary dinner at his table would have comprised four removes, i.e. a dish removed when finished and replenished, sixteen dishes, and desserts on certain weekdays (Robins 2001: 36–38).

Public dining, of necessity, required a larger number of more sumptuous dishes. Greater pomp and abundance surrounded public dining as the court became grander and more sophisticated under successive viceroys, reaching its apogee towards the end of the eighteenth century. The rich, varied cuisine that was served was produced by cooks who had trained in royal and aristocratic kitchens in England and France. Having a private cook had become essential for the Irish élite (Mac Con Iomaire 2009: 50). Mrs Mary Delany (cited in Cahill 2005: 68), a contemporary social arbiter, was amazed to find that even a modest Anglo-Irish gentleman kept a 'man cook'. Employing a French cook carried the greatest cachet, and Charles Lennox, the 4th Duke of Richmond & Lennox was bitterly disappointed when a perceived dearth of Italian opera in Dublin dissuaded a prominent, clearly melomanic French chef from accompanying him to the Castle in 1807 (Robins 2001). The absence of a French chef, however, never precluded the sating of the appetites of viceregal guests. All public dinners given under Chesterfield, for instance, provided 'two courses of twenty-one dishes each, not including removes and a generous provision of desserts' (Robins 2001: 39).

Great dinners coming together

Married to an Irish dean and a friend to Jonathan Swift, Mrs Delany is renowned in her own right for her fascinating floral découpage and incisive letters. She had occasion to entertain viceregal guests in her home, Delville, so she was *au fait* with the prerequisites of contemporary hospitality at the highest level. In 1752, she observed that the Irish gentry were too fond of 'high living'. Coming from England, Delany (cited in Cahill 2005: 77) was amazed to find that in Ireland 'you are not invited to dinner to any private gentleman of £1000 a year or less, that does not give you seven dishes at one course, and Burgundy and Champagne: and these dinners they give once or twice a week.' That same year, she considered inviting the current viceroy and his wife (the Duke and Duchess of Dorset) to breakfast, reasoning that 'dinners are grown such luxurious feasts in this country ... and our viceroy loves magnificence too well to be pleased with our way of entertaining company' (Delany cited in Cahill 2005: 54). Nevertheless, she sometimes enjoyed the opulence on offer at Dublin Castle:

> The grand ball was given last Wednesday ... musicians and singers were dressed like Arcadian shepherds and shepherdesses, and placed among rocks. If tea, coffee or chocolate were wanting, you held your cup to a leaf of a tree, and it

was filled; and whatever you wanted to eat or drink, was immediately found on a rock, or on a branch, or in the hollow of a tree. (Cahill 2005: 87)

Rare was the lord lieutenant who conceded defeat in the face of a virtually uninterrupted onslaught of gargantuan repasts. In 1781, however, Lord Carlisle admitted that his constitution was suffering, complaining that '… two great dinners coming together (for almost before I have lost sight of the knives and forks of one, the soup of the other makes its appearance) fatigue me very much' (Robins 2001: 66).

The Duke of Rutland recognized no such limits. His predilections as a gourmet have been noted, but, more prosaically, he was also famed as a man 'who dearly loved a good dinner' and set a record for dining out which remained unequalled by subsequent viceroys (O'Mahoney 1912: 191). In 1787, he undertook a tour of the estates of Irish noblemen, during which he astonished his hosts by the staggering – even by contemporary standards – quantities of food and wine he consumed. Gamble (1810: 59) opined that Rutland attempted to drink – and, it appears, to eat – himself 'into the hearts of the Irish', but that 'he fell a martyr to his exertions, and died of a fever, brought on by carousing and hard drinking'. The Duke did fall ill and died immediately after returning to Dublin Castle from his three-month-long immersion in excess. An autopsy showed his liver to be utterly decayed; he was thirty-three years old!

Robert Smith (1725), a former cook to the 2nd Duke of Ormond, published a book of recipes of court cookery which provides an insight into the variety of rich dishes which would have graced viceregal dining tables in the early eighteenth century. Smith had trained under Patrick Lamb, who had served as Master Cook to reigning monarchs from the time of Charles II to that of Queen Anne (Mennell 1996: 93). Smith was well versed in the preparation of dishes for courtly feasts. Numbering amongst these must surely have been the intriguingly named 'surpriz'd fowls' who find themselves stewed along with oysters, cockscombs, morels, and anchovies, to be garnished with 'truffels' (Smith 1725: 14). Many of his recipes are categorized as 'royal' – an adjective that appears to apply to dishes with a multiplicity of costly ingredients. 'Royal Sausages' provide one such example, with partridge, quail, snipe, pigeon, chicken, veal, ham fat, chives, parsley, mushrooms, truffles, mace, eggs, cream, cinnamon, onion, beef, and bacon all to be formed into sausages 'about six inches in Length, and three in Thickness' (Smith 1725: 99). Custards, very popular at this time, were displaced by ices at viceregal suppers by the 1750s (Barnard 2004: 144).

Accustomed to high-caste guests – including viceregal couples – and a regular at Castle entertainments, Mrs Delany is an excellent source for detailing the range of dishes typical of élite Georgian Irish households. The list of dishes she served to visiting 'grandees' in 1747 demonstrates the necessary components of a menu 'as showy as any eighteenth-century chatelaine could wish' (Cahill 2005: 69–70). The first course included fish, beef, rabbits, steaks, soup, and veal. The second course comprised grilled salmon; young turkey; pickled salad and quails; dishes of peas, onions, and mushrooms;

and savoury pies. Desserts, of which nine were offered, consisted of four types of fruits, served with or without cream, blamange (sic), sweetmeats and jelly, and Dutch cheese. Delany (cited in Cahill 2005: 78), though quite proud of her own table, disapproved of high ecclesiastics aping 'the fantastical luxuriances of fashionable tables' by serving culinary show-stoppers such as Perigord pie.

This rich game and truffle-laden pastry would certainly not have appeared incongruous at a viceregal entertainment, nor would it have been difficult to obtain its ingredients since an extensive range of imported foods and wines were widely available from specialist merchants in Georgian Dublin. Robins (2001: 54) relates that a merchant at The Blue Door on Abbey Street stocked 'Bayonne hams, Parmesan cheese, peaches in brandy, West Indian sweetmeats, green ginger, truffles, olives, macaroni, anchovies, Muscatel raisins, and Marseille figs.' A broadsheet entitled 'The Dublin Cries', printed sometime between 1773 and 1793, shows the types of foods and beverages that would have been available from street hawkers operating in the vicinity of Dublin Castle. Dairy products like milk, butter, curds and whey were on offer, as were fish (Dublin Bay herrings, Boyne salmon) and shellfish (Carlingford oysters, cockles, crabs, and lobsters). A range of fruit and vegetables, including cherries, gooseberries, Windsor beans, peas, green sprouts, cabbage, cauliflower, and artichokes – not to mention the now-ubiquitous potato – round off the list of some of the hawkers' edible merchandize (Panter 1924: 70). As Barnard (2004: 191) points out, the desire amongst the gentry and the aristocracy to make a grand figure played a key role in fruit and vegetable cultivation in this period. In 1759, Mrs Delany was impressed when served a pineapple 'ready pared and cut, all served in fine old china' (cited in Cahill 2005: 50). By 1772, however, a guest entertained at a nobleman's country seat in county Down had become sufficiently accustomed to such exotica that he was able to observe that the pineapple served there was below par (Barnard 2004: 191).

Private papers from various Irish estates also provide insight into food and wine purchases typical of the upper class in this period. A list of accounts in the Wicklow Papers at the National Library of Ireland (Dublin, NLI, MS 38,575/6) details payments made in 1746 for items such as '6 Trowts [sic], a kid, caraway seeds, a stone of salt, 3 pair of rabbits, sack and brandy, a half sammon [sic]'. A very early nineteenth-century cellar-book from the Clonbrock Estate Papers (NLI, MS 19,504) reveals purchases from several different wine merchants. The following marginal notation within it highlights the discrimination of the Anglo-Irish palate: 'Oct. 24th 1814: 23 doz. Sneyd's claret. Stated to be prime Chateau Margaux vint. 1811, also 3 magnums of same'.

Native hospitality and Castle celebrations

Whilst the Irish gentry generally seemed uninterested in the appearance of their homes and the poor impression this might make upon visitors, this apparent defect as hosts was counterbalanced by lavish displays of hospitality. After a round of visits in 1732, amongst which one to 'a gentlemen of fifteen hundred pounds a year' appeared typical,

Celebrations and Hospitality in Georgian Dublin

Mrs Delany wrote her sister that:

> I have not seen less than fourteen dishes of meat for dinner, and seven for supper … they not only treat us at their houses magnificently but if we are to go to an inn, they constantly provide us with a basket crammed with good things; no people can be more hospitable or obliging. (Glin and Peill 2007: 60)

The same year, an Englishman travelling in Ireland observed that 'the Irish Gentry are an expensive People; they live in the most open hospitable manner, continually feasting with one another' (Markham 1984: 124).

The singularity of Irish hospitality has long been remarked upon by visitors. In the sixteenth century, Stanihurst noted that Gaelic Irish chieftains were 'the most hospitable of men, nor could you please them more in anything than by frequently visiting their houses willingly of your own accord, or claiming an invitation from them' (1584: 33). Simms (1978: 94–95) opines that the 'riotous hospitality' exhibited throughout the Georgian era by members of the Ascendancy was not, in fact, an English import. Over time, the Protestant ruling class had assimilated traditional Gaelic standards of hospitality. Commentary by contemporary English observers supports the proposition that the ruling class emulated the native Irish in their displays of generous hospitality; English visitors invariably remarked upon the overwhelming level of Irish hospitality in comparison to the prevailing English norms (Barnard 2004; Mac Con Iomaire 2009; Maxwell 1946; O'Mahoney 1912).

Towards the end of the eighteenth century Lord Harcourt distinguished himself by the magnificence of his viceregal court. The results of his munificence were quite extraordinary. In attempting to emulate and even supersede the standards of Dublin Castle, important families actually 'beggared themselves, spending in a few years the income of a whole generation' (O'Mahoney 1912: 179). A vicious cycle became established; as reigning viceroys strove to outdo the Irish peers in their displays of hospitality, the latter were forced to ever-escalating degrees of excess in reciprocation. The *Gentleman's Magazine* (November 1785: 913) noted that while touring Ireland the Duke and Duchess of Rutland 'visited the principal seats … of this country, where they have been received with that magnificence and hospitality which has ever distinguished the nobility and gentry of Ireland'. O'Mahoney (1912: 191) later pointed out, however, that the cost to these honoured hosts ran to thousands of pounds. Gamble (1810: 82) mused that 'The usages of Dublin make it necessary to give dinners, often beyond the income of the entertainer; who, in his ordinary mode of living, probably pays the penalty of his … profusion'. Clarkson (1999: 101–102) assumed that upper-class expenditure on food at this time amounted to thirty per cent of total income, but it appears likely that this must have been exceeded by the Irish élite in their Georgian heyday. Ireland's premier peer, the Duke of Leinster, and many other members of the Irish aristocracy, such as the Marchioness of Antrim, matched the viceroys in the scale of their entertaining (Maxwell 1946: 111). Visitors to the private houses of Irish grandees were struck by their 'peculiarly splendid way of living – a multiplicity of servants, great profusion of dishes on the table, abundant wine' (Maxwell 1946: 101). Some, however, disapproved of a noticeable tendency towards one-upmanship, suggesting that assemblies in the private residences of the quality 'would have been agreeable enough if they did not vie with one another in expense' (Guy 1990: 40). The Duchess of Northumberland, a vicereine, expressed shock in her diary at the 'luxury of both rich and poor … The people in Trade generally keep one, nay some have 2 livery servants and they give dinners, Balls, Routs and suppers' (Glin and Peill 2007: 115).

The end of an era

Dublin Castle really only commenced to offer the exaggerated level of hospitality expected by the Irish in the 1670s, when Lady Essex became the first vicereine to provide truly lavish entertainments (Robins 2001: 6). Rising to the demanding standards of Gaelic hospitality which had been imbibed by the Ascendancy, succeeding viceroys continued in like mode. The implementation of the Act of Union in 1801, however, which resulted in the dissolution of the Irish Parliament, put an end to the halcyon days of Dublin's viceregal court and the more outrageous excesses of Georgian hospitality.

Within ten years of the Act, Gamble (1912: 58) opined that the lord lieutenant's role was reduced to keeping 'the people … in good-humour, if he can'. Rapidly changing social mores and turbulent political and economic realities put paid to the viceregal court's glory days. Levels of over-indulgence that were once aspired to were now, generally, viewed with disapproval. Maria Edgeworth (cited in Maxwell 1946: 117–118) welcomed the fact that 'to make the stranger eat or drink to excess … to set before him old wine and old plate, was no longer the sum of good breeding'. Guests, she enthused, now 'escaped the pomp of grand entertainments'.

Bibliography

Barrington, Jonah T. 1826. *Recollections of Jonah Barrington* (Dublin: The Talbot Press).
Barnard, Toby 2001. '"Grand Metropolis" or "The Anus of the World"? The Cultural Life of Eighteenth-Century Dublin', in *Two Capitals: London and Dublin, 1500–1840*, Clark, C. and Gillespie, R. eds. (Oxford: Oxford University Press for the British Academy), pp. 185–210.
—— 2004. *Making the Grand Figure: Lives and Possessions in Ireland, 1641–1770* (New Haven: Yale University Press).
Cahill, Katherine 2005. *Mrs. Delany's Menus, Medicines and Manners* (Dublin: New Island).
Clarkson, L.A. 1999. 'Hospitality, housekeeping and high living in eighteenth-century Ireland', in *Luxury and Austerity*, Hill, J. and Lennon, C. eds. (Dublin: University College Dublin Press), pp. 84–105.
Faulkner's Dublin Journal, September 1772, p. 188.
Fitzgerald, Brian 1949. *Correspondence of Emily, Duchess of Leinster, 1731–1814*, vol. 1 (Dublin: Stationery Office).
Gentleman's Magazine, November 1785, p. 913.
Gamble, John 1810. *Sketches of History, Politics and Manners in Dublin and the North of Ireland in 1810* (London: Baldwin, Cradock and Joy).
Glin, Knight of and J. Peill 2007. *Irish Furniture* (New Haven: Yale University Press).
Guy, Alan J. (ed.) 1990. *Colonel Samuel Bagshawe and the Army of George II, 1731–1762* (London: The Bodley Head for the Army Records Society).
Hibernian Magazine, February 1780, p. 85; —— March 1784, p. 154.
Huth, Henry and W. Carew Hazlitt (eds) 1869. *Narrative of the Journey of an Irish Gentleman through England in the Year 1752* (London: Chiswick Press).
Mac Con Iomaire, Máirtín 2009. 'The Emergence, Development and Influence of French Haute Cuisine on Public Dining in Dublin Restaurants 1900–2000: An Oral History', vol. 2 (doctoral thesis, Dublin Institute of Technology).
Markham, Sarah (ed.) 1984. *John Loveday of Caversham, 1711–1789: The Life and Tours of an Eighteenth-Century Onlooker* (Norwich: Michael Russell Publishing).
Maxwell, Constantia 1946. *Dublin Under the Georges, 1714–1830* (London: Faber and Faber).
Mennell, Stephen 1996. *All Manners of Food: Eating and Taste in England and France from the Middle Ages to the Present*, 2nd edn (Chicago: University of Illinois Press).
National Library of Ireland, Dublin. The Wicklow Papers: MS 38,575/6
—— The Clonbrock Papers, MS 19,504 (Dublin).
O'Mahoney, Charles 1912. *The Viceroys of Ireland: the Story of the Long Line of Noblemen and their Wives who have Ruled Ireland and Irish Society for over Seven Hundred Years* (London: John Long).
Parkinson, R.E. 1957. *History of the Grand Lodge of Free and Accepted Masons of Ireland*, vol. 2 (Dublin: Lodge of Research, CC).
Panter, George W., 'Eighteenth Century Dublin Street Cries', *The Journal of the Royal Society of Antiquaries of Ireland*, 6th ser., 14, (1924), 68–86.
Robins, Joseph 2001. *Champagne and Silver Buckles: The Viceregal Court at Dublin Castle 1700–1922* (Dublin: The Lilliput Press).
Simms, Katharine, 'Guesting and Feasting in Gaelic Ireland', *The Journal of the Royal Society of Antiquaries of Ireland*, 108, (1978) 67–100.
Smith, Robert 1725. *Court Cookery: or, The Compleat English Cook*, 2nd edn (London: T. Wotton).
Somerville-Large, Peter 1996. *Dublin: The Fair City* (London: Sinclair-Stevenson).
Stanihurst, Richard 1584. *De rebus in Hibernia gestis* (Antwerp).

The Unavoidable Ham Biscuit

Mark McWilliams

> Whenever a genuine country ham can be found,
> it is a cause in itself for joyful celebration.
>
> *John Egerton*

In the American South, it is difficult to imagine a celebration of any kind that does not feature ham biscuits. At country club wedding receptions and debutante balls, ham biscuits. At church luncheons and country revivals, ham biscuits. At birthday parties and graduation galas, ham biscuits. And at funeral receptions of high and low, black and white, ham biscuits. Pairing Smithfield or country ham with biscuits whose variety has changed across the region and over time, the ham biscuit has long been the essential food of Southern celebration. To explain this ubiquity, this paper will examine the history of the ham biscuit, consider changes to both country ham and biscuits over time, and briefly explore the nature of celebration itself.

Indeed, the ham biscuit has become almost a kind of shorthand for either Southern hospitality – witness Julia Reed's book entitled *Ham Biscuits, Hostess Gowns, and Other Southern Specialties* – or even a whole approach to life, as in Nani Powers' attempt to explain her upbringing in small-town Virginia: 'It's a funny world I come from. Nobody cries, at funerals or anywhere, dry little conversations, handshakes, ham biscuits, bourbon. Things need to be pleasant.' Where I come from, in big-town Virginia, we may cry at weddings and funerals, but we eat the same ham biscuits afterward.[1]

Surely that shorthand stems from the ham biscuit's ubiquity. As Jill Baughan learned when she moved to the South, 'no one is married, buried, or invited to any special occasion when two or more people are gathered without ham biscuits. And if you run out of ham biscuits, you might might as well send everybody home, because believe you me, they won't be staying.' James Villas insists, 'Country Ham biscuits are still a cocktail staple of the South.' As Jeanne Voltz and Elaine Harvell explain, 'A holiday party is hardly legal without trays piled high with the delicious mini-sandwiches.' And the funeral guide from the Old City Cemetery in Lynchburg, Virginia, guides those in mourning: 'Ham Biscuits are the quintessential offering at bereavement. They abide by all the rules of Funeral Food. They are pickup food that require no additional fussing over. They can be eaten for breakfast, lunch or supper. They are familiar and comforting. Virginia ham does not require refrigeration, though it would be a good idea to refrigerate if they last overnight.'[2]

The biscuit has a special place in Southern foodways, but the country ham itself is the secret of the ham biscuit. John Egerton calls country ham 'an ancient and inimitable

The Unavoidable Ham Biscuit

treasure, the highest form of the Southern gastronomic art'; James Beard wished that more of his countrymen were familiar with 'the most elegant of all American foods.' Country ham is special, the key flavoring to greens and beans as well as 'festive food for holidays and celebrations' – as a result, Voltz and Harvell explain, 'Country ham brings a warm feeling of home to us; we grew up with it.' And Southerners have been eating a lot of it for a long time. In the 1720s, Virginian William Byrd wrote of neighboring North Carolinians: 'The Truth of it is, these People live so much upon Swine's flesh, that it don't only encline them to the Yaws, & consequently to the downfall of their Noses, but makes them likewise extremely hoggish in their Temper, & many of them seem to Grunt rather than Speak in ordinary conversation.'[3]

The special history and qualities of country ham may be the root of the ham biscuit's popularity, by it is still unusual for a food to stay so common across time and, more strikingly, class, especially when the preparation as well as the ingredients of a dish remain constant. More often, particular foods mark celebrations of one segment of society – recall the tagline of the television show *Lifestyles of the Rich and Famous*: 'Caviar Wishes and Champagne Dreams' – while others vary in ways that reveal differences in class as well as taste, as Jean-Anthelme Brillat-Savarin explained by describing versions of roast turkey in his native France:[4]

> When the vine-grower or the ploughman wants a treat on some long winter evening, what do we see roasting over a bright fire in the kitchen where the table is laid? A turkey.
>
> When the hard-working artisan invites a few friends to his house to enjoy a holiday which is all the more precious for being rare, what is sure to be the principal dish of the feast? A turkey, stuffed with sausages or Lyons chestnuts.
>
> And in the high places of gastronomy, at those select gatherings where politics are forced to give way to dissertations upon taste, what do the guests hope for and long for as the second course? A truffled turkey!

As Brillat-Savarin notes, changing the technique and ingredients alters the dish; altering the dish changes the meal's cultural associations.

Pierre Bourdieu reminds us that such differences precisely mark class status: 'In cultural consumption, the main opposition ... is between the practices designated by their rarity as distinguished, those of the fractions richest in both economic and cultural capital, and the practices socially identified as vulgar because they are both easy and common, those of the fractions poorest in both these respects.' Thus we would expect the foods of the rich – especially celebratory foods – to be far removed from those of the poor, and yet there remains no consistent difference between the ham biscuits served at a cocktail party at the Country Club of Virginia and those served at a funeral reception a few miles away in Richmond's lower class Oregon Hill neighborhood.[5]

Its universal status may be surprising, but the ham biscuit has become a celebratory food in the American South for good reasons. First, the combination is exquisite.

The Unavoidable Ham Biscuit

Though rarely recognized in the same breath, American country ham falls into the same category of 'sublime hams,' as Harold McGee calls them, as Italy's *prosciutto di Parma* or Spain's Serrano and Iberico hams. And the biscuits themselves, whether the increasingly rare and labor-intensive beaten biscuit of tradition or today's more common risen biscuits, are at their best similar examples of culinary excellence. Second, the flavor is so intense that the relatively expensive meat must be served in small quantities. A good country ham may be 'as different from the ordinary ham perpetrated by pork packers as beer is different from champagne' – note how this description turns precisely on different class associations – but the small serving sizes mean, effectively, champagne on a beer budget. In other words, ham biscuits are both good enough for the wealthy and affordable enough for special occasions among the less affluent.[6]

That intense flavor is difficult to describe and impossible to equal: 'As a result of curing and aging hams, marvelous new flavors and textures unlike those in any other food are created. The first taste of country ham is salty. The flavor is big and complex in the mouth. The texture is firm with a richness unrivalled by any other meat. Even the tiniest sliver of country ham contributes rich flavor to a simple dish.' Peter Kaminsky tries to summarize the processes that produce such flavor, but he soon melts, like ham fat in the mouth, into romance and desire:

> Time, and with it, heat, salting, smoking, and cold will produce hundreds of flavor compounds – too many for the lay person to keep straight: amines, ketones, aldehydes, aclcanes, aldols, melanoids, and scores of the subsets. Each influences the progression of flavors that begins with the insistent and decadent bouquet that is released into the air when a slice of ham is cut. As the ham comes into contact with your tongue, the punch of salt pushes forward wave after wave of subtler notes – smoky, floral, fruity. Finally, as your teeth come together and you breathe out, you smell the return, only deeper, of that initial aroma of flesh and sweet decay. You would think this last might be off-putting, but in the right balance, it is a heady perfume, just this side of rancidness. Most mammals recognize it as a turn-on.

As John Egerton points out, country ham has the same hybrid origins as all the best American foods: 'English hogs fattened on African peanuts and cured by Indian methods of salting and smoking were the source, around 1650, of the first Smithfield hams.'[7]

Smithfield, Virginia, is, as Egerton puts it, 'the undisputed birthplace of Southern-style country ham.' By the mid-1600s, hams were already being sent back to Europe in trade. Soon individuals like Captain Mallory Todd could make a good living by exporting ham, and Smithfield grew up around the pig trade: 'Ample docking space for clipper ships on the Pagan River, a tributary of the James, was a crucial feature of the town plan. Arthur Smith donated land and probably his name, though some say the town was named for Smithfield, the meat center of London.' Certainly the town quickly became an American meat center. Production accelerated after the Civil War,

The Unavoidable Ham Biscuit

when 'P.D. Gwaltney, Jr., first with his father and then with his sons, turned from tobacco and peanut farming to meat packing, and the Gwaltney name is still prominent in the industry. By 1907, Smithfield ham producers were shipping forty thousand hams a year.' While that growth has skyrocketed – now that 1907 production takes a single day – there are still traces of the town's early history: Berry Hill Farm's smokehouse, for example, has been in operation since the 1700s.[8]

Though Smithfield became known for its hams, the pigs themselves were widespread long before the town was settled. The first pigs arrived in Florida with the Spanish in 1539, and the Spanish spread them through the region. Soon 'the progeny of these hogs probably populated the mountains and wooded areas of present-day Virginia, Georgia, and the Carolinas and roamed the cypress swamps of Florida.' The hogs' spread was also aided by Native Americans, who 'soon learned to eat the meat and became so fond of it that they raided the de Soto camps to capture wandering pigs, starting skirmishes that erupted into major battles from time to time. By the time de Soto died in 1542, the pig herd that had landed with his troops had multiplied to seven hundred, some of which were kept by the natives while others roamed the countryside.' As the hog population grew through both Native and European efforts, more pigs were arriving: '[a]lmost every shipload of immigrants brought pigs to add to the growing population of porkers.'[9]

Recognizable descendants of Spanish swine still exist in America, notably the Ossabaw Island breed, named for the island off Georgia on which the Spanish left pigs as a food supply for explorers and colonists in the 1500s. Since the island remains accessible only by boat, the pigs there today resemble the pigs that would have been common in colonial America. Indeed, Mount Vernon maintains an Ossabaw herd, as does Colonial Williamsburg, which uses Ossabaws for their annual demonstrations of pig butchery and ham production. In the colonial period, hogs were so common that '[t]he people of Williamsburg complained about dodging swine on the footpaths of the town' and attempted to banish the pigs to an island on the nearby James River.[10]

The hogs may have been resented on Williamsburg's streets, but they were welcome on its tables. Ham production grew from its early roots in nearby Smithfield, and '[b]y the end of the eighteenth century, cured ham was widely praised as a coveted Southern delicacy.' The reputation of the Smithfield hams continued to grow, and '[b]y the middle of the nineteenth century, Queen Victoria had put in an order for six hams a week for the palace kitchen.' But Smithfield was hardly the only source of good country hams. As the colonies expanded, ham production did too. All the states of the upper South can claim a strong country ham tradition, and 'even the deepest South had farm-cured hams. One of the best-known ham producers, Talmadge, was in central Georgia.' Even there '[a] well-made ham survived the heat of summer and could sit on a table for hours with little worry about spoilage.'[11]

The legendary taste of the Smithfield ham resulted from the hogs' diet and processing. The traditional diet seems remarkably similar to that of pigs producing legendary Spanish hams. As *The Smithfield Cookbook* explains, 'after a spring and summer of foraging in the woods for acorns and other wild nuts, hogs on the farms around Smithfield are turned into the fields to root for the peanuts that have been left behind by the harvesters.' John Egerton notes that '[s]uch a diet is said to make the meat redder, the fat yellow, and the taste slightly oily – all considered positive qualities of Smithfield distinction.'[12]

Indeed, in 1926, a Virginia statute regulated the Smithfield name, limiting its use to hams 'cut from the carcasses of peanut-fed hogs, raised in the peanut-belt of the State of Virginia or the State of North Carolina, and which are cured, treated, smoked, and processed in the town of Smithfield, in the State of Virginia.' But the law was later changed to remove the requirement that the hogs be peanut-fed and locally raised (although it still stipulates 'hams processed, treated, smoked, cured by the long-cure, dry-salt method of cure and aged for a minimum period of six months'), and, according to some, the legendary foraging methods had been long-abandoned. Tommy Darden, a Smithfield ham maker featured in an important *New York Times* article, claimed that 'Nobody fattens hogs on peanuts around here anymore … . I never cared much for that taste anyway – too soft, too oily. And that business about hogs being turned into the peanut field to fatten, that was always more of a fairytale than the truth, even in the old days' – although the 1926 law's specificity, let alone Darden's own sense memories, suggests that his explanation might be somewhat defensive. Certainly some well-respected country hams result from hogs that are not finished on nuts, like those of Kentucky's Trigg County Hams, which are corn-fed.[13]

As such variations suggest, the curing methods specified in the Virginia laws may be even more crucial to the distinctive taste of a country ham than diet. Once the hogs are butchered, they are salted, a process that requires an experienced touch; (usually) smoked; and then aged at least through the crucial summer months. But each step in that sequence must be properly executed to end up with a country ham worth the time and care it takes to make one.

Salt does more than protect and flavor the ham. Harold McGee explains that '[h]igh salt concentrations cause the normally tightly bunched protein filaments in the muscle cells to separate into individual filaments'; this process produces the characteristic translucence of fine hams. In addition to the salt, many ham makers add other ingredients to the mix that is carefully applied to the hams, including sugar, pepper (common in Smithfield), and saltpeter. Trigg County Hams is among this group, adding sugar and 'a tiny amount of saltpeter' to the all-important salt. McGee explains that, while nitrates from saltpeter have long been believed to produce the 'characteristic rosy color' of the best hams, that color actually results from 'the presence of a particular ripening bacteria.' McGee even speculates that curing hams without saltpeter, including the best *prosciuttos* as well as some country hams, might be part of why these hams are so good. While '[n]itrate protects meat fats from oxidation and the development of off-flavors,' it is precisely 'fat breakdown' that serves as 'one of the sources of desirable ham flavor.'[14]

The Unavoidable Ham Biscuit

Smoke contributes flavor too – hence the careful selection of woods like oak, hickory or apple – but it also contributes to preservation. McGee notes that smoke 'has long been used in conjunction with salting and drying – a happy combination because salted meats are especially prone to developing rancidity.' As Voltz and Harvell insist, though, 'not all smoked hams have the traditional cure and aging, and a country ham is not necessarily smoked. Smoking alone does not produce the elegant, complex flavor of a dry-cured, well-aged ham.' Nevertheless, the image – and aroma – of the smokehouse is as evocative to many Southerners as the distinctive sight of a hanging country ham.[15]

Time matters too. The hogs are butchered and salted in the late fall, when the temperature drops. The hogs are then smoked before the summer, when the hams undergo a crucial change. During the 'July sweats' or 'summer sweats,' as Kaminsky summarizes, 'the flesh of the ham expands into the outer covering of mold. In the winter, the meat contracts, drawing with it the taste-enhancing enzymes.' After the summer, the ham may be considered ready, although many makers age their hams far longer.[16]

The whole process takes somewhere from a minimum of six months – although purists scoff at anything less than nine months – to several years. The process has been around for centuries, but it meets at least the spirit of USDA regulations (although few country hams are inspected): over the length of the process, hams 'will lose 25 to 30 percent of their weight … and that is more than the minimum required … . They will also take on at least the minimum amount of salt … and they will get hot enough in the smokehouse in July and August to exceed the government's temperature standard for killing disease-carrying bacteria.'[17]

While the famous Smithfield name is protected by law, other country hams made in similar ways – and indeed many made to higher standards – have to rely on their reputations, since there is no official definition of country ham. Indeed, as Egerton points out, 'Most commercial firms now use some or many of the modern short-cut methods: immersion in brine or injections of brine instead of dry-salt curing; liquid smoke or no smoke at all; and a combination of refrigeration and heating rather than natural temperatures for aging. Instead of hams produced in nine months, many companies are now turning out "90-day wonders".'[18]

The same drive toward modern convenience has dramatically affected ham's partner, the biscuit. The traditional beaten biscuit is rarely seen any more. Beaten biscuits are exactly what they sound like, made from dough that has been beaten for half an hour or more. Because of the sheer work required, beaten biscuits are a prime example of John Egerton's description of Southern food: 'Most of what [Southerners] consumed cost them little or no money – just energy, of which they had an abundance.' Bill Neal explains:

> Beaten biscuits are, like grits, very much of a mystery to the uninitiated. They may be the forerunner of the modern raised biscuit, but these chewy, unleavened morsels resemble more the hard tack produced by early European bakers for armies and navies than anything else served up in the modern South. …

Country ham was for some time wedded to the beaten biscuit in Southern cuisine. At the most traditional fancy parties and weddings, biscuits no bigger than a quarter are invariably served up with baked, cured ham sliced as thin as imaginable sandwiched inside and spiked with mustard. Otherwise, beaten biscuits are rarely seen anymore.

They sound harder to make than they are. ... [T]hose who enjoy a physical relationship with their doughs should be in heaven here. There is no getting around the activity. Fifteen minutes of heavy, consistent abuse is the minimum. You can use a rolling pin, a hammer, the side of an axe; whatever, it must be heavy. ... When properly beaten, the dough will blister at each blow. It will develop a strange plastic quality and be smoother than any other bread dough you have ever seen ... .

As the dough was beaten, the cook would also be 'continuously folding and flattening the dough until it became soft and smooth. This layering and pounding process introduced air into the dough and gave the biscuits a lift in the oven.' It is no wonder that, despite being 'the most glorious bread with ham,' beaten biscuits 'almost disappeared when servants became scarce' (note here the traditional euphemism for slaves).[19]

Beaten biscuits were almost saved by technology, as Egerton explains: 'In 1877, when the labor involved ... came to be viewed as too burdensome and time-consuming, Evelyn L. Edwards of Vineland, New Jersey, received a patent for a dough-kneading machine.' The biscuit brake, as such machines became known, 'utilized a hand crank to turn two rollers, between which the dough could be passed repeatedly until it reached the desired smoothness. Like the cotton gin, this Yankee invention swept through the South, and for another half-century or more, it not only saved beaten biscuits from extinction but actually made them smoother, prettier, and more popular than before.' Soon several types were available, and today '[a] lover of beaten biscuits is lucky to inherit or find a biscuit brake.'[20]

The beaten biscuit's origins seem unclear, as Egerton writes:

There is something mysterious and intriguing about beaten biscuits. Where did they come from? England? The British had unleavened breads, of course, but nothing quite like this. Africa? John and Karen Hess suggest that possibility in their book *The Taste of America* – but again, there is no clear evidence. The Indians? Mary Randolph, in her *Virginia House-Wife* (1824) had an unleavened biscuit recipe that called for beating the dough with a pestle, and she gave it an Indian name: Apoquiniminc cakes. No connection has been found, though, between recipes for beaten biscuits and any breads baked by the Indians.

But there are early English recipes that seem remarkably like the beaten biscuit, like the 1596 recipe from *The Good Housewife's Jewel* for 'Fine Biscuit Bread.' The cook is to combine flour, sugar, aniseed, eggs, and rose water in 'an earthen pan and with a slice of wood beat it the space of two hours' before baking the biscuits in buttered tin moulds.[21]

Not everyone was fond of beaten biscuits. Indeed, Eliza Leslie interrupts her recipe for 'Maryland Biscuits' to complain:

> This is the most labourious of cakes, and also the most unwholesome, even when made in the best manner. We do not recommend it; but there is not accounting for tastes. Children should not eat these biscuits – nor grown persons either, if they can get any other sort of bread. When living in a town where there are bakers, there is no excuse for making Maryland biscuit. Believe nobody that says they are not unwholesome. Yet we have heard of families, in country places, where neither the mistress nor the cook knew any other preparation of wheat bread. Better to live on Indian cakes.

Leslie's complaint reminds us of Neal's comparison of beaten biscuits to hard tack, and yet it seems drowned out by the many reveries celebrating the same dish, especially when glorified with country ham.[22]

While the beaten biscuit largely died out after the Civil War, it remained popular in the upper South through the 1940s, 'and it was no mere coincidence that the same territory was also known as the country ham belt, for the combination of country ham and beaten biscuits was a culinary delight that many people considered without peer. … Southerners who could resist paper-thin slices of prime country ham piled high between halves of a beaten biscuit were few and far between,' insists Egerton (who adds, 'They still are'). Frederick Philip Stieff, who collected Maryland recipes in the early twentieth century, includes one for 'Maryland Beaten Biscuit': '3 pints winter wheat flour, 1/4 lb. Lard, one-half ice water and milk to make a stiff dough, 1 heaping teaspoon salt. Work in the lard, add the liquid and beat with a club for twenty-five minutes. Make in small biscuits and bake in a hot oven.'[23]

The beaten biscuit can still be found, but others have long replaced it as country ham's celebratory partner. Almost anything can serve, from common risen biscuits (those made with lard are superior to many tastes) to the twice-leavened angel biscuits (with both yeast and baking powder, a recipe 'often called Bride's biscuits'). Indeed, in many places the dinner roll has replaced the biscuit as the desired bread, though the resulting combination is still uniformly called 'ham biscuits.'[24]

Variations on the ham biscuit go beyond the bread. Many prefer the biscuit (or its substitute) to be heavily buttered, but a spread made of butter, mustard, Worcestershire, onion, and poppy seeds has become common in many places, often those which have adopted the dinner roll. Perhaps there is some compensation here for the lost biscuit, but the spread offends purists as much as the substitution of city ham for country ham. Other variations come from baking the ham into the biscuit. In *Pig: King of the Southern Table*, James Villas includes a recipe for West Virginia Ham and Grits Biscuits, a sort of hand-held Southern breakfast. These 'memorable biscuits' made from 'zesty' country ham results from mixing cooked grits and diced country ham into the dough: 'The trick to making this style of biscuit … is leavening the dough with enough baking powder and lard (not butter), and because the biscuits are not intended to be light and fluffy, the dough can be kneaded till pliable.'[25]

But despite such variations, the ham biscuit itself presides over Southern reception tables. It might be argued that the very affordability that helps make the ham biscuit ubiquitous also challenges the Bakhtinian nature of celebration: times when, spare no expense, excess and desire are often given free rein. Indeed, the ham biscuit seems opposed to excess: the few thin slices of country ham in each biscuit almost seem an attempt to stretch the meat in obvious economical ways, ways not far removed from the old custom of sharing a ham hock so that neighbors could season their bean pots.

And yet focusing on expense misses the excess represented by a platter loaded with a tower of ham biscuits. For Bakhtin, celebratory feasts share with the carnival '[t]he mighty aspiration to abundance and to a universal spirit.' Feasts connect us with excess and the body – or, as my great uncle used to say after a good meal, 'I hurts much better now.'[26]

In fact, the ham biscuit's popularity may rely more on Southern history than economy. Both the country ham and the biscuit evoke the region's contested yet shared past. In this context, it matters that country ham has the same hybrid origins that produced Southern food in general. The collision of English, African, and Native peoples resulted in unspeakable tragedy, but also in resilience, and the resulting foodways transcended hybridity to become a shared tradition. With such influences, the country ham seemed destined to become the pinnacle of pork, the meat Americans ate so often that the country might better be called 'the great Hogeating Confederacy, or the Republic of Porkdom,' as one commentator said in 1860. Nani Powers notes that ham biscuits thus became a 'food that has survived the Civil War' to become 'the quintessential southern delight.'[27]

Finally, though, it's the taste that keeps the dish on Southern tables: 'For a pork lover, the ineffable smoky, salty, funky, meaty mix of flavor from the long-cured hindquarters of a peanut-fed hog is the dining experience against which one measures all others,' and there's no better way to savor that flavor than in a biscuit. Good thing you can find them at every celebration.[28]

The Unavoidable Ham Biscuit

Notes

1. Julia Reed, *Ham Biscuits, Hostess Gowns, and Other Southern Specialties* (New York: St Martin's, 2008); Nani Powers, *Feed the Hungry: A Memoir with Recipes* (New York: Free Press, 2008): 27.
2. Jill Baughan, *Born to Be Wild: Rediscover the Freedom of Fun* (Birmingham, AL: New Hope Press, 2006): 124; Villas, *Biscuit Bliss: 101 Foolproof Recipes for Fresh and Fluffy Biscuits in Just Minutes* (Boston: Harvard Common Press, 2004): 113; Jeanne Volz and Elaine J. Harvell, *The Country Ham Book* (Chapel Hill, NC: U. North Carolina P., 1999): 59; Jessica Bemis Ward, *Food to Die For: A Book of Funeral Food, Tips, and Tales from the Old City Cemetery, Lynchburg, Virginia* (Lynchburg, VA: Southern Memorial Association, 2004): 131. Country ham is often referred to as Virginia ham and Smithfield ham, although the meaning of those names is becoming less precise with time.
3. John Egerton, *Southern Food: At Home, on the Road, in History* (New York: Knopf, 1987): 263; Beard qtd. Voltz & Harvell 2; Voltz & Harvell 1; William Byrd, *William Byrd's Histories of the Dividing Line Betwixt Virginia and North Carolina* (Mineola, NY: Dover, 1967): 55.
4. Jean-Anthelme Brillat-Savarin, *The Philosopher in the Kitchen*, trans. Anne Drayton (New York: Penguin, 1970): 76.
5. Pierre Bourdieu, *Distinction: A Social Critique of the Judgment of Taste*, trans. Richard Nice (Cambridge, MA: Harvard UP, 1984): 176.
6. Harold McGee, *On Food and Cooking: The Science and Lore of the Kitchen* (New York: Scribner, 2004): 174; *The Knoxville Cook Book* (1907) qtd. Egerton 256.
7. Voltz & Harvell 1; Peter Kaminsky, *Pig Perfect: Encounters with Remarkable Swine and Some Great Ways to Cook Them* (New York: Hyperion, 2005): 7; Egerton 256.
8. Egerton 256; Voltz & Harvell 10, 13; Egerton 257; *The Smithfield Cookbook* (1978) qtd. Egerton 256.
9. Voltz & Harvell 9, 12.
10. Ed Crews, 'Ossabaw Island Pigs: Feral American Breed Provides 400-Year-Old Genetic Link between Past and Present,' *Colonial Williamsburg: The Journal of the Colonial Williamsburg Foundation* (Winter 2010): http://www.history.org/foundation/journal/winter10/pigs.cfm; Voltz & Harvell 23, 12.
11. Egerton 256; Voltz & Harvell 13, 15, 2.
12. Qtd. Egerton 256, Egerton 256.
13. Qtd. Egerton 256, qtd Egerton 261, Egerton 258.
14. McGee 174; Voltz & Harvell 8; Egerton 258; McGee 174.
15. McGee 175; Voltz & Harvell 27.
16. Kaminsky 21.
17. Egerton 261.
18. Egerton 257.
19. Egerton 27; Bill Neal, *Biscuits, Spoonbread, and Sweet Potato Pie* (Alfred A. Knopf: New York, 1996): 39; Egerton 219; Voltz & Harvell 60.
20. Egerton 219; Voltz & Harvell 60.
21. Egerton 219; Thomas Dawson, *The Good Housewife's Jewel*, ed. Maggie Black (Lewes, East Sussex, UK: Southover Press, 1996): 79.
22. Eliza Leslie, *Miss Leslie's New Cookery Book* (Philadelphia: T.B. Peterson, 1857): 432.
23. Egerton 219; Frederick Philip Stieff, *Eat, Drink and Be Merry in Maryland* (New York: G.P. Putnam, 1932): 186.
24. Neal 50.
25. James Villas, *Pig: King of the Southern Table* (Hoboken, NJ: John Wiley & Sons, 2010): 400.
26. Mikhail Bakhtin, *Rabelais and His World*, trans. Hélène Iswolsky (Bloomington, IN: Indiana UP, 1984): 278; see also 8–9.
27. John S. Wilson, MD in *Godey's Lady's Book* (1860) qtd. Egerton 259; Powers 43.
28. Kaminsky 6.

North and South: Two Banquets Given to Promote the Great 1851 Exhibition

Valerie Mars

Prince Albert's proposal for a great 'Exhibition of the Works of Industry of all the Nations' in 1851[1] needed support from both established and newly-created economic interests. To promote this project two banquets were given during the preceding year, with the Prince as guest of honour at both.

These banquets were more than just two notable dinners. In their presentation and bills of fare[2] they represented two distinct constituencies: the City of London, the traditional hub of the establishment, represented by the Lord Mayor of London;[3] and a new alliance of British civic leaders, chiefly mayors, headed by the Lord Mayor of York.[4] Tension between these two economic – and socially – based constituencies was a dominant feature of the period as Britain went through fast industrial and social change. Prince Albert was ideally placed to accommodate these differences in his promotion of the Exhibition.

The first banquet was given by the Lord Mayor of London at the Mansion House[5] on Thursday, 21 March 1850. It was both an imposing and traditional feast. The second, on Friday 25 October, was a surprisingly spectacular banquet held at the York Guildhall by the Lord Mayor of that city with other British mayors.

Both banquets were reported at length in the press.[6] Giving such complete accounts incorporated the greater mass of those uninvited into these great occasions, thereby encouraging wider interest in the Exhibition. The *Illustrated London News* included lavish engravings of both banquets and, with other reports, gave guest lists, accounts of the speeches, and descriptions of the scene and bills of fare. Both banquets had décor specially designed for the occasion, augmenting displays of plate and culinary skills that were demonstrated in *pièces de résistance* and overt plenty.

Setting the scene
The importance of the London banquet was announced by the Lord Mayor's elaborately gilded and embossed invitations sent to members of the nobility, ambassadors, the mayors of Britain's major towns and cities,[7] as well as other distinguished and influential men. Women were not invited. Nor, on this occasion, do they appear even to have been spectators.

Both banquets included music and substantial speeches from the hosts and their principal guests. *Punch* praised Prince Albert's speech at the 'Knife-and-Fork Exhibition

North and South: Two Banquets

at the Mansion House': 'Indeed *Punch* has rarely witnessed – with all his knife and fork experience – such emotion; such enthusiasm.'[8]

On arrival at the Mansion House's Egyptian Hall, guests saw décor more elaborate than usual, designed by the City Architect and described as being 'in a most appropriate manner'. Flags representing British counties hung from the pillars. At either end of the hall were large pictorial transparencies, including one above the royal table representing 'the genius of Great Britain presiding over the commerce and industry of the country'. At the opposite end of the hall, the transparency of a proposed exhibition building[9] did not obscure the Egyptian Hall's familiar classic design.

Guests saw tables set in the usual style with the royal table placed at right angles to those which extended down the body of the hall. The *Illustrated London News* noted 'a magnificent display of plate on the sideboards with the tables having a profusion of plate, costly vases, fruit, and rare exotics, [with] many beautiful emblematic devices of art, trade and manufactures being interspersed with more substantial viands.' The whole gave an impression of long-established wealth.

Elaborately engraved and gilded bills of fare were printed for both banquets. Usually the Lord Mayor of London's banquet bills were simply printed in blue ink on white paper within a stamped and cut border. The York banquet, unlike the London banquet, was a unique event. It was catered and designed by the well-known cook and entrepreneur, Alexis Soyer, who had been cook at the Reform Club. The Reform, founded by and for Whigs and Liberals, was open to the manufacturers and men of business whom the Exhibition was intended to encourage.[10]

For the Lord Mayor of York, Soyer produced a re-interpretation of tradition that was intended to amaze. The *Illustrated London News* reporter noted that Prince Albert 'appeared to be much struck with the magnificent *coup d'oeil*' as he entered the hall. Earlier, in 1848, the Prince had been to the Royal Agricultural Society's dinner in the same Guildhall. On that occasion the hall had been unadorned; only the illuminated great gothic stained-glass window had relieved the plain stone walls.[11] On this occasion however, the hall had been especially enlarged, and Soyer rearranged the seating to give all the diners a view of the royal table. He followed this with a complete make-over of the Guildhall: now crimson drapery covered the walls and the gothic window's local heraldry, so that this new focal point behind the top table was filled with a monumental gilt tribute incorporating portraits of Victoria and Albert, the heraldic shields of London and York, and as many other apposite allusions as there was space to accommodate them. Displayed on a purple cloth on a raised dais in front of the royal table were the host mayors' insignia, swords and maces: 'in a fanciful and elegant arrangement … some indeed almost grotesque in their antiquity.'[12]

Flags from the host cities and greenery decorated the pillars. On the royal table, unique red and green cut-glass goblets had been made for Prince Albert and the two Lord Mayors. On other tables glittering mirrored globes reflected extra-bright gaslight, as it illuminated the lavish silver plate.[13]

Figure 1. The Banquet in the Guildhall at York, Illustrated London News, *2 November 1850.*

North and South: Two Banquets

The banquet cuisines

Feast foods celebrate the specifics of time, place, and occasion, and so both these banquets required dishes that defined them as Lord Mayors' banquets: they required turtle and roast beef or venison.[14] In London a baron of beef was preferred. Large cattle were bred to produce these great double sirloins. At York haunches of venison were served. Turtles from the West Indies reflected colonial trade,[15] while baron of beef represented domestic wealth. Alternatively, haunches of venison reflected nature captured, offering an image of abundant landscape.

The Mansion House banquet in London followed in the continuous tradition of commensal expression consolidating established wealth and power. Beef, as a feast dish, did not, like turtle and venison, have exclusively élite associations, being more widely served.[16] It had been depicted throughout the eighteenth century in patriotic painting,[17] lampoons and songs,[18] as superior to anything French. This banquet was distinctive in having a more elaborate bill of fare than their more regular banquets. All were catered by the mayor's usual caterer, Ring and Brymer. To emphasize continuity they noted their place at the foot of the bills of fare as being successors from 1836 to the famous city caterers Birch, Birch & Co.[19] Birch's connection with the Mansion House had been strengthened when Samuel Birch was made Lord Mayor in 1814.

Unfortunately Ring and Brymer have left no information about their cooks or the sources of their recipes, so that it is not possible positively to locate them, but it is possible to suggest some sources for their 1850 bill of fare. Almost all of it can be found in Charles Elmé Francatelli's *The Modern Cook*, published in 1846. This is not to claim that Francatelli cooked for Ring and Brymer since many other versions of his recipes can be found in earlier books, but it is possible to reconstruct most of the 1850 London bill of fare from the precise instructions in this work. However, *The Modern Cook* does not include the more traditional English recipes that appear on the bill. These can be found in eighteenth – and earlier nineteenth – century books, particularly those by two cooks who had connections with the City:[20] William Gelleroy's *The London Cook*[21] and Richard Briggs' *The English Art of Cookery*.[22] Again, their recipes are not exclusive, but do offer possible sources and indications of City tastes[23] for dishes such as trifles and hunting pudding on the bill of fare.

Francatelli had cooked under Antonin Carême,[24] maintaining a long tradition of French *haute cuisine* produced for the English élite. Louis Eustache Ude,[25] who had cooked in England from the early nineteenth century, also includes some of the regular Mansion House banquet dishes that were typically anglicized by Ring and Brymer, such as 'Filets de Merlans à la Horley' originally in Ude as *Filets de Merlans à l'Orlie*. Here, whiting fillets are marinated in lemon juice, onion, and parsley stalks then dried, coated in egg-white, flour, and breadcrumbs, deep-fried, and served with a sharp sauce.[26]

All these cooks catered dinners and banquets for male élites. But these sources can but offer conjecture about how the recipes were actually cooked and presented, since unpublished cooks' work is as finite as diners' memories.

North and South: Two Banquets

London and York's bills were presented as two differently arranged *à la Française* services. London's bill simply listed a 'First Course' of soups and fish dishes followed by the 'Sideboard' with a range of dishes both savoury and sweet – suggesting they were available on request after the soup and fish. The bill then lists 'Removes' which were roasts that replaced the soup and fish on the tables. These ranged from sirloins of beef to goslings.

At the head of the sideboard items were puff-paste *Petits Pâtés* filled with meat, fish, or fowl forcemeat. These are also to be found in Briggs' and Gelleroy's books, among many others. Soyer, in his *Gastronomic Regenerator,* advises 'the hors-d'œuvres, or flying dishes, to be handed round the table during the time the removes and entrées are placing upon it.'[27] Next to *Petits Pâtés* at the head of the sideboard list came the baron of beef, the double sirloin that, unlike the smaller removes that were carved at the tables, would have been served by waiters directly to the diners from the carver. After the removes, dessert was served, comprising fresh and preserved fruits with a selection of cakes including imposing Savoy cakes. The bill concludes with ices.[28] There is nothing written about the drinks that were served at the London banquet, either on the bill or in the reports. This suggests that a usual selection of drinks was available on request while decanters of *vin ordinaire* may have been set on the tables.

The 1850 London bill is longer and has more French-named dishes than appeared at more routine Mansion House banquets. In 1850 both the first course and the sideboard items were in French. French-named dishes were part of élite dining while paradoxically these co-existed with long-held chauvinist attitudes to French *haute cuisine*. In Eustache Ude's opinion, 'It [French] is necessary for French dishes, and particularly for making a bill of fare, to retain the French names of sauces &c. as the bill of fare of a grand dinner is always French.'[29]

On this occasion, instead of the usual 'Turtle and iced punch', the first items of the first course are *Tortue Clair* and *Tortue à l'Anglaise*. However, Soyer's York bill is uncompromisingly French. He was engaged for the occasion as a 'French cook' and the turtle soup he serves is *Tortue Transparente*.

Banquets were ranked in quantity and elaboration as were other celebratory meals illustrated in eighteenth- and nineteenth-century cookery books. These Lord Mayors' Mansion House banquets were similarly subtly graded in elaboration, as appropriate to the occasion and as part of a succession of feasts. Three lesser Mansion House banquets were held one and two years before the 1850 event: the Lord Mayor and Lady Mayoress's Easter banquet on 25 April 1848;[30] the Lord Mayor's banquet given on 15 June 1849,[31] and another on 25 July 1849.[32] At the same time many items were regularly offered by Ring and Brymer, even when allowing for seasonality. Those that appear on one or all of the 1848 and 1849 bills are underlined on the 1850 bill.[33] Regular banqueters, the City's great and good, were going to be served much that was familiar, even at this special Ring and Brymer event, described as of 'the most sumptuous order, fully sustaining the character of their establishment.'[34]

North and South: Two Banquets

In London the first course after the soup offers a range of fish including *Turbots Boullis à la Sauce du Homard*, more often billed as 'Turbot and lobster sauce', and the popular *Turbans de Filets de Soles*, a complex and elegant dish illustrated in *The Modern Cook*.[35] Fillets of sole are diagonally wrapped around forcemeat, covered with slices of bacon, and baked in a copper mould. The mould is turned out, the bacon removed, and a final garnish, such as mussels with a sauce round the turban's base, is added. It may not be possible to find out if the turbans were made as shown in *The Modern Cook* or followed Soyer's recipe in his *Gastronomic Regenerator*. Soyer's interpretation of this dish was simpler than Francatelli's. His fillets were masked with a sauce and surrounded with a border of potato.[36] This plain style was typical of Soyer's standard recipes.

Abram Hayward, a noted epicure and critic, admired Francatelli, and commented on the dinners that he had created at Chesterfield House as being 'the admiration of the gastronomic world of London'. He did not however, have the same regard for Soyer, noting that although his 'name has been a good deal before the public' and that 'he is a very clever man, of inventive genius and inexhaustible resource … his execution is hardly on a par with his conception.'[37]

The York banquet offered Soyer the opportunity to demonstrate his well-known talents as a cook of original gourmet dinners,[38] grand banquets,[39] and everyday bills for the Reform members' coffee-room.[40] As the most entrepreneurial of Victorian cooks, Soyer was in close accord with the innovative tastes of Reform Club members, and was therefore an ideal candidate to offer York his distinctive re-interpretations of tradition.

The *Illustrated London News* described the York banquet as 'very *recherché*'[41] – a favourite term applied at the time to exquisitely refined food, usually French or French-style. As a great self-publicist, Soyer was a ready subject for *Punch*'s puns and xenophobic remarks. Thus: 'Soup à la PRINCE OF WALES which we presume is an elegant little idea of SOYER'S who has given to hare soup the title of what he, in his foreign accent, might call the hare apparent.'[42] Soyer gives us two bills of fare:[43] one for the royal table and a general bill for the other guests.[44] Many items appear on both bills, and most of them are from his *Gastronomic Regenerator*.[45] Some of the recipes are re-named for the occasion, such as *Blancs de Volaille à la York Minster* which could have been any one of the seven recipes for *Blancs de Volaille* in the *Regenerator*. Soyer's York bill includes several other similarly re-titled dishes. Among these is *Salade de Grouse à la Soyer*. No Ring and Brymer anonymity for him.

Whereas the London banquet had a sideboard with both sweet and savoury dishes, the York banquet had only a side table of vegetables for those not at the royal table. None of the original bills printed for the occasion has survived, but they can be found in press reports and in *The Pantropheon*.

Soyer's final chapter of *The Pantropheon*,[46] entitled 'Modern Banquets', gives an account of the York banquet as an example of contemporary culinary improvement. His spectacular dish *L'Extravagance Culinaire à la Alderman*, especially created for the royal table, is illustrated to reveal its extraordinary structure and is accorded its later title *The*

Figure 2. The Hunded Guinea Dish, Illustrated London News, *2 November 1850.*

*One Hundred Guinea Dish,*⁴⁷ together with a list of the costly ingredients. Soyer was later to comment: 'The opportunity of producing some gastronomic phenomenon for the royal table on such an occasion as the York banquet was irresistible.'⁴⁸ Other spectacular items included *Chapon à la Nelson*, a capon embellished with a model ship's prow, and *Paon à l'ancienne Rome garni d'Ortolans*. In London there had also been peafowl among the roasts but not in ancient Roman style nor garnished with tiny ortolans.

Another surprise among the three relevés that preceded the dessert was a boar's head made of sponge-cake, decorated with chocolate icing, and filled with lemon cream ice. London's modest Decorated Trifles and Chantilly Baskets suggest something simpler than Soyer's relevés. This may be a misunderstanding. The city caterers Purssell illustrate their 1849 brochure⁴⁹ with an ornate Chantilly Basket and a trifle crowned with a pagoda. Ring and Brymer's shop was in the same street as Purssell, Cornhill, who offered similar items to those on Ring and Brymer's bills. Were these caterers rivals or is it possible that Purssell supplied these special items for the banquet?

North and South: Two Banquets

Figure 3. Decorated Trifle from Messrs Purssell's 1849 brochure (Museum of London).

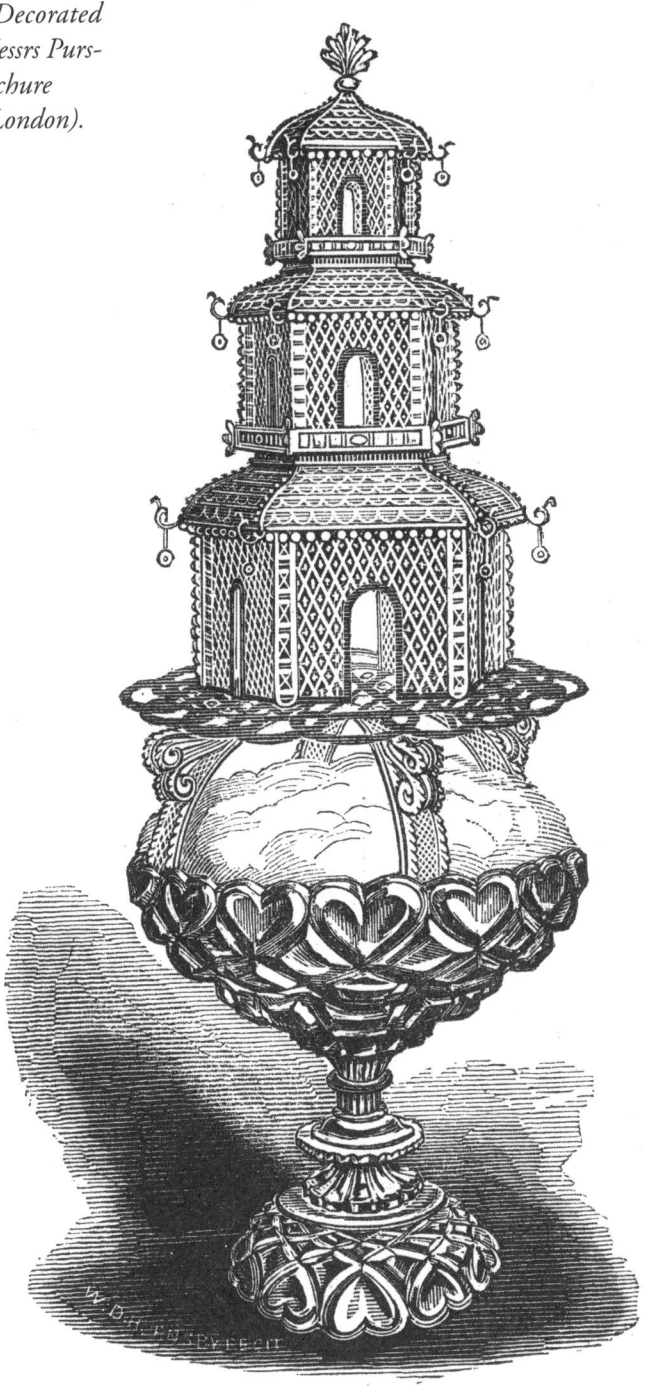

TRIFLE.

North and South: Two Banquets

Soyer also offered conventional dishes that accorded with more everyday tastes. He included his well-known *Cotelettes de Mouton à la Réforme*[50] among the entrées on the royal table. Soyer took this traditional English taste for mutton chops and added just enough elaboration to satisfy his club diners. Grilled or fried mutton cutlets were one of those basic bachelor foods that could be cooked over a room fire and were of course eaten in chop houses. Soyer gives these mutton chops a coating of finely-chopped ham and bread-crumbs, fries them, then dishes them with the usual potato border and *sauce à la Réforme*,[51] based on brown or *espagnol* sauce garnished with egg-whites, mushroom, gherkin and Indian pickle.[52]

All the bills of fare discussed in this paper included some simpler recipes and familiar roasts to please those who might not care for more complex dishes. As unity is an overriding theme of banquets, all must be satisfied.

Finale

These banquets certainly increased publicity for the Great Exhibition of 1851, although its eventual success was to be uncertain until Henry Cole, the great organizer, became involved. He had been at the Mansion House banquet, the first time he had dined there, describing it, 'As good as it can be.'[53]

Ring and Brymer continued to serve the City of London until the late 1980s when they were taken over by the Compass Group, which still operates. Soyer went on to offer Exhibition visitors his own spectacular themed restaurant at Gore House, called the Symposium. Unfortunately it lost money and had to close. Soyer, however, lived on as a great Victorian culinary entrepreneur both in contemporary print and in a succession of posthumous biographies.

These banquets, representing two constituencies, were able to express their distinct identities – not only in their décor and ceremony but particularly through their bills of fare. Those who were at both banquets could readily recognize the similarities that defined them as Lord Mayors' banquets while appreciating the differences expressed in their distinctive cuisines. Unity through banqueting offered the necessary collective support for Prince Albert's all-inclusive 'Exhibition of the Industry of All Nations'.

North and South: Two Banquets

APPENDIX I
Mansion House 21 March 1850

FIRST COURSE

TORTUE CLAIRE, TORTUE A L'ANGLAISE
TURBOTS BOUILLIS A LA SAUCE DE HOMARD
TURBANS DE FILETS DE SOLES, SAUMON DE GLOSTER BOULLIS
MACKEREL EN MATELOT, ANGUILLE AUX TOMATO
TRANCHES DE SAUMON A LA TARTARE, FRIED FISH
FILETS DE MERLANS A LA HORLEY

SIDE BOARD

PETITS PATÉS, BARON OF BEEF
FILLETS DE POULETS AU SUPREME, RIS DE VEAU A LA ST. CLOUD
HOMARDE A LA INDIENNE, FRICANDEAU DE VEAU
PIGEONS AUX CHAMPIGNONS, COTELETTES HOMARD
GRENADINES DE VEAU, TURBANS DE FILLETS LEPREAUX
CHICKENS, CAPONS, TURKEY POULTS LARDED
HAMS AND TONGUES ORNAMENTED, RIBS OF LAMB
RAISED ORNAMENTED PIES, LOBSTER SALADS, PRAWNS
CHANTILLY BASKETS, ORNAMENTED TRIFLES
PINE, STRAWBERRY, NOYEAU, RHENISH AND ITALIAN CREAMS
DANTZIG, NOYEAU AND MARASCHINO JELLIES
NOUGAT WITH CREAM, CHARLOTTE A LA RUSSE
GATEAU DE POMME, GATEAU A LA DUCHESSE
APPLE TARTS, FANCHONNETTES, BOUDIN ST. CLAIR
RASPBERRY, APRICOT AND GREEN GAGE TOURTES
HUNTING PUDDINGS, TRIFLES, CABINET PUDDINGS
NESSELRODE PUDDINGS, CREAMED TARTS

REMOVES

HAUNCHES MUTTON, CHINES MUTTON, SIRLOINS BEEF
QUARTERS LAMB, GUINEA FOWLS, DUCKLINGS
GOSLINGS, TURKEY POULTS, PEA FOWLS

DESSERT

PINES, GRAPES, ORANGES, APPLES, NUTS, DRIED FRUITS
PRESERVED GINGER, BRANDY AND CHERRIES
SAVOY CAKES, ALMOND CAKES, MIXED CAKES, WAFERS

ICES

PINE, MILLEFRUIT, RASPBERRY,
LEMON, GINGER, CHERRY, &C.

North and South: Two Banquets

APPENDIX II
Bill of Fare for the Royal Table

FIRST COURSE.

Trois Potages.
Potage à la Victoria.
Id. à la Prince of Wales.
Id. Tortue Transparente.

Trois Poissons
Turbot à la Mazarine.
Rougets à l'Italienne Blanche.
John Dory à la Marinière.

Trois Relevés.
L'Extravagance Culinaire à l'Alderman.
Chapons à la Nelson.
Quartier d'Agneau de Maison à la Sévigné.

Quatre Flancs.
Timballe de Riz à la Royale.
Jambon à la York.
Vol au vent à la Tallyrand.
Cannetons Canaris, Macédoine de Légumes.

Six Entrées.
Sauté de Faisans au fumet de Gibier.
Blancs de Volaille à la York Minster.
Turbans de Quenelles de Lapereaux aux Truffes.
Côtelettes de Mouton à la Réforme.
Riz de Veau à la Palestine.
Filets de Canneton à la Séville

SECOND COURSE.

Trois Rôtis.
Paon à l'ancienne Rome garni d'Ortolans.
Bécasses aux Feuilles de Céleri.
Guillenôts des Ardennes.

Dix Entremets.
Crême de la Grande Bretagne à la Victoria.
Galantine d'Oisons à la Volière.
Gelée de Fraises Françaises à la Fontainebleau.
Miroton de Homard.
Tartelettes pralinées aux cerises de Montmorency.
Crême de la Grande Bretagne à l'Albert.
Salade de Grouse à la Soyer.
Chartreuse de Fruits aux Pêches.
Gâteaux crêmants à la Duke of York.
Rocailles aux Huîtres gratinées à l'Ostend.

Trois Relevés.
Hure de Sanglier à l'Allemande en Surprise.
Jambon Croquant aux Abricots.
Paniér de Fruit glacé à la Lady Mayoress.

Dessert Floréal à la Watteau.
Raisins de Fontainebleau.
Fraises des bois Françaises.
Pêches de Montreuil.
Ananas.
Raisins Muscats.
Melons.
Bananas.
Compote de Chaumontelle.

North and South: Two Banquets

General Bill of Fare for 248 Guests

FIRST COURSE.

Trente-deux Potages.

Quatre Potages à la Victoria. Huit Potages à la Tortue Transparente.
Quatre Id. à la Prince of Wales. Seize Id. à la Moderne.

Trente-deux Poissons.

Huit Turbots à la Mazarin. Huit Filets de Merlans à la Crême.
Huit Truites Saumonées à la Marinière. Huit Crimp Cod aux Huîtres .

Trente-deux Relevés.

Six Chapons à la Nelson. Six Quartiers d'Agneau de Maison à la Sévigné.
Six Saddleback de Mouton Gallois. Quatre Aloyaux de Boeuf au Raifort.
Quatre Dindonneaux en Diadême. Six Haunches de Venaison.

Trente-deux Flancs.

Huit Jambons à la York. Huit Timballes de Riz à la Royale.
Huit Poulardes à la Russe. Huit Pâtés chaudes à la Westphalienne.

Quarante-huit Entrées.

Huit Sautés de Faisans au fumet de Gibier aux Truffes.
Huit de Côtelettes de Mouton à la Vicomtesse.
Huit Blancs de Volaille à la York Minster.
Huit de Riz de Veau à la Palestine.
Huit de Rissolettes de Volaille à la Pompadour.
Huit de Salmi de Gibier à la Chasseur.

SECOND COURSE.

Quarante Rôtis.

Huit de Perdreaux aux feuilles de Cêleri. Six de Grouses à l'Ecossaise.
Huit de Faisans bardés au Cresson. Six de Levreaux au jus de Groseilles.
Six de Cannetons au jus d'Oranges. Six de Bécasses et Bécassines au jus

Cent Entremets.

Dix Chartreuses de Pêches Dix Crevettes au Vin de Champagne.
Dix Gelées de Fraises Françaises à la Fontainebleau. Dix Gâteaux crêmants à la Duke of York.
Dix Petites Macédoines de fruit cristallisé Dix Salades de Grouses à la Soyer.
Dix Mirotons de Homard aux Olives. Dix Galantines Aspiquées à la Volière.
Dix Tartelettes pralinées aux Cerises de Montmorency. Dix Crêmes transparentes au Kirchenwaser.

Vingt Relevés.

Dix paniérs de Fruits Glacés à la Lady Mayoress.
Dix Jambons en Surprise à l'Ananas

Side Table – Vegetables.

Cêleri à la Crême. Cêleri à la Crême.
Choux Fleurs au beurre. Choux Fleurs au beurre.
Haricots Verts. Sea Kale.
Choux de Bruxelles. Choux de Bruxelles.

Grand Dessert Floréal à la Watteau.

North and South: Two Banquets

Notes

1. Later known as 'The Great Exhibition'.
2. The *Illustrated London News* uses 'bills of fare', although 'carte' and 'menu' are both cited before 1850 in the *Oxford English Dictionary*. See Appendices I and II for complete bills of fare.
3. Thomas Farncomb, Lord Mayor of London, 1849–50.
4. George Hicks Seymour, Lord Mayor of York, 1849–50.
5. The Mansion House, completed by 1754, is the official residence of the City of London's Lord Mayors, Jeffery (1993) p. 99.
6. *The Times*, 22 March 1850 and 26 October 1850. *Illustrated London News*, 23 March 1850 and 2 November 1850. Also local papers.
7. To which they were asked to send an immediate reply so they could be sent an admission ticket, the tickets to be checked and given in as they arrived. The invitation could then be kept as a souvenir.
8. *Punch*, vol. xviii, January to June 1850, p. 123. The following year Prince Albert's speech was published in several languages for the benefit of Exhibition visitors.
9. This was not the final design. By the time of the York banquet, Paxton's Crystal Palace was under construction. *Illustrated London News*, p. 350.
10. The Reform Club was founded at 104 Pall Mall in 1836, after the Reform Act of 1832.
11. Royal Agricultural Society of England's meeting at York, banquet 12 July 1848. *Illustrated London News*, 15 July 1848.
12. *The Times*, 26 October 1850.
13. Gas gives a brighter, harsher light than candles or oil lamps.
14. A Lord Mayor's feast from 1761 includes olio turtle pottages and roast venison. Reproduced in a commemorative booklet produced by Ring and Brymer in 1921, William Gelleroy's banquet that Sir Samuel Fludyer Bt. gave for the King and royal family at the Guildhall on Lord Mayor's Day the same year has no turtle. Both of these banquets have roast venison. Guildhall banquets were not comparable with Mansion House banquets. See the 1850 bill for the new Lord Mayor's banquet. There is a copy in the bar of Le Gavroche, London W1.
15. From the middle of the eighteenth century, West Indian green turtles had been imported live across the Atlantic. Lehmann (2003) describes turtle as 'the key dish of grand English cuisine in the second half of the eighteenth century', p. 258.
16. Brears (1987) notes roast beef and plum pudding were often part of celebratory feasts during the first half of the nineteenth century. He quotes John Yewdale's account of a Leeds clothier's coronation feast for his family and workers: 'The table was made, upon which were laid, | Twenty four plum puddings compact; | Roast beef and good beer, that old English cheer, | Were placed in their order exact.' p. 155.
17. William Hogarth, *O the Roast Beef of Old England (The Gate of Calais)*, 1748, oil on canvas, Tate Britain, N01464.
18. *The Roast Beef of Old England*, a patriotic ballad by Henry Fielding, first performed in 1731.
19. Samuel Birch (1787–1840). Birch's business, at No. 15 Cornhill. was celebrated for supplying turtle soup.
20. Recipes that were not necessarily exclusive to these books but by being included it suggests they were popular with City men.
21. Gelleroy (1762). William Gelleroy was cook to Sir Samuel Fludyer, Lord Mayor, 1761. Details of this Guildhall banquet are included in his book. See Lucraft (1992) pp. 7–24, and Lucraft (1993) pp. 34–46.
22. Briggs (1788). Richard Briggs was the cook at the Temple Coffee House.
23. The appropriately titled *The London Art of Cookery*, (1st edn 1783), is attributed to John Farley, cook at the London Tavern, but research in *Petits Propos Culinaires* ascribes it to the publisher and not the cook. See Lucraft (1992) pp. 7–24, and Lucraft (1993) pp. 34–46.
24. *Dictionary of National Biography* (1889) p. 163.

25. Ude (1841) p 287.
26. Ibid., p. 282.
27. Alexis Soyer (1846) p. xii.
28. Ring and Brymer appear to serve the same selection of ices. See Appendix I.
29. Ude, op. cit., p. 41.
30. *The Times*, 26 April 1848, p. 5.
31. Mansion House bill, Museum of London, Acc. No. 37, 146/20.
32. Mansion House bill, from Andrew Black's private collection.
33. See Appendix I.
34. *The Times*.
35. Francatelli, op. cit., No. 802, 'Turban of Fillets of Soles à la Ximenes', pp. 242–3.
36. Soyer (1846) p. xxiv. Soyer gives exact instructions for making this mashed potato with butter, salt and milk, and rolling the resulting paste in a cloth 'to the circumference of a fourpenny or sixpenny piece', to form a border for an entrée.
37. Hayward (1852) pp. 75–77.
38. Voland & Warren (1859), 'Diner à la Sampayo', pp. 92–95.
39. Ibid. 'Dinner for 150 given by members of the Reform Club to Ibraham Pacha, 3 July 1846', pp. 87–89.
40. The coffee-room offered daily meals to members. There were also complaints which members entered in a book.
41. *Illustrated London News*, 1850, p. 350.
42. *Punch*, vol. xix, July to December 1850, p. 191.
43. See Appendix II.
44. Soyer (1853) p. 406. The main body was by Albert Duhart-Fauvet not Soyer. Only the last chapter, 'Modern Banquets' is Soyer's. Bills of fare and descriptions, pp. 401–7. See McKirdy (1988) pp. 18–21
45. Soyer (1846).
46. Soyer, (and Duhart-Fauvet, 1853) p. 406.
47. Ibid.
48. Ibid.
49. Messers Purssell (1849).
50. Soyer (1846) op. cit., No. 698, pp. 294–5.
51. Ibid. No. 1299, 'Hure de Sanglier glacé en surprise', pp. 549–50.
52. Ibid. No. 35, p. 17.
53. *Henry Cole's Diary*, 21 March 1850.

Bibliography

Peter Brears, *Traditional Food in Yorkshire* (Edinburgh: John Donald, 1987).
Richard Briggs, *The English Art of Cookery* (London: G. G. and J. Robinson, 1788).
Henry Cole's Diary (Nat. Art Lib. 45.c, 112, 1850).
Dictionary of National Biography, ed. by Leslie Stephen, Vol. XX (Smith Elder & Co., 1889).
Charles Elmé Francatelli, *The Modern Cook: a practical guide to the culinary art in all its branches* (London: Richard Bentley, first published 1846).
William Gelleroy, *The London Cook* (London: S. Crowder & Co., 1762).
Abraham Hayward QC, *The Art of Dining, or Gastronomy and Gastronomers* (London: John Murray, first published 1853, this edn 1883).
Illustrated London News, 15 July 1848, 23 March 1850, 2 November 1850.
Gilly Lehmann, *The British Housewife, Cookery Books, Cooking and Society in Eighteenth-Century Britain* (Totnes, Devon: Prospect Books, 2003).
The London Art of Cookery, attrib. John Farley (London: Scatcherm and Letterman, 1783).
Fiona Lucraft, 'The London Art of Plagiarism, Part One', *Petits Propos Culinaires* 42 (December 1992) pp. 7–24.
Fiona Lucraft, 'The London Art of Plagiarism, Part Two', *Petits Propos Culinaires* 43 (May 1993) pp. 34–46.
Michael McKirdy, 'Who Wrote Soyer's *Pantropheon*?', *Petits Propos Culinaires* 29 (July 1988) pp. 18–21.
The Modern Method of Regulating and Forming a Table, by several eminent cooks and others acquainted with the art (London: J. Hughes and S. Crowder, 1760).
Punch, vol. xviii, January to June 1850.
Messrs Purssell, Biscuit Bakers for Families or Exportation, Cooks, Confectioners and Contractors for Dinners, Wedding Breakfasts, Ball Suppers or Fetes of Any Kind. 50, Cornhill, London. October 1849, Museum of London, Acc. No. Z2996.
Ring and Brymer, commemorative booklet produced in 1921.
Alexis Soyer, *The Gastronomic Regenerator* (London: Simpkin, Marshall & Co., 1st edn 1846, 4th edn 1849).
Alexis Soyer, *The Pantropheon: the History of Food and its Preparation in Ancient Times* (London: Simpkin Marshall, 1853; facsimile London: Paddington Press Ltd, 1977).
The Times, 22 March 1850 and 26 October 1850.
Louis Eustache Ude, *The French Cook: a system of fashionable, practical and economical cookery* (London: Ebers and Co., 1841).
F. Volant and J. R. Warren, *Memoirs of Alexis Soyer* (London: W. Kent & Co., 1859; this facsimile edn Rottingdean, Sussex: Cooks Books, 1985).

Dining with the Drapers: The Drapers' Company 1564 Election Day Feast as a Map of Elizabethan London

Sarah Ann Milne

If the London Livery Companies take us straight to the heart of the metropolis, then feasts are a fast-track to the core of the company. A close reading of these feasts affords unprecedented access to one of London's most powerful livery companies at a crucial point in the city's history. Re-mapping the city of London through the feasts of the Drapers' Company, this paper will be driven by the exceptionally detailed and unstudied 'Dinner Book', which presents the only coherent accounts of feasting in the city for the Elizabethan period.

Plunging into the largely unexamined archives, one particular feast in 1564 will act as the focus for an interrogation of how the ever-advancing scholarship of Tudor food history and established theories of the social production of space meet within the context of the city.

Having transcribed the carefully notated records of the 1564 feast found in the dinner book, significant weight will be ascribed to this empirical material. And while the scope of the wider project is defined by the extent of the feast as an entirety, this paper will focus on specific episodes buried within the text. Navigating through key themes of feasting, the Livery Company, and the city, this paper will place evidence from the dinner book at the centre of its discourse, employing other archival material where appropriate to investigate implications and claims embedded within the dinner book's pages.

Introduction

'The Master and Wardens and Brethren and Sisters of the Guild or Fraternity of the Blessed Virgin Mary of the Mystery of the Drapers of the City of London'[1] was granted its formal charter in 1364 – although it had existed since 1180. As early as the twelfth century, craft 'guilds' began to form in London.[2] Members became known as liverymen due to their colourful and distinctive uniform. Initially united by their common trade, the guilds quickly became multi-faceted organizations with interlinked aims and fulfilling a wide variety of purposes. Their most visible function was the close monitoring of economic activity; guilds inspected and controlled the working conditions of apprentices, assessed quality and regulated prices, with the power to discipline any found practising in violation of the codes of the city.[3] The monarch granted each company a generally fluid position in the 'order of precedence'. However, by the advent of the sixteenth century the arrangement was fixed, and twelve companies had become recognized as the 'Great' companies as a rough result of their power, wealth and age. The Drapers' Company is third in order of precedence, a position of distinct prestige within the city.

For every guild the annual celebration of the patronal feast day was the event that, above all, gave it visible definition. A carefully constructed mesh of identities, ideologies, memories, and tastes, the banquet offers a fast-track route to the heart of the guild. The feast is a tangible expression to outsiders of the companionship apparently inherent in the guild and a means of reinforcing rituals of submission and hierarchy from within. The act of dining together, as in the familial setting, is a strong symbol of a united body. A close reading of these feasts offers unique access to one of London's most powerful livery companies at a crucial point in the city's history. Allowing food presented at the table to sit within a broader context of the city, this paper will draw upon the feast as a basis for a wider consideration of the guild's role and relationship to the city.

The dinner book

Owing to its more extensive resources, the Drapers keep their own archive, separate from that in the Guildhall Library where most companies have deposited theirs. The Drapers' Hall is located on Throgmorton Street, a stone's throw from the Bank of England, and is the base for all guild activities and functions. The corporate archives include the charters (1364) and grant of arms (1439), the minutes of the court (1515–), accounts (1475–), and membership records from a later date, as well as extensive documents and drawings relating to the Drapers' property and estates throughout Great Britain and Ireland.

Within the archive a special place is reserved for DB1, referred to as the 'Dinner Book' as if no others existed. And indeed this particular document is unique in its age, breadth, consistency and detail. It records the cost, content, and management of the annual election feast and quarter day dinners for the period 1564–1602. The book is unique not only within the Drapers' Company but in London as a whole. For while other companies, such as the Fishmongers', similarly possess many colourful menus from the eighteenth and nineteenth centuries, as far as can be known no other company possesses a document quite like the dinner book.

The book has no title page and there is no explanation as to the purpose of its contents, or whether it is one volume in a longer series. It appears some information regarding company feasts had been gathered and noted in the court minutes in an ad hoc manner up until this time. If it were to have been part of an older series, this volume's particular survival is even more curious. The Great Fire of London in 1666 proved devastating for the city as a whole, and among the widespread destruction of homes and businesses many livery halls were burned down, including the Drapers' Hall on Throgmorton Street. Not a tremendous amount survived from the original building, although clearly efforts were made to protect the company records. The dinner book itself would have been 100 years old at the time of its rescue.

Dining with the Drapers

Due to the exacting nature of the costs and payments of servants and products, it is impossible for the records to have been completed beforehand. The dinner book would never have been a working document. Interestingly, the Drapers' Company archivist notes that there would have been no real need, from an administrative point of view, for keeping such a record of feasts after the fact. Did it begin as a labour of love for one clerk? Or was it requested as a reference for the planning of future feasts by the court? Either way, the dinner book's comprehensibility is remarkable – correlating all the constituent parts for forty years of feasting in this one place. It contains information concerning what food was purchased from whom, how it was presented, to which table, in what order, who guarded it, cooked it, served it, how much of it was eaten, what happened to the leftovers, how much the brooms for sweeping the floor cost, how many padlocks were purchased and so on, supporting all this with the separate items of account.

It is possible to argue that these particular feasts could only happen in this particular context, at this particular time, because of a certain amount of communication, trade and access. In this way the city can be seen in full flow of its operation, not as a static object, but a living organism of habitations, relationships, and exchanges.

The feast of 1564

Held to enable the election and appointment of the next year's officers, three dinners were provided on three consecutive days. However, relatively modest meals were consumed in the run up to the feast, designed not to spoil members' appetites for the great feast itself. The dinner book gives an especially elaborate account of the election day feast, in August 1564, given for 89 guests. The total expense for the three-day event – Sunday, Monday, and Tuesday – came to £82–9s.–4d. This would be the equivalent, at today's values, of £15,236.17.[4]

In contrast to the contemporary royal feasts in palaces such as Hampton Court and Westminster, which could be uprooted from their context with relative ease, the Livery Company feast was linked inextricably to the unique economic environs of the city in which it was held, and the Drapers' Hall embedded within the city. The intimate connection between the fortunes of the Guild and that of the London economy can be seen in the late 1570s when a succession of bad harvests affected the feasts, to the extent that there was indeed no feast to be had.

Much can be made of the trade links through members of the Company (foods from afar are plentiful on the table), however this paper will not examine these in detail. Let us instead briefly examine one example: a key ceremonial drink named 'ypocras'. The variety and quantity of spices from the East used in ypocras, such as musk, pepper, and cardamom, designated it as a drink of the upper classes only. Only Londoners with access to such international trade would be able to enjoy such a privilege.

Not only was the symbiotic relationship between the city's economy and the Guild made visible at the feast table, but on the election day itself the Guild liveryman could be seen parading through the city in their finery to the sound of ringing bells from St Michael's Cornhill (payment scrupulously recorded in the dinner book); a powerful symbol of a united body. In very good years, the brightly coloured and fur-trimmed gowns would have been given an extra vibrant upgrade, and in bad years, the city would lack this promenade of colour altogether. Immediately after promenading back and forth to the church on election day, the Company filtered into the Hall and the annual banquet got underway.[5]

Beauty and the beast

The sheer energy embodied in creating this magnificent feast is laudable, and the records of 1564 point to a definite struggle to ensure the feast offered an evening of some beauty amid the intensity and grime of everyday life in the city. In 1550 London's population, still confined largely within the medieval city walls, was approximately 120,000. By 1600 this had grown to 200,000.[6] The city was becoming increasingly characterized by a swelling population and exponential commercial growth, experiencing the growing pains of modernity. Nevertheless, spatially, the city walls still bound a metropolis of over 200,000 into the area of only a large village.

While the tentacles of London stretched ever deeper into the countryside, in the city retailers were increasing in number to cope with demand. In 1550, for example, there were 89 butchers. By 1599 this number had grown to 113.[7] The spatial effects of increased food distribution within the city walls also can be seen in the steady increase of grocers in London, rising between 1550 and 1599 from 280 to 377.[8] Space was at a premium. Not only was there demand for more housing but commercial and retail entities also were left wanting. Pressure on commercial premises led the butchers on Eastcheap to encroach on the street in front, first building roofs over their stalls, then upgrading those to larger sheds, finally building houses on those sites.[9] The city was becoming further condensed and spaces miniaturized.

And yet, Orlin observes, 'Company halls, equally implicated in the competitions of self-representation and status, were media through which innovation was transmitted to the large populations of their merchants, traders, craftsmen, and apprentices.'[10] With no plans of the Drapers' Hall from this period in existence,[11] it is possible to use the evidence in the dinner book to inform our understanding of the prestigious setting in which this feast took place, for the court knew that the corporate space of the Drapers' Company was a powerful tool in a condensed city.

Beginning with candles from the chandler, almost 7 metres of candles are accounted for, over and above everyday purchases. However, a further £2 worth of candles are noted in extraordinary charges, being supplied through other tradesmen. This is significant – for functional eating dictated the main meal of day should be eaten in the light at midday, although some historians report that those with more fashionable aspirations were beginning to dine later and later.[12] The ability to provide for artificial light (through candles) was a sign of prestige and wealth. Meals of this sort would begin around 3 p.m., in context, quite late and, with the sun going down at 6 p.m., no doubt much of the feast was conducted in the warm glow of candlelight.

Without a doubt the feast would have taken place in the largest room of the company house, aptly named the great hall. Although the exact size and dimensions of this grand apartment are not known, it can be estimated through a reading of the size and number of its tables, and the guests who dined at them. With three tables and eighty-nine guests, it surely deserved its imposing name. If we afford each guest 2.4 square metres of space, the hall must have been, at the very least, 212.4 square metres in extent, approximately the size of a tennis court.[13] Modern ears might dismiss this as a rather pokey room for the splendour which was on show within, and yet, it must be remembered that Tudor London was an extremely confined environment. Large interior spaces were rare, so no doubt the Drapers' Hall was indeed 'great' at the time.

Judging from other accounts, the hall must have been set up to maintain the exclusivity of the high or cross table on the *haut pas*, then the 'second table' or tables would have been located in the centre of the hall, and below them a final table for those further down the pecking order.[14] The top table was principally reserved for members of the court and notable guests of high standing, while the second table was more often furnished with the senior livery, their wives, and other guests. Orlin speculates that the table with the most important guests, in this instance the high table, would have been placed significantly adjacent to the cupboard or buffet. A key piece of Tudor furniture, the cupboard was used to house and show off silver and silver-gilt plate.[15]

A concern for all scales of representation can be found in the dinner book, from the display and presentation of high-status foods, to the service of the same and dressing of the hall itself. For those members of the livery that did not warrant an invitation there was always the opportunity to show their face as waiters on tables, for even at this superficially low level the livery hall was the place to see and be seen. The 1564 feast describes how 24 of the 'best & comely of that could be founde and best apparelled' bachelors were selected to wait on the tables. Further selection was made from this pool by the Master Bachelor to attend to the high table; evidently appearance was important for even the waiters were considered part of the corporate image. These yeoman waiters were effectively joining the 'waiting-list' for an invitation to the main event, fraternizing with some of the most influential Londoners of the day.

The presentation of the dishes seems to have occurred in procession-like fashion with the lead dish consisting of 18 stuffed ornamental swans from the Thames. Another clearly theatrical moment can be found with the possible enclosure of live birds within pastry coffins. The accounts for the 1564 feast record fifteen pigeons. The birds were the preserve of the rich, being kept tame in dovecotes on country estates.[16] And yet, at this feast, the pigeons were only served to the lower tables of the lavish hall! Elizabethan cookery text abound with such conceits, hence the old rhyme 'four and twenty-black birds, baked in a pie'.

Again, it would have been a breath-taking moment when the decorative marchepanes (essentially marzipan confections) appeared, fashioned into all manners of shapes, colours and sizes, named 'sotelties'. The Drapers probably stipulated particular designs and colours, perhaps relating to company imagery. In 1570 the dinner book details a wax chandler commissioned to make 'three standing dishes': a model of a boars head, the helm and crest of the company, and the arms of it.

With the vast array of dishes it seems remarkable that only nine workers are noted in the kitchen; the master cook Stephen Treacle had under him lesser cooks, scullions and 'tourne-brouchers' (small boys employed to take on the labour-intensive job of turning the spit(s)). The 18 swans eaten at the feast probably roamed the internal courtyard or garden of the Hall before being killed, as payment for oats to feed them is found in the accounts. After being slaughtered messily by the cooks, their rejected parts were probably flung onto Throgmorton Street. The dinner book documents a large amount of breakages in the kitchen: 21 out of 24 'green' pots, 7 out of 24 pottle pots, 8 gallon pots out of 24 and 1 pan out of 6, painting a lively picture of a working kitchen full of activity and no doubt extremely warm!

The distribution of pasties

The dinner book also holds details regarding events after the feast. Amusingly, an entire chapter of the documentation of the 1564 feast is devoted to the creation and distribution of venison pasties from the leftover meats. The disbursement of these to families, small businesses, and neighbours is an example of the wide-ranging Drapers' patronage networks, which spread throughout the Elizabethan metropolis. The episode illuminates the role of food in the process of exchange within the city at large, showing the Drapers' relationship with the all levels of city society to be both intimate and readable at street-level.

Caught outside the city walls, wild game was considered the height of luxury. As a display of prestige and wealth, nothing was more impressive than a table full of game. In addition to wild boar, the 1564 feast relied heavily upon venison, coming from that of bucks (male deer) that would have been presented by members of the Guild. At the time, bucks, along with swans, appear to have been used almost as currency within livery companies. For example, the Carpenters had two tenants who paid partly in money and partly on the promise of a buck to be delivered 'on the next dinner day'.[17] The dinner book notes that Peter Smyth and 'Clyff' provided four swans between them, this being noted next the quarterage totals, suggesting the provision might have been a gift in place of monetary payment. Only considered fit for consumption in the most lavish circumstances, swans were the ultimate indicator of prestige; all unclaimed swans being owned by the Queen.

Food was clearly viewed as an exchangeable commodity. A tradition in place since much earlier times, hunting gifts were frequently given in order to cement social relationships between individuals. Bucks in particular were traded as a precious commodity, sometimes being given to the Company in lieu of monetary redemption, payment for tenancy, or in return for a favour. The brunt of the provision of such animals for the feast, however, was shouldered by the Wardens, who coordinated the event. Although it is difficult to unpick the precise background of the other gifts from specific individuals, it is clear an intricate system of exchange based on close networks of people was in action. The three biggest players in attendance at the feast, the Lord Mayor, Sir William Chester and Sir Richard Champion, each gave a token buck towards the feast, perhaps as an act of goodwill, conveying their patronage on the Company. Altogether 40 bucks were collected. Liverymen at the three noted feasting tables were then apportioned a carefully considered amount of the meat in accordance with their standing in the Company. However, despite leftovers from Monday's feast being served again on Tuesday, enough meat was left over to produce 168 pasties; the election day was obviously hugely over-catered. One especially illuminating incident carefully recorded from the 1564 feast is the laughable allocation of every single one of these pasties to the wider community. The loss of these individual pasties was clearly a matter of concern for the clerk; perhaps he had a particular penchant for venison pasties and bemoaned his own rather measly allocation of a single pasty.

One of the perks of holding the position of Warden was the prerogative to distribute such pasties. It seems, aside from feeding themselves and other servants the wardens repaid favours or rewarded particularly hard workers. However, more obviously, their wives, families, and neighbours appear to have been first in line to receive the pasty gifts, perhaps in lieu of a place at the dinner table itself or for putting up with the disruption planning such an event must have inevitably caused. It is unlikely that those unable to attend through infirmity were forgotten either, as later there is mention of 'Brawne sliced, a boyled Capon, a rost capon, a pastrie of venison of a syde, a swanne, a pye of goose giblette, a custard, a tarte, ffrenche wynne and claret of each a gallon' being sent to Lord George, specially delivered by a 'handsom' bachelor.

Also widely rewarded for their services were the small businesses who supplied the feast: the poulterer, chandler, baker and brewers being given one pasty each. As previously noted, such suppliers were often referred to as 'ower' baker and 'ower' butcher throughout the text. Clearly the Drapers had built up good relationships with those they came into contact with, bestowing their patronage on the same. The livery companies often also patronized their local inn, regularly holding 'search dinners' there, and several pasties were gifted in 1564 to the 'Bisshopes Headd' by Mr Mynors. Stowe notes this tavern could be found on Lombard street, a street full of merchants from 'divers nations' and in an area predominantly 'possessed by rich drapers'.[18] Members of similar trades gathered together on London streets, areas being characterized by the commerce they accommodated.

It had by this time become tradition for paupers to loiter by the hall gates in the realistic hope that they might receive remnants from the feast or kitchen leftovers. Indeed fifteen pastries were kindly donated 'to the Neighbours afore our gate'. However it seems there was a more formalized process of distribution to the poor already in place, the purchase of onions 'to make porridge for poore folks' being noted earlier. This was not a one-off display of charity; the warden's accounts of 1566, 1569, and 1571 relate the regular giving of such gifts, roasted beef and venison pasties often being distributed the following day.[19] The delivery of these miniature embodiments of the feast would surely have been amusing, carts overflowing with pasties slowly making their way around the city streets pushed by harassed porters. Before the feast the transport of food from the dock and markets reminds us how closely the physical space in London has always been tied to commerce; it appears no different with the disposal of leftover meat after the act either.

Conclusion

It is possible to look at neither Guild nor London in isolation from the each other. In this way, just as London cannot be seen as a static entity, the Guild must not be seen as stagnant. The dinner book presents a snapshot of the Guild in motion, a dynamic organization differing from year to year. A feast in 1518 would have differed from the one in 1564, which again would have differed from that held in 1580. One consistent aspect of the feast, however, can be identified in show of wealth and power of the fraternity. The dinner book illuminates the extent to which the Guild was essentially the sixteenth-century equivalent of a major City corporation flexing its muscles. From the size of the great hall to the use of expensive candles and spices from the East, on many levels the Guild was using the feast to demonstrate its position as third-ranking guild in the city. The showy nature of the feast can also be read in the presentation of marzipans, chandler-sculptures, game and pigeons at the table. The grandeur of the feast is abundantly clear – something which is in stark contrast to the unassuming dinner book with no title page.

Although the dinner book, through the 1564 feast, offers the reader valuable insight into the city as a living organism, there is still much to be done to fully understand the forces at work shaping its transformation. A transcription and examination of a series of the feasts presented in the dinner book would perhaps reveal further the extent of trade routes, and facilitate greater access into arguments regarding social mobility. However, not only would the performative space of the feast vary from year to year, but from guild to guild and city to city. By looking at the feast in this way, food takes us right to the heart of the metropolis.

Notes

1. M. Brentnall, *The Old Customs and Ceremonies of London* (London: B. T. Batsford Ltd, 1975), p. 31.
2. B. Weinreb and C. Hibbert, p. 161
3. Ibid., p. 161.
4. National Archives, 'Currency Converter': http://www.nationalarchives.gov.uk/currency/default0.asp#mid.
5. 'Ordinances and Oaths of Officers and Freemen 1541–1560', as quoted in Johnson, *HWCDL*, Vol. II, p. 284
6. A.L. Beier and R.Finlay, p. 37.
7. L. Picard, *Elizabeth's London* (London: Phoenix, 2004), p. 167.
8. Ibid., p. 170
9. C. Hibbert, *London: the Biography of a City* (London: Longmans, 1969), p. 38.
10. Orlin, *LPTL*, p. 112.
11. Except a 1620 plan of the Hall.
12. Orlin, *LPTL*, p. 31.
13. G. John and K. Campbell, *Handbook of Sports and Recreational Building Design* (London: Architectural Press, 1996), p. 102.
14. W. Herbert, *The History of the Twelve Great Livery Companies of London*, Vol. I (Published by the author, 1837), p. 465.
15. E. Ehrman, H. Forsyth, and J. Pearce, p. 19.
16. Thirsk, *FEME*, p. 28.
17. M. Bower, ed., *Records of the Worshipful Company of Carpenters* (Oxford, 1915) as quoted in Picard, *EL*, p. 181.
18. J. Stow, *Survey of London* (1603), ed. C. Kingsforde (Oxford: Clarendon Press, 1908), p. 171.
19. Drapers' Warden's Accounts, 1566, 1569, 1571.

Bibliography

Ackroyd, P., 2001: *London: The Biography* (London: Vintage).
Ackroyd, P., 2007: *Thames: Sacred River* (London: Chatto and Windus).
Archer, I., 2003: *The Pursuit of Stability: Social Relations in Elizabethan London* (Cambridge: Cambridge University Press).
Barron, C., Coleman, C., Gobbi, C. (eds.), 'The London Journal of Alessandro Magno 1562', *The London Journal*, vol. 9, no.2, (1983).
Beier, A.L., Finlay, R. (eds.), 1986: *The Making of the Metropolis, London 1500–1700* (London: Longman).
Brears, P., Black, M., Corbishley, G., Renfrew, J., Shead, J., 1993: *A Taste History: 10,000 Years of Food in Britain* (London: British Museum Press).
Brentnall, M., 1975: *The Old Customs and Ceremonies of London* (London: B. T. Batsford Ltd)
Brigden, S., 1989: *London and the Reformation* (New York: Clarendon Press).
Certeau, M. De, 1984: *The Practice of Everyday Life* (Berkeley: University of California Press).
Chamberland, C., 2009: *Honor, Brotherhood, and the Corporate Ethos of London's Barber-Surgeons' Company, 1570–1640* (Oxford: Oxford University Press).
Davies, M., (ed.), 2000: *The Merchant Taylors' Company of London: Court Minutes 1486–1493* (Lincolnshire: Richard III and Yorkist History Trust).
Dodd, G., 1856: *The Food of London* (Longmans).
Ehrman, E., Forsyth, H., Pearce, J., 2003: *London Eats Out 1500–2000: 500 Years of Capital Dining* (London: Philip Watson).
Epstein, S.R., Prak, M. 2008: *Guilds, Innovation and the European Economy 1400–1800* (Cambridge: Cambridge University Press).
Fisher, F.T., 1935: 'The Development of the London Food Market', *Economic Hist. Rev.*, vol. 5, No. 2.

Giard, L (ed.) 1998: *The Practice of Everyday Life*, vol. 2 (Minneapolis: University of Minnesota Press).
Hanson, M., 1969: *2000 Years of London: an Illustrated Survey* (Country Life).
Harrison, W., 1877: *Description of England*, (ed.) Furnivall, J. (London: F.J. Early English Text Society).
Heal, F., 1990: *Hospitality in Early Modern England* (Oxford: Claredon Press)
Herbert, W., 1837: *The History of the Twelve Great Livery Companies of London*, vol I (London).
Hibbert, C., 1969: *London: the Biography of a City* (London: Longmans).
Hickman, D., 1999: 'Religious Belief and Pious Practice among London's Elizabethan Élite', *Historical Journal*, vol. 42, no. 4, p. 941–960.
Home, G., 1927: *Medieval London* (E.Benn).
Hope, V., Birch, C., Torry, G., 1982: *The Freedom: the Past and Present of the Livery, Guilds and City of London* (London: Barracuda Books).
Horowitz, J., Singley, P., (eds) 2004: *Eating Architecture* (Cambridge, Mass.: MIT Press).
Howes, E., (ed.), 1615: *Stowe's Annals* (London).
Inwood, S., 1998: *A History of London* (London: Macmillian).
James, M., 'English Politics and the Concept of Honour, 1485–1642,' *Past & Present*, supplement no.3, (1978) p. 1–92.
John, G., Campbell, K., 1996: *Handbook of Sports and Recreational Building Design* (Architectural Press).
Johnson, A. H., 1922: *The History of the Worshipful Company of the Drapers of London* (Clarendon Press).
Jordan, W.K., 1960: *The Charities of London 1480–1666* (London).
Lang, J. 1975: *Pride Without Prejudice, The Story of London' Guilds and Livery Companies* (Perpetua Press).
Orlin, L. C., 2007: *Locating Privacy in Tudor London* (Oxford: Oxford University Press).
Paston-Williams, 1993: *The Art of Dining, A History of Cooking & Eating* (London: National Trust).
Pearce, A., 1929: *History of the Butcher's Company* (London).
Pepys, S., 1898: *The Diary of Samuel Pepys* (London: Macmillan & Co).
Picard, L., 2004: *Elizabeth's London* (London: Phoenix).
Platter, T., 1970: 'A Swiss Tourist in London' (1599), in Brooke, T., *Shakespeare of Stratford: a Handbook for Students* (London: Ayer Publishing).
Rappaport, S., 1987: *Worlds Within Worlds: Structures of Life in Seventeenth-Century London* (Cambridge: Cambridge University Press).
Rendell, J., 2002: *The Pursuit of Pleasure: Gender, Space and Architecture in Regency London* (London: Continuum).
Schofield, J., 1984: *The Building of London: From the Conquest to the Great Fire* (London: British Museum).
Schofield, J., 1987: *The London Surveys of Ralph Treswell* (London: London Topographical Society).
Sheppard, F., 2000: *London: A History* (Oxford University Press).
Simmel, G., 1994: 'The Sociology of the Meal' (1910), Symons, M. (trans.), *Food and Foodways*, Vol. 5, No.e, pp. 345–50.
Skeel, C.J., 1926: 'The Cattle Trade between Wales and England from the Fifteenth to the Nineteenth Century', *Trans. R. His. Soc.* (series iv, vol. ix).
Steel, C., 2008: *Hungry City How Food Shapes Our Lives* (London: Chatto & Windus).
Stow, J., 1908: *Survey of London* (1603), Kingsforde, C., (ed.) (Oxford: Clarendon Press).
Thirsk, J., 2007: *Food in Early Modern England* (London: Continuum Academic publishing).
Unwin, G. 1908: *The Gilds and Companies of London* (London: Frank Cass).
Ward, J. 1997: *Metropolitan Communities: Trade Guilds, Identity, and Change in Early Modern London* (Stanford: Stanford University Press).
Weinreb, B., Hibbert, C., 1983: *The London Encyclopaedia* (London: Macmillan).
Whittingham, C., 1839: (ed.), 1568, *Institution of a Gentleman* (Cambridge: Cambridge University Press).
Wilson, C.A., 1991: *Food and Drink in Britain from the Stone Age to the 19th Century* (Chicago: Academy).
The Worshipful Company of Drapers Warden's Accounts: (Reps E–F).
The Worshipful Company of Drapers Court of Assistants Minutes: (Reps D–E).
The Worshipful Company of Drapers Dinner Book I: (D.B.I).

Feast for a King: The Wine and Food Society's Carême Banquet at the Royal Pavilion, Brighton

Joan Navarre

On 20 October 1934, at eight o'clock in the evening, 200 distinguished guests, including Mr H.G. Wells, gathered in the banqueting room of the Royal Pavilion, Brighton, for a Regency Banquet. This was the most sumptuous and elaborate feast held in Britain for more than a century. The purpose was twofold: to celebrate the first anniversary of the founding of the Wine and Food Society and to honor the memory of Marie-Antoine Carême, 'the chef of kings and the king of chefs.' This paper addresses the Wine and Food Society's Carême Banquet at the Royal Pavilion. I describe the setting (Great Kitchen, Banquet Hall, and Music Room), menu, and results. I also explore the contributions of André Simon and A.J.A. Symons, co-founders of the Wine and Food Society. As this paper reveals, the banquet – a feast for the senses – honored a great chef and great artist, signaled the start of a gastronomic revolution, and celebrated the art of good living.

There are no original documents relating to the Carême Banquet in the archives of the Royal Pavilion. However, early issues of *Wine and Food: A Gastronomical Quarterly*, contemporary newspapers, and volumes of Wine and Food Society memorabilia shed light on the preparation for and success of the banquet.[1]

Founding of the Wine and Food Society

André Simon and A.J.A. Symons co-founded the Wine and Food Society on 20 October 1933. Simon served as President, and Symons as Secretary. At the end of the first year, the Society had more than 1,000 members. The foundation was, as A.J.A. Symons documents in his Secretary's Report of 1934, 'a result of the deliberations of a small group of enthusiasts who desired to improve the standard of eating and drinking in this country.' The goal: 'to promote the art of good living in England.'[2]

The mission of the Wine and Food Society was to make people aware of what they were eating and drinking and to encourage changes to the quality of food and wine. As A.J.A. Symons reported, the objectives of the Society were as follows:

1. To promote a greater interest in, and knowledge of, food, wine, and the arts of the table.
2. To organize, periodically, luncheons, tastings and dinners at which experimental and inexpensive dishes will be tried, accompanied by suitable wines.

3. To supply advice and assistance in all matters relating to food and wine.
4. To publish books and pamphlets relating to food and wine, and their history.
5. To collect from members, and publish, information as to hotels and restaurants where good food and wine may be enjoyed.
6. To oppose legislative restrictions prejudicial to the enjoyment of good food and wine.
7. To organize tours by members of the Society to the Vineyards in vintage time under favourable conditions.

Symons concludes, 'the Society's aims go far beyond the arrangement of gastronomic gatherings, important and interesting though these are. It intends to oppose and stop misdescription of wines which has become increasingly common; it intends to work for the relaxing of the present unduly stringent licensing laws; and above all, it intends to work for a better standard of food and wine in country inns.'[3]

The Wine and Food Society promoted the art of good living by publishing a journal: *Wine and Food: A Gastronomic Quarterly*. The editor, André Simon, encouraged readers to send reminiscences of gastronomic tours; records of memorable meals, out-of-the-way recipes, or information; and (not necessarily for publication) reports on hotels and inns visited, good or bad. The objective of the publication was to 'put forward the point of view of the amateur of good living, as well as that of the expert.'[4]

The Wine and Food Society prepared members and the public for the banquet at the Brighton Pavilion by dedicating the autumn number of *Wine and Food* (1934) to Carême's life and work. André Simon contributed.[5] So did Eugène Herbodeau, chef at the Carlton Hotel.[6] According to Herbodeau, 'Carême was a great artist and a great teacher.' His mission in life was 'to raise the standard of living, to teach his own people and all the peoples of the earth how to eat with greater elegance, sense and dignity, in order to be healthier in body and mind and to lead lives at once more pleasurable to themselves and helpful to others.'[7] Another contributor was Ambrose Heath, who addressed the language of cookery and described details of dishes 'dignified by the description *à la Carême.*'[8]

The autumn number also presented the schedule for the meeting in Brighton. According to Simon, two events would occur on 20 October 1934. First, the annual conference (also the 10th meeting) of the Wine and Food Society would be held at 3 p.m. in the Royal Pavilion. The first item on the agenda was the Secretary's report on the past year's activities. The next item was a talk by J. Irving Davis: 'Observations on the Present State of Gastronomy in England, with Some Proposals for its Amendment.' Members were invited to attend and consider the first year's results and the future policy of the Society. Moreover, they were invited and urged to take part in the discussion which followed the talk. There was no charge for admission, either for members or guests, but only members were permitted to take part in the discussion and vote.

Feast for a King

A few hours after the annual conference concluded, the Carême Banquet (the 11th meeting of the Wine and Food Society) would commence. Simon declared: 'It will be one of the most noteworthy functions arranged by the Society; the menu will be an imposing one, served in the fashion of a hundred years ago, in two 'services', each with about twenty different dishes. The wines presented will also be typical of those that were served during the Regency – Bordeaux, Burgundy, Champagne, Hock, Moselle, Port, Madeira, Brontë, Constantia, Brandy, and Curaçao.'[9] Finally, the evening would conclude with a concert of Regency music.

The cost for a ticket to the banquet: 2 guineas.

Celebrations: first anniversary and Carême centenary

The Wine and Food Society celebrated its first birthday in style. This was a double celebration: the first anniversary of the Wine and Food Society and the 100th anniversary of the death of Carême (1784–1833), the 'most illustrious chef of the nineteenth century, having known and served Napoleon I, George IV, the Emperor of Russia, and a host of illustrious people in Paris, London, Vienna and St Petersburg.' As Simon states, 'He cooked and he taught, and he left at his death a number of books on cooking and the art of good living which have been a source of inspiration for cooks and all students of the art of good living during the last one hundred years.'[10]

Carême was chef to the Prince Regent for eight months, from the summer of 1816 until the spring of 1817. The actual menus served by Carême to the Prince Regent at Brighton had been preserved.[11] Thus it was decided to hold the banquet at the Royal Pavilion in Brighton where Carême prepared the Prince's dinners and pleased his master, who told him one day: 'Carême, you will be the death of me; you send in such appetizing fare that I cannot help overeating,' to which the master chef replied, 'Sir, my duty is to tempt your appetite; yours, to control it.'[12]

The Royal Pavilion was the perfect setting. It was here that Carême performed gastronomic feats of magic for the Prince Regent, later George IV, with the most memorable meal being the Regent's Banquet of 1817. Carême's celebration of the art of good living was a feast for the senses. In addition to creating over twenty dishes, Carême constructed a four-foot-high Turkish mosque made entirely of marzipan. Because the place resonated with the memory of Carême, Brighton's municipal authorities allowed the Society to celebrate at the Royal Pavilion. The Wine and Food Society returned to the Royal Pavilion to reconstruct the manner and proportions of Carême's Regent's Banquet.

After the conference, but before the banquet began, guests were invited to visit the Great Kitchen. One photograph published in the 22 October 1934 edition of the *Sussex Daily News* documents this visit. Roasts were cooked on spits before a great fire in the Pavilion kitchen – the first time in half a century that a fire had been lit in the kitchen. André Simon stands near the joints as they cook before the huge open fireplace. Also pictured are chefs wearing tall white caps. According to Herbodeau, in his essay on

Carême published in *Wine and Food*, the chef's tall white cap worn when working was introduced by Carême to replace the cotton 'night cap' worn in his days; old prints of the Brighton Pavilion kitchen show Carême's influence.[13]

The vast E-shaped banqueting hall was illuminated by thousands of tallow candles in 80 great candelabra. According to *The Times* (22 October 1934), 'When the guests entered the Chinese dining-room points of flame from hundreds of tallow candles standing in branched candlesticks threw a soft light on silver, glass, and china, and mellowed the colours of the panelled pictures and the dragon in the dome. This scene could not be retained as with the beginning of dinner the electric lamps in the great chandelier blazed into stronger and more revealing light; and the candles were snuffed.' Even the lights, though, had ties to the past: 'the chandeliers, designed as part of the original furniture for the room, formerly worked by gas but now converted to electricity.'[14] In a similar attempt to control the meal's mood, cigarettes were not allowed (too modern an invention), but snuff was handed round.[15]

The menu was modeled on dishes served by Carême to the Prince Regent. The banquet was divided into two services, with 42 dishes and 16 specially chosen wines and liqueurs. Rare dishes were served on china once owned by George IV. Some of the dishes were meant to be a visual feast. For example, there was a boar's head and two models in iced sugar. The sugar models were christened *Le Temple de l'Amour* and *La Frégate 'La Gourmande'*.

The arrangement in two services followed the custom of Carême's day. So did the food and wine, all specially chosen in accord with historical precedent – especially with respect to the Constantia, one of the favourite wines of the Regency which was imported from the Cape for the occasion.[16]

There was a royal toast. Then, during dinner, the toast of 'Carême' was proposed by Simon and received with acclamation. Finally, there was a toast to the chef: 'The health of the Chef of the evening, Mr. L.W. Thomas, was drunk with at least equal enthusiasm.'[17]

After the banquet, guests retired to the Music Room. A special concert had been arranged of chamber music by Arne, Boyce, Handel and Vivaldi, of the type that would have been played before the Prince Regent in the Pavilion 100 years before. According to a report from *Wine and Food*, 'The lateness of the hour made it necessary for a number of the diners to forgo the final pleasure of the concert, but those who were able to remain were richly rewarded.'[18]

Results: 'A gastronomic cavalcade'

The meal took two and a half hours to serve. The Pavilion formed an ideal background; the banquet was a great success. *The Caterer* reported:

> One of the most remarkable catering feats of recent years was achieved by a British firm with a British chef in the Royal Pavilion at Brighton last Saturday.

Feast for a King

MENU

PREMIER SERVICE

QUATRE POTAGES

La Tortue Royale   Le Potage à la Jardinière
La Purée du Gibier   La Crème de Homard

SIX HORS-D'ŒUVRE

Les Petits Vols-au-Vent
    en maigre: à l'emincé de saumon
                aux crevettes roses
                à la purée de champignons
    en gras: à la purée de gibier
                aux foies de volaille
                aux rognons hachés

DEUX RELEVÉS DE POISSON

Les filets de sole à l'Orly   La Barbue farcie au four

QUATRE ENTRÉES

Les cuisses de poularde en ballotte
Les filets de canard à l'orange
Les noisettes d'agneau persillées
Les escalopes de veau au citron

LES BOUTS DE TABLE

au naturel: La Hure de Sanglier
                Le Faison Doré
en sucre: Le Temple de l'Amour
                La Frégate 'La Gourmande'

VINS

Vins stomachiques avec les potages
L'Amontillado de Duff Gordon, Port St. Mary
Le Madère St. John de Leacock
Le Marsala Virgin d'Egidio Vitali

Le Vin blanc de Graves avec les Petits Vol-au-Vent en Maigre
Le Rosechâtel de Schröder et Schÿler, Bordeaux

Le Vin blanc de Bourgogne avec les petits Vol-au-Vent en Gras
Le Meursault St. Pierre de Geisweiler, Nuits St. Georges

Le Vin blanc de la Moselle avec les Relevés de Poisson
Le Berncasteler Berg de 1932 (Blue Label)

Le Vin blanc du Rhin avec les Entrées
Le 1929 Senator's Hock, Cabinet Wine, Gold Seal, de Sichel söhne, Mayence

DEUXIÈME SERVICE

DEUX GROSSES PIÈCES
Le Rosbif d'aloyau à l'Anglaise
Le Quartier de Chevreuil Mariné

QUATRE PLATS DE RÔTS
Le Dindonneau aux Marrons	Le Perdreau au Jus
Le Faisan au Cresson	La Grouse d'Ecosse

LE RELEVÉ DE RÔT
Le Jambon de Sanglier à la Gelée

DEUX ENTREMETS DE LÉGUMES
Les Epinards au Velouté	Les Harricots Verts à l'Anglaise

SIX ENTREMETS AU SUCRE
La Gelée au vin de Madère	Les tartelines mélées
La Gelée au marasquin	Les Profiterolles au chocolat
Le nougat aux avelines	La Crème à la vanille

SIX ASSIETTES DE DESSERT
de pommes	de Noix	de Biscuits
de Poires	de Fromages	de Mendiants

VINS

Le Vin rouge de Bordeaux avec les Grosses Piéces
Le Château Pontet-Canet 1928 des Frères Cruse, Bordeaux

Le Vin rouge de Borgogne avec les Rôtis
Les Clos Lamarche 1926 de Bouchard Aîné, Beaune

Le Vin rouge de Champagne avec le Relevé de Rôt
Le Bouzy 1929 du Propriétaire

Le Vin blanc du Sauternais avec les Entremets au Sucre
Le Cru Bousela 1929 de Barsac

Les Vins capiteux avec le Dessert
Le Vin de Porto de 1933 frais et puissant
Le Vin de Constantia du Cap de Bonne Espérance
Le Vin de Malvoisie de Blandy

Le Liqeurs d'après-diner
Le Cognac vieux de Pinet Castillon
Le Curaçao de Bols, Amsterdam

Feast for a King

> This was the Carême Centenary Banquet of the Wine and Food and Society .... A typical Carême menu ... consisted of 42 dishes in two services, with 16 specially chosen wines and liqueurs. This had to be served to a company of nearly 200 epicures within the space of two and a half hours. Yet the whole affair went through as efficiently as a modern luncheon. All the food was brought from London, while the staff, consisting of nine chefs, six commis, 28 waiters, and 12 wine waiters, these dressed in Georgian livery, only 'took over' the day before. Some idea of the equipment necessary can be gathered from the fact that 2,700 wine glasses alone were needed!
>
> ... The roasts, incidentally, were cooked before the great fire in the kitchen actually used by Carême, the great chef in whose memory the banquet was held.[19]

The London and provincial press also offered high praise. The *Daily Telegraph* hailed the meal as a 'gastronomic cavalcade'.[20]

Another article trumpeted: 'Gourmets Honour Famous Chef'.[21] A third article paid homage to the chef:

> Shyly from the kitchen came Mr. Thomas, looking so typically English that his chef's cap seemed incongruous. He stood bowing under the great glittering chandeliers of the banqueting room of the Royal Pavilion, while the guests clapped their hands. Garnished dishes of boar's head and succulent pies surmounted by golden pheasants in all their brilliant plumage were by the banqueting boards.[22]

As to the most interesting dishes, opinion varied. However, the boar's head was greeted with cheers on its appearance.

According to Patrick Morrah, biographer of André Simon, 'The lavishness of the entertainment provided, coupled with the splendid setting and its historical significance, caught the public imagination and many who would not otherwise have heard of the Society picked up their ears and took an interest. Gastronomic revolution was on the way, and its undisputed leader was André Simon.'[23]

Conclusion

On 20 October 1934, just after eight o'clock in the evening, at the Royal Pavilion in Brighton, the doors of the Banqueting Hall closed, the fires in the Great Kitchen blazed, and time turned back. The Carême Banquet at the Royal Pavilion honored a great chef and great artist, promoted the mission of the Wine and Food Society, and signaled the start of a gastronomic revolution. This feast for a king and feast for the senses was unforgettable: a celebration of the art of good living.

Notes

1. I am grateful to Philip Cark, International Secretariat of the International Wine and Food Society, for access to the A.J.A. Symons volumes of memorabilia.
2. Symons, A.J.A., 'Secretary's Report,' 'Proceedings of the Society: The Tenth Meeting,' *Wine and Food*, No. 4, Winter Number, 1934: 51.
3. Ibid., 54.
4. André L. Simon, 'Editorial,' *Wine and Food*, No. 3, Autumn Number, 1934: 3.
5. André L. Simon, 'Carême', *Wine and Food*, No. 3, Autumn Number, 1934: 4–12.
6. Eugène Herbodeau, 'Carême: The Prince Regent's Chef', *Wine and Food*, No. 3, Autumn Number, 1934: 16–22.
7. Ibid., 16.
8. Ambrose Health, 'A La Carême', *Wine and Food*, No. 3. Autumn Number, 1934: 28–29.
9. Simon, 'Editorial,' 2.
10. Ibid., 4.
11. *Maître d'Hôtel* (Vol. II).
12. Herbodeau, 'Carême,' 18.
13. Herbodeau, 'Carême,' 19.
14. 'Proceedings of the Society: The Eleventh Meeting,' *Wine and Food*, No. 4, Winter Number, 1934: 73.
15. 'Proceedings of the Society: The Tenth Meeting,' *Wine and Food*, No. 4, Winter Number, 1934: 51–67.
16. 'Proceedings of the Society: The Eleventh Meeting,': 71.
17. Ibid., 71.
18. Ibid., 73.
19. 'Carême Banquet – A Catering Feat – By a British Firm and Chef.' *The Caterer and Hotel-Keeper*, No. 750, Vol. 69, 26 October 1934: 819.
20. 'A Gastronomic Cavalcade,' *The Daily Telegraph*, 22 October 1934: 8.
21. 'Gourmets Honour Famous Chef,' *The Morning Advertiser*, 22 October 1934: 4.
22. 'Brighton Pleases 200 Epicures.' *The Daily Mail*, 22 October 1934: 23.
23. Patrick Morrah, *André Simon: Gourmet and Wine Lover*, 114.

Bibliography

'Brighton Pleases 200 Epicures,' *The Daily Mail*, 22 October 1934: 23.
Carême, Marie-Antoine. *Le maître d'hôtel française*. Paris: L'auteur, Imprint de Firmin Didot, 1822.
'Carême Banquet – A Catering Feat – By a British Firm and Chef.' *The Caterer and Hotel-Keeper*, No. 750, Vol. 69, 26 October 1934: 819.
'A Gastronomic Cavalcade,' *The Daily Telegraph*, 22 October 1934: 8.
'Gourmets Honour Famous Chef,' *The Morning Advertiser*, 22 October 1934: 4.
'Great Chef and Great Artist. Notable Brighton Banquet,' *Sussex Daily News*, 22 October 1934: 7.
Morrah, Patrick. *André Simon: Gourmet and Wine Lover*. London: Constable, 1987: 116–138.
'A Regency Banquet,' *The Times*, 22 October 1934: 8.
Simon, André L., ed. *Wine and Food: A Gastronomical Quarterly*, No. 3, Autumn Number, 1934.

Keeping Kosher: Cause for Celebration?

Felicity Newman

> I have come to the reluctant conclusion that the most Jewish part of many people is their stomach, and the Olam Haba (world to come) will be crowded with Jewish stomachs which have passed muster, well ahead of their souls and their minds.
>
> Rabbi Ronald Lubovsky 1995, 24

Rabbi Lubovsky's comments reflect the widely held view that the Jews are a people obsessed with food. While most people know that observant Jews don't eat pork, the intricacies of kosher observance are not well known. In this paper I demonstrate what every Jewish cook knows: that keeping kosher is costly and time-consuming. However there are also social costs and consequences of keeping kosher. Keeping kosher and enforcing community standards of *kashrus*, as it is known in Hebrew, can be divisive. Diasporic Jewish communities separate themselves from host communities as a result of kosher observance. In addition, intra-community divisions reflect the diversity of kosher practices, including both regional differences and varyingly strict observance. It is not my intention to criticize the motives of those who are responsible for kosher certification or indeed the consumers, merely to point to the obvious conclusion that kosher food provision is no longer a community-based practice: it has become big business.

Many Jews are nostalgic for a world destroyed by the Holocaust and the subsequent dispersal of centres of Jewish learning and culture. These were tight-knit communities where female family members and friends provided food for social occasions and migrants brought these practices to their new homes. This is no longer the case, and the informality, exchange and commensality that bind communities have been lost. These social costs seem not to be highly valued among Orthodox communities. As the divisions between secular and religious attitudes grow, there appears to be no impetus amongst Orthodox communities to return to more inclusive practices.

This paper begins with a description of the practices of keeping kosher before discussing differences in kosher observance. Readers who are familiar with Jewish food may know this, but it is my experience that most Gentiles, and indeed many Jews, are not familiar with the intricacies of keeping kosher. The paper then considers the reasons for buying kosher food products and the costs involved. Finally I argue that the communal nature of food cooked in the home and shared has been sacrificed to the quest for perfection, for doing things 'by the book'.

Keeping Kosher: Cause for Celebration?

A feminist reading of what is required in order to keep kosher reveals other concerns. Women have always practised keeping kosher within the home. Strict injunctions are open to interpretation; however, these interpretations have been written by (male) Talmudic scholars. Women's religious obligations revolve around three *mitzvot*, the acts that fulfil the requirements of Orthodox Jewish practice. Only three *mitzvot* are normally associated with women, though men must perform some six hundred and thirteen. Women's *mitzvot* are: lighting Sabbath candles; *niddah*, the ritual purification a woman performs at the completion of her menstrual period; and the third *mitzvah* is *challah*, when baking the Sabbath twisted loaf (or other foods categorized as bread) one must tear off a small piece and burn it in the oven while saying a blessing. 'While this act is reminiscent of the ancient priest's act at the sacrifice at the Temple, it is appropriate to women because they are associated with the domestic realm and food preparation' (Prell 1978, 79). Overseeing the production of kosher food is men's business, while cooking kosher food is women's business.

What is kosher?

'Kosher' literally means 'fit' or 'acceptable', hence *kashrus* refers to the food considered 'fit' or 'acceptable' for Jewish consumption. In order to keep kosher, observant Jews must eat only animals considered to be fit or clean, that is animals killed in accordance with kosher practices and drained of all blood. Milk products and meat products must not be eaten in the same meal, and must be separated on the plate and in the home.

In accordance with the laws of *kashrus*, there are three categories of food. Meat (*fleichig*) refers to all kosher animals and fowl slaughtered in the prescribed manner, and their derivative products. Dairy foods (*milchig*) must be separated from meat. The third category is *pareve* (or *parve*). *Pareve* foods, which are neither dairy nor meat, include fruit and vegetables but most important are eggs and fish.

Avoidance of non-kosher animals is relatively straightforward though the preparation of meat is not. Blood, and the prohibition on its consumption, is a core tenet of *kashrus*:

> The story of the Flood also lays down one of the fundamentals of the dietary laws: 'but the flesh within the life, which is the blood, you shall not eat' (Genesis 9:4). Blood lies in the centre of the Jewish dietary prohibition. Blood is the essence of being, it is the property of God; it is both holy and sinful, therefore out of bounds to humans. The rejection of blood in the Jewish tradition comes from a basic cultural abhorrence of paganism which was associated with blood-drinking rituals. Only by dedicating blood to God, by spilling it on the ground and covering it, can a man come to terms with the killing of another of God's creatures. This concept of the sacredness of all of God's creation was probably as important as the belief in a single God in setting the Jews apart from all their pagan neighbours. (Schwartz 1992, 13)

Keeping Kosher: Cause for Celebration?

To '*kasher*' the meat, all blood is removed. After the animal has been ritually slaughtered, the blood is drained from the animal. Then the meat is soaked and salted:

> This process, namely broiling, or soaking and salting, is meant to drain all blood (which symbolizes life) from the meat, and thus ease the conflict we humans have, when satisfying our carnivorous need. Kashering is often done routinely now by most kosher butchers. Pre-packaged, frozen, kosher chicken has been salted. To remove salt, soak in cold water, changing water three times in one hour, or remove skin whenever appropriate. Adjust salt in recipes accordingly. (Bornstein 1994, 17)

Note that 'broiling', or what we call grilling, is a suitable process as the blood will be released and drain away. There are many questions of law that have arisen from these interpretations of what is kosher. Most of these questions concern this separation of milk and meat products. The division of milk and meat, more than the injunction on certain animals and the prescription for ethical slaughter, is most contested because it performs the greatest leap of interpretation:

> The prohibition of cooking a baby goat in its own mother's milk developed into the complete separation of all milk and meat products. This is clearly a case of adaptation, of interpretation. The use of different sets of dishes, as well as pots and pans, developed in order to ensure complete separation of milk and meat products, as did the practice of waiting at least three hours after eating a meat dish before eating a dairy product. The two types of food should not even mix together in Jewish stomachs.
>
> At the end of the repetition of the kosher laws (Deuteronomy 14:21) there is a reference to the most curious law of all: 'Do not cook kid in its mother's milk.' This law is mentioned twice before in Exodus 23:19 and 34:26 and always in connection with the celebration of the harvest festival. (Schwartz 1992, 17)

Schwartz and others argue, after Maimonides, that this derives from the desire to distance the Jews from pagan practices in the region: 'There was an express injunction for these worshippers to seethe a kid in its mother's milk in order to become one with Dionysus and the goat goddess his mother' (Koval 1993, 8). However, the motivation for this prohibition is neither entirely clear nor agreed upon. It could be argued that this command comes from a position of sensible nutrition and animal husbandry. To consume the products from the animal in the same meal as the animal itself, in a marginally sustainable community, is poor use of scarce supplies of protein. Orthodox Jews will not even consider these arguments, nor the notion that the rabbis of the *Gemarra* may have known that it is unwise to eat fat with fat. (The composition of the Talmud is complex, consisting of Rabbinic commentary on the Mishnah, also known as the Oral Torah – the original law. This commentary is known as the *Gemarra*.) However, Schwartz makes the point, 'Meat was seldom eaten amongst nomadic people, as sheep, goats and cattle were much too important for their milk production and monetary value to be killed for everyday use. They were slaughtered only in religious celebration or for entertaining important guests' (1992, 13). He concludes that 'Maimonides, an important medieval Jewish physician and scholar, discusses the milk/meat prohibition thus; "Meat boiled with milk is undoubtedly gross food and makes a person feel overfull"' (ibid. 17). The resulting concern with separation has spawned a massive industry in processed and other foods which are manufactured and overseen to ensure *treyf* (forbidden) substances do not contaminate them and that milk and meat have not met. Since most homes no longer have a dedicated cook, the demands for prepared and processed foods is ever increasing.

Pareve foods may be mixed and served with either category. However, having contacted meat they cannot be eaten with milk. This problem of contamination provides the greatest complications for kosher observance. It is crucial that readers understand the intricate problems this practice gives rise to. For example when interviewing my kosher home cook, I asked what happens when this injunction is broken? Her response illustrates this intricacy:

> It all depends on the temperature – it depends if it's something spicy like an onion. If you cut an onion with a milk knife that means that onion cannot be used to cook meat with, but you can use it to make a salad you're going to have or make a quiche or something like that so it's not a problem, but there are a lot of things that are variables.

In order to avoid contamination when shopping, two general methods are practised: keeping ingredient kosher, and what is called keeping *heksher* kosher. Ingredient kosher observance is possible if one is cooking from scratch or is very familiar with manufacturing processes in order to ensure there are no animal products used.

Heksher kosher means that, when shopping, one must check the packages of all products to insure that they bear a symbol known as a *heksher*. Derived from the word 'kosher', a *heksher* is a symbol, usually the letter K and a surrounding design, or a large letter U surrounded by a circle which denotes that the product has been processed under the supervision of a rabbi and is guaranteed to be strictly kosher. Depending on the product, the *heksher* design will usually indicate whether the product is dairy, meat, or *pareve*.

Observance of *kashrus* becomes even more complex during the eight days of Passover when no leaven (*chametz*) may be kept in the home. Leaven refers to any grain product that is already fermented (yeast-based breads, many alcoholic drinks) or substances that can cause fermentation (yeast, sourdough, corn syrup, etc.). The issues involved in keeping kosher for Passover provide a layer of concerns beyond the scope of this paper.

The experience of the Diaspora has meant that Jewish food is regional and diverse leading to differing practices and varied levels of observance, especially regarding

Keeping Kosher: Cause for Celebration?

Passover. Most of what Gentile readers assume is Jewish culture is in fact *Ashkenazi*. *Ashkenazi* Jews originate from, or are the descendants of those who emigrated from Central and Eastern Europe, from the area known as the Pale of Settlement, referred to as the Pale, that area of Eastern Europe where Jews were permitted to settle. *Ashkenazim* form the majority of Jewish migrants to the US, UK, South Africa and Australia.

The second largest group are the *Sephardim* whose origins are Southern European, Middle Eastern and North African. There is considerable tension between these communities. The minority *Sephardi* culture and history has been subsumed by the dominant *Ashkenazi* community particularly in Israel, but also in the US, UK, and Australia. There are many other communities including the *Mizrahi* Jews of the Middle East, the Jews of Bukharin, the *Bene Israel* of Bombay, and the Jews of Cochin. Little is known about these diverse groups even amongst Jewish communities. When we think of popular images of Jewish life they are of *Ashkenazi* life.

Kosher observance varies between these communities, as do ingredients, techniques and recipes. The result is a fabulously diverse and regional cuisine. Claudia Roden observes:

> The concept of separating *milshig* (dairy) and *fleyshig* (meat) in different parts of the kitchen emerged in Europe in the Middle Ages, when public bakehouses in the ghettos were divided into two parts. In the *shtetl*, those whose ways of observance were different were scorned and considered as kinsmen who had assimilative tendencies and wandered from the fold. The Sephardim usually managed a synthesis between religious consciousness and the world around them and had little time for hairsplitting pilpulistic arguments about the law. European travellers to Egypt and Syria in medieval times were shocked to see local Jews buying cooked food such as *harrissa* … as well as pastries and sweetmeats, from non-Jews in the bazaar for their evening meals.
>
> Jewish tradition always attached great importance to the local customs of a community. These local customs, although not based on the written law, and varying from one community to another, were regarded as binding. Most *Sephardi* communities allowed the eating of rice during Passover and still do, whereas *Ashkenazim* do not. (20)

Roden demonstrates that there is no sense of right or wrong in this context, just that 'we do this, while they do that'. So there is diversity in terms of the ethno-cultural make up of the various communities but there is a great deal of variety *within* these groupings. In Jewish life authority is always local – one's rabbi will be the final arbiter of all issues. The *Ashkenazi* Jewish community is further split according to levels of observance which range from the extreme Orthodox position, through Modern Orthodox to Liberal/Progressive practices adopted by more Liberal-leaning congregations, to Jews who do not observe any Jewish religious practices but identify on an ethno-cultural basis.

Keeping Kosher: Cause for Celebration?

As (Progressive) Rabbi Jacqueline Ninio of the Emanuel Synagogue in Sydney explained:

> So within the Orthodox community there are different authorities, even what's kosher in Melbourne, there are two different *kashrut* authorities and in America hundreds of them. You have to decide which one you're going to follow. Some would say 'if *they* say it's kosher then it can't be', and 'if *they* say it's kosher then it is' and everyone sort of finds their own way and I think that's what the Talmud is all about, right?

Here Rabbi Ninio supports the view that Talmudic law is interpretative, evolving, and dynamic. This Progressive/Liberal view is ignored by more Orthodox authorities, who would not acknowledge the authority of a female rabbi. Secular Jewish life is the result of the influence of the liberal Kantian thinking of the Enlightenment and the subsequent understanding that though Jewish life is based on the principles of Judaism, the resultant Jew is someone for whom this is an inheritance rather than an injunction.

Though the origins of kosher practice are to be found in the Bible, there is much speculation about the reasons people continue with it. Health benefits are often cited: clearly there was a logic in avoiding pork in a hot climate with no refrigeration just as there is a logic to avoiding any combination of milk and meat. Considering the 'why' of keeping kosher, rather than the 'how' is, however, to some extent irrelevant. As Leon Kass explains:

> Moreover, from the point of view of the tradition whose laws these are, it is a questionable practice to raise questions about the why of the dietary laws. The first and last thing to be said about them is that they are laws, to be obeyed; that they are commanded by God is the sole and sufficient reason for obeying them. Like law in general, the dietary laws are to be kept, not interrogated. To inquire about the reason or meaning of the law – any law – threatens to weaken its force, given that its binding power lies mainly in its *being* law, rather than in the reasonableness of its content – all the more so in this case, its being a divine commandment. (1999, 197)

Kass has, however, attempted the task anyway, arguing that it is necessary in order to achieve cultural understanding. Kass shows how integral Jewish dietary practices are to an understanding of a Jewish way of being when he says:

> The Jewish dietary laws reflect – and mirror – a comprehensive anthropological and cosmological teaching, one that can still command assent. They embody and reflect more-or-less true understanding, first, of the problematic character of eating, but, more significantly, of the nature and of the place of man within the whole. (ibid. 198)

Keeping Kosher: Cause for Celebration?

Keeping kosher is a challenge. Adaptation has always been the key. Despite advances in technology, it is becoming more difficult to adapt Jewish foodways to modern lifestyles. Keeping kosher was easier in a rural Jewish community, as was the case in the villages of Europe. Food was produced and exchanged within the community; one could trust the source. Increased Jewish awareness, as witnessed in the burgeoning *heksher* industry, may be seen as a Jewish reflection of global concerns about food sources. Certainly during my youth, friends whose families observed *kashrus* did so in rather haphazard fashion. As my friend Belinda Epstein-Frisch said:

> When I was growing up in Sydney, packaged food was assumed to be kosher unless the labelling indicated a non-kosher product such as meat shortening. We didn't worry about *heksher*s but now there is a strong *Kashrus* Authority that reviews packaged products and designates them kosher or un-kosher, but we never worried much about that.

This view is echoed by Mrs Bronia Sharp who is a noted cook and authority within Perth's Modern Orthodox community. Mrs Sharp practises a sufficiently high degree of *halachic* (Jewish Law) observance to be held in high esteem by the Jewish community of Perth. She does, in fact, share responsibility for the running of the Perth *mikvah* (ceremonial bath). As there are no kosher restaurants in Perth she only eats away from home when invited to other kosher homes and at celebrations. Her grandparents ran a restaurant and kosher butchery in Poland, and her mother cooked traditional Ashkenazi and Polish food but did not keep kosher. 'I suppose after all that happened during the war, they lost their faith', she told me with heart-rending understatement. Mrs Sharp tells us:

> Keeping kosher is from the Bible, and it's mentioned three times and keeping kosher to me is, first of all if you believe that the Torah came from *Hashem*, from Moses ... . There's no real reason to keep kosher, I mean apart from the fact that it says to keep kosher. Some people try and rationalize keeping kosher – that it's healthy, that it's better – but bottom line is, you keep kosher because it says so.

However this display of piety serves a social purpose. As Eleni Litt (1996) expresses it:

> While intermarriage was the way the group boundary was maintained by our parents' generation, adherence to *kashrus* is the way it is maintained by some of us today. Kashrut, as one aspect of Jewish particularism, emerges as a way of creating new group boundaries and reconstructing a Jewish identity in a postmodern world.

An increasingly popular way to maintain a kosher home is by adopting vegetarianism. Vegetarianism does not mean vigilance may be abandoned – the problem of contamination by non-kosher foods must still be considered – but it does avoid using two sets of dishes and the attendant complications. This begs the question: if keeping kosher, with all its complications, is an act of devotion, is it 'kosher' to avoid these?

Keeping Kosher: Cause for Celebration?

Even in a vegetarian home the high cost of kosher products remains an issue. Rabbi Menachem Genack, Rabbinic Administrator of the Kosher Certification Division of the Orthodox Union of the USA claims:

> There is usually no increase in the price of the product due to its kosher certification, because the cost of certification is generally met by increased sales. In over 45 years, fewer than 12 companies discontinued their certification programs because sales did not increase. Thus, kosher supervision benefits the manufacturer and the consumer, who can be confident that foods may be consumed without violating the kosher standards. (http://www.kosher.org.au/kosher_market.htm).

The Australian Kashruth authority makes the claim that 'A recent survey of Kosher Australia clients found that the ongoing cost of certification on average represented less than one tenth of one percent in the dollar cost of production.' However, some examples of food prices I found online suggest a marked increase in cost. One can purchase 25 Wissotsky kosher English Breakfast tea bags for $A11.85, as compared with 100 Twinings English Breakfast tea bags for the same price. A 200g packet of 'Osem' brand Cremugit Hazelnut Cream Filled Kosher Cookies could be purchased for $A11.30. I do not need to remind Australian readers that a non-kosher packet of cream-filled biscuits would cost no more than $A3.

A visit to the shelves of Perth's Kosher Food Centre revealed items which were cheaper than those online, but I found none that were as cheap, or cheaper, than non-kosher. Indeed I found 1 kilo of kosher tasty cheese at $18.45, while my local supermarket charges between $7.99 and $10.80 for non-kosher cheese; a 400g tin of peeled tomatoes for $3.95 while my local supermarket charged between $1.09 and $1.97 and so it went.

Presumably readers will ask, what makes a tea bag kosher? Being produced in an observant business environment and having been certified kosher means there is no possible contamination by *trefe* ingredients:

> So even in the process of buying various batches – for example Vegemite – it has to be a certain batch; because what happens, on a regular basis, the factories will clean the machinery down, put hot water over it and then leave it for 24 hours and then that kosher batch we can use. So it's not just buying something that doesn't look like there's anything else in it because there is a certain percentage that does not necessarily have to be on the labels. So, there are lots of things involved in keeping kosher. (Bronia Sharp)

The notion of separation dominates Jewish thought and practice. Though many would argue that monotheism is the overarching concern, this monotheism is expressed via separation as a practice. The laws of *kashrus* act to reinforce separation of Diasporic Jewish communities from host communities. As Rabbi Alfred Kolatch expresses it:

Keeping Kosher: Cause for Celebration?

One additional value of the dietary laws is reflected in the attitudes of the early rabbis. They believed that the secret of Jewish survival was separatism. Holiness means being separate. Being a holy people, to them, meant being a people apart.

Adhering to dietary laws keeps the observant Jew apart form those who have rejected him. He cannot mingle freely because socializing together often means dining together. And the Rabbis, taking this point to its outer limits noted, in effect, 'if we cannot eat with them, our sons will not marry their daughters and Judaism will be preserved.'

This may well be the underlying reason for all dietary laws: to ensure Israel's survival by keeping it holy that is, separate. (1988, 85–86)

Perth's Jewish community provides an excellent example of what is lost in the zealous process of enforcing *kashrus*. Because of the remoteness of this community, adaptation and making do have always been evident in Jewish life. An extreme example of this is that kosher meat supply from the 1920 to 1960s was provided by a brash, cockney, Yiddish-speaking Gentile who was happy to trade on a Sunday for his Jewish customers. He supplied both kosher and non-kosher meat from his premises – something that simply couldn't happen these days. Though there was distrust of his produce, women were happy to buy his meat as long as the Rabbi said so.

During this period the Perth community was led by Rabbi Freedman, followed by Reverend Rubin-Zacks in 1939. Reverend Rubin-Zacks accepted Freedman's liberal practices: 'He accepted the communal catering service which, while it gave general satisfaction, deviated from the requirements of *kashrus*' (Mossenson 1990, 163). Mossenson refers here to the catering provided by the WIZO (Women's International Zionist Organization) ladies for weddings and other occasions. Since these women cooked at home and their homes were not subject to rabbinic scrutiny, they would not pass muster as 'strictly kosher'. These women had no need for male authority and if things weren't quite by the book, they certainly knew where to draw the line.

All this changed with the arrival, via Sydney, of a South African rabbi, Dr Shalom Coleman, in 1965. Coleman first insisted that all catering by the Synagogue Ladies Auxiliary be kosher. He demanded measures be introduced to ensure kosher catering for communal functions. Coleman was also far less liberal on other issues, such as conversion, than his predecessors. However:

> Catering for communal functions was the issue which kindled most heat and ill-feeling. Over many years the women of WIZO had established a popular and effective service for the provision of morning and afternoon teas, suppers as well as lunches and dinners for weddings and barmitzvahs. The baking and cooking were performed by a large number of volunteers working in their own homes at times to suit their convenience. With negligible costs, and heating and ingredients largely donated, the exercise was a highly lucrative source of Zionist fund-raising.

Keeping Kosher: Cause for Celebration?

> However, few of the participating homes could be classified as strictly kosher, and with no supervision in force the enterprise, despite its strengths, could not satisfy religious dietary requirements. That the system had prevailed unchallenged for so long rendered its cessation more disagreeable. (ibid. 189–190)

The rabbi insisted that hosts provide kosher catering for their celebrations. The Synagogue board insisted that synagogue services would be available for all but it backed the rabbi's decision that no clergy should attend non-kosher catered functions. The WIZO women were unable to establish a central kitchen and after a time kosher caterers were found.

During an extended conversation with the National Council of Jewish Women, Shalom Group, I was regaled with tales of community, competition and commensality from this era. The stories were all told with some nostalgia if not regret. It is these precious encounters, this enacting of extended family – that is, one's community – which has been lost. Now Jewish families all over Australia must gird their loins in anticipation of the costs involved in providing a catered, kosher meal for their celebrations. Perth's Jewish community's main caterer, Aviv Catering, is run by two Scottish Presbyterian gentlemen and, though their menu includes some traditional dishes, it resembles any other 'Modern Australian' function menu.

We cannot turn back the hands of time. A fundamentalist tide has swept through many religious communities. I do not argue against this: I merely point to the costs, financial, cultural and social. A friend of mine recently celebrated her daughter's batmitzvah at Perth's Progressive Temple David. On such occasions the parents will provide a light lunch for the entire congregation. These are usually catered and therefore kosher. However her friends offered to provide the food and the Temple is happy to accommodate *milchig*-only meals. We proudly brought along our various specialities and laid them out in a most impressive display. The generosity and love expressed by this was widely observed. However, the traditional recipes cooked by the WIZO ladies, the sense of engagement with, and contribution to their community, the marvellous rivalry and showcasing of women's skills that such occasions elicit, are gone. Perhaps this spirit will reside within less Orthodox communities.

References

Bornstein, Miriam, 1994 : 'Comments on *Kashrus*', in *The Reasoning and the Seasoning of Jewish Cooking*. Malibu: Pangloss Press, 1994. 17–18.

The Columbia Encyclopaedia sv 'Halakah'. Sixth Edition. Retrieved 3 Oct. 2001: <http://www.bartleby.com/65/ha/halakah.html>.

Epstein-Frisch, Belinda. E-mail to the author. 17 November 2001.

Henkin, Alan. 1999: '*Kashrus* and Autonomy', *CCAR Journal: A Progressive Jewish Quarterly*, Fall, 2–6.

Kass, Leon. 1999/94: *The Hungry Soul: Eating and the Perfecting of Our Nature*. Chicago: University of Chicago Press.

Kolatch, Rabbi Alfred J. 1988: *The Jewish Book of Why*. New York: Jonathon David Publishers Inc.

Kosher Australia. 'Overview of the Kosher Market – from 'Paddock to Plate''. <http://www.kosher.org.au/kosher_market.htm>

Koval, Ramona, 1993: *Too Many Walnuts: Jewish Cooking, Jewish Cooks*. Port Melbourne: Heinemann.

Litt, Eleni Zatz, 1996: 'Assimilation and Digestion: An Anthropology of *Kashrus* in Postmodern America', *The Reconstructionist, A Journal of Contemporary Jewish Thought & Practice*. <http://www.rrc.edu/journal/recon61-2/litt.htm>

Lubovsky, Ronald, 1995: 'Manduco Ergo Sum: I Eat Therefore I Am', *Generation: A Journal of Australian Jewish Life, Thought and Community* 5.2: 21–24.

Mossenson, David, 1990: *Hebrew, Israélite, Jew: The History of the Jews of Western Australia*. Perth: University of Western Australia Press.

Prell (Prell-Foldes), Riv-Ellen, 1978: 'Coming of Age in Kelton: The Constraints on Gender Symbolism in Jewish Ritual', in *Women in Ritual and Symbolic Roles*. Ed. Judith Hoch-Smith and Anita Spring. New York: Plenum Press, 75–99.

Schwartz, Oded, 1992: *In Search of Plenty*. London: Kyle Cathie.

Wissotsky Tea: http://www.wtea.com/.

The Midwinter Celebration in Antarctica: Feeding Body and Soul

Diana Noyce

We are half-way through our long winter. The sun is circling at its lowest; each day will bring it nearer our horizon. The night is at its blackest; each day will lengthen the pale noon twilight. Until now, the black shadow has been descending on us; after this, day by day, it will rise until the great orb looms above our northern horizon to guide our footsteps over the great trackless wastes of snow. If the light-hearted scenes of to-day can end the first period of our captivity, what room for doubt is there that we shall triumphantly weather the whole term with the same general happiness and contentment?

Captain Robert Falcon Scott, 1905

The celebration of Midwinter's Day is a holiday unique to Antarctica, and marks the halfway point in the polar night, on or around 22 June. By the late nineteenth century, Antarctica was the last unexplored continent on earth. The geographical prize was the South Pole – the most remote spot on earth. The 100th anniversary of reaching the South Pole will be commemorated in 2011, which means Midwinter's Day will be keenly celebrated this year by those who winter on the ice.

Over those 100 years, the celebration of the winter solstice has evolved into a festive and often lavish holiday for those who spend the winter season in Antarctica. It is an occasion to decorate the mess with the flags of the Antarctic Treaty nations, send greetings, in some cases have a midwinter swim, and to consume a special feast – the Antarctic Midwinter Dinner. It is a formal affair; the tables are laid with the best table cloths, glassware, and cutlery. The dinner is probably the only time that the men in the expedition will appear in a suit and tie. Meals are generally served by waiters. Part way through the meal there is the presentation of gifts sent by families, followed by toasts to families and loved ones, as well as the traditional toast to past explorers of Antarctica. From there on into the evening, formality is progressively abandoned. The evening is traditionally one of home-grown entertainment, which might include poetry reading, music (if there are any musicians on station), skits, and the traditional play (Rich 2002). It is the most important day in the polar calendar, as it marks a turning point in the time of waiting and preparation for the active summer season, with the dark days beginning their progressive recession as the sun makes its return journey.

A number of governments maintain permanent research stations, purpose-built for conducting scientific research throughout Antarctica and its surrounding oceans. A

The Midwinter Celebration in Antarctica

total of 29 out of 48 countries, comprising 37 stations, all signatories to the Antarctic Treaty ratified in 1961, operate seasonal (summer) and year-round research stations on the continent and in its surrounding oceans. The population of persons doing and supporting scientific research on the continent and its nearby islands varies from approximately 4,400 during the summer season to around 1,100 persons during winter (CIA 2011). Midwinter's Day in Antarctica is perhaps the most international of holidays, celebrated equally by people of all nationalities, regardless of politics, ideology, or religion – an event that has become an integral part of Antarctic culture: 'Midwinter is like any celebration you remember as a child. You start thinking about it well in advance. There is an incredible build up to it. It is discussed, planned, talked about and anticipated as a special day' (Rich 2002).

Akin to Thanksgiving and New Year celebrations, the Midwinter's Day celebration is an invented tradition that has strong social and cultural ties. But why was it necessary to invent such as tradition in a land that had no human history? The answer is rooted in the history of Antarctic exploration. Fortunately, the early explorers kept meticulous records of their expeditions in diaries, including midwinter celebrations. Narratives were written from these diaries, and it is from these accounts that the traditions of the midwinter celebrations unfold.

Polar night

> The pleasures of the table belong to all times and all ages, to every country and every day; they go hand in hand with all our other pleasures, outlast them, and remain to console us for their loss.
>
> Jean-Anthelme Brillat-Savarin, 1825

A constant theme in the narratives of the early explorers who wintered on the frozen continent was the destabilizing effect the long polar night (24 hours of darkness) had on both the body and the soul. In the closing years of the nineteenth century, a little-known expedition sailed from Belgium and became the first to endure (albeit inadvertently) an Antarctic winter. The *Belgica* expedition (1897–99) was locked in the ice of the Bellingshausen Sea for over a year. The ship became a virtual laboratory of human endurance for its 19-member crew. 'It was a new human experience in a new inhuman experience of ice,' wrote the ship's doctor, Frederick Cook (Cook 1900, 23). In contrast to Scott's description of midwinter, Cook describes the long polar night as a soul-despairing darkness, 'The curtain of blackness which has fallen over the outer world of icy desolation has also descended upon the inner world of our souls' (Cook 1900, 282). The isolation, tinned foods, low temperatures, and increasing storms reduced 'our systems' to what Cook described as 'polar anaemia', whereby the skin became pale with a greenish hue (Cook 1900, 303). Two sailors went mad.

The *Belgica* expedition began the flurry of exploration that was prompted by an announcement at the Sixth International Geographic Congress in 1895. The Congress proclaimed the 'exploration of the Antarctic Regions [was] the greatest piece of geographical exploration still to be undertaken' (Martin 1996, 106). Scientific societies and organizations around the world were encouraged to organize scientific and geographic expeditions to Antarctica. The British, Germans, Swedes, Scots, French, Norwegians, Japanese, and Australians joined the retinue of Antarctic exploration.

The men who went south represented their nation, sought out excitement, and carried desires for the heroic status then accorded explorers. Until the 1960s, Antarctica was an exclusively male domain. It was the twentieth century's prime site for boys' own adventures. The ice was a masculine place where women might be imagined and missed, but never seen (Griffiths 2007, 203). The prestige of men and nations crystallized in the race for the last great geographical achievement – the journey to the South Pole. No longer an abstract spot on the map, it became a goal of heroic struggle. However, it was not merely a geographical race; it had strong nationalistic overtones. Antarctic exploration was a fully fledged cultural experience. Scientists were part of the south polar expeditions sent from these countries in the period that followed, but in the public eyes, and in those of expedition promoters, the South Pole remained the principal objective – exploration's last great prize (Martin 1996, 127).

Britain planted the first flag on the Antarctic continent and made the first attempt to reach the Pole. The British *Southern Cross* expedition (1898–1900), led by the Norwegian Carsten Borchgrevink, reached 78°50'S. Living in dark claustrophobic winter quarters no bigger than a garden shed, it was necessary to create diversions from the darkness and silence that weighed heavily on the minds of the men, as well as the monotonous diet of tinned food. 'There was very little to break the monotony or to create excitement,' said Australian physicist Louis Bernacchi, and relations among the men became strained (Bernacchi 1901, 137).

Seal soup

Subsequent expeditions organized games, lectures, and music to help enliven their stay, and celebratory feasts were organized on special days such as the Queen's birthday, national festivals, and individual birthdays. When birthdays failed to materialize at the correct time, other anniversaries were sought. Charles Laseron, who went south with the Australian explorer Douglas Mawson, said, 'for want of better, we kept up the anniversary of the lighting of London by gas' (Laseron 1957, 93). These men recognized the value of a feast as a psychological boost and as a surrogate for social pleasures lost to them in an inhospitable environment. Food became fundamental not only to feed the body, but also to nourish the soul. Midwinter dinners evolved out of this need to lift the spirits, to help maintain relationships that may have become strained during the suffocating winter, and to encourage a sense of solidarity.

The National Antarctic Expedition (1901–04), commonly known as the *Discovery* expedition led by Robert Falcon Scott, made a second unsuccessful attempt at the Pole. Although the first German Antarctic expedition, the *Gauss* expedition (1901–03) led by

The Midwinter Celebration in Antarctica

Erich von Drygalski, had made preparations before departure to celebrate the solstice (Drygalski 1989, 199), it was Scott and the men of the *Discovery* expedition who were the first to initiate an elaborate midwinter celebration. Antarctica has no ecosystem to sustain expeditions – its natural resources include seals, birds, penguins and whales, but these are confined to coastal areas, only to disappear in winter. Once the coast is crossed, there is nothing except ice and more ice. It was therefore necessary to take to the continent all the provisions, as well as the comforts, of civilization required for the length of the expedition. Arrangements had been made in New Zealand before arriving in Antarctica for a live turtle and a sheep to be sent down by the relief ship *Morning* from New Zealand. The livestock was killed within the Antarctic Circle and then frozen in the Antarctic ice for winter consumption.

Scott writes of the *Discovery* expedition 1902 midwinter dinner:

> At six we had our dinner in the wardroom with the table decorated and the display of all our plate. Starting with turtle soup, we passed on to a generous helping of mutton, and from that to plum pudding, mince pies, and jellies, all washed down with an excellent champagne. With a largely assorted dessert of crystallized fruits, almonds and raisins, nuts, &c., came the port and liqueurs, which brought us into good form for the enthusiastic speeches that followed. With such a dinner we agreed that life in Antarctic Regions was worth living. (Scott 1905. II: 254)

Dr Edward Wilson, who accompanied Scott on both the *Discovery* expedition and the subsequent *Terra Nova* expedition (1910–13), referred in his diary to the midwinter feast as 'Christmas dinner': 'The table was decorated with bunches of holly (artificial) and berries, and a lot of union jacks and printed menus, and then there were Christmas cards' (Savour 1966, 155). The meal was traditional British Christmas fare. Turtle soup, the quintessential Victorian dish, was not tinned, but made fresh with the frozen turtle. Singing, recitations, and readings followed the feast.

The initial midwinter dinner on the *Discovery* expedition was, to some extent, a postponed Christmas, which itself had mutated from pagan origins into Christmas. Pagan festivals were rituals to banish darkness and cold (death) and reawaken life: light, fire, dance, noise, greenery, warming food and drink were common features (Fletcher 2004, 205). Antarctica's elongated seasons meant that the men had to take every opportunity during the Antarctic summer to accomplish scientific and exploratory work. The severity of the polar winter made any extensive outside endeavours virtually impossible. Most men were out sledging on 25 December, so Christmas Day was modestly celebrated among the sledging parties.

The British launched another unsuccessful attempt on the Pole with the *Nimrod* expedition (1907–09) led by Ernest Shackleton, which reached within 180 kilometres of the Pole. Fuelled by his first failure to reach the South Pole, Scott made another attempt with the *Terra Nova* expedition. To reach the South Pole meant that expeditions had to

Figure 1. Frank Hurley's Midwinter Dinner Menu, 1912. Aurora Expedition (1911-14). State Library of New South Wales.

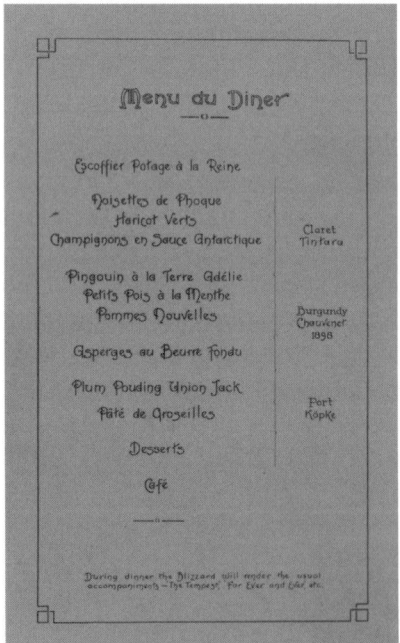

Figure 2. First midwinter dinner at the South Pole, 1957. Photograph by Cliff Dickey, National Science Foundation.

The Midwinter Celebration in Antarctica

establish bases on the continent. New communities, albeit isolated, were created and prefabricated huts were shipped to Antarctica on the expedition ships. The structures were used as bases during winter while their occupants participated in scientific endeavours and made preparations for the trek to the South Pole in the summer months. It was in these wooden huts that the tradition of celebrating the winter solstice evolved.

By 1910, according to Raymond Priestley, a geologist and meteorologist for Scott's northern party stationed at Cape Adare during the *Terra Nova* expedition, the Midwinter's Day celebration had become an event. Several days before the occasion, signs of its approach were visible everywhere. Parcels that had been sent by friends and family from home were opened and examined, a menu prepared, menu cards drawn, decorations made, and the champagne organized. According to Priestley, the dinner 'would not have disgraced a London restaurant' (Priestley 1914, 309).

For the 1911 midwinter dinner, members of Scott's *Terra Nova* expedition stationed at Cape Evans exchanged gifts and improvised a Christmas tree. According to Scott, 'it was observed with all the festivity customary at Xmas at home' (Scott 1996, 238). Union Jacks and sledge flags were hung about the large table, which was laid with glass and a plentiful supply of champagne bottles instead of the customary mugs and enamel lime-juice jugs. 'After all we celebrated the birth of a season which for weal or woe must be numbered amongst the greatest in our lives,' said Scott (Scott 1996, 241). Thomas Clissold was the cook who prepared the meal.

> At seven o'clock we sat down to an extravagant bill of fare as compared with our usual simple diet. Beginning on seal soup, by common consent the best decoction that our cook produces, we went to roast beef with Yorkshire pudding, fried potatoes and Brussel sprouts. Then following a flaming plum-pudding and excellent mince pies, and thereafter a dainty savoury of anchovy and cod's roe. (Scott 1996, 238–239)

Herbert Ponting, the expedition photographer wrote, 'Those who have never been deprived of it (roast beef and Yorkshire pudding) for many months have never relished the national dish of Old England as we did that day. It was food for the gods' (Ponting 1922: 141).

It is apparent from the bill of fare that the men were taking advantage of the natural resources. Although eaten during the earlier *Discovery* expedition, the 'wild' foods of Antarctica were now exalted, being included in the midwinter menu and served along with traditional British fare. The seal soup was, according to Scott, an excellent palate-pleaser, 'very much like thick hare soup' (Scott 1996: 211).

The midwinter dinners provided a means by which the men could emulate the social pleasures lost to them and the dinners they would have enjoyed at home. Where possible, linen and silverware were used on the tables and a special menu card was designed and printed for the occasion. Menu cards were a popular feature of British dinner parties of the Victorian and Edwardian eras. The menu, alongside the Christmas

The Midwinter Celebration in Antarctica

decorations, cards, gifts, and champagne, exuded a sense of civilization and familiarity despite the wildness and desolation of their Antarctic surroundings. However, the seal soup linked the men strongly to their present situation.

If commensality promotes a feeling of togetherness, it can also proclaim the separateness of a group. The expedition huts were arranged and organized along naval lines, a tradition that lasted well into the 1950s. The floor plan of Scott's hut at Cape Evans shows that the officers and men ate and lived separately. Packing cases separated the 'men' from the 'officers'. These eating arrangements emphasized the lower status of the 'men'. Only the officers partook of the midwinter dinner with Scott, or the 'owner' as he was known. The 'men' ate their meal separately and at lunchtime. They enjoyed much the same meal, but the champagne was substituted by whisky and beer (Scott 1996: 44).

Roald Amundsen, now Scott's rival in the race to the Pole, had more egalitarian living arrangements. The Norwegians had arrived in Antarctica on the *Fram* and set up a base at the Bay of Whales 644 kilometres west of Scott's base. Amundsen's team erected a small hut where all nine men ate and lived together. On Midwinter's Day the hut was decorated with small Norwegian flags everywhere, on the table and walls. The festival began at 6 p.m., when all the 'Vikings' came merrily in. The Norwegians also ate plum pudding, and Lindström, the cook, made a traditional favourite, 'Napoleon' cakes, which were made with the 'finest puff-pastry, and filled with mouth-watering layers of vanilla custard and cream'. The cakes were followed by Benedictine and punch (Amundsen 1913: 335).

A few months later both Amundsen and Scott set out for the South Pole. It was Amundsen and four others who were the first to stand at the South Pole on 14 December 1911, a month before Robert Scott. Reaching the Pole after Amundsen was a dispiriting experience for Scott's party, and they turned wearily home. The expedition party never reached home base, perishing on the way from cold and starvation.

At the same time Amundsen and Scott were racing for the Pole, the Australasian Antarctic expedition (1911–14), known as the *Aurora* expedition, led by Douglas Mawson, landed on Antarctic shores. Mawson's main objective was to explore the Antarctic coast directly south of Australia. Frank Hurley, the Australian photographer who accompanied Mawson, compiled the menu for the expedition's midwinter dinner celebrated on 22 June 1912. On the cover page, one of Hurley's famous photographs of Antarctica's harsh environment links those participating in the meal to their present situation. The menu, with the arbitrary mixture of English and French, is typical of the day. Places and people were commonly celebrated on Edwardian menus, a custom that lingered on until the Second World War (Fletcher 2004: 153). Walter Hannam and Francis Bickerton prepared the meal.

The menu features a mixture of local and imported delicacies. The first dish on the bill of fare is named after the most famous celebrity chef of the day, Auguste Escoffier, who was living in London at the time. Naming dishes after a famous person was something

The Midwinter Celebration in Antarctica

Escoffier himself liked to do when creating dishes. *Escoffier Potage à la Reine* was royal soup, a popular cream soup offered at dinner parties among the wealthy throughout the period. *Noisettes de Phoque* was a second course of seal meat dished up with French green beans and mushroom sauce, and served with claret. *Pingouin à la Terre Adelie* was penguin meat served with green minted peas and new potatoes, accompanied by an 1898 Burgundy Chauvénet. The fourth course, *Asperges au Beurre Fondu*, was another favourite of the Victorian and Edwardian period. The white sauce that garnished the asparagus was traditionally made using shallots, white wine, fish stock, and lots of butter. The grand finale before dessert was plum pudding and currant jelly.

The *menu de diner*, which Mawson described as 'a marvel of gorgeous delicacies', was followed by a toast to King and country and, as tradition dictated, past explorers, as well as to the success of their own expedition (Mawson 1996: 111). To theme the menu in this way effected a cohesion of the meal and the event, and created a strong emotional bond between the food served and the people consuming it (Olive 2004).

Hoosh

The midwinter celebrations were not always celebrated with large quantities of sumptuous food. Hunger can be a spur to appetite, which helps us to relish food and can transform the simple into the sublime. Midwinter's Day was duly observed even when members of Shackleton's ill-fated Imperial Trans Antarctic Expedition (1914–17) were stranded on Elephant Island after their ship the *Endurance* was crushed by the ice. A 'magnificent breakfast of sledging ration hoosh' (a hot soupy stew eaten during sledging expeditions or field trips), 'full strength, and well boiled to thicken it' was served with hot milk. Luncheon consisted of a pudding, made of powdered biscuit boiled with 12 pieces of mouldy nut-food. Supper was a very finely cut seal hoosh flavoured with sugar (Shackleton 1999: 200).

Raymond Priestley from Scott's northern party celebrated midwinter in an ice cave during the winter of 1912. Sea ice prevented them from being picked up by the *Terra Nova* in February 1912, and they were forced to overwinter in an ice cave on Inexpressible Island. Scott's marooned party of six men wintered for six months on half-rations of monotonous food, at 'which any English tramp would have turned up his nose', said Priestley (Priestley 1914: 309). Nevertheless, the men saved their meagre rations for the special day. The midwinter dinner of four biscuits, four sticks of chocolate, 20 raisins, and 14 lumps of sugar per man, and a full ration of cocoa with four lumps of sugar per man, as well as hoosh flavoured with seal's brain and penguin's liver was 'sublime', said Priestley. The Wincarnis tasted strongly of muscatel grape and, 'the sweet cocoa was the best drink I have had for nine months', recorded Priestley (Priestley 1914: 308–310).

By concocting a menu out of such simple, meagre ingredients in the most adverse conditions, tradition and Western culinary ideals could still be doggedly maintained. Psychologically, maintaining tradition was a 'victory' over a hostile environment. The midwinter celebration was not simply an opportunity for extravagant eating, but a deliberate attempt to help cope with psychological stress caused by the harsh and unwelcoming environment.

The pleasures of the table belong to all nations

While most expeditions from the Heroic age onwards were comprised of men of different nationalities, the first official international expedition was in 1949–52. Men from Norway, Sweden, Britain, Canada and Australia made up the expedition team. The menu of the midwinter dinner of 1951, still referred as the 'southern Christmas', reflected the international flavour of the expedition. The Scandinavian open sandwich, the Swedish *smörgås* consisting of pieces of bread topped with an array of toppings from tinned shrimps, cold steak, caviar, hard boiled eggs, bacon, herring, fish fillets, small meatballs, and pickled beets was served with drinks. A traditional celebratory cake of Norway, a macaroon tower cake or *Kransekake,* made with almonds and egg whites, made a suitable centrepiece for the table. The Norwegian cook Bjarne Lorentzen saluted the occasion, serving roast chicken and mushrooms for the main course, followed by a 'symphony' of Christmas pastries. The British provided candied fruits (Giaever 1954: 192).

As the last place on earth to be colonized, the International Geophysical Year of 1957–58 inaugurated the full-scale exploration and occupation of Antarctica. Individual nations including France, Germany, Australia, Britain, New Zealand, the Soviet Union and the United States established permanent bases on the continent, adding to the ethnic mix. A total of 40 stations were eventually set up on the continent, with another 20 on sub-Antarctic islands (Martin 1996: 208). The ethnocentricity of Western exploration was now a thing of the past. The midwinter dinner ceased to be referred to as a 'southern Christmas', and became a secular celebratory meal.

Greenhouse greens

When Scott arrived at the South Pole he found Amundsen's tent. Today, Scott would find something resembling a small town. The South Pole, which is no longer an abstract spot on the map, or a goal of heroic struggle, is today a posting for scientists and support personnel. They live in permanent quarters known as the Amundsen-Scott South Pole Station. The image on the 2009 midwinter dinner menu at the South Pole Station puts the meal in context. In the background are a map of Antarctica and an image of Scott and his team standing in front of Amundsen's tent at the South Pole.

The 2009 menu reveals a changing culinary culture. As midwinter is now a secular celebration the traditional plum pudding is no longer served. To commemorate the centenary of Amundsen and Scott reaching the South Pole, however, sous chef Wil Watkins resurrected the plum pudding (to represent Scott) and Napoleon cakes (to represent Amundsen) for the 2011 midwinter dinner. The image of the modern day South Pole station again puts the meal in context. Furthermore, the wildlife of Antarctica is notably absent on menus – intrepid gourmets are no longer able to sample the wild foods of Antarctica, as the Antarctic Treaty's 1991 Protocol on Environmental Protection prohibits 'disturbing' any wildlife, let alone eating them, except in case of life-threatening emergency (Rubin 2003: 37).

While the seal and penguin meat found on the previous menus may not be offered now, the menu has become more elaborate. Noted on the 2009 menu are greenhouse greens. Most of the larger stations have sealed and insulated greenhouses (food growth chambers) providing hydroponic vegetables grown under high-intensity discharge lamps. A variety of vegetables such as tomatoes, cucumbers, peppers, lettuce, and herbs, as well as flowers are grown for the table. The hothouses are mainly used for the winter crew. Fresh vegetables are flown in from New Zealand during the summer months.

Advances in technology have not only influenced what is dished up on the midwinter menu, but have also created new traditions affiliated with the midwinter celebration, which have helped to alleviate feelings of isolation. Since the mid-1990s, e-mail has provided a psychological boost to those who are over-wintering. Across the continent, messages of greeting and goodwill are sent via e-mail to everyone celebrating the special day, with an open invitation to drop by if you happen to be passing – a highly unlikely event, of course, with the exception of a few bases in close proximity, such as McMurdo and Scott Bases. Nevertheless, delicious-sounding menus are sent from various stations to tempt visitors.

Conclusion

For those over-wintering in Antarctica, the Midwinter's Day celebration marks a major milestone in their stay. Through the tradition of the feast and the elaborate preparations, the celebration provides a psychological boost to the monotony of the endless night. It is a marker that signals that the worst is over and the light of day is dawning, and an opportunity for relieving the emotional stress caused by the dark, thereby allaying tensions and disagreements. The camaraderie restored by the feast carries over to the ensuing weeks, helping to maintain the stability of the isolated communities of Antarctica.

The Midwinter Celebration in Antarctica

South Pole Midwinter Dinner ~ 2009 Menu

Old Dome Cocktail with Homemade Ginger Ale
Champagne Cocktail with Raspberry & Orange Infused Vodka

Midwinter '09 South Pole Brew

Salmon Gravlaax with Dill Yogurt & Pickled Onion
Pork Rillettes with Orange Marmalade
Country Paté
Warm Artichoke Fromage
Baguette Toasts

Midwinter Toast with House Made Mead

Greenhouse Greens with Dijon Chive Vinaigrette & Goat Cheese Croûtes
Fresh Rolls

Pumpkin Cream Soup with Fried Onion, Yogurt Creme & Garlic Toast Spears

Warm Crab-Stuffed Crab Puffs with Mornay Sauce & Arugula
Warm Vegetarian Puffs with Cheeses, Mornay Sauce & Arugula

White & Red Wine

Grilled Duck Breast with Dark Cherry Balsamic Vinegar Glaze
Roasted Lobster Tail with Garlic Smoked Paprika Cream
Handmade Gnocchi in Herbs & White Truffle Oil
Warm Porcini & Button Mushroom Salad
Garlic Spinach Timbales
Oven-Charred Carrots

Baked Alaska

Stilton Platter
Homemade Candies

Figure 3. The 2009 midwinter dinner menu.

The Midwinter Celebration in Antarctica

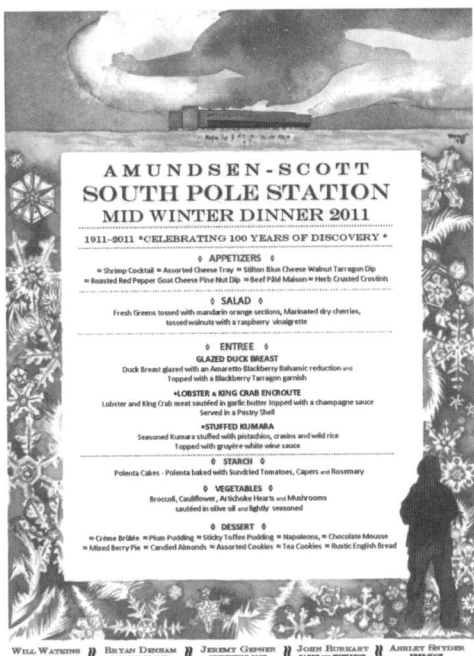

Figure 4. The 2011 midwinter dinner menu. Menu compiled by sous chef Wil Watkins.

Figure 5. (below). Table setting and menu for the 2011 Midwinter dinner held 18 June. Photograph by Wil Watkins.

References

Amundsen, Roald, 1913: *The South Pole: An Account of the Norwegian Antarctic Expedition in the 'Fram' 1910–1912*. Translation by A.G. Chater. Volumes I & II (London, John Murray).
Armitage, Albert B. 1905: *Two Years in the Antarctic* (London, Edward Arnold).
Bernacchi, Louis, 1901: *To the South Polar Region: Expedition of 1898–1900* (London, Hurst & Blackett).
Brillat-Savarin, Jean-Anthelme, 1994: *The Physiology of Taste* (England, Penguin Books).
Borchgrevink, Carsten Egeberg, 1901: *First on the Antarctic Continent: Being an Account of the British Antarctic Expedition* (London, Newnes).
Brown, R.N. Rudmose, J.H. Pirie, H. and Mossman R.C. 1906: *The Voyage of the 'Scotia': Being the Record of a Voyage of Exploration in the Antarctic Seas* (Edinburgh, William Blackwood and Sons).
Bruce, William Speirs, 1992: *The Log of the Scotia Expedition, 1902–04* (Edinburgh, Edinburgh University Press).
Charcot, Jean-Baptiste, 1978: *The Voyage of the 'Why Not?' in the Antarctic. The Journal of the Second French South Polar Expedition, 1908–1910*. Translated by Philip Walsh (London, C. Hurst & Co.).
Cherry-Garrard, Apsley, 1994: *The Worst Journey in the World: Antarctic 1910–13* (London, Picador).
CIA World Factbook and other Sources (2011). Available at: http://www.theodora.com/wfbcurrent/antarctica/antarctica_people.html. (accessed January 2010)
Cook, Frederick A. 1900: *Through the First Antarctic Night 1898–1899* (New York, Doubleday & McClure Co.).
Drygalski, Erich von, 1989: *The Southern Ice-Continent: The German South Polar Expedition Aboard the Gauss, 1901–03*. Translated by M.M. Raraty (Norfolk, Bluntisham Books).
Evans, Admiral Sir Edward R.G.R. 1956: *South with Scott* (London, Collins).
Farb, Peter and Armelagos, George, 1980: *Consuming Passions: The Anthropology of Eating* (Boston, Houghton Mifflin).
Feeney, Robert, 1997: *Polar Journeys: The Role of Food and Nutrition in Early Exploration* (Washington, D.C., & Fairbanks, American Chemical Society, University of Alaska Press).
Filchner, Wilhelm, 1994: *To the Sixth Continent: The Second German South Polar Expedition*. Translated by William Barr (Norfolk, Bluntisham Books).
Fletcher, Nichola, 2004: *Charlemagne's Tablecloth: A Piquant History of Feasting* (New York, St Martins Press).
Giaever, John, 1954: *The White Desert: The Official Account of the Norwegian British Swedish Antarctic Expedition*. Translated from the Norwegian by E.M. Huggard (London, Chatto and Windus).
Griffiths, Tom, 2007: *Slicing the Silence: Voyaging to Antarctica* (Sydney, University of New South Wales Press).
Laseron, Charles Frances, 1957: *South With Mawson* (Sydney, Angus and Robertson).
Martin, Stephen, 1996: *A History of Antarctica* (Sydney, State Library of New South Wales Press).
Mawson, Douglas, 1996: *The Home of the Blizzard* (South Australia, Wakefield Press).
Migot, Andre, 1957: *The Lonely South*. Translated from the French by Richard Graves (London, Rupert Hart-Davis).
Nordenskjöld, Otto, 1977 [facsimile of 1905 edition]: *Antarctica, or Two Years amongst the Ice of the South Pole*. Translated by Edward Adams-Ray (St Lucia, University of Queensland Press).
Olive, Sarah, 4 July 2004: 'Eating Your Heart Out: The Emotional Aspects of Menus', *NLA News, National Library of Australia*, Volume XIV, Number 10. Available at http://www.nla.gov.au/pub/nlanews/2004/jul04/article2.ktml (accessed 4 October 2008).
Paston-Williams, Sara, 1993: *The Art of Dining: A History of Cooking and Eating* (London, National Trust).
Ponting, Herbert, 1922: *The Great White South: Being an Account of Experiences with Captain Scott's South Pole Expedition* (London, Duckworth & Co).
Priestley, Raymond E. 1914: *Antarctic Adventure: Scott's Northern Party* (Victoria, Melbourne University Press).

Pyne, Stephen J. 2003: *The Ice* (London, Weidenfeld & Nicholson).
Rich, John, 2002: 'Reflections on Midwinter'. Australian Government, Department of Sustainability, Environment, Water, Population and Communities. Australian Antarctic Division. Available at: http://www.antarctica.gov.au/about-antarctica/this-week-in-antarctica/2002/reflections-on-midwinter, accessed January 2011.
Rubin, Jeff, 2003: 'Train Oil and Snotters: Eating Antarctic Wild Foods', *Gastronomica, The Journal of Food and Culture*, Vol. 3, No. I, 37–57.
Savour, Ann (ed.), 1966: *Edward Wilson. Diary Of The 'Discovery' Expedition To The Antarctic Regions 1901–1904* (London, Blandford Press).
Scott, Robert Falcon, 1905: *The Voyage of the Discovery*, Volumes I & II (London, Smith Elder).
——, 1996: *Scott's Last Expedition: The Journals* (New York, Carroll and Graf Publishers Inc.).
Shackleton, Ernest, 1909: *The Heart of the Antarctic*. Volumes I & II (London, William Heinemann).
——, 1999: *South: The Endurance Expedition to Antarctica* (Melbourne: Text Publishing).
Swithinbank, Charles, 1999: *Foothold on Antarctica: The First International Expedition (1949–52) Through the eyes of its Youngest Member* (Sussex, The Book Guild).
Wilson, Edward, 1972: *Diary of the 'Terra Nova' Expedition to the Antarctic 1910–1912* (London, Blandford Press).

The Bull's Head Breakfast in Old Los Angeles

Charles Perry

A century ago, Los Angeles' special occasion food *par excellence* was barbecued ox head: a whole head, with the skin and horns removed, cooked by a process we would not call barbecuing today. It was in effect baked in a sealed pit dug in the ground.

This earth-pit oven is the oldest special-occasion cooking method. Our Stone Age ancestors cooked large quantities of meat this way – when they had it, always a special occasion. It is a laborious method, because it requires a lot of digging. The typical Los Angeles barbecue pit was about 1.5 meters in diameter and 2 meters deep.[1] And it's expensive, because it takes about 1.25 cubic meters of hardwood to fire this sort of oven.

And it's time-consuming. The fuel needs to burn for about seven hours, followed by another hour's wait for the flames to die down to a thick bed of coals so that the meat can be laid on it, wrapped in something to prevent scorching. Finally the pit has to be covered and hermetically sealed for at least seven hours.[2]

At the time the pit is sealed, the temperature inside is around 290ºC, and seven hours later it's around 95ºC. If left sealed, it will hold at that temperature for at least 12 hours longer – the one convenient thing about this method. The cooked meat, so tender it falls apart at a touch, has a rich flavor and a suave smoky note quite lacking the hint of soot present in other smoked foods (the smoke flavor is produced by gases from the hot coals; there is no flame in the sealed pit). It gives a very juicy effect, produced by melted connective tissue rather than moisture.

People have used this cooking method on every continent, and archaeologists consider the characteristic ash bed it leaves as prima facie evidence of human habitation. It has tended to die out in densely populated areas such as China and western Europe, partly because the roaring fire is a danger to crops and buildings, but perhaps mostly because it's so laborious, expensive, and time-consuming. It survives today notably in parts of Oceania, Latin America, and the Middle East.[3]

In the eighteenth century, Spanish colonial authorities determined that California was to specialize in cattle ranching. Along with their herds, the Spanish *rancheros* brought the earth-pit oven technique, which happened to be very suitable for cooking the proverbially tough meat of their longhorn cattle.

Since the technique had died out in Europe, they had learned it afresh in Mexico, where the Aztecs called it *nacacoyonqui*, 'meat that has been dug up.' Rather confusingly, the Spaniards called it *barbacoa*, a Caribbean word which had previously meant meat smoked or grilled above ground on a framework of sticks.[4]

Since there was no way to transport fresh meat to market, the Californios were raising

The Bull's Head Breakfast in Old Los Angeles

their cattle for their hides and tallow, and the meat was virtually a free by-product. Parties at the *ranchos* typically featured a *barbacoa* of generous quantities of beef.

After California was admitted to the United States, earth-pit barbecue continued to be practised around the state in a relatively sporadic way. Los Angeles, however, embraced it passionately and made it a centerpiece of local pride. To a degree, this reflects the fact that Los Angeles had been the barbecue capital of old California, simply because it had been the ranching capital – by 1830 some 80,000 head of cattle were already roaming the area and cowhides from Los Angeles, known as 'California bank notes,' were being used as currency up and down the west coast of the Americas.

But it also served a spiritual need for the newcomers from the eastern United States who started thronging in once a rail connection went through. Between 1876 and 1890, the city's population grew six-fold to over 50,000, and by 1900 it had doubled again. The newcomers wanted a sense of local identity in their new home. San Francisco could boast heady memories of the wild Gold Rush days, but Los Angeles had nothing in its past but cattle ranches and Franciscan missions.

The city decided to romanticize precisely the Days of the Dons, which seemed long ago and far away to the newcomers, though Spanish had been the city's everyday language as recently as 1870. *Barbacoa*, as a genuine heritage of old Los Angeles, was seized on as the city's unique sort of celebration (some people considered it appropriate to wear a sombrero to one). These barbecues became huge events, typically serving between 500 and 1,500 people, very often more. A barbecue had to draw over 5,000 to be considered really noteworthy.

Europeans are familiar with the connoisseurship of pork head meat – the boar's head was a lordly adornment to a medieval feast. In the old ranching territories of New Spain – California, Texas, and northern Mexico – baked or roasted beef head (*barbacoa de cabeza*) has always been known, though these days it's nearly always cooked in a conventional oven rather than an earth pit. You can get about four kilograms of meat from a head, and it includes both very tender and very flavorful muscles. Beef tongue cooked in an earth pit is exceptionally tender and luscious.

On the old *ranchos*, however, beef had been so abundant that bony cuts such as ribs were considered a waste of space in the pit. The *rancheros* typically cooked whole shoulders or rounds weighing 15 kilograms or more. It's not clear when anybody started making a point of adding a bull's head to the pile of boneless beef.

How did this massively bony cut become the centerpiece of a barbecue at all? Perhaps people simply liked the flavor. Perhaps it was because of the need to have a special-occasion dish; on the *ranchos*, earth-pit barbecues had become commonplace, often weekly events.[5] The head accounts for only about 10 per cent of the barbecue-able meat on the animal and there's only one head to an ox, so it had that distinction. For some people it was probably simple exoticism – your relatives back East had never heard of eating bull's head.

At any rate, by the 1880s, the bull's-head breakfast (usually served at 10 a.m. or later) was established as the supreme Los Angeles feast. The flavor of these celebrations can be gleaned from this report of a relatively small 1901 breakfast attended by 400 politicians and other eminentoes, which was followed by speeches in English, Spanish and Basque:

> The special train provided for the invited guests reached the Puente station between 12 and 1, at which point a cavalcade of Spanish-Californian horsemen was in readiness to escort the crowd to the scene of the festivities. At the head of the troop was a Mexican band, and at the head of the band a stalwart trooper carried the American flag. The road from the station to the objective had been thickly strewn with barley straw, the bell of the adjacent schoolhouse was merrily rung, and the belles of the neighborhood, neatly arrayed in white, greeted the procession by the waving of parasols and handkerchiefs.
>
> Soon the orange grove was reached – as the distance was less than one eighth of a mile – and here, upon an esplanade between two rows of lemon, pomegranate, and magnolia trees, there were two long tables loaded with imported condiments of every kind, red-hot native sauces, and the necessary table implements and all the other articles, except the tamales, frijoles and the pièces de résistance – the tantalizing aroma from which freighted the air. ...
>
> At about 1 o'clock orders were issued 'Be seated,' and then occurred the most enlivening episode of the day – the consumption of tamales, frijoles, (red beans,) tortillas (big wheaten griddle cakes,) fricassed chicken, enchilladas, barbecued beef and mutton, and the bulls' heads, in about the order presented, accompanied by white and native wines and beer, and water and coffee as well.[6]

Bull's head breakfasts were particularly popular with fraternal organizations. Here is a sampling of events recorded in the *Los Angeles Times*:

> On May 30, 1885, 1,000 members of the Emerald Club attended a bull's-head breakfast at Arroyo Seco Grove, a popular picnic spot north of town.

> In 1887 the Bull's Head Club of Los Angeles was formed in Arroyo Seco, its semi-secret membership alone being permitted to attend the regular bull's-head breakfasts.

> For September 10, 1891, the Native Sons of the Golden West promised a bull's head breakfast 'on a mammoth scale.'

> In 1895, on the 20th anniversary of Sheriff William Rowland's capture of the notorious bandit Tiburcio Vasquez, six rail coaches of his friends attended a bull's-head breakfast in Rowland's honor where 'beneath the shade of an osage orange grove the long table was laid for the fiesta, and where from the glowing pits there drifted the savory odors of the barbecue – the roasting beeves and sheep and the toothsome bulls'-heads.' Reflecting the barbecue's Spanish heritage, every guest

received a souvenir reading 'Tenja V. la bondad de acompanarnos al desentierro de una cabeza de novello en mi casa, servido en el Arroyo de San Jose, sin falta, para el diez y siete del Agosto, 1895.'

September 21, 1898: a bull's head breakfast for the Hickory Club, a Democratic Party organization.

June 17, 1900: a bull's-head breakfast by a Spanish-American group called the Tecolote Club.

July 13, 1903: the 'mysterious Mulligan Club' to host a bull's-head breakfast in Santa Monica Canyon.

April 15, 1904: 2,500 members of the Brotherhood of Locomotive Engineers having a bull's-head breakfast in Playa del Rey.

On December 24, 1905, visiting newspapermen were treated to a bull's head breakfast and a performance of Spanish rancho dances.

July 19, 1908: A party of hunters traveling by auto enjoyed a bull's head breakfast at Wadley's Ranch, Conejo Pass.

August 5, 1911: A bull's-head breakfast was served to 400 auto dealers in the hills above Calabasas.

May 10, 1912: A picnic for the Ancient Arabic Order of the Nobles of the Mystic Shrine (Shriners) featured 4,000 pounds of beef, 50 yearling lambs and 40 bulls' heads – the largest number on record for a single event.

These last two events were catered by the city's leading barbecue chef, Joe Romero, who organized an average of 25 barbecues a year during a career that lasted from 1885 to 1932. The typical number of diners at one of his events was 5,000, but he once fed 30,000 on a single day, for a 1909 Elks Club convention.

The late 1900s and early 1910s proved to be the high-water mark for bull's-head barbecue. After that time, bulls'-head barbecues quickly became rare, the last one being reported in 1928.

Earth-pit barbecue itself continued to be Los Angeles's favorite public party down to through the 1930s for occasions such as Independence Day and Admission Day, and at conventions, charitable events, and in particular real estate sales. A pit barbecue could still draw diners by the thousands, and it remained a point of local pride. Angelenos still claimed to disdain grilling as an amateurish sort of cookery, suitable only for Boy Scout campouts, and Southern pit barbecue as a coarse, if clever, way of rendering cheap cuts palatable.

But then earth-pit barbecue died with shocking suddenness in the late 1930s. Beginning in the early 1920s, there had been a trickle of stories about socialites and

The Bull's Head Breakfast in Old Los Angeles

Hollywood people grilling in their back yards (in the beginning, the meat was always beefsteak).[7] By the mid-1930s, the backyard barbecue grill – occasionally referred to at the time, most inaccurately, as a 'barbecue oven' or even 'barbecue pit' – had an established design that survived almost without challenge until the late 1950s. It was a hulking structure constructed from 1,000 bricks, four sacks of cement and a ton of sand, loosely modeled on the old wood-burning kitchen range, complete with a chimney and dampers. It looked more or less like a fireplace elevated about three feet above the ground.

Originally one assigned one's household cook to flip the steaks on it, but in 1934 the film composer Billy Hayes was reported to enjoy doing his own grilling, wearing a white apron and chef's hat, the future uniform of backyard chefs everywhere.[8] As the decade progressed, the practice rapidly built momentum as more and more celebrities were in the news hosting home barbecues.

The pivotal year was 1939, when being able to grill in your back yard was referred to as the leading reason to buy a house.[9] That was also the last year a public earth-pit barbecue was advertised within the city of Los Angeles (true, it was a large one which drew 30,000 people). Afterward, the practice lingered only in outlying areas or as a fundraiser for certain Catholic parishes. By 1940, backyard grilling was being casually described as 'real California hospitality,'[10] as if earth-pit barbecue had never existed.

How quickly the city had forgotten. How could this have happened?

There had been a cultural shift at the end of the Twenties. The frenzy of the Jazz Age no longer appealed during the Depression, because when you're struggling to keep your head above water, it becomes very important to maintain your dignity. Elegance and easy grace were now the ideal, and they were incompatible with an event serving hundreds or even thousands, to say nothing of having to fire up a pit for hours and eventually digging your meal out of the dirt. Far more appealing was the prospect of calling up a few friends and casually, as if on the spur of the moment, inviting them over for drinks and steak.

However, there was certainly another factor in this decline, which had been foreshadowed two decades earlier when bulls' heads went out of fashion. The bull's-head breakfast had been only the most emphatic culinary form of the romance of the Days of the Dons, and its popularity tracks fairly well with the feverish cult of *Ramona*, a sentimental novel of the *rancho* days. During the Teens, and ever more rapidly during the Twenties, it dawned on Los Angeles that it now had a far more potent focus of local pride than dusty old cattle ranches: Hollywood. The city no longer needed the Dons. It had the Stars.

The Bull's Head Breakfast in Old Los Angeles

Notes

1. The minimum diameter was imposed by the logistics of using a shovel. When a larger pit was required, the diameter could be increased, though in Los Angeles it was more usual to turn the pit into a trench three or four meters long. The bottom of the pit had to be lined with a layer of rocks about a third of a meter deep. Some Los Angeles barbecue chefs used discarded iron railway rails instead because they were convenient to reuse.
2. The Stone Age method was to shovel dirt, ashes and hot rocks onto the bundles of meat, but it was eventually discovered that the meat is cleaner and easier to remove if the pit is covered with a lid of some sort before shoveling. A hundred years ago, Los Angeles barbecue chefs wrapped the meat in cotton sacking and stuffed it into wetted burlap sacks, rather than wrapping it in thick leaves, the Stone Age method.
3. E.g. some varieties of North African *méchoui* and the Omani *shuwa*. The thirteenth-century Arabic cookery book *Kitāb alWuṣla al-Ḥabīb* associates earth-pit cooking with the Bedouins, e.g. *nau' tu'ānīhi al-'arab* (MS Fatih 3617, Süleymaniye Library, Istanbul, p. 31b–32a). In this recipe, a pit was fired until the stones lining it turned red. The meat was set over the hot stones on a framework of green canes and the pit was covered with a special copper lid. Like the Turkish *kuyu tandir*, this is a modification of the ancient technique, because the coals were removed and as a result the meat would not have the smoke flavor.
4. Sometimes they called the meat *carne tatemada*, having coined the verb *tatemar* from the Aztec *(tla) tema*, 'to bathe (someone) in a *temascal* (*temaxcalli*)' or sweat lodge, the indigenous equivalent of a sauna. In the tequila industry, the word for baking the heart of an agave plant is still *tatemar*.
5. Louie and Annie Yorba, personal communication 5 July 2011. They have continued their family tradition of pit barbecue but are unaware of the special role of ox head, which tends to suggest that it was something developed by newcomers to Los Angeles in the 1880s.
6. *New York Times*, 6 October 1901, p. SM4. In an omitted paragraph the reporter claims, 'parts of half a dozen fat steers and as many select muttons were being roasted on improvised spits,' which is certainly a misunderstanding. This was an earth-pit barbecue, as the presence of bulls' heads proves. On internal evidence I suspect he never strayed very far from the 60-gallon 'majestic reservoir' of punch, 'the delectable contents of which told truthfully and augustly of a blend of not too dainty proportions of whiskey, rum, champagne, sugar, lemon, ice, pineapple, orange and banana slices, and the noblest berry of them all [viz. grapes].'
7. The earliest I have found appeared in the *Los Angeles Times* 1 September 1922, p. I18: 'Dr. and Mrs. Henry Lissner are to give a barbecue supper party next Tuesday evening at their summer home on the Palisades, Santa Monica… The barbecue will be prepared in the patio, which has a large fireplace and grill.'
8. *Los Angeles Times*, 25 July 1934, p. 14.
9. *Los Angeles Times*, 22 November 1939, p. 5: 'Fun begins with a home of your own. Barbecue, badminton, ping-pong, flower culture, amateur carpentry, photography … a thousand little hobbies and pleasures are made possible when you move into your own home.' The accompanying illustration shows a deeply contented papa in an apron and chef's hat grilling steaks for his guests, a pipe clenched in his teeth.
10. *Los Angeles Times*, 19 July 1940, p. 14: 'Not Suzy-Q but Barbecue is the last word in entertaining and good times. Everything from swank patio party to beach or mountain picnics turns into an outdoor barbecue. This is real California hospitality for you, informal, gay, and loads of fun.'

Underground Restaurants – A New Way to Celebrate with Strangers

Heike Pethe and Sabine Cikic

Secret supper clubs are gaining in popularity in Western metropolises. These novel celebratory social events are organized by amateur chefs who aim to prepare an ambitious menu. Hosts find strangers to be their guests by posting invitations to the public at large via the Internet. Guests usually pay a previously agreed amount – often between €20.00 and €100.00 – to cover the host's costs, and are normally allowed to bring their own alcohol.

This trend originated in the Americas where a particular busy supper club scene emerged in Buenos Aires. In the US, supper clubs are well visited and the concept is firmly established. In March 2011, a first cookbook was even published (Rodgers 2011), introducing the concept of underground restaurants and containing recipes from what is probably London's most famous supper club.

Berlin, Germany's exciting and historic capital, is not only a city with a turbulent past but is nowadays a dynamic and ever-changing creative and cultural melting-pot. It is known for an almost unceasing succession of festivals and events, but for some time now Berlin has lagged somewhat in the field of culinary innovation. The city is the site of Germany's first fast-food restaurant, Aschinger, which had huge success selling pea soup to passing factory hands and office workers. Other quick bites consumed standing up are the omnipresent *currywurst* and *doner kebab*. Although in Europe Germany is second only to France in the number of Michelin-starred restaurants, *haute cuisine* is not a significant part of Berlin's culinary scene.

But still, in Berlin the last few years have seen the emergence of a small but lively supper club scene. In this paper we will look at the identity of the main players who are establishing not only a new form of hospitality but also celebrating pure culinary pleasure. We will focus particularly on the extent to which modern rituals correspond to those of the past, and what role is played by the particular occasion behind the event and by the community that attends it. For our research, in March and April 2011 we visited five out of the ten functioning supper clubs in the city. We used the method of participant observation to collect our information. In addition, we interviewed the hosts of one other club that only posted their menus sporadically.

Celebrating and eating: the search for a definition

The secret cooks hosting a supper club may choose any or no particular occasion to celebrate, and generally are not guided in the scheduling of their events by any festive calendar dictating the communal and social commitments of a certain group, nation or church. Rather the focus is on 'celebrating' one's own ability and performance as a cook. The key benefit to the guests is that they can enjoy a restaurant-quality dining experience at a much lower cost than usual, as well as offering them the opportunity to participate in a gathering of a more adventurous nature, and one that still offers a certain clandestine *frisson*. The guests and their chef for the evening form a conspiratorial community which is united by a love of good food – one in which they are active participants rather than passive customers.

At first glance it may not be entirely clear to the observer to what extent events of this kind can be classified as celebrations in the usual sense, but although many characteristics differ, the parallels are strong. In this paper we argue that this new way of 'underground' feasting might be an answer to post-modern society's need for sociability, eating, and self-determining festive occasions. By bringing together a new community of participants in cities where family, religious and other social commitments play a diminishing role in determining social interaction, one's ability to select one's own social environment for festive occasions is here asserted. The once-strong connection between the celebration itself and the guests chosen to share in its observance – traditionally determined by the social, political, economic, and religious identity of the host – is thus broken down. Strangers are granted access to the private sphere and together assume the role of guests, although they are still selected in one sense by virtue of their expertise and sympathy for the culinary celebration being performed.

Perhaps surprisingly, the secret dinners display all the familiar characteristics one would usually expect to find in any communal dining ritual: a well-prepared table, due diligence in composing the menu and selecting the food, a thorough display of the cooks' technical abilities, and finally an orderly procedure in inviting and hosting guests. All these measures go beyond what is normally necessary in everyday meals. Although the hosts might be freer to determine the course of the ritual than conventional hosts who are bound by a specific occasion and the social expectations of their peers, the self-selected hosts appear to be more conservative in this respect. They tend to follow traditional rules and rituals of hospitality with some degree of rigour.

Celebrations in literature

German literature on celebrations and festivities touches only lightly on the relationship between celebration and eating (Bausinger 1987; Bubner 1989; Dewald 2008; Hugger 1987; Hugger et al., 1987; Lipp 1987, 1989; Marquard 1989). This may be due to the fact that, more than their neighbours, Germans typically draw a distinction between work and leisure time, and similarly between the everyday and the special occasion (for a comparison of Germany and the Netherlands see Linthout (2006)). As there is practically no precise definition of the function and meaning of food at festivals and celebrations, in our analysis we will make use of the very broad definition of a celebration in the Brockhaus *Lexicon* (1989): 'Celebration: a ceremonious event distinguished from the everyday, to mark a notable private or public, secular or religious occasion, usually a communal event; ...' (own translation). The execution of such celebrations is defined by three definitive elements: an occasion, a festive community and an appurtenant ritual (cf. Hillmann 1994). This will be discussed in greater detail below.

Occasions for celebrations

It is probably nigh on impossible to list all the many and various occasions which, throughout history, people have marked with feasts and celebration. They are too diverse and, above all, too numerous. From the bacchanalia of antiquity to medieval tournaments, courtly banquets to revolutionary celebrations, birthdays, graduation parties and receptions – there are many occasions to celebrate individual or collective events (Gebhardt 1987: 35 and 63–64). They are an expression of the individual and collective search for meaning – no wonder there are so many of them.

Making up a festive community

The nature of the festive community is generally determined by the nature of the event: at Christmas the family is invited, local inhabitants come to the neighbourhood street party, funerals are attended by family, friends, acquaintances, colleagues, etc. A hobby or interest, a political persuasion or sexual identity, or the place of residence can be the determining factors. At most celebrations, participants share either a common interest or the same family origin. Thus it is not surprising that in his study of French society Pierre Bourdieu found that in all social classes more than two-thirds of all invitations are directed to close family and friends. Only in bourgeois circles are professional colleagues invited to any significant extent (Bourdieu 1987: 318–19).

In summary it can be stated that in this context celebrations serve to reinforce social structures and to consolidate social groups (Bell and Valentine 1997: 204). Therefore a festive meal will generally be conservative in its design, and the composition of the flavours used is even called old-fashioned by some. According to this argument, culinary innovation is hardly to be expected at celebrations. Although most celebrations are actually relatively predetermined in their selection of guests, and homogeneous in terms of their culinary expectations, there is a trend that runs counter to this. The traditional circle of guests at the table is breaking up, and a space is emerging in which the closed collective can be dissolved.

As long as twenty-five years ago researchers were surprised to discover that only one in two families were still following a fixed order for meals, and only one in four were still eating meals together. The increase in take-away food was a factor in this process of dissolution (Gedrich and Oltersdorf 2002: 17; Lincke 2007: 9). Although we have not yet looked in detail at how traditional festive communities have changed, it can be assumed that their composition is opening up to new forms of membership, while at the same time old forms are becoming obsolete (Bell and Valentine 1997: 65).

The change in social structures is accompanied by a change in the food people

Underground Restaurants – A New Way to Celebrate

regularly consume. Although in general eating habits change far more slowly than other forms of behaviour, the availability of foreign cuisines in Western Europe, culinary souvenirs from foreign travel, and the wide range of food-related content in the media – from cookery programmes, recipe books, and cooking magazines to cooking videos on the Internet – have all greatly added to the culinary options available. Although ethnic cookery remains for most people, particularly the educated middle class (Bell and Valentine 1997: 193 and 202), limited to what is available in supermarkets and restaurants, many people who have partners, parents, friends or neighbours from other cultural backgrounds are already experiencing a much more diverse and multifarious dining experience than was possible even for their parents' generation (ibid.: 117 and 191).

Finally, there is another line of argument to support the point that festivals function not only to reinforce existing communities but also contain a multiplicity of elements which would indicate that they contribute to forming new communities. The philosopher Odo Marquard (1989: 685, own translation) summarizes the significance of festivals as follows: 'In the everyday, people are involved with just living their lives. In celebrations, people take a step back from their usual lives'. There is a long list of philosophers and social scientists who describe the 'celebration' as something 'eccentric' (Marquard), 'unrestrained' (Mauss, Freund), 'subversive' (Duvignaud), or as the 'very epitome of intoxication' (Nietzsche) (Hugger 1987; Lipp 1989: 665 and 671; Marquard 1989: 656, own translations). As people open themselves up to the unexpected, celebrations become places of encounter, an antidote to routine social conventions. People open themselves up to new experiences. It is through eating that people forge new personal connections. The feeling of pleasure created by eating becomes a means to shared learning, creating meaning, and to participation (Lipp 1989: 673–681). In the introduction to his recipe book, Paul Bocuse (1999: 15, own translation) describes the table as an altar, 'only set and decorated to celebrate the cult of friendship'. New communities are created.

Celebratory rituals

In his analysis of the various elements that make up a celebration, Hugger comes to the conclusion that, particularly at modern celebrations, the act of eating is excluded as a subject for discussion. The purpose of the celebration, the type and form of the related cultural manifestations, and the type of festive community involved are often the subject of lively debate, but the actual eating is hardly mentioned (Hugger 1987: 17). This may be down to that inherent conservatism already mentioned. Thus Teuteberg (1993: 119, own translation) reports that the formation of taste, like the behaviour of feeding, is 'an extremely tough process' which only gradually changes 'after certain feelings of reluctance have been overcome'. On the other hand even a brief glance at the history of art shows that the aesthetics of culinary taste, ever since the Italian Futurists and the principles they established for 'The Taverna of the Holy Palate' and the Restaurant Spoerri in the old town centre in Düsseldorf, has been seen as a critical space for revolutionary interventions (Lemke 2007). One does not perhaps have to be quite as radical as the activists of Eat Art, who continue to want to break completely with traditional habits surrounding dining, but giants of social sciences such as Norbert Elias do point out that the changes in eating rituals have mainly been due to changes in the progress of civilization (Elias 1992) and not due to technical or hygiene-related achievements. In spite of medical progress, new kitchen and cooling technology, and the increase in the production of processed products for the kitchen and cooks, the ritual of eating remains much more a civilizational consensus than a product of knowledge transfer, or of the increasing importance of technology and hygiene in world societies.

The supper clubs in Berlin

Although there may at first appear to be little reason to choose Berlin in which to look for food trends or the particularities of culinary celebrations, hospitality and festiveness do in fact have a long-standing institutional tradition in the city, in the form of the Berlin salons, in which high-society ladies, before World War II, would open their houses to select social gatherings, offering people of all kinds of backgrounds a space for discussions, readings, or musical performances, wrapped in hospitality of every imaginable kind. They opened their houses to guests in order to share in celebration and entertainment (Sombart 2002, 52–61; Wilhelmy-Dollinger, 2000). These salons are unfortunately long gone from Berlin, as they are from other cities such as Paris. Inviting strangers into your house to eat now seems to be an extremely rare occurrence. So it is even more surprising that, as we now observe, a new and public form of hospitality is again being cultivated in today's Berlin, and one in which eating is a central part of the event.

There are currently in Berlin ten active supper clubs, offering events at more or less regular intervals, often maintaining thoroughly professional standards. Most supper clubs have specialized in five-course menus, but three- and four-course menus as well as buffets for a larger number of guests are occasionally offered.

The occasion

Opinions on whether our modern society celebrates too much or too little (Lipp 1987: 231; 1989) are many and contradictory. In contrast to the normal calendar of festivities, supper clubs are not bound to any fixed date, and so are not linked to traditions, religious occasions or other ideological belief systems.

The occasion is mostly determined exclusively by the hosts' ambitions. When they have time to play the role of a host and/or have collected and tested enough recipes, it is again time to invite strangers to their supper club for a five-course meal. As these hosts are generally not professional cooks, and the focus is not on earning money, the preparation needed for the dinners determines how often people are invited. And as the hosts are not dependent on income from these events, they do not need to make compromises. At this point we should mention that while this applies almost across the board for Berlin supper clubs, different circumstances are at least as common in other cities. In New York, for example, many professional cooks who have lost their jobs in the recession set up a supper club on the one hand to secure a half-decent regular income and on the other to add lustre to their reputation. As far as we can determine, there seems to be only one such profit-oriented supper club in Berlin. Though hosts in this case were not dependent on the income (at least they said as much), the value for money on offer was extraordinarily poor. But as we only experienced such a negative result once, we tend to count this host and event as the exception that proves the rule!

Festive communities at the Berlin supper clubs

In supper clubs, it is entirely up to the host to select who will be part of the festive community. They are not bound to any occasion, nor obliged to take account of any ideology or function. And in fact many cooks make explicit mention of this new degree of freedom. They are relieved not to have to cook for a specific festive community whose expectations they have no desire to comply with. On the contrary, the supper club cooks have every possible freedom to design a meal according to their own interests, and to select the festive community themselves. In these respects they are truly autonomous.

Berlin clubs have, however, so far proved quite reserved/conservative when it comes to selecting their guests. As hosts, they seem to make little use of their rights to determine who enters their home: applications are often dealt with on a first-come, first-served basis. And hosts continue to uphold this principle even when for example the mixture of guests that results may not appear particularly favourable, or one demographic group appears to dominate more than would be ideal to ensure a truly sociable atmosphere. Thus to a large extent they surrender the social-organizational aspect of their roles as hosts, as is confirmed by an additional factor: interaction between the organizers of the supper club and their guests is generally limited. This is of course due to the fact that they are busy cooking during the evening, but they do always appear briefly to both welcome their guests and often to present the various dishes as the meal progresses. These moments could be used to get to know their guests better, but in fact usually are not. Most hosts are quite reserved in their behaviour, to the point of seeming almost shy. They usually join the company after the dessert, at which point they might discuss their motivations and their menu. By this point in the evening, of course, the guests will have formed a social group of their own accord.

How keen are those invited to get to know other guests, and how important is the level of sociability at the table to them? We found that the guests in this respect behave very similarly to their hosts. As they also tend to focus on the quality of the five-course menu on offer, the social aspect of the meal is deemed of secondary importance. This does not however mean that guests are insensible to the social aspects. Especially when compared to restaurants, where guests have no obligation to engage with each other, these emphasize how pleasant they find it to come into contact with other people at these supper clubs. Those who were visiting the supper clubs as tourists were hoping for a good introduction to the city and to have an opportunity to meet with locals. Others were anxious to escape from the anonymity of restaurants and desired a more open and friendly interaction with other guests than is possible in professional establishments. In our observations we did, however, also determine that although a communal meal can encourage interaction and mutual openness, the results may vary according to the composition of the group in question. Friendly reserve is the dominant mood, which is quickly dissolved as soon as interests or factors in common are discovered. But it remains intact as the basis of the interaction. Some guests, particularly those of German origin, are not especially outgoing and will arrange their evening to ensure they have limited contact with strangers. They tend to bring friends with them in large numbers, and to only make a limited and select use of any foreign language skills they possess. An open and easy manner, which many people in Germany value in Americans, for instance, does not come easily to people like this and they find it difficult to assume such a manner even at the communal evenings we describe here. For these individuals, getting to know other people is not the main aim of their visit to the supper club, but is rather a fortunate happenstance if the circumstances are right.

So although supper club organizers play a very low-key role among their guests, the type of people who are involved in supper club activities is relatively homogeneous. As stated above, most participants share an intense interest in sophisticated, exotic, high-level cookery. The majority have an academic degree, and often a career in the media. In contrast to most Berlin events, most participants here are of an international background. The clubs are most frequently visited by English-speaking guests, generally (doctoral) students or young professionals relatively new to the city. An older international group visit as tourists. This predominantly international background may partly be related to the hosts' own social circles, but is also of course at least in part due to the fact that supper clubs as a form of event are much better established in English-speaking countries than they are in Berlin.

Many of the Germans are frequent guests, evidently finding this form of dining interesting enough to sample it repeatedly. We found scarcely any repeat visitors amongst the non-German guests. This may well also be due to the prices associated with the supper clubs. Most German guests were over forty years of age, and well established in their careers, whereas the non-Germans tended to still be in education, and were presumably unable or unwilling to afford such events on a regular basis, which were often not inexpensive in relation to the local restaurant scene.

The demographic profile of the supper club guests tended to confirm Bourdieu's analysis of the relationship between social class and food consumption (Blasius 1990; Bourdieu 1987: 288–323 and 830–31), whereby consumers of simple, attractively presented, local and highly nutritious dishes tend to belong to the working class, while the upper and middle classes tend to prefer original, exotic, sensually appealing, refined and elegant food (Bourdieu 1987: 830–31). In transposing Bourdieu's themes to German society (Köln-Nippes) Blasius pointed out that students and young educated professionals with a lower income tend to gravitate to more artistic and improvised forms of dining much more frequently than wealthier older groups with a comparable level of education (Blasius 1990). This factor is clearly discernible in the ritual elements of the supper club, as we discuss below.

Rituals at supper clubs in Berlin

Menu design proved surprisingly conservative, with most hosts presenting a five-course menu. Nearly all supper clubs offer an accompanying series of wines as an optional extra, but guests are generally free to bring their own drinks.

The event usually starts with a welcome from the host, after which an (alcoholic) aperitif is offered. Guests then have chance to introduce themselves to each other, and in some cases to take time to appreciate the setting, which is after all an integral part of the event. At this stage in the evening conversation tends to centre on where the guests come from and whether they have taken part in a supper club before. If they are present for aperitifs at all, the host usually takes a back seat. Guests are summoned to table after no more than half an hour, and the first course is then presented.

Guests are generally seated around one large table, in some cases with the rest of the room's furniture cleared away to make space. As far as we were able to observe, table decoration is kept simple. Tablecloths and place cards are not generally used, but fresh flowers are always in evidence. Crockery and glasses sometimes seem to have been assembled from a variety of sources, but often matching glasses and silverware had been provided.

From the point of view of Berlin's contemporary standards, the menus composed are strikingly international and often innovative, typically featuring for example fusion cuisine with inspiration drawn from Asian and American traditions: Californian / Mexican cooking of a kind that is scarcely to be expected in any of Berlin's 'Mexican' restaurants, Basque tapas (called '*pintxos*' – which again are not to be found in Berlin's usual tapas bars), or Caribbean jerk chicken, etc. It does seem that guests can reliably expect new and unfamiliar dishes and flavours at each event, and ones which are not to be found in conventional restaurants. In conjunction with the also novel five-course menu form, and the (varyingly) complementary selection of wine and drinks on offer, the supper club's culinary aspect is for most guests very much the highlight of the evening. This is perhaps the reason why most participants (in fact almost all, at all the supper clubs) seemed to be relatively unconcerned with dressing in an elegant manner. It could not be ignored that most were dressed much more casually than one would expect for a visit to a conventional restaurant.

Conclusion

In this article we have shown that supper clubs have established a new kind of culinary celebration in a city more usually known for its fast-food culture. But will the supper clubs, being private events, have a comparable influence on Berlin's cuisine and society

Underground Restaurants – A New Way to Celebrate

as did the private literary and artistic salons of the eighteenth century and onwards on the cultural life of the city? In Berlin perhaps more than in other cities, supper clubs have developed as an initiative on the part of hobby-chefs in search of an audience for their talents. With this type of celebration, food is much more a focal point than in other kinds of festive gatherings. The cooks determine their schedule, and thus are not obliged to follow any conventions linked to any specific occasion or specific festive community. The promise of a high-quality menu, in a five-course format that is rare in Germany, is occasion enough to bring a group of celebrants together. In this context, hobby-cooks from English-speaking countries go beyond the local international community to attract more and more Berliners with the offer of new dishes of a kind that is extremely uncommon in the Berlin culinary landscape. A new festive community is brought together by food. For the guests, the charm of the supper club is that it offers a way to escape from the anonymity of professional gastronomy, to meet new people and to sample the cook's own domestic environment. The new interaction is more intense than would be experienced in a restaurant but much more reserved than is usual at other celebrations, where guests often already know each other and sociability is the focus. We see much more potential in the culinary aspects of the event. It can still be hoped that Berliners too will gradually allow themselves to be tempted by the gastronomic delights on offer, as this is an area in which the supper clubs truly are breaking new ground. The innovative cuisine prepared with so much commitment and dedication, and served in the format of a five-course menu, is certainly unusual for the city, and is the focus of much attention in the media and amongst the international (and increasingly also native) public at large. The celebrations that arise in the private framework of the supper clubs may very well contribute to raising the standard of the culinary landscape in Berlin, and the concept of unusual dishes served as an evening-long ritual may in the longer term have the effect of increasing the quality of Berlin's cuisine in general. In order to ensure that this contribution is effective, further German and international adherents still need to be attracted both as hosts and as guests to the supper club scene.

Underground Restaurants – A New Way to Celebrate

References

Bausinger, Hermann, 1987. 'Ein Abwerfen der großen Last …', in *Stadt und Fest*, ed. Paul Hugger, Walter Burkert, and Ernst Lichtenhahn (Unterägeri and Stuttgart: W&H and J.B. Metzler), 251–267.

Bell, David, and Valentine, Gill, 1997. *Consuming geographies* (London: Routledge).

Blasius, J. 1990. 'Gentrification und Lebensstile', in *Gentrification. Die Aufwertung innenstadtnaher Wohnviertel*, ed. Jörg Blasius and Jens Dangschat (Frankfurt/Main: Campus), 354–375.

Bocuse, Paul, 1999. *Das Paul Bocuse Standardkochbuch* (München: Heyne).

Bourdieu, Pierre, 1987. *Die feinen Unterschiede* (Frankfurt: suhrkamp taschenbuch wissenschaft).

Bubner, Rüdiger, 1989. 'Ästhetisierung der Lebenswelt', in *Das Fest*, ed. Walter Haug and Rainer Warning (München: Fink), 651–662.

Dewald, Markus, 2008. *Trend zum Event* (Ostfildern: Thorbecke).

dtv-Brockhaus-Lexikon, 1989: s.v. 'Feier' (Mannheim and München: Brockhaus dtv), 251.

Elias, Norbert, 1992. *Wandlungen des Verhaltens in den weltlichen Oberschichten des Abendlandes* (Frankfurt am Main: Suhrkamp).

Gebhardt, Winfried, 1987. *Fest, Feier und Alltag. Über die gesellschaftliche Wirklichkeit des Menschen und ihre Deutung*, Europäische Hochschulschriften Reihe 22, Soziologie, Bd. 143 (Frankfurt/Main: Peter Lang).

Gedrich, Kurt and Oltersdorf, Ulrich (eds.), 2002. *Ernährung und Raum: Regionale und ethnische Ernährungsweisen in Deutschland* (Karlsruhe: Bundesforschungsanstalt für Ernährung).

Hillmann, Karl-Heinz, 1994. 'Fest', in *Wörterbuch der Soziologie*, ed. Karl-Heinz Hillmann (Körner: Stuttgart), 221–222.

Hugger, Paul, 1987. 'Einleitung', in *Stadt und Fest*, ed. Paul Hugger, Wolfgang Burkert and Ernst Lichtenhahn (Unterägeri and Stuttgart: W. & H. and J.B. Metzler), 9–24.

Hugger, Paul, Burkert, Wolfgang, and Lichtenhahn, Ernst (eds.), 1987. *Stadt und Fest* (Unterägeri and Stuttgart: W. & H. and J.B. Metzler).

Lemke, Harald, 2007. *Die Kunst des Essens* (Bielefeld: transcript).

Lincke, Hans-Joachim, 2007. *Doing Time* (Bielefeld: transcript-Verlag).

Linthout, Dik, 2006. *Frau Antje und Herr Mustermann* (Berlin: Ch. Lincks Verlag).

Lipp, Wolfgang, 1987. 'Gesellschaft und Festkultur', in *Stadt und Fest*, ed. Paul Hugger, Wolfgang Burkert, and Ernst Lichtenhahn (Unterägeri and Stuttgart: W. & H. and J.B. Metzler), 231–249.

——, 1989. 'Feste heute', in *Das Fest*, ed. Walter Haug and Rainer Warning (München: Fink), 663–683.

Marquard, Odo, 1989. 'Moratorium des Alltags', in *Das Fest*, ed. Walter Haug and Rainer Warning (München: Fink), 684–691.

Rodgers, Kerstin, 2011. *Supper Club: Recipes and Notes from The Underground Restaurant* (London: Collins).

Sombart, Norbert, 2002. *Jugend in Berlin 1933–1943* (Frankfurt/M: Fischer).

Teuteberg, Hans J. 1993. 'Prolegomena zu einer Kulturpsychologie des Geschmacks', in *Kulturthema Essen – Ansichten und Problemfelder*, ed. Alois Wierlacher and Gerhard Neumann (Berlin: Akad.-Verlag), 103–136.

Wilhelmy-Dollinger, Petra, 2000. *Die Berliner Salons* (Berlin: de Gruyter).

On *Mfúúmbu, Nkasa*, and Whisky: A Wedding Celebration in Kimbonga-Louamba (Congo-Brazzaville)

Birgit Ricquier

It is often stated to be 'the happiest day of one's life'. Couples spend months if not years to prepare for that one day when they will publicly vow to spend a lifetime together, in good times and bad. Relatives and friends gather to witness this culmination of romance. An indulgent wedding meal is the stage for the reunion with distant relatives and for new encounters – sometimes resulting in other unions. In July 2010, I was more than delighted when I was invited to attend a wedding in Kimbonga-Louamba. I stayed nine days in this village in order to collect culinary vocabulary in Kikaamba, and my hosts thought this feast would be a good moment for me to observe their culinary traditions. Mama Honorine, mother of the bride, was kind enough to let me attend all the preparations for the wedding. What follows is an account of the wedding that focuses on its food-related aspects.[1]

Kimbonga-Louamba is a village in the Bouenza province of the Republic of the Congo (often dubbed Congo-Brazzaville after its capital and to distinguish it from the Democratic Republic of the Congo or Congo-Kinshasa). The village is situated some twelve kilometres from the town of Nkayi. The inhabitants of the village are members of the Kaamba ethnic group. Most, if not all, are Christian – belonging to different churches, however. Kimbonga-Louamba is situated in the savannah, one of the most fertile parts of the country. Cultivated crops include cassava (the staple of the region), yams, peanuts, plantains, and diverse vegetables. At the back of the houses several fruit trees are planted, for instance mangoes and oranges, as well as palm trees. The latter supplies amongst other things palm wine and the palm nuts used to make the sauce *mwáamba*. Chickens run free around the house. The Kaamba also keep sheep and, to a lesser extent, pigs. An important source of cash income is the sale of tomatoes grown on large fields some kilometres from the village. Many men also get an income from work on the SARIS sugar-cane plantations which surround Nkayi.

A wedding in Kimbonga-Louamba

On Sunday, 11 July 2010, Missie Théophile Thomas and Bidounga Nzoussi Chimène got married according to local customs. The civil and the Christian marriages were concluded in 2006, but it took the groom some time to save enough for the bride-wealth that is essential for the traditional marriage. The couple already had three children. The village chief or *président* jested that you need to test whether the match is fertile before getting married. However, since Théophile had asked Chimène's hand in

On *Mfúúmbu, Nkasa,* and Whisky

1997, after which they were allowed to live together, the children were not actually born out of wedlock. It must be observed that the match is intercultural. Missie Théophile Thomas is of the Teke ethnic group; his bride is Kaamba.

Although the couple, like many members of the family, lives in Brazzaville, the marriage took place in Kimbonga-Louamba. This is where Mama Honorine, the bride's mother, lives and she was in charge of the wedding meal.[2] It is the bride's family that welcomes the family of the groom, who will arrive with the bride-wealth. Mama Honorine had to take care that food was tasty and sufficient for the entire party. Not succeeding would mean an embarrassment to her family. In sub-Saharan Africa, most food items are difficult to preserve. As such, no feast meal can be prepared in advance and many hands are needed to compose the meal right before serving. To organize a feast, one thus needs to be a good manager (Dietler 2001, 80–81). Mama Honorine had solicited the help of daughters, relatives and friends. The preparations started on Saturday, at noon. Once they had said a prayer, a first team started cooking huge volumes of *kikwánga*, one of the staple dishes of the region. This took the entire afternoon. When dusk fell, the team ended the day by preparing peanut butter which would be used in the preparations of the other team. The first team was cooking at Mama Honorine's home; the second in the village centre. The second team first took care of a meal for all the women. They fried *makwáálu*, smoked fish from Pointe Noire, the main harbour and second city of the country. This was served with *kikwánga*. Next, they started cooking cassava leaves and beans. Both preparations are time-consuming and thus needed to be made in advance. The last task of the second team was cutting up the frozen chicken. The chicken was purchased in Nkayi. Around 7 p.m., the women suspended preparations. The cassava leaves and beans were left to 'sleep on the fire'.

Sunday, in the early morning, activities were resumed. Two men slaughtered and butchered a pig and a sheep. The meat was used for the wedding meal, but the entrails were prepared for the butchers. In the meantime, several fires were lit and the women started composing the various dishes. These were as follows:

Ntoobá ya bisúlu: cassava leaves prepared in peanut butter
Ntoobá ya máámba máámba: cassava leaves prepared in a bouillon
Salade ya ngúlu: pork salad (with vinaigrette, fresh tomatoes, peppers and onions)
Bíindya byá mbote: pork in tomato sauce
Mádeeso: beans in tomato sauce
Dímeeme dya sauce: mutton in tomato sauce
Midyá mya dímeeme: mutton entrails
Mfúúmbu yá nsyesi: *Gnetum africanum* with Duiker meat (*Cephalophus* sp.)[3]
Kinkúla: 'sorrel' (leaves of *Hibiscus* sp., with an acidic taste)[4]
Makwáálu má kaangu: fried fish
Nsusu zá kaangu: fried chicken
Nkasa za mwáamba: peas in palm-nut sauce
Ngulú ya musóngi: pork (ears, feet, etc.) prepared in stock (butcher's meal)[5]

These dishes would be served with rice, *kikwánga* and bread. The bread in the Republic of the Congo is the French-style baguette introduced during colonization.

In the meantime, the groom and his family had arrived. Around 1 p.m. it was announced that the wedding would soon begin. The women dispersed to get dressed, leaving just a few to finalize the dishes. The marriage ceremony was a *coup de théâtre* in which the family of the groom presented the bride-wealth to the bride's family. A family member of the bride took up the role of negotiator and embroidered the enactment with comments and jokes. Whenever gifts were well received he incited the women to sing and dance. After the presentation of the bride-wealth, some marital advice was formulated and then the bride's family offered gifts to the newly married couple. The ceremony ended with the wedding meal.

The cooks and the diners

This description of the events depicts a strict labour-division during the preparations. In most societies, cooking is a female activity, but certain tasks, for instance roasting and butchering, are reserved for the men (Goody 1982, 71). Indeed, all preparations were in the hands of the female relatives and friends of the bride's mother. However, the killing and butchering of the pig and sheep were carried out by men. As soon as the meat was cut up in smaller pieces, it was handed over to the women who continued its preparation.

Also during the wedding and the meal, men and women fulfilled different roles and respected a specific hierarchy. A distinction was made between three groups. The first consisted of the relatives of the groom, regardless of gender. They were seated at the left side of the bride and, together with the married couple, they were served before the others. The second group was formed by the male relatives of the bride and other male guests.[6] They sat on the right hand side of the groom and were second to be served. Finally, the female relatives of the bride and other women of the village constituted the third group. Many of them had taken part in the preparations for the wedding meal, but they were the last to eat. Consequently, they had to content themselves with leftovers. During the wedding ceremony, they were seated opposite of the couple, thus closing the square, and they animated the event with songs and dancing. In sum, the women of the village were cooks, singers/musicians and dancers. This stands in contrast with the female relatives of the groom who, for the occasion, acted out the same role as the men. For once, they were not the cooks but the diners (cf. Dietler 2001, 91).

Pork, wine and Maggi cubes

Hayden (2001, 28) defines feasts as 'any sharing between two or more people of special foods (i.e. foods not generally served at daily meals) in a meal for a special purpose or occasion'. But what are 'special foods'? In his famous monograph on cuisine and class (Goody 1982), Goody stated that culinary practice in sub-Saharan Africa is not differentiated and that a high-class cuisine or *haute cuisine* is virtually absent. Indeed, the Kaamba wedding meal was not an example of gastronomic excess as might be expected in Europe. At first glance, the dishes served could have appeared at a weekday supper. I had been served *ntoobá* and *nkasa* only a few days before. However, also in sub-Saharan Africa, feasts are marked by food specificities. Luo feasts, for instance, differ from daily meals by the presence of beer and beef (Dietler 2001, 96), and Yassa and Mvae feasts are marked by domestic meat, game, large smoked snapper, plantains, and alcoholic beverages like beer and whisky (de Garine 1996, 211).[7] Similarly, meat and alcohol were abundant at the Kaamba wedding, but the dishes served were also out of the ordinary, having been prepared in a more elaborate fashion.

For the wedding, a pig and a sheep were slaughtered, frozen chicken was purchased at the market in Nkayi, and smoked Duiker appeared on the menu. The guests thus had the choice between two pork dishes, two mutton preparations, fried chicken and a Duiker stew, in sum six meat dishes. On top of that, there was also fried fish available. This multitude of proteins is not served on a daily basis. Only fish appears regularly on an everyday menu. From time to time chicken or game might be offered, but quite often people content themselves with a vegetarian meal. Consequently, the wedding was an occasion during which the guests could literally feast on meat and fish.

Secondly, there was a plethora of drink, alcoholic as well as sodas. Local beverages included palm wine and sugarcane wine. Then there were bottled beers and sodas. Finally there were the much-appreciated bottles of red wine and whisky. These were part of the bride-wealth which will be discussed further below. Even if alcoholic beverages and sodas are an occasional treat for many at the wedding, by and large they would quench their thirst with water alone. The presence of these drinks at the wedding, therefore, marked out the event as a special celebration.

The meal's preparation was special too. Even if the dishes concerned are not exclusive to festive occasions, they were prepared with a celebratory twist. The preparation of cassava leaves, for example, clearly was out of the ordinary. Usually, these greens are seasoned with palm oil and peanut butter only and, when available, fish is added. For the wedding meal, the cassava leaves were prepared with the addition of eggplants, cabbage, onion, peppers, garlic, scallions and Maggi cubes. The mixture was seasoned in two different ways: a hearty version with palm oil and peanut butter, and a lighter version with peanut oil. No fish was added since plenty of fish and meat was served on the side. The other dishes were also more elaborately flavoured. Most included the quartet of onion, garlic, scallions and peppers, as well as Maggi cubes, which are readily available at town markets but hardly used in villages (cf. Ricquier 2011, 33, 34). In sum, the higher number of different and more exclusive ingredients set the dishes of the wedding meal apart from daily fare.

Mfúúmbu versus *nkasa*, and a salad on the side
Dietler notes that '[c]oncepts of ethnicity … very frequently involve beliefs (of variable accuracy) about distinctive food tastes and culinary practices', and that '[f]easts can be

a theatre for the symbolic manipulation of such culinary distinctions' (Dietler 2001, 89; cf. also Fribourg 1996, 349). The marriage under discussion being intercultural, it was the perfect stage to express views on Kaamba and Teke culinary identities. Mama Honorine explained that she wanted to please the in-laws by serving them a dish that she considered to be typically Teke. However, she also wanted them to have a taste of Kaamba culinary practice and chose a dish that could represent Kaamba culinary traditions.

The signature dish of the Teke, according to Mama Honorine, was *mfúúmbu* (*Gnetum africanum*). *Gnetum africanum* is a leafy vegetable found in tropical Central Africa, from Nigeria to Angola, and it is usually collected in the wild (Latham 2004, 141). Its leaves are cut into fine strips and prepared in stock or peanut sauce. Mama Honorine had the vegetable prepared with Duiker meat (*Cephalophus* sp.) in a stock with tomatoes, onion, scallions and salt. The idea that this vegetable may represent Teke culinary traditions was confirmed by Teke women when I visited the town Ngô on the Teke Plateau four weeks later. Asking one of the women there to prepare a signature dish, she settled on this leafy vegetable. She prepared it with fish and peanut sauce. It should be observed that this is not a cultural variation but simply another version of the dish, also prepared elsewhere in the region.

Kaamba cuisine was represented by *nkasa za mwáamba*, i.e. 'peas' in palm-nut sauce. Even if my informants called these legumes *petits pois*, i.e. *Pisum sativum* or peas, it probably concerns *Cajanus cajan* or pigeon pea, a cultivated legume of African origins (cf. Latham 2004, 64). In other interviews with Kaamba women, this legume was also tied to local food customs.

Mfúúmbu and pigeon peas are by no means exclusively Teke or Kaamba dishes. Each vegetable is prepared by the other ethnic group, as well as by other Central African peoples. Not even the preparation method can be claimed by one or the other ethnic group. The link between the food item and ethnic identity is rather a matter of food preferences.

Food preferences also mark the opposition between city and village. In the village, people mainly rely on local foodstuffs which are prepared in a traditional way, but city-dwellers experiment with introduced foodways, mostly of European origin. As mentioned, many members of the family live in the capital, Brazzaville, and one of the sisters of the bride decided to prepare for the party a dish from her 'urban' culinary repertoire. She prepared a salad with pork, tomatoes, peppers, onion and (canned) vegetable macédoine, in a vinaigrette composed of peanut oil, mayonnaise, vinegar and salt. She had planned to garnish the salad with parsley but none was found in Nkayi. Salads are a European introduction. Raw foodstuffs, except for fruits, are not consumed in the region. Consequently, with the salad she added a city flavour to the meal.

Since the marriage took place in the village, the other food served was *a priori* local and traditional. This was in sharp contrast with the food served at an engagement ceremony that I had attended the previous month in Brazzaville. That match was

On *Mfúúmbu, Nkasa,* and Whisky

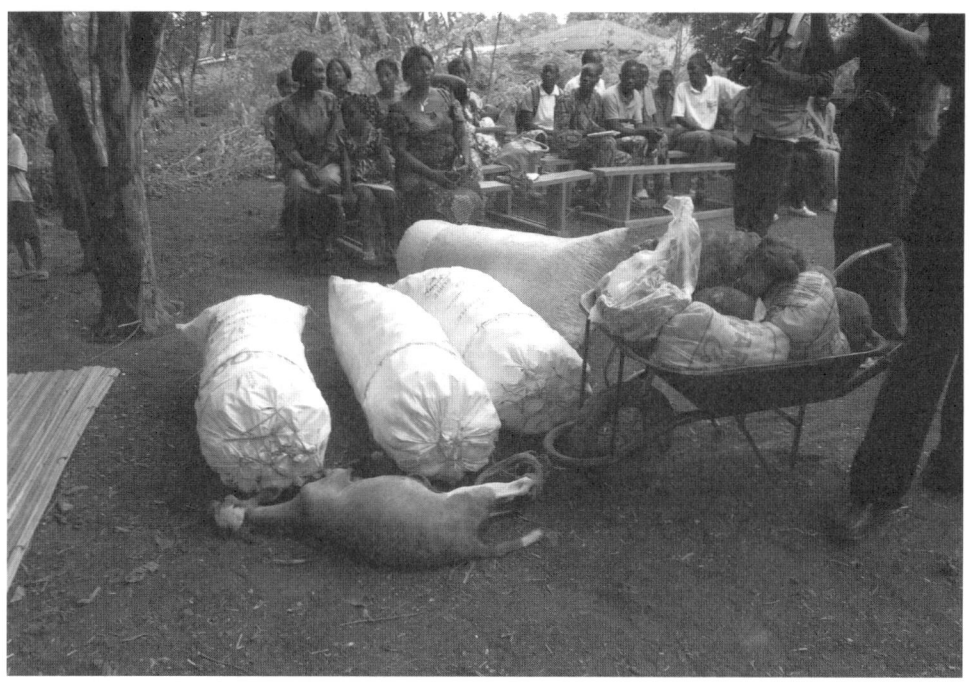

equally intercultural, between a girl of Kunyi origins and her fiancé from the north of the country. The dishes served were essentially 'urban': sardine sandwiches, lemon cake, and sachets filled with biscuits, popcorn, and grilled peanuts. Only the last-named is not a European import. This difference in food choice was not linked to the importance of the occasion, as in a custom that a wedding meal needs a traditional approach, for instance. Instead, I was told that choosing city-fare in Brazzaville and local foods in the countryside was simply a matter of convenience. Since many of the necessary ingredients and foods are only available in cities, an 'urban' wedding meal in the village would have demanded more organization.

Whisky and soda

Celebrations such as a wedding are the stage for reciprocal gift-giving (cf. Mauss 1923–1924). On this particular occasion, the family of the bride was the receiving party. However, it did not make them much richer (cf. the observation made for Polynesian birth celebrations in Mauss 1923–1924, 42–43). They had the obligation to prepare the wedding meal and they also presented gifts to the newly married couple. In this exchange of gifts, food played a major role, and not only in the form of the meal.

A traditional marriage is concluded by the presentation of the bride-wealth. It is the family of the bride that decides what the price will be. As mentioned, Missie Théophile Thomas had spent many years of saving to be able to pay the bride-wealth. The family of the bride had demanded a large sum of money, amongst other reasons to compensate the father of the bride for the expense of a suit.[8] They had also asked for clothes, jewellery and cooking pots for the mother and aunts of the bride. Finally, the groom needed to bring along the drinks for the celebration, specifically six crates of soda, six crates of beer, three demijohns of red wine, four demijohns of sugarcane wine, and five of 'local wine', as well as two bottles of whisky.[9] The whisky is especially important, being the subject of jokes and negotiations during the *coup de théâtre* that accompanies the presentation of the bride-wealth. The chosen brand must be of good quality, otherwise cash compensation may be requested. The family of the bride had also asked for four demijohns of palm wine, but this was delivered in cash instead.[10]

The bride-wealth was exchanged for the wedding meal and gifts from the family of the bride to the newlyweds. The gifts mainly consisted of food: one sheep, a few roosters, cassava flour, dried cassava sticks, and yams. All these food items can be stored or, in the case of the animals, slaughtered whenever necessary. As such, the couple was provided with a food supply to start their married life. In sum, the expenditure of the groom's family on the bride-wealth was well compensated.

Conclusions

Soon after they had eaten, the family of the groom left the village. The marriage was concluded, the gifts exchanged. Maybe slightly disappointingly for a European guest, no dancing followed. Instead, the remainder of the food was shared between the relatives of the bride and their friends in Kimbonga-Louamba, and then the close relatives of the bride retired to discuss the events of the day. The wedding had been a success: the bride-wealth had met their expectations, and the food that had been offered in return had been ample.

Back in my room I also reflected on the feast. Since my fieldwork was concerned with culinary traditions, it had been a wonderful occasion to witness the out-of-the-ordinary, a meal prepared with great care, the best of Kaamba cuisine. It had taught me what foods are appreciated and considered appropriate for a celebration, and it provided me with clues on the link between food and ethnic identity. Of course, I had offered the married couple a small present out of gratitude for letting me attend the celebration and its preparation, and my gift had been returned twofold: in the form of a great meal and extraordinary fieldwork observations.

Notes

1. In total I conducted two months of fieldwork in the south of Congo for the PhD project 'A Comparative Linguistic Approach to the History of Culinary Practice in Bantu-Speaking Africa' (Université Libre de Bruxelles – Royal Museum for Central Africa, with a grant from the Fonds de la Recherche Scientifique – FNRS). I wish to thank Milondo Honorine, Missie Théophile Thomas and Bidounga Nzoussi Chimène for having me at the wedding ceremony, as well as Mama Jacquis, Papa Philippe, and many others in Kimbonga-Louamba for their hospitality and for letting me savour their culinary traditions. I am very grateful to Guy Blaise Ndouli, Bernard Babingoula, and Mboungou Léonard for bringing me into contact with all people mentioned in this paper. Finally, I wish to thank Pierre de Maret and Pierre Petit for suggestions and comments on an earlier draft.
2. All women are called 'Mama' as a sign of respect. It can be compared to 'Mrs'. In the same way, all men are called 'Papa'.
3. I wish to thank Jan Kennis for identifying the antelope species.
4. It might be *Hibiscus mechowii* (cf. Latham 2004, 150), a plant of which both leaves and fruits are prepared.
5. The names of the dishes are written in Kikaamba and were offered to me by Mama Honorine. Kikaamba is a tone language. The high tones are marked with an acute accent (´). Low tones are not marked.
6. I was invited to sit with the male relatives of the bride, meaning that as a foreign female visitor I was accorded a different role to the women of the village.
7. The Luo people live in western Kenya, and the Yassa and Mvae in southern Cameroon.
8. Because the father of the bride had passed away since his daughter's engagement and the formulation of the bride-wealth requirements, he was represented by another male member of the family.
9. In the end, the 'local wine' was mostly sugarcane wine. As for the whisky, being rather focused on the preparations of the wedding meal, I did not pay attention to the brand. Hence, it might well have been 'whiskey'.
10. Palm wine needs to be fresh, preferably tapped from the tree the same morning. It was not possible to be certain that the quantity required could be obtained on the day of the wedding. Moreover, the family had to come a long way, from the Lékoumou department, and they had stayed the night in Nkayi. Palm wine is usually purchased in the countryside rather than in town. Cash was thus a more convenient choice.

References

de Garine, I. 1996: 'Food and the Status Quest in Five African Cultures', in Wiessner, P. & Schiefenhövel, W. (eds.), *Food and the Status Quest. An Interdisciplinary Perspective* (Providence – Oxford, Berghahn Books), 193–217.

Dietler, M. 2001: 'Theorizing the Feast: Rituals of Consumption, Commensal Politics, and Power in African Contexts', in Dietler, M. & Hayden, B. (eds.), *Feasts. Archaeological and Ethnographical Perspectives on Food, Politics, and Power* (Washington – London, Smithsonian Institution Press), 65–114.

Fribourg, J. 1996 'Fêtes et cuisine traditionnelle en Espagne', in Bataille-Benguigui, M.-C. & Cousin, F. (eds.), *Cuisine, reflets des sociétés* (Paris, Éditions Sépia – Musée de l'Homme), 349–358.

Goody, J. 1982: *Cooking, Cuisine and Class. A Study in Comparative Sociology* (Cambridge, Cambridge University Press).

Hayden, B. 2001: 'Fabulous Feasts: A Prolegomenon to the Importance of Feasting', in Dietler, M. & Hayden, B. (eds.), *Feasts*, 23–64.

Latham, P. 2004: *Useful Plants of Bas-Congo Province, Democratic Republic of Congo* (DFID, London).

Mauss, M. 1923–1924: 'Essai sur le don. Forme et raison de l'échange dans les sociétés archaiques', *L'année sociologique* 1, 30–186.

Ricquier, B. 2011: 'Central Africa', in Albala, K. (ed.), *Food Cultures of the World Encyclopedia*. Volume 1: *Africa and the Middle East* (Westport, Greenwood Press), 31–41.

Tableware and Taste: Ceramic Production and the Presentation of Banquet Food

Gillian Riley

> Thou shalt break them with a rod of iron;
> thou shalt dash them in pieces like a potter's vessel.
>
> Psalm 2:9

This paper was inspired by a profound dislike of maiolica, an ornate, richly coloured ceramic style developed in Renaissance Italy. Nineteenth-century collectors in England, and later in the United States, bought the stuff and amassed vast displays of it. Scholarship followed in their wake, cravenly attentive to the need to authenticate and provide details of provenance and ownership – and of course market value – a symbiotic relationship that brought lustre and lucre to all parties, encouraging a reputation based on a skewed perception that obscured and ignored the output of other work from the same potteries.

I use the word potteries, with its vulgar commercial associations, because the production on an industrial scale of serviceable and attractive tin-glazed ware was the economic reality behind the phenomenon of the garish *istoriato* (narrative or history) style of maiolica. There were many versions of the simpler, less expensive 'white ware', 'white on white' *bianchi di Faenza*, either completely plain or decorated with rapidly executed patterns and figurative subjects in a style later called *compendiario*, sketchy, as Wendy Watson, historian of maiolica, neatly puts it. The city of Faenza was only one of the many centres in Italy for the production of maiolica, but the ware took on the name, which in France became known as faience. This everyday pottery made the most of the newly invented brilliant white glaze, enhancing it with subtle decoration rather than obscuring it with galumphing imitations of the works of major artists. The clear simplicity of this plainer style appealed to both lovers of refined gastronomy and those wishing to show off this novel tableware. Popes and cardinals bought it and used it as a sort of trendy alternative to precious metals, not, as has sometimes been said, as a cheap substitute. In 1528 the agent of Eleanora della Rovere in Urbino wrote to her of how Pope Clement VII was observed dining off plain white on white Faenza maiolica:

> Vedendo mangiare Nostro Signore su piatti di terra in biancho sopra biancho, ho dimandato al suo siscalco perchè la Santita Sua non mangiava in quelli depinti a figure. Hamme detto lei non mangiare in altro, reservando quelli per uso di Cardinale.

Tableware and Taste

(Seeing our Master eating off white on white glazed earthenware dishes, I asked his steward why His Holiness did not eat from ones decorated with figures. He said to me that he never ate off anything else, keeping the other kind for cardinals.)

So if he preferred plain white dishes, what did his interlocutor mean by 'decorated with figures'? The full monty, the *istoriati*, or the *compendiario*? Some dishes survive with Clement's coat of arms in the centre, painted in a pleasantly free style, which would have been obliterated by any food on them, leaving us to assume that the decoration would have looked good on the credenza, but not have been visible at table, and still wondering exactly what the cardinals ate off. There was the posh *istoriato* stuff, the lightly decorated *compendiario* and the white on white, completely pure unembellished crockery. None of this was rustic pottery, and for the first time people had the choice of refined and sophisticated, not always expensive, easily available, tableware. This paper tries to find out how the different kinds of maiolica were manufactured and made available for banquets and everyday dining, and if this might have brought about changes in gastronomy.

The *bianchi* were by their very nature ephemeral, fragile and replaceable, thrown away when worn and damaged, not preserved and handed down, like the precious *istoriato* ware: 'Dashed in pieces like a potter's vessel', battered and chipped, like the fruit bowls in a Giovanna Garzoni still life, or the bowls in Vicenzo Campi's *Fruit Vendor*. Some versions had no decoration at all, and impressed with their dazzling, almost unearthly, purity, like the display to be seen today at the castle at Fontanellato, not far from Faenza. In 1581 Montaigne was impressed by the 'cleanliness of this earthenware pottery, which seems like porcelain, so white and pure, and such good value, that they seem to me so much nicer to eat off than the unpleasant metal ware in French hostelries'. And in 1580 there was a comment, quoted by an eighteenth-century writer, on a cardinal who offered a banquet to Henri III where there were two long tables covered with eleven to twelve hundred '*vaisselle de faïenze*', most of which were smashed by the pages and valets, 'a real shame, since they were really magnificent specimens.'

It looks as if there was a taste for whiteness in the presentation and serving of food, where exquisite white tablecloths were removed after each course to reveal another layer of pure white. This purity was hard to achieve in linen, tableware, and food. The usual sludge colour of the coarse clothing and food of the lower classes was inevitable, grains and pulses boiled up with the odd herb to make a sort of porridge-coloured mush, whereas white food and white clothing involved time and effort and expensive materials. The traditional *biancomangiare* was a luxury dish which was an almost dazzling white, made from chicken breasts, ground almonds, perhaps starch, but carefully excluding the off-white tones of everyday broth, spices, and flesh of meat or fowl.

Tin-glazed earthenware pottery was developed from the eleventh century in the Arab world, where craftsmen were inspired to attempt to copy the fine exquisite finish of imports of porcelain from China and the Far East. Both the resultant pottery and the technique came to Italy from Spain, and also from North Africa via Sicily. Maiolica, the name that we now give to the painted *istoriato* ware, might derive from Majorca, the port through which consignments passed on their way from Spain to Italy, but in the sixteenth century it was used to describe imported lustre ware. The smooth white glaze provided the ideal surface, once fired, for detailed work by craftsmen, whose glowing colours gained in richness when the surface was glazed and fired again. There were many styles of ornamentation, often influenced by Arab products, derived from late Gothic patterns. But the potters, or rather their clients, also wanted images like those made by the great artists of the time, especially Raphael. The skills involved in getting the work of painters of biblical and mythological themes onto plates and dishes were not inconsiderable; a steady hand and a trained eye, working from a stock of engravings or drawings after the great masters of the time, were needed by the craftsmen who worked either on their own or as part of a production line. New techniques made possible the pigments which, when fired, have the brilliant, not to say strident, colours that clients admired. It still seems perverse to us that, having achieved the hitherto unobtainable luminous white purity of finish, they then slathered it with often clumsy imitations of the work of artists. However the potteries also made a wide range of objects decorated in a looser style, that did not ape the work of painters, and had a verve and freedom that today we find more appealing than the up-market stuff. These were the 'white on white' and 'sketchy' versions of maiolica.

It is not at all clear what the owners of the *istoriato* maiolica did with them. Some dishes have bases pierced for the means of suspending them on walls, others would have been displayed on the credenza, but it is impossible to tell if food was actually eaten off them. Meat was usually cut up by the *trinciante*, the carver, and presented on serving dishes from which diners helped themselves, with the aid of a spoon if the food was sloppy. Eating with the fingers does not have to be messy and has a voluptuous appeal, a tactile charm, where touch stimulates taste and texture enhances flavour. This would not have marked the glaze the way energetic work with knife and fork does today, so it is hard to find evidence of use on *istoriato* dishes. John Varriano argues with characteristic verve that the intellectual élite of the Renaissance enjoyed the cut and thrust of discussing the mythological and biblical scenes on their maiolica in the course of the elaborate meals described by Scappi and Messisbugo. You could discuss Ovid as you mopped up the gravy to reveal the stories lurking beneath; that is if your erudition was less wonky than that of the pottery painters, who were not all that well-informed, relying on woodcuts and engravings, and so prone to getting aspects of the stories wrong. The exquisite tedium of all this might have been endured for one or two dinner parties, but what about the next one, and the one after that? The mind boggles. Discussion of the use of the ornate maiolica is difficult because surviving written evidence about who bought what, and how much, is not plentiful. Household inventories mention maiolica sets, but rarely give details. We know of an expensive set commissioned for the Gonzaga family in Mantua, of which 23 pieces survive, but it is hard to reconcile this with a letter to Isabella d'Este from her daughter Eleonora in Urbino: 'Thinking of visiting Your Excellency with some of the products of this country, which might please you ... I have had made a *credenza* of earthenware vessels, and I am sending it to Your Excellency by Battista, my steward, the bearer of this letter, since the *maestri* of this country of ours have some reputation for good work ... you might make use of it at Porto, since it is a villa thing (*cosa da villa*) ... it is my wish to think of nothing more than to please you.' But crockery suitable for 'the villa' might have been the more humble *compendiario* white ware, not the ornate expensive d'Este set, for which there is no documentation. The cringing tone of the daughter is understandable, her mother Isabella candidly described herself as '*appetitosa*', a state of mind between greedy and acquisitive, with cultural overtones. Eleonora might have cautiously offered a gift that was agreeable but not competitive, a tactful contrast to the *istoriato* set, for the pretty white ware, with its frill of decoration, was indeed just right for a rustic setting. We have no means of knowing for sure if this letter from Eleonora refers to the ornate *istoriato* set, with the Gonzaga arms in the centre of each dish, of which 23 examples survive in various collections, but it is prudent to keep our options open. Seriously posh dining would have used the items displayed on the banquet scene in the Palazzo Te, where a display of gold and silver plates and vases is shown on a credenza, alongside gods and goddesses disporting themselves with abandon at the banquet table. Isabella's correspondence shows how she was an avid collector of silverware for the table and fretful about its upkeep and security. But she ordered maiolica tiles for her studiolo and appreciated the work of the potteries.

In 1559 or thereabouts Cipriano Piccolpasso wrote a treatise on the manufacture of ceramics, *Il tre libri dell'arte del vasaio*, with detailed descriptions of all the processes of the potter's art. His manuscript was never published. It is now in the Victoria and Albert Museum, and a translation and facsimile edition are available. Piccolpasso described the preparation of pigments, the construction of kilns, the working of the clay, and its shaping on the wheel or in moulds. He included life-sized diagrams of the dimensions of various objects, explaining how standardization of sizes made stacking the kilns more efficient. Although he does not say so, it would also have streamlined marketing and distribution. These sizes and dimensions are likely to be a fairly accurate indication of usage.

Piccolpasso lists the dimensions of a range of plates, bowls, and dishes – six different sizes of at least fifteen different objects – all standardized to fit the kilns of Casteldurante in the Marche, where he studied the potter's art and was probably owner of the business. His diagram shows the different circumferences of different objects – from cups and small bowls to large serving plates and dishes, stemmed bowls and raised salvers. The largest, approximately 274 mm in diameter, are *tazzini*, platters with or without a rim, *piatti detti da carne*, platters called meat dishes, *canestrelle da frutti*, basket work (pierced or lacy) containers for fruit, and *aborchiati*, raised salvers; the next size down is 250 mm, and includes *copette, canestrelle, aborchiati*, drinking bowls, pierced fruit bowls, other bowls; the third category, 162 mm, are *ongaresche*, bowls on a foot, *piatti da insalata*, for salads, *piatti cavati dalo argento per minestre*, for stews (based on silver models), *schudelle da lorlo della magior grandezza*, bowls with a wide rim, of the largest size; 187 mm *piatti da salviette o da savore*, dishes for napkins and relishes; *schudelle* 162 mm, *da l'orlo, da limpagliata, schudelini da lorlo*, bowls with a rim, bowls for childbirth sets, smaller bowls with a rim; and finally 120 mm *tazzine*, small drinking bowls. The impossibility of translating the names into accurate English language versions is evident. The sizes too are approximate. His many mentions in the text of different items shows what a wide range was available:

> Schudelle, con orlo e senza; Schudelini; Boccali, con bocca e senza fogliette; Baccile, cavati da l'argento; Tazzoni o vogliam confetiere; ongaresche dette, in Vinegia, piadene; Piatti strati o vogliam piani; Piatti con fondo piede e senza; Tondi con il fondo e senza; Saliere a fonghi; Tazine o vogliam ciotolette; Fiale da tener olio, acceto et aqua; Fiaschi da vino, acceto et aqua; Albarelli da spetiarie et da confetioni, lettovari et unguenti; Diversi vasi cavati dall'antico; Vasi a pera et a palla; Vasi da dua corpi; Vasi a torre.

In the Victoria and Albert catalogue quoted below, Reino Lifkes points out that historians have difficulty in correlating this repertoire of the dimensions of the Casteldurante pottery with surviving items in collections of maiolica and with archaeological remains. But it does indicate how pots of all kinds for everyday domestic use were being made on a large scale, not just as collectors' pieces for the élite.

Piccolpasso gives several pages of popular designs, with arabesque patterns and landscapes, but it is significant that his text does not mention the *istoriato* ware. Can one conclude from this that these luxury items were merely an expensive and labour-intensive spin-off from the everyday production of these potteries, that *istoriato* was the icing on the cake?

It is the cake that we are concerned with here, and so this paper attempts to look at the ornate and expensive maiolica in the context of plainer crockery made for daily use in sixteenth- and seventeenth-century Italy. There is information about this in household inventories, in archaeological researches, surviving items in fine art collections, as visual clues in paintings and engravings, and in printed banquet menus. These show changes in taste from the new cuisine of Maestro Martino and Platina in the 1460s, to the banquet menus of Messisbugo and Scappi a century later, and in the exquisite displays, at once refined and highly elaborate, of the Baroque banquet as depicted by Pierre Paul Sévin for Christina of Sweden on her visits to Rome in the seventeenth century.

It is possible to argue that the technical breakthrough that made moderately priced but beautiful tableware available to a wider public was in response to changes in gastronomy, but it could also be argued that this profusion of cheap and replaceable crockery made it possible to cook and serve a vast number of items in each course of a banquet, with small amounts of delicious food served in a pile-up of plates, bowls, and dishes overlapping each other on hugely overpopulated table surfaces, a style that influenced menu planning, serving, eating, and cooking.

The catalogue of the exhibition *At Home in Renaissance Italy* at the Victoria and Albert Museum in 2007 gives detailed insight into records of commissions for sets of maiolica and pieces that have survived. Marta Ajmar Wollheim writes of household inventories which list the crockery displayed on the credenza or sideboard, a feature of reception or dining-rooms where the wealth and taste of a prosperous family was ostentatiously on show. The Salviati family in Florence owned in the 1530s a service of which six pieces survive, with the family coat of arms and the deep blue and white patterned plates, fruit bowl, and oil jar, all fully functional. They commissioned a service of 180 pieces in about 1559, decorated with landscapes. This would have done for about 24 guests. They also owned by 1583 a big set of 272 *bianca di Faenza*, the plain white ware.

One of the more interesting uses of maiolica was the manufacture of 'childbirth sets', *da parto* or *impagliata*, various bowls and dishes for serving, eating and drinking, which were intended to be stacked in a 'nest'. Childbirth was something of a growth industry in sixteenth-century Italy where civil strife and epidemics of the plague had caused a drastic fall in population. Consequently this joyful and perilous experience was surrounded by concern and rejoicing. The expectant mother was cherished and presented with the maiolica birth sets by way of encouragement and celebration: the bowls and dishes would be used for nourishing food after her confinement and treasured as reminders of the event. They were often decorated with scenes of childbirth, showing the items in use. Piccolpasso devoted a whole page of his treatise to explaining how the five items in a set were manufactured to be fitted together: the *scudella*, a bowl on a foot, was covered by a *tagliere*, a flat, rimmed dish, which in turn had an *ongaresca*, an upturned flat bowl with a small base, placed upon it, and perched on top of that a small salt cellar, *saliera*, with its separate lid. Jacqueline Musacchio has studied the surviving examples and compared them with the wooden birth-trays, *deschi da parto*, which were used earlier to carry food and gifts for the mother. From such research we get glimpses of what might have been ordinary crockery, for the trays, bowls and dishes, although special possessions, were examples of things in everyday use. A maiolica inkstand shows a couple having a meal, using everyday items of maiolica.

One might try to correlate Piccolpasso's standard sizes with the likely dimensions of the plates and bowls needed to serve the dishes presented in every course of some of the banquet menus in printed texts, especially those listed by Bartolomeo Scappi, whose monumental *Opera* was published in 1570, when production of the *compendiario* style of pottery was at its peak. The amount and texture of each dish would require a particular size and shape of bowl or plate (Scappi uses the word *piatti* as a generic term, giving no information about dimensions or form): some of the food was dry, carved from roasts or boiled ingredients, some included their cooking juices, dense or runny, and some were whole, like pies or tarts or moulded dishes. Whoever planned and implemented the menus would have specified the appropriate serving dishes, but Scappi simply lists the number of items in a course, a brief description of each recipe, and the quantity of dishes to serve them on. His concern is with the food, and the recipes used to prepare it; the appearance mattered, as we can deduce from many of the lists and recipes, where Scappi describes the garnishes – blue borage flowers or red pomegranate seeds – but the logistics of dishing up and serving were not the subject of his book but rather the responsibility of the *scalco* or head steward.

An analysis of just one of his banquet menus might give us some clues as to the size and shape of dishes on which the food was presented. For example, a meal for 50 guests on the last day of February at some point in the mid-sixteenth century, consisting of 3 cold services from the sideboard and 4 hot ones from the kitchen, was served by 10 carvers and 10 waiters, with 10 dishes for each item, with each waiter and carver looking after 5 people, using a total of 963 serving dishes, not counting the plates the food was eaten off. Scappi lists the food and the number of dishes needed to serve it in each course. The number of guests can be deduced from the number of perfumed toothpicks, *stecchi profumati*, supplied for use during the last course, when the dual purpose of the little skewer was to attend to teeth, and spear sticky fruit in syrup, not a job for the fingers. One could tot up what was likely to be on each dish, and so calculate the size of dish needed, referring to Piccolpasso for approximate sizes. This is hard going. Here are a few insights: the very first item in the first course is 20 lb (a Roman pound was about 12 oz) of sugared comfits in 10 dishes, requiring some fairly large kind of bowl to take 2 lb of the tiny white sugar-coated spices; then come 50 biscuits (Pisan and Roman) with glasses of malvasia to dunk them in, which could have needed flat rimmed dishes or platters to take the biscuits and 5 glasses; next came 50 *ciambelle*, bagel-like bread rings made with egg and milk, 5 to a dish; then various kinds of spiced biscuits, 5 to a dish, (another 20 dishes); followed by some ham cooked in wine and sliced (into finger-food portions) in 10 dishes holding 2 lb each; next cured salt pork, served in slices with mild mustard, 10 dishes of 2 lb each; then some Milanese flaky pastries (10 more dishes); followed by little portions of clotted cream, *capi di latte*, sprinkled with sugar, 5 to a dish (like small fresh cream cheeses, drained in little pierced moulds or reed baskets, like ricotta), 10 dishes; next come 10 pasties of shin of goat, weighing 6 lb each, 10 more dishes; 300 Sicilian olives in 10 dishes, (these could be quite small); marinated pork chops grilled over coals, 4 to a dish; 10 dishes of salad of sliced citron dressed with sugar, salt and rosewater (shallow bowls perhaps); calissons of marzipan, 10 dishes of 5 to a dish; 10 open tarts of prunes and marzipan, 1 to a dish; sausages cooked in wine and sliced, 15 lb in 10 dishes and finally 30 lb of various kinds of fresh grapes (in February?) in 10 dishes. This course needed 170 dishes, not counting plates for the guests to eat off, and containers for salt, relishes, and so forth.

The next course, the first service of hot food from the kitchen, consisted of 12 dishes, served on 144 plates, starting with tarts of kids' sweetbreads and pigs' cheeks, one to each of 10 plates; then 40 spit-roast partridges finished with chopped *limoncelli* (probably limes or small lemons) and rosewater (this would need a bowl with room for the liquid); 80 spit-roasted woodcock and lapwings, sprinkled with sugar and capers, served in 20 dishes (4 small birds to a dish); meatballs of pork meat and liver, wrapped in caul fat and fried, served with sliced lemons and dusted with sugar (if the sliced lemons were to decorate the dish they might have been arranged round the wide flat rim of a serving platter, big enough for 15 meatballs of 3 oz each); 50 little tarts of chopped veal sweetbreads in flaky pastry, 5 to a dish; 200 spit-roast ortolans (with their dredged crust of seasoned breadcrumbs and butter) on 10 dishes; 50 turtle doves (similar to squabs) interleaved with slices of *gola di porco* (*guanciale*, cured pig's jowl) and sage leaves, spit-roasted and served with sliced lemons and sugar (this seems to call for a wide-rimmed dish); 17 dishes of mild mustard; 10 small kids, skinned and stuffed and spit-roasted, one to a dish; 300 olives from Bologna in 10 dishes; 10 *pollanche d'India*, turkeys, finely larded, spit-roasted and served with capers and sugar, one to a dish; the course ending with 17 dishes of jelly cut into squares.

The second service from the kitchen begins with 30 boned and stuffed kids' heads, served covered with *biancomangiare* decorated with pomegranate seeds and sprinkled with sugar, 2 to a dish (one assumes that each head was cut into bite sized portions before serving, then covered with the sauce); a 60 lb loin of wild boar, marinated, then spit-roasted and served with the marinade (probably used to baste the beast) and a sprinkling of sugar and cinnamon, in 10 dishes; 10 pigeon pies (tame not wild), 4 birds to a pie, one pie to a dish; 30 pheasants, breasts studded with cloves, paper wrapped and spit-roasted, served with capers and sugar; 20 spit-roasted rabbits, with a mirause sauce, decorated with pine nuts and sprinkled with sugar and cinnamon, 2 to a dish; a *minestra Ongaresca*, 17 dishes of Hungarian stew with sugar and cinnamon; a fricassee of 4 hindquarter of hares, with fried baby onions, served sprinkled with sugar and cinnamon, served in 19 dishes; 50 boned and stuffed pigeons, stewed then fried, and served sprinkled with sugar and cinnamon, 5 to a dish; 60 portions of amber coloured jelly in morsels, 6 to a dish; 60 lb of pieces of calves liver larded in the French fashion, spit-roasted and served covered with *sapor reale*, on 10 dishes (hard to comprehend the quantity); 10 pasties of cow's udder, first stewed, 5 lb to a pasty, served hot, one to a dish.

The third course from the kitchen, boiled dishes, began with breast of veal, stewed, then marinated, then fried, and served with the marinade as a sauce, 60 lb on 10 dishes; next came 20 stewed capons, 2 to a dish, with cardoons and sliced *cervellate* sausages (perhaps as decoration round the rim) sprinkled with sugar and cinnamon; 10 plump stewed ducks covered with *anolini* (small twisted filled pasta) seasoned with cheese, sugar, and cinnamon, one to a dish; 17 dishes of coloured jelly set in moulds; 10 veal meat balls in pasties, each weighing 5 lb, one to a dish; lumps of wild boar, stewed in the Hungarian manner, 50 lb in 10 dishes; 10 Milanese *tortiglioni* (filled pastries), one to a dish; 150 thrushes stewed with bacon, 15 to a dish; 17 dishes of *biancomangiare* sprinkled with sugar; 50 pigeons stewed with prunes and dried cherries, 5 to a dish;

10 capon pies, two birds to a pie, served hot; stuffed veal bellies, stewed and served decorated with flowers.

The fourth and final course from the kitchen was similar to the previous ones.

The second course from the sideboard began with raw cardoons with salt and pepper, 15 plants in 10 dishes; then 20 lb of raw truffles with salt and pepper in 10 dishes; 10 custard tarts with pine nuts in 10 dishes; 10 herb tarts in the manner of Bologna; 10 tarts of turnip tops; 10 quince pasties with 4 to a pasty; 50 pear pasties, 3 to a pasty; 150 pears in red wine, in 10 dishes served with sugar; 50 cooked baby artichokes served with vinegar and pepper in 10 dishes; 50 raw artichokes with salt and pepper; 100 pears, Florentine and *riccarde* on 10 dishes; 100 red and green apples on 19 dishes; 10 *marzolini* cheese, in chunks, on 10 dishes; 20 lb of *romagnolo* cheeses in 10 dishes; 300 roasted chestnuts with salt, sugar and pepper in 10 dishes; 20 lb of truffles stewed in oil with bitter orange juice and pepper; 17 dishes of frothed milk; 450 wafers made in heraldic irons in 10 dishes; 300 cookies made by nuns (*ciambellette di monache*).

The final course of the banquet was served on a fresh clean tablecloth after the guests had rinsed their fingers in perfumed water. They had trimmed raw fennel bulbs, 8 lb in 10 dishes; perfumed toothpicks (this was a grand enough meal to warrant small forks and spoons for the sweetmeats as well); 10 dishes each of various candied and preserved fruit and nuts; and farewell offerings of silk flowers with golden stems, one for each guest.

Even allowing for a team of scullions washing up the dishes as they were removed after each course, we are looking at hundreds of serving dishes of different sizes to be recycled according to the menu. Plate had the advantage of being almost indestructible, but harder to clean, The lightly decorated *compendiario* ware had the advantage of providing an attractive foil to the food, where a decorated rim might enliven a dull dish, or a large plain white rim was a surface for sliced oranges or olives or other garnishes. The extracts from Scappi quoted above give some idea of the different kinds of container needed for all the dishes in a grand banquet, but in his text Scappi makes no mention of all this crockery or plate; its availability is taken for granted. His illustrations show kitchen equipment and some serving dishes, but not in a way that we can link with Piccolpasso's treatise. But a little vignette, in the foreground of one of his kitchens, shows a key personality in the drama that was the Renaissance banquet – the dishwasher, hard at work at a sink with the benefit of a flow of fresh water, perhaps from one of the fountains restored and replenished as part of the papal strategy for the renewal of Rome. The restoration of aqueducts and the complex hydraulics that supplied them was part of a great vision of urban renewal and deliberate self promotion, in which a lavish supply of pure fresh water was an outward and visible sign of the power and magnanimity of the popes. This beneficent flow would naturally have found its way into their private kitchens, as well as impressing and refreshing the populace. This would have helped the constant recycling of crockery which must have been a big part of a Renaissance banquet. The myth of the gold and silver plate being heaved into the Tiber during one of Agostino Chigi's banquets in his gardens alongside the Tiber, is endearing, when we know that they were later collected by his servants in carefully concealed nets. But the miracle of a flow of constantly renewed plates and dishes for Scappi's banquets is even more impressive.

Attempts to count them, guess at their sizes and shapes, can be assisted by images from paintings and actual objects in collections, but much still needs to be done, and this paper is a tentative approach to an aspect of maiolica production which might have had an influence on the development the structure and contents of Renaissance and later banquets.

Bibliography

The literature on maiolica is immense. Here are some of the works consulted:

Ajmar-Wollheim, Marta and Dennis, Flora, eds., *At Home in Renaissance Italy* (London: V & A Publications, 2006).

De Pompeis, Vincenzo, ed., *La Maiolica Italiana di stile Compendiario, I Bianchi* (Umberto Allemandi & C. Turin: 2010).

Malacarne, Giancarlo, *Sulla Mensa del Principei* (Il Bulino, Modena: 2000).

Musacchio, Jacqueline Marie, *The Art and Ritual of Childbirth in Renaissance Italy* (London: Yale University Press, 1999).

Watson, Wendy M. *Italian Renaissance Maiolica from the William A. Clark Collection* (London: Scala Books, 1986).

——, *Italian Renaissance Ceramics* (Philadelphia Museum of Art, Philadelphia: 2002).

Wilson, Timothy, *Maiolica: Italian Renaissance Ceramics in the Ashmolean Museum* (Ashmolean Museum, Oxford: 1989).

Þorrablót – Icelandic Feasting

Nanna Rögnvaldardóttir and Michael R. Leaman

Þorri is the fourth winter month in the old Icelandic calendar. It always begins on a Friday between 19 and 25 January and ends on a Saturday between 18 and 24 February, and its start signifies for Icelanders the middle of winter. The name *Þorri* (Thorri) has been known since the twelfth century, but its origin is unclear. There have been suggestions that *Þorri* may be related to the name of the heathen thunder-god Þór. The *Þorrablót* (literally, perhaps, Thor's Blood) goes back to pre-Christian sacrifices and a time when there probably was also some kind of mid-winter celebration. It is mentioned in the Icelandic Sagas. So *Þorri* feasts are an ancient tradition, but their links to the present are by no means so clear, and no doubt the ways in which they are celebrated have changed over the years. The intriguing history of *Þorrablót* tells us much about Icelandic society and customs as well as the way food cultures can adapt to harsh environments.

Þorri himself is found in medieval Icelandic literature through to the nineteenth century and is represented as the personification of winter – an old man, with an icy grey beard who needs to be treated as an honoured guest unless one wants to risk violent weather or worse. Sources from the early eighteenth century related by the ethnologist Árni Björnsson mention eccentric local customs associated with *Þorri*. One custom, described in 1728, is that the woman of the house should go outdoors the evening before the beginning of *Þorri* and bid him welcome, and ask him not to be harsh. According to a mid-nineteenth century source, it was the man of the house that should bid *Þorri* welcome on the morning he arrived. This should be done in the following manner: The master of the house should rise first thing in the morning and wear only his shirt; he should be barefoot and bare-bottomed but should put on one leg of his trousers and drag the other trouser leg behind; then he should go outside and hop on one foot around the farmhouse, bidding *Þorri* welcome all the time (and this in the middle of the Icelandic winter!). The first day of *Þorri*, called *Bóndadagur* or Husband's day, was supposed to be a day of reverence from the wives. It was the man's day; he was often brought food in bed, the best that was available in the house: the best cuts of a lamb or mutton; soured lamb's heads; or some bread, cakes or pancakes were baked. Everybody was served something, but the man of the house could stuff himself with all he could eat. It is celebrated today by wives, who buy flowers or small gifts for their husbands and cook their favourite foods.[1]

In the seventeenth and eighteenth centuries any revival of pagan feasts would have been thought anti-Christian in Iceland – any hint of paganism could have been thought destabilizing. By the late nineteenth century, however, much had changed:

Þorrablót – Icelandic Feasting

in 1874 Denmark granted Iceland limited home rule and there was a new Icelandic constitution. A nationalist movement was formed that aimed to wrest independence from Denmark, and a revival of old pagan customs was in the air.

*Þorrablót*s were held both in Iceland and Copenhagen between 1867 and 1874, and the custom spread. The earliest source mentioning them is the meetings book of a secret society in Reykjavík recording their *Þorrablót* on 2 March 1867. It is not known if any food was served, but the participants probably drank quite a lot, and a drinking song composed especially for the occasion does survive. Singing and poetry played a big role in those feasts, as several of Iceland's best poets were members of the society. It continued to hold *Þorrablót*s for several years, and in 1873 Icelanders in Copenhagen held a *Þorrablót að fornum sið* (in the ancient style). Icelanders did not gain religious freedom until 1874, but as soon as the religious restrictions were lifted the first public *Þorrablót* was held in Reykjavík and soon spread to other villages around the country. In 1880 the Archaeological Society in Reykjavík held a *Þorrablót* that was intended to simulate a Viking feast, with fires burning in long hearths; the guests drank to Odin, Þór, and other pagan deities. These early gatherings were exclusively for well-educated, upper-class males. It was only much later that *Þorrablót* became a feast for all sexes and all kinds of people in Iceland.

Around the turn of the century the *Þorrablót*s waned in Reykjavík and other towns in Iceland. In the following decades people who had migrated to Reykjavík from various parts of Iceland began to organize gatherings for those that came from the same region. They would hold an annual dinner, serving food from their home region, old-fashioned country fare. But those gatherings were not called *Þorrablót*, and the food was not called *Þorramatur* (usually just 'Icelandic food', in contrast to the Danish-influenced cuisine that had taken over by then the towns and villages, at least). So *Þorrablót* as such declined, or perhaps more exactly never became properly established in Iceland. All this changed in the 1950s when a limited revival took place in certain locations. That was followed in 1958 by the true rebirth of the *Þorrablót* when a traditional Reykjavík restaurant called Naust reintroduced the *Þorri* feast to the Icelandic public. It served traditional Icelandic foods in a publicity coup that caught the nation's attention by offering dishes like smoked lamb, pickled ram's testicles, cured shark, pickled lamb's heads, etc. The foods were served at Naust in a traditional wooden tray or trough. This is also the origin of the term *Þorramatur* (*Þorri* food). There was an emphasis on stuffing oneself, even overeating – in the early years Naust had an offer: they gave you a tray with lots and lots of *Þorramatur* (2.5 kilos), and if you could consume it within two hours you got it free; if not you had to pay. *Þorrablót*s became all the rage, and within a few years Icelandic stores were carrying an abundance of *Þorri* food for a month or two each winter. That continues to this day, and means that everyone can hold a *Þorrablót* in his own home without having to make the traditional food for him or herself.

*Þorrablót*s today are a standard feature of the Icelandic social calendar, and have thrived since the late 1950s. (Icelanders have a number of other special days which

Þorrablót – Icelandic Feasting

are exclusive to Iceland, and associated with food and drink, like *Bolludagur*/ bun day during Lent and Sun coffee to celebrate the reappearance of the sun after the winter's darkness in the narrow fjords of north-western and eastern Iceland.) *Þorrablót*s are held all over Iceland during the month of *Þorri*. In smaller communities, people simply come together to celebrate, but in Reykjavík and the larger towns the feasts are held by various clubs, associations, groups, or workplaces. These are almost always catered, the food is bought and is fairly standardized, but in the countryside and in many smaller communities every family brings an abundance of their own food, more or less homemade, to the feast, often in the traditional wooden troughs, and although people sit together at communal tables they eat their own food (although neighbours may be invited to taste some special dishes). At a bring-your-own *Þorrablót* you will see more variety, both in the recipes – your neighbour's *súrt slátur* may taste quite different from your own – and in the things being offered; people from the Breiðafjörður region may indulge themselves on soured seal flippers; in the Mývatn region they serve pickled eggs; on Melrakkaslétta there may be smoked male lumpfish; some may serve soured lamb's trotters or trotter cheese, smoked home-made sausages, etc.

In many smaller communities around Iceland, the annual *Þorrablót* is the main gathering (feast), and people look forward to it all year. They begin preparing the food they are bringing months ahead. Whole families (teenagers, grown-ups, grandparents) often attend together. Everybody is dressed in their finest clothes, which can make quite a contrast to the rather crude food, usually packed in plastic tubs and bags, aluminium foil and such, and more or less eaten with the fingers.

*Þorrablót*s have even been exported to countries that have Icelandic communities (for example, the UK, Canada and USA) and foreign friends and spouses are often taken along to these bewildering events, which really can be reimagined as the modern equivalents of ancient feasts. In Iceland, as in foreign *Þorrablót*s, there is usually music, dancing, and feasting (and serious drinking) until the early hours of the morning. In the past the music used to be supplied by an accordion player, but today it could be by a band or even a rock group, and traditionally there is quite a lot of singing as well as special *Þorri* poetry recited, in praise of *Þorri* and other pagan gods. *Þorri* songs are often composed by a local poet for a specific town or rural community.

Nowadays it is only during *Þorrablót* that most people will eat many of these old-fashioned foods (although in the countryside many have been long-standing staples), and most of the foods served at the feasts have been preserved in some way: by pickling in whey (*súrmatur*), salting, smoking, drying, or fermenting. Some foods at the *Þorrablót* are quite challenging to the modern palate, but they usually include some items that are eaten throughout the year across Iceland, and nowadays some other foods like pickled herring, lamb stew, roast lamb, maybe even chicken are also present in order not to drive away those who can't stomach such traditional Icelandic delicacies.[2]

The following are some of the traditional offerings at a *Þorrablót*:

Þorrablót – Icelandic Feasting

Hákarl (fermented shark), is perhaps the most extreme food on offer. The shark is placed in a shallow hole and then covered with sand and gravel. Stones are then placed on top in order to squeeze out the shark's fluids. The shark ferments in this fashion for 6 to 12 weeks, depending on the season, to allow certain unhealthy substances to leak out, and then it is air-dried. Without this process the ammonia in the shark could be harmful or even deadly. The reason for this is simple: in Iceland sharks are mostly Greenland or basking sharks, which do not have urinary tracts and, therefore, must secrete their urine from their skin. As a result, high amounts of uric acid become so concentrated that eating even a small part of a shark can cause people to vomit blood. By allowing the shark to fully decay and be cured, the acid is removed from the flesh, thus making it easier to digest.

Following this curing period, the shark is cut into strips and hung to dry for several months. During this drying period a brown crust develops, which is removed by commercial outlets prior to cutting the shark into small pieces and serving, although some people get hold of the meat with the crust. The modern method is just to press the shark's meat in a large plastic container with drainage holes. *Hákarl* is divided into two types, *Glerhákarl* (glass shark) – the part closest to the skin which is chewy and semi-opaque – and *Skyrhákarl* (skyr shark) from the soft inner parts. It is usually served in small chunks and washed down with ice-cold *brennivín*. Both kinds are extremely pungent and reek of ammonia, which is worse than the actual taste. People either love it or hate it. Some people think it is good for the digestive system. Chef Anthony Bourdain has described it as 'the single worst, most disgusting and terrible tasting thing' he has ever eaten.

Harðfiskur is fish that has been dried, then (traditionally) beaten on a stone with a mallet until soft. Nowadays, though, this is done mechanically. It is often eaten with butter. *Harðfiskur* (usually haddock but possibly another kind of fish) is one of the old delicacies that has survived and is now sold in many shops, usually as a popular snack for eating on the move. It is spread with butter because in former times it was consumed in place of bread which was an expensive commodity (owing to most wheat having to be imported).

Whey-preserved whale blubber (*súr hvalur*) used to be a staple at the *Þorri* feasts. It disappeared when whaling declined, but it is now available again. One side of a piece of sour blubber is very stringy and tough, then the texture changes gradually and the other side becomes so soft it can be cut with a fork.

Hangikjöt, literally 'hung meat', is one of the most popular offerings. This usually refers to smoked lamb or mutton. It is served cold and cut into thin slices.

Magáll is a thin fat-streaked slab of meat off a sheep's belly. It is usually smoked and cut into thin slices. *Lundabaggar* used to be a piece of lamb meat, often the heart, rolled in a lamb's intestines and suet before being cooked. It was eaten fresh or whey-preserved, and sometimes smoked. Now the name seems to have been transferred to rolled, fatty flank of lamb, soured in whey. *Bringukollur* is fatty meat from the breast of the lamb, usually on the bone. The meat is cooked, then preserved in whey. *Hrútspungar* are lamb's testicles, pressed and preserved in whey.

Svið, singed sheep's head halves, are sometimes served. The name refers to the tradition of burning away all the hair from the head before cooking (boiling). This gives the meat a smoky flavour. The heads are cut in half lengthwise and the brains removed before cooking. All the meat around the head, including the ears and eyes, can be eaten. *Sviðasulta*, head-cheese, both fresh and whey-preserved, is a must at a *Þorri* feast. The head is boiled until the skin falls off and the meat (with eyes, tongue and everything else) is pressed into a mould to set, along with a little of the gelatinous cooking liquid which holds it all together once set.

Slátur in two types, *Blóðmör* (blood pudding) and *lifrarpylsa* (liver sausage), both fresh and whey-preserved, are always to be found at these feasts. They are served cold in slices. Both contain rye meal, which contributes to the souring process and gives rise to a special kind of taste that's hard to describe.

Selshreifar, seal's flippers, are rare, except at some family feasts where the participants have hunted the seals themselves.

Brennivín (caraway-flavoured Icelandic schnapps, known locally as *Svartidauði*, or Black Death) is provided to drink with the shark, along with other strong spirits and, in latter years, quite a lot of beer. Several Icelandic breweries now make special *Þorri* beer.

Some of the processes involved in the preservation of such foods evolved because of Iceland's historic lack of salt. Iceland is a country completely surrounded by saltwater, and it is probably surprising that one of the things that had a great impact on Icelandic food culture was salt-poverty. When salt is harvested from the sea, it is usually done by evaporation, either naturally, by using the heat of the sun to dry up shallow pools, or by boiling the water until only salt crystals remain. The first option is clearly not very viable in Iceland, as the climate is neither hot, sunny, nor dry. Boiling the salt was possible at first, and consequently the early settlers will have been able to use salt in broadly the same manner to which they had been accustomed. But after a few centuries, maybe a few decades, lack of firewood became a problem. So people tried to economize. In winter, barrels could be filled with seawater and left until a thick layer of ice had formed. This was then removed and the process was repeated a few times, until the salt in the remaining water was so highly concentrated that it didn't freeze.

Then it was boiled, but the process took much shorter time than usual and less fuel was needed. Another common method was to gather seaweeds and dry them. They were then burned and the salty ashes used to preserve food. This was called 'black salt' and was used when nothing else was available, but of course the food was contaminated with ash and dirt.[3]

Despite these procedures, the lack of salt became a problem early on. Salt could of course be imported but that was very expensive – in the mid-fifteenth century the price was one dried cod for a pound of salt. Most people couldn't really afford that. So other methods had to be found, and Icelanders developed their own systems of preservation that did not rely on salt. They used one of the few things they had more than enough of, whey. Fermented whey is an excellent preservation agent, and it can even add nutritional value, since vitamins from it seep into the preserved food. It also tenderizes and softens the meat and gradually softens and dissolves bones. Food that is kept in fermented whey for some time will gradually acquire a more sour taste. It is sometimes said that all food will eventually taste the same if it is kept in whey for long enough. Food that was preserved in this manner was usually boiled and cooled before being submerged in the whey. A lid was then placed on top and, if the barrel was to be kept undisturbed for some time, some tallow was usually melted and poured over the rim to seal it.

Much of the so-called *Þorri* food can be bought throughout the year, with the notable exception of the soured stuff. That doesn't mean it isn't eaten, but you probably have to make your own if you want it to taste good. The biggest challenge to the *Þorrablót*s of today is that the industrialized production of traditional foods has created a rather bland collection of mediocre (or worse) specialities and those people who have not eaten such foods from childhood tend not to like them. This is especially the case with the soured food: the other stuff fares much better. Many – maybe most – young people have no taste for whey-preserved food or find it disgusting, and even those who eat it sometimes say it all tastes the same. There is some truth in that, not least because now everyone uses whey from the same producer and Iceland has lost the varieties of flavour that abounded when people made their own skyr at home and every farm had their own *sýra* (fermented whey), with varying qualities and tastes. Yet it is possible to buy decent soured *slátur* if you know where to go, and some people still make their own.

Since many of these things are only eaten once a year, and mostly by people who have grown up with them, Icelanders seem to lack motivation to improve on them. This is not the case with items like *hangikjöt*, which is also eaten at Christmas and other times in the year. For these, producers (both larger companies and individual farmers with small smokehouses) have experimented with traditional and regional methods with the result that you can now choose between many excellent varieties of smoked lamb and mutton, which is usually the most popular offering at a *Þorrablót* anyway.

To conclude, *Þorrablót* is an intriguing feast with a history entwined with Iceland's unique society. Its foods seem strange to outsiders but make sense when one considers how resourceful people were obliged to be in order to preserve foods. Iceland's recent economic crisis has brought with it a new appreciation of such traditional Icelandic foods, some of which are cheap and wholesome. Iceland is a country which has in recent years imported more and more luxury goods as well as foreign foods. These have contributed to its high inflation rate. Going back to basics, to traditional foods, and to a greater self-reliance is one outcome of the crisis, both material and psychological, which many may see as a positive development and, wider still, may provide a possible example for other nations.

Notes
1. Björnsson, Árni: *High Days and Holidays in Iceland* (trans. Anna H. Yates), Mál og menning, Reykjavík 1995.
2. http://www.gestgjafinn.is/english/nr/352.
3. http://www.gestgjafinn.is/english/nr/349.

Bibliography
Björnsson, Árni: *High Days and Holidays in Iceland* (trans. Anna H. Yates), Mál og menning, Reykjavík 1995.
——: *Þorrablót*, Mál og menning, Reykjavík 2008.
——: *Saga daganna*, Mál og menning, Reykjavík, 1993.
Gísladóttir, Hallgerður: *Íslensk matarhefð*. Mál og menning, Reykjavík, 1999.
Guðjónsson, Skúli V.: *Manneldi og heilsufar í fornöld*. Ísafold, Reykjavík, 1949.
Rögnvaldardóttir, Nanna: *Cool Cuisine*. Vaka-Helgafell, Reykjavík, 2004.
——: *Icelandic Food and Cookery*. Hippocrene Books, New York, 2002.
——: *Matarást*. Reykjavík, Iðunn, 1998.

Celebrating Life in Multicultural Rotterdam: A Visual Approach

Linda Roodenburg

Over the last 50 years the population of the city of Rotterdam has changed dramatically. Now almost 50 per cent of the inhabitants are immigrants. These newcomers brought their own food habits, adapted them to their new urban lives and so changed the food culture of the city as a whole. Nowadays everybody eats pasta, rice, and potatoes, and the Turkish pizza is as common as the Dutch new *haring* or the Vietnamese spring roll. Dutch Turks have adopted 'Surinam potatoes' (sweet potatoes); Cape Verdeans are fond of Dutch *erwtensoep* (pea soup); which reminds them of their national dish *cachupa*; Caribbeans are getting used to exotic vegetables like cauliflower; and the Dutch-Indonesian *rijsttafel* – a result of the colonial past – is recommended in every tourist guide as typical Dutch food.

Recently traditional Dutch (Christian) celebrations have been changing into more neutral intercultural events. In schools and community houses in migrant neighbourhoods, for example, people are looking for common elements in their celebrations. Thus specific religious aspects may be left out or reinterpreted as universal symbols. In December many Moroccans and Turks decorate their homes with Christmas trees and candles, symbolizing the lengthening of the days and the coming New Year.

Celebrating Life in Multicultural Rotterdam

Celebrating Life in Multicultural Rotterdam

People from all creeds participate in Easter celebrations with chocolate hares and painted eggs as symbols of fertility and the beginning of spring. And when Ramadan ends around 5 December, the Sugar Feast is easily combined with the Dutch *Sinterklaas* feast as both Muslim and Dutch traditions use it to shower children with sweets and presents. In a sense, Christmas and Easter are returning to their pre-Christian roots of celebrating midwinter, the New Year, and the beginning of spring.

Department stores gladly support this trend because they don't want to exclude customers unfamiliar with Christmas songs or other biblical references. At the same time migrants cherish their own separate feasts, especially at home when they are among family and friends. Then they will have traditional dishes with flavours that evoke memories of celebrations like birth, marriage, and New Year or religious high-days like Easter, Ramadan, and Divali. So every Moroccan *iftar* meal should start with dates and *harira*, an Aruban Christmas dinner needs a *ham di pascu*, and a Chinese New Year without fish doesn't portend any good for the coming year.

These images show the power of imagery in invoking the joy and social importance of eating. Most of them are part of the *Rotterdam Cookbook,* a project about the variety of food cultures in Rotterdam. For this project I interviewed families of different cultural backgrounds about their food traditions and how these survived in Rotterdam's urban environment. Together with photographer Carel van Hees, I enjoyed the hospitality of these families and joined them at the special meals they served for their family and friends. We also followed the cooks doing the shopping, selecting the proper ingredients and preparing the dishes.

Celebrating Life in Multicultural Rotterdam

This paper ends with a striking example of the mutual interference of separate food traditions in the Netherlands. Recently young Rotterdammers have discovered street-food with the very un-culinary name of *kapsalon* (hairdresser's). It has nothing to do with eating hair, but everything to do with an extremely nutritious mix of Cape Verdean, Turkish and Dutch food.

Chinese New Year with the Chau family

Born in Hong Kong, as a young man Mr Chau immigrated to the Netherlands in the 1960s. Like many other Chinese men he started working as a waiter in Chinese-Indonesian restaurants. Now he is head waiter at one of the best Chinese restaurants in Rotterdam. Mr Chau is married and has four children. He is a very good cook himself, a specialist in slaughtering and preparing lobster. On this special day Mister Chau is cooking at home a New Year's meal for his wife and children.

MENU
Steamed chicken feet with sweet and sour sauce
Peking dumplings
Wintermelon soup
Fried shrimp with 5-spice powder
Steamed tilapia with coriander, ginger and spring onions
Choi sum with oyster sauce
Fried lobster with ginger and spring onions
Fried chicken wings
White rice

Celebrating Life in Multicultural Rotterdam

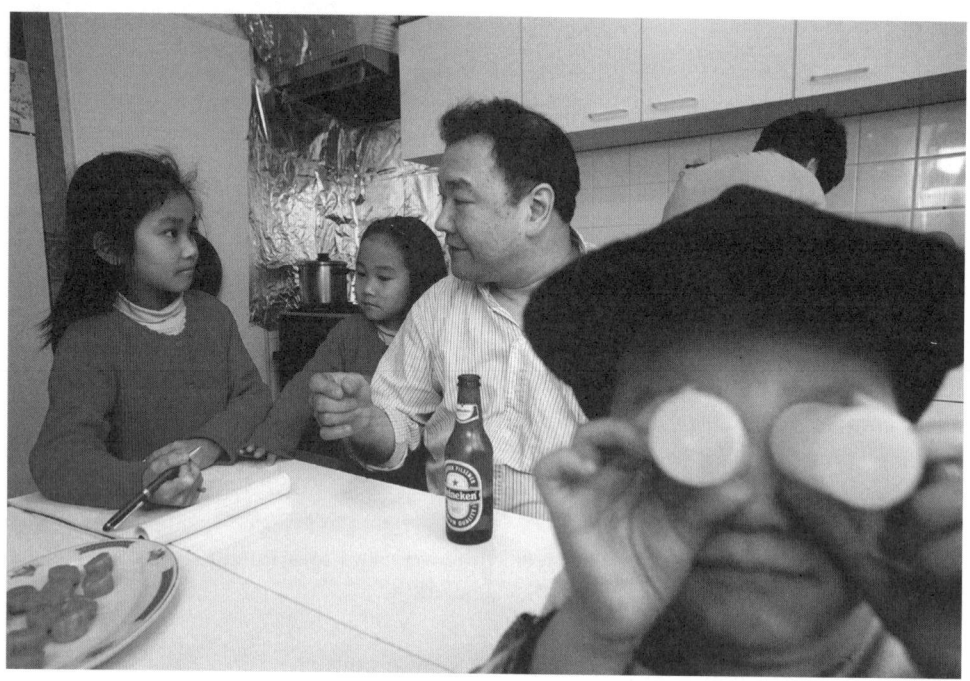

Celebrating Life in Multicultural Rotterdam

Eritrean women celebrating New Year

Haile Selassie, Emperor of Ethiopia, annexed Eritrea in 1962, which was the start of a long war between both countries. As with many other men and women, Haimanot Salvatore had to leave Eritrea because the danger of being arrested for her political activities. After a long detour she arrived in Rotterdam, a city in a country she had never heard of before. She built up a new life in Rotterdam. Now she has a job as a coordinator of projects for refugees.

New Year is the most important feast of the year in Eritrea and Ethiopia. It is always celebrated on 11 September. In Rotterdam, Haimanot and her friends have their festive meal in the sports hall of the community house. In the well-equipped kitchen they cook as many traditional dishes as they can afford. They use the hot and spicy *d'leg* or *berbere* as the base of many dishes, herbs and spices like ajowan, fenugreek, and *corrorima* (grains of paradise), well known in Europe in classical times, but now hardly used any more. Of course there will be *injera* on the menu as well, the soft and sour flat bread made of *teff* (a special grain), which accompanies every traditional Eritrean (and Ethiopian) meal.

Their feast ends with singing, dancing, jumping over a fire and a coffee ceremony.

Celebrating Life in Multicultural Rotterdam

MENU

Injera
Zigni (meat stew)
Tumtumoh (cooked lentils with *berbere*)
Helbet (hand-whipped bean flour with fenugreek)
Humutoh (braised sheep's stomach and liver)
Silsi (hot sauce)
T'ihlo (barley flour balls)
Shiro (chickpea sauce)
Alicha (mixed vegetables)

Celebrating Life in Multicultural Rotterdam

Junion Hanenberg and Agnes Vreugd cooking a Surinamese meal

In 1975, when he was six years old, Junion moved from Surinam to Rotterdam. There he joined his mother, Agnes Vreugd, who had come to Rotterdam two years earlier to seek out the the father of her children and a house with enough space for the family. Years later, Junion and his Dutch partner Rob bought an apartment in the centre of Rotterdam where they transformed the kitchen into a high-tech stainless steel laboratory.

Junion likes to experiment with new ingredients, cooking techniques and food styling. But his African-Surinamese roots are still recognizable in the cooking he learned from his mother Agnes. Together they prepare a festive meal for the family, inaugurating the new kitchen.

MENU

Djiendja bierie (home-made ginger beer)
Tajersoup with lamb
Chicken and caper pie
Kouseband (string beans) with balsamic
Fried drumsticks
Agnes' '*sambal sjippie*' (potato sticks with chilli paste)
Cucumber salad
Baka bana (deep fried plantain)
Sweet potatoes
Fruit soup
White rice

Celebrating Life in Multicultural Rotterdam

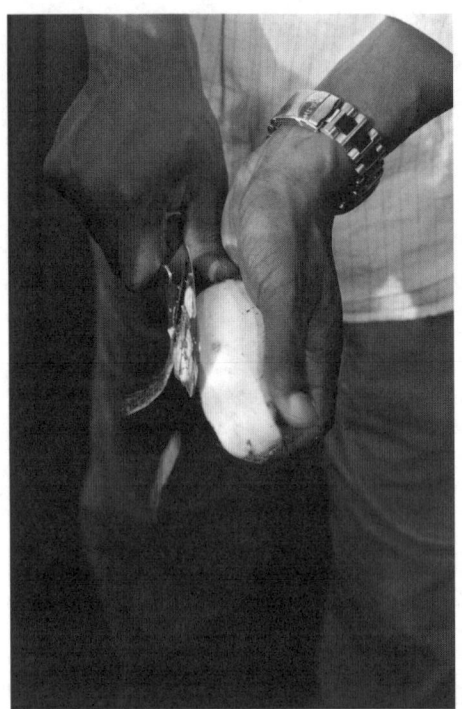

Celebrating Life in Multicultural Rotterdam

The Çoban family on a sunny summer afternoon.
Emine and her husband Sefer Çoban grew up in central Anatolia. They moved to the Netherlands in the 1970s. Sefer worked in a factory; Emine in a bakery where she became a specialist in Turkish pastry. They have five sons, two of them born in Turkey, the others in Rotterdam. Every morning, in summer and winter, Emine and Sefer leave their apartment in the centre of Rotterdam and drive to a small piece of land alongside the railway track behind the Mevlana mosque. There they have built their own paradise. They grow flowers, fruits, vegetables, and herbs, and there are goats for their grandchildren to play with.

The interior of their shed is dominated by a *soba*, a wood-burner that functions as an oven for baking pastry and bread and as a hot-plate for cooking soups and stews – the traditional food deeply rooted in the traditions of the eastern part of Turkey.

MENU

Köfte (roasted minced lamb)
Ispanek börek (pastry stuffed with spinach and goat cheese)
Sis Kebap (roasted beef)
Bazlama and *yufka* (breads)
Manti (dough stuffed with minced lamb)
Domates salatesi (tomato salad with mint)
Gözlemeh (pastry stuffed with egg, cheese and parsley)
Yaprak sarmasi (grape leaves stuffed with rice, raisins and pine seeds)
Raw chili peppers, fresh grapes
Tea with baklava

Celebrating Life in Multicultural Rotterdam

Celebrating Life in Multicultural Rotterdam

The boy and the *kapsalon*. An urban legend

> *The first* kapsalon *(hairdresser's), a street-food mix of Cape Verdean, Turkish and Dutch foods, was eaten in Rotterdam some years ago. Since then it has rapidly conquered the rest of the country, especially in neighbourhoods near train stations and discothèques.*

Once upon a time there was a boy. He lived on an island in the ocean, far away from the African coast. Long ago it was a desert island, until the Portuguese arrived. They called the small archipelago *Ilhas de Cabo Verde,* and it became a transit port for the slave trade. They laid out sugar plantations that African slaves were brought to work. Traders from Europe and the Far East procreated with African women, and that is how Cabo Verde got a population.

The island where the boy grew up was not fertile. There was little food to eat. Usually his mother cooked beans with some vegetables and fish. Sometimes there was meat on the island, dried or salted, brought in by ship from Portugal. Then she made a special dish by putting all things available in a pot and cooking it slowly until everything was done. She called it *cachupa*. The boy loved *cachupa*, he could eat it every day, but that wasn't possible of course.

One day their neighbours made *cachupa* as well, and then their neighbours, and so on. *Cachupa* became the national dish of Cabo Verde. They even made a postage stamp with a hefty portion of *cachupa* on it.

One day the father of the boy announced to his family that he was going to leave the island. Like many other men he had no job. He had met a man from Holland who invited him to work in the port of Rotterdam. There were more Cape Verdeans working in the docks, and the father decided to join them. He was going to send money to the family, and as soon as he had found a place to live, the boy, his sisters and mother could come to Holland as well.

The father said goodbye and left the island. After two years he had not yet found a good place for the whole family to live, and there was not always enough work for him in the docks. Father became homesick. He longed for his island and the *cachupa* of the mother.

The boy missed his father. He dreamed of the big city with shops where you could buy all kinds of things like nice clothes and shoes. When he was seventeen years old he decided to follow his father. He could sail by ship to Holland, and on board he had to give haircuts and shaves to the men and help the cook in the kitchen.

When the ship arrived in Rotterdam, his father was waiting for him on the quay. The boy could move into his father's place. He wasn't suited for work in the docks, so he went downtown looking for a job, which he found at a hairdresser's.

Next to the hairdresser's was a cafeteria. One day the boy entered and asked the Turkish owner what he could eat. There was kebab and *patat* (French fries), cheese, salad, and all kinds of sauces. The boy asked if he could have it all together. The Turkish owner made something special for him. He took a big aluminium box, started with a layer of kebab, then *patat,* and covered it with a thick slice of Gouda cheese. He put the box under the grill till the cheese was melted. As a finishing touch he added some green salad, a few slices of tomato, garlic sauce and chili paste. A new dish was born. The boy loved it. From that moment his daily lunch was this special box filled with delicacies.

One day it was very busy at the hairdresser's. The boy asked a younger boy to bring his daily lunch from the Turkish cafeteria. 'Order *kapsalon* (hairdresser's), then he will know what you mean', he said. When it was his turn, the younger boy asked for *kapsalon*. The Turkish owner knew what he meant and started preparing it. A group of Surinamese boys watched with interest what he was doing. 'That looks good man, for me *kapsalon* as well please', one of them said. His friends ordered the same. They all loved the *kapsalon*. They came back, and more and more clients asked for *kapsalon*. The owner wrote *kapsalon* on the menu: small (€3), medium (€4), and large with extra meat (€5). Other cafeterias followed, and it became the favourite food of young Rotterdammers before and after a night of heavy drinking and dancing.

Now, a few years later, *kapsalon* is well known throughout the Netherlands. There are rumours that *kapsalon* has reached Brussels and Antwerp, and the first organic *kapsalon* (€6) has been spotted at a farmers' market.

In real life the boy's name is Nataniël Gomes. The name of the hairdresser's is Kapsalon Tati, and the cafeteria where kapsalon *was born is El Aviva at the Schiedamseweg in Rotterdam.*

Photographs
The Rotterdam Cookbook: Carel van Hees; '*Kapsalon*': Linda Roodenburg.

M.F.K. Fisher, W.H. Auden, and *Thanksgiving for a Habitat*

Seth Rosenbaum

In 1970, just three years before his death, W. H. Auden published *A Certain World*.[1] Organized alphabetically by subheadings such as 'Goat, Nanny,' 'Man,' 'Mnemonics,' 'Spoonerisms,' and 'World, End of the,' the commonplace book 'is a sort of autobiography,' as Auden writes in his foreword to the volume.[2] The collection of quotations impresses with its literary and historical scope, but with a poet and prose writer of Auden's range and skill, it hardly surprises that he had such myriad literary material in his 'personal planet' on which to draw. Auden writes, 'I have tried to keep my own reflections ... to a minimum, and let others, more learned, intelligent, imaginative and witty than I, speak for me.' The foreword, in fact, is one of the longest prose passages written by Auden in the entire book, and it is revealing to examine the metaphor the poet deploys to sketch the skeleton structure of Auden's own imagination:

> Biographies of writers, whether written by others or themselves, are always superfluous and usually in bad taste. A writer is a maker, not a man of action. To be sure, some, in a sense all, of his works are transmutations of his personal experiences, but no knowledge of the raw ingredients will explain the peculiar flavor of the verbal dishes he invites the public to taste ...

These lines immediately recall one of the most famous lines in twentieth-century verse, written by Auden in his 1939 elegy for Yeats: 'Poetry makes nothing happen[.]'[3] The poet should *make*, true to the etymology of the Greek word, *poieisis*; 'a man of action' makes something happen, and that is not Auden's conception of the poet's office. The distinction between the poet as maker and the man of action was a nascent idea to Auden in 1939, but in the following three decades it evolved into one of Auden's immutable ideological principles. So we should pay careful attention to Auden's 'maker,' who in his foreword is not the plastic or traditional verbal artist we might expect – not a sculptor, not a painter, not even a writer. Auden's artist is, decidedly, a cook, serving forth a verbal meal. The gustatory language of 'bad taste,' 'raw ingredients,' 'peculiar flavor,' 'verbal dishes,' and public 'taste,' gluts the first paragraph of the foreword. It is no surprise to discover that the entry on 'Eating' is one of the longest in *A Certain World*.[4]

Immediately after the cluster of gustatory references, Auden quotes Chesterton to provide a different angle on the poet as maker: 'There is at the back of every artist's mind something like a pattern or type of architecture ... the strange flora and fauna of his own secret planet. ... This general atmosphere, and pattern or structure of growth, governs all his creations, however varied.' Auden affirms Chesterton's stress on 'architecture,' 'atmosphere,' 'flora and fauna,' 'pattern or structure of growth,' calling *A Certain World* 'a map of my planet,' a guide to the architecture of his complex environment. The poet-maker as a cook and as the designer and denizen of a personal habitat are the two governing metaphors Auden utilizes to introduce his commonplace book. Enter my personal planet, Auden invites; taste the fare.

What role did food and taste play in Auden's structural imagination? The opening lines from the foreword are not simply dismissible, metaphoric language. In a book that includes so little of Auden's own prose, but claims autobiographical status, the logic behind the foreword intimates a deep significance to the idea of man as a maker, taster and eater of food, but also a builder and inhabitant of a small, semi-private environment. In this paper I trace the roots of that significance to Auden's poetry in the late 1950s and early to mid-1960s, when Auden composed a series of poems that he ultimately collected into the sequence *Thanksgiving for a Habitat*, published in 1965 in *About the House*.[5] The sequence demonstrates how Auden uses food not only symbolically, but structurally as well to ask the classical questions: 'Who is the happy man?' 'What is the *summum bonum*?' Auden answers in a new voice, 'the happiest [in which] he had ever written,' according to Edward Mendelson, but also through a contemporary interlocutor, whom he hides in plain sight: the great American food writer, M.F.K. Fisher.[6] I will argue that Fisher teaches Auden to celebrate and give thanks in his extended sequence.

Thanksgiving for a Habitat comprises twelve poems, each prefixed by a Roman numeral. The sequence operates both chronologically and spatially, chronicling a typical day in Auden's Kirchstetten 'habitat' from morning to evening, as well as taking the reader on a walking tour of the only home Auden ever owned. The sequence as a whole divides itself into distinct groups of poems. The following grid will, I hope, illuminate the basic structure and rooms of the poem:

Genre	Poem	Précis / Location
Introduction	I. Prologue: The Birth of Architecture	Human time is distinct from 'natural' time
	II. Thanksgiving for a Habitat	The poet describing his place in the 'Habitat'
Solitary	III. The Cave of Making	Elegy for Louis MacNeice, the writer's study
	IV. Down There	Cellar
	V. Up There	Attic
Transition	VI. The Geography of the House	Toilet
	VII. Encomium Balnei	Bathroom

M.F.K. Fisher, W.H. Auden, and *Thanksgiving for a Habitat*

Social	VIII. Grub First, Then Ethics (Brecht)	Kitchen
	IX. For Friends Only	Guest-room
	X. To-night at Seven-Thirty	Dining-room
Solitary & Social	XI. The Cave of Nakedness	Bedroom
	XII. The Common Life	Living-room

Auden criticism has noted the dedication of one of the twelve poems to Fisher, and identified a passage in Fisher's *The Art of Eating* that Auden used as a source text, but has not considered other strong references to Fisher's work or how Fisher's influence extends beyond the single poem, 'To-night at Seven-Thirty,' and into the sequence as a whole.[7] Auden's debt to Fisher, I will show, is a systemic one that had a notable effect on the structure of *Thanksgiving for a Habitat*, as well as on Auden's imagination more generally. I will focus first on the social, gustatory poems of the sequence ('Grub First, Then Ethics (Brecht)' and 'To-night at Seven-Thirty'), and then explain their relationship to the sequence as a whole. Edward Mendelson, Auden's literary executor and greatest critic, identifies Dante as the major influence on Auden's verse of the 1930s. Shakespeare replaced Dante in the 1940s, and Goethe replaced Shakespeare in the 1960s.[8] I argue that in the late 1950s and early 1960s Auden adopts Fisher's ideas of food, taste, and the rites of the table. Auden's adaptation of Fisher enabled him to re-imagine the relationship between self and other, between man and environment, in an intermediary period between the titanic influences of Shakespeare and Goethe. I am arguing for an influential place for Fisher amidst canonical authors of Western literary history, but I will demonstrate that she deserves recognition in Auden's planet, and Auden suggests the same in his 1958 essay, 'The Kitchen of Life.'[9] In reviewing Fisher's magnum opus, *The Art of Eating*, Auden writes that 'Mrs. Fisher is as talented a writer as she is a cook. Indeed, I do not know of anyone in the United States today who writes better prose.' Auden supported himself by his own prose, lectures, and teaching, and the sometimes curmudgeonly Auden was no hollow flatterer. We should take Auden's praise, and his thanksgiving, at face value, and investigate how the best prose writer in the United States might have influenced pervasively one of the great poets of the twentieth century.

Saying grace

A reader of *Thanksgiving for a Habitat* would not be unjustified in asking, at least through the first seven poems of the sequence, just why Auden is thankful. The opening poems show glimmers of happiness, but only in absurd, literally parenthetical asides: '(I am glad/ the blackbird, for instance, cannot/ tell if I'm talking English … that what he utters/ I may enjoy as an alien rigmarole)' (689). Just lines later Auden considers a 'drawn-out' death or an instantaneous translation 'in a nano-second/ to a c.c. of poisonous nothing/ in a giga-death' of atomic warfare. The poem purportedly of thanksgiving is saturated with death from its very first line, 'Nobody I know would like to be buried/ with a silver cocktail-shaker' (687). Is Auden grateful for his 'habitat?' Hardly, it seems, as he trivializes and criticizes his fellow inhabitants, the animals, insisting that 'a pen/ for a rational animal/ is no fitting habitat for Adam's sovereign clone' (688). The 'magic Eden' is not a habitat but the home, and yet the transition in the poems from habitat to home proper shows little promise of thanksgiving. Death, loneliness, and fear continue to dominate as we enter the house, and Auden provides no obvious relief until the social poems, specifically in the poem he dedicates to Fisher, 'To-night at Seven-Thirty.'

   The first stanza of the poem reprises the question Auden raises in the opening poems: Why should humans, who are distinct from animals, be thankful? Auden's question in the opening poems, which provides melancholic humor as an insufficient response, gives way to a substantive and satisfying answer, at last:

> The life of plants
> is one continuous solitary meal,
>   and ruminants
> hardly interrupt theirs to sleep or to mate, but most
>   predators feel
> ravenous most of the time and competitive
> always, bolting such morsels as they can contrive
> to snatch from the more terrified: pack-hunters do
>   dine *en famille*, it is true,
> with protocol and placement, but none of them play host
> to a stranger whom they help first. Only man,
>   supererogatory beast,
> Dame Kind's thoroughbred lunatic, can
>   Do the honors of the feast …   (707)

Auden begins with the familiar habitat outside, moving from plants to herbivores, then to carnivorous predators, and finally to humans. The common thread through the different forms of life is an analysis of their respective foodways. '[S]olitary' eating is rejected out of hand, an important point to which we will return in the penultimate poem of the sequence, and 'predators' in the habitat or wild lack the capacity for empathy and hospitality that Auden valued so highly. Auden's human might be a beast, but he is a 'supererogatory' one, bestowed with extraordinary favor; the very philosophic opulence of Auden's adjective, 'supererogatory,' cancels the crudeness of its noun, 'beast.' Man is an animal, but the difference is one of kind, not degree. The celebratory, carefully chosen feast Auden goes on to describe in the poem is literally the Thanksgiving meal we have been awaiting in *Thanksgiving for a Habitat*.

M.F.K. Fisher, W.H. Auden, and *Thanksgiving for a Habitat*

A word must be said about the form Auden chooses for the poem. No two poems in the sequence share a common structure, and 'To-night at Seven-Thirty' and 'Grub First, Then Ethics (Brecht)' are undoubtedly the most complex poems with respect to form. Though 'Grub First' has clear, repetitive features in its isometric stanzas, the 16-line stanzas lack a coherent, repeating rhyme scheme, but this is appropriate for the rough 'grubbiness' implicit in the title. I will return to 'Grub First' but want to note at this point that, at the beginning of the social, eating poems, Auden's is a first and incomplete gesture toward celebration and thanksgiving from the perspective of form. 'To-night at Seven-Thirty' solves the looseness of the earlier poem with its precisely crafted 14-line stanzas, based on the traditional sonnet structure. Auden renovates one of the core forms of English literature by installing a new rhyme scheme, *abacbddeecfgfg*, and metrical variation (not merely iambic pentameter). Where the sonnet typically divides, Auden deliberately creates coherence between octave and sestet, not a turn or break. The *ddee* rhymes in lines 6–9, flush in the middle of the stanza, build continuity through rhyme, and are flanked by quatrain rhymes that, atypically, close the stanza.

The formal strictness of 'To-night' underscores the coherence Auden finds in the act of social eating without sacrificing the humble, conversational tone that has been consistent throughout the sequence. Auden's appreciation for that act of eating comes from his reading in Fisher's *The Art of Eating*. Auden writes that 'doters who wish / to tiddle and curmurr … belong in restaurants' (708); Fisher that 'I prefer not to have among my guests two people or more, of any sex, who are in the first wild tremors of love.'[10] Auden describes his kitchen and decides that 'six … is now a Perfect / Social Number,' and he renders the strict poem in 6 stanzas, going so far as to identify the six guests: '**I** see [at] a table … the **youngest** and **oldest** present … **one raconteur, one Gnostic** with amazing shop … and **one wide-travelled worldling**'[11] (709); in 'Sing of Dinner in a Dish,' Fisher too describes her ideal chef's space, listing a number of small details. But, all those things, she writes,

> are relatively unimportant. There are only three things I need, to make my kitchen a pleasant one as long as it is clean. First I need space enough to get a good simple meal for six people. More of either would be wasteful as well as dangerously dull … Most of all I need to be let alone. I need peace.[12]

Thanksgiving for a Habitat asks for the same basic requirements, only in reverse order – in the opening poems Auden asks to be let alone; only then is he prepared for a 'good simple meal for six.' But where the opening poems of the sequence find Auden alone, he is not yet at peace. From a rhetorical perspective Auden, and the poem, must arrive at peace in the social poems. As Mendelson writes on the first page of *Early Auden*, 'Auden begins alone,' and in this late sequence he accepts loneliness as necessary to the social cohesion found later in the sequence.[13] What was once so estranging is now the precondition for the social activity that separates man from the animal world. We recall that '[o]nly man, / supererogatory beast … can / do the honors of a feast' (707). Fisher rendered the idea in prose first: 'When we exist without thought or thanksgiving we are not men, but beasts.'[14]

Mendelson, Fuller, and Callan have noted similar allusions to Fisher, found in 'The Perfect Dinner,' Fisher's closing essay in *The Art of Eating*, excerpts of which appear in *A Certain World*. But the above references, scattered throughout Fisher's magnum opus, have gone unnoticed.[15] They begin to speak to the thoroughness of Auden's engagement with Fisher, that he did not merely recall the final pages of Fisher's 800-page volume. Fisher's presence in this intensely personal poem is, in and of itself, curious and telling. Of the other eleven dedicatees, the Kronenbergers, Weisses, Clarks, Neil Little and John Bayley were friends and even visitors to Kirchstetten; Isherwood, Macneice, Gardiner, and Gorer were a group ranging from close friends to those with a long and personal history with Auden. Chester Kallman, Auden's longtime lover, stands in a category of his own. The eleven as a group suggest a wide range of friendship and intimacy, but Fisher decidedly does not fall within that range. Auden's biographers make no mention of Auden and Fisher ever having met.[16] M.F.K. Fisher's biographers record neither acquaintanceship nor correspondence between the two.[17] But there was correspondence, at least one letter, and perhaps more. On 18 August 1963, Auden wrote the letter reproduced here.[18]

> Dear Mrs Fisher:
>
> The enclosed poem is one of a series I am writing about what a house is, room by room. I should like your permission to dedicate it to you because, as you will see when you read it, it owes such a lot to you.
>
> Congratulations on *A Cordiall Water* which Faber's have just sent me. I enjoyed it immensely.
>
> Yours sincerely
> Wystan Auden

M.F.K. Fisher, W.H. Auden, and *Thanksgiving for a Habitat*

Auden typed many of his letters, but he wrote to Fisher in his own hand, a sign of personal address.[19] The formal address, however, 'Dear Mrs. Fisher' and not 'Mary Frances,' suggests that Auden and Fisher were not intimate. Auden makes clear that *Thanksgiving for a Habitat* is a poem about the house, not the habitat; that 'To-night at Seven-Thirty' 'owes such a lot' to Fisher is an understatement. It is curious that Auden asks Fisher's permission, as an afterthought no less (shown by the inserted superscript edit in the letter), to dedicate the poem to her. In requesting permission to dedicate the poem to Fisher Auden is really asking permission to translate Fisher's prose into poetry, and the dedication serves as the 'plagiarist's' citation.[20]

Fisher earned her way into Auden's poem as the other dedicatees did not insofar as she directly influences Auden's notion of thanksgiving and celebration. Though Auden wrote the letter to Fisher in 1963, he had her prose in mind at least as far back as July 1958 when he wrote 'The Kitchen of Life,' the essay in which Auden reviewed glowingly *The Art of Eating*. The timing of the essay is crucial because that same year Auden wrote 'On Installing an American Kitchen in Lower Austria,' which was published two years later in *Homage to Clio*.[21] Auden had food and eating on the brain, certainly because of Fisher, but he didn't quite know how to incorporate Fisher into his own work. By 1962, however, Auden found his solution – the sequence that would become *Thanksgiving for a Habitat*. 'On Installing an American Kitchen in Lower Austria' reappears in the 1965 publication *About the House*, under a new title, as the eighth poem of *Thanksgiving for a Habitat*, 'Grub First, Then Ethics (Brecht).' Mendelson writes that in 'the summer of 1962 Auden decided that his poem about the kitchen belonged in a sequence of poems about each room in his house[,]' which the letter to Fisher confirms, but Mendelson also cites a note Auden attached to 'Grub First,' stating that Auden 'did not realize that … [the] proper place of ['On Installing an American Kitchen in Lower Austria:] was in a cycle.'[22] The cycle, from an imaginative perspective, begins with the American kitchen, which begins with Auden's reading and reviewing of Fisher.

Auden tells us that *Thanksgiving for a Habitat* is a poem that describes 'what a house is,' and in 'Grub First, Then Ethics (Brecht)' Auden writes that '[t]he prehistoric hearthstone … is numinous and/ again the centre of a dwelling' (703). Auden, who was a connoisseur of music, but no chef, calls the 'cook a pure artist/ who moves Everyman / at a deeper level than / Mozart' (704). The kitchen is the center of Auden's home economics and ethos, where 'all we ask for … is a good dinner' (705). Auden agrees with Brecht that we need to satisfy basic human needs, like eating, before we can discuss abstract 'ethics,' but Auden doesn't dedicate this, or any other poem, to Brecht. *Thanksgiving for a Habitat* is not a cycle about the civic virtues and intellectualized ethics; it is a private poem about the house, and Auden makes a clear distinction between man, who creates the bourgeois feast, and the beasts, who do not know how to 'play host' (707). 'Grub' is important, but Auden's Edenic 'habitat' centers on the home, which is centered around the kitchen, comity, and the human privilege of choice dining. But why do the social, eating poems I have been analyzing in Auden's carefully divided sequence fall just off-center in the cycle, when Auden stresses the centrality of the kitchen? How does Auden reconcile the chef and the architect in *A Certain World* in this cycle?

Off-center, *en route*

In the second half of the sequence, as we have seen, Auden concentrates the distinction between man and animal through Fisher's culinary emphasis, but that distinction is expanded more generally into the architecture of the early poems with carefully placed culinary references. If we revisit the beginning of the sequence we will find that Fisher has been with Auden, and with us, all along. In 'Thanksgiving for a Habitat,' Auden recognizes that, because humans are atop the food chain, 'I shall not end/down any oesophagus' but Auden will 'anyhow, stop eating' when he dies (689). In the elegy for MacNeice, the first of the private poems, 'a starving ear is as deaf as a suburban optimist's,' which anticipates Brecht. In 'Down There,' Auden reminds the reader that

> we dine at street level:
> But, deep in Mother Earth, beneath her key-cold cloak,
> Where light and heat can never spoil what sun ripened,
> In barrels, bottles, jars, we mew her kind commons,
> Wine, beer, conserves and pickles, good at all seasons.   (695–6)

The cellar keeps the preserves of the summer harvest fresh for consumption, but there will be no dining at street level for quite some poems yet. The raw ingredients for 'To-night at Seven-Thirty,' however, are stored here, waiting to be opened and shared. Though food is represented in the cellar, it is literally conserved for later in the poem. The elegy and the attic poems speak specifically to hunger, the latter describing 'a starving spider spin[ning] for/The occasional fly' (696). All these poems, as I said earlier, show no signs of Thanksgiving, but rather depict a solitary and starved Auden.

The turn or change from fasting to feasting begins in the transitional center, 'The Geography of the House' and 'Encomium Balnei.' Auden's move from solitude to a social atmosphere is thrilling, if moderately disgusting. The four stanzas of 'Down There,' written in six-line dodecasyllabics, narrow into the three stanzas of 'Up There['s]' hendecasyllables. The physical width of the stanzas then thins radically in 'The Geography of the House,' in which a pair of six syllable lines (the broken twelve-syllable lines of 'Down There') precede a six-syllable and then five-syllable third and fourth line, respectively (the broken hendecasyllables of 'Up There'). Auden's intestines in 'Geography' literally digest the preceding poems of loneliness and starvation, 'Down There' and 'Up There.' Auden 'leave[s] the dead concerns of/Yesterday behind' in order to 'face with ... courage/What is now to be.' 'Geography' excretes the two poems in regular stanzaic strips at the sequence's center, making space for a different kind of nourishment.

'Geography' also resets the diachronic clock on the sequence, beginning as it does '[s]eated after breakfast.' 'A satisfactory / Dump is a good omen,' and a fresh beginning, but still a private, concentrated act of waste disposal, even if it is an 'ur-act of making' (697–8). In moving from 'Geography' to 'Encomium' Auden moves from the pristine, 'white tiled cabin' of the toilet to a 'carcallan acreage' of Roman baths, so lavish against a modern bathroom (700). It is all very funny, and yet serious, too. Baths are now private affairs, but Auden recalls them in their public, Roman glory. The turn from the toilet to the tub makes possible an imaginative opening from the singular sphincter to the multitudinous pores of the skin, exfoliation rather than excretion.

Solitary excretion and then bathing enable the plural companionship that follows in the poems of actual thanksgiving and grace. The 'mallarmesque / syllabic fog' in which Auden casts the poem creates the visual effect of a steamy, foggy bathroom and its mirror, permitting the aesthetically visual turn Auden begins in 'Geography' to move from caves, cellars, and attics to kitchens, bedrooms, and dining-rooms (702). 'Geography' condenses and narrows in order to excrete; 'Encomium' expands in preparation for social contact. Though, as I have argued, Fisher's gastronomy is the intellectual and imaginative center of *Thanksgiving for a Habitat*, rhetorically it made more sense to Auden to place the bathroom at the physical center of poem and house, deferring the eating poems until body and mind are cleansed and prepared to dine. 'Brains evolved after bowels,' Auden writes in 'To-night,' but 'they are not essential like artful cooks / and stalwart digestions' (709). As the poem is organized, Auden performs an aesthetically and rhetorically convincing move from the solitude of the opening five poems of the sequence, in which there is no living human population with whom Auden can interact, to the final five poems in which Auden converses with the living, not the dead.

Following the pomp and arrangement of Auden's ideal dinner in 'Tonight,' it would appear that the poem moves away from Fisher's influence. While critics have noted the many influences of Fisher's 'The Perfect Dinner' on 'Tonight' in the details of the feast, they have not seen that Auden copies Fisher's consideration of the solitary and 'the category of Two' in order to close his sequence. At the end of her essay, Fisher describes a meal she might make for herself to eat alone. She writes,

> I close the refrigerator door firmly … and go to bed, bolstered by books to be read …
>
> The slightly depraved ramifications of dining alone are plainly limitless. I have savored many of them and do not feel myself the loser. In the main, though, I prefer the category of Two … above all the company of One other, making the rarest kind of Two …[23]

In 'The Cave of Nakedness' Auden retreats from the perfect meal for six to 'the pleasure of reading in bed,' just as Fisher suggests. Alone in his bed, Auden's return to the solitary is bittersweet. He is an 'unwilling … celibate[,]' but he is grateful for the experience of life displayed throughout the sequence, both the solitary and the convivial: 'Age, despite its damage,/ is well off.' It is better to be old, more often than not alone, and to have experienced the world, Auden writes, than to return to a youth in which 'Junior has daily to cope/ with ghastly family meals' (711).

Auden's movement from consideration of six to one follows the precise trajectory of Fisher's essay. What is more, the final poem, 'The Common Life,' is a meditation on Auden's life with Kallman. It is a poem in which Auden, like Fisher, says that he prefers 'Two' to one or six, an affirmation of Auden's life with Kallman 25 years in the making. Fisher subtly plays with 'One' and 'Two,' using capitalization to draw attention to the distinction and to force the reader to linger over the numbers. When we reread closely, we see she is not talking about two people eating, per se, but about 'the *category* of Two,' category suggesting terrain that Fisher's essay barely begins to cover.[24] She merely intimates, at her conclusion, a different kind of perfection, one that goes beyond the pleasures of the table. Auden develops Fisher's 'One' and 'category of Two,' rewriting Kallman and himself as '*Thou* and *I*' in 'The Common Life' (713).[25] What conclusions does he reach?

> Howbeit,
> fasting or feasting, we both know this: without
> the Spirit we die, but life
>
> without the Letter is in the worst of taste,
> and always, though truth and love
> can never really differ, when they seem to,
> the subaltern should be truth.   (715)

Auden ends with a bold final stroke, transcending the flesh and body he has worked so hard to defend in this sequence for the sake of love. Fasting, feasting, and the Spirit are put on level ground: they are akin to Brecht's Grub, necessary but insufficient for the good life, a tasteful life, Auden concludes. In the foreword to *A Certain World* Auden was concerned with 'bad taste,' and the precedent for those lines appear here in the closing of 'The Common Life.' Auden ultimately relies on Fisher's sense of good taste to guide him. When Auden sent Fisher a letter to request permission for a dedication, he had Fisher's 'Letter[s]' in his mind. 'Art is our chief means of breaking bread with the dead,' Auden once said, but *Thanksgiving for a Habitat* shows that Fisher's prose, in conjunction with bread and food, was, for a period, one of Auden's chief means of making art.

M.F.K. Fisher, W.H. Auden, and *Thanksgiving for a Habitat*

Notes

1. Auden, W.H., *A Certain World: A Commonplace Book*. New York: Viking Press, 1970.
2. *A Certain World*, vii–viii.
3. Auden, W.H., and Edward Mendelson, *Collected Poems*, The Centennial Edition, edited by Edward Mendelson. New York: Modern Library, 2007, p. 246. All subsequent citations will be in the main text.
4. *A Certain World*, 134–142.
5. Auden, W.H., *About the House*. New York: Random House, 1965.
6. Mendelson, Edward, *Later Auden*. New York: Farrar, Strauss and Giroux, 1999, p. 440.
7. See *Later Auden*, 443; Fuller, John, *W.H. Auden: A Commentary*. Princeton, N.J: Princeton University Press, 1998, p. 493; Callan, Edward, *Auden, a Carnival of Intellect*. New York: Oxford University Press, 1983, especially pp. 241–50.
8. *Later Auden*, 448.
9. Auden, W.H., *Forewords and Afterwords*. New York: Random House, 1973, p. 485. First publication in *The Griffin*, June 1958. See Auden, W.H., and Edward Mendelson, *Prose*, Volume IV. Princeton, N.J: Princeton University Press, 2010, pp. 166–172.
10. Fisher, 43.
11. I have used boldface to indicate the six guests Auden imagines at the table.
12. Fisher, 106.
13. Mendelson, Edward, *Early Auden*. New York: Viking Press, 1981, p. 3.
14. Fisher, 188.
15. See *Later Auden*, 443; Fuller, 493; Callan, 249.
16. See Davenport-Hines, Richard P., *Auden*. New York: Pantheon, 1995; Osborne, Charles, *W.H. Auden: The Life of a Poet*. New York: Harcourt Brace Jovanovich, 1979; Carpenter, Humphrey, *W.H. Auden, A Biography*. Boston: Houghton Mifflin Co, 1981.
17. See Zimmerman, Anne, *An Extravagant Hunger: The Passionate Years of M.F.K. Fisher*. Berkeley, CA: Counterpoint, 2011; Reardon, Joan, *Poet of the Appetites: The Lives and Loves of M.F.K. Fisher*. New York: North Point Press, 2004. In personal correspondence Reardon confirmed with me that she knows of no record of Auden and Fisher having met, let alone having corresponded with one another. I, too, in my archival work in Schlesinger Library, was unable to find references to Auden in Fisher's papers.
18. Auden's letter copyright by the Estate of W.H. Auden; reprinted by permission.
19. Auden, W.H. Letter to M.F.K. Fisher, 18 August 1963. W.H. Auden Papers, MS 89-03, Box 1, FF20. Wichita State University Libraries Special Collections, Wichita State University, Wichita, KS.
20. To my knowledge the letter from Auden to Fisher has not been analysed in Auden scholarship. It is listed in 'Published letters by W.H. Auden: A Bibliography,' as a sale item in 1986 and 1989. See Auden, W.H., Katherine Bucknell and Nicholas Jenkins, *In Solitude, for Company: W.H. Auden After 1940, Unpublished Prose and Recent Criticism*. Oxford, England: Clarendon Press, 1995.
21. Auden, W.H., *Homage to Clio*. New York: Random House, 1960.
22. *Later Auden*, 442.
23. Fisher, 744.
24. Italics mine.
25. See Fuller, 494 for discussion of Auden's '*Thou and I*' and Martin Buber's *I and Thou*.

Cake: The Centrepiece of Celebrations

Marietta Rusinek

Celebrations have always been closely connected with food and eating. Although the types of foods that are used in celebrations vary from home to home and from country to country, it appears that cake has always played a vital role in celebrating special occasions, holidays, and festivals. This paper examines the symbolic and ritual aspects of cake, viewing it as an intrinsic element of celebrations.

The paper briefly discusses the history of the word *cake*, drawing on the data provided by the *Oxford English Dictionary* (*OED*), and then traces the origin of celebration cakes by considering the relationship between cake and celebrating dating back to the times of ancient Greece, Rome, and Israel. Furthermore, the paper identifies the significant and predominant role that cakes play in events marking the progress of time or the transition from one status to another, e.g. festivals marking cycles of the calendar, agricultural as well as liturgical, and rites of passage such as birth and marriage. Therefore, the paper will highlight the intertwining relationship between cakes and the following festivals: the Mid-Autumn Festival, Maslenitsa, Twelfth Night, and Easter. Since birthday and wedding cakes seem to be the most heavily ritualized contemporary celebration cakes, the primary focus of the present paper is to examine their origin and symbolism as well as rituals accompanying both birthday and marriage celebrations.

The origin of cake

According to one of the major etymological sources, the *OED*, the origin of the word *cake* is uncertain. Not related to Latin *coquěre* 'to cook', as formerly supposed, *cake* probably derives from Old Norse *kaka*. When it first entered the English language in the early thirteenth century, the word denoted 'a small, flat and round loaf of bread'. It was not until the beginning of the Modern English period in the fifteenth century that *cake* started to denote and more or less resemble our contemporary cake, eventually becoming a celebratory elaboration of bread.

Ancient offertory cakes

It appears that cakes have long been associated with celebrating. As Humble (2010, 14) points out, the origins of the celebration cakes date back to the ancient tradition of offering cakes to gods or higher powers during religious ceremonies to celebrate their good deeds. If we look closer at the history of ancient Greece, we immediately notice the tradition of baking round or moon-shaped honey cakes for Artemis, the Goddess of Moon. As Dalby (2003, 69) observes, the roundness of the cakes symbolized the full phase of the moon, considered a symbol of good luck. What is more, it was often lit by burning candles so that it glowed like the moon, which led to today's custom of decorating birthday cakes with candles.

When it comes to Roman traditions, it is important to mention *libum*, a sacrificial cake offered of the altars of household spirits. First mentioned in Cato's *On Agriculture*, *libum* was probably a precursor of modern cheesecake since it was a small cheese bread served on fresh bay leaves, which must have imparted an interesting aroma to the *libum* (Dalby 2003, 69).

The importance of cakes in a religious context can be also traced back to ancient Israel, where women used to make cakes for Aserah, the Queen of Heaven. (The term Queen of Heaven, in a context unrelated to Virgin Mary, was a title given in the ancient Near East to a number of goddesses: Anat, Aserah, Isis, and Innana. In the Old Testament the prophet Jeremiah refers to the 'queen of heaven' when he scolds people for worshipping the goddess and therefore having sinned against the Lord (Beal and David 1997, 60–61).) The cakes that depicted the goddess were offered with wine at her temple. It appears that this tradition derived from the Hebrew belief that the goddess deserved veneration, hoping that in return for this veneration the Queen of Heaven would secure their well-being, give them food, and improve their lives in general (Chas and Harvey 2004, 9–10). Thus, it seems that the earliest celebration cakes were in fact sacrificial cakes offered to the gods. Therefore, we may draw a comparison between the ancient use of cake as a religious offering in the literal sense, and the later function of cake as a symbolic offering at celebrations of birthdays or weddings. For this very reason, ancient offertory cakes must have contributed significantly to cake becoming the ultimate food in various celebrations throughout the world.

Cakes in festivals

Cakes have always accompanied events which mark the progress of time or transition from one status to another. This part of the present paper is devoted to annual festivals which mark the cycles of the calendar, agricultural as well as liturgical. The Mid-Autumn Festival, also known as the Moon Festival, is a harvest festival celebrated by the Chinese, dating back more than 3000 years. Held on the fifteenth day of the eighth month in the Chinese calendar, this important festival is celebrated by the custom of eating moon cakes whose origins are traced back to the fourteenth century (see Figure 1). Traditionally made from lotus seed paste with a thin crust of pastry, moon cakes have developed over time into many regional variants, differing in the type of filling and crust, the latter being soft, chewy, or flaky. As Gunde (2002, 207–8) points out, this old festive speciality is more than just a small, sweet confection eaten by families while watching the moon. More importantly, it symbolizes family reunion and perfection, and therefore is undoubtedly a central element of the Moon Festival.

Another festival whose celebration is naturally intertwined with the presence of a cake is Maslenitsa. A Russian holiday with both religious and folk origins, Maslenitsa immediately precedes the seven-week Lenten fast before Easter and signals at the same

Cake: The Centrepiece of Celebrations

Figure 1. (above) Chinese moon cakes baked for the Mid-Autumn Festival.

Figure 2. (below) Bliny *served with cream – a Russian speciality during Maslenitsa.*

time the end of winter. Because of the fact that Great Lent imposes strict fasting, Maslenitsa is a time of feasting and enjoying the last days of eating meat, dairy and confectionery forbidden during Lent. The name of the festival derives from *masło*, the Russian name for 'butter', in reference to rich and fat foods eaten during the period (Schultze 2000). Therefore, it is not surprising that people celebrate this holiday by indulging themselves in consuming the richest foods. The most characteristic delicacy and the absolute necessity is *bliny*, the hot, yellow Russian pancakes served with melted butter or cream, as seen in Figure 2. Hudgins (2003, 199) explains the symbolic dimension of *bliny* – because of the fact that they are made warm, round and golden, they resemble the sun and symbolize rebirth with the beginning of spring.

When it comes to the celebration of Easter, *paskha*, a rich Russian cheesecake or dessert, is undoubtedly a cake worthy of note. The name of the confection comes from *paskha*, a term for Easter in the Eastern Orthodox Church. *Paskha* originated in the Eastern Orthodox countries, such as Russia, Ukraine, and Belorussia, and was originally made during the Holy Week and then brought to church on Great Saturday to be blessed (Hudgins 2003, 201–3). Interestingly, the cake in question is made from foods which are forbidden during the fast before Easter: cottage cheese, sour cream, eggs, butter, raisins and dried fruit. Thus, it appears that *paskha* is more than just a cake baked for Easter. First, its white colour symbolizes the purity of Christ. What is more, moulded into the shape of a truncated pyramid, it stands for the symbol of the Eastern Orthodox Church. Moreover, paskha is decorated with religious symbols such as a cross and the letters X and B meaning in Russian 'Christ is Risen!' (see Figures 3 and 4). For this very reason, *paskha* may undoubtedly be conceived of as an important element of celebrating Easter (Hudgins 2003).

Twelfth Night is a holiday celebrated by some branches of Christianity on the night of January 5, the eve of the Epiphany, concluding the Twelve Days of Christmas. It is observed as a time of merrymaking, and in some countries it marks the beginning of the Carnival season. In the past, the festival would start with eating the Twelfth Night Cake, also known as King Cake. As Davidson (1999, 817) observes, Twelfth Night Cake was a rich cake which contained a bean. It was believed that a person who received the slice containing the bean would be the king for the night and rule the feast. With time the cake in question started to be decorated with symbolic figures, often representing elaborate scenes. Twelfth Night Cake is considered to be complexly symbolic; in many countries there used to be different traditions concerning the cake. As the tradition of Twelfth Night faded, Twelfth Night Cake was replaced by Christmas cake, this, in turn, becoming an intrinsic part of Christmas celebrations.

Finally, it is worth noting other examples of cakes baked for festivals in different countries all over the world. Christmas specialities, among other things, include Italian *panettone* (a kind of sweet bread), *pandoro* (a yeast cake), and *torrone* (nougat), Spanish *polvorón* (a shortbread) and *turrón* (nougat), German *Christstollen* (a fruitcake), Portuguese *bolo rei* (a fruit cake), French *la bûche de Noël* (sponge cake roll), Polish

Cake: The Centrepiece of Celebrations

Figure 3. (above) Paskha decorated with the symbol of a cross.

Figure 4. (below) Paskha embossed with the letters 'XB'.

makowiec (poppy seed cake) and *piernik* (gingerbread) and Swedish *pepparkakor* (gingerbread cookies). As to Easter cakes, worth mentioning are Italian *cuzupe di Pasqua* (Easter bread with coloured eggs) and *colomba Pasquale* (a dove-shaped yeast cake), Spanish *la mona de Pascua* (a Spanish equivalent of Italian *cuzupe di Pasqua*), German *das Gebackene Osterlamm* (a lamb cake), Portuguese *pão-de-ló* (a sponge cake), and Polish *mazurek* (a flat cake with various toppings) and *babka drożdżowa* (a yeast cake).

Cakes in rites of passage: birth and marriage

Cakes also play an essential role in celebrating rites of passage. Since birthday and wedding cakes are thought to be the most heavily ritualized contemporary celebration cakes, they will be the focus of the remainder of this paper: their origins, traditions, and rituals. Let me start with the birthday cake.

'Birthdays are nature's way of telling us to eat more cake' – this anonymous quotation aptly illustrates the importance of cake to birthday celebrations (http://quotations.about.com). Its origin is a matter of doubt. It is linked by some food historians to the moon cakes of ancient Greece, especially because of the tradition of putting candles on the cakes adverted to above. Others believe, however, that the cradle of the contemporary birthday cake is medieval Germany, where sweetened bread dough was given the shape of baby Jesus to commemorate his birthday (Cunningham 2002, 62–3).

In the course of time, rituals arose which were centred on birthday cake such as placing candles, making wishes, or singing the 'Happy Birthday' song. These have been investigated by Katz (2003, 212–14). More specifically, customs surrounding the candles include making wishes over the flaming candles and blowing them out. Although the origin of the candle-blowing ritual is dubious, it is worth noting that it could have stemmed from the ancient practice of praying over flames, which led to pagan beliefs that by lighting candles people send signals to the gods: the smoke carrying their prayers heavenward. Today the custom of placing candles on the cake and making a silent wish before blowing out the candles is still popular. It is also believed that if you blow out all the candles with one breath, your wishes will come true. Another ritual related to birthday cake is singing the 'Happy Birthday' song which accompanies the appearance of the cake. Although in English, this song has become popular all over the world and is sung even in non-English-speaking countries. After singing the song, making a wish, and extinguishing the candles, the cake is cut and distributed among the guests (Katz 2003, 212–14).

Apart from these rituals, a number of superstitious beliefs related to the birthday cake have developed. As Smaridge (1978, 36) observes, in the Middle Ages people in England used to put symbolic objects such as coins and thimbles into the batter of the cake. Thus, it was believed that the person who found a coin in the cake would be wealthy, whereas those who got a thimble would never marry. Even today some people continue this old tradition by placing small figures, fake coins, or candies inside the cakes. One more superstition related to birthday cake is the belief that dropping the cake was an omen of bad luck in the following year. The rich traditions surrounding birthday cake show that it has become an integral part of birthday celebrations.

As far as wedding cake is concerned, its significant role at the wedding reception is encapsulated in the following sentence: 'A competent young anthropologist arriving on this planet from Mars … sooner or later … would start being invited to weddings and there he would be perhaps baffled to make up his mind whether the central focus of the ceremony was the marriage or the cake' (Douglas 1982, 105). A common myth which has grown up about the wedding cake is that certain rites can be traced back to ancient Rome, for example the practice of breaking the cake over the bride's head by the groom. However, this account of the history of wedding cake, popularized by Jeaffreson (1872) in his *Brides and Bridals*, is nowadays considered a myth created in the Victorian era based on the assumption that almost every contemporary practice must have originated in ancient Rome. Jeaffreson's fanciful story does not supply a cogent link between Roman practice and later traditions (Charsley 1992, 29–32). Nevertheless, as Day (2002, 56–57) observes, a number of nineteenth-century folklorists from northern England and Scotland provide reliable evidence of the rite of breaking the cake over the bride's head by the groom. They believed the crumbs of the cake that landed on the floor symbolized happiness and fertility for the newlyweds. Since the crumbs of the wedding cake were viewed as tokens of good luck, the guests would eat them. This rite may be the source of the modern custom of sharing and distributing wedding cakes. As the cake grew larger and larger, so breaking it over the bride's head became less feasible (indeed, more dangerous). Another reason for the demise of this tradition may be that it was felt that breaking the cake over the bride's head stood also for breaking the bride's hymen and such symbolism was in a sense improper (Ingoldsby 2006, 142).

Because the cake has become the focal point of wedding ceremonies, a number of rituals have developed, the most important of which is its cutting. Originally, wedding cake was cut by the bride then shared with the guests. However, nowadays it is cut by the bride and groom together. More precisely, the first piece of the wedding cake is cut by the bride with the groom's hand placed over hers. Symbolically, this is the first task that the bride and groom perform jointly. After that, they feed one another with the first slice to make manifest their mutual commitment. Then, it is divided into small portions and shared with the guests (Charsley 1992, 112–117).

Another ritual connected with wedding cake surrounds its display. In the past it was often allocated its own table, to be shown off to the guests. Thus, it appears that the cake, apart from being designated for cutting and sharing, also functions as an object to be admired for its elegance and decoration. Humble (2010, 86) argues that this perplexing function of wedding cake, i.e. to be seen rather than to be eaten, is best demonstrated by modern Japanese Western-style wedding cakes that are entirely inedible: the point is to make a good show in the wedding pictures.

Both birthday and wedding cake traditions, handed down from generation to generation, have become an indispensable part of the contemporary birthday and marriage celebrations to such an extent that birthday and wedding cakes have become symbols rather than delicacies. What is more, the cakes have acquired such significance that today they are the elements least likely to be omitted from any celebration of birthday or marriage.

References

Beal, T. K. and M. David (eds.), 1997: *Reading Bibles, Writing Bodies: Identity and the Book* (London & New York, Routledge).
Charsley, S. R. 1992: *Wedding Cakes and Cultural History* (London & New York, Routledge).
Chas, S. C. and G. Harvey (eds.), 2004: *The Paganism Reader* (New York & London, Routledge).
Cunningham, S. 2002: *Cunningham's Encyclopedia of Wicca in the Kitchen* (Saint Paul, Llewellyn Publications).
Dalby, A. 2003: *Food in the Ancient World from A to Z* (London & New York, Routledge).
Davidson, A. 1999: *The Oxford Companion to Food* (Oxford, Oxford University Press).
Day, I. 2002: 'Bridecup and cake: The ceremonial food and drink of the bridal procession', in Mason, L. (ed.), *Food and the Rites of Passage* (Devon, Prospect Books), 56–57.
Douglas, M. 1982: 'Food as an art form', in Douglas, M. (ed.), *The Active Voice* (London, Routledge and Kegan Paul), 105–113.
Gunde, R. 2002: *Culture and Customs of China* (Westport, Greenwood Publishing Group).
Hudgins, S. 2003: *The Other Side of Russia. A Slice of Life in Siberia and the Russian Far East* (Texas, Texas A&M University Press).
Humble, N. 2010: *Cake. A Global History* (London, Reaktion Books).
Ingoldsby, B.B. 2006: 'Mate selection and marriage', in Ingoldsby, B.B. and S.D. Smith (eds.), *Families in Global and Multicultural perspective* (Thousand Oaks, Sage Publications).
Katz, S.H. (ed.), 2003: *Encyclopedia of Food and Culture,* Volume 1 (New York, Charles Scribner's Sons).
OED = *The Oxford English Dictionary* http://www.oed.com/
Schultze, S. 2000: *Cultures and Customs of Russia* (Westport, Greenwood Publishing Group).
Smaridge, N. 1978: *The Story of Cake* (Nashville, Abingdon).

Celebrating Purim and Passover:
Food and Memory in the Creation of Jewish Identity

Georg Schäfer and Susan Weingarten

In this paper we look at two Jewish festivals, Purim and Passover, where eating and drinking play an important part in the celebrations, in order to see how food is used to establish the identity of the Jews at two critical periods of their history. Susan Weingarten concentrates on the Jewish side; Georg Schäfer brings pagan parallels and contrasts to point up the differences between them. Both festivals have textual and material aspects: the texts dictate (or appear to dictate) practices of eating, but clearly practices evolve outside the texts as well.

Together with the function of forging a Jewish identity, the biblical and Talmudic accounts of these festivals demonstrate the deliberate attempt to build a prospective communal memory, so we shall also be examining the function of history and memory as related to food in these contexts.

The biblical books of Leviticus and Deuteronomy have details of the foods forbidden to Israel. Mary Douglas and Marvin Harris have written famously about these laws and attempted to pose a rationale, and there have been at least a dozen other scholars who have joined in the fray.[1]

How far the dietary laws were instrumental in forming Jewish (or Israélite or Judaean) identity in early Jewish history is debatable. David Kraemer suggests that since meat-eating was rare and confined to national and local festivals, most of the time there would have been little to differentiate Jew from non-Jew.[2] But it is clear that from the time of the Seleucid Greek conquest of Palestine, and the subsequent Jewish uprising under the Maccabees, food began to serve as an important marker of Jewish identity. Both in Palestine and in the Diaspora, 'tell me what you eat and I will tell you what you are' separated Jew from non-Jew: Daniel refuses the King's food in Babylonia; Judith takes her own food with her when going to meet the enemy general Holophernes; in the books of the Maccabees the revolt against the Seleucid Antiochus IV is epitomized in the Jews' refusal to eat pork. The food of the Babylonian and Greek 'other,' then, is refused by the Jew, who sometimes goes further than the basic requirements of the dietary laws in refusing all non-Jewish food.

We turn now to look at the food of Purim and Passover. The story of the foundation of the festival of Purim is told in the biblical book of Esther, probably written in Palestine, although the setting of the book is in the Persian Diaspora.[3] There are ten feasts described in the book, beginning with the King's feast (Esther 1.4), which goes on for 180 days, and continuing with other lavish Persian feasts. No food is mentioned, only drink. Esther herself gives two feasts in this mode, for herself, the King, and Haman, and it is at the last of these that she denounces her enemy and the Jews are saved.

Esther was probably written in Hellenistic times (around the second century BCE): there is a longer Greek version extant in the Septuagint. Scholars have noted how it uses Greek perceptions of Persian drinking and excesses to depict the king and his court's 'conspicuous consumption.'[4] Esther tells us of King Ahasuerus who ruled over 127 provinces 'from India to Ethiopia.' Ahasuerus has been identified with the Persian Xerxes, of whom Athenaeus tells us he would have the choicest fruits of every one of his many provinces placed before him on his table.[5] The biblical text satirizes the Persian King: after his wife disobeys him at his feast, he sends out an order that all wives should obey their husbands! From early times Greek writers had related to the Persian 'other' as a way of defining Greekness. For example, Herodotus tells a story of the Spartan general Pausanias who, seeing the foods of the Persians set out splendidly on gold and silver, ordered his men to prepare a standard Spartan meal for them – presumably the notoriously horrid black broth made of pork and blood.[6] This serviceable but unappetizing food is clearly used here to establish Spartan identity against Persian self-indulgence. Thus in establishing his/her own Jewish identity, the author of Esther seems to have used handy local Greek 'we are not Persian' tropes, expressed in these pictures of drunken excesses. The Hebrew text does not mention any problems for Esther with the King's food, unlike Daniel, but the Septuagint version has a prayer where she expresses her sadness at having to share a table with the King.[7]

In contrast to Persian over-indulgence, the Jews in the book are initially shown as fasting – for three days.[8] This becomes feasting after their victory. However, while Persian feasts are described as *mishteh*, from the root 'drink,' the Jewish feasts which end the book are described as comprising *mishteh* and *simhah*, celebration. *Simhah*, celebrating before God in the Hebrew Bible, often includes eating a festive meal.[9] Esther also includes a prescription for future Jewish celebrations by eating quite differently from Greek or Persian banquets. Here the food is not provided by those above, king or municipal benefactor: it is to be given in mutual portions, *manot*, by each Jew to her/his neighbour. Individual Jewish identity through food is being established with a moderate and equal feast, and a Jewish communal identity is being forged, using food to create memories in the future.[10] The vocabulary here is the same as in Nehemiah 8:10–12, when Nehemiah and Ezra make a feast of rejoicing over the *Torah* (Law), with *mishteh*, *simhah*, and *manot*.[11] Jewish eating and identity, even in Esther where God is not mentioned, is allusively linked to the *Torah* and its prescriptions.

* * * * *

We move now to the feast of Passover, held every spring a month after Purim. Passover is recorded in the Bible as first marking (Ex 12.1–13), then commemorating (Ex 12.14; Deut 16.1f) the Exodus from Egyptian slavery to freedom. In Egypt, immediately before the Exodus, God had differentiated between Egypt and Israel in killing the firstborn of Egypt and sparing Israel. Israel is to sacrifice the 'abomination of Egypt,' later specified as a lamb.[12] Thus they are to establish themselves as distinct from Egyptians by sacrificing the lamb, sprinkling its blood on the threshold of their houses, roasting it, and eating it. The other foods are also part of this identity: *matzah* (unleavened bread), called the 'bread of affliction,' and bitter herbs. The slavery they are leaving is signified by the taste of the bread of affliction and the bitterness of the herbs. Eating the meat of the lamb signifies their freedom from the Egyptians, who consider lamb an 'abomination.' The text then adds, 'This day shall be to you for a memorial; and you shall keep it as a feast to the Lord; throughout your generations you shall keep it as a feast by ordinance for ever' (Ex 12.14). The biblical feast is said to be there to create a historical memory for the future, just as we saw for Purim. Both in Exodus and in Deuteronomy, food is used to underline this: each Jewish family was to take their lamb to the place ordained by God (later identified with the Jerusalem Temple), offer it as a sacrifice, and eat it with bitter herbs and *matzah*. The text makes it clear how far this is part of creating a Jewish (Israélite) identity. Both freedom and the memory of slavery are a part of Jewish identity, which separates the Jew from the people around (whom we presume would not celebrate with bitter herbs and bread of affliction). According to later Talmudic sources,[13] the rules about ritual purity in eating, which during the rest of the year separated strict observers of purity from those who were less strict, were suspended on festivals, so that Jews were not separated from other Jews, but equal with them.[14] Thus the celebration of Passover with its distinctive foods according to the biblical prescription became a part of being Jewish.

The Jerusalem Temple was destroyed in 70 CE, facing Jews with a serious identity crisis. The centre of Judaism, which had been the Temple cult, was no more, and a vacuum was left at the heart of Judaism. In addition, Palestine was subjected to Roman rule, made even harsher by the failure of the nationalist Bar Kokhba revolt a generation later, which brought violent repercussions. The rabbis who took on the leadership of the Jewish people had to restructure Judaism and fill the gap.

They did this by centring Jewish life on a text on the page, on the study of the *Torah*, rather than on the cult in the Jerusalem Temple. The celebration of Passover was no longer communal, national and public, but moved into the home. And they made brilliant use of food and eating to establish a new individual- – and family- – centred Jewish identity. They appropriated local Graeco-Roman meal practices, all the while differentiating them from Jewish eating, to create the Passover *seder*. Thus the process here is similar to that at Purim: just as Jews used Greek models of Persian others to express their own identity, while expressing their differences from the Hellenistic world through their food at Purim, so the Passover *seder* appropriates the model of the Greek symposium to show how Jews were different.[15]

What is a Greek symposium? *Symposion* in Greek means 'drinking together.' Strictly speaking it refers to the second part of the Greek evening banquet, which was devoted to drinking and conversation. Often, however, it denotes the entire meal. The customary order of the classical symposium as described by Plato and Xenophon is as follows: The participants washed with the assistance of slaves, then reclined on pillowed couches. In the first part, food was eaten. Then the symposium proper, the drinking party, started: libations were offered to the gods; some wine was poured on the floor and a paean was sung. In some cases a libation was made to a particular god from every bowl mixed at the party. Sometimes a symposiarch was elected, to decide about mixing the wine. During the drinking party the participants engaged in conversation, literary works were read for their entertainment, and there was singing and artistic musical presentations. Unlike the Passover *seder*, the classical symposium was not a family meal, but was restricted to men. Only flute girls or courtesans took part in the all-male banquets.

It is unlikely that the leading Jews in the second or third century who created the Passover *seder* were directly influenced by the literary symposia of classical Athens. They would seem to have been more influenced by later developments of the banquet culture, for the symposia of the high and late Roman empire differed from the earlier model. Not only were respectable women now allowed to attend the meals together with men, but the separation between meal proper and the drinking party became blurred: participants drank wine throughout the meal. At the Socratic symposia, the participants hardly talked about the food itself, whereas in Plutarch's *Table Talk* and Athenaeus' *Deipnosophists*, the food served could spark a discussion. Here there are parallels to the interpretation of the foodstuffs at the Passover meal.[16] However, the symposium of classical times still remained the reference point for writers like Plutarch and Athenaeus, so that it is perhaps more likely that the *seder* was influenced by contemporary meal practices rather than by literary models.

There were, indeed, a variety of meal practices in the wider social environment of the ancient Jews, and it is possible to identify two types of meals which may have influenced the creation of the Passover *seder*: firstly, festive dinners hosted by private individuals, and, secondly, meals of pagan associations – funeral clubs, professional guilds, and religious associations. The influence of association meals is quite possible: not only pagans, but also ancient Jews formed associations which held communal meals.[17] Even the paschal meal was not always celebrated within the family everywhere. During the Second Temple period, the paschal lamb was eaten within fellowship groups.[18]

Let us look first at private meals. It is possible that Jews and pagans socialized at banquets in the cities of third-century Galilee, where the élite classes comprised both pagans and Jews, and it was precisely there that the Mishnah was compiled, including tractate Pesahim, the oldest treatise on the celebration of the *seder*. Although a Jew who wanted to avoid idol-worship could not take part in a cult meal, he could have attended private dinners together with pagans.

A fascinating insight into banquet culture contemporary with the Mishnaic tractate dealing with the *seder*, is to be found in the so-called 'House of Dionysos' in Sepphoris, Galilee, dating from the third century CE. This residential building has a splendid mosaic in its *triclinium* (dining-room). The panels of the mosaic show scenes of the myth of Dionysos, god of wine, and dionysiac festivals. These images were visible to the banqueting guests, reclining on couches around the panels. They may even hint at the discourses held and the performances given at dinner.[19]

Rabbi Judah haNasi, the redactor of the Mishnah, lived in Sepphoris at the beginning of the third century. We have no way of knowing whether he was ever a guest at the 'House of Dionysos,'[20] but it is possible that he visited similar dining-rooms. He was celebrated for his close relations with the Roman authorities, and we can presume that other Jews also maintained contacts with their pagan neighbours and knew how they celebrated their meals. Thus it is not surprising that they should take over and adapt some of their neighbours' ritual practices, all the while maintaining a cultural distinction. According to Baruch Bokser, one of the boundaries between *seder* and symposium is expressed in a rule in Mishnah Pesahim 10, 8: 'After eating from the Passover offering, one does not end with the *afiqimon*.' Nowadays, the term *afikoman* is used to refer to a piece of unleavened bread eaten ritually at the end of the *seder*. This term may be derived from the Greek *afikomenos*, 'the one who comes.' If so, the *afikoman* might allude to the coming of the Messiah.[21] But according to another theory, the word *afikoman* was originally modelled after the Greek *epikomion*, the after-dinner revelry, when the symposiasts roamed the streets, going from one party to another.[22] So it is perhaps not a mere coincidence that the Sepphoris mosaic features a related noun, which at the same time denotes the dionysiac procession, and the act of drinking: *komos*.[23] One panel shows a satyr and two maenads, one of whom is playing a flute. The inscription above reads simply KWMOS. If we add the prefix *epi*, this would give *epikomos*, which may also denote the festal procession.[24] But *epikomos* can also refer to the roaming around in groups after a private party, or simply the revelling.[25] The festivals of Dionysos, as they appear on archaic Greek vessels and reliefs of the Roman period, included wild and ecstatic dancing. The *komos* of the mosaic, however, is of a gentle and restrained nature: the maenads are not dancing wildly, and no naked satyrs with phalloi are depicted in the mosaic.[26] It seems, therefore, as if neither the pagan upper class of Sepphoris nor the rabbis in Mishnah Pesahim approved of drunken revelry.

We also know of restrictions on disruptive behaviour among pagan associations.[27] The attempt to check all the undesirable effects of wine consumption is not simply a peculiarity of the Jewish *seder*: a ban on unruly behaviour at dinner was a common feature of ancient table fellowships.[28] Even the conversation was sometimes regulated: speaking in turn at the banquet was part of the moral code.[29] In religious associations, the regulated discourse also had a cultic significance.

At the meetings of some of these guilds, specific roles were assigned to the participants. For example, the Iobakchoi were an association of worshippers of Dionysos in Athens.[30] The ordinance of their guild, which dates from the late second century CE, stipulated '… they shall speak and act their allotted parts under the direction of the priest or the *archibakchos*' (l. 63–67). The guild ordinance of the Iobakchoi also rules on the distributions of sacrificial meat during the Dionysos festival: 'And when portions are distributed, let them be taken by the priest, vice priest, *archibakchos*, treasurer, cowherd, Dionysos, Kore, Palaimon, Aphrodite, and Proteurythmus' (l. 121–125). The first names refer to office-holders of the association. The last five are names of deities which certain members represented at the ritual drama. Another role play in which the participants acted as gods is known from the Roman cult of Mithras. Here, on the banquet benches of their *mithraeum*, the initiates replicated the mythic feast of Mithras and the Sungod, which took place after Mithras had slain the bull. A relief in Konjic in present-day Herzegovina and some frescoes in Santa Prisca in Rome show the initiates participating in roles defined by their positions within the hierarchy of mithraic grades: the Father (Pater) and the Sun-Runner (Heliodromus) represented Mithras and Sol reclining at their feast, and the other grades serving them at table.[31]

Thus the participants imitated in ritual the mythological deeds of their gods. In other cases, the cult-myth was represented in a formal speech. At *Katagogia*, the yearly festival of the Arrival of Dionysos, the priest of the Iobakchoi gave a speech called *theologia*, the word of the god (l. 115). This clearly commemorated the special occasion within the liturgical year: the celebrations were linked to the annual calendar of the cult.

Thus amongst the pagan associations, the representations at dinner were linked to the foundation myth. The deeds of the gods were visualized through the medium of ritual drama or glorified by a speech.

In Graeco-Roman pagan society, then, in some cult associations, the loose conversation at the symposia became fixed according to ritual patterns, and the dinner-entertainment was converted into ritual drama. Discourse was not open to personal choice, since the ritualistic requirements of the respective cult had to be fulfilled. The leaders of pagan guilds – like the Jewish rabbis – used the conventions of the Graeco-Roman banquet to create a new form in order to meet the necessities of their religion.

Returning now to the Jewish Passover, we do not know when the *seder* took its main shape that it has today, formed by the recitation of the text of the *haggadah*. The Mishnah and Tosefta contain some elements which are the same as today's *haggadah*, but others are different or absent. All the rabbis mentioned in the text of the *haggadah* (except for one) belonged to the group from Yavneh who engaged in re-inventing Judaism after the destruction, so it would seem reasonable to think that it was they who were responsible for some of its present form. Thus just as the cult at the Jerusalem Temple was replaced by study of the written *Torah* in any place, so the Passover sacrifice and meal in Jerusalem were eventually replaced by the ritual of a new text, the *haggadah*, in every Jewish home. The associations or family groups around the paschal lamb became family groups around a table. We have looked at the some of the practices of talking or acting according to fixed roles at the pagan club banquets of the Iobakkhoi and the worshippers of Mithras. There are some similarities in these role-plays to the dialogues of father and son at the Passover *seder*: indeed, some pagan communal meals had a convenor referred to metaphorically as a 'father,' but children were not present.[32]

The Jews differentiate themselves from these pagan contexts now by making the metaphor literal: the ritual recitation of texts and ingestion of foods is begun by a child questioning his father about similarity and differences.

> 'How is this night different from all [other] nights?', asks the child.
>
> 'For on all the [other] nights we dip once, this night twice.'
>
> 'For on all the [other] nights we eat either bread or *matzah*. Tonight we eat only *matzah*.'
>
> 'For on all the [other] other nights we eat meat roasted, steamed or boiled, this night only roasted.' (MPesahim 10,4)

Later, questions were added about the bitter herbs, and about eating while reclining, instead of the question about the roasted meat, when the rabbis decided that the memory of the Passover sacrifice should be only textual.

Thus non-Jews may eat bread or *matzah*, meat cooked in various ways, all kinds of herbs, sitting or reclining, but only Jews specifically eat *matzah*, roast meat, and bitter herbs and recline as part of their Passover celebrations. Indeed, Rabban Gamaliel tells us that an individual who does not mention the Passover offering, bitter herbs, and *matzah* has not had a *seder* at all (MPesahim 10.5). Thus the participants are differentiated from their non-Jewish neighbours, and eating symbolic foods (and drinking the four prescribed cups of wine) while reclining on Passover becomes part of Jewish identity throughout the generations.[33] And while there are similarities with the role-plays of some pagan associations, there are clear differences: Jews could not play the role of gods, which association members certainly did.

Recently anthropologists have begun to discuss memory as a cultural, rather than an individual faculty, distinguishing between 'inscribed' memories in texts, and performed or habitual memories, 'incorporated' in the body.'[34] Sutton has discussed memories of eating as the ultimate incorporated memory.[35] Applying these theories to the celebration of Passover, it becomes clear that the text of the Mishnah and later the *haggadah* use the ceremonial eating of ritual foods to incorporate the inscribed memories for the whole Jewish community.

Sutton also discusses 'prescribed memories:' the creation of future memories. We noted that the biblical text prescribed eating patterns for the future in memory of the past: this is continued by Mishnah and *haggadah*. The Mishnah prescribes the text read in reply to the child's questions – the so-called 'small historical creed' – the few verses in Deuteronomy (26.5f) that sum up the history of the Jewish people, beginning with 'my father,' the forefather of the Jewish people. Indeed the *haggadah* says that 'in every generation a person is obliged to regard himself as if he went out from Egypt.' Thus we have an identification of individual, family, people, as well as a telescoping of past, present, and future. Just as the pagan associations commemorated their foundation myths in their yearly banquets, so the rabbis ascertained that God's saving deed is remembered in the *haggadah* narrative at the *seder* table.

We saw that pre-destruction Passovers included the eating of the paschal lamb. Once the Temple was destroyed, sacrifices could not be brought there, and eventually the rabbis instructed the participants to substitute a symbolic piece of *matzah* when talking about the Passover sacrifice. This *matzah* is broken off from a larger piece: memories are being fragmented. And new memories are being created. *Haroset*, originally a Graeco-Roman dip for bitter lettuce and endives called *embamma*, is added, probably because in Roman times eating bitter herbs was believed to be harmful unless modified by a sauce.[36] The rabbis give this new addition symbolic significance: it is a memorial of the clay the Israélite slaves made bricks with in Egypt, or of the blood shed there.[37] Once again an ordinary foodstuff is distinguished by being given special significance and the Jew who eats it is eating his/her own history, and thereby building a Jewish identity, distinct from the pagan or Christian neighbours.

Postscript: Jewish and Christian identities
Thus after the destruction of the Temple and the ending of the sacrifices, the rabbis created a new Jewish identity and a prospective communal memory by prescribing the ritual eating of foods, old and new. Emerging Christians engaged in a similar, parallel process, using communal meals to define and differentiate themselves from Jews and others.[38] If Jews incorporated symbolic foods to successfully re-create their identity and communal memory, Christians go further. Thus Christians symbolically eat *matzah* and drink wine, thereby incorporating the body and blood of Jesus to express their communal identity, as differentiated from that of Jews. They abandon the Jewish eating customs of bitter herbs and reclining, but keep the basic *matzah* and wine, giving them new meaning, built on the old. Jews substituted *matzah* for the paschal lamb sacrifice after the destruction of the Temple. For Christians, Jesus is the last sacrifice, and eating the *matzah* which substitutes for the lamb is a symbolic incorporation of his body for the Christian celebrant. For them, incorporating the special foods of Passover becomes the incorporation of the divine.

Food and Memory in the Creation of Jewish Identity

Acknowledgement
Georg Schäfer and Susan Weingarten are working in Germany and Israel respectively on a joint project on Food in the Ancient World, supported by the German-Israel Fund (GIF).

Notes
1. A convenient summary with detailed bibliography is to be found in N. MacDonald, *Not Bread Alone: The Uses of Food in the Old Testament* (Oxford, 2008) chapter 1.
2. David Kraemer *Jewish Eating and Identity through the Ages* (NY, 2007).
3. On the place and date of *Esther*: J.-D. Macchi, 'Le livre d'Esther: écrire une histoire perse comme un Grec', in *Comment la Bible saisit-elle l'histoire?* (Issy-les-Moulineaux, 2005) 197–226; idem., 'L'identité judéenne au banquet: le défi de la commensalité à l'époque hellénistique selon le livre d'Esther', in O. Artus and J. Ferry (eds), *L'identité dans l'Écriture : Hommage au professeur Jacques Briend* (Paris, 2009) 227–260.
4. Macchi, 'Écrire comme un grec', above. Esther certainly uses Greek literary forms (it has been called a *novella*) to build its picture of Persia, but this is not to deny that the Persian circumstances it depicts must have been familiar to the exiled Jewish community.
5. *Deipnosphistai* xiv, 652b, citing Dinon's *Persian History* (C4 BCE).
6. *Histories* ix 82. On the Persian 'other,' see François Hartog, *Le miroir d'Hérodote. Essai sur la représentation de l'autre* (Paris, 1980). Hartog also analyses the ultimate barbarians, the Scythians, who are the 'other' for the Persians, just as the Persians are the 'other' for the Athenians (36): they don't know the proper way to sacrifice and may not even have a communal meal afterwards (185–186). On black broth see Michael Beer, *Taste or Taboo? Dietary Choices in Antiquity* (Totnes, 2010) 108.
7. See on this Macchi, 'Identité judéenne' (above n.3).
8. MacDonald, *Not Bread Alone* sees this as a sign of Jewish 'moderation,'(209, 212–6) but elsewhere makes clear that this is only in contrast with early Christian extreme asceticism (210). Fasting for three whole days without food and water is clearly an extreme to contrast with Persian excesses.
9. MacDonald 79 citing Deut 14.26; 16.11; ib. 14; and cf. Macchi on Nehemiah 8.10–12. The Babylonian Talmud Pesahim 109a says that before the destruction of the Temple there was no celebration without meat, but that after the destruction, celebration was with wine.
10. The carnivalesque aspects of the celebration of Purim do not seem to antedate the mediaeval period.
11. Macchi, 'Identité judéenne' (above n.3).
12. Exodus 8.22.
13. For a brief explanation of the Talmudic literature, see S. Weingarten, 'Nuts for the children: the evidence of the Talmudic literature,' in R. Hosking (ed.) *Nurture: Proceedings of the Oxford Symposium on Food and Cookery 2003* (Bristol, 2004).
14. BT Betzah 11b; BT Niddah 34a: A. Oppenheimer, *The 'Am Ha'aretz* (Leiden, 1977).
15. This paradox explains why there has been wide scholarly disagreement over the relationship of the *seder* to the Graeco-Roman *symposium* : S. Stein 'The influence of symposia literature on the literary form of the Passover haggadah', *Journal of Jewish Studies* 8 (1957) 13–44 and J. Tabory, *The JPS Commentary on the Haggadah: Historical Introduction, Translation and Commentary* (Philadelphia, 2008) claim that the *seder* is based on the *symposium*; B.M. Bokser, *The Origins of the Seder: the Passover Rite and Early Rabbinic Judaism* (Berkeley etc., 1984) claims the *seder* rejects the *symposium*; Dennis Smith, *From Symposium to Eucharist: the Banquet in the Early Christian World* (Minneapolis, 2002) tries to harmonize, suggesting both used the same cultural background.
16. Tabory, *History*, 65–67. The food served is also important in the *cena Nasidieni* by Horace and the *cena Trimalchionis* by Petronius.
17. Josephus, *Antiquities* 14, 213–216 (Paros); 227 (Ephesos); 259–261 (Sardis); *Corpus Papyrorum Judaicarum* I 139; *Corpus Papyrorum Judaicarum* I 138.
18. A. Oppenheimer, '*Haburot* in Jerusalem at the End of the Second Temple Period', in N. Oppenheimer

ed., *Between Rome and Babylon, Studies in Jewish Leadership and Society* (Tübingen, 2005), 109.
19. C.L. Meyers, E.M. Meyers, E. Netzer, Z. Weiss, 'The Dionysos Mosaic,' in R. Martin Nagy, C.L. Meyers, E.M. Meyers, Z. Weiss, *Sepphoris in Galilee. Crosscurrents of Culture* (North Carolina, 1996) 111 ff.; R. Talgam, Z. Weiss, *The Mosaics of the House of Dionysos at Sepphoris*, (Jerusalem, 2004), 47 f.; for a similar mosaic at Antioch: C. Kondoleon, 'Mosaics of Antioch,' in C. Kondoleon, *Antioch, The Lost Ancient City*, (Princeton, 2000), 63 ff.
20. S. S. Miller, 'Jewish Sepphoris: A Great City of Scholars and Scribes,' in Nagy et al., *Sepphoris in Galilee* 59 ff. especially 60; Talgam, Weiss, *Mosaics*, 128 ff.
21. David Daube, *He that Cometh* (London, 1966).
22. Bokser, *Origins* (above, n.15) 65.
23. K. Vössing, 'Das römische Trinkgelage (*commissatio*) – eine Schimäre der Forschung?' in K. Vössing (ed.), *Das römische Bankett im Spiegel der Altertumswissenschaften. Internationales Kolloquium 5./6. Oktober 2005 Schloß Mickeln, Düsseldorf* (Stuttgart, 2008), 169ff.
24. *LSJ*, New Edition 642.
25. REAC 1267: cf. Clement of Alexandria *Paedeia* 2, 4, 40, 1.
26. Talgam, Weiss, *Mosaics* (above, n.19) 69.
27. C. Roberts, T.C. Skeat, A.D. Nock, 'The Gild of Zeus Hypsistos,' *Harvard Theological Review* (1936), 40ff (PLond VII 2193).
28. See CIL XIV 2112; PLond VII 2193 l.15–17 = SB V 7835; PMich V 243, p. 96, l,.4; BGU XIV 2371 l.4–5; IG II² 1368 l.63–67; 72–83; 107–110; SEG XXXI 122, l.6; LSCG 53, l.40–45. P.A. Harland, *Associations, Synagogues and Congregations. Claiming a Place in Ancient Mediterranean Society* (Minneapolis 2003) 75f.
29. P. Berol 13270 = H. Froschauer, C.Römer, *Mit den Griechen zu Tisch in Ägypten* (Wien 2006) 7.
30. IG II² 1368= SIG³ 1109=LSCG 51. For interpretation and bibliography: E. Ebel, *Die Attraktivität früher christlicher Gemeinden. Die Gemeinde von Korinth im Spiegel griechisch-römischer Vereine* (Tübingen 2004) 87ff; also Dennis Smith, *Symposium to Eucharist* (above, n.15), 116ff. and 129ff.
31. CIMRM1895 (Konjic); M.J. Vermaseren, C.C. Van Essen, *The Excavations in the Mithraeum of the Church of Santa Prisca on the Aventine* (Leiden, 1965), 150, Pl. LVI–LVIII and 152f. See also R. Beck, 'Ritual, Myth, Doctrine, and Initiation in the Mysteries of Mithras: New Evidence from a Cult Vessel', *Journal of Roman Studies* 90 (2000), 145.
32. Philip A. Harland, 'Familial dimensions of group identity(II): "mothers" and "fathers" in associations and synagogues of the Greek world', *Journal for the Study of Judaism* 38 (2007) 57–79.
33. See now J. Rosenblum, *Jewish Eating and Identity in Early Rabbinic Judaism* (Cambridge, 2011).
34. Paul Connerton, *How Societies Remember* (Cambridge, 1989).
35. David Sutton, *Remembrance of Repasts: An Anthropology of Food and Memory* (Oxford/NY, 2001).
36. S. Weingarten, 'How do you say *haroset* in Greek?' in B. Isaac and Y. Shahar (eds.) *Judaea-Palaestina, Babylon and Rome: Jews in Antiquity* (Tübingen, 2012).
37. Jerusalem Talmud 37d. These explanations are not included in *Mishnah* or *haggadah*
38. There is apparently general scholarly agreement that not all the elements of the ritual of the *haggadah* as we know it were extant at the time of Jesus, but the writers of the Gospels felt they needed to use the form of whatever Passover celebration was extant at the time to structure their account of Jesus' Last Supper.

Prints Charming: Nineteenth-Century New York Cake Boards and New Year's Cake

Kimberly Sorensen

Introduction

My first encounter with cake boards occurred at the Luce Center of the New-York Historical Society (New York, New York). I was browsing the museum collection for inspiration for a paper I intended to write on forms of early American cookery, and though I had been warned that it can often be difficult to glean rich cultural information from kitchen tools, since they were seldom meant for display, here I found two large, intaglio carved wooden boards depicting important figures – Lafayette on one, and firefighters on the other. They suggested that baked goods could participate in the festivals and celebrations of nineteenth-century America not just as refreshments, but also as a form of edible print culture.

Figure 1. Cake board carved with Lafayette, ca 1824. Mahogany, 15 x 26 x ½ in. New-York Historical Society. Purchased from Elie Nadelman, 1937 (1937.592). Author's photograph.

Figure 2. Double-sided cake board carved with fire engines. Possibly mahogany, 8 x 14½ x 1 in. New-York Historical Society. Purchased from Elie Nadelman, 1937 (1937.1562). Author's photograph.

The name 'cake board' is a bit misleading because they were used to print malleable dough, and not a runny cake batter as the name might imply. The final product resembled something closer to a cookie, albeit a very large cookie (the modern notion of spongy, soft cake only emerged in the middle of the eighteenth century, and the word 'cake' continued to be used for both kinds of confection into the nineteenth century).[1]

Nineteenth-Century New York Cake Boards

The carving on the two New-York Historical Society boards had decidedly different styles, yet they shared the same shaped framing device – a pointed oval – suggesting a traditional, distinct form of baked good made by different bakers.

Indeed, they were used for printing caraway-flecked New Year's cake, to be served at open house on New Year's Day in New York. Several key sources make this connection clear. In Eliza Leslie's recipe for 'New York Cookies,' published in 1840, the author instructed to 'stamp the surface of each with a cake print,' and explained, 'They are similar to what are called "New Year's cakes".' The cake print appeared again in 1857 in Leslie's recipe for 'New-Year's Cake,' where she wrote that 'The bakers in New York ornament these cakes, with devices or pictures raised by a wooden stamp.'[2] A 1905 kitchenware trade catalogue also labeled their illustrations of large carved wooden molds as 'New Year prints'. These cookbooks and trade catalogues indicate that 'cake board' is a modern term; 'cake print' would have been used in the nineteenth century. Finally, two cake boards in the collection of the Albany Institute of History and Art (Albany, New York) were donated by the descendants of bakers, who remembered their use for printing New Year's cakes.[3]

As I went through books on American woodcarving and auction sales of Americana, more and more cake boards turned up with the characteristic pointed oval border (and also sometimes a round border). The cake boards range in size from several inches to up to three feet long, and set themselves apart from European cookie molds in that the American carving is shallow, meant to print the surface of the dough which is then cut out according to the shape of the design, rather than mold the dough in a deeply carved recess. Revolutionary War heroes, presidential candidates, opera singers, political slogans, fire engines and horse races appear as subject matter, surrounded by motifs of cornucopias, roses, thistles, scrolling foliage and birds. The finished cakes must have made a striking display on the New Year's table, though changing fashions also humbled the old-fashioned New Year's cake.

New Year's Day in New York City
In an 1873 engraving titled 'New-Year's Calls – the Knickerbockers of 1650 and 1873,' *Harper's Weekly* compared New Year's Day in old New York with New Year's Day in nineteenth-century New York. The Knickerbockers of 1650 sit around a rustic table laden with food and drink in earthenware containers. A seated woman, in a simple dress, bonnet and wooden clogs, contrasts with the woman seated in the 1873 version, dressed in layers of precious material and sporting a complicated hairdo. In the modern interior, the table is covered with a cloth; delicate glassware has replaced the homely earthenware, and a chandelier composed of rococo curves drops down from the ceiling. While the humble interior of 1650 was based more on a nineteenth-century imagination of the past than on reality, nevertheless, the illustration comments on the increasing sophistication of the domestic interior and its inhabitants in nineteenth-century New York City, and the fact that New Yorkers acknowledged the Dutch origins of New

Year's visiting, yet understood it to be different in modern times.[4] This paper will investigate how these changes influenced New Year's Day celebrations in the course of the nineteenth century, before considering how New Year's cake operated as a symbol of the past and a mode of communication in these celebrations.

New Year's Day was a major holiday in nineteenth-century New York City, celebrated by going door-to-door visiting friends and acquaintances. These visits served to reinforce friendships and commence the year on a positive note. As one writer put it in 1868, 'It is the day of social atonement. Neglected social duties are performed; acquaintances are kept up; a whole year's neglect is wiped out by a proper call on New Year's.'[5]

Accounts of New Year's Day visiting appear frequently in diaries, newspapers, and memoirs, and practically all of these sources express the immense popularity of the holiday, which was described as 'the happiest day of the year.'[6] For example Philip Hone, a prominent New Yorker and mayor from 1826 to 1827, wrote in his diary in 1844, 'this fine old custom, almost peculiar to New York, does not lose favor in the eyes of our citizens, and foreigners are delighted with it.' Women stayed at home to host visitors, and men went visiting, either on foot, or by carriage, omnibus, cab, or curricle; pedestrians and vehicles thronged thoroughfares such as Broadway. For someone like Hone, it was typical to spend about five hours visiting friends, and to receive over a hundred guests at one's home; his wife and daughter counted 169 in 1844.[7] The Irish novelist Samuel Lover (1797–1868) described the considerable amount of effort involved in visiting as many acquaintances as possible: 'Your visiting must be done systematically, or it would never be done at all. You must range addresses in their localities, and make your calls in such regular order that time and space may be economized.'[8]

This sort of strategizing was due to the expanding size of New York City, and had reverberations outside of New Year's Day visiting. Beginning in the 1830s, increasing distances between the home and the office had altered meal times. It had become difficult to return home midday for dinner, which had traditionally been served at two or three in the afternoon to the whole family, so instead dinner was pushed back to the evening, when the father returned home from work. Dining became 'an emblem of gentility,' and, more and more, home and work came to occupy distinct, gendered social spheres, the former belonging to women and children, and the latter to men.[9]

These changes influenced the way the ritual of New Year's Day visiting was acted out. Wives and their daughters were to remain at home to host guests. One writer remarked, 'It is a rare thing to see a woman on the streets on New Year's Day. It is not genteel, sometimes not safe.'[10] More importantly, in a culture where the domestic interior embodied gentility, New Year's Day, as the most social day of the year, was the supreme occasion for display, and the New Year's table was the centerpiece of these sophisticated interiors. A culture of consumption and competition grew up around the New Year's table: 'Great rivalry exists among people of style about the table – how it shall be set, the plate to cover it, the expense, and many other considerations that make the table the pride and plague of the season.'[11] Throughout the nineteenth century, descriptions of the New Year's table came to include not just simple New Year's cake, but also ice-cream, charlotte russe, and molds of jelly. Sumptuous presents also entered the scene. In 1847, Philip Hone observed on New Year's Day that 'New Year's presents have abounded this year. This is the Parisian mode of celebrating *le jour de l'an*, and we are getting into it very fast.'[12] The presents he saw included costly cashmere shawls, silver tankards, toy watches, and children's rattles. Indeed, in an 1859 illustration of New Year's Day in New York, the foreground is littered with children's toys, while elegant confectionary pyramids peek out from the table in the background. Similarly, the rococo chandelier in the *Harper's Weekly* 1873 illustration mentioned above nods to Parisian fashions.

Period advertisements were in keeping with these illustrations and Hone's observations. In an advertisement posted on 23 December 1856, A.E. Dean announced his stock of 'boned turkeys, game, oysters, pyramids, ice cream, Charlotte russe, jellies, blanc mange, meringues, ornamented plum, almond, citron, fruit, pound, sponge, New-Year and other cakes.'[13] On the same day, John Taylor & Co. advertised, in addition to fancy boxes and baskets, their 'cakes, ornaments, jellies, chicken salads, boned turkeys, pickled oysters, dishes of game, boeuf à la mode, and other delicacies for New Year's tables.'[14] The days leading up to New Year's Day must have been a frenzy of shopping and errands. As a journalist for the *New York Times* observed in 1860, '[the ladies] were preparing for New-Year's as most of them had been doing for a week past, and were, as an artist might say, giving the final touches to their work of love.'[15]

New Year's cake

How did New Year's cake fit into these elaborate celebrations? Though beautifully ornamented with raised decoration, they must have paled in comparison to the tall, glistening confectionary pyramids and the brightly colored molded jellies. New Year's cake came to represent older, simpler traditions and people. This can be seen, for example, as early as 1808 in Washington Irving's satirical portrayal of a disgruntled Dutch New Yorker. The character deplores the fact that 'our respectable new-year-cookies have been elbowed aside by plum-cake and outlandish liqueurs in the same way that our worthy old Dutch families are out-dazzled by modern upstarts, and mushroom cockneys.'[16]

There were two different sizes of New Year's cake: the large examples, originally given by bakers to their patrons, and the smaller 'cookies' which were originally formed in wafer irons, but which by the mid-nineteenth century were also formed in smaller wooden cake boards. Hands-on experimentation with recipes for New Year's cake has shown that both versions were relatively flat like a cookie (no more than ½ inch thick). They would have been sweet and crumbly, yet tinged with the fragrant, savory note of caraway seed. Sometimes, cake boards were carved on one side with a large design, and with many smaller designs on the reverse, allowing the baker to print both versions of New Year's cake at the same time. The large versions served as display pieces. For example one writer wrote of New Year's Day in 1839: 'On a side table reposes in great state, a large New Year's cake.' He did not go into further depth, confessing that 'I would fain enlighten you upon the subject of New Year cookies, if it were not a very busy day, and I have scarcely time to eat one, much less tell you how they are made.'[17] In the novel *The Last of the Knickerbockers*, New Year's cakes appeared on the piano: 'Decanters stood upon the piano and beside them in a lordly dish some long cakes molded into patterns and savory with caraway seed.'[18]

Housewives served the smaller cookies with a glass of wine, raspberry brandy, or cherry-bounce, or dispensed them to children.[19] As Frederick W. Seward (1830–1915) described New Year's Day in 1840: 'Immediately after sunrise children began to perambulate the streets, to ring or knock at each door, wish the inmates a "Happy New-Year," and receive in return a New-Year's cake stamped with "pictures." Many thrifty housewives had a basket of these standing in the hall, to supply the juvenile demands.'[20] It makes sense, in light of the baskets filled with cookies, that one housewife's recipe for New Year's cake called for twenty-eight pounds of flour.[21] According to Seward, at the Governor's house 'Barrels of New-Year's cakes stood at the door, to be handed out to children.'[22]

Surplus cookies were donated to local orphanages or handed out to 'street urchins.'[23] The *American Female Guardian Society, and Home for the Friendless,* reported in 1852 the donation of 'One large basket of new year's cake from R.M. Walduck,' as well as 'A large new year's cake and one hundred small ones from Mr. W. Sampson.'[24] In 1853 the Society reported similar donations from Mr W. Sampson,[25] and in 1855 the Society reported the donation of fifteen New Year's cakes from 'Mrs. Walduck 6th Ave., per Mrs. Buchanan.'[26]

An account by Arthur Cleveland Coxe (1818–1896) of an annual sermon held for the children of New York during Easter week suggests that in some cases, bakers continued to produce New Year's cakes after 1 January:

> In 1831, I again attended the festival in Saint John's Chapel. It was the custom as the children passed out of the Church, on these occasions, to give each of them a little book and a New Year's cake. The New Year's cake, or 'cookey' of New York was inherited from the original Dutch settlers of Manhattan Island. Imitations abound; but even in New York I know of only one baker who can produce the genuine article at the present day. The cookey was generally stamped with Christmas devices, and was not much in vogue after Septuagesima. I never saw one at Easter, except at these festivals and the custom of giving New Year's cakes at this time was a survival from the earlier use of Innocents' Day, or Childermas, for this celebration.[27]

This sermon had originally taken place on Innocents' Day, but the bad weather and general hectic nature of the Christmas season caused the church to change the festival to the 'happy season of the Resurrection.'[28] Thus from this passage we learn that bakers continued to bake New Year's cake until Septuagesima (the ninth Sunday before Easter, Septuagesima can fall between 18 January and 22 February), and as late as Easter, in the case of special Church festivals.[29] Coxe was thirteen years old in 1831, and thus like the Frederick Seward passage quoted above, this is a childhood memory of old New York traditions. In the same passage he went on to describe in palpable detail the 'two enormous baker's baskets, filled with the crisp and fragrant cakes,' which were located under the 'great tower-door of Saint John's.' One can imagine the children restlessly waiting inside the doors for the sermon to finish so they could redeem their cookie, which the Sunday School authorities handed over on the condition that they read the little book that accompanied it.

New Year's cake as a mode of communication

The New Year's cakes have long since been consumed, but many cake boards survive to show the messages they conveyed. In museums, books, auction records, and other sources, I have uncovered 141 cake boards in the New York style. The majority of these boards depict the same kind of popular commemorative imagery that would have been found in broadsides, maps, newspapers, and transfer printed pottery, and indeed, cake board carvers probably copied directly from these sources.

In the period following the American Revolution, commemorative prints and art served to reinforce the republican system, and express the immense pride that Americans felt for their country. For instance, Lafayette's farewell tour in America between 1824 and 1825 had huge reverberations in the material world. It was the main event of the fifty-year anniversary of American independence, and Lafayette was the ideal icon. Not only was he the only surviving general from the Revolution, he loved being the center of attention. Artists and manufacturers collaborated to capitalize on the event, producing items such as silk badges, scarves, pottery, and kidskin gloves imprinted with the likeness of Lafayette.

A cake board in the collection of the New-York Historical Society, which features the inscription 'Lafayette, defender of American and French Liberty,' may have been made at this time, but not necessarily. Another cake board depicting Lafayette, in the collection of the New York State Historical Association, is dated 1834 on its edge, which was the year Lafayette died. The latter cake board was undoubtedly made to memorialize the late general. At 2½ feet long, the New Year's cake formed in this cake board would have certainly made a striking display on the piano or sideboard. New Yorkers must have been extremely proud of the fact that their city was Lafayette's first stop on his grand farewell tour of the United States (he landed at Castle Garden on 24 August 1824).[30]

Other cake boards represent similar themes of civic pride, featuring subject matter such as George Washington, firefighters, horse races, political campaigns, patriotic themes, and civic organizations. For example, one cake board features the famous horse race between Eclipse (a Northern horse) and Sir Henry (a Southern horse) over the

Long Island Course in 1823, which was later seen as a foreshadowing of the Civil War.[31] Eclipse won, to the great pride of New Yorkers – and indeed, the board depicts Eclipse in front of Sir Henry. Another fascinating example, which was probably made between 1850 and 1852, depicts the Swedish opera singer Jenny Lind, who toured America during these years under the auspices of the New York promoter P.T. Barnum. Her grand opening took place at Castle Garden in New York, the same location as the gala organized for Lafayette 26 years before.[32]

While one might argue that the political imagery often found on cake boards, such as George Washington or the Marquis de Lafayette on his horse, seems to evoke an occasion other than New Year's Day, political subject matter was in fact common on this holiday. In his diary entries on 1 January, Philip Hone frequently reflected on the political events of the year, so why not ornament the New Year's table with the same kinds of themes? In fact, the imagery found on the elaborate displays for New Year's Day lunches served at hotels in New York is quite similar. In an article from 2 January 1896, The *New York Times* reported 'A winter scene in sugar, and among the other decorations ... a portrait of Washington' at the Plaza Hotel. Similarly, the Murray Hill Hall concocted 'a beautiful representation in sugar of the fountain in the Vatican Square in Rome, one showing the meeting of Washington and Lafayette, and an artistically formed cornucopia filled with fruits and flowers.'[33]

The cornucopia is a common motif on cake boards, many of which do not feature a particular subject, but rather bring together a number of festive motifs. In addition to cornucopias, baskets of fruits or flowers; perching birds; sheaves of wheat; scrolling foliage and bunches of grapes all appear frequently. These motifs operated as symbols of plenty, representing an optimistic, fruitful outlook on the New Year.

Cake boards were often self-consciously historicizing. Many feature beekeepers, shepherdesses, and other figures in old-fashioned dress, as well as American Indians. This is in keeping with the fondness that shines through in writings by Washington Irving and other New Yorkers for upholding the traditions of the Dutch colonists around the holidays. Indeed, the key flavoring agent in New Year's cake is caraway seed – an ingredient distinctly associated with Dutch cuisine. Yet in the course of the nineteenth century, New York City rapidly industrialized and witnessed the introduction of waves of immigrants from diverse cultures. In this light, the old-fashioned imagery on the cake boards is a form of colonial revival, representing nostalgia for an agrarian past in a city with one foot planted firmly in the future.

Nineteenth-Century New York Cake Boards

Notes

1. For a careful history of the historical and linguistic roots of cake, see: Nicola Humble, 'Cakes Through History,' chapter 1 in *Cake: A Global History* (London: Reaktion Books Ltd., 2010).
2. Eliza Leslie, *Directions for Cookery in its Various Branches* (Philadelpia: Carey & Hart, 1840), 360; Eliza Leslie, *Miss Leslie's New Cookery Book* (Philadelphia: T.B. Peterson and Brothers, 1857), 605.
3. Object files, Albany Institute of History and Art, Albany, New York.
4. Perhaps Washington Irving's characterization of the old Knickerbockers influenced these later illustrations. The character in the doorway in the illustration of 1650 is comparable to Irving's personification of the New Year in his essay on New Year's Day: 'An honest rosy-faced New-Year comes waddling in, like a jolly, fat-sided butler.' Irving, 'The New Year,' 98.
5. Matthew Hale Smith, *Sunshine and Shadow in New York* (Hartford: J.B. Burr and Company, 1868), 351.
6. 'New Year's Day in New-York' in William D. Gallagher, ed., *The Hesperian: A Monthly Miscellany of General Literature*, 2 vols. (Columbus, Ohio: John D. Nichols, 1838), 2:224.
7. Bayard Tuckerman, ed., *The Diary of Philip Hone, 1828–1851* (New York: Dodd, Mead and Company, 1889), 204.
8. Samuel Lover, 'New Year's Day in New York' in Bayle Bernard, *The Life of Samuel Lover, R.H.A.: Artisic, Literary, and Musical with Selections from his Unpublished Papers and Correspondences*, 2 vols. (London: Henry S. King & Co., 1874), 2:75.
9. Edwin G. Burrows and Mike Wallace, *Gotham: A History of New York City to 1898* (New York: Oxford University Press, 1999), 460–61.
10. Smith, *Sunshine and Shadow*, 353.
11. Ibid., 351–52.
12. Tuckermam, *The Diary of Philip Hone*, 291.
13. *New York Times*, Classified Ad, 23 December 1856, 3.
14. *New York Times*, Classified Ad, 23 December 1856, 8.
15. *New York Times*, 'A Happy New Year,' 2 January 1860, 5.
16. Irving, 'The New Year,' 99.
17. Gallagher, 'New Year's Day in New-York,' 2:224.
18. Herman Knickerbocker Vielé, *The Last of the Knickerbockers: A Comedy Romance* (Chicago: Herbert S. Stone & Company, 1901), 148.
19. Irving, 'The New Year,' 99; Tuckerman, *The Diary of Philip Hone*, 241.
20. This quote is taken from an autobiography of William H. Seward that Frederick W. Seward completed on behalf of his father. As Seward Jr. explains in the preface, Seward Sr. had begun his autobiography in 1871, but had only managed to tell his story up to 1834 when he died in 1872. Therefore, it is more likely that this quote draws on Seward Jr.'s childhood memories than on Seward Sr.'s observations. See: Seward and Seward, *William H. Seward: An Autobiography*, 458.
21. See: 'Mrs. Lefferts' Book' (unpublished manuscript, *ca.* 1786–1865, Lefferts House, Prospect Park, Brooklyn). See also: Rose, *Food, Drink and Celebrations*, 140. A curator discovered this tiny book in the attic of the Lefferts House in Brooklyn, New York. It belonged to Maria Lott Lefferts (1786–1865), who married John Lefferts, a descendant of one of the earliest settlers in Brooklyn. Her terse recipe called for '28 lb of flour 10 lb of Sugar 5 lb of Butter carraway seed and Orange peal.' With its '28 lb flour,' this recipe was almost certainly meant to nourish the crowds that came to visit the prominent Lefferts family on New Year's Day; none of her other recipes call for such large proportions of ingredients.
22. Ibid.
23. Ibid.
24. 'Donations of Clothing, Provisions, &c., Received since 1 May 1852,' in *Nineteenth Annual Report of the American Female Guardian Society, and Home for the Friendless, for the Year Ending May, 1853* (New York: Stephen Angell, Printer, 1853), 25. Accessed via Google Books, 23 February 2011.
25. 'Donations of Clothing, Provisions, &c., Received since 1 May 1853, in New York and Vicinity,' in

Twentieth Annual Report of the American Female Guardian Society, and Home for the Friendless, for the Year Ending May, 1854 (New York: Stephen Angell, Printer, 1854), 28. Accessed via Google Books, 23 February 2011.

26. 'Donations of Clothing, Provisions, &c., Received since 1 May 1855 to 1 May 1856 in New York and Vicinity,' in *Twenty-Second Annual Report of the American Female Guardian Society, and Home for the Friendless, for the Year Ending May, 1856* (New York: Stephen Angell, Printer, 1856), 25. Accessed via Google Books, 23 February 2011.
27. Dix et. al., *A History of the Parish of Trinity Church* (New York: G.P. Putnam's Sons, 1898), 108–109. This account by Coxe is part of a series of recollections. Coxe would have been thirteen years old in 1831, and thus like the Frederick Seward passage quoted above, this is a childhood memory of old New York traditions.
28. Ibid.
29. Francis Mershman, 'Septuagesima' in *The Catholic Encyclopedia*, ed. Charles G. Herbermann et. al., 17 vols. (New York: Robert Appleton Company, 1912), 13:721–22.
30. Ibid., 106.
31. John Eisenberg, *The Great Match Race: When North Met South in America's First Sports Spectacle* (Boston: Houghton Mifflin Co., 2006).
32. Gladys Denny Schultz, *Jenny Lind: The Swedish Nightingale* (Philadelphia: J.B. Lippincott Company, 1962).
33. *New York Times*, 'New Year's Day Lunches,' 2 January 1896, 6.

The Festive Fruit: A History of Figs

David C. Sutton

The festive fruit

Figs are the supreme festive fruit, and in western civilizations they have played that role for thousands of years. This essay explores the historical background and analyses fig-eaters through history: their role in society, their religions, and, in particular, the balance between the rich as eaters of figs and the poor as eaters of figs.

Figs have typically been the fruit of winter festivals, because in most of Europe the fig fruits from late summer into the autumn. Baskets of fresh figs are seen in the iconography of European festivals from the earliest times (there are some beautiful examples on the walls of Pompeii), but dried figs also became a characteristic winter festival fruit.

In England figs became the typical fruit of the post-Dickensian family Christmas. Along with Christmas trees, Christmas stockings, Santa Claus, tinsel, and images of robins in snow-covered gardens, dried figs were an essential component. Indeed, in many English families in the nineteenth and twentieth centuries, dried figs were eaten only on Christmas Day and the days following. A contemporary of Dickens tells us that in the 1830s the best dried figs in England were held to come from Turkey, Italy, Spain, and Provence, in that order.[1]

Long before Dickens, figgy pudding was established as an English Christmas treat. In some homes it may still be. As Christmas 2008 approached, the *Daily Telegraph*, that bastion of true Englishness, ran an article (12 December 2008) headed 'Figgy pudding's welcome Christmas return', telling us 'From the 16th century, figgy pudding traditionally appeared at the end of a Christmas meal – it is on the table of Bob Cratchit in *A Christmas Carol* – though it used to be served on Palm Sunday.'

The most famous commemoration of figgy pudding at Christmas is surely from the well-known song 'We Wish You a Merry Christmas', which appears to be a secular hymn dating to the sixteenth century. This is its most Christmassy refrain:

> Oh, bring us a figgy pudding
> Oh, bring us a figgy pudding
> Oh, bring us a figgy pudding
> And a cup of good cheer.

The festive figs of English Christmases were following long-established traditions. In the ancient world, the fig tree and its mature fruit were venerated.

The Festive Fruit: A History of Figs

Fig tree worship ... is credited to the people of an ancient race whose birthplace was in the country of Mt Ararat, and who were the first Phrygian worshippers of household fire. It was preceded by the worship of the oak tree and of the almond tree. The fig tree was held sacred in all countries of southwestern Asia, and in Egypt, Greece and Italy.[2]

The Romans in particular had a number of sacred fig trees in their city and used figs in religious celebrations for the start of a new year. Roman religion was often delightfully functionalist: in Ovid's *Fasti* Janus explains that gifts of dates, dried figs, and honey to propitiate the gods as the year opened were omens to ensure that the year would begin in sweetness so that it could continue in sweetness.

Before the Romans the fig had always been a fruit with festive and symbolic significance: in its Mesopotamian prehistory, in biblical Palestine, in ancient Greece and then from the very beginnings of Rome. Most famously, it is present in the biblical Eden, where Adam and Eve sewed fig-leaves into aprons to hide their nakedness.

Palaeobotanical and prehistoric origins

Botanically, the fig has two peculiarities. First, it is not strictly a fruit so much as a tiny cluster of ingrowing flowers:

> Considered botanically, the Fig, as we eat it, is a very remarkable form of fruit. It is actually neither fruit nor flower, though partaking of both, being really a hollow, fleshy receptacle, enclosing a multitude of flowers, which never see the light, yet come to full perfection and ripen their seeds. ... In the Fig, the inflorescence, or position of the flowers, is concealed within the body of the 'fruit'. The Fig stands alone in this peculiar arrangement of its flowers.[3]

The second peculiarity is that many varieties of fig tree bear fruit in two different seasons: a spring crop and a late summer crop. In the Spanish language, the two crops are considered to be different fruit, the spring fruit being known as *brevas* and the later, sweeter fruit as *higos*. Illustrations in Spanish textbooks show *brevas* with harder, greener skins and paler interiors while ripe *higos* have softer blue-black skins and ripe red contents. In Italian, the word used for the early and often inedible fruit of the fig tree is *fioroni*. Although most languages distinguish between green and violet figs, many appear not to have a *higos/brevas* distinction (in Turkish, for example, both are covered by the word *incir*). Even in fig-rich Menorca, the Menorcan version of Catalan does not use a word for *brevas*, but distinguishes June-fruiting varieties, principally *figaflor* (cognate with the French *figue-fleur*), from October-fruiting trees, such as *coll de dama*.[4]

The principal works on the history of the fig[5] have indicated the probable origins of the tree in Arabia and its cultivation as a fruit crop in Mesopotamia over 5000 years ago. Botanical texts regard the tree as indigenous to Asia Minor, Iran, and Syria. The working consensus has been that the fig developed in Arabia, was then improved by

Sumerian and Assyrian fruit-farmers, before becoming a mainstream crop across Iraq, Greater Syria and Anatolia.

More recently archaeologists working in the Jordan Valley discovered remains of carbonized figs which they believe to have been cultivated and which have been dated to around 9300 BC. These finds were part of the excavations of an early neolithic village known as Gilgal I and were reported in *Science* in 2006, attracting widespread coverage on the BBC and elsewhere. Later in 2006, unnoticed by the BBC and other media, another group of scientists published a refutation in *Science*, suggesting that what had been found were not (at such an improbably early date) cultivated figs but unpollinated female spring figs, which they refer to as 'breba'.[6]

With the present state of archaeological research, it is safest to retain for the origins of cultivated figs a date some time before 3500 BC. As we shall see, figs became a major feature in everyday life in 'the cradle of civilization' in Iraq, and spread to all the emerging civilizations in neighbouring lands, notably Egypt and Turkey. A Turkish food writer tells us that the Ancient Egyptians 'broke their fasts by eating figs'.[7]

Climatic factors appear to be the major reason why fig cultivation (which is adversely affected by high humidity) did not thrive in India nor in China, but succeeded particularly in Turkey, Syria, the Crimea and southern Italy. In northern Europe the fig tree had to fight a different struggle – against the winter cold. Matthew Paris reported that in the severe weather of 1257 in England 'the fig trees were almost all destroyed'.[8]

The fig is above all a characteristic fruit of the dry lands in and near the eastern Mediterranean:

> Figs ranked next to olives as an article of food. They were grouped with bread and oil in the diet of the common people throughout the Mediterranean lands. Cato advised that farm slaves should be fed chiefly on figs from the summer solstice, when the first crop came in, till late autumn. Dried figs were eaten by the country folk all winter in Italy, they were welcome as army rations in ancient Palestine, and once served instead of grain for the forces of Philip of Macedon in western Asia Minor, doubtless owing to their sugar content.[9]

Figs in the Bible

An excellent source for ancient Arabia, Iraq, and the Jordan Valley is the Old Testament, which contains many references to figs – beginning with the fig-leaves covering the nakedness of Adam and Eve. Most archaeologists trace the early stories of the Book of Genesis to Mesopotamia, at least in the chapters up to and including the flood story apparently derived from the epic of Gilgamesh. If, following the researches of the archaeologist Geoffrey Bibby, we see the shadowy origins of the figure known in the Bible as Adam in a leader or ruler who first moved from Bahrain/Dilmun to present-day Iraq, then the presence of figs in an Iraqi Garden of Eden some 6000 years ago would be credible. Credence could also be given to the accounts which suggest that the original forbidden fruit was not the apple (an important crop in Iraq but mostly in the north of the country) but an Iraqi fig.

The fig also plays an emblematic role in the following, Palestine-specific sequences of the Bible. When spies return to report on Canaan as the 'promised land' (Numbers 13:23) they bring with them grapes and pomegranates and figs; and elsewhere the land promised to the Israélites is described (Deuteronomy 8:8) as a good land, of wheat and barley and vines and fig trees and pomegranates. There is a similar prominence for the fig in the Song of Songs (2:12–13):

> Flowers are appearing on the earth,
> The season of glad songs has come,
> The cooing of the turtledove is heard in our land,
> The fig tree is forming its first figs
> And the blossoming vines give out their fragrance.

And the fig tree is portrayed as having a wisdom based on its place in the natural order in Judges 9:12–13:

> Then the trees said to the fig tree, 'You come and be our king!' The fig tree replied 'Must I forgo my sweetness, forgo my excellent fruit, to go and hold sway over the trees?'

The exchange is subject to several possible interpretations, but the biblical primacy of the fig tree, at least, is clear.

When Abigail went out to meet King David, a man of great and sometimes dubious appetites, she offered him a hundred clusters of raisins and two hundred cakes of figs (1 Samuel 25:18). Of the many references to figs in the Old Testament, these are perhaps the two most attractive:

> But they shall sit every man under his vine and under his fig tree; and none shall make them afraid. (Micah 4:4)

> All thy strong holds shall be like fig trees with the first-ripe figs: if they be shaken, they shall even fall into the mouth of the eater. (Nahum 3:12)

Figs and the ancient Greeks

Figs were a constant presence in Greek society, with the first Greek cultivation of figs being probably around 900 BC. It appears that in earliest times figs may have been an exclusive food in Greece, a food for the rich and for religious use, but that in later centuries figs became more easily available and hence a staple food of the poor. Plutarch believed the tradition that Solon forbade the export of figs, some time around 590 BC, and that the law was rigorously enforced. Those who tried to smuggle figs (συκή or *syke*) out of Attica were liable to be reported to the authorities by 'those who reveal figs' (*sykophantes*), an intriguing etymology for sycophancy.[10]

The Festive Fruit: A History of Figs

Several writers emphasize that although the Greeks defined themselves principally by the olive, the gift of Athena, they sometimes defined themselves also by the fig. References can be found contrasting the civilized fig-eating Greeks with the barbarous Medes and Persians 'who know neither wine nor figs'. In Book three of *The Deipnosophists*, amongst many pages on the glories of Greek figs, Athenaeus quotes Herodotus as believing that the fig is the most useful to man of all the fruits which grow on trees, and quotes a certain Magnus as saying 'the fig tree, my friends, is the guide to men to lead them to a more civilized life'.

Once Solon's prohibition on export of figs had expired, we find numerous examples of Greek figs being sought by representatives of other civilizations, including those in India.

> 'Nothing is sweeter than figs', Aristophanes declared, and their reputation spread far beyond the lands in which they grew until, in the third century BC, Bindusara, king of the Maurya dominions in India, wrote to Greece asking for some grape syrup, some figs and a philosopher. Grape syrup and figs, he was told with cool courtesy, would be sent to him with pleasure, but it was 'against the law in Greece to trade in philosophers'.[11]

We are told that by this period 'the two top items of Ancient Greek exports were olive oil and wine, followed by figs and walnuts'.[12]

Figs in the Roman Empire

The Romans were also worshippers of figs. They especially celebrated the first day of the year with figs:

> It was customary to carry a basket of figs next to the vessel of wine used in the Dionysia, or festivals in honour of Bacchus. The fig is related to have been the favourite fruit of Cleopatra, who was the most luxurious queen the world ever produced. The asp with which she terminated her life, was conveyed to her in a basket of figs.[13]

In the Introduction Ovid was cited on the Roman idea that beginning the year with figs, dates and honey might lead to a year of sweetness. Gillian Riley, in *The Oxford Companion to Italian Food*, notes that related celebratory traditions continue in some parts of Italy:

> Ancient Romans initially marked the beginning of the New Year at the spring solstice; then in 153 BC, it was moved to 1 January. They exchanged glass jars full of dates and figs in honey so that the year would be sweet, and a bay branch so it would bring good fortune. The tradition is still honoured in Naples, where people exchange figs wrapped in laurel leaves, and in Campania and Abruzzo, where dried figs stuffed with almonds are gifts of the season.[14]

The Festive Fruit: A History of Figs

Although figs grow perfectly well in Italy, they ripen even better in the warmer lands to the south and east. The ancient Romans imported figs, notably from north Africa; and Plutarch and others tell the story of how Cato the Elder deliberately dropped some 'Libyan' figs from his toga onto the floor of the Senate. When the senators admired the size and beauty of the figs, Cato agreed but then pointed out their source in Carthage – only three days' distance from Rome – underlining his constant theme: Carthage must be destroyed.[15]

Virgil does not mention figs in the *Georgics*, but this is no great loss given his notorious ignorance about trees and grafting. His contemporary Varro was better informed. Varro believed that fig culture was part of the earliest way of life on Rome's Palatine Hill [16] and, like Pliny, saw a close association between figs and milk. Romulus' sacred fig tree was closely associated with Rumina the milk goddess (it was called interchangeably the *ficus Ruminalis* and the *ficus Romularis*). Three main reasons have been suggested for this: confusion between the names; the compatibility of figs and milk as foodstuffs; and the homeopathic connection between milk and the milky sap which flows from fig-wood. All three may contain some truth. In any event, figs, fig-wood and the sacred fig tree were seen as defining elements in religious celebrations in ancient Rome.

Figs in medieval Europe

Figs became more widely available across Europe during the medieval period, and attempts were made to extend the growth of fig trees into the countries of northern Europe. This may have partly reflected the love of figs which had been developed by returning crusaders. The figs of the Disiboden cloister garden in Germany, for example, are attributed to crusader influence. (The crusaders found that all too few of them could gain ownership of the Palestinian land around Acre and Tyre, which was 'famous for its lemons, oranges, almonds, and figs'.[17]) In northern Europe figs would be grown principally in the sheltered special orchards of palaces, great houses and religious foundations. Matthew Paris' comment, quoted above, illustrates that fig trees had been planted in England some time before 1257. A fig tree in Lambeth Palace is said to have been planted by Cardinal Pole around the 1520s, and a fig tree in Archbishop Cranmer's estate is said to have been planted by the Archbishop himself, probably in the 1530s. Nonetheless these were special cases, and figs were not considered to be an English fruit. Figs are not mentioned at all in the general works of Thomas Tusser and Francis Bacon, and several of their contemporaries commented upon the difficulty of getting figs to ripen in England.[18]

For Britain, northern France, and all of northern Europe, transportation was the key to access to figs. For as long as transport was difficult, they remained a rare and luxurious product. When transport improved, or when a military alliance was formed with a fig-producing country, access became easier.

In southern Europe, figs were grown extensively in most Mediterranean countries

The Festive Fruit: A History of Figs

at the time of the fall of the Roman Empire. The fig-growing zone was extended by the Moorish conquests, notably into Portugal and across north Africa. Fig-production in Spain and Portugal came to be even more important than in Italy and Greece. Figs grew well in the south of France, and Thomas Jefferson, visiting Marseilles and Toulon in 1787, suggested that the French figs were the most delicately flavoured of all.

Figs went from Spain to the Americas, and it is claimed that the oldest fig tree in the New World is the Pizarro tree in the governor's palace in Lima, probably planted around 1540. Figs were introduced to Mexico by Hernán Cortés, perhaps in the 1530s, and it was soon discovered that Mexico and California provided good climates for fig-production.

Figs were seen in England in the Middle Ages as an exotic Mediterranean fruit. For Shakespeare the fruit was 'the fig of Spain' (*Henry V*, 3.7.50). He also associated figs with Egypt, having Charmian say 'I love long life better than figs' (*Antony and Cleopatra*, 1.2.34). Connections were made with figs from Palestine through the story that Jesus Christ desired to eat figs along the road to Bethany, leading to the medieval English tradition of eating figgy pudding on the Sunday before Easter.[19]

Looking at English archival sources, port records show that figs (presumably dried) were being extensively imported into England by the mid-fourteenth century and then through the fifteenth century. Ports such as Sandwich and Exeter (both much more important in medieval times than now) record cargoes of figs, especially from Italy. A more exclusive archival source, the privy purse accounts of King Henry VIII, records a gift to the king from a Mr Worsley of Portuguese figs. It is probable that these were fresh figs – truly a dainty dish to set before a king.[20]

From the fruit of the gods to 'not worth a fig'

There is a curious ambivalence about the status of the fig in Western cookery and food habits. On the one hand, it was a luxury product and a prized festive fruit with a long history of religious and celebratory significance. On the other hand, it became a byword for a food which is so common as to be almost valueless – 'not worth a fig'.

The expression 'not worth a fig' existed in ancient Greek (it is found in Athenaeus, despite his great love of figs), and now exists in many languages, notably in Turkish, where the movie *İncir Çekirdeği* (*Not Worth a Fig*, directed by Selda Çiçek, 2009) is regarded as a new landmark in Turkish cinema. It finds its way into several memorable Spanish proverbs:

> *Amigo sin dinero, eso quiero; que dinero sin amigo no vale un higo* (a friend without money, that I love; money without a friend is not worth a fig).

> *Blanca con frio no vale un higo* (a fair woman in cold weather is not worth a fig).

> *Oficio que no da trigo no vale un higo* (trade which provides no wheat is not worth a fig).[21]

Figs, then, are paradoxical: so commonplace as to be worthless, so exotically delicate as to be a gift fit for a king. They appear on both sides of the great food divide, as an exquisite food of the rich, but also a proverbial food of the poor.

The paradox is explained in various ways. The first explanation lies in the two forms of the edible fig: fresh and dried. The fresh fig is an archetypal luxury food because of its perishability; it can be sublime one day and rotten the next. The true exquisiteness of flavour (which is enhanced by pure water) belongs only to the fresh fig on its day of perfect ripeness. By contrast, the dried fig is durable – a cheap source of summer sweetness all through the winter, and an ideal staple food.

The second explanation of the paradox is geographical. Figs grow easily and copiously in Mediterranean and Levantine lands, but are exotic imports to northern Europe. Figs grown to the north of, say, Bordeaux or Bologna never have that taste of the southern sun, which led the Prophet Mohammed to say 'If I should wish a fruit brought to paradise, it would certainly be the fig'.[22]

Despite their omnipresence in the Mediterranean region, figs retain their exotic status – touched by strange stories from the Bible, by comments in the Koran, by memories of the Crusades and the Ottoman wars. In more recent ideas of gastronomy, they have added a form of exoticism by association. For example, the combination of figs and Parma ham is often described as a marriage made in heaven, while the French have long given special status to *foie gras* from geese fed on figs.

Conclusion: proverbs and strategies

In an earlier presentation to the Oxford Symposium I underlined the importance of proverbs in food history, in providing a real historical insight into everyday life and feelings in centuries long ago.[23] This is also true for figs, although our sources have to come from the Mediterranean countries. There are very few English proverbs about figs, but, as we have begun to see, Spain provides many evocative fig-proverbs.

For the time of ripening, we find:

Por San Miguel, los higos son miel (for St Michael, figs are honey-sweet [St Michael's day is 29 September])

There is a powerful proverb on perishability, of figs and human beings:

Los hombres somos como los higos: el que no cae hoy cae mañana (we men are like figs; those who don't die today will die tomorrow)

The proverbs also refer to the abundance of figs:

Al tiempo de higo, no hay enemigo (at fig-time, there are no enemies [because there is food for everyone])

and tell us that fig trees need to mature, although not to the same extent as olive-trees:

The Festive Fruit: A History of Figs

Olivares de tu abuelo; higueras de tu padre, y viñas de ti mismo (your grandfather's olive-trees; your father's fig trees; your own vineyards)[24]

In his wonderful book about the relationship between pears and cheese,[25] Massimo Montanari provides us with thoughts about both proverbs and the shifting status of the foods of the rich and the foods of the poor.

Montanari's starting point is an Italian proverb which says 'Don't let the peasant know how well cheese accompanies pears' (*Al contadino non far sapere quanto è buono il formaggio con le pere*). This leads him to a series of reflections on the exclusiveness of the food of the rich and on specialness, illuminated by Italian proverbs. For the fig, one of the proverbs he cites is

Al fico l'acqua, e alla pera il vino (drink water with figs and wine with pears)

with a Campanian variant

Con i fichi l'acqua, e con le pesche il vino (drink water with figs and wine with peaches)

These proverbs place figs in the tradition of luxurious foods which do not take wine, but are enhanced by water – such as artichokes and asparagus. And we should remember that clean drinking water itself was a luxury product in medieval times.

Montanari stresses how difficult it was for peasant foods to be accepted at the tables of the rich. In order for this to happen there had to be, in his terminology, 'strategies' for making the peasant food different, special and hence acceptable. He uses in particular examples from amongst cheeses and fruits. Mushrooms provide another example (classed as food from dirt, even food from excrement, when eaten by the poor; irresistibly earthily delicious in exotic forms such as *cèpes*). Salt-cod (*bacalao*) has a similar ambiguity (the *brandade de morue* is a peasant dish still found in backstreet French cafés, but also an exquisite mix of flavours found in all the aristocratic cookbooks from Escoffier onwards).[26] Cheese, soft fruit, fungus food, salt-cod: these are foods of the common people, folk foods, everyday foods, which have such tempting characteristics of deliciousness that the rich need to reclassify them so that they can grace their own tables.

Forms of specialness could include perishability; delicacy and exquisite subtlety of flavour (too subtle to be appreciated by crude peasant palates); exotic origins; and exceptional individual characteristics. In the case of cheese, there was a long struggle of reclassification before it could become accepted as a food for the tables of the rich. It was necessary to establish the clearest of distinctions between the rock-hard long-life peasant cheese and the soft luxury cheese whose excellence would remain only for a short period of time.

Perishability, delicacy, subtle flavour, exotic origins, exceptional characteristics: all of these forms of specialness apply to figs and allow them to be acceptable food for the rich, in spite of their easy accessibility.

The Festive Fruit: A History of Figs

Fresh figs are seasonal, perishable and delicate; they are not quite ripe on a Monday, at their perfect best on a Tuesday, and beginning to collapse on a Wednesday. Although the flavour of figs continues to be excellent when they are over-ripe, for their appearance on aristocratic tables they must be served on their perfect day.

In northern Europe, fresh figs are exotic: Portuguese figs made a regal gift to King Henry VIII. In this respect they can sit on aristocratic tables alongside fruits which have no European folk traditions attached, such as pineapples.

Even in countries where fresh figs are common and abundant, they are treated as special. In Istanbul in August and September the contrast between delicate finesse, on the one hand, and sheer abundance, on the other, is seen to the full. Although fresh figs are sold in the bazaars for less than half the price per kilo of dried figs, they are displayed arranged with as much care and precision as if they were of antique glass. And sold with love and reverence, as befits a divine festive fruit.

The Festive Fruit: A History of Figs

Notes

1. Henry Phillips: *The Companion for the Orchard: an Historical and Botanical Account of Fruits Known in Great Britain*. London: H. Colburn & R. Bentley, 1831, p. 160.
2. Ira J. Condit: *The Fig*. Waltham, Mass.: Chronica Botanica, 1947, p.2.
3. From www.botanical.com.
4. *Minorca: Cooking and Gastronomy/* [text by Xim Fuster, Manel Gómez et al.]. Sant Lluís, Menorca: Triangle Postals, 2005, p. 134.
5. The principal source is Ira J. Condit: op.cit. Condit cites as his own main sources the works of H. G. Solms-Laubach (essays in German published in 1882 and 1885) and Gustav Eisen (essays published in the USA in 1885 and 1896, and *The Fig*, bulletin published by the United States Department of Agriculture, 1901). All of these works are now difficult to locate.
6. Mordechai E. Kislev, Anat Hartmann, Ofer Bar-Yosef: 'Early domesticated fig in the Jordan Valley', *Science* 312 (2 June 2006), pp. 1372–1374; and Simcha Lev-Yadun, Gidi Ne'eman, Shahal Abbo, Moshe A. Flaishman: 'Comment on "Early domesticated fig in the Jordan Valley"', *Science* 314 (15 December 2006), p. 1683.
7. Denis Gürsoy: *Turkish Cuisine in Historical Perspective*. Istanbul: Oğlak Güzel Kitaplar, 2006, p.30.
8. Ira J. Condit: op.cit., p. 12.
9. Ellen Churchill Semple: 'Ancient Mediterranean agriculture', *Agricultural History* 2 (1928), p. 89.
10. Plutarch: *Solon*, 24; A. B. Cook:'СΥΚΟΦΑΝΤΗС', *Classical Review* 21 (1907), p. 133.
11. Reay Tannahill: *Food in History*. New ed. New York: Three Rivers Press, 1989, p. 51, citing Athenaeus.
12. Denis Gürsoy: op.cit., p. 33.
13. Henry Phillips: op.cit., p. 150.
14. Gillian Riley: *The Oxford Companion to Italian Food*. Oxford: Oxford University Press, 2007, p. 195.
15. See F. J. Meijer: 'Cato's African figs', *Mnemosyne* 37 (1984), pp. 117–124.
16. G.D. Hadzsits: 'The *Vera historia* of the Palatine *Ficus ruminalis*', *Classical philology* 31 (4) (1936), pp. 305–319. On tree-worship more generally see Sir James George Frazer's *The Golden Bough*.
17. Frederic C. Lane: *Venice: a Maritime Republic*. Baltimore: Johns Hopkins University Press, 1973, p. 72.
18. Henry Phillips: op.cit., pp. 152–153.
19. For these three paragraphs, see Ira J. Condit: op.cit., pp. 8–14, and Ira J. Condit: 'Fig history in the New World', *Agricultural History* 31 (2), April 1957, pp. 19–24. (The date of 1560, given by Condit for Cortés' introduction of figs into Mexico, is not possible, however, as Cortés died in 1547.)
20. See Joan Thirsk: *Food in Early Modern England: Phases, Fads, Fashions, 1500–1760*. London: Hambledon Continuum, 2007, especially pp. 10, 17, 21.
21. See Juliana Panizo Rodríguez: 'Algunos frutos del campo en el refranero', *Revista de folklore* 214 (1998), pp. 134–139.
22. Quoted in many places, e.g. Ira J. Condit: *The Fig*, p. 11.
23. David C. Sutton: 'The language of the food of the poor: studying proverbs with Jean-Louis Flandrin', in *Food and Language: Proceedings of the Oxford Symposium on Food and Cookery 2009*, edited by Richard Hosking. Totnes: Prospect Books, 2010, pp. 330–339.
24. Juliana Panizo Rodríguez: op.cit.
25. Massimo Montanari: *Il formaggio con le pere: la storia in un proverbio*. Bari: Editori Laterza, 2008.
26. David C. Sutton: 'The stories of bacalao: myth, legend and history', in *Cured, Fermented and Smoked Foods: Proceedings of the Oxford Symposium on Food and Cookery 2010*, edited by Helen Saberi. Totnes: Prospect Books, 2011, pp. 312–321.

Be Merry, Around a Wheat Berry! The Significance of Wheat in Anatolian Rituals and Celebrations

Aylin Öney Tan

Background of wheat cultivation and its significance in Anatolia

Anatolia is home to wild wheat, and the first domesticated species, einkorn (*Triticum monococcum*) and emmer (*Triticum dicoccum*), were used as food circa 10,000 BC. Until a decade ago, archaeobotanical knowledge for neolithic Anatolia was confined to findings from the settlements of Çatalhöyük in Konya, Çayönü in Diyarbakır and Cafer Höyük in Malatya. Four recently discovered settlements in south-eastern Anatolia, Göbekli Tepe and Nevali Çori in Urfa and Hallan Çemi and Demirköy in Batman, revealed new findings.[1] It seems that at settlements like Hallan Çemi and Demirköy, wild wheat was still gathered but not yet cultivated. In Göbekli Tepe, which is one of the most exciting new archaeological sites in Turkey, barley and einkorn seeds and husks have been found. Meanwhile, the Çatalhöyük excavation team is conducting research to compare archaeological findings with the wild and domesticated wheat varieties still growing in Turkey.

The domestication of wheat and other grains brought about the establishment of farming communities, which later gave rise to the great civilizations of Mesopotamia and Anatolia. The abundance of wheat also facilitated the transition from the village to the city and led to the emergence of city-states and regional powers. Peoples of Anatolia acknowledged their debt to wheat by incorporating it in their celebrations and rites of passages, in a way mirroring in their own lives the role played by wheat in the history of their civilizations.

Recent ethno-archaeological studies reveal an unbroken cultural chain in agricultural practices. There are surviving clues of this continuity in local names. For example, the word *siyez,* used locally for emmer or einkorn in the vicinity of the city of Kastamonu, strongly resembles the Hittite word *zēz* or *ziz* for wheat. Depictions of wheat ears can be seen on finds from all the early civilizations, such as the Hittite Kingdom, the Hellenes, and Romans. All deities related to fertility bear the symbol of wheat corn, such as Tammuz, Kybele, Kubaba, Ceres, and Demeter, to name a few.

Celebrating with wheat berry

Much has been said about the sacredness of bread in religious rituals and mythology, but the use of the whole wheat berry in ceremonial dishes is rarely mentioned. In today's Anatolian communities, the presence of wheat dishes at almost all occasions marking critical stages of life like birth, death and marriage is quite remarkable. Furthermore, whole berry or sprouted wheat also takes the stage on occasions marking seasonal changes, particularly in rituals celebrating the end of winter and the welcoming of spring. The fact that wheat figures in both testifies to the interconnectedness of individual and communal life and has deep roots in past agrarian societies who depended on the rhythms of the nature for their survival. From the perspective of their celebratory dishes, the rituals of the various religions of Anatolia greatly resemble each other, and festive foods are shared across all kinds of communal boundaries.

Ceremonial wheat berry sweets and dishes can be grouped under two kinds of celebrations: rites of passage and seasonal changes.

Rites of passage

Wheat dishes figure prominently on occasions marking significant stages in life like birth, the first tooth, circumcision, engagement, marriage, death, and important occasions like going on pilgrimages, starting military service, or any other happy event.

Keşkek: Wheat Berry Stew for Weddings. The most joyous of all festivities are weddings. The custom of preparing *keşkek*, a communal wheat and meat stew, remains a strong tradition today, with almost all rural weddings featuring huge cauldrons of the ritual dish as the centrepiece of the feast. The wheat in wedding ceremonies symbolizes fertility and prosperity for the newly established family, while the meat demonstrates the wealth of the wedding host and stands as a sacrifice to ward off all evil forces that may darken the happiness of the married couple. *Keşkek* is not only confined to matrimonial weddings. The term 'wedding' (*düğün*) is used for many occasions, including engagement or circumcision celebrations. *Keşkek* is the quintessential *düğün yemeği*, the 'wedding dish', and also the traditional ceremonial dish at circumcision feasts marking the passage from boyhood to manhood.

Keşkek is also prepared for farewell gatherings. Any member of the community leaving the village for an honourable purpose, such as pilgrimage to Mecca or military service, is sent off with a feast. In this case, there is no particular symbolic significance, but obviously, the preparation and eating of the dish is a communal practice, repetition of which reinforces bonds between the participants. In this case *keşkek* serves as a means to give spiritual support to those parting from loved ones. Other occasions like religious holidays, the month of Ramadan, the birth of a long-awaited baby, or the prayer of *Mevlid*, held for the deceased, are also opportunities for a *keşkek* feast. Due to the influence of court cuisine, the more expensive and prestigious rice pilaf and roast lamb began to appear more frequently in rural weddings, but the role of *keşkek* as the centre of celebrations and the communal ritual of preparing it remained unchanged.

The dish may be named differently according to region, such as *haşıl, herise, helise, harissa, gölle, köle,* or the many variations on the word *keşkek* in different dialects, but the role of wheat as the backbone of the dish remains unchanged. In other countries, similar words may refer to completely different dishes. Françoise Aubaile-Sallenave gives an extensive list of dishes in various cultures and the variations in name.² *Keşkek* is similar to Middle Eastern *harissa* and Iranian and Afghani *halim*, or *haleem*. This ritual is not only confined to Muslims. Anatolian Christian communities share the same tradition. The only remaining rural Armenian village, Vakıflı, close to Antakya (Antioch), celebrates Surp Asdvadzadzin, honouring the Virgin Mary on 15 August, with the same ceremonial dish along with the first grapes of the season. Claudia Roden mentions a slow oven cooked wheat porridge *harissa* with chopped meat, pounded later in the same fashion as *keşkek*, as a typical Saturday dish of Spanish Jews in medieval Spain,³ but there is no record of such a dish in contemporary Sephardic cooking in Turkey. In all these celebrations, the basis of the community is reasserted and the deep-rooted agrarian foundations of the society are reestablished through shared labour in preparing *keşkek* and by feasting on the ever-present traditional dish.

There are two basic methods of preparing *keşkek*. The more common method is open-fire cooking in cauldrons with continuous stirring and pounding of the wheat and meat until they form a homogeneous mass. The other involves hours of oven baking: the pots of wheat and meat are put into the communal oven a day in advance and ceremoniously taken out the next day. When it is prepared for a wedding, preparations start with a prayer and the pounding of the whole wheat in stone mortars. This process marks the start of the wedding and once the wheat husk is completely removed, the cooking starts. The dish cooks on an open fire overnight. The pots are often left untouched but the fire is monitored, and the next day, the stew is pounded for several hours to achieve a sticky porridge-like consistency.

While basic cooking methods remain simple, variations of the dish are numerous. The type of meat used may differ: lamb, mutton, goat, beef or poultry like chicken, turkey, goose or, on rare occasions, game can be used. In the past, dried meat or just dried bones could be used to give the taste of meat, but this is getting rarer. There are also cases where no meat is used. Nowadays the most commonly used meat is lamb or chicken. Along with the wheat, other grains or pulses might be added, the most common being chickpeas. In the Black Sea region where wheat is scarce, dried corn replaces wheat. Another common practice is to caramelize chopped onions for a final finish. The central Anatolian city Çorum, home to the Hittite Kingdom, with its chief god Kumarbi always carrying a wheat stalk, has astonishing varieties of *keşkek*. In a recent cooking contest in May 2011, 17 different versions appeared, all traditional. In all cases, a dose of sizzling clarified butter or olive oil with powdered chilli peppers is poured over the finished dish before serving. The dish can vary in consistency; some remain slightly soupy and sometimes wheat berries remain intact like in a pilaf, but mostly the wheat and meat amalgamate into a thick, sticky purée and no meat can be seen in the final serving. The meat practically dissolves into the dish, broken down into threads, and the wheat releasing all its starch to form a porridge-like mass. This homogeneous character makes the dish very democratic: no one gets the better part or the privileged cut or more of the meat, but every single member of the community has an equal share of the feast, enjoying the egalitarian taste of the common dish.

Hedik: First Bite in Life. The appearance of a baby's first tooth is an opportunity to celebrate. There is joy and excitement generated by the bud of tooth and the family prepares a hasty celebratory sweet made of boiled whole wheat berries. The sweet is called *diş buğdayı*, literally meaning 'tooth wheat'. The baby is not expected to eat it of course, but the whole wheat berries stand for the expected passage from mother's milk to solid food and eventually having a row of firm healthy teeth. The tooth wheat is distributed to neighbours, sent to relatives and friends, and served to all guests visiting the proud mother and baby. The recipe is simple: boiled wheat is sweetened with sugar or sometimes with grape molasses or honey, often sprinkled with cinnamon and ground walnuts. The dish may also be called *hedik, haşıl,* etc., and in this case it is not necessarily prepared for first tooth, but as an enjoyable snack, usually shared around the stove during long winter nights. *Hedik* often includes crunchy seeds like flax, poppy, hemp or nigella, and might be not sweet but savoury, perhaps with the addition of a knob of butter.

Koliva: Last Taste of the Mortal World. In contrast to the first tooth celebration, a very similar wheat berry sweet is prepared for funerals by the Greek communities. *Koliva* is a mixture of boiled wheat berries, pat-dried with napkins until all the moisture is removed, with an addition of pan-roasted flour or powdered biscuits to keep it dry, which is then mixed with sugar and spices, mainly cinnamon and coriander seeds. It is pressed into flat trays, covered with a layer of icing sugar, and decorated with sugared almonds, pomegranate kernels, or raisins. The initials of the deceased are written on the finished tray with an omnipresent Orthodox cross and sometimes floral motifs are made with sugared almonds. Even the preparation is a ritual in itself: nothing, not even the water used to wash the wheat, is wasted, but instead poured out to sea or into flower pots, as Rena Salaman notes.[4] *Koliva* is also prepared on the day of Ton Psihon, dedicated to all the deceased. Christian Gagauz Turks also follow the same ritual, as do the Bulgarians and Rumanians, making *Zito* or *Vareno Zhito*.[5] The term *koliva* does not come from *helva*, another funeral sweet in Turkey, as some suggest, but from *kollybos*, as Charles Perry explains:

> originally *kollybos* probably came from a Semitic word meaning 'to exchange,' such as the Hebrew *khalap*. The Greek word for someone who made change was a *kollybistes*. In later times, *kollybos* meant something that people could exchange that was of less value than any coin, so if you wanted somebody to pay you something more than 5 of the smallest coins but less than 6, you would ask for 5 coins plus *kollybos*, which would generally be some grains of wheat or barley. When Christians started making their ritual dish of whole grain, they called it *kollybos*.[6]

Be Merry, Around a Wheat Berry!

Seasonal celebrations

Anatolia is often called the cradle of civilization, as it has been home to numerous religions and communities over the course of its long history. Each community has its own important dates in the yearly calendar: Christmas and New Year vary according to the different calendars used, and there are numerous spring festivals like Easter, Pesah, Tu Bishvat, Nevruz, Hıdrellez, and Aya Yorgi (St George's) day. It is also possible to see these dates as variations of celebrating the change of seasons, with the coming of the spring being a particularly festive occasion. Wheat berry is a symbolic ingredient that keeps reappearing on many of those seasonal festive occasions.

Aşure: Mourning and Celebrating. Aşure is a sweet pudding made of wheat berries, pulses like beans and chick peas, and dried fruits and nuts, traditionally eaten on the tenth day of Muharrem, the first month in the Islamic lunar calendar. The day of Ashura (in Turkish: Aşure Günü), marks the remembrance of the battle of Kerbela, but the ritual apparently has deeper roots back in history.

The ritual of preparing the sweet wheat berry pudding *aşure* is a very strong tradition observed by various ethnic and religious communities in Turkey. The richness of the dessert is mirrored in *aşure* celebrations and the stories about its origin. Traditionally, it is important to fast for the first ten days of Muharrem and prepare the pudding as a feast for the last day of fasting. The term Ashura actually means the tenth in Arabic, so the name of the dish is taken from the date it is prepared and shared. The Semitic root for ten, *ashurah,* and the fasting on the tenth day of the first month, obviously has connections with the fast of Yom Kippur, on the tenth of Tishri, the first month of the Jewish calendar. Interestingly, 'the tenth' also refers to the tithe (*öşür*, deriving again from *aşar* meaning ten), the tenth of the harvest traditionally collected as tax.

Once prepared, a dishful of *aşure* is distributed to as many neighbours, friends, and relatives as possible. Being a very popular pudding, nowadays it is widely available in local eateries, pâtisseries, and pudding shops throughout the year. It is usually described as Noah's Pudding in English-language books on Turkish cookery, because a legend attributes its origin to Noah's Ark. The dish is said to have been created with whatever stored food remained on board once the ark finally landed in the aftermath of the disastrous flood. Here, it symbolizes a new beginning. It can also be called *tatlı çorba*, meaning sweet soup, like its Armenian counterpart *anuş abur*, or *şükran çorbası*, meaning Thanksgiving soup. It is decorated with dried fruits, nuts, and pomegranate kernels, another symbol of fertility and prosperity, and perfumed with rosewater. Less often, a piece of meat is added to the pudding, and it is more like a soup, not sweet but savoury or, rarely, both sweet and savoury.

The *aşure* ritual is particularly important for the Alevi Muslims of Turkey, a community that has created a unique synthesis of different sects of Islam with older pagan traditions. As the tenth of Muharrem marks the tragedy of Kerbela, where the Prophet's grandsons were killed, it is a day of lament for the Alevis. For them, *aşure* symbolizes mourning rather than celebration, but this is a mourning that also includes joy and hope in rebirth and future. The Alevis fast for twelve days and include twelve ingredients to commemorate the twelve imams martyred at the tragedy of Kerbela. Sunnis sometimes try to bring the number of ingredients to seven or even to forty or forty-one, as these numbers are considered lucky. If there is a shortage of ingredients, a pinch of salt may even be used, or a spoon of honey is added, as bees take nectar from at least forty flowers. The Kerbela remembrance of the Shiites, in contrast, is laden with agony and mourning, so it is notable that they never prepare the otherwise essential wheat pudding of *aşure* for the occasion. As in homes, *aşure* is also prepared and distributed to visitors at *Cemevi*, the spiritual centre for Alevites, literally meaning 'house of gathering'. Some Sunni sects also distribute *aşure* on the tenth of Muharrem in soup kitchens, the most famous one being the Kadiriler Asitanesi in Istanbul.[7] As in *koliva*, *aşure* is considered sacred, and even if it goes bad, it is never thrown out as waste, but fed to birds or given back to nature, to the sea or back to mother earth.

Aşure is about sharing and it is always made in vast amounts and distributed to neighbours, friends, and relatives or even to strangers, and definitely to the poor. It signifies both death and rebirth, mourning and celebration, and stands for a new beginning and hope and, needless to say, also for fertility and prosperity. The *aşure* tradition was so important at the Ottoman court that a special carafe-like porcelain pot called *aşurelik* was used for its distribution. Court cuisine refined *aşure*, making it as smooth and white as possible by sieving the wheat to obtain a jelly-like consistency. Mary Işın gives various examples of this type, called *süzme aşure*, which literally means 'sieved'.[8] The refinement comes from extracting the starch within the wheat to achieve a smooth version. In this way, while remaining loyal to the original roots of the dessert and keeping the essential core ingredient, they were elevating it to a finer state.

Anuş Abur: Welcoming the New Year. The Armenian version of wheat berry pudding, *anuş abur* (sometimes written *anuşabur*) is an essential part of the Christmas and New Year's Eve feasts, again symbolizing a new start and hope for prosperity for the coming year. *Anuş abur* means 'sweet soup,' and has a slightly jelled consistency of soft pudding. It is almost identical to *aşure* but without pulses. Similarly to *aşure,* it is decorated with pomegranate kernels and perfumed with rosewater. As the new year is about to dawn, the dinner table is cleared and converted into the *anuş abur* table, with the pudding as the centrepiece and dried fruits, nuts, and pomegranates as decoration. Like the New Year table, no Christmas Day is complete for Armenians without *anuş abur*, whether it is celebrated on 25 December as by the Catholic Church or on 6 January as by the Orthodox Armenian Church. Actually, the period between these two dates is in a way like an *anuş abur* season, with every house preparing the pudding and exchanging it with neighbours. Like *aşure*, it is essential to share *anuş abur*.[9]

Be Merry, Around a Wheat Berry!

Golifa: Turkish Cypriot Koliva of New Year. Cypriot *golifa* is a cultural hybrid. It is actually a version of *hedik*, the tooth-wheat dish, but made for a seasonal occasion, in this case welcoming the New Year. The Cypriot Turkish term '*Golifa gibi dağıtmak*' is widely used, meaning to give away for free. It often appears in political debates: one opposition leader once accused his political rival of arranging EU passports from the Greek side for their supporters, saying they were giving away passports like *golifa* to gain votes.

Trigo Koço: Boiled Wheat Berry of Tu Bishvat. The Jewish sweetened boiled wheat, *trigo koço,* literally meaning cooked wheat, is made by Jewish communities of Thrace, Gallipoli, and the Aegean region, particularly in Izmir, for Tu Bishvat, marking the beginning of spring.[10] The boiled wheat is sweetened with sugar and mixed with ground walnuts and cinnamon, and the final sweet is almost identical with *hedik*, made for the first tooth of a baby. It can be argued that, although the name is Ladino (Judeo-Spanish), the language of Sephardic Jews, the ritual may have been a very old Anatolian tradition embraced by various cultures sharing the same geography and that over time the dish was given a Ladino name. It has to be noted that before the Sephardic Jews arrived in Anatolia, especially on the Aegean coast, there were other Jewish communities, mostly Greek-speaking Romaniot Jews, living in the region, and one of the oldest synagogues is in Sardis dating from the third century AD. *Trigo koço* is served along with dried fruits and nuts, the table is adorned with wheat and barley grains, dried figs and sultanas, dates, olives and pomegranates, and children are given small gift sacks filled with dried fruits, nuts, candy, sweets and little surprises. Tu Bishvat is also known as the festival of trees, and it is customary to plant new trees on this day. The Jews of Salonika had a very interesting tradition regarding Tu Bishvat, worth mentioning, since there are many Jews and Muslims living in Turkey who were originally from Salonika. According to Nicholas Stavroulakis, the traditional Tu-Bishvat sweet is *assuré,*[11] and he provides two recipes, one very similar to Turkish *aşure,* the other more close to Armenian *anuş abur,* but both being drier versions, actually resembling *hedik*.

Sümenek, Samani, Uğut, Uhut: Sweetness of New Life in Nevruz. Another New Year celebration where wheat plays a leading symbolic role is *Nevruz*, literally meaning 'New Day', nowadays celebrated not at the New Year but as a spring festival. Celebrated on the 21 March, on the day of spring equinox, a potent sweet paste, *sümenek,* is prepared by pounding freshly sprouted wheat and cooking it to a thick paste. Wheat grass sprouted in shallow trays, surrounded by dried fruits and nuts, is placed on tables together with dyed boiled eggs. This is a tradition observed by Turkic countries and communities with Turkic roots living in Turkey, like Azeris, Turcomans, etc., and also by the followers of the Bahai faith, who have strong Iranian cultural connections. Needless to say, sprouting wheat for Nevruz and preparing *samanak* is a robust tradition in Iran. Helen Saberi points out the Zoroastrian root of the Nevruz celebrations and mentions *samanak,* the wheat sprout sweet pudding, in Afghanistan.[12] The tradition of preparing wheat sprout *halva* survives in many regions of Turkey, not necessarily related to Nevruz and under different names such as *uhut* or *uğut*. The Ottoman court tradition of having a very potent spicy sweet paste, *Nevruziye,* for the day of Nevruz, probably has roots in the Central Asian tradition of the wheat sprout paste. The tradition survived in the Aegean city of Manisa, where it is now called *Mesir Macunu,* often marketed under the nickname Turkish Viagra for obvious reasons. Kurds consider Nevruz their most important festival day, but no tradition related to wheat is observed, possibly because Kurds were traditionally pastoralists rather than farmers.

Hedik Aşı: Spring Festival of Hıdrellez. There are cases where wheat berries are cooked together with chickpeas and beans for the spring festival of Hıdrellez on 5 May, a Muslim variation of St George's day, Orthodox Greek Aya Yorgi. When prepared for Hıdrellez, the dish is called *hedik aşı,* and is sometimes sweetened with grape molasses and spiced with cloves.

Varvara: Boiled Wheat for St Barbara. Orthodox Greeks have sugared boiled wheat for Varvara Day, St Barbara's Day to Catholics, on 4 December, and distribute it to families with small children or to unwed girls. Marianna Yerasimos records another St Barbara celebration among Anatolian Greeks, when a sweet is prepared by the village women, each bringing a different ingredient (wheat, sugar, walnuts, dried sultanas, spices, or pulses) to a junction of three roads. Yerasimos points out the similarity between St Barbara's wheat and *koliva*.[13] Likewise Anissa Helou gives a recipe remarkably similar, but obviously different in taste, for a boiled wheat dessert and explains, '*Qameh* or *qamhiyyeh* (which means wheat in Arabic) is made for the first teeth of babies as well as for Eid el-Berbara which is our halloween.'[14] Claudia Roden records a similar sweet, *belila,* made for happy events or a baby's first tooth in Syria.[15]

Shared cultures, reflections and similar practices beyond borders

Bowls of boiled wheat appear as *hedik, trigo koço, golifa, koliva, zito,* or *vareno zhito* in Muslim, Christian, and Jewish celebrations. Marie-Hélène Sauner-Leroy explains the desired dryness of wheat in *koliva* by the fear of it rotting and decaying, in contrast to *aşure* and *anuş abur,* which are soupy puddings.[16] The dryness of the wheat berry is believed to prevent decay and sustain hope in the sprouting of a new life. Whereas the wheat in the others is swelled and full of life, just as a pregnant woman ready to give birth. *Koliva* is distributed in the cemetery in paper cones; ironically, in the past, Muslim friends of the family used to take their share and convert it into *aşure*. Cypriot Turks make a similar *golifa* for New Year's Eve, more in the context of *aşure* as a symbol of a new start, and distribute it to all in the same manner.

Variations on the theme go as far as Sicily, where *Cuccìa di Santa Lucia,* a wheat berry sweet, is prepared to honour the miracle of Santa Lucia on 13 December, *Festa di Santa Lucia*. The significance of wheat on that day is attributed to the miracle of St Lucia, when ships loaded with grain suddenly appeared in the harbour after the long famine of 1582. Hunger-stricken Sicilians did not have the patience to grind the grain into flour and directly boiled it, which is why the day is celebrated with boiled wheat soups, dishes, and desserts. No Sicilian worth his salt touches bread or eats pasta on Santa Lucia's Day.[17]

One early example of *cuccìa* is a very simple boiled wheat with *vin cotto* (grape must), amazingly similar to Anatolian *hedik* sweetened with *pekmez* (grape molasses). In Calabria, Ottavio Cavalcanti records *cuccìa salata*,[18] celebratory wheat porridge with goat meat, almost identical to Anatolian *keşkek*, a tradition passed on to Italy by Albanians. Obviously, wheat berry and meat porridges spread over a vast area, from *harissa* to *haleem*, many being amazingly similar to Anatolian *keşkek*. Similarities concerning the significance of wheat continue with the tradition of offering sprouted wheat to St Mary in Easter, just like the sprouts of Nevruz, the spring rite. This last tradition can be found as far away as southern France. Sauner-Leroy points out that in Provence, also on St Barbara's day, wheat grains are soaked in water and left to sprout on wet cotton to be ready as green shoots for the Christmas table. As mentioned, sprouting wheat for Nevruz is very important in Iran, Afghanistan, and Central Asian Turkic countries and *samani* or *samanak* is the traditional sweet that gets its unusual sweetness from the high sugar content of the young shoots.

Similar dishes can also be found deep in Central Asia and China. Sweet congee eaten for the Chinese New Year and even the famous eight jewel rice pudding bear similar symbolism for New Year, expressing hopes for sustaining prosperity and good crops. The variations on all these wheat dishes and related rituals are endless, but one thing remains unchanged regardless of religion, ethnic roots, or geography: wheat stands for hope in the future and a profound belief in the renewal of the life-cycle in all communities and cultures in Anatolia and beyond.

Notes

1. Willcox, G. and M. Savard 2007, pp. 427–440.
2. Aubaile-Sallenave, Françoise 2000, pp. 105–139.
3. Roden, Claudia 1997, p. 377.
4. Salaman, Rena 1990, pp. 213–215.
5. Kaneva-Johnson, Maria 1999, pp. 208–212.
6. E-mail correspondence with Perry, 18 July 2010.
7. İşli, Necdet 2008, pp. 941–954.
8. Işın, Priscilla Mary 2008, pp. 267–272.
9. Cook book/memoir writer Takuhi Tovmasyan recalls her family exchanging the pudding for *vasilopita* with their Greek neighbours.
10. Antebi, Ester, et al. 2004, pp. 104, 113.
11. Stavroulakis, Nicholas 1986, pp. 131–133.
12. Saberi, Helen 2000, pp. 23–24.

13. Yerasimos, Marianna 2008, pp. 110–114.
14. Helou, Anissa 1994, pp. 243–244.
15. Roden, Claudia 1997, p. 494.
16. Sauner-Leroy, Marie Hélène 1987, pp. 8–9.
17. Farina, Salvatore 2009, pp. 106–112.
18. E-mail correspondence with Cavalcanti, 16 June 2010: 'Di 'cuccìa' esistono due versioni: a) una dolce, che si ottiene utilizzando prevalentemente la melassa (o miele di fichi), oppure vino cotto, zucchero, gherigli di noci, cioccolata, acini di melagranata, ma anche crema bianca di latte e ricotta. Si prepara per il 13 dicembre, festa di S. Lucia, nel calendario cattolico, ed è presente in diverse regioni italiane, soprattutto meridionali, come Basilicata, Calabria, Campania e Sicilia; b) una salata. La seconda presenta diverse varianti. È, infatti, pietanza di carne di capra e maiale con grano; ma anche minestra di farinacei e legumi. Un'ultima preparazione vuole la presenza di grano, messo a bagno e fritto con cipolle, olio di oliva e sale.Il complesso rituale esaminato, rientra nell'ambito delle feste per il raccolto del grano ed è di lontanissima origine precristiana, richiamandosi al mondo greco-romano e alla sua cultura.'

Bibliography

Antebi, Ester, Sara Enriquez, Lina Eskinazi, Nüket Franco, Ora K. Gürkan, V. Jinet Sidi Sarfati 2004. *Kaybolan ve Yaşayan 100 tarifiyle İzmir Sefarad Mutfağı* [Izmir Sephardic Cuisine – 100 Lost and Surviving Recipes]. ed. Nedim Atilla, İzmir,.

Aubaile-Sallenave, Françoise 2000. 'Al-Kishk: the past and present of a complex culinary practice', in Sami Zubaida and Richard Tapper (eds.), *A Taste of Thyme-Culinary Cultures of the Middle East,* Tauris Parke.

Bozis, Sula 2000. *İstanbul Lezzeti /İstanbullu Rumların Mutfak Kültürü*. İstanbul: Tarih Vakfı Yurt Yayınları.

Eksen, İlhan 2001. *Çok Kültürlü İstanbul Mutfağı*. Istanbul: Everest.

Farina, Salvatore 2009, *Dolcezze di Sicilia-Storia e Tradizioni della Pasticceria Siciliana.* Edizioni Lussografica.

Helou, Anissa Helou 1994. *Lebanese Cuisine,* Grub Street.

Işın, Priscilla Mary 2008. *Gülbeşeker-Türk Tatlıları Tarihi*.Istanbul: YKY, 2008.

İşli, Necdet 2008. 'Kadirihane'de Aşure', in *Yemek Kitabı I*, ed. Sabri Koz, 3rd edn., Istanbul.

Kaneva-Johnson, Maria 1999. *The Melting Pot Balkan Food and Cookery,* Totnes: Prospect Books.

Roden, Claudia 1997. *The Book of Jewish Food – An Oddyssey from Samarkand and Vilna to the Present Day.* London: Viking.

Saberi, Helen 2000. *Afghan Food & Cookery*. Totnes: Prospect Books.

Salaman, Rena 1990. 'Wheat, Staple Food for the Dead', in Harlan Walker ed., *Staple Foods. Proceedings of the Oxford Symposium on Food and Cookery 1989.* Totnes: Prospect Books.

Sauner-Leroy, Marie Hélène 1987. 'Türk Aşuresi, Ermeni Anuşaburu ve Rum kolivası: Yaş mı, Kuru mu?', *Tarih ve Toplum*, 20 April.

Stavroulakis, Nicholas 1986. *Cookbook of the Jews of Greece*. Athens: Lycabettus Press.

Tan, Aylin Öney. 'Aşure'nin Halleri', *Cumhuriyet*, 29 February 2004; 'Buğdayın Dirilişi', *Cumhuriyet*, 20 February 2005; 'Nurlu Azize', *Cumhuriyet*, 11 December 2005; 'Hayat Aşı', *Cumhuriyet*, 04 February 2007.

Tovmasyan, Takuhi 2004. *Sofranız Şen Olsun*. Aras Yayıncılık.

Üçer, Müjgân 2006. *Anamın Aşı Tandırın Başı-Sivas Mutfağı*. Istanbul: Kitabevi.

Willcox, G. and M. Savard 2007. 'Güneydoğu Anadolu'da Tarımın Benimsenmesine İlişkin Botanik Veriler'. in M. Özdoğan and N. Başgelen (eds.) *Anadolu'da Uygarlığın Doğuşu ve Avrupa'ya Yayılımı-Türkiye'de Neolitik Dönem – Yeni Kazılar, Yeni Bulgular*. Istanbul: Arkeoloji ve Sanat Yayınları.

Yerasimos, Marianna 2008. 'Ölümle İlgili Törensel Bir Yiyecek: Koliva', *Yemek ve Kültür*, 13, Istanbul.

The Rise of Taste and the Rhetoric of Celebration

Viktoria von Hoffmann

When considering the word 'celebration', defined by the *Oxford English Dictionary* as 'the action of celebrating an important day or event', the first idea that comes to mind is usually the ritual of a feast taking the form of a celebratory moment, such as an extraordinary meal. However, if one considers the word 'celebration' as referring to the general act of celebrating, it can then suggest a range of other possible interpretations.

In this paper, I would like to explore another possible meaning of the idea of celebration. Rather than studying celebratory events, I propose to analyse the celebratory dimension of discourses. Discourses, as well as specific events that frequently occur outside everyday life, can also reveal peculiar strategies of celebrations, informing us about the representations and cultural identities of a given society. Of course, in this case the decorum of celebration is different – words being used instead of material objects – but the purpose can sometimes be very much the same. What people choose to celebrate through discourses – in this case, the written discourses of early modern history – indicates a lot of how they think about the world. What is considered important enough to be celebrated in a literary way? Which rhetorical shifts can be observed? When analysing discourses, one must indeed pay special attention to the movement of words and rhetoric, permanencies and ruptures within discourses and ideas, stereotypes appearing or disappearing, since these often reveal larger social and cultural changes, as well as provoking them.

I would like to illustrate the celebratory dimension of discourses using the example of the history of taste. We know that celebrations seem to be closely connected to food and eating, hence also to taste and identities. This paper will however not really be about food nor about meals, but about taste and its relations to the other senses. The history of taste appears to be an interesting case study, since it shows an evolution of the rhetoric used to qualify this sense. There is a progression from the silences regarding a lower animal and corporal sense, to celebratory discourses that appear in the seventeenth and eighteenth centuries, leading on to the invention of gastronomic literature.[1] Discourses on taste have a history of their own, closely linked to food history of course, but not limited to this field alone. When being understood as the history of a sense, the study of taste goes far beyond the history of food practices, to which it is most often confined.[2]

The cultural construction of the senses is always accompanied by a set of discourses, the later testifying to, as much as elaborating on, the former. To understand the position of taste within representations of early modern times, one needs to go back to antiquity and consider the traditional hierarchy of the senses. This classified all five senses from the lowest (touch and taste) to the higher ones (hearing and sight), with smell being in

The Rise of Taste and the Rhetoric of Celebration

the middle of these two pairs. This structure also designated each as senses of contact and of distance. The highest position of sight within the hierarchy of senses was obvious and unquestioned for centuries. The superiority of sight was justified and reinforced by a repeated celebrative rhetoric. 'Sight is the most noble of all senses',[3] and the eye was considered the most beautiful organ of all. This sentiment was repeated for centuries by scholars. Descriptions of the 'Beauty of the Eye' and the higher value of sight over the other senses took place within a rhetoric of celebration, which revealed and also constructed the domination of visuality within European cultures.

If the celebrative dimension of discourses on sight is clear, the same cannot be said for those on taste. Taste hasn't always been considered in the very positive way it is today. For a long time, taste, placed between touch and smell, was located toward the bottom of the traditional hierarchy, and was closely linked to gluttony. Taste was therefore considered a lower and despicable animal sense, that appeared to be more material, more corporeal than the higher senses, such as sight and hearing.[4] The baser senses revealed the animal in human beings, which men of the *ancien régime* tried so hard to hide by developing manners and civility, thought to distinguish men from beasts, but also the élite from less educated people. At that time, taste appears to have been the least noble sense of all. As a result, it has not been a topic of scholarly debate. In most *traités des sens* – treatises on the senses – from the early modern period, the longest chapters are the ones related to sight and hearing. These were considered as more noble in the traditional system of naturalism as they were thought to be more valuable bearers of knowledge and more closely connected to the divine and spiritual aspects of humanity. The discrimination is plain for all to see: these works sometimes contain two hundred pages on sight, but only five on taste. Scholars working on the five senses usually considered sight and hearing more worthy of interest. For a long time, taste seems to be left aside, always on the periphery of discourses. One can find small details, sometimes a few sentences about it, rarely a whole book on a subject that appears to be insignificant. It's as if there's nothing to say on that subject, taste being a pure physical sense, only destined to help us fulfil a corporal act essential for survival: feeding.

As a consequence, discourses on taste were at first rather negative, revealing all the dangers and disorders that could be caused or provoked by this corporal sense. Moreover, not only were discourses on taste not always celebrative, but for a long time they hardly existed. The silence on this topic was a sign of the disqualification of a sense perceived as too animal or too material to be considered positively or of interest to scholars and members of educated society. There are no specific discourses on taste – meaning related to this sense alone – to be found before the seventeenth century. During the classical period, books of manners indicated clearly that it was very rude to testify to one's personal preferences at table and that was unacceptable to talk about taste in society. As Antoine de Courtin explains it, 'constantly speaking of grub is an obvious mark of a sensual soul & of lower education'.[5] The nineteenth century, in contrast, witnessed the

The Rise of Taste and the Rhetoric of Celebration

rise of specific celebrative discourses on taste in gastronomical literature. The invention of this new literary genre was linked to a specific cultural context in which taste had become an important subject of concern.

But the emergence of positive discourses on taste took centuries. In the French cultural arena, the first real celebrative accounts are found during the seventeenth and eighteenth centuries. Unsurprisingly, they are in cookbooks, which were intimately linked to the universe of taste and *cuisine*. What's interesting, though, is that these discourses appear for the first time in a totally new generation of recipe books. This period witnessed the progressive development of a new modern way of cooking, leaving behind the culinary habits of the Middle Ages.[6] For instance, cooks tended to use a smaller amount of spices, suggest buttery sauces, grill meat – these techniques supposedly respected and revealed what cooks then called '*le vray goust*'[7] (the real authentic taste) of each ingredient.

The first new cookbook demonstrating these changes was *Le Cuisinier François*, published by La Varenne in 1651, after almost a century without any novelty in this area of publishing.[8] Not only did it show a new way of cooking, but it also revealed a new way of writing about *cuisine*. A totally new genre of recipe book was born. For a long time, cookbooks had been brief. Written by professional cooks and addressed to other professional cooks, they went straight to the point and lacked unnecessary details. Cookbooks printed after 1651 were totally different. They were more precise and also better organized, because the readership had changed and extended. One of the major innovations was the preface, in which cooks, after being silent for centuries, began to write a few pages about their own way of thinking about taste and *cuisine*. These introductions can be considered as the first real celebrative discourses on taste, preceding the invention of gastronomic literature in the nineteenth century. They testify to the emergence of a new modern way of cooking and writing about *cuisine*, of which the authors' contemporaries were very well aware.

The new recipe books printed after La Varenne started to offer small discourses on taste and *cuisine* within their introductions. At first limited to a few discrete comments by the cook himself, they became more and more elaborate in the eighteenth century. In the late 1730s *Nouvelle Cuisine* arose, which claimed to be better, both for health and taste, and more sophisticated than the cooking practices of the mid-seventeenth century. Lightness and simplicity of dishes were the recurrent themes of this new way of cooking, which was presented as closely linked to modernity. Some novelties can indeed be observed in food practices at this time, such as the importance given to *coulis, bouillons,* and other *quintessences*, supposedly concentrating the essences of foods. But the changes observed in cooking practices are far less significant than the ones that occurred during the previous century. The major development of the late 1730s was located in discourses. New cookbooks are printed, such as for instance *Les Dons de Comus*, attributed to François Marin, or *La science du maître d'hôtel cuisinier*, supposedly written by Menon.[9] This new generation of recipe books had a totally different style.

The Rise of Taste and the Rhetoric of Celebration

There was a material difference that distinguishes them from the ones published in the seventeenth century: they were bigger, often consisting of several volumes, and they also contained illustrations, which was something new. Moreover, the prefaces had changed dramatically. The preliminary pages now occupied much more space and took the shape of real celebrative discourses on taste, which will later influence the birth of gastronomic literature. No longer written by cooks, the prefaces were undertaken by professional writers or intellectuals who were not themselves culinary professionals.[10] Under these erudite pens, these introductions took on the form of serious historical and philosophical dissertations on food, taste and cooking, some of them more than fifty pages long. These discourses, written by scholars, were even more celebrative than hitherto, presenting taste and *cuisine* as much as an art [11] as a science,[12] and seeking to prove the superiority of the moderns to the ancients. The former, they claimed, were more refined and more informed about taste.

The claim of *cuisine* to be considered as an art was something new that couldn't have been seriously considered two centuries earlier, as we see when Montaigne laughed about the supposed '*science de gueule*' [13] (science of the mouth) of arrogant cooks. Now, culinary art dared to compare itself to painting [14] or music.[15] Taste had the audacity to measure itself against sight or hearing, which blurred the traditional categories of the hierarchy of senses. But new values don't necessarily always remove more ancient concepts. The history of taste is the history of a very slow evolution, of new representations that coexist with earlier ideas. Contradictions were inevitable: polemics as well. One can see for instance that the audacious claims of the advocates of *Nouvelle Cuisine* would lead to gastronomical disputes, one of the numerous forms of the general battle between the Ancients and the Moderns at this time. Discourses on taste were not always celebrative, but even negative discourses tended to reveal the new position and status of taste.

This new celebration of taste wasn't restricted to the culinary field but was linked to the more general rise of Taste at the end of early modern times. New discourses on taste can be found in many different kinds of sources, not just in recipe books.

One of the turning-points in this history is the invention of a figurative sense for the word 'taste' that can be seen developing from about the middle of the seventeenth century. Until then, the term 'taste' was only used to describe the physical process of distinguishing the flavors of food. But during the seventeenth century, intellectuals started to use this word more and more frequently as a metaphor, inventing an entirely new non-material sense. This new use became increasingly popular, inspiring writers and scholars who published a large number of books on the subject to explain where the new figurative sense of the word came from and why it seemed particularly useful to describe an immaterial reality. At the same time, many metaphors of the word appeared in different contexts: we can find 'taste of god' in mystical writings,[16] '*bon gout de l'honnête homme*' so intimately linked to the *beau monde*, and the aesthetic taste, chosen to refer to the judgment of Art and Beauty during the eighteenth century. At

The Rise of Taste and the Rhetoric of Celebration

first one might think that these very different metaphors have nothing in common with each other. But a more thorough analysis of the sources (mystical texts, taste treatises, aesthetics, etc.) demonstrates that these concepts were more closely related than one might have thought. Together, they testify to the emergence of a spiritual taste, a sort of taste of the mind that was now not only grounded in the body, but which also required the intelligence. It's also the invention of a proper human taste linked to interiority and separated from the earlier animal sense. Only once this had been accepted did taste start started to interest scholars. Books were published on the subject; intellectual debates on the topic involved the most famous minds of the times, such as Voltaire, Montesquieu, Diderot, David Hume and even Emmanuel Kant. This metaphor, that is so obvious to us today, was a novelty for readers of these earlier periods and authors had often to explain to them whence it came. In their texts, they tried to show how closely allied were physical and intellectual taste, even if the former was still considered inferior. Most of any ensuing book would then be devoted to the taste of the mind.

As a result, this celebration of taste can be observed within the *beau monde*. If it was considered rude to talk about food during the seventeenth century, in the eighteenth century, on the contrary, educated people didn't hesitate to talk about the pleasures of eating. Some of them, like the Regent Philippe, Duke of Orléans, even tried to cook themselves. Many philosophers, like Voltaire, became real gourmets, caring about the quality of their table. They provided philosophical dinners, where the pleasures of the tongue were as important as the joys of the mind and good conversation, developing an ideal of conviviality, that was, however, reserved for an élite of men of taste – this combined taste of the body with taste of the mind.[17] It is clear that this new understanding of taste fits perfectly with the new aesthetic of life that appeared during the Enlightenment, when the issue of happiness and the pleasure of living on earth took on a totally new importance.

As soon as taste ceased to designate only a corporeal sense and became associated with a form of human interiority, this inferior sense was seen as far more positive and valuable. After being largely ignored, taste enters the social stage and begins to interest intellectuals and people of the *beau monde*. The birth of this figurative taste is interesting because such choices of words and expressions are often signs of new ways of thinking about the world. This is clearly the case for taste.

What's interesting is that, in order to make taste more noble, a rhetoric was constructed using various kinds of discourses which together, despite their many differences, celebrated taste. For a long time it had been limited to the culinary field, but now, during the seventeenth and eighteenth centuries, taste was progressively inscribed within a broader cultural register. This involved the deployment of a celebrative rhetoric, which demonstrated the new position of taste on the social stage. Discourses cannot be considered only as vehicles of representations or ways of expression, but must be seen also as actors: not only witnesses but also agents of a new cultural dispensation. Celebrative discourses hence need to be seen as performative.

The Rise of Taste and the Rhetoric of Celebration

During the eighteenth century, celebrative discourses on taste, at first restricted to the culinary field, were found in a much broader set of discourses discussing, for instance, aesthetics, as well as physics, medicine and chemistry. The scholarly introductions to cookbooks explaining the *Nouvelle Cuisine* reveal this new general interest in taste, as they refer to books in these other intellectual fields. Foncemagne, for instance, mentions the *Traité des alimens* (1702) of Lemery, recommending it to cooks who want to know more about all properties of foods.[18] He was also very much aware of contemporary debates in aesthetics, as he shows in his references to Francis Hutcheson, Bayle, Crousaz, Du Bos, Lévesque de Pouilly and many others.[19] In the same fashion, Meusnier de Querlon announced the forthcoming publication of a 'New essay on human understanding', demonstrating that 'food is the source and unique origin of ideas and thoughts', which was an obvious allusion to John Locke, though it was expressed in a rather ironic way.[20] Thus, these intellectual discourses published within cookbooks use a range of wide general knowledge to reinforce their arguments. One can find many allusions to contemporary aesthetics, chemistry, and philosophy. Even though published in a recipe book, the question of taste, as an art and a science, was no longer restricted to the culinary field. Increasingly, contemporary works on medicine, philosophy, and aesthetics mentioned taste and cuisine in books that were not about cuisine. It was a general cultural system of representations of taste that can be seen when one compares these very different kinds of sources that, together, reveal the new position of taste, established through a celebrative set of discourses.

In conclusion, the example of the history of taste shows that discourses, as much as social events, can be considered as very powerful vehicles of celebrations. Celebrations of taste can be expressed through banquets as well as through culinary discourses. Just as the celebratory meals themselves, discourses on taste and cuisine seek to demonstrate something about social and cultural identities. The example of the introductions of French recipe books published in the seventeenth and even more in the eighteenth centuries shows that cookbooks can also be read as celebrative rituals, revealing a specific and modern rhetoric of celebration of taste. Taste is an interesting example because its history starts with silences about an inferior sense that progressively develop into very positive discourses celebrating a new sensorial modality at the meeting of body and mind. Taste is then considered important by scholars. Its articulation becomes a distinctive mark of high society consisting of men of taste with a delicate judgment in the matter, who know not only what and how to eat, but also how to talk about taste and cuisine. This celebration of taste is also a celebration of the modernity of cooking and thus of those who can follow it, and as such also a form of aesthetics of life. Celebrative discourses, just like celebratory events, tend to bring people together and demonstrate and reinforce the identity of a group, in this case that of highly educated members of eighteenth-century French fashionable society.

The Rise of Taste and the Rhetoric of Celebration

Notes

1. von Hoffmann, V. 2010: *Goûter le monde. Pour une histoire culturelle du goût aux Temps modernes* (Thèse en Histoire, Art et Archéologie, unpublished, University of Liège).
2. Sensory studies are a very prolific research field. Among others: Howes, D. (ed.). 2005: *Empire of the Senses. The sensual culture reader* (Oxford-New York, Berg [Sensory Formations Series]); Korsmeyer, C. 1999: *Making Sense of Taste: Food and Philosophy* (Ithaca–London, Cornell University Press); Havelange, C. 1998: *De l'œil et du monde. Une histoire du regard au seuil de la modernité* (Paris, Fayard).
3. « Que la veuë est le plus noble de tous les sens ». Du Laurens, A. 1598, 43: *Discours de la conservation de la veuë : Des maladies melancholiques : des catarrhes : & de la vieillesse, Reveus de nouveau & augmentez de plusieurs chapitres* (s. l., Théodore Samson). All translations of sources are mine.
4. « (…) l'homme est composé de deux parties, du corps & de l'âme : La veuë & l'ouye servent plus à l'ame qu'au corps, le goust & l'attouchement servent plus au corps qu'à l'ame : l'odorat sert à tous les deux également ». [(…) the human being is composed of two parts, body & soul: Sight & hearing are more useful to the soul than to the body, taste and touch are more useful to the body than to the soul: smell serves both]. Du Laurens, A. (1598, 36).
5. « (…) parler sans cesse de mangeailles, c'est une marque évidente d'une ame sensuelle, & d'une éducation basse ». [de Courtin, A.] 1728 [1st ed. 1671], 176: *Nouveau traité de la civilité Qui se pratique en France parmi les honnêtes-gens. Nouvelle édition revuë, corrigée, & de beaucoup augmentée par l'Auteur* (Paris, Josse, L. and Robustel, Ch.).
6. Albala, K. 2003: *Food in Early Modern Europe* (Westport, Greenwood Press); Ferguson, P. 2004: *Accounting for Taste. The Triumph of French Cuisine* (Chicago-Londres, University of Chicago Press); Fink, B. 1995: *Les liaisons savoureuses. Réflexions et pratiques culinaires au dix-huitième Siècle* (Saint-Etienne, Publications de l'Université de Saint-Etienne); Flandrin, J.-L. and Montanari, M. (ed.). 1996: *Histoire de l'alimentation* (Paris, Fayard); Wheaton, B.K. 1983: *Savoring the Past: The French Kitchen and Table from 1300 to 1789* (New York, Touchstone); Pinkard, S. 2009: *A Revolution in Taste. The rise of French cuisine, 1650–1800* (Cambridge, Cambridge University Press).
7. [Bonnefons, N. de]. 1655, [209]: *Les Delices de la Campagne. Suitte du Jardinier françois, ou* (sic) *est enseigné a preparer pour l'usage de la vie, tout ce qui croît sur Terre & dans les Eaux* (Amsteldan (sic), Raphael Smith).
8. La Varenne, P.-F. de. 1651: *Le Cuisinier françois, enseignant la manière de bien apprester & assaisonner toutes sortes de Viandes grasses & maigres, Legumes, Patisseries, & autres mets qui se seruent tant sur les Tables des Grands que des particuliers. Par le Sieur de LA VARENNE Escuyer de Cuisine de Monsieur le Marquis d'Uxelles* (Paris, David, P.).
9. [Marin, F.] 1739: *Les Dons de Comus ou Les délices de la table. Ouvrage non seulement utile aux officiers de bouche pour ce qui concerne leur art, mais principalement à l'usage des personnes qui sont curieuses de savoir donner à manger, et d'être servies délicatement, tant en gras qu'en maigre, suivant les saisons, et dans le goût le plus nouveau* (Paris, Prault Fils); [Menon], 1749: *La Science du Maître d'Hôtel Cuisinier, avec des Observations sur la connoissance & propriétés des Alimens* (Paris, Paulus-du-Mesnil).
10. For instance, Etienne-Laureault de Foncemagne, member of the Académie française, is said to be the author of a 'Dissertation préliminaire sur la cuisine moderne', used as a preface to the cookbook of [Menon], 1749. The prefaces of the first editions of *Les Dons de Comus* (1739, 1742, 1750) are attributed to the journalist Anne-Gabriel Meusnier de Querlon. The longer introductions published within later editions are attributed by food historians to Pierre Brumoy and Guillaume-Hyacinthe Bougeant, two Jesuits.
11. [Marin F.] 1739, 30.
12. Idem, 29.
13. Montaigne. 1727 [1st ed. 1580], t.1, 609: *Essais* (La Haye, Gosse, P. & Neaulme, J.).
14. « On ne s'est peut-être jamais avisé de chercher du rapport entre deux objets aussi éloignés que paroissent l'être l'art de la Peinture & de la Cuisine. Mais sauf la hardiesse de la comparaison, & à l'irrévérance près, je n'ai point trouvé d'image plus propre à rendre mes idées sensibles. L'union & la

rupture des couleurs qui font la beauté du coloris, représentent assez bien, ce me semble, ce mélange de sucs & d'ingrédiens dont le Cuisinier compose ses ragoûts. Il faut que ces ingrédiens & ces sucs soient noyés & fondus de la même manière que le Peintre fond ses couleurs, & que la même harmonie, qui dans un tableau frappe les yeux des connoisseurs, se fasse sentir aux palais fins dans le goût d'une sauce ». [One may have never tried to find a link between two objects as far from each other as the art of Painting & of Cooking seem to be. But besides the audacity of the comparison & if I may say so, I haven't found any better image to show my ideas. The union and the rupture of colors that makes the beauty of colour, represent pretty well, as I tend to think, this mixture of juices & ingredients of which the Cook composes his ragouts. These ingredients & these juices need to be blend & melt the same way as the Painter blends his colors, & the same harmony, that in a painting strikes the eyes of connoisseurs, needs to be felt by delicate palates in the taste of a sauce.] [Marin, F.]. 1758, t. 1, xxij–xxiij: *Les Dons de Comus, ou l'art de la cuisine, réduit en pratique* (Paris, Pissot).

15. « (…) il peut donc y avoir une Musique pour la langue & pour le palais, comme il y en a une pour les oreilles » [(…) there can thus be a Music for the tongue & for the palate, as well as there is one for the ears]. Poncelet, P. 1766, xviij–xx: 'Dissertation préliminaire sur la salubrité des Liqueurs, & l'harmonie des saveurs', in [Poncelet, P.], *Chymie du gout et de l'odorat, ou principes pour composer facilement, & à peu de frais, les Liqueurs à boire, & les Eaux de senteurs* (Paris, Pissot).

16. As, for instance, in Thérèse d'Avila or Jean de la Croix.

17. Mervaud, C. 1998: *Voltaire à table. Plaisir du corps, plaisir de l'esprit* (Paris, Ed. Desjonquères).

18. Lemery, L. 1705: *Traité des alimens, où l'on trouve par ordre, et separement, La difference & le choix qu'on doit faire de chacun d'eux en particulier ; les bons & les mauvais effets qu'ils peuvent produire ; les principes en quoi ils abondent ; le temps, l'âge & le temperament où ils conviennent* (Paris, Witte, P.). [Menon], 1749, xxv.

19. He mentions for instance the book of Hutcheson entitled *An inquiry into the original of our ideas of beauty and virue* (1725), that had just been translated in 1749 [*Recherches sur l'origine des idées*].

20. « (…) essay nouveau sur l'Entendement humain » démontrant « d'une façon nouvelle & Métaphysico-géométrique, que la diversité de nos opinions ne vient que de la différence de nos nourritures, & qu'en un mot nos alimens sont la source & l'unique origine de nos idées & de nos pensées, par où on peut juger de quelle importance l'Art de la Cuisine est dans un Etat, puisque la santé & la façon de penser des Sociétés en dépendent ». [Meusnier de Querlon, A.-G.] 1981, 36: 'Apologie des Modernes ou Reponse du Cuisinier françois auteur des Dons de Comus, à un patissier anglois', in Mennell, S., *Lettre d'un pâtissier anglais, et autres contributions à une polémique gastronomique du XVIII*e *siècle* (Exeter, University of Exeter).

Celebrations and the Torrid Pleasures of an Ice-Cream and Sorbet Tree in Rome in August 1714

Robin Weir

Ice or compacted snow was used for centuries to chill food and drink, but it was not until the discovery in the mid-seventeenth century of the endothermic effect of salt on ice that ice-creams and sorbets were made and enjoyed, first as an aristocratic delicacy and later as a popular treat. This paper outlines some of the ways in which the trickle-down of ices brought pleasure to the many and the few, concentrating on one of many festive events of which descriptions survive. The talk emphasizes the hands-on skills required to construct elaborate ice-cream constructions. Demonstrations of techniques and a display of some of the different kinds of moulds used in the past and today contribute to a painstaking reproduction of just part of the amazing 'ice-cream tree' which was the star of the celebratory events in 1714. This paper delivers information about two events in Rome in that year, in August and November, when ices were served in the context of a prestigious celebration of an imperial birthday; we give a summary of the document describing the events, providing the relevant information about the ice-creams and their production, but leaving out some of the rather long-winded accounts of the entertainments on offer. The talk and presentation offer additional information about the hard craft involved in all this, a glimpse of the hopefully not too deliquescent 'ice-cream tree' and some hands-on demonstrations of its construction.

In *Harvest of the Cold Months*, Elizabeth David pointed out that 'once given the successful breakthrough in the technique of creating ice, no part of the saga is more striking than the dazzlingly simple idea of the man, whoever he was, who thought of applying the technique of metal-casting to the production of ice bowls, drinking goblets, and fruit dishes.,

The development of moulds in silver, copper and pewter, shaped in a variety of increasingly complex shapes, probably peaked in late nineteenth-century America with a multiple hinged mould in 20 pieces of the Statue of Liberty containing 17 litres (4 ½ US gallons) of ice-cream. Such moulds were a result of the popularity of ice-cream as décor.

Thus an old technology and a new one were harnessed in the service of the great baroque tradition of complex food and table settings, with their ornate silver and gold tableware, sugar and butter sculpture, and *trionfi*, jellies, and elaborate pastry work, and moulded foods from blancmanges to mousses and pâtés. Descriptions of important events made much of all this expensive pomp, and we gain a lot of information from this indefatigable listing of entertainments, décor, food and drink. Ices and their

Torrid Pleasures of an Ice-Cream and Sorbet Tree in Rome

presentation were edible art of a hugely ephemeral kind, fraught with possible pitfalls for both producers and consumers. The logistics of keeping moulded ices cold and solid in temperatures of 70 degrees or more, in a typical Roman summer, are not explained in surviving documents. We can assume that the ice houses and ice pits that were in use since Roman times all over Italy provided sufficient amounts of ice and compacted snow to keep the great cooling basins full and overflowing, as the cacophony of shapes, sizes, and flavours were stashed up ready to display and then serve.

This paper is based on a contemporary account of a celebration in Rome in 1714 to welcome a visit from the Empress Elisabetta Cristina:

> Relazioni della sontuosa Festa celebrata nel felicissimo giorno Natalizio della Sacra Cesarea Real Cattolica Maestà d'Elisabetta Cristina Imperadrice nel giorno Festivo de Glorioso Nome della Sacra Cesarea Real Cattolica Maestà di Carlo Sesto Imperadore e terzo re cattolico dall' Illustrissimo ed Eccellentisimo Signor Conte Giovanni Vincislao di Galasso Ambasciador Cesareocattolico in Roma.

The background to all this is political: the Treaty of Utrecht of 1713 ended the War of the Spanish Succession, curbing the expansionist ambitions of France, and keeping Austria, Spain, and France from ganging up together to nibble away at the rest of Europe. Spanish possessions in Italy passed to Austria, the Duchy of Milan, the Kingdom of the Two Sicilies (Naples and Sicily), and other areas. One should not perhaps read too much into the fact that the organizers of the festivities were Austrian, English, and a

Torrid Pleasures of an Ice-Cream and Sorbet Tree in Rome

Roman. No hint of French or Spanish input. Was this also reflected in the menu? The offering of these two magnificent festivities by the Austrian Ambassador comes then as no surprise; he wanted to be known and loved, and what better place to make his mark than Rome?

The somewhat long-winded account of the event is too lengthy to transcribe here, so we quote relevant information from it. It is significant that the organizer of these events drew on *bottiglieri* from the noble households of Rome; there is no mention of the professional ice-cream makers who had Latini worried in Naples.

Trying to link the descriptions with the engravings is tricky, since the engraver may have simplified things. God rot his cotton socks. The long table is the illustration of the refreshments for the firework display.

An account of the sumptuous celebration for the most joyful birthday of Her Sacred Catholic Majesty the Holy Roman Empress Elisabetta Cristina, on the day of the feast of His Sacred Majesty Charles VI Emperor and Catholic Sovereign, offered by the most Excellent and Illustrious Lord, Count Giovanni Vincislao of Galasso, Catholic Ambassador in Rome

The events took place in Rome on 28 August and 4 November 1714. The text describes the setting and the music in some detail. What follows is a translation and summary of the parts that describe the refreshments.

At the second hour after sunset the gentlemen and pages of his Excellency distributed beautifully printed sheets of the evening's entertainment to all the guests ... and the concert began.... Meanwhile Signor Domenico Tosi, Steward of the Count and of the foreigners [the Emperor's retinue] in the palace, had prepared the first *gran rifresco*, to be distributed half way through the entertainment. From the early morning until evening sixty-five *bottiglieri* [wine stewards, or rather perhaps still-room staff] from the noble households of Rome, together with their assistants, had been working in the palace garden, there being nowhere else to go, sheltered from the sun by a large awning, preparing the *acque agghiacciate* [chilled drinks] of more kinds than their skills had ever provided before. The second musical chorus of the evening came to an end, to universal applause, and the gentlemen and pages of his Excellency began to hand out refreshments in regular order to the nobility in the loggia and within the palace. At the same time four gentlemen, preceded by hussars followed by one hundred persons with covered dishes containing large *giare* [ice-cream containers] distributed the rest of the refreshment to all the people sitting in their carriages [onlookers allowed into the limited space]. The refinement and fine flavour of the *ghiacciati liquori* [iced water or ices] and the abundant quantity can be deduced from the number of *Officiali*, hard at work all day without a break, and the skilled organization of Signor Domenico Tosi, worthy of the generosity of his

Torrid Pleasures of an Ice-Cream and Sorbet Tree in Rome

Excellency the Count, who during this time circulated with great benevolence from one side to the other of the Great Loggia, greeting the Ladies and Cardinals whom he had honoured with an invitation, and showing them the particular inventiveness with which he had embellished his dwelling.

When the first refreshments were over, the rest of the evening's entertainment proceeded with music from the second Choir, while in the huge hall that faced onto the piazza to the left of the Sala, lit by four great crystal candelabras, and with torches upon silver triangles set on silver columns, was the second service of refreshments, laid out on five tables, as can be seen in the illustration. The inconceivable artistry of the sugar work, the preparation of fruits, and the freezing of the juices of the same, set solid in moulds with the power of snow, with the colours of all apples; a profusion of everything was displayed in neat order for the delight of the guests. There was an enormous *trionfo* placed in the middle of the central table, which with its four *cartelloni* and foliage, extended as far as each corner. In each of the four centrepieces was a niche in which could be seen four conch shells made of Japanese porcelain full of pyramids of choice iced fruit, and on another similar shell in the middle, raised up on a pyramid [perhaps a structure of tiered dishes] of Bohemian crystal, was a vast profusion of sweetmeats, pastes, jellies, jams, biscuits, candied citron and oranges, and every kind of candied fruits and flowers. There were eight similar, but smaller, *alzate* to the sides of the larger ones, with as many smaller vases of the same porcelain, each containing four fresh citrons with a pretty posy of flowers. Two cornucopias emerged from each side of the centrepieces, with as many porcelain platters, which bore pyramids of *sorbetto* of peaches, *pappina*, fresh almonds, citrons, which had enclosed within them the same fruits in syrup. The volutes of the first order or level supported two basins of the same porcelain, on one of these was a little pyramid of *botiro ghiacciato*, and on the other a pyramid of *frutti gelati*. [Could this be a little pyramid of chilled butter, or a buttery custard ice? Fruit juice frozen in moulds and piled in a pyramid?] The porcelain on the second level had on each side a pyramid in the middle, made of a verjuice jelly flavoured with jasmine, with whole sour green grapes in syrup inside it; and on the two sides two small pyramids of *crema* [custard ice] with citron marmalade. Those on the third level had in the middle a pyramid of raspberries with the same fruit in syrup, and some made of jelly, and at each side two *formagetti di crema* [custard ices made in moulds]. A beautiful vase sculpted from ice the colour of alabaster, two and a half *palmi* [a *palmi* in Rome in 1714 measured 22.8cm/9 inches] high, was on a base in the middle of the *gran Trionfo*, and from it emerged a counterfeit green tree, from whose branches hung one hundred and fifty *frutti gelati*. [This improbable tree was partially reconstructed for the Symposium, and displayed together with a selection of the moulds and equipment used.] Six *palmi* away from the main *trionfo* were the four central tables that surrounded it. Each table

Torrid Pleasures of an Ice-Cream and Sorbet Tree in Rome

had in the centre, as is customary, a large gilt and inlaid filigree basket, from which emerged a good hundred Bohemian crystal glasses filled with perfect comfits and fresh candied citron. Four lesser baskets of various shapes, had at either side two saucers of whipped cream, and *spuma di cioccolate* [whipped chocolate], were placed at the four sides of the big basket, near to whose lower and upper sides were placed two stemmed dishes with crystal saucers full of little biscuits and *formagetti di ghiaccio framezzati di ciocolate* [little moulded custard ices mixed with bits of chocolate], and *latte alla portoghese gelato in pezzi* [milk in the Portuguese manner, with eggs, frozen in moulds]. Between these saucers there was another *conca*, basin, of the same porcelain, with pyramids of *pappina* and full of *frutta di gelo* [moulded fruit ices]. Then the *vani* [edges?] of the tables were covered with gilt bowls with the thinnest napkins, silk handkerchiefs, little gold spoons and forks, and knives. Everything, in short, was in such refined and delicate taste, to please the palate and the eye, that the ladies were equally surprised and delighted. When the pleasing concert was finished, the Nobility were ushered into the room where this second *rinfresco* was laid out, and circulated freely among the tables, sampling and admiring the artifice, the delicacy and the splendour. [The rest of the account deals with games of cards, more music, and praises for the splendour of everything.]

An account of the fireworks display on 4 November 1714

It has been a long time since Rome endured such a rainy autumn as the present year, so much so that as the Feast of San Carlo Borromeo approached, the same day as the birthday of the most glorious Emperor [of Austria], it was greatly feared that the preparations ordered by His Excellency Signor Conte Giovanni Vincislao di Galasso, Ambassador to his Imperial Majesty at the Holy See, might not have taken place as planned for that particular day. Then it seemed that the nearer the festive day approached, the more the rains decreased, and a few days before the event the importunate clouds and squalls completely disappeared, and pure calm weather settled in for some time, to the delight of the earth and its inhabitants. [Details of the rapid organization of the firework display and the structures for it are omitted.]

The sound of the countless spectators among the populace, along with the music of trumpets and drums, generated unaccustomed cheerfulness. While waiting for the start of the fireworks, his Excellency's gentlemen and pages continuously handed round delicate *sorbetti* and *acque agghiatte* to the invited guests. This went on more or less continually from the start to the finish of the noble entertainment, with great abundance and equal variety and delicacy. [… After the firework display came the refreshments … displayed in a huge hall, concealed behind damask curtains, which were drawn back to reveal the spectacle.]

Torrid Pleasures of an Ice-Cream and Sorbet Tree in Rome

The refreshments depicted in the above plate: the table was 84 *palmi* [19.2m/63'] long, in the middle of it was a *trionfo*, 8 *palmi* high, whose base was 4 *palmi* square. Six steps of candied sugar were the base for 4 columns, made of red and white sugar, whose capitals supported four arches ornamented with every kind of sweetmeats from France, and on top of these arches an Imperial eagle of candied sugar. At each of the four sides of the *trionfo* rose a pyramid 5 *palmi* high, with 4 levels, on each of which were various coloured Venetian glass bowls and little dishes with comfits, candied sweetmeats of every colour and flavour. Two larger pyramids were placed at either end of the table, also decorated with the same delicacies, but from the summit of each arose a beautiful tree, one with candied oranges, and one with limes. On either side of these pyramids there were four beautifully engraved vases, placed on pedestals with two levels, each containing a tree, one citron, one sweet orange, one peach and one pear. From the branches of each, covered with natural-looking foliage, were suspended 50 of each kind of fruit, made of ice, with life-like colouring [*frutti gelati, ed al vivo coloriti*]. The soil in the vases was *spuma di cioccolate* [whipped chocolate? frozen chocolate froth?]. The first level of the pedestals of these vases had at each angle 4 crystal saucers, from which arose 4 pyramids, two large ones, and two truncated, of *sorbetti* of various flavours, with festoons of a variety of *frutta gelate* [moulded fruit ices?], and *biscottini agghiacciati* [iced biscuits?], and each of the four sides had two smaller crystal saucers of *spuma di cioccolate*, and *latte gelato* [gelato here is an adjective, frozen, not a noun, but is this an early sighting of the word?]. At the angles of the second level [of the pedestal] were placed four crystal saucers full of *frutti di cioccolate* in *tavolette* [solid chocolates in the shape of fruit?], and other flavours of *pezzi di gelo* [frozen moulded ices], and on every side were 4 small plates, also of crystal, with little pyramids of *butiro gelato all'Inglese* [custard ices, English style]. The grand table had 16 quadrangles [convex curved edges in the engraving], with stepped plates on two levels, the first four of which had crystal saucers of *formagetti gelati* [custard ices in moulds], and four porcelain dishes of cinnamon biscuits, and on the second level a big dish of *pan lavato gelato ad uso di Polonia* [frozen filled sponge cake in the Polish manner]. Another four [of the curved areas] had, in similar containers, *frutta, e cioccolate in pezzi* [frozen fruit ices in moulds? moulded chocolate ices?] , and *biscottini in gelo*, [biscuit ices?], and in the middle could be seen a bowl sculpted out of ice with *botiro gelato*. The saucers on the other four [curved areas] were full of *latte freddo alla portoghese* [a chilled custard or cream], with little dishes of *ova* [ices made in egg moulds], and frozen cinnamon biscuits, and in the middle a *spuma di cioccolata, e di lattemiele agghiacciato* [whipped chocolate and frozen milk sweetened with honey]. On the last four were pyramids of *botiro gelato* on saucers, and *pezzi di cioccolata*, and *crema* [custard, or custard ice?] and in the centre a green pyramid of pistachio, surrounded by numerous smaller pyramids of various flavours on silver dishes.

Torrid Pleasures of an Ice-Cream and Sorbet Tree in Rome

[The rest of the description is of the fruit, furnishings, etc.]

The organizer of the refreshments was Signor Enrico Dienebier of Prague, highly experienced manager, the *confezzione* [confectionery?] was by Signor Arnoldo Ritfelt, an Englishman, and the *geli* [ice-creams, or moulded sweets?] were by Michele Ansidei, Roman and *bottigliere*.

It is helpful at this point to compare the Roman event with less grandiose feasts that happened in Naples a couple of decades earlier, organized by Antonio Latini, and described in his great work *Lo Scalco alla Moderna* of 1692. By its very nature ice-cream was an ephemeral treat, and not suitable for being part of a display of cold food on a buffet, sitting around and waiting to be handed out in between courses of food hot from the kitchen. So many other kinds of cold or chilled food were more suitable, junkets, jellies, moulded mousses and custards, and so forth. This must be why Latini hardly ever lists ice-creams or sorbets in his serious banquet menus. But he does offer ices, in enormous quantities, on more relaxed occasions, like the expeditions to informal meals in the countryside outside Naples, when the Viceroy's chief political advisor, Don Stefano Carillo Salcedo entertained a group of Spanish notables in the stables of his country estate in Torre del Greco, where his guests, after a massive lunch and a little lie-down, had a happy time hunting semi-wild game in the nearby game park, then refreshing themselves with a vast array of sorbets before returning home to the city.

Latini tip-toed with tact around the sensibilities of the professional ice-cream makers of Naples, a closed shop that he had no wish to antagonize, and although one can assume that he had the gear to make his own, he must often have needed to rely on their services. On this occasion providing enough ices to offer, not just to the gentry, but to the lesser nobles, the servants, horsemen, grooms, and the ever-present Neapolitan rabble, must have been a well-coordinated effort in mass production. And politically astute, for the Spanish ruler and his associates needed to placate the local populace. What better than with ice-creams?

Latini said in Book II of *Lo Scalco alla Moderna* of 1692, 'Although I have given the ingredients for several chilled waters and sorbets I had no notion of displeasing the Professionals, Pantry Stewards or Officials of the Buffet; but merely to inform those ignorant of these professional skills, but needing background information. In fact it seems as if here in Naples everyone is born with the instincts and genius to make sorbetti.'

An anonymous little booklet published about the same time confirms this. Its 24 recipes are the basic information about what goes into a range of exquisite and imaginative ice-creams, with precious little about the 'how to' aspect, taking for granted all the skills, equipment and know-how that the gifted Neapolitan ice-cream makers were blessed with. Those of us who have followed these recipes to the letter (Ivan Day and the author) were amazed at the accuracy, originality, and deliciousness of the results. This modest little book gives us the chance to experience the variety of

Torrid Pleasures of an Ice-Cream and Sorbet Tree in Rome

subtle and delicious ices available in late seventeenth-century and early eighteenth-century Rome and Naples. This paper provides some of the context of the practical demonstrations at the Symposium.

List of ices in the order in which they are mentioned
[N.B. some of these might be custards, creams, mousses, jellies]

Acque agghiacciate
Ghiacciate liquori
Acque agghiacciate
Ghiacciati liquori
… agghiacciamento de'sapori delle medesime [frutta] stretti a forza di neve in forma,
… scelti frutti tolti della neve
sorbetto di persico
… di pappina
… di mandole fresche
… di di cedrati
[all of which chiudean dentro le loro frutta siroppate]
botiro ghiacciato
frutti gelati
gelo d'agresta con odore di gelsomino, e con agresta intiera siroppata demtro
crema con marmellata di cedrato
frambues col medesimo frutto intiero siroppato, e di gelo
formagetti di crema
frutti gelati
spuma di pana
spuma di cioccolate
biscottini e formagetti di ghiaccio framezzati diciocolate
latte alla portoghese gelato in pezzi
piramide di pappina
frutta di gelo
delicati sorbetti
acque aghiacciate
frutti gelati (cedrati, portogalli, persiche, pere)
spuma di cioccolate
sorbetti di diversi sapori
spuma di cioccolate
latte gelato
frutti di cioccolate in tavolette
pezzi di gelo
butiro gelato all'Inglese

Torrid Pleasures of an Ice-Cream and Sorbet Tree in Rome

formagetti gelati
pan lavato gelato ad uso di Polonia
cioccolate in pezzi
biscottini in gelo
botiro gelato
latte freddo alla portoghese
piattini d'ova
biscottini di cannella gelati
spuma di cioccolata
lattemiele agghiacciato
botiro gelato
pezzi di cioccolata e di crema
piramide verde di pistacchi
piramidine di diversi sapori

Acknowledgements

I would like to thank Gillian Riley for all the help and encouragement and also for her translation. I would also like to thank Ivan Day and John Gauder for help and advice.

The Origins of the Celebration of St Cosmas and St Damian in Rio de Janeiro

Marcia Zoladz

The city of Rio de Janeiro is famous for its flair for enjoying and celebrating life. Where else in the world do the inhabitants of a major city gather on the beach to applaud the sunset? Where else do they celebrate Carnival so seriously? Mardi Gras or Fat Tuesday is merely the end of a gigantic feast that starts ten days before. But this celebration is so well publicized, it could almost be said that Carnival in Rio is the world's best-known celebration.

Even in Brazil, though, most people are not familiar with the celebration dedicated to St Cosmas and St Damian that happens in the streets of that same city. It is completely different from Carnival, which only took today's format in the second half of the twentieth century: its exuberance hides equally important festivities in Brazilian culture that are also part of the city's calendar. Sts Cosmas and Damian is one of them.

The feast is a major element in forging the cultural identity of the *cariocas* – the name given to the inhabitants of Rio de Janeiro. This popular feast is dedicated solely to the celebration of the children of the city. Although it was not part of the official calendar of either the Catholic Church or the colonial government, it was introduced quite early in the colonial period, during the sixteenth and seventeenth centuries.

The feast's origin lies in Portugal and Spain at the time of the Reconquista, when the Moors where expelled and conversion to Catholicism was imposed on the local population. In Brazil, the festival honoring St Cosmas and Damian began with the arrival of the first Europeans in the late sixteenth century. Today, unknown to foreigners and celebrated in *carioca* homes, the feast was absorbed by the *Umbanda*, the Brazilian religion influenced by African religious cults and the *Candomblé*, an Afro-Brazilian religion with even stronger ties to the African continent.

To understand this feast and how it influences the lives of children in Rio de Janeiro, one has to

Figure 1. The most commonly used image of Sts Cosmas and Damian in Brazil.

understand the importance of the first European inhabitants of the city. The beauty of this feast is that it can be looked at as snapshot of Portuguese life in the Americas, which at first were settled mainly by Portuguese and Spanish New Christians. The festival shows also the effort of the new converts to maintain their original religious and cultural traditions, sometimes without deep knowledge of them, since the first conversions had happened in some cases in 1494 or even earlier and the city of Rio was not founded until 1565.

These converts were forbidden to study or practise the liturgy and laws of Judaism and forced to behave like Christians. It was such a complex situation that after a while they had to be legally classified as a separate group – they were neither 'old' Christians nor Jews, they were 'new' Christians.

Since they were aware of their origin, many clung to the possibility of one day returning to Judaism. To keep their memories alive, they either maintained or established a series of practices linked to their interpretation of Judaism. Nowadays, one can hardly imagine the effects caused by the forced conversion enforced by the Church, which created massive disruptions in the lives of the Jewish community, of the ex-Jews – now New Christians – and, of course, also of the Christians and Muslims still living in Spain. These were very old communities. There are documents that attest the existence of Jews in the Iberian Peninsula since the sixth century BC.

Although equally disruptive in Portugal, the Inquisition courts and the forced conversions happened there a little later. Since the Crown needed the Jewish/New Christian community to finance its colonial expansion, it accepted 200,000 converts, some of whom emigrated to Brazil.

The city of Rio de Janeiro, where colonists began to arrive from Portugal after 1565, developed around a well-protected, deep, quiet bay. The main activity at that time was the exportation of sugar and the importation of slave labor from Africa. These early European inhabitants left some traces that indicate a possible crypto-Judaic origin of the feast dedicated to St Cosmas and St Damian.

The feast today

The feast – or what is left of it – is still a very exciting experience for children. The celebration has been moved inside buildings, schools, and the cult centers of the *Umbanda*, mainly due to changes in the city's architecture as the construction of high-rise buildings have replaced rows of houses with small front gardens.

The celebration starts with the excitement created a few days before the feast day of Sts Cosmas and Damian, when signs are hung around the neighborhood with the addresses of the houses where candies will be given away. Some schools even liberate the students from classes. The children stand in line in front of these houses, and then the doors open and they start picking up small paper bags filled with candies and sweets.

They rush from one house to the next, as if they were on a battlefield, to get as many candy-filled paper bags as possible. Traditionally, when they get home this sweet

Celebration of St Cosmas and St Damian

Figure 2 (above). The entrance of the Guanabara Bay with the Sugar Loaf at the right.

Figure 3. (above, left). Mugunzá, a corn and coconut cream.

Figure 4. (above). Purple potato paste.

Figure 5. (left). Different sweets that will be distributed.

treasure is emptied into a bowl to be shared by all the children in the family. The paper bags carry all sorts of inexpensive candies and sweets, such as '*pé de moleque*' – peanut brittle, '*doce de leite*' – a caramel-like milk-based sweet, '*doce de banana*' – a hard paste made with banana and sugar, different flavored toffees, sugar candies that resemble glass beads from Murano, and lollipops for the younger children. Less frequently today than in the past, the bags sometimes include small portions of sweets made of purple sweet potato, '*cocada preta*' – dark coconut patties, and '*cocada branca*' – white coconut patties. Because of the hot climate of Rio, chocolate was never part of the treats distributed.

The image of the saints stamped on the paper bags portrays, in an anachronistic way, the two Saints dressed as citizens of ancient Rome, standing next to each other.

The remains

To discover the origin of this feast, it is necessary to view it as if it were a painting and ask whether the artist has painted over another painting underneath it, as interesting – or even more interesting – than the visible painting. In this case, some vestiges have remained.

The first vestige is the choice of the saints that are honored. In Brazil, there are many popular and religious feasts that honor at the same time a Catholic saint and an African spirit or entity. This syncretism was often based on a coincidence of dates in the calendar. Other feasts merged certain aspects of a given saint into Afro-Brazilian religions, as, for example, Sts Cosmas and Damian. In the African tradition, these two saints are portrayed as being small, like children. Actually their images are used instead of what they really represent: the free spirits, referred to as the 'Ibejis' and 'Erês' – the children that exist in all of us and that look after the small details of daily life.

Prior to this, the first act of official camouflage, in Brazil, can be traced to the sixteenth century, and coincidentally, to a chapel built in honor of Sts Cosmas and Damian in Brazil's north-east, right at the beginning of the colonial times, in 1535. The date of the chapel's construction indicates that the celebration already existed in Portugal. The chapel was built by an early governor, Duarte Coelho, a New Christian who established himself in Pernambuco. The local population readily accepted this celebration, since as that time there were no collective festivities as they are known today, such as Carnival. There were, instead, moments of social gathering occasioned either by secular and colonial considerations – the king's birthday, for instance – or by the Church and its calendar. These are the roots of many typically Brazilian festivals, but because neither government nor church offered enough opportunities to have a good time to its Brazilian subjects, whether free-men, natives, or slaves, they created their own.

The choice of Sts Cosmas and Damian probably resulted from overlapping dates. The day established by the African religions in Brazil to commemorate them is 27 September; in Portugal and in the Catholic Church calendar it is the 26th. Both dates correspond approximately to the fifteenth day of the month of Tischrei, the day when Sukkoth, one of the major Jewish holidays, is celebrated.

This date does not entirely mean that the festival for Sts Cosmas and Damian is a syncretic celebration of Sukkoth, but it may well be camouflage for what was by then, more than one hundred years after the first mass conversions in Spain, the safeguarding of a common memory for a group of people in a foreign land.

Cosmas and Damian were martyred in the fourth century AD, at the beginning of Christianity. They were both physicians and were worshipped as protectors of people from epidemics, hunger, and from dying when giving birth to twins. Their cult was encouraged by the Church because they represented an ideal behavior for early Christians – these were more than good people: they refused to charge for their services, they were possibly from well-off families, and, moreover, they spread the word of Jesus.

Later on, as the pressure for conversion of Muslims and Jews arose, celebrations in the saints' honor expanded in many New Christian communities in Portugal and in Spain. For example, the city of Albaran, in central Spain, has a celebration of Sts Cosmas and Damian that began prior to 1505, the year the last mosques in the region were converted into churches. About this time, most of the Spanish Jews had left the country, and converted families who remained close to their origins were secretly practising some Jewish rituals. In the streets they behaved like Christians, but at home they developed another culture, no longer Jews, but following the Old Testament as much as the Inquisition allowed.

In Brazil, the older chapels dedicated to Sts Cosmas and Damian are in the regions where the first sugar-cane mills were built by the *conversos* in and around Rio de Janeiro. For a heterogeneous group of people forced to go into exile in a colony on the edges of a mercantile empire such as the Portuguese, celebrating Sts Cosmas and Damian made sense. Also, in a world full of sickness, as seen in so many satires that poked fun at physicians' inability to cure the sick, praying to saints that protected people's health was easily accepted by the Church.

The second sign of the origin of the feast is its geographical range: the celebration takes place only in the neighborhoods that, though they look towards the Bay of Guanabara, are not close to the open sea. The port, with its warehouses and social and religious life, developed far from the Atlantic Ocean. Even today the feast is still restricted to this older region. The Rio de Janeiro famous for its Copacabana and Ipanema beaches was only urbanized in the late nineteenth century.

The third sign of origin is the fact that, in a Portuguese colony dominated by a Catholic Church that controlled the daily life and habits of an entire population, this is the only Catholic feast that was never celebrated inside the city's churches. The celebration is held in front of peoples' homes, where the children get candy-filled paper bags in recognition of a request that has been granted. That this feast for Sts Cosmas and Damian takes place outside church buildings is nothing new; many Christian

Celebration of St Cosmas and St Damian

Figure 6. A family eating in a Sukkah, Amsterdam, 1722. Engraving by French artist Bernard Picard.

celebrations take place in squares or streets close to a church. Except this one neither began nor ended in a church. This contradicts the religious practice of fifteenth-century Portugal, when processions were important for the reaffirmation of the Christian faith, and were at the same time the cradle of the Portuguese theater, since the lives of the saints were told as dialogues along the processions. The uniqueness of the St Cosmas and St Damian festival lies in this difference; and up to today this celebration, as part of the Umbanda, still takes place in the porches and front yards of houses, nurseries, and schools.

The fourth clue, although a little more difficult to grasp, is that in Brazil – a country first inhabited by indigenous people, followed by many New Christians, Africans, exiles, French and Dutch invaders, pirates, and even a shipload of orphan girls (the Catholic Church's last attempt to reduce the number of marriages with indigenous women) – not everything is as it seems.

Traditions camouflaging under other traditions, most of which related to religious syncretism, were revealed only in the second half of the twentieth century, when the African religions were officially recognized and distanced their festivities from those of the Church. By that time, the feast of Sts Cosmas and Damian had already become part of the city's tradition, included in the calendar of the *Umbanda* and the *Candomblé*, but its origin had been forgotten.

It was not easy to be a New Christian

Life in early Rio de Janeiro was full daily challenges. In addition to the need of organizing themselves as a group to help each other and avoid isolation, the *conversos* had to deal with conflicts with the native population as they were occupying their lands. Furthermore, they had to look after their food that, at that moment, remained highly influenced by the Jewish tradition, despite their new religion.

Many of these new inhabitants were New Christians who secretly kept the religious habits of their ancestors while living an apparently Christian life. In some cases, conversions had taken place more than a generation earlier, which means that a process of religious dilution had begun. Therefore, these people knew, for example, that they had to follow a familiar calendar. However, as Catholicism was the only religion allowed at the time, they had to resort to subterfuge to worship and celebrate their feasts.

The fact that these people lived far from the center of persecutions in Lisbon was very helpful; their private religious habits were changing but still had many Jewish influences that could be denounced to the Inquisition tribunals. They were therefore going through a process of interiorizing, almost submerging, their private lives and habits, in order to keep their interpretation of their original religious practices.

In Brazil, although no longer Jewish, they kept so much in their New Christian habits, despite the religious persecution by the Inquisition, that recently – three centuries later – three communities in the State of Bahia renewed their ties with Judaism, much like their ancestors had done in Holland in the sixteenth and seventeenth centuries.

During the Inquisition in Brazil, eating habits were frequently the reason for accusations, as official documents attest. Such accusations were less frequent in Rio de Janeiro during the sixteenth and seventeenth centuries, when many of the New Christians were involved in growing sugar-cane and producing sugar; many others were physicians, lawyers, and traders. Brazil never had an official Inquisition tribunal, but they did have two so-called visits that resulted in many accusations against families with Jewish habits.

A 1636 report by the chief rabbi of Recife describes the complexity of the covert actions, the camouflages, and the confusion of the New Christians and of those who secretly still worshipped in the Jewish faith in the New World, even in an area where the Jewish religion had not been banned while it was under the domain of Holland from 1630 to 1654. In his report, the rabbi describes how the New Christians made serious efforts to go back to their Jewish religious practices. However, he had a problem – it was difficult to convince them to come to the synagogue to observe Shabbat on Fridays at sunset, as this was the day when they and their families would get together to light candles, eat dinner, and then play cards. This was a different version of Shabbat.

Celebration of St Cosmas and St Damian

What were the sweets like?

Of the many new products the Europeans found in Brazil, two were soon adopted as natural substitutes for foods normally eaten in Europe: *mandioca* (cassava) and corn. Cooked *mandioca* roots were served as bread, and the flour and the starch were used instead of wheat flour in cakes and sweets. A huge number of new desserts were created with the new ingredients, especially after the introduction of coconut palms in the seventeenth century.

Corn, a staple food in Brazil since pre-Colombian times, was part of the native diet and consumed as very thin flour (*fubá*) cooked with water. This flour, mixed with other ingredients, was used by the Europeans in cakes and in pastries. The dried corn grains were broken and cooked with meats and vegetables.

Hearts of palm and cashew nuts were novelties. The almonds common in Portuguese sweets were replaced by peanuts. To this day, peanuts are consumed either lightly toasted or used as one of the ingredients in cakes and sweets. The use of peanuts to make sweets was first described in the sixteenth century by Gabriel Soares, a sugar plantation owner, in his report on life in the tropics: '(with peanuts) … the Portuguese women make all kinds of sweets that would normally use almonds; the peanuts are chopped and covered with sugar and confections.'[1]

One of the few recipe books published in the nineteenth century, *Doceira brazileira*, includes a compilation of recipes from the early eighteenth century, as attested to by the very old spelling and measures:

'In a pint measure of purified honey [sugar cane molasses was also referred to as honey] mix in a selamin [a measure used in the early eighteenth century, equivalent to 2.28 liters] of peanuts toasted, shelled and pressed with the fingers in order to halve the kernels. Wait until the syrup has thickened. Take the pan from the stove and spoon the mixture on a wooden board or on a table that has been dampened with water so that the mixture does not stick to the surface; it is ready when it has cooled off.'

'*Paçoca*' is another adaptation of a food conservation method employed by the native population. The original recipe calls for dried meat or fish mixed and kneaded with cassava flour. The Portuguese settlers created a sweet version, by mixing ground peanuts, cassava flour, and sugar. The oil exuded from the peanuts helps shape the mixture into small cylinders. This is a typical sweet eaten by children or when one wants to eat a little something both sweet and strong.

If there was a banquet in honor of Sts Cosmas and Damian, maybe some of the dishes resembled one from the *Recipe Book of the Infanta D. Maria*, a Portuguese princess from the sixteenth century. Nowadays, the taste of this concoction seems rather strange, but at that time, the boundary between sweet and savory was not clearly defined:

Celebration of St Cosmas and St Damian

Roast a chicken and cut it into pieces. Beat an egg and dip the pieces of chicken in it. Fry the egg-coated chicken pieces in butter. Dip some slices of day-old bread in the egg and fry them in butter, like the chicken. Dip everything in sugar, place the bread slices in a bowl and place the pieces of chicken on top of them. Sprinkle them with sugar and cinnamon.

A paste of guavas cooked with sugar was exported to Portugal by the Jesuits, but many fruits were eaten raw or cooked in sugar syrup. Travelers describe beautiful gardens with fruit trees and many domestic animals, such as chickens, ducks, and geese. The same Gabriel dos Santos writes about recipes with native fruit used in a very creative manner for baking and frying cakes and for making peanut and cashew nut confections.

In the following two centuries three species – bananas, mangoes and coconuts – were introduced. Guava paste, banana paste, *cocada* and *doce de leite* in different versions – softer, harder, with more sugar, with less sugar – are still the country's favorite treats.

Peanuts instead of almonds

Once the Portuguese colonists arrived, it took them a very short time to adapt to their new environment and to native products. In spite of many conflicts, the settlers maintained very close contact with the natives. There was an enormous gap between Renaissance Europe and Rio de Janeiro: therefore there is a moving aspect in this change of continents by such a large group of exiles and in their ability to build a new life in the Atlantic forest despite the Inquisition.

It is impossible to state definitively that the festival of Sts Cosmas and Damian in Brazil masked an original feast dedicated to Sukkoth. After a while the settlers distanced themselves from Europe. Their relation with a country they had not chosen changed, especially with miscegenation through intermarriages and the absorption of cultural habits from both African and local populations. It may have been a rather slow process, but change became faster and more intense as time passed.

Nowadays, it cannot be said definitively that the colonists built sheds in their backyards as part of the celebration of Sts Cosmas and Damian; however, their stoves were often placed under a covered area outside the house. Therefore, it is very likely that they ate next to the stoves, as seen in the houses from that era. If they actually did it only during Sukkoth, or simply had their meals outside, nobody would have said anything in a hot city located over marshes. Likewise, using a palm branch, a willow branch, and a periwinkle branch (*lulav*) and a lemon (*ertrog*) as part of the Sukkoth ceremony would go unnoticed, even though it was not that easy to get them for these were not tropical products. But because the Church was a major power in the Portuguese colonial world, actions relating to the celebration not only of Sukkoth, but other religious festivals too, changed, becoming increasingly more discrete, timid, actually hiding behind other rites and customs acknowledging Catholic saints.

Although under surveillance, the colonists led a very productive life. First they

Celebration of St Cosmas and St Damian

Figure 7. The Tupinamba Indians celebrating, dressed with feather capes.

survived religious persecution in Portugal. Then, in taking part in the colonial business, they managed to leave the Iberian Peninsula, opened a huge farming area – larger than some countries in Europe – constructed sugar mills, established the port in Rio, and built the city itself. It was a very united group, with frequent marriages and business partnerships, which usually met to celebrate with their own rituals and songs, as attested by documents of the Inquisition.

Because the country's main crop was sugar, an emphasis on sweet food could not be easily denounced as a Jewish habit. After all, consuming sugary concoctions at festivities was not originally only a Jewish habit. The difference in this celebration from the Christian ones was where it took place.

Sukkoth has many aspects with different religious and historical interpretations. One of them tells about how God guided his people from the desert to the promised land. In an enormous gesture of faith, the Israélites, despite living in a desert where they could not plant and feed themselves without difficulty, were able to believe they would achieve a future of plenty.

In colonial Rio de Janeiro this faith was translated into the habit of giving away candies as a way of sharing abundance. The tradition was kept and these children, initially of Jewish descent, also share their 'bounty', at first with their siblings and cousins, and later with their own children, thus renewing their loyalty to their cultural and distant religious traditions.

By creating the feast of Sts Cosmas and Damian, this group of people made it

Figure 8. A Tupinamba Indian cape, today at the Department of Ethnography of the National Museum of Denmark.

possible for the culture of the city to absorb the meaning of Sukkoth, even though the meaning was a hidden one, and they also made it possible for the feast to persist largely unchanged until today. The noisy children standing in line and waiting for their bag of candy were honored as representatives of the people who took their harvest to the Great Temple of Jerusalem and followed the Jewish tradition that said: 'You shall rejoice on your festival … for the Lord will bless all your undertakings'.

Today's festival of Sts Cosmas and Damian is still a celebration of the future, represented by children. But instead of remembering the ancient festival with different crops, they use sugar, the largest harvest of the country. The New Christians commemorated two aspects of Sukkoth, the harvest represented by sugar produce and the children, celebrated as a metaphor of the future. Establishing the festival represented the first step toward celebrating their past – and also the possibility of undoing the effects of the Inquisition 450 years after their arrival in Rio.

Bibliography

Basto, Constança, *Doceira Brazileira* (Rio de Janeiro: Laemmert e Co., 1896).

DaMatta, Roberto (author), Drury, John (translator), *Carnival, Rogues, and Heroes: an Interpretation of the Brazilian Dilemma* (Notre Dame: Helen Kellog Institute of International Studies, 1991).

Freyre, Gilberto, *Assucar* (Rio de Janeiro: Jose Olympio Editora, 1939).

Hue, Moura Sheila, *Delícias do descobrimento, a gastronomia brasileira no século XVI* (Rio de Janeiro: Zahar, 2009).

Knobel, Peter S., *Gates of the Season* (New York: Central Conference of American Rabbis, 2007).

Melammed, Renée Levine, *A Question of Identity: Iberian Conversos in Historical Perspective* (Oxford: Oxford University Press, 2004).

Illustrations

1. The most commonly used image of Sts Cosmas and Damian in Brazil. (Brazil: http://eliseteart.blogspot.com/2007/09/27-de-setembro-dia-de-so-cosme-e-damio.html, 2011)
2. The entrance of the Guanabara Bay with the Sugar Loaf at the right. Photo: Marcia Zoladz
3. Example of the sweets served to celebrate the Saints day. Photo: Marcia Zoladz
4. Mugunzá, a corn and coconut cream. Photo: Marcia Zoladz
5. Purple potato paste. Photo: Marcia Zoladz
6. A family eating in a Sukkah, Amsterdam, 1722. Engraving by French artist Bernard Picard. http://commons.wikimedia.org/wiki/File:Sukkah_meal_Amsterdam_1922_Bernard_Picart_Wigoder_editor_Jewish_Art_Civilization_1972_p60-1.JPG (http://bit.ly/pWWOSB). Published with the permission of Wikimedia, Creative Commons.
7. The Tupinamba Indians celebrating dressed with feather capes. Engraving by Theodor de Bry from 'History of a voyage to the land Brazil, also called America by Jean de Léry', 1578. http://www.cemobafluminense.com.br/cemobafotos/displayimage.php?album=6&pos=5 (http://bit.ly/pB9MZ9). Published with the permission of Wikimedia, Creative Commons.
8. The Tupinamba Indians cape, Department of Ethnography of the National Museum of Denmark. http://www.cemobafluminense.com.br/cemobafotos/displayimage.php?album=6&pos=4 (http://bit.ly/r54PnU). Published with the permission of Wikimedia, Creative Commons.